The Concise Handbook of Management

The Concise Handbook of Management

A Practitioner's Approach

Jonathan T. Scott

ATLANTIC®
PUBLISHERS & DISTRIBUTORS

Best Business Books®
The Haworth Reference Press™
New York • London • Oxford

ATLANTIC®

PUBLISHERS & DISTRIBUTORS
7/22, Ansari Road, Darya Ganj
New Delhi – 110 002
Tel: 2327 3880, 2327 5880, 2328 0451
Fax: 91-11-2328 5873
E-mail: info@atlanticbooks.com
Website: www.atlanticbooks.com

Published in India by
Atlantic Publishers and Distributors, New Delhi
in association with
Best Business Books®, and The Haworth Reference Press™,
imprints of The Haworth Press, Inc.
10 Alice Street, Binghamton, New York 13904-1580

First published 2005 by Best Business Books® and
The Haworth Reference Press™
First Indian Reprint 2006

ISBN 81-269-0618-9

Printed in India by
Nice Printing Press, Delhi

To George G. Scott Jr.,
a successful executive, manager, and turn-around specialist
in the highly competitive American wire rope and cable industry
(and a great dad too!)

ABOUT THE AUTHOR

Born in Trenton, New Jersey, **Jonathan T. Scott** grew up in nine different states before attending Brevard College (Brevard, North Carolina) and graduating from Florida State University (Tallahassee, Florida) in 1987. He has since earned a language certification from the Universite de Bourgogne (Dijon, France), an MBA from Western International University (at its former London, UK, campus), and a teaching certificate from Oxford Brookes University (Oxford, UK).

Scott worked in the leisure and recreation industry for over twenty years before becoming a teacher. As a manager he earned his stripes, and a reputation, for turning around three separate businesses under difficult circumstances (the first occurred in a war zone). Currently on his third passport, he has lived and worked in eight different countries. He now lectures on business and management issues in Europe.

Apart from his numerous internationally published management articles, Scott's books include *Fundamentals of Leisure Business Success,* the highly acclaimed novels *Expedition* and *Days Captive,* and the upcoming *On Wings*—the story behind the most successful fighting unit in all of human history.

If you are interested in having Jonathan Scott speak with your employees or students about work and management issues, or simply wish to share your comments about this book, please feel free to send him a message via the following address:

Jonathan_T_Scott@hotmail.com

I slept and dreamt
that life was joy.
I woke and saw
that life was duty.
I acted, and behold!
Duty was joy.

Rabindranath Tagore
Calcutta, India

CONTENTS

PART II: BASIC THOUGHTS ON AND THEORIES OF MANAGEMENT

PART IV: THE BASICS OF BUSINESS

Preface

Why Another Book About Management?

My induction into teaching was a sink-or-swim affair. While investigating a business opportunity in Warsaw, Poland, I learned that a former corporate executive had "pulled a runner" at the country's most prestigious private business school (unable to cope with the responsibilities of teaching, she'd simply disappeared). Although I'd never taught anything before, someone asked if I'd be interested in replacing her. Simply put, no one else could be found at such short notice. I said yes even though it was three weeks into the semester and neither syllabus nor lecture notes could be found. Because I didn't know quite how to approach the job, I took a few minutes during the first class and asked the students to explain their expectations.

"Well, so far we sat through two boring lectures based upon nothing more than theory and definitions," one student said. He cast his eyes to the ground as if he'd blurted out something wrong.

"Do you know anything about management?" asked another.

"When is someone going to teach us something we can actually use?" muttered a third.

The rest of the class, an intriguing mixture of young men and women from half a dozen different countries, nodded their heads in agreement.

My head reared back. After more than twenty years of working as a business practitioner I couldn't believe my ears. These students were displaying the typical signs of customer disgruntlement. It was apparent that most of these students were eager to learn, desperate even, but after suffering from a stream of lecturers who seemed to put teaching at the bottom of their priority list, they were losing interest.

"The problem with universities today," stated a friend (an Ivy League University lecturer) to me in an e-mail later that week, "is that they're full of professional researchers who are amateur teachers."

From that moment on I decided to revert to basic business sense. I would listen to my customers' (the students') wants and needs and *act upon them.* Every theory or academic point I introduced in class would be accompanied by an interesting highlight or example of practical application that brought the point home. The way I figured it, the onus was upon me to have my students *want* to come to class and do well. Thankfully, as a part-time lecturer, I had no publishing pressures placed upon me. My emphasis could therefore be placed on preparing students to be good managers—not in having them memorize abstract theories or in using them as cheap labor to gather research data. Now all I needed was a good management book.

Teachers (including myself) notoriously turn into prima donnas when it comes to selecting course texts and now I know why. As I looked through the piles of available material, I could see only the faults. Most textbooks were incredibly verbose and full of hyperbole and/or questionable profiles (remember when **celebrity CEOs** such as Jeff Skilling, Bernie Ebbers, and Dennis Kozlowski were heralded, and when Enron, WorldCom, and Arthur Andersen were considered excellent companies?). Others had graphs and models that were either so oversimplified they were meaningless or needed the explanation of entire chapters to comprehend. Many more books were dead boring or contained Disneyesque-styled writing and explanations. Too many of them placed far too much emphasis on big corporations when more than 90 percent of the world's working people are employed by small to midsized businesses (I suspect it is big corporations that are doling out research grants so they get studied more). In addition, the voices behind these books were not bold enough. In other words, the people who wrote them didn't appear to have much management experience. But what really irked me was how most of these books gave little or no attention to the importance of customers. Everything, and I mean *everything,* a manager does must be customer oriented. Yet it's difficult to come to that conclusion when reading most management books. The word *customer* is barely mentioned. Undaunted, I continued searching. One book seemed to suggest that children's stories could solve business problems (it was actually a pretty good book, but a management course can't be based on children's stories). Others appeared to be designed as an author-publishing vehicle or as a means of self-promotion. A few did nothing but disparage opposing thinkers. Still more were based on a catchy title and/or a marketing gimmick. The majority were ridiculously overpriced. At one point I considered photocopying relevant academic papers and passing them out to students, but so many of these papers are written in such an unnecessarily complex manner that I soon thought better of burdening students with them.

My mind went back to the MBA program I attended in London, England, at Western International University. On the first day of a class titled "Finance and the Corporation," the instructor limped into the room (he was awaiting hip replacement surgery) and blinked at us through spectacles the thickness of Coke-bottle bottoms. We, the assembled students, were reduced to a hush. This man was rumored to be a part of almost every piece of accounting legislation passed in the United Kingdom and he was very intimidating.

"Over the past several decades, I've worked in over a dozen companies, not to mention five different countries," he stated in his introduction. "And every few months it seems some bright spark publishes a new theory about determining costs in a business. Indeed there are too many of these formulas out there now, each one more complex than the last. Yet despite this proliferation, only two are ever really used outside academia. And by the end of this term, those two—and only those two—are what you're going to know inside and out."

I decided to apply this type of thinking to my new teaching position. I concluded to keep it simple and give the students bits and pieces from my first book, *Fundamentals of Leisure Business Success* (The Haworth Press), combined with what readable and applicable material I could find from around the world. After two years of this process I'd gathered enough fundamental material to write a book on management in much the same way my finance professor had approached his subject: by sticking to the basics. And so, *The Concise Handbook of Management* was born. Is it biased? Yes. Is it scientific? No. Is anything new being presented? Not really. The vast majority of information contained in this book is, similar to most management books, a rehash of everything else that's out there. The difference is that this book approaches the subject from a practitioner's viewpoint. In other words, it discusses management with customers in mind. I didn't write this book to pitch a new management theory but to present the practical necessities of management from a manager's perspective.

Please note that nothing in these pages is designed to be prescriptive or omnipotent. Rather, *The Concise Handbook of Management* is meant to

- be motivating—to whet the appetite of readers and get them interested in probing further into the subject of management (which really is fascinating);
- be supplemental to and balanced against other management books (because what's presented here is certainly not definitive or all-encompassing);
- approach management in a way that is understandable, practical, and, yes, somewhat entertaining;
- not overload the reader (management is *not* a complicated subject); and
- be affordable.

To accomplish these objectives, this book has been laid out in short, condensed chapters that include many true stories and renowned case studies designed to assist in highlighting each section's main points. Important terms have been highlighted in bold print and included in the glossary. Topics are approached with the attitude that you, the reader, have enough intelligence and ability to determine if or how the issues raised can be applied to current or future work challenges. In the end, I suppose proof of the book's success will be measured by the sales figures. I hope you find the information presented here to be useful.

Acknowledgments

Many thanks are owed to those at The Haworth Press, whose efforts helped make this a better book. These people include Donna Biesecker, Tara Davis, Peg Marr, Jillian Mason-Possemato, Julie Bednar, Lindsey Lewis, and Dawn Krisko.

PART I: BUILDING THE MANAGEMENT FOUNDATION

Chapter 1

What Is Management?

1: the act or art of managing: the conducting or supervising of something (as a business) **2:** judicious use of means to accomplish an end **3:** the collective body of those who manage or direct an enterprise

Merriam-Webster's Collegiate Dictionary

1: the control and organizing of a business or other organization **2:** . . . also refers to the people who do this **3:** the way you control someone or something

Collins Cobuild English Language Dictionary

1: the art or practice of managing (especially a business or money) **2:** the people in charge of a company or industry **3:** skill in dealing with people or situations (judgment)

Longman Dictionary of Contemporary English

1: the application of skill or care in the manipulation, use, treatment, or control of things or persons, or in the conduct of enterprise, operation or organization of commercial enterprise

The New Oxford English Dictionary

1: planning, organizing, leading and controlling the use of resources to accomplish goals

A popular definition seen in many textbooks

1: overseeing the work of others

A classic definition

By any stretch of the imagination, there will probably never be a shortage of management definitions or management job titles (see Exhibit 1.1). The problem with most definitions of management is that they only tell part of the story. For example, in the definitions previously mentioned (indeed in every definition of management I've ever seen) the word *customer* isn't seen. This is astonishing because servicing customers is the crux of *every* business organization. Equally as remiss is that most writers neatly filter out human nature in their descriptions of management. Let's face it, aseptic words and terms are great for dictionaries and academic tomes but they're terrible when it comes to explaining, warts and all, the full scope of what management entails. So how can the art and science of management be summed up in a few succinct words? Well, truth be told, it can't. Management is about more than leading, controlling, planning, organizing, and setting goals and objectives. Much more.

EXHIBIT 1.1. Three Basic Categories of Management Positions

TOP MANAGERS (ADMINISTRATORS)

Presidents
Managing directors
Vice presidents
CEOs (chief executive officers)

MID-LEVEL MANAGERS

Department heads
District managers
Unit chiefs

FRONTLINE MANAGERS

Supervisors
Foremen
Coordinators
Team or project leaders

Perhaps the best way to present a richer and more accurate concept of management is to look at what good managers do—or are *supposed* to do—in the course of a typical working day. Good managers constantly streamline their organizations toward making a sale. In other words, good managers keep their organizations on track by ensuring that everything that's being done is geared toward providing what customers want. In this regard, a good manager is responsible for reducing ambiguity, keeping costs down, and motivating others to do the same. In the same vein, good managers regularly take educated risks and exercise good judgment. These risks include trying new approaches, successfully adjusting to constant change, developing subordinates (good managers aren't afraid of letting other people shine—in fact they encourage it), and improving their own skills.

Since most managers are responsible for more work than one person can normally perform, a good manager delegates and integrates the work of others by acting as a clear channel of communication within the businesses they serve. Good management is about rising above the often monotonous grind of a working day and injecting motivation, creativity, discipline, and enthusiasm into areas in which they either don't exist or they're not wanted. It entails doing things you don't want to do in order to get and do the things you want. And while all this is occurring, the ups and downs of life in general must be successfully dealt with, such as fear, insecurity, births, deaths, romances, divorces, physical injuries, bad-hair days, bad-manner days, personal failings, and attitude problems to name a very few. Again, I'm talking about *good* managers. These are the men and women who face problems, put in long hours, set a good example, and have an inherent knack to create something from nothing. Good managers work well with others (including those they don't like) and can be counted on to be honest and upstanding. They concentrate on goals and results rather than showing who's boss, because the creed they live by is *integrity, responsibility,* and *maturity.* This means financial figures aren't manipulated and production numbers aren't fiddled with. That's not to say that good managers always score; they most certainly do not, but when good managers don't succeed the first time they pick themselves up, brush themselves off, learn from what happened (without blaming others), and *then* score. Good managers create value. In other words, they don't make excuses; they produce results.

Sound like a tall order? Well, it's not so high that it can't be reached. The truth is that there are tens of thousands of good managers in this world quietly going about their work and performing admirably. That most of them don't attract attention to themselves, in part, shows their management acumen and the dedication they have for their craft. Good managers understand that management isn't merely a rank; it's a responsibility, and they more often than not let their work speak for itself. They don't need to be charlatans, actors, or showpeople. Yes, a little bit of flashiness sometimes goes a long way in business; nevertheless, *prioritizing* showmanship is not the mark of a good manager.

Now let's look at the other side of the coin. What constitutes bad management? Simply put, bad managers are insecure, overbearing, dictating bosses who, in the long run, do little more than manage to get to work on time, instill fear in others instead of respect, barely put in an eight-hour day (or less) of real work, collect a paycheck, and/or maintain the status quo when opportunities abound. At an administrative level, bad managers tend to see their profession as only a game of acquisitions and mergers or act as though what they do involves only numbers.

Calling yourself a manager doesn't make you one in the same manner that cooking dinner doesn't make you a chef, penning a letter doesn't make you a writer, and going jogging doesn't make you an athlete. For those of you who think management is glamorous, well, placing the word *manager* on your door or a business card isn't an invitation to a gold-encrusted club and a bottomless expense account. Most management positions, particularly those in small to midsized businesses, aren't glamorous and don't come with perks. A business's resources are best spent serving *customers*—not managers—and that involves deflating one's ego,* rolling up one's sleeves, and working with everyone in an organization's hierarchical structure. In this regard, management is not about you. It's about serving others.

I often tell anyone who'll listen that although managing a business isn't the easiest thing in the world to do, too many teachers and students try to make it as complex as brain surgery. Certainly management, like so many other tasks, can be made as complicated as you'd

---

*Winston Churchill was once asked if he was flattered by the size of the crowds that came to hear him speak. "Yes," he replied, "but then I remind myself that if I was being hanged the crowds would be twice as big."

like, but the truth of the matter is that it needn't be complex. Nor is it dry and boring. In most cases management is fascinating—or at least it should be. (It's based on the study of human nature for heaven's sake. Who among us isn't intrigued by money, influence, passion, achievement, success, failure, greed, good deeds, and similar emotions, attributes, and weaknesses?) What else besides management demands the successful maneuvering of the strengths and weaknesses of those who perform it alongside those being managed? What else besides romance, sport, and warfare constantly tries and tests an individual both personally and against others?

Suffice it to say that all these factors combined with planning, organizing, leading, and controlling is a tough, relentless, and time-consuming job that demands regular assessment, constant improvement, and the ability to give more than is taken. And that, in part, is what makes management so difficult to define—let alone do.

Chapter 2

A Brief History of Management

> Because before taking any journey, it's important to know where you've been, where you are, and which direction you're going.

Every day new technologies and innovations make our world a better place. Advancements on almost every front are being made at an astonishing rate. Yet when it comes to management, there isn't much that's new under the sun. If you traveled back in time thousands of years you'd probably be surprised to discover that we're really no more intelligent than our ancestors (i.e., our tools have changed, but human behavior hasn't). We live in a rather arrogant age in which too many people believe we have nothing to learn from the past. For a species that constantly relives its mistakes, this is a disturbing trend. Long before skyscrapers, multithousand-employee corporations, and the computer, people, not unlike us, built the great pyramids, the Great Wall of China, sailed the seas, explored the earth, and traded with far away lands. It took highly intelligent brains to do that.

Consider the pyramids, designed and built approximately 5,000 years ago by *people*—not a super human race of beings, not individuals anointed by Gods, and certainly not by alien intervention, but people—regular people who sat down, thought through, and carried out the entire process. Experts today concede that this monumental achievement, still unsurpassed today, was primarily the result of a well-managed, orderly system of volunteerism and rotating conscription. As proof of this, the ruins of medical facilities, housing areas, recreation grounds, kitchens, communal eating locations, and other remnants of a vibrant community project are scattered over the vast area surrounding the pyramids' bases. The general belief today is that it took 10,000 people twenty years to build the great pyramid—or perhaps 20,000 people ten years. Other sources state it took many more people and much more time. Either way, it took scores of competent managers to organize the stone cutters, labor crews, artists, and planners, as well as those who fed thousands of people every day, provided medical assistance, ran the housing areas, and so on. Force and fear alone cannot be attributed to the successful completion of such a massive project. Good management techniques had to be preeminent.

The same applies to the Great Wall of China, built thousands of years ago and still one of the only reported man-made objects (apart from light) observable on earth from space.

And what about the Romans? In their day the Romans conquered and governed most of Europe and parts of the Middle East and North Africa. After the Romans had conquered an area, the locals more often than not assimilated to the "enemy" way of life because the Roman lifestyle was much more advanced, better managed, and more comfortable than theirs.

The great cathedrals and artworks of Europe make for additional managerial examples. Take Michelangelo for example. It's been reported that when he died his house was virtually empty except for a bed alongside which stood a locked iron strongbox filled with today's equivalent of $8 million in gold coins. Did he acquire this breathtaking fortune from single-handedly sculpting and painting portraits? No. Michelangelo was an accomplished manager. When a work was commissioned (such as the Sistine Chapel, the Medici Chapel, or the Laurentian Library), he hired dozens, sometimes hundreds, of skilled workers, trained them to do exactly what he wanted, and kept meticulous employee timesheets and payment records. In fact, when he wasn't involved in his own personal artistry, much of Michelangelo's day was spent visiting and supervising his various project sites.

Then, after all of these accomplishments, in the course of numerous cycles of war, disease, religious intolerance, corruption, apathy, and famine, the managerial skills used to create the pyramids, the Greek temples, Rome, and most of the European masterpieces seemingly vanished—only to be reinvented by future generations in much the same way that concrete, formerly introduced by the Romans, had to be reinvented when it was needed again.

THE INDUSTRIAL REVOLUTION AND THE DIVISION OF LABOR

In 1776, economist Adam Smith, in his famed treatise, *The Wealth of Nations,* advocated that dividing labor into manageable stages would greatly improve a business's production. No doubt some former civilization had previously reaped the benefits of this simple idea, but Smith had the good sense to write it down and publish it. His proposal centered on the idea that ironworkers made approximately 10 to 200 pins per day when they worked individually. However, he argued, if these workers were split into separate units with each unit responsible for a specific task, around 48,000 pins could be produced (e.g., one man would keep the fire stoked, another would operate the molds, and a third would extract the cooled wire and pass it onto others who cut, shaped, and sharpened the wire into pins).

So began the industrial revolution.

Some one hundred years later, Samuel Colt reinvented division of labor processes to mass produce firearms. Fifty years after Colt, Henry Ford reinvented the division of labor process by applying it to the building of automobiles.

THE STUDY OF MANAGEMENT BEGINS

From 1776 onward, the study of management continued in fits and starts right up to the twentieth century, specifically, 1911, when industry really took off. At that time a man named Frederick Taylor published a book titled *The Principles of Scientific Management.*

Taylor was by most accounts a rigid, prickly, and highly religious man (he was both a Quaker and puritan) who firmly believed that most workers were inherently lazy. Unable to bide this, he made it his mission to rectify the situation. It should be noted that in this period of history, Taylor had a point. Workers tended to take as long as possible to complete a job and management usually consisted of on-the-spot decisions made by an untrained foreman. Little or no emphasis was made to match worker skills with the job at hand and any sense of personal responsibility was virtually nonexistent. Apart from trained craftsmen, unskilled workers had a reputation for caring little about their work.

In response, in 1901, at the Midvale Steel Company in Pennsylvania, using workers loading iron ore (in units that weighed ninety-two pounds each) into boxcars as his core project, Taylor began experimenting with his theories. On one day he had a worker (a man named Schmidt) use one type of tool to load the boxcars. On another day a different tool would be used. The following day, Taylor would tell Schmidt to walk while bending his knees. The next, he would be asked to keep his legs straight. On and on it went.

In the meantime, Taylor calculated the number of minutes it took Schmidt to perform each task as well as the total amount of iron ore he could load onto the trains. After much experimentation, Taylor concluded that there was one most effective method of loading boxcars. As he predicted, taking the time to figure this out resulted in a 400 percent increase in productivity! Word spread. By 1908 Harvard University declared Taylor's methods of scientific management to be the basis upon which all its business courses would be set. However, the ball didn't really start rolling until 1910. In that year the United States convened a court trial to determine why the country's railroad owners wanted to raise transport rates. During the subsequent hearings, a disciple of Taylor took the stand and testified that the railroads didn't need to raise their rates. Instead, if they employed scientific methods of management, they could save $1 million a day. This was an inconceivable amount of money at the turn of the twentieth century, and the gasp of astonishment that arose in the courtroom spread like wildfire across the United States, as well as overseas. The age of efficiency had begun.

THE EVOLUTION OF SCIENTIFIC MANAGEMENT

In the decades that followed, Taylor's work was examined, used, and enhanced by many others. Included in this frenzy is the work of Frank and Lillian Gilbreth. Early in their careers the Gilbreths attended one of Taylor's lectures and decided to join the cause. They were among the first to use motion pictures to study and improve human movement in the workplace, and they became famous for reducing the amount of motions necessary for laying bricks from eighteen to five, thereby tripling productivity. They also championed the development of specialized tools to improve worker performance.

Through their work the notion of scientific management continued to spread.

At about the same time, management studies began spiraling off into different areas. Whereas Frederick Taylor concentrated on mid- to bottom-level management, others began looking at top-level administration and management as a whole. Equally as important, the classification of management split into separate directions. For the sake of discussion, these two approaches can be considered the *administrative approach* (which views management as something akin to a caste system that focuses on tasks) and the *humanistic approach* (which envisions management as a means of motivating others to increase productivity).

The administrative approach had in its corner an academic named Max Weber (pronounced *vay-ber*). Writing in the early 1900s, Weber's idea of management involved a strict hierarchy of authority that he named **bureaucracy.** It's important to remember here that Weber conceived his theory in a different time and age than exists today. In part, bureaucracy was created as a means of eschewing nepotism and favoritism. Then, as now, these unfair practices denied too many people a place in the employment loop. Weber also realized that his ideas would probably never work in the real world—something few academics ever admit. Instead, his intention was for managers to focus on the positive aspects of bureaucracy (rationality, technical competence, authoritarianism, and impersonality) via the following practices:

- Jobs should be broken down into simple, routine, and well-defined tasks (division of labor).
- Offices and positions should be arranged in a hierarchical order.
- All managers and workers should be selected on the basis of their qualifications.
- Formal rules and regulations should be used to ensure uniformity and discipline.
- Rules and controls should be impersonal and applied uniformly.
- Managers should be hired from within.

Around this same period a man named Henri Fayol took a different approach. Unlike Weber, Fayol was an actual practitioner (he was the managing director of a coal mining firm) who developed a list of points designed to improve an organization's efficiency. He called them the fourteen universal truths or principles of management. They are as follows:

- Work should be divided into specializations (division of labor).
- Managers must have the authority to make **rules** and give orders.
- Employees must obey and respect these orders.
- Each employee should receive orders from only one superior.
- Each set of activities should be directed by one manager with one plan.
- The interests of one employee or employee group cannot take precedence over an **organization.**
- Workers must be paid a fair wage for the jobs they perform.
- A business must determine beforehand if employees can do a job on their own or if a managerial hierarchy is needed.
- Communication should follow a **chain of command.**
- People and materials should be in the correct place at the correct time (i.e., **planning** is essential).
- Managers should be kind and fair to their employees.
- A high rate of employee turnover is inefficient and should be avoided.
- Employees who are allowed to actively participate in the design and implementation of their work will work harder.
- Promoting team spirit will build harmony and unity within a business. (Fayol, 1916)

Today, many of these points seem so patently obvious that, again, it must be remembered that both Weber and Fayol were making bold statements for their time. Simply put, the industrializing world was ripe with the stench of inhumane practices—child labor and twelve-hour workdays being only two. Most employees lived and worked in appalling conditions and both Weber and Fayol, in their own distinct way, wanted to introduce improvements that benefited worker, manager, and business owner alike.

Other Movers and Shakers of Note

If Frederick Taylor can be called the "father of management," then Mary Parker Follet is almost certainly its mother. At the time of

World War I, when most workers were considered little more than uneducated servants, Follet, working out of Boston, preached the unpopular idea that employees were valuable assets who had the ability to add greatly to their work if their ideas and complaints were listened to. Her conclusion was that managers and workers should operate as a team. The result, she said, would be an increase in workplace harmony and productivity. At a time when most people thought workers should neither be seen nor heard, her thoughts were not welcomed with open arms.

Hugo Munsterberg is another management scientist worth mentioning. As early as 1913, Munsterberg recommended that businesses should adopt psychological testing as a means of selecting the best employee for a job. He also used testing to determine the best training methods and motivation techniques for use with employees. Nearly one hundred years later, many of Munsterberg's ideas, or variants of them, are still in use today.

Last on this list, Chester Barnard, then president of the New Jersey Bell Telephone Company, advocated in 1938 that businesses were social environments that not only had responsibilities to their workers but also to customers, communities, suppliers, investors, and other stakeholders. Again, at a time when most people viewed a business as the personal property of an owner with which he or she could do whatever he or she wanted, this was not a popular notion. Despite Barnard's teachings, the human element is today still taken for granted in most businesses.

PERHAPS THE MOST IMPORTANT STUDY OF ALL

Between 1924 and 1932, the Western Electric Company, operating out of their Hawthorne Works factory in Chicago, Illinois, began a series of revolutionary experiments. Hawthorne Studies, as they came to be called, began with the desire to discover what made employees more productive (the Hawthorne plant assembled telephone equipment and similar electrical components). Researchers began their experiments by trying to ascertain whether a connection existed between environment and productivity.

The first observations began with an increase in factory lighting. Several tests were conducted in which the brightness of the room was intensified. The conclusion was that brightening the workroom did indeed cause an increase in productivity. Incredibly, worker absences decreased as well. However, when researchers later turned down the lights they discovered that the same thing happened! Furthermore, as the lights were turned down lower, productivity continued to increase until it became so dark no one could see.

In another experiment, a silent person did nothing but sit and take notes in a room full of workers. Again, researchers watched in amazement as productivity increased and worker absences decreased.

In a third experiment the workers were told that if productivity increased their wages would increase proportionately. In other words, the harder each person worked, the more he or she would be paid. Astonishingly, productivity levels decreased.

Years later, it was determined that what had made the workers in the first two experiments more productive (and more apt to come to work) wasn't due to the amount of lighting or the act of being observed. Instead, the workers had been made to feel important, more secure, and in some ways more accepted by their company by taking part in the experiments. These factors made them work harder. The third experiment took longer to analyze. In the end, interviews with the employees concluded that because they were being paid more to produce more, a feeling was generated that perhaps management was trying to weed out slower workers. As a result, the employees had banded together when not being observed in order to come up with their own idea of what constituted a proper work output. That way, everyone could meet an agreed-upon target and no one would be reprimanded or fired. Money, that recreant, age-old, cure-all proved to be less of a motivator than job security.

Those Who Don't Study History Are Doomed to Repeat It

In the early 1990s, an American company bought a boiler factory in Warsaw, Poland. Armed with technology and the latest managerial practices the company set out to make their new acquisition more productive and cost efficient. In the process, just as in the Hawthorne experiments, factory employees were told that the harder they worked the more they would be paid. This concept usually worked in the United States so it was bound to work in a country where the average monthly paycheck was less than what most Americans made in a week. Right? Wrong! Productivity in the factory took a downward turn until, months later, someone took the time to get to know the employees and ask them what it was they most wanted from their job. Job security was their reply.

To Be Continued . . .

Although the Hawthorne Studies were instrumental in shattering the notion that employees are nothing more than servants who should be devoid of emotion, feeling, and the need to be respected—and should therefore be treated as such—many academics still see the studies as unscientific, flawed, inconclusive, and just plain dumb. The truth is that they opened the door to understanding that every workplace is unique, every group of people is unique, and every manager has his or her work cut out for him or her in determining what works best for business improvement. They also helped prove the old maxim "management seeks efficiency; workers seek motivation."

And so it continues today as managers and management researchers continue to take sides, denounce others, and disregard history when insisting that business success results only from one of the two age-old managerial categories: administrative or humanistic.

Chapter 3

The First Three Steps to Becoming a Good Manager

An ancient Chinese proverb suggests that a journey of a thousand miles begins with a single step. We're going to begin with three.

STEP 1: MIND-SET

Nothing occurs in a vacuum. In business, this means that above-average amounts of the following attributes are needed before anyone can become a good manager:

Ambition: an overwhelming desire to succeed
Commercial intellect: the ability to scan business environments for weaknesses, threats, and opportunities
Perseverance: being steadfast and consistent (not stubborn) with your goals no matter what happens
Resilience: the capacity to learn from mistakes, brush off adversity, and pull yourself together
The will to win: the commitment and dedication to make real sacrifices and come out on top rather than merely participate*

In other words, the first step toward becoming a good manager is to have a good attitude. How is a good attitude acquired? Much the way most achievements are accomplished: through practice and refinement. To be a good manager you have to want to successfully control

*The will to win is aptly depicted in modern-day, big-city marathons. Although thousands of people participate in these marathons, realistically only a dozen or so can expect to win. The others are happy to just finish the course. As a manager, it's not enough to finish the course. Each and every day a good manager must set out to win.

your life and its direction. It also helps to know and care about the industry you've chosen to enter. You should learn about its history as well as the heroes, villains, and everyday people who comprise it. You need to formulate an idea for where you and the industry want to go and establish a concept for the role you want to play. A successful attitude, if it's to grow at all, will come from these interests.

Many years ago I attended a seminar presented by a man widely regarded as one of the world's foremost authorities on throwing the javelin. Potbellied, chain-smoking, and possessing an astonishingly colorful vocabulary, this man looked as different from an athlete as anyone could possibly be. Indeed, during the question-and-answer session that followed, an attendee asked him point-blank how he had become such an expert.

"Well, I certainly didn't set out to be," he replied, "In fact, I'm a house painter and have never attended college. But when my son announced that he was taking up the sport, I decided to look into it. At that time I didn't know anything about the javelin so I read a couple of books. That led to attending seminars and contacting experts in the field—all of whom were quite keen on sharing their passion. One step led to another and before I knew it I was hooked. Years later, the words 'leading authority' were used in conjunction with my name. I guess it all comes down to the fact that instead of sitting on the sidelines I got interested. That led to getting involved, and once I got involved I didn't want to stop."

STEP 2: INTEGRITY

Simply put, good managers are honest people; they don't lie to others and they don't lie to themselves. It's been said that for every corporate crook there are at least ten corporate deceivers: people who fool themselves into thinking that situations are different from what they appear to be. Deception or dishonesty—call it what you want—either way, it constitutes bad management. Remember the corporate scandals of 2002 and the around-the-clock media coverage of dozens of disgraced companies? In a perverted desire to excel, the managers running these businesses somehow made conscious decisions that the ends were more important than the means. Greed and unchecked ambition became their measure of success. Ironically, before these scandals broke, many respected media outlets repeatedly told viewers and readers that these companies as well as their managers should be admired and emulated. Unfortunately, the people managing these highlighted businesses turned out to be nothing more than charlatans. In every conceivable way they lacked the stoic integrity and quiet pragmatism that good managers radiate.

As a former business practitioner I'm completely baffled whenever I see managers throwing honesty by the wayside. In business, honesty isn't an option; it's an imperative. If you don't think this is true ask yourself the following question: If I have a choice between doing business with an honest person (or business) or a dishonest one, which will I choose? The following story illustrates this point.

I once led a firm that oversaw approximately two dozen business sites scattered across a large Middle-Eastern city. One of these sites consisted of a cavernous building hired out to organizations for corporate affairs, art exhibits, fashion shows, product displays, children's programs, theater groups, film showings, and so forth. One day I was approached by a group of men interested in setting up a three-day trade show to kick off a new product line. I greeted them and gave them directions to the building's booking office.

"Thank you," they replied. One of the men then extended his arm and a brand new, wide-screen color television was pushed into my office.

"As a token of our appreciation," he said.

For several seconds I gazed at the television in amazement. "That's not necessary," I finally stammered.

The men stared back.

"Really, it's not necessary," I insisted. "If you want to book the exhibition hall all you need to do is put down a deposit."

The men glanced at each other, shrugged their shoulders, and left with the television.

Confused by this, I told my employees what had happened at the next staff meeting.

"You mean you didn't take the television?" they asked incredulously.

"Of course not," I replied.

They laughed. Apparently, my predecessors had all demanded gifts *in addition to a rental fee* as their regular way of conducting business. It suddenly became apparent why exhibition hall bookings were so difficult to procure. A few weeks later, a Persian rug seller also tried to give me a gift before renting out the hall, which I turned down as well. Two months passed before I was next approached, but this time it was under vastly different circumstances.

"Your cashier has informed us that there is a three-month waiting period for booking your exhibition hall," a visiting sales team said. "Unfortunately, we can't wait that long."

"Three months? That's impossible," I replied. I asked them to follow me to the office.

"What's going on?" I whispered to the cashier. "We can't afford to turn business away. For crying out loud, if these people want to book the building, do it."

"But sir," the cashier replied, "the building *is* fully booked for the next three months."

Stunned, I reached across her desk to check the calendar. Indeed, every available time slot was taken for the following twelve weeks. My head reeled with astonishment. "What's prompted this?" I mumbled.

"Word's gotten around that no one has to pay us a bribe anymore," she explained.

STEP 3: TRAINING

It's been said that the only situation in which one starts at the top is when digging a hole. In management, as with so many other career options, if one begins at the top with no experience that hole usually becomes the digger's grave. Training helps resolve problems of inadequacy and ignorance. Because the best indicator of future behavior is past behavior, and the road to good management is paved with past mistakes and failures, it is crucial to want to continuously learn and do better. The reason for doing so is not to draw up a plan so you can charge into the future, but to develop enough skills so that almost *any* plan can be put into action. One of the essentials in becoming a good manager is to be flexible and sustain the ability to rapidly take action. Only then can you handle almost anything the future may throw at you.

To put it differently, good managers, like good athletes, continuously hone their skills while carrying in their gut a desire to go for it. Good managers aren't interested in maintaining the status quo. They want to shake things up and seek out new opportunities—not in a sloppy, fanatical, all-out campaign that withers away after a few days or weeks—but rather in a series of actions that lead to small, achievable successes from which they and the people they manage can gather encouragement. Please note that this is not something that can happen overnight. It takes patience and much practice in

- dealing with others (motivating people and successfully playing politics);
- handling responsibility;
- wringing as much as possible out of a business's culture (working *within* an established system and knowing when and how to bend the rules without breaking the law, without being unethical, or without acting selfishly);
- establishing market share (ethically taking no prisoners) and looking ahead; and
- understanding, accepting, and *acting upon* the concept that a manager's duty is to serve others.

In essence, upon becoming a manager you learn that you've begun to have control over your work. Not all of it, but some of it. Through trial and error you learn that you *can* make a difference and that you *can* do things differently. Just as important, good managers must take into account the motivation and well-being of others—actions that don't come naturally in a world in which we're all fighting for our professional lives. A man that spent his life building a successful business once summed this up beautifully when asked how he had accomplished so much. "The way I look at it," he replied, "is that I didn't build this business. It built me."

I'll finish this chapter with an illustrative joke:

Two men run into each other thirty years after attending the same university. One is a college professor. The other is an extraordinarily wealthy businessman.

"How did you do it?" asked the professor. "Of all people, how in the world did you end up succeeding at business?"

"Well," replied the other man, "somewhere along the way I learned to buy things at one dollar and sell them for two dollars. And it's that one percent difference that's made me what I am today."

The point is that genius doesn't guarantee managerial success. More often than not it's attitude, integrity, and school-of-hard-knocks training that matters most.

Chapter 4

Understanding the Importance of Customers

In the summer of 2001, I began a new job as the general manager of a $15 million water park nearing completion in the Far East. Within a week of arriving I knew much work lay ahead. For instance, although the children's swimming area was designed for 400 occupants, I was told that only two lifeguards would be employed. "Two lifeguards is a start," I suggested to the woman who, up to this point, had been overseeing the project, "but two people watching over four hundred children is difficult to do on dry land. If water is added to the equation, there's an even greater risk of—"

The woman spun around as if she'd been slapped. "Hiring more lifeguards is not in the plan," she snapped.

We continued our tour in silence. Looking around, I noticed that the park, designed to accommodate 6,000 people, contained only three small food kiosks set up in short-order-cook style. A fourth operation was envisioned as a luxurious restaurant complete with linen tablecloths and uniformed waiters. The small area it encompassed could serve only fifty customers at a time. In a bid to be diplomatic I pointed out the many good things that were being done in the park before mentioning the food service issue. "Most people eat lunch around noontime, and with thousands of people in attendance that'll put a huge demand on the food kiosks," I said. "Maybe if the kiosks are redesigned in a fast-food-restaurant style we can resolve any problems before they occur."

"But we don't want fast food here," the woman interjected. Her eyes narrowed. "The people on this island don't eat hamburgers and french fries."

"No, no," I said, "I'm talking about a fast-food *setup*. The kiosks can serve anything customers wish. It just needs to be served quickly."

"But that's not what we want," she retorted.

I carefully mentioned a few more positive things before continuing. "In water parks," I said, "almost everyone is wearing a bathing suit. So is a restaurant with linen tablecloths and uniformed waiters our best option? With only fifty customers serviceable at any one time, not to mention the children running around—"

"But this type of restaurant is what our chairman wants," she explained.

"Of course the wants and needs of the chairman are important," I replied, "but at the end of the day everything a business does must be designed with its customers in mind."

She stared at me for ten long seconds before uttering the most astonishing words I've ever heard in my professional life. "That's no way to run a business," she snorted. "In a proper business, everything must come from the top down."

Needless to say, I didn't last long at the job. By the end of the month the woman had me kicked off the island and soon another general manager took my place. He lasted six months. Some time later I received an e-mail from the recreation director of a resort close to where the waterpark had opened. "The park is a complete disaster," he stated, "so much so that we've decided not to send our guests there." Another e-mail, from the liaison company that had set up my initial interview for the job, was even more specific. "No one has been paid, many people are angry, and the government is opening an investigation. To top it off, 'Mrs. X' [the woman who'd showed me around] has disappeared."

Fifteen years before accepting the waterpark job I worked for a fitness club that decided to change its billing operation to a direct debit format. At the time, direct debit was a new concept and most customers were reluctant to sign over authorization giving a business the right to automatically deduct monthly fees from their bank accounts. The manager, however, was adamant. One day a man came in to buy a year's membership for his son. As I began to explain our direct debit policy, he pulled out a wad of cash. "I'd like to pay with this if you don't mind," he said.

At that moment the club's manager walked by. "What are you doing?" he asked.

"I'm signing this man's son up," I said.

"Is everybody around here deaf?" he bellowed. "Payments can be made only by direct debit."

Of course the customer left. And so did I two months later. Not long after that the business collapsed. But I guess the manager had shown everyone who was boss.

LOSING TOUCH

What is it that causes so many otherwise intelligent people to lose sight of the fact that to make money and survive a business must focus on its customers? Perhaps this rather astonishing oversight can be attributed to *sensory adaptation*. **Sensory adaptation** is the human body's inclination to eventually ignore the stimulus of clothes, smells, eyeglasses, wristwatches, contact lenses, and almost anything else we need, get used to, and forget is there—until it's gone.

UNDERSTANDING EXTERNAL AND INTERNAL CUSTOMERS

Getting Back to Basics

According to Oakland (1993), a **customer** is everyone that an organization serves. Read this definition carefully because it includes *everyone* we come into contact with at work—not just the people whose money we take in exchange for a product or service. For reasons of clarity these people can be labeled as

external customers: those who buy a business's products and services, and

internal customers: those who are either employed by, use, or rely on the work of others within an organization (including suppliers, contractors, shareholders, the community in which the business is located, and other stakeholders).

Management 101

Lesson 1

The reason why external customers are important is because the money they exchange for goods and services pays for everything in the business (the taxes, bills, rent, salaries, materials, insurance, pensions, medical plans, equipment, and so on).

Lesson 2

The reason why internal customers (employees) are important is because without them business will not take place. Equally, *how internal customers are treated has a direct bearing on the way external customers are treated.* In other words, the basic responsibility of every person in any business is to serve everyone else. Think of the individuals within an organization as links in a chain. Now form a picture of a chain in your mind. Which link is the least important?

Lip Service versus Customer Service

External and internal customers are essential to every business. It doesn't take fancy schemes or dramatic expenses to win them over. Usually all that's needed is the human element: acknowledgment, respect, a smile, a listening ear, politeness, and honesty. Gimmicks, slogans, or the latest trendy management theory rarely amount to much when attracting or retaining customers.

Not long ago I stood in line at a library waiting to check out a book. Behind the counter a group of employees earnestly attended to their duties. In the background a phone rang incessantly while one employee organized books on a trolley, a second typed on a computer, and a third searched for something in a drawer. So I stood there, along with four other customers, waiting for these people to finish whatever it was they were doing in order to get some service. One customer simply wanted to return a book (there were no convenient after-hour book drops). Another was trying to herd her kids together. Behind me an old man glanced at his watch. You would have thought we were invisible. The puzzling thing is that this was the most well-staffed library I'd ever seen. Employees were literally all over the place. And above them all hung a yellowing sign that read: THE CUSTOMER IS #1.

When budget cuts hit this library, the result was predictable. The knee-jerk reaction to money loss in so many businesses is to cut staff. Rarely does *improving service to attract more customers* come into play. Doing so involves too much hard work. Instead, employees and training are eliminated from the budget and customer platitudes are nailed to the wall. Some of the more popular include

OUR CUSTOMERS ARE OUR FAMILY.
WE ARE CUSTOMER DRIVEN.
PEOPLE ARE OUR MOST IMPORTANT ASSET.
THE CUSTOMER IS ALWAYS RIGHT.
THE CUSTOMER IS KING.

The list is endless, yet, when you think of your own experiences as either an internal or external customer, how many times have you been subjected to rudeness, glued-on grins, unhappy repetitive responses, lies, or a generally uncaring or patronizing manner?

THE TEN COMMANDMENTS OF BUSINESS SUCCESS

One of the best examples in understanding the importance of customers was written by Graham Brooks, Managing Director of Dowman Car and Trucks in Stockport, England. His principles are difficult to contradict:

1. Customers are the most important people in our business.
2. Customers are not dependent on us; we are dependent on them.
3. Customers are not people with whom to argue or match wits.
4. Customers bring us their needs; it is our job to fill those needs.
5. Customers are not an interruption of work; they are the purpose of it.
6. Customers do us a favor when they call; we do not do them a favor by serving them.
7. Customers are part of our business; they are not outsiders.
8. Customers deserve the most courteous and attentive treatment we can give them.

9. Customers are the individuals who make it possible to pay our wages.
10. Customers are the lifeblood of this and every other business. (Scott, 1998)

Elementary Customer Mathematics (or Penny-Wise and Pound-Foolish)

Make no mistake, if customers are not happy with the service they're given they *will* take their business elsewhere. Studies show that a business can lose 20 percent of its external customers if its products are of poor quality, but 66 percent will be lost if the service itself is perceived as poor. Some estimates claim that it costs anywhere from five to ten times as much trying to attract new external customers than it costs to retain old ones. Also, keep in mind the costs of finding, hiring, and training internal customers (employees). I know many practitioners who quietly lament the fact that their companies spend a fortune finding and educating good people only to have them lured away by other businesses that appreciate them more. The message is clear: Winning over customers (both internal and external) is not only a necessity, it's an ongoing process requiring *regular* fine tuning and attention.

WHAT IS GOOD CUSTOMER SERVICE?

Profitable customer service begins with good ethics and includes truthful advertising, good phone etiquette, sincere attempts at quality, and *giving immediate attention*. In other words, it starts before the customer arrives at your business and continues long afterward. Everyone is ultimately responsible for creating a positive image. *No one is too busy to help*. No customer should be abandoned, or be made to feel abandoned, during or after they make contact with you. If you don't already know this then you need to memorize and practice it until it becomes second nature.

Dealing with Difficult Customers

Generally speaking, difficult customers are people whose cost of service outweighs what they generate in terms of revenue. Every business has them. Whether internal or external, there are several ways to treat difficult customers before taking the irrevocable step of showing them the door. When pride, the need to maintain dignity, or temper threaten to contaminate a customer relationship, a few proven tips may help diffuse the situation:

1. *Listen to the customer.* Don't just let the customer talk. *Listen.* The customer may have a valid point and is merely not presenting it appropriately. Don't interrupt and don't trivialize the problem. Instead, let the customer run out of steam.
2. *Remain calm.* Speak softly and directly. Lowering your voice almost always results in the person to whom you are speaking doing the same. Don't exacerbate the situation by becoming excited, matching wits, or trying to get the upper hand. Control the situation by controlling yourself. It's very difficult for difficult customers to play their "game" if the opposition refuses to play.
3. *Don't take any remarks or behavior personally.* Leave personal traits out of the situation. If you maintain your professionalism you will not lose dignity—no matter how much the other person is carrying on.
4. *Attempt to solve the problem.* Do not pass the buck by sending the customer away on a wild goose chase. The goal is to solve the problem quickly and directly. Remember that the customer may not know your organization's setup and may be frustrated because it's not obvious where to go for help.
5. *Apologize for any inconvenience and thank the customer.* Acknowledgement is a powerful tool for disarming aggression.

Something to Consider

If the importance of maintaining good, all-around customer service still hasn't sunk in, consider the story of Ray Kroc.

In the 1960s, Mr. Kroc was a salesman who sold milk-shake makers and other restaurant appliances. He became intrigued by a large order that a California customer made for milk-shake mixers and traveled across the country to find out why so many were needed. Ray thought that perhaps he could figure out why this customer needed more than the average number of mixers and use this reasoning to sell more mixers to other restaurants. The name of the restaurant he visited was called McDonald's (at the time a small chain of burger stands), and in no time at all Kroc became enamored of its simplified menu philosophy and the speed with which it served customers. As a result, he established such close relations (as a supplier) with the McDonald brothers that he was the first person they approached when they decided to sell their business and retire. The rest is history. Kroc took the ball and ran with it and McDonald's became what it is today. The moral of the story? It was good customer service, both internal and external, that provided the means of forming what eventually became one of the most successful businesses in the world.

THE FINAL WORD

In an age in which acquisitions, mergers, and artificially inflating the price of stocks can take center stage (thereby taking management's eye off the ball), it's crucial to remember that creating a product or service and selling it to customers forms the essence of what business is about. Therefore, the purpose of the manager is to serve others (i.e., find customers and keep them). Put another way, fancy gimmicks, glitz, underhandedness, sleight-of-hand tricks, and fiddling with statistics are no match (or substitute) for shoe leather and elbow grease when it comes to running a business. Nothing in a business supersedes paying customers—and employees are the people who serve paying customers. Interpreting business any other way is a complete and utter waste of time and resources. Period.

PART II: BASIC THOUGHTS ON AND THEORIES OF MANAGEMENT

Chapter 5

Management Competencies and Styles

Despite evidence to the contrary, many businesses are under the impression that good managers come only from within one industry. In other words, good hotel managers must come from the hotel industry, good retail managers must be trained in the retail trade, and so on. Although promoting from within is a noble and sometimes appropriate policy, doing so blindly without considering the talents and freshness that an outsider brings to a managerial job can lock an organization into a cyclical course that merely repeats its bad habits. The leisure industry for example (hotels in particular), is rife with this practice, which in some cases amounts to little more than managerial incest. The truth is that good managers can be competent in a variety of fields if they concentrate on two overriding factors: (1) the ability to get the most from employees, and (2) the needs and wants of customers.

Many years ago, British Airways suffered from one of the worst reputations in the airline industry. For the most part this notoriety was attributed to poor service. Desperate to make improvements, the company's chairman decided a radical change was in order. Shock waves resulted as the former head of an American rental car agency was named as British Airways' new CEO.

"Ridiculous!" screamed the critics. "Ludicrous!"

But British Airways was soon on the mend and eventually found itself at or near the top of several "World's Best Airlines" lists (it has since run into other difficulties, but that's another story). Bear in mind that before this turnaround occurred most airline CEO's were either former pilots or had worked in the flight industry all of their lives. But British Airways' new CEO didn't have a pilot's license or indeed any aviation experience. Apparently, British Airways thought there were enough people in the company who could advise him on things of that nature. Instead, his strengths lay in being competent, which was just what the airline needed.

MANAGERIAL COMPETENCIES

Competencies in management can more or less be classified into the following two categories:

1. General management skills:
   - *Conceptual skills:* the ability to comprehend complex situations
   - *Interpersonal skills:* the ability to work with, understand, and motivate other people
   - *Political skills:* the ability to network as well as gain allies and gather power
   - *Technical skills:* the ability to understand and apply specialized knowledge or expertise
2. Specific management skills:
   - *Exercising good judgment:* the ability to plan and prepare for the future, respond to change, be held accountable for decisions made, and stay focused on objectives
   - *Organizing and coordinating:* the ability to organize tasks and their interdependent relationships
   - *Handling information:* using and communicating information
   - *Fostering personal growth and development:* encouraging both managers and employees to increase their knowledge and better themselves personally and professionally
   - *Handling conflict:* understanding the need for, and potential destructive force of, conflict

Take a look at the two lists again. Note that the emphasis of good management is placed on what a manager can *do* rather than what a manager knows. Yes, having specific expertise is often a precious commodity. But a good manager doesn't need to have a higher grade point average or more industrial experience than his or her subordinates. The ability to serve others, produce results, and get employees to do the same is what matters most.

Another Primary Managerial Skill: Keeping Costs Down

Cutting costs refers to the practice of constantly striving to reduce a business's costs and using resources sparingly *without sacrificing quality.* From a manager's standpoint, the reason behind this is to create an atmosphere in which waste and excess are considered unacceptable. Wal-Mart is a good example of this practice. For instance, I've been told that it is Wal-Mart's policy to not provide its store managers with offices. Instead, every store's administrative staff shares a common work area. The absence of an office ensures that store managers walk the floor in a constant state of vigilance to ensure that everything is running smoothly. Just as important, eliminating offices keeps costs down. For the same reason no Wal-Mart manager can authorize payments above petty cash limits without first seeking approval from head office. It's also been reported that Wal-Mart managers are encouraged to take away free pens and other freebies when participating in training seminars and workshops. "For every dollar we save," the company keeps reminding its employees, "so too will our customers." Although such stringent measures might be considered draconian in other businesses, the clear message Wal-Mart sends out is that cutting costs is everyone's job. Perhaps a better way to successfully apply this concept is to make cutting *waste* a priority before hacking away at costs—costs that should have been kept to a minimum in the first place. Cutting too many costs almost always leads to a reduction in quality somewhere along the line, and that's just the tip of the iceberg. For an excellent article on how an obsession with cutting costs can lead to all sorts of "knock-on effect" problems, including company closures, job losses, and more, read the article "The Wal-Mart You Don't Know" by Charles Fishman (2003).

MANAGERIAL STYLES

How Does a Manager Obtain Results?

For many managers power is mostly wielded through trial and error. The style that worked best in the past is then dragged out and used again and again. There are probably as many management styles as there are streets in New York. Acclaimed management researcher Charles Handy has condensed the lion's share of these styles into six methods of influence:

1. *Force:* This is the crudest method. It is derived from pure authority and can range from outright threats to bullying.
2. *Rules and Procedures:* Setting down concrete rules and guidelines that everyone must follow is a time-honored way to control others. This is often the favored method of bureaucracies.
3. *Exchange:* Bargaining, negotiating, cajoling, and bribery fall under this category. Promotions, pay increases (bonuses), rewards, and recognition are more subtle examples.
4. *Persuasion:* This is usually the first method of choice. However, as Handy suggests, in practice it's usually contaminated by one of the other methods.
5. *Ecology:* This occurs when a manager uses his or her surroundings to exercise influence. The use of a crisis is a good example. (A colleague once relayed to me that in every job, most managers have three power-holding ecological moments: [1] when negotiating a contract, [2] during the first six months of employment, [3] during any moment of crisis.)
6. *Magnetism:* Sometimes witnessed in its abuse stages by salespeople, faith healers, religious fundamentalists, and so on. Personal charisma and obtaining followers are the keys to magnetism. (Handy, 1993)

One of the biggest dilemmas managers face is when to use these styles (or a variant thereof) to maximum benefit. Unfortunately, all succesful solutions are relative to the people involved and the situation encountered. What works for one manager may or may not work for another. What works one day may not work another. Therefore, instead of trying to establish a management cure-all (which doesn't exist), an emphasis should be placed on managers' choices and the consequences of those choices. For example:

- Using force or fear may achieve immediate results, but the results could be short-lived and lead to high employee turnover.
- Rules and procedures can effectively control behavior, but may drain a workplace of creativity, spontaneity, and morale.

- The exchange method can prove to be a good motivator, but can lead to problems when everyone expects some type of reward in exchange for doing a task. The result can be expensive, time consuming, and produce a lack of respect for management.
- With excessive use of the ecology method, managers might be seen as opportunistic or conniving.
- As for magnetism, well, as the expression goes, you can fool some of the people some of the time . . . but not all of the people all of the time.

So Which Style Is Best and When?

Management style theories tend to ebb and flow like tides, but one of the best (and one that I have personally used to great effectiveness) is known by the acronym MBWA (**m**anagement **b**y **w**alking **a**round). The idea behind MBWA is simple: to reduce the distance between manager and employee and strengthen the relationship (and understanding) between them. Just as the name suggests, MBWA demands that a manager get out of the office and walk around the shop floor. As acclaimed management consultant Richard Pascale explains, the point is not to interfere with employees but to draw management into reality (or, as he puts it, *get grounded*). Too often management lives and operates within its own perceptions of what is right or wrong rather than in what is real. The result manifests itself into various forms of misunderstanding, miscommunication, anger, and resentment. However, when contact between a manager and an employee is void of fear and apprehension, communication is strengthened. The result for the manager is a clearer understanding of what best motivates the employee, thereby suggesting a style of management that best suits the situation.

MBWA has other positive effects. It tends to reduce managerial arrogance as well as generate experience in influencing others. Not surprisingly, it's difficult to remain a liar or a control freak when face to face with employees every day. In addition, MBWA allows managers to see firsthand what's happening in their businesses without having it **filtered** by someone else. If what is seen is far enough out of line with what was previously believed, then management will be forced to update its thinking. That's when progress is made. Bear in mind that MBWA is not designed as a means of looking over employee's shoulders or becoming "the man who came to dinner." The idea is to facilitate cohesiveness, communication, cooperation, and improvement, and produce results.

TO RECAP

Good managers can be competent in a variety of fields if they posses above-average skills in (1) getting the most from employees, and (2) identifying (and acting upon) the needs and wants of internal and external customers. How a manager decides to handle this balancing act will result in a style or styles that greatly affect the business, the employees involved, and, most important, the paying customer.

Chapter 6

Getting the Most from Employees

In the About the Author on page *vi* of this book, much is made about the fact that I turned around three businesses. The statement is accurate, but in each of these businesses I probably came up with only a half dozen solutions to the seemingly infinite number of problems that were faced. The staff conceived the remaining ones. Yes, you read correctly—the *employees* had more to do with these business turnarounds than I did. As their manager I merely let them succeed—something none of my predecessors had allowed. Mind you, it took months to train these employees to be responsible (and brave) enough to solve their own work challenges, but after that mountain was climbed, situations improved in leaps and bounds. Simply put, as a manager I did not have a monopoly on intellect.

TAPPING INTO THE WORKFORCE

"Many hands make light work" says a popular proverb and the same can be said about many brains. Let's use a factory as an example. If employees are asked to clean and provide basic maintenance to their workstations on Mondays and Thursdays, they'll probably clean and provide basic maintenance to their workstations on Mondays and Thursdays. If a large order comes in on Tuesday and workstations become untidy, employees may wait until Thursday before attending to them. However, if they're told that *they alone are responsible* for ensuring that their workstations are *always* clean and well maintained, something different happens. By leaving the job up to the employees, their expertise and judgment has been applied.

Since most organizations are comprised of a number of employees, there are bound to be several interpretations of what constitutes an orderly workstation. Therefore the solution to ensuring that workstations remain appropriately clean and properly maintained depends on the organized transition of responsibility, outlined as follows:

Workstation Example	*Transitional Steps*
Informing employees of exactly what needs to be done	Creation of responsibility
Providing employees with relevant information	Training
Discussing with employees how they are to achieve their objective	Establishing work perimeters
Giving employees the tools necessary to accomplish their objective	Handing over authority
Reviewing the results	Enforcing accountability

Is it important to judge the method an employee uses to carry out a task? In certain cases yes—certain procedures must be followed due to safety and other factors. Otherwise, no. It's sometimes pointless to compare what an employee does with what a manager would have done in similar circumstances. In most cases a *result* is more important and should suit the task's purpose. In other words, if the solution is not contingent upon the process then the talents and abilities of employees should be left to their own accord. This is more than just a philosophical argument. If the right people were hired, trained accordingly, and provided with whatever is necessary to complete their jobs, then managers need to be extracting as much from these people as they can. The word for this is **delegation**.

DELEGATING RESPONSIBILITY

Delegation involves transferring a manager's decision-making authority and ability to act to a subordinate. The point is to get something done by someone else. This does not simply translate into assigning someone else to do a task. Delegation usually also allows employees to choose and implement *how* that task will be done. In doing so, an extraordinary sense of achievement is created. Delegation lets employees show the world what they are capable of accomplishing. Again, if the right people were hired to begin with then quite a lot should be accomplished.

To Delegate or Not to Delegate?

For most managers, delegation is not a choice. Most managers simply have more work than one person can be expected to perform. Thus the question is not whether one *should* delegate but *how.* Figuring out how can be quite intimidating. Perhaps the intimidation comes about when one imagines the negative consequence that can occur if an employee screws up a delegated task.

Taking the Fear Out of Delegation

As with most management subjects, the challenge behind delegation lies in its implementation. Many years ago I worked with a man who said that his father tried to teach him to swim by dragging him to a lake and throwing him in. He ended up thrashing around in the water before he was finally rescued. Ridiculous? Yes. But for many managers this "sink or swim" philosophy represents the very essence of how they delegate.

Another impedance to proper delegation is insecurity. Insecure managers don't trust others and often try and do everything themselves while complaining (or bragging) that they're overworked. Again, the result is that employees aren't used to their full potential. Here are some typical arguments used to avoid delegating:

Myth 1: Delegation undermines a manager's position. Some managers believe that if tasks are routinely delegated to employees the employees will gain experience and skills, which will eventually enable them to steal their manager's job.

The Reality: Good managers bolster their reputation and effectiveness by developing the people below them. Managers don't usually lose their jobs because they find and develop good people.

Myth 2: Because a manager is ultimately responsible for every delegated task, it's easier and safer for most managers to do everything they're responsible for themselves.

The Reality: A manager's time is limited. It's not possible for managers to do by themselves everything they're responsible for. Therefore, certain tasks and responsibilities *must* be handed to others.

Myth 3: A manager gives up power when delegating, thereby decreasing his or her effectiveness and authority.

The Reality: Delegation increases a manager's influence among employees. This enables most managers to widen their span of control, usually resulting in an increase in their powerbase.

Myth 4: Delegation demoralizes employees because most managers delegate the most boring tasks to their subordinates and leave the best stuff for themselves.

The Reality: Ironically, the fun tasks are usually the easiest to delegate. Besides, if managers chose to only do the fun things they wouldn't also be able to perform the tasks for which they alone are responsible.

Putting It All Together

Delegation need not be a fearful process. Using the following twelve steps should help eliminate most pitfalls:

1. *Don't assign duties because you don't want to perform them.* This includes managerial functions such as providing feedback, reprimanding, hiring and firing, training, motivating, handling sensitive issues, team-building, and so on.
2. *Clarify the assignment before it's delegated.* Determine what is being delegated, the results expected, and any time limitations. Again, unless specific methods must be adhered to, concentrate on the end results the employee must achieve instead of the means of doing so.
3. *Choose the right person for the right job.* Ensure that the employees have the time and motivation to complete it. Delegation, by its very nature, is designed to provide opportunities—not teach employees a lesson or put them in their place.

Know who is ready to handle more responsibility as well as how hard this person can be pushed.

4. *Determine work perimeters.* Let employees know *exactly* what they can and cannot do as well as what will make their job easier and any potentially damaging avenues they should avoid.
5. *Make delegation a gradual process by giving employees time to gain confidence.* The key is to provide employees with enough rope to be constructive without having them hang themselves. Ask yourself this: Can the task be done in stages?
6. *Discuss the tasks with the employees.* Allow employees to participate in discussions concerning what they are expected to do, how much authority they have, and by which standards they'll be judged. That way there will be fewer surprises in the end for both parties.
7. *Inform others about the delegation.* Failure to inform other employees of an impending delegation increases the likelihood of conflict and decreases the chance that the delegated task will be done efficiently.
8. *Allow the employees to make as many decisions as possible.* Unless your decisions are significantly better than the employees', let them use their own. Doing so is highly rewarding and deeply motivating for employees.
9. *Expect a mistake or two.* With appropriate monitoring you should be able to catch mistakes before they get out of hand. Remember that mistakes are a part of every learning process and tend to show at the very least that something is being done.
10. *Establish feedback controls.* Regular monitoring will help identify important problems or expensive mistakes at an early stage. Keep your office door open, but don't let this become a situation in which the employee is made to feel a constant, overshadowing presence. Let the employee know that help is available if needed or additional information/training is required (the catchy phrase for this is, "delegate don't abdicate").
11. *When problems arise, insist on solutions.* Along with ensuring that the employee does not feel abandoned, it is equally important that he or she does not keep running back to you with

each and every problem encountered. Insist that whenever a problem arises, the employee come to you with possible solutions rather than just the problem.

12. *Review results and reward good performance.* Let the employee know how he or she is doing. Praise any progress and politely address any setbacks. More often than not, people hunger for the chance to show how much they can accomplish. After employees have successfully completed a delegated task, act appropriately so that you can continue to get the most from your employees and ensure that they'll keep coming back for more.

THE EMPLOYEE-CUSTOMER CONNECTION

In the 1970s and early 1980s, the American car industry was in a crisis. How was an industry virtually invented by Americans brought to its knees? It's partly because when a rise in inflation and oil prices occured that dealt a massive one-two punch to every motor industry in the world, the administrators at the helm of the American car companies put their finance people in the driver's seat. Once the bean counters took control, they did their jobs wonderfully. Stopping financial losses became not only the end desire but also the means to achieving that end. Jobs were eliminated, production methods were squeezed, purchasing costs were reduced, new projects were canceled—everything was looked at through a microscope except the most important issue of all: what customers wanted in a car. However, the accountants can't be blamed. They did what they were supposed to do. They avoided risk. Accountants are supposed to steer a company away from all the attributes that can't be worked into a calculator. Intangibles such as innovation, style, and value were thrown to the wayside because they didn't fit into a ledger book. Time went by and employee morale decreased as the heart and spirit essential to manufacturing automobiles was smothered by the risk-free, concrete inflexibility of a finance company. Financial targets took priority and no one would listen to what those on the front lines (the dealers) had to say. Yet it was the car dealers who knew exactly what paying customers wanted, and who would eventually save the day.

Back to Basics (Again): Who's Most Important?

If external (paying) customers are the lifeblood of every business, then internal customers (employees) are its brain and muscle. Employees are the people who carry out the activities that make up an organization and ultimately determine a company's direction. Yet, before employees can, or will, work together, some sense of order and discipline must be established. Traditionally, this includes formulating a business **hierarchical pyramid** (see Figure 6.1).

The problem with this view, however, is that there's no room for external customers. It can probably be assumed that they're languishing somewhere below service-level employees. What would happen if a different approach were taken? What if management inverted this pyramid so that paying customers become the most important element? (See Figure 6.2.)

Showing a pyramid-shaped organizational chart from this perspective graphically displays the importance of the often disregarded service-level employee. In terms of who works for whom, it demonstrates that the group at the bottom should focus on providing for the group above. Every employee therefore shares a common purpose: to

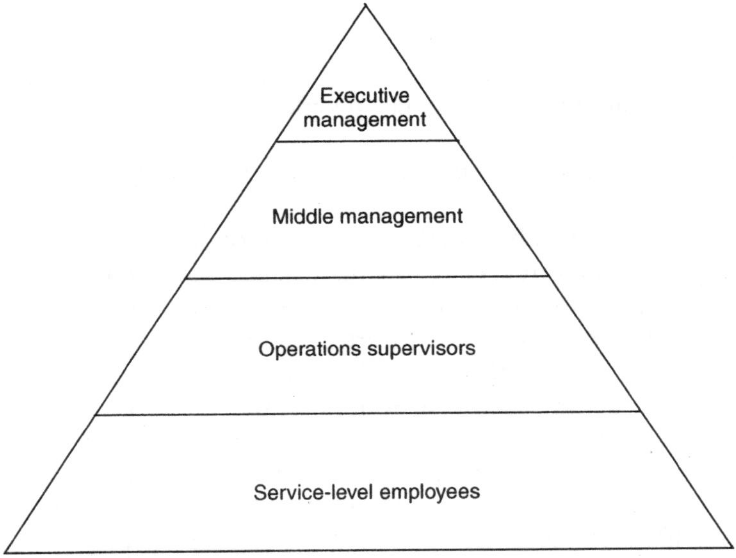

FIGURE 6.1. Traditional Business Hierarchical Pyramid

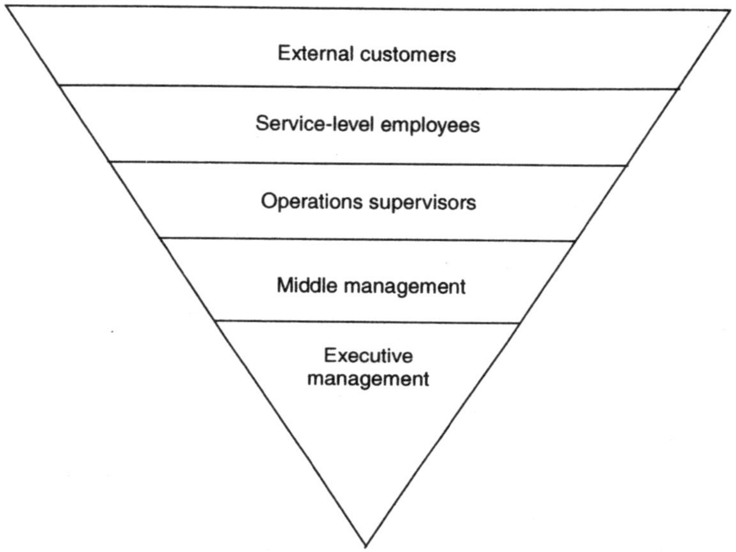

FIGURE 6.2. Inverted (or Customer-Oriented) Business Hierarchical Pyramid

work together to serve and satisfy his or her customers (a lesson lost on the car manufacturers' finance people).

Looking After Your People So That They'll Look After You

There's no doubt about it, the security, emotions, and well-being of employees have a direct effect on the service given to paying customers. Motivating employees becomes more difficult as employee numbers increase. Accepting the inverted hierarchical pyramid and the previously explained principles behind delegation are the first important steps in getting the most from employees, but they're only the first of many. In most organizations, different departments are constantly battling over territory. Each department is confident that their input and sense of direction is the most valid (as the finance people thought in the car industry). Within these departments, ambitious individuals are doing much the same thing. In fact, one of the greatest challenges of management lies in understanding that people are motivated for their *own* reasons, not a manager's reasons. In other words, ideas, rules, and regulations cannot be implemented unless the employees who must work with them *will* work with them. Thus, it is dependent on managers to provide employees with incentives for self-motivation. Years ago (and still today) this could be accomplished through fear. However, a better method is to go beyond delegation by allowing employees to make their own decisions and to some degree control their own destinations. This doesn't mean that everyone is allowed to go off in different directions. Strong leadership must be shown and it must be emphasized that employees will face the rewards or consequences of whatever they choose to do.

EMPLOYEE EMPOWERMENT

Transferring *ongoing* job-related authority and responsibility from management to workers is the way to **employee empowerment.** Similar to delegation, it's primarily done to motivate employees by allowing them to develop their own self-worth and, to some degree, operate with **autonomy.** The purpose of employee empowerment is to keep a company customer driven. First, management must start the process by (1) establishing clear, uncontested goals and guidelines, and (2) accepting that someone gaining power does not mean that someone else has to give it up.

Empowerment in Action

In Brazil, a country wracked by severe economic problems, one company keeps chugging along. Its name is Semco and it produces (among other things) turnkey biscuit factories, giant marine pumps, and industrial mixers that blend everything from rocket fuel to bubble gum. Before it acquired its fame, Semco suffered the usual rundown of corporate problems. Only after collapsing twice from stress-induced illnesses did CEO Ricardo Semler realize that something radical had to be done. In his book *Maverick* he describes how, over a period of several years, he gradually handed over his power and authority to company employees. This included allowing machine operators to lease Semco's expensive tools and machinery for their own purposes as well as assisting skilled employees to use the company's equipment and materials to set up their own businesses. Company executives at first derided this decision, predicting that chaos—or worse—would ensue. Semler thought differently. He began by teaching his workers accounting. This brought many to the previously inconceivable conclusion that the company's profits did not go straight into the bank accounts of top managers. They also learned to make their own decisions, quickly realizing that everyone ultimately benefited when the company did. Thus, workers were assured of job security if they prudently solved their own problems, cut waste, increased quality and production, worked together as a team, and weeded out laggards. Incredibly, employees grew so adept at this they eventually set their own salaries! In effect they had become the caretakers of the company that employed them and they alone became accountable for its success. Put simply, given a choice between success and failure, they chose success. Give a man a fish, suggests an age-old philosophy, and he has a meal. Teach him how to fish, and he will feed himself for the rest of his life.

Making Empowerment Work for You

How does a manager introduce the concept of empowerment? Obviously it doesn't happen overnight. It's a long process that demands strong leadership, honesty, cooperation, courage, and a commitment to serve. It necessitates cooperation from all involved as well.

For nonmanagers, empowerment means

- learning to take and handle responsibility (*warning:* be aware that some employees don't enjoy responsibility and prefer the safety of dead-end jobs);
- realizing that constant learning and training are a part of every job;
- understanding that the ownership of problems and solutions belongs to everyone in the business (i.e., problem prevention and work ownership);
- accepting that everyone needs to pull in the same direction (i.e., serve others);
- showing up for work and performing bottom-line duties is not enough—wages are given for value created; and
- displaying caring, integrity, and trust.

For managers, empowerment involves

- viewing workers as assets (not expenditures) and recognizing their value;
- sharing information and providing good training;
- listening, asking, valuing, and then acting on other's viewpoints and ideas;
- creating a motivating environment conducive to creativity, participation, and innovation;
- working toward preventing problems—not just battling them;
- rewarding good performance;
- displaying caring, integrity, and trust;
- prudently choosing the right people for the right jobs; and
- ensuring that employees and departments serve each other (pull in the same direction).

Another, Simpler Example

Years ago, a well-known retail operation in the United States watched its sales plummet. Managers blamed it on the faltering economy, yet in the same area of the country another retail operation prospered. Investigations later revealed that the first retailer used an employee manual the size and thickness of a phone book. In militant detail it dictated to employees how to think, dress, behave, and carry out their duties. The second retailer had a different approach. Its employee manual is written on a single 5 × 8 inch card that reads:

Welcome to Our Company. We're glad to have you with us.
Our number one goal is to *provide outstanding customer service.*
Set your personal and professional goals high; we have great confidence in your abilities.

Our Rules:

Rule 1. Use your good judgment in all situations.

There will be no additional rules.
(Please feel free to approach the department manager, store manager, or division manager if you have any questions at any time.)

If you're still not convinced that empowerment works, ask yourself the following questions: (1) Which of these companies would you rather work for, the first or the second? and (2) Do you think that allowing employees to use their own judgment means that management has lost control, or gained it?

SUMMARY

Delegation involves assigning an employee a specific responsibility and having that person use his or her talents to successfully complete it. In other words, delegation is task related. Empowerment goes beyond that. Empowerment is an ongoing process that involves the *complete* transfer of job-related authority and responsibility from managers to workers. With delegation there is a foreseeable end to an assigned task. Empowerment has no end. Once a goal (such as providing 100 percent satisfaction to customers) has been established, it's up to the employee to march toward it and keep marching toward it. Both *delegation and empowerment are designed to motivate employees* by allowing them to show others what they can do, to be creative, and seek out their own sense of fulfillment. However the onus is upon the manager to set the stage for success by taking these steps:

1. *Assigning responsibility.* Explain exactly what needs to be done as well as any work perimeters.
2. *Granting authority to act.* Spend money, direct the work of others, use resources, and so on.
3. *Creating accountability.* Have the worker agree to become directly obligated to the task as well as be responsible for any outcomes and performance results.
4. *Not abandoning (or abdicating) his/her position.* Management's office door is kept open to any problems, concerns, or needs.
5. *Maintaining trust.* Like freedom, once empowerment has been bestowed upon people it cannot be taken away without repercussions. When employees have shown that they can handle responsibility they should be congratulated and directed toward other endeavors. Only then can a manager truly begin to
   - reduce his or her workload,
   - tap into the company workforce,
   - create an atmosphere of problem prevention and personal responsibility (work ownership), and
   - provide the ultimate in human motivation.

Chapter 7

Organizational Structures and Cultures

BUREAUCRATIC AND ADAPTIVE ORGANIZATIONS

Organizational structure refers to how a firm is organized. In graphic terms, this means how the chain of command is arranged in a hierarchical pyramid. Diagramming a business in this manner shows how its entities are tied together and, in part, how information moves (or doesn't move) within it. Generally speaking, there are two kinds of business structures: **bureaucratic** (or mechanistic) **organizations** and **adaptive** (or organic) **organizations**. Bureaucratic (mechanistic) organizations thrive in stable environments. Adaptive (organic) organizations do best in dynamic or rapidly changing environments.

Figure 7.1. dramatically illustrates why the process of going from a bureaucratic organizational structure to an adaptive one—as most current management trends are designed to do—is often referred to as *flattening* an organization. Flat organizations have fewer layers of management that are replaced by autonomous (empowered) employees. Fewer managers and fewer chain-of-command restrictions create an environment that increases managerial responsibility. The idea behind creating an organization such as this is twofold: (1) autonomous employees can react to changes in the marketplace faster when fewer managers, fewer piles of paperwork, and fewer rules and regulations stand in their way; and (2) flat organizations bring managers (and everyone else) closer to their customers. Figure 7.2 showcases the differences between bureaucratic and adaptive organizations.

Which organizational structure is best? That depends on a business's nature and needs. The ultimate purpose of organizational design is to put into place a structure that enables the implementation and achievement of key goals and objectives. Some employees enjoy the safe, slow pace, the comfort of rules and regulations, and the from-the-top-down authority of bureaucracies (probably because bu-

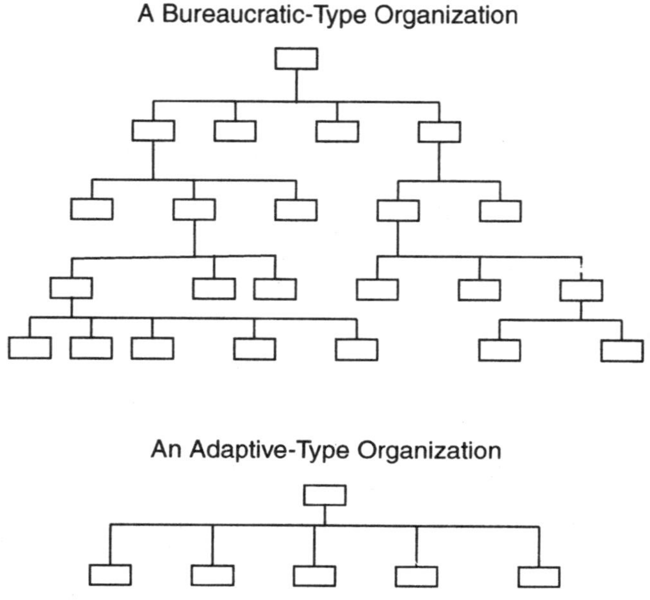

FIGURE 7.1. Comparison of Bureaucratic and Adaptive Organization Diagrams

reaucracies discourage risk or performance above the norm). Others thrive on the freedom, constant changes, and ability to make decisions inherent in adaptive organizations. Many business practitioners (and academics) advocate the flexibility and speed inherent in adaptive organizational structures.

The IBM Story

Business tales are notorious for being so full of hyperbole that it's often difficult to separate fact from fiction, but the lessons they generate are usually reason enough to repeat them. One case in point, and a good way to bring to life the importance of organizational structure and culture, is the story behind how IBM, who invented the first office computer, developed its first personal computer for use at home.

Prior to the development of the world's first personal computer (PC), IBM was a large and powerful corporation. Affectionately referred to as "Big Blue," it dominated the international business ma-

Bureaucratic organizations (mechanistic design)				*Adaptive organizations* (organic design)
Centralized (power comes from the top)	⟵	**Authority**	⟶	Decentralized (employee empowerment)
Many	⟵	**Rules and procedures**	⟶	Few
Small	⟵	**Span of control** (the number of people reporting to a manager)	⟶	Large
Specialized	⟵	**Tasks**	⟶	Shared
Few	⟵	**Teams and task forces**	⟶	Many
Formal and impersonal	⟵	**Coordination**	⟶	Informal and personal

FIGURE 7.2. Bureaucratic and Adaptive Organization Policy Spectrum (*Source:* Adapted from Burns and Stalker [1994]. *The Management of Innovation*. Oxford: Oxford University Press.)

chine market. Yet when the personal computer was invented and began demonstrating its potential, IBM famously decided to ignore this "fad" and stick to manufacturing typewriters, calculators, and adding machines. In fact many years earlier the CEO of IBM had publicly proclaimed that computers were a dead-end market because the world would only ever need five or six of them! Of course by the time IBM realized this wasn't the case, it was too late. Like a giant ocean liner the IBM bureaucracy was so intransigent and colossal (for instance, a great deal of effort was spent enforcing a strict dress and behavioral code) it simply couldn't change its course quickly. As a result, dozens of smaller companies sprang up, each taking advantage of the rapidly expanding home-computer market.

In desperation, IBM's top administrators gathered together a team of the company's best people and sent them to Florida to design a marketable home computer. As legend has it, freed from the company's binding bureaucracy, they designed the IBM personal computer in record time. Unfortunately, when these people returned to their posts they were once again chained to the same unyielding rules and procedures that had prevented IBM from developing a home computer in the first place. As a result, every one of them quit the company within a year. IBM did, of course, survive thanks to its new PC, but by then too many competitors had entered the market and as a result it never regained the reputation or market share it once enjoyed. It has since dedicated itself to becoming flatter.

ORGANIZATIONAL CULTURES

In continuing with the theme of organizational structure, it's important to note that every business also has its own unique culture, which dictates to some degree, either by rule or example, the way the business is organized, how people think, and how things are done. This is called **organizational culture**. The culture a business practices is defined as a system of shared values held by an organization that distinguishes its methods of operation from others. These methods include the following:

- *Innovation and risk taking:* the level to which employees are encouraged to take risks and/or do new things

- *Attention to detail:* the degree to which employees are expected to exhibit precision and/or analysis in their work
- *Outcome orientation:* whether management focuses more on results and outcomes or on the techniques and processes to achieve those outcomes
- *People orientation:* the importance the organization places on its people
- *Team organization:* the degree to which an emphasis is placed on teams rather than individuals
- *Aggressiveness:* the level of "hunger" and competitiveness that exists within the organization
- *Stability:* the emphasis placed on maintaining the status quo in contrast to growth

Subcultures

In many organizations, usually larger ones, there also exist **subcultures.** These are found in different departments, branches, and/or work groups. Subcultures operate similar to organizational cultures but on a smaller scale. For example, the precision and formality of an accounting department usually induces operating under a stricter system than the looseness, innovation, and creativity needed in a product design department. To accomplish their goals and develop their people, each department must establish its own distinct rules and procedures (culture) in order to facilitate success.

Cultural Classifications

There are probably as many different organizational cultures as there are organizations, but in 1972, management researcher Roger Harrison identified four distinct types. Again, the type of culture a business establishes should be contingent upon the product or service it offers and what it hopes to achieve. Harrison's designations are as follows:

1. The *power culture* is based on key individuals who generate control from their center. There are few rules and little bureaucracy. Power cultures can move quickly and react well (if they are inclined to); however, if key individuals are removed the or-

ganization is extremely vulnerable to collapse. (Examples of this include companies with celebrity CEOs, companies for which the CEO either invented or innovated the product, or, in general, any company in which the CEO has high levels of control.)

2. The *role culture* is rigid and formal, often stereotyped as bureaucracy, although not always in its negative sense. Coordination is maintained by a narrow band of senior management. Performance above and beyond the established guidelines is not needed. Personal power is frowned upon. Rules and procedures are the major methods of influence. (Examples of this include the military, government, and large corporations.)
3. The *task culture* is project oriented. The emphasis is on getting the job done. Attention is given to skills, and to putting the right people in the right job and letting them get on with it. Task cultures are results-oriented and usually very adaptable. They tend to thrive where creativity, competitiveness, and speed are required. (Examples of this include advertisement teams, computer software developers, construction contractors, etc.)
4. The *person culture* has the individual as the center point. Person-culture organizations exist because the people within them are doing their own thing yet still pulling in the same direction. (Examples of this include lawyers, physicians, university professors, etc.) (Harrison, 1972)

Where Does Company Culture Come From?

Company culture can derive from a number of sources, but the three important ones follow:

1. *The environment.* Whether in the city or the countryside, landlocked or on the sea, a business's location can have a profound influence on culture. A country, its customs, technology, the levels of available education, local and national politics, the economy, even climate can influence human interaction and development. The result is a marked influence on organizational culture. For example, when I was working on my bachelor's degree at Florida State University I had a roommate from New York City who took as many classes as he could fit into his schedule. His idea was to graduate quickly and head back to

New York. When I asked him why, he said he couldn't bear the thought of slowing down. "And if I stay here too long that's exactly what's going to happen!" he insisted. He firmly believed that people in Florida (or the entire southern United States for that matter) were too laid back. "If I get back to the rush and bustle of New York and I've become a Floridian," he told me, "I'll be eaten alive!"

2. *Leadership (and in particular, company founders).* When it comes to establishing company priorities or setting a work ethic, the influence of a business leader can last for an organization's lifetime. For example, Ray Kroc of McDonald's fame didn't found the company, but his legendary obsession with hygiene and cleanliness exists long after his death. Today, regardless of what you think of the food, it's difficult to fault the high sanitary standards of most McDonald's restaurants.
3. *Past successes or failures.* How a company treats its successes is equally as important as how it behaves when it fails. A good example of this is reflected in Coca-Cola's disastrous decision in the 1980s to change its centuries-old formula. The vice president who initiated this change (and conducted the $4 million in research that supported it) was a lifetime employee who had worked his way to the top of the company the hard way. Coca-Cola was his life, but his decision was nevertheless a bad one. Pepsi, Coke's biggest competitor, pounced on the change, claiming that it meant something was wrong with the original formula and that it was being altered to more closely mimic Pepsi. Whether Pepsi was right or wrong is irrelevant; the result was that Coke's market share plummeted. Desperate to stop its hemorrhaging, the company reintroduced its old formula and fired the vice president who had instigated the change. Morale at Coca-Cola reportedly went south as employees came to the realization that new ideas (and the mistakes that sometimes result from them) were not tolerated. Seven years later, a newly appointed CEO rehired the vice president. The intended message was to let employees know that moving forward meant taking risks—and that mistakes, as long as they're learned from, are acceptable. (It wouldn't be surprising if the CEO also realized that of all the people in the world who had the least chance

of making another mistake of epic proportions, it was that vice president!)

The Two Levels of Organizational Culture

In every business, culture exists on two separate levels. The first is **observable culture,** or what one sees and hears when walking around the company's premises. This includes:

- *Stories:* the tales told again and again about dramatic incidents within the company
- *Heroes:* the people singled out for special attention (and whose stories are told again and again)
- *Rites and rituals:* ceremonies, meetings, and celebrations (e.g., the annual company award banquet)
- *Symbols:* the use of language or nonverbal expressions to communicate important themes (An example of this is reflected in the Polish university where I began teaching. The corridors are lined with photographs of presidents, prime ministers, Nobel Laureates, and other people of distinction—all of whom have taught or spoken at the school. Other examples include corporate logos, charity funding, public relations campaigns, and even architecture.)

The second level of a business's culture is unseen. This is called the **core culture,** and it reflects the values or underlying beliefs that influence employee behavior. Examples include:

- *Performance excellence* (the way employees are judged)
- *Innovation* (if or how new ideas are welcomed)
- *Social responsibility* (the importance placed on environmental and social ethics)
- *Worker involvement* (the level to which employees are involved in decision making)
- *Quality of work life* (the state of general working conditions)

How Is Company Culture Maintained?

Culture is usually maintained in three no-nonsense ways:

1. Hiring people who think the way management does and firing those who do not (e.g., some organizations make candidates go through as many as twelve interviews before being selected).
2. Indoctrination (the types and levels of employee training).
3. Having management set an example.

Strong versus Weak Organizational Cultures

Culture plays a significant role in a company's work climate. Strong cultures often influence the behavior of employees more than weak cultures because a high degree of shared values tends to create an atmosphere of control. In other words, if more employees accept a company's values the company's culture, as well as its influence on employees, will be stronger.

A good way to demonstrate this is with Disney World in Orlando, Florida. Disney World has an extraordinarily strong culture. Apart from the lingo (uniforms are called *costumes,* employees are *cast members,* being at work is considered being *on stage,* and so on), employees are told what color underwear to wear, how much jewelry can be worn, the type of hairstyles allowed, the intensity of perfume or cologne, and many other restrictions. The purpose of this is to establish a strict "Disney look" and ensure unity. It sounds awful, but the company balances these rather militant demands with a welcoming attitude that's hard to beat. On my first day at work there (all new employees attend two days of Disney University prior to beginning their jobs), the manager in charge of training cheerfully announced, "Welcome to Disney World! I want you to know that for every person sitting in this room more than 200 applicants were turned down. Why? Because we wanted *you!*"

No company had ever said that to me before and it made me (and everyone else) feel very good. I was ready to toe the line.

Of course that doesn't mean strong cultures are for everyone. The days are long gone when IBM employees had to stand beside their desks each morning and sing the corporate anthem, but some companies still vigorously encourage unity and high morale via similar actions (something that tends to be accepted more readily in America than in other countries). Having workers stand in a circle while clapping and chanting uplifting slogans ("We're number one, we're number one") is but one example. Personally, I'd rather have needles stuck in my eyes. However, if employees respond to this style of morale building, then it's certainly worth doing.

CAN STRUCTURE AND CULTURE BE CHANGED?

Organizational structure and culture are powerful manipulators of employee behavior and success, but what if they adversely affect a company? How can an organization's culture be changed into something more suitable? Although some people feel that it's easier to work within a company's culture rather than try to change it, the issue of change, which can be applied to organizational structure and culture, is nevertheless addressed in the next chapter.

Chapter 8

Managing Change

> There is nothing more difficult to take in hand, more perilous to conduct, or more uncertain in its success than to take the lead in the introduction of a new order of things.
>
> Machiavelli

In words difficult to improve upon, writer Bruce Chatwin once suggested that a fundamental contributor to all-around good health is experiencing **change**. "Diversion, distraction, fantasy, change of food, fashion, love and landscape; we need them as the air we breathe," he wrote. "Without change our bodies rot. The man who sits quietly in a shuttered room is likely to be mad—tortured by hallucinations and introspection" (Chatwin, 1996).

Chatwin went on to say that changes of scenery and the passage of seasons have been proven to stimulate the rhythms of the brain as well as contribute to a sense of well-being and an active purpose in life:

> Monotonous surroundings weave patterns that produce fatigue, nervous disorders, apathy, self-disgust, and violent reactions. It is hardly surprising then, that generations cushioned from the cold by central heating, from the heat by air-conditioning, and carted in aseptic transports from one identical house or hotel to another, should feel the need for journeys of mind or body, for pep pills or tranquilizers, or for the cathartic journeys of sex, music and dance. We spend far too much time in shuttered rooms. (Chatwin, 1996)

It's tough to argue with this sentiment, yet, ironically, although change is inevitable and indeed necessary, when it comes to management, it's almost always resisted.

In his book, *Management: Theory and Practice,* author Gerald Cole sums up the change process well. To change something, he says, implies altering it, varying it, or modifying it in some way. Some organizations change mainly in response to external circumstances **(reactive change);** others change principally because they have decided to change **(proactive change).** Some businesses are conservative in outlook, seeking little in the way of change; others are entrepreneurial in outlook, always seeking new opportunities and new challenges. Some organizations are constructed in such a way that change and/or adaptation is a slow and difficult process. Others are designed with built-in flexibility—enabling adaptation to take place regularly and relatively easily. There is not much point in change for change's sake, and most people need to be persuaded of the need for change. The reality is that every group has forces within it that keep it together and provide it with stability and others that provide it with reasons to change and adapt.

PREPARING FOR ORGANIZATIONAL CHANGE

For too many companies the buzzwords *reengineering, restructuring,* and *downsizing* are the only methods of change. Unfortunately these methods of change usually amount to little more than laying off scores of employees. Saving money by eliminating workers is a timeless act, but it shouldn't be the sole device of organizational change. Besides, the practice of casting adrift large numbers of employees often returns to haunt a business. Imagine the captain of a ship eliminating a large number of his crew to enable his provisions to last longer. Sure, he'll save money, but when the first storm hits (as storms eventually do) his ship will most assuredly suffer because there aren't enough people on board to sail it.

Introducing change into a business, therefore, should be a *proactive process that focuses on customer needs.* This includes

- cutting waste,
- reducing customer waiting time,
- increasing product or service quality,

- eliminating unnecessary paperwork, and
- generally streamlining operations to serve customers better.

In order for *effective* change to be implemented and take hold within an organization **breadth** and **depth** are required. *Breadth* means that change must take place across the entire organization (i.e., every department and area from the executive offices to the stockroom). *Depth* means that everyone within these departments must be aware of why change is occurring and *be involved* in the change process. Getting employees involved in change (having them become part owners in the process by asking for their input) is a powerful way to win them over. Yet, for many, the fears that changes bring are valid. These fears include job loss, embarrassment at not being able to adapt to new technologies or new practices, and so forth. The result usually manifests itself into some form of resistance—either seen or otherwise.

UNDERSTANDING RESISTANCE TO CHANGE

Probably the Most Important Management Theory Ever Developed

In the 1950s Kurt Lewin developed a model (the Force-Field Theory) that helps explain organizational change and its resistance (see Figure 8.1). Lewin states that there are two forces at work in change situations. The first comes from those who are trying to instigate change *(driving forces)*. The second results from those who are resisting it *(restraining forces)*.

Lewin says that most people prefer to use force (or power) to bring about change. This means that they try to "win" by exerting pressure on those who oppose them. In practice, though, the more one side pushes the more the other pushes back. Therefore, the better way of overcoming resistance is to concentrate on the removal or weakening of the objections and fears of the opposing side. The question management should be asking isn't "How can we persuade these people of our arguments for change?" but rather, "What are their objections and fears and how can we deal with them?"

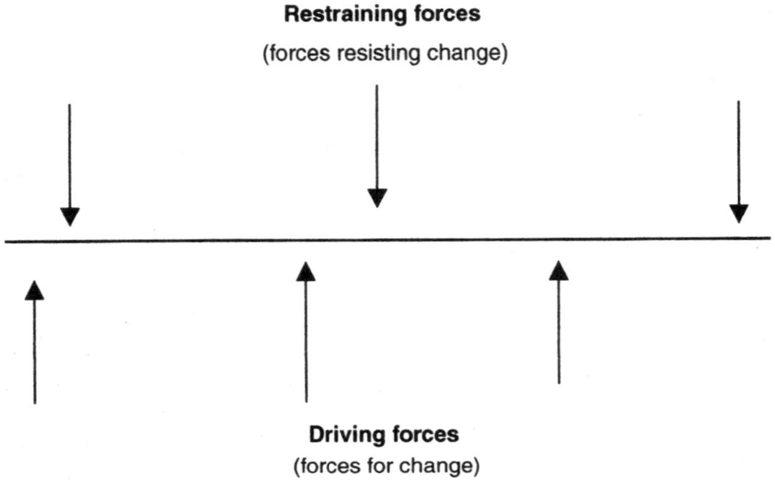

FIGURE 8.1. Kurt Lewin's Force-Field Theory Model (*Source:* Adapted from Lewin [1951]. *Field Theory in Social Science.* New York: Harper Press.)

Understanding Human Nature

Initiating change can be such a gut-wrenching experience that it's been known to reduce seasoned executives to tears. This is because the comfort of old habits and protective barriers are broken down and rearranged during the change process, leaving everyone feeling stranded and fighting for their professional lives. The following text is adapted from *Creating Value for Customers* by William Band. It adequately explains the feelings a business is likely to encounter when dealing with change:

- *Fear of loss of control:* People feel that things are being done *to* them rather than *by* them.
- *Too much uncertainty:* The future is not obvious, and every day feels like walking off a cliff. This can lead to people wanting excessive details, contingency plans, and other procrastination techniques (i.e., paralysis by analysis).
- *Too many surprises:* People like novelty, but hate surprises. Early warnings are necessary to avoid unwanted shocks.

- *Letting go of habits:* Habits are efficient, effective, and mindless. Change will be uncomfortable.
- *Need for familiarity:* Everybody likes what is familiar. We feel comfortable going to places and doing things we are familiar with.
- *Fear of more work:* True, implementing new ideas means more work, especially at the beginning of change, but this often subsides, and tasks can become easier and more efficient (usually the reason for change).
- *Concern for competence:* People often question their ability to master new skills, particularly if training and ongoing support are not provided or are viewed with skepticism.
- *Time to adjust:* Saying "Let's do things differently" is not enough. It takes time for new skills and a sense of comfort to develop. Rushing through the change process can lead to disruption, sabotage, foot-dragging, and poor performance. (Bard, 1991)

BUILDING THE COMMITMENT TO CHANGE

With Kurt Lewin's Force-Field Theory in mind, there are seven ways a manager can reduce the fears that change creates:

1. *Involve as many people as possible.* Participation leads to ownership, enthusiasm, and motivation.
2. *Communicate clearly and often.* Provide as much information as possible.
3. *Divide changes into manageable, comprehensive steps.* Make these steps as familiar as possible and make them small and easy. Also, ensure each step is deemed a success.
4. *Never surprise anyone with change.*
5. *Let commitment grow.* Don't ask for immediate allegiance to new and untried ways (you won't get it).
6. *Make clear what will be expected of people during and after the change.* Communicate standards and requirements.
7. *Provide as much continuous training as needed.*

Change from Another Angle

In 1952, Kurt Lewin developed a Three Stage Approach to Change Behavior that was later elaborated upon by Edgar Schein in 1969. Since good habits are recognized as being just as difficult to break as bad ones, Lewin makes the analogy of unfreezing (or breaking) bad habits and then freezing good habits once they've been established:

1. *Unfreeze existing behaviors.* Gain acceptance for change by reducing fear.
2. *Change existing behaviors.* Implement change through breadth, depth, and work ownership.
3. *Freeze new behaviors.* Reinforce new patterns of thinking and working via rewards and praise. (*Note:* if this is not done, employees *will* revert to their old ways.)

Remember: Different Strokes for Different Folks

No solution to change is all-encompassing. In 1996, Paul Strebel, working out of the Institute of Management Development in Lausanne, Switzerland, came up with a diagram (modified in Figure 8.2) that demonstrates that one, never-fail solution does not exist. Instead, there are many.

Strebel's point is that every type of situation that requires change is different. Therefore, managers cannot expect to blindly apply a one-size-fits-all strategy. In the diagram I've labeled the boxes with numbers 1 through 9. The greater the number, the more drastic are the actions needed to implement change. For example, managing a crisis in the face of strong forces against change (box 9) often requires radical action (firing people), which is completely different from trying to stimulate change when things are going well (box 1).

CHANGE MANAGEMENT: SOME EXAMPLES

A Personal Look

When I entered business school I'd just completed my second business turnaround and had found the experience excruciating. Naturally, because it had been so difficult (much more difficult than my

Type of change

	Proactive	Active	Rapid
High resistance to change	7 Radical leadership (charisma)	8 Reassigning people and responsibilities	9 Eliminating jobs and/or people
Medium resistance to change	4 Management-led changes	5 Redesigning of processes	6 Autonomous restructuring
Low resistance to change	1 Employee-led changes	2 Goal setting (creating incentives to make changes)	3 Rapid adaptation to change
	Weak	Moderate	Strong

Perceived need to adapt to change (change force)

FIGURE 8.2. Paul Strebel's Change Willingness Grid (*Source:* Adapted from Strebel [1996]. Choosing the Right Change Path. *The Financial Times,* 14 [February]: 5.)

first turnaround, which involved little more than setting improved quality standards for a half dozen highly skilled technicians in a television studio—something they readily agreed to undertake), I thought I'd done a number of things wrong. After looking into the matter, however, it became apparent that few, if any, business turnarounds are easy. In fact, it was shocking to learn that I'd actually done most things right. More astonishing was finding out that many business turnaround successes, as with mine, are not the result of a master plan. Concentrating on formulating and carrying out plans too easily leads to restrictive procedures that can suffocate the change process. Instead, when it comes to implementing change, most successful managers (as business guru Richard Pascale says) set out into the unknown with the heart of an explorer and the mind of a business contractor, armed with common sense, a basic understanding of their business and customers, and an overwhelming desire to excel.

Does This Stuff **Really** *Work?*

Perhaps the best testimonial I can offer comes from an executive earning his MBA through a postgraduate program I was helping to teach in Europe. Change management was one of the first subjects I introduced when my section of the program began. At our next meeting several weeks later, the executive stood and announced, "That change management stuff is fantastic! I've been using it at work and believe it or not it produced results. No kidding." He stopped and laughed. "Imagine that," he continued, "we've finally iearned something in an MBA program we can actually use!"

Chapter 9

Managing Conflict

In the 1980s, management gurus Tom Peters and Robert Waterman published a book titled *In Search of Excellence: Lessons from America's Best-Run Companies*. The book immediately stormed onto the best-seller lists. It became one of the top sellers of all time, racking up sales of more than 8 million copies. Basically, *In Search of Excellence (ISoE)* examined some of the most successful businesses in America and identified eight common traits, which are explained as follows:

1. *They were action oriented.* Management placed an emphasis on production and performance (i.e., made things happen).
2. *They were close to their customers.* Each sold what customers wanted to buy rather than what the business wanted to sell. In order to do this, the business listened to their customers and then created an environment that could deliver what their customers wanted.
3. *They were autonomous and entrepreneurial.* To a certain degree, each business let its employees call the shots. In doing so employees tried new things and took measured risks.
4. *They believed that productivity came through people.* Each business operated under the concept that if people are treated well, they will reciprocate in kind.
5. *Managers had a hands-on, value-driven style.* Managers didn't sit in an ivory tower and they didn't consider nonmanagement employees to be beneath them.
6. *Each business stuck to what it knew best.* As a rule, most companies didn't diversify into areas in which they knew nothing.
7. *Each organization had a lean staff.* Each business tended to adapt a flat organization structure (no bureaucracy, red tape, or

top-heavy management structure). Also, communication channels were clear and accessible.

8. *They each had simultaneous loose-tight properties.* Autonomy was given to employees on the shop floor, yet each business was firmly "grounded" and committed to its core values.

Of course many companies, when studied, claim that they're doing everything right, but about ten years after *ISoE* was released, one of its contributors (Richard Pascale) decided to take another look at the companies he and his colleagues had studied to see how they were doing. What he found shocked him. About two-thirds had lost huge amounts of market share. Several appeared on the verge of bankruptcy. What in the world had gone wrong?

On a side note, it's interesting to mention what happened when this information surfaced. Human nature being what it is, *ISoE* was derided, sneered at, and attacked by almost every business writer and academic that had failed to make the best-seller lists (and many more to boot). It's a shame because *ISoE* is a well-written book that makes many valid claims.

The problem for the companies examined in *ISoE* was that they had probably taken too much of a good thing and gone overboard—not unlike a person who is issued a drug prescription to take one pill every 24 hours and decides to take the whole bottle under the assumption that it will induce recovery faster, or a person who decides to lose weight and becomes anorexic. In addition, in a slash-and-burn fervor to become lean and mean, many of the companies had effectively eliminated one ingredient crucial to every business's success: **conflict.**

THE VALUE OF CONFLICT

The Best Business Story Ever

The quality of Honda products is legendary, but who would ever believe that this quality was born out of conflict? The Honda Motor Company has been listed as one of the best-managed companies in the world for so long that few people take notice of it anymore, and even fewer remember the company's dramatic history. One of the stories behind the company's success (which I'm sure has inflated over the years) rarely fails to reduce an audience to utter silence.

As a young man, the company's founder, Soichiro Honda, had a fascination with small engines and motorbikes. Keep in mind that this was in the days following World War II. As a Japanese man, Honda had huge obstacles to overcome. Yet, despite these setbacks, his reputation for producing engines of superior quality grew. Beside him every step of the way stood Takeo Fujisawa, a man who became Honda's longtime friend and business partner. Success followed success until Honda decided that the future of motors lay with air-cooled engines. His partner disagreed, insisting that water-cooled engines were the only way to go. Thus began a disagreement of epic proportions. Eventually, the two men could no longer work together because of their arguments. "It's my company, we're going with air-cooled engines, and that's final!" Honda shouted. As a result, Fujisawa stormed out of the company and quit. Sometime later, Honda came to the sobering realization that the future of the combustion engine did indeed lay with water-cooled engines—and that he had driven away the only person in his company who had the guts to tell him so. Aghast at what he'd done, he went to find his friend. As legend has it—and here's where the story starts sounding biblical—he eventually found him in a monastery; apparently, Fujisawa was so angry he was considering becoming a monk. Honda then did two of the most astonishing things any company CEO has probably ever done. (1) He apologized and admitted he'd been wrong, and (2) he vowed that from then on he was going to create a company in which *anyone* would be able to look their boss in the face and say, "You're wrong" without suffering any consequences.

Think about it. Soichiro Honda worked during a time when *nobody* in any Japanese company dared question his superior. Yet he decided to break away from this accepted way of thinking (as well as popular hierarchical business practices) and create a work environment that embraced the one thing that almost everyone tries to avoid with a passion. Soichiro Honda wanted a company that welcomed, and in many instances *encouraged,* conflicts. By doing so, he felt that his employees would forever be able to safely question one another, thereby helping to eliminate any future bad decisions.

THE NATURE OF WORK-RELATED CONFLICT

Major Truths Behind Conflict

Why is handling conflict important? As the Honda case shows, having everyone toe the company line can result in disaster—particularly when the company is heading for a cliff. There are other reasons as well. According to the American Management Association, 20 percent of a manager's time is spent dealing with conflict situations. That's one out of every five hours. With this in mind, here are some important points to remember:

- Not all conflicts are worth a manager's time and effort (conflicts can be trivial).
- Some conflicts are unmanageable (they may be outside management's sphere of influence, or the involved parties may not be interested in a resolution).
- Conflicts have causes (they don't spring up out of thin air). So it's in management's best interests to dig for the sources of disagreement and know the players. What are their interests, feelings, values, and personalities?

Major Causes of Work-Related Conflict

Most work-related conflicts do not transpire into open dramatics or fistfights. Instead, they fester under a thin veil of civility that invisibly consumes energy, productivity, and money. Beginning the process of conflict resolution involves accepting that solutions tend to fall into two categories: *cooperating* (the desire to satisfy another person) and *assertiveness* (the desire to satisfy the self). First, it's important to ascertain what type of conflict exists. Types of conflict are as follows:

Communicative conflict results from misunderstandings or crossed wires (but not, as many people believe, a lack of communication, because in most conflicts a lot of "talking" is going on).

Substantive (structural) conflict involves differences in goals, allocation of resources, distribution of rewards, policies and procedures, and job assignments.

Emotional (personal) conflict results from feelings of anger, distrust, dislike, fear, resentment, and personality clashes.

Two Directions Conflict Can Take

Conflict can make or break a business depending on how employees perceive it. With **dysfunctional conflict,** everyone either avoids or sadistically prepares for the imminent confrontation of those with opposing views. Issues are constantly seen as black or white, or right or wrong. The result, more often than not, is that tempers run high, battles erupt, and employees end up canceling each other out.

With **functional conflict,** people have been trained to respect opposing views and agree not to be threatened by them (suggestions on how to do this are mentioned in the next chapter). Establishing a company culture that can cope with disagreement in the form of functional conflict helps emphasize the importance of individual input and creativity. Conflicts can then take the form of civilized (if not animated) discussion, thereby clearing the air and lowering an organization's collective blood pressure. In other words, disagreement does not mean that war has been declared. Instead, employees learn to express their views without attacking others, and to listen to others without taking offense.

DEALING WITH CONFLICT

Typical Options Taken When Conflict Arises

Following is a list of options we've all resorted to at one time or another when trying to handle conflict. Which method best suits the needs of your internal or external customers?

1. *Avoidance:* best used when the conflict is trivial, when emotions are running high, or when attempts at resolution can be more disruptive than the conflict itself.
2. *Accommodation:* placing another's needs or interests ahead of one's own. **Accommodation** is useful when the issue under dispute is not of great interest to you or if you need to build up credits for later use.

3. *Forcing:* getting your way at the expense of another. Forcing your views on others becomes necessary when a quick resolution is needed, when unpopular actions must be taken, or when commitment by others is not critical.
4. *Compromise:* requires each party to give up something of value. Usually compromise can only be used when all parties are of equal power, when time pressures are being felt, or when a temporary solution is needed for a complex problem.
5. *Collaboration:* ends in a win-win solution for all parties. This can only occur when honesty, trust, and empathy are an integral part of discussions.

Making Conflict Work for You: Conflict Stimulation

Functional conflict is healthy and stimulating, but, again, employees must be trained in its implementation before it can produce results. It should be introduced in these situations:

1. When subordinates believe it's in their best interests to maintain the appearance of peace and cooperation (i.e., when "yes-men" dominate)
2. When employees show high resistance to change
3. When there is a general lack of ideas in the business
4. In a business that has unusually low employee turnover and/or an emphasis is placed on maintaining the status quo

Playing with Dynamite (or How to Stimulate Conflict)

1. *Tossing communicative grenades.* When things need to get moving quickly, one way of lighting a fire under everyone is to state something ambiguous (money is being lost, two departments are merging, people are going to be laid off), or send out a nasty memo and wait for the reaction. Be careful with this though. You may be the one who ends up getting burned.
2. *Bringing in outsiders.* Bringing in people whose backgrounds, values, attitudes, and styles are different often helps shake things up.
3. *Restructuring.* Reassigning jobs and responsibilities can really get the ball rolling. This is vividly displayed in governmental cabinet reshuffles.

4. *Playing the devil's advocate (particularly in meetings).* Assigning a person(s) whose job is to counter every argument or decision is another way to discover different options and get people communicating.

BATTLING THE STRESS THAT WORK AND CONFLICT CREATE

Few would dispute the fact that conflict produces stress, or that stress in the form of safe and regular physical exercise is good for you. However, physical exercise is voluntary and by its very nature allows the body to rest and rebuild afterward. Work-related stress is different. It grips and doesn't let go, thereby grinding the mind and body down day after day after day. Don't be someone who dies at age thirty-five but isn't buried until eighty-five. Here's how to cope with workplace stress:

- *Take control of your situation and life.* Know your limits and avoid unrealistic deadlines.
- *Pace yourself.* Try to do high-priority tasks first. Stay flexible and slow down.
- *Periodically stop and relax.* It's a mystery as to when we ever got it into our heads that work is something we can escape from each evening (historically, when has that ever happened?). So find time(s) to relax throughout the day, even if all you can muster is fifteen minutes with your eyes closed (some studies suggest that the best way to optimize this is to do so on your back on the floor).
- *Open up to others.* Discuss problems, fears, and frustrations with those you can trust.
- *Do things for others.* Selflessness is a great stress alleviator. If you want to reduce your own tensions, think about someone else's needs and satisfy them.
- *Exercise.* Engage in regular, measured, physical activity.
- *Balance work and recreation.* Schedule periods of recreation and quality time apart from work. No one can give 100 percent of his or her physical and intellectual time day after day, month after month, without some form of down time. To do otherwise

invites anguish, sickness, disability, and perhaps even death. Few people die uttering the words, "I wish I'd spent more time at the office."

- *Don't look for relaxation in the form of a bottle.* Whether through pills or alcohol, don't try to escape work pressures via chemically induced means. It doesn't work.

PUTTING IT ALL TOGETHER

The reason why the founding fathers of the United States felt so strongly about freedom of speech is because they fully understood the need for debate and dissent. Yet of all human trials and tribulations, wisely catering to differences of opinion must certainly be among the most difficult. For more ideas on how to harness conflict and make it work for you, reconsult: Chapter 4, "Understanding the Importance of Customers" (particularly the section titled "Dealing with Difficult Customers"); Chapter 6, "Getting the Most from Employees"; Chapter 7, "Organizational Structures and Cultures"; Chapter 8, "Managing Change"; Chapter 10, "Managing Teams and Work Groups"; Chapter 15, "Management: Theory versus Practice"; and Chapter 19, "Dealing with People in the Workplace."

Chapter 10

Managing Teams and Work Groups

Apart from the word *quality,* perhaps no other word in management is used and abused more frequently than *team.* In a business sense, the word **team** refers to a group of people who get together (or are forced together) to accomplish a **goal.** Using the word implies that everyone in an organization is happily working to fulfill a common purpose. The truth of the matter can be somewhat different.

For the most part, the reason for forming teams is to produce **synergy**—often explained via the mathematical equation that 2 + 2 = 5. Put another way, the caliber of a team's work is usually expected to exceed the sum of what each individual can produce on his or her own.

A **work group** is defined as two or more individuals who get together to accomplish a task or goal. Although it may be fine to make a distinction between teams and work groups in an academic setting, in a business organization the expectations for both are the same. In any company, whether you're assigned to a team or a work group, you will be expected to perform as a unit and produce results. Common sense dictates that the wider skill and knowledge base of a group of people has a distinct advantage over that of one person. Although no one in the real world—apart from motivational speakers and consultants—believes that 2 + 2 = 5 (or that 110 percent of anything can be achieved), the purpose of a team *is* to

- bring out the best in each member (motivate),
- help formulate ideas **(brainstorming),**
- conduct feasibility checks on ideas (reality test), and
- in general, complete a task better (or perhaps more uniquely) than can reasonably be expected of an individual.

Teams work best in environments requiring change or innovation, but the key to their performance hinges on cooperation, coordination, conflict handling, and commonality. In other words, teams work only when the basic social skills taught in kindergarten are put into practice. The problem is that many of us all too often need to relearn these basic manners. This means that time and effort is needed before teams can be relied upon to run smoothly and produce results, because the people within them will usually, at first, seek to satisfy personal ambitions.

TYPES OF TEAMS

Teams or work groups (the terms will be used interchangeably from here on) usually fall into three categories:

1. *Cross-functional teams* (also known as *committees* or *task forces*) consist of individuals who come from different departments, different schools of thought, and/or different work areas. The idea is that different mind-sets working together have a better ability to see the bigger picture. Cross-functional teams are known to work particularly well when it comes to product development as well as large, complex situations. The downside, however, is that they tend to take a great deal of time to manage and "get the ball rolling."
2. *Problem-solving teams* are designed to solve problems or give suggestions, not to implement these solutions. Historically, solving problems is the reason teams and work groups were first formed in business environments.
3. *Self-managed teams* are problem-solving teams that have the ability (and authority) to regulate themselves and enforce decisions. Studies show that self-managed teams work best when handling equipment purchases, customer problems, establishing departmental policies, scheduling jobs, and enforcing rules. Although self-managed environments can lead to an increase in work satisfaction (and has led to much positive press), the jury is still out regarding their long-term effectiveness. Absenteeism and high turnover are sometimes common with self-managed groups.

DEVELOPING A FUNCTIONAL TEAM

Teams generally develop in five stages:

1. *Forming* or selecting the people who will be on a team. During **forming** everybody is usually very polite and quiet. Group members will want to know what they will be asked to contribute and what the group will offer them. Conflict is seldom voiced and is usually suppressed. Since the grouping is new, most people are guarded and reserved in their comments and opinions and may defer to those who appear to be leaders.
2. *Storming* is characterized by personality clashes, faction forming, fights for domination, and much talk with little listening. During **storming** the group splits into separate factions and battle lines are drawn. Most important to note is that very little communication occurs at this stage. In most businesses, this battlefield scenario rarely erupts into a readily observed situation. Instead, emotion and conflict seethe beneath a veil of civility and are transformed into sarcasm and innuendo. Failure to pass through this stage without intense conflict resolution may result in lasting liabilities.
3. *Norming* begins when a team settles down and begins to work toward its goal. During **norming** the group finally recognizes that it must work together, or perhaps it's told that it must—or else. In-fighting subsides. Bickering, fighting over turf, playing politics, and, in effect, canceling each other out, reduces. **Norms** (acceptable standards of behavior) begin to be established. Most important, people start to listen to each other.
4. *Performing* develops when the group begins to work within a system that allows it to get the job done, and when everyone's input culminates into a single, shared outcome. During **performing** individuals feel free to express their views and support one another. In doing so, a clear and stable structure develops. More to the point, this is the stage during which the elevated performance of each individual emerges.
5. *Adjourning* involves reviewing results and disbanding the group. During **adjourning,** particularly with temporary or task-oriented groups, a time always comes for group members to disband and return to their former positions within the business.

Ideally, the group does so with a sense of accomplishment. Although adjourning may sound like the easiest of the five stages, it is not. In the IBM story discussed in Chapter 7, the employees who had saved the day returned from their liberating assignment only to be shoehorned back into the rigid folds of the company—and as a result (or so the story goes), each one quit within a year.

Making Groups Work

During any of the five stages of team development, problems can occur. For this reason, many groups need a *facilitator*—a person whose role is to draw the group's attention to any agreed-upon norms as well as keep them on track toward their agreed-upon goal. Bear in mind that this person does not have superiority over the rest of the group; that would diminish the reason for forming a group in the first place. Merely having *respect* for this individual is the operative issue.

In theory, groups are supposed to work toward their own norms; however, when putting a group together, most managers should establish a few ground rules beforehand, such as

- the group's purpose (posted for all to see);
- attendance expectations;
- a few behavior rules (show respect: no laughing, eye-rolling, or criticism that is focused on personality rather than the task);
- work performance expectations (the standards that will determine if members are pulling their own weight and what will be done if they are not);
- methods of agreement (or dissent);
- clarity of task(s) and responsibilities; and
- handling deadlock (for example, will lots be cast or will a coin be flipped?).

These topics must be discussed, agreed upon, and written down before a group can perform. As progress is made, all decisions should be recorded on a large display board on which they can be clearly seen and referred to. Concentrating on the positives is essential. Staying upbeat is the best way to build group morale and reinforce cooperation and participation. Indeed, it may be necessary to insist that every negative criticism be accompanied by a positive suggestion for improvement.

And Now the Bad News

Despite the proliferation of stories about the success of teams and work groups, they are not a cure-all. Just as it would be absurd to ask a group of people to do something as simple as make a cup of tea, the same applies in business. Teams usually don't work well in environments requiring simplicity, speed, strong leadership, and/or cost minimizing. Waterman and Peters (1980) cite a classic example when they discovered a large corporation that had 325 task forces, none of which had completed its specified duties in three years and none of which had been disbanded.

To add to this, strong evidence has shown that assigning people to groups can sometimes decrease their performance. **Social loafing** is defined as the tendency for some individuals to reduce their efforts when working with others. Perhaps the reasoning is that they hope to disappear into the crowd—or maybe they think that since others aren't pulling their weight they don't have to either. The result is that a few lazy individuals enjoy the hard work of others. The larger the group, the greater the chance for social loafing to occur. So what possible solutions are there to help combat this?

OVERCOMING THE OBSTACLES OF A TEAM

From time to time, every group must avoid the danger universally known as **group think.** This is best illustrated through the stereotyped "committee mentality" in which too much analysis leads to paralysis and nothing gets done. Likewise, a committee's solutions may not appeal to anyone, or be so far removed from the initial problem that they're meaningless. Group think or stagnation occurs when the smug air of superiority creeps into a team and the team refuses to consider what it feels are different or disturbing viewpoints from outsiders. As a result, contradictory data is ignored or shelved, other alternatives are not considered, and jumping to conclusions or inactivity may dominate. Group think and social loafing are best avoided by

- assigning a team member to play devil's advocate at each group meeting;
- holding second-chance meetings after a consensus has supposedly been achieved;
- not being partial to only one course of action (perhaps make it a rule to always come up with two or three alternatives);
- going "around the table" with assembled team members and insisting on **feedback** (this helps prevent quiet people's opinions from being withheld and bigmouths from dominating discussions);
- encouraging team members to do their own research and conduct their own fact-finding investigations;
- remembering that the point of formulating a group is to *produce results*—groups are not automatically a solution in themselves; and
- understanding that since every group is unique, each one will require a different start-up, functional style, and form of leadership.

Although it may be true that "many hands make light work" and "two heads are better than one," whenever two or more people work together the notion that "too many cooks spoil the broth" must be considered. In this regard, some academics make a distinction between teams and work groups—and that's fine. In the world of business, however, the concept of teamwork (the process of people working together as a unit to achieve common goals) applies to both terms. Whether you wish to call a functioning unit of employees a team or work group is up to you. The point is that in every business, employees must make a commitment to work together, serve one another, fulfill a common purpose, and hold themselves mutually accountable. Anything less and the group of employees is merely a crowd.

Chapter 11

Managing by Objectives

Of the many management fads that have surfaced over the decades, *goal-setting* is one of the hardiest. Formulated in 1968, it continues to be the basis behind many modern management techniques. Goal-setting makes three important claims:

1. Specific goals increase performance more than ambiguous goals.
2. Difficult goals, when accepted, result in a higher performance level than easy goals.
3. Providing good feedback produces more results than not saying anything.

As it so often happens in management literature, someone somewhere along the way took this proven formula, hung a few baubles on it, renamed it "management by objectives," and pretended something new had been discovered. But I digress.

As with much in management theory, the idea behind goal-setting or management by objectives is a simple one: People work better when they know *exactly* what is expected of them. Before that can happen, however, these same people need to know where they are as well as the direction they're going. With that in mind, the following three-step process should help create a starting point and bearing.

GOAL SETTING: A THREE-STEP PROCESS

Step 1: Create a Vision

In business, the word **vision** is usually so clouded in hyperbole it's misinterpreted as being synonymous with either a fantasy or predicting the future. Vision has nothing to do with a crystal ball. Rather, it's a clear and vivid idea of how things should be. When written down, a good vision is a simple yet highly motivating means of uniting people toward a common purpose and direction. This does not pertain to pie-in-the-sky dreams or financial goals ("We will reduce costs 14 percent by next quarter," or "Our aim is to increase production by 8 percent"). Instead, visions tend to move hearts and minds.

Dr. Martin Luther King Jr., one of the world's greatest speakers and humanitarians, said in his famous speecn in August, 1963, "I have a dream that my four children will one day live in a nation where they will not be judged by the color of their skin but by the content of their character." Note that he did *not* say, "I would like to see a future in which 32 percent of our nation's congressional representatives are people of color." Instead, Dr. King relayed the direction he thought his country should go in a way that most people could passionately understand—using children as an example of how things should be instead of the way they were. That's vision.

The story behind the personal home computer provides another good example. For a long time most people believed that only universities and/or government organizations had a use for computers. But Stephen Jobs (the inventor of the personal home computer) thought differently. Instead of dreaming about quarterly earnings, cost reductions, or annual percentages of growth, he envisioned computers being reduced in size, simplified, and made available to everyone. Then he did something about it. That's vision too.

Step 2: Decide on a Mission

Once a vision has been formulated, the next phase is to come up with a company **mission statement.** A mission statement individualizes a business by clearly defining its purpose and uniqueness. In doing so, mission statements usually share four common traits:

1. They set tough, but obtainable, standards.
2. They relay basic beliefs, values, and priorities.
3. They are measurable.
4. They clearly explain what business the company is in.

Mission statements can be a page or two in length or a simple, one-sentence statement proclaiming that a company will surpass its main competitor in two years. Either way, they should avoid generic blurbs. Mother and apple pie platitudes such as, "we will not just compete, but advance," "our purpose is to satisfy our customer's needs and wants," "we will provide even better service in our field," and "our mission is to be number one" look great, but are hardly inspiring. In place of these worn-out clichés, a clear, unique, and unambiguous message should be made that everyone takes seriously. An example of this comes from the Newport Shipping Company of Rhode Island: "We will build great ships. At a profit if we can. At a loss if we must. But we will build great ships."

It can be argued that this statement is as bad as the previous examples (why mention operating at a loss?), but the statement still gives me pause. In all my years in business I've never heard the mission of a business put quite this way and it leaves me with no doubt that the Newport Shipping Company places a heavy emphasis on quality, pride, and teamwork.

Years ago the Ford Motor Company came up with its own version of a marketable mission statement that was used to create improvements in many of its operations: "Quality is Job 1." Note that an emphasis wasn't placed on sales figures or cost cutting or production quotas. Instead, the mission was *quality*. Everything else was done in pursuit of this. Just as important, concentrating on this one attribute prevented the company from spreading itself too thin by trying to be all things to all people—which no organization can do.

Step 3: Breaking the Mission Down into Achievable Objectives

Objectives are blueprints for achieving a mission. They address both financial and nonfinancial issues, incorporate concepts of time and measurement, and are designed to be more concrete and action-oriented. If, for example, a company's mission includes "making our product(s) accessible to everyone in Central Europe," the company's objectives may be "to have employees focus on sales and marketing strategies," or "for our factories to eliminate waste by 6 percent," or "to provide better home delivery service to our customers."

These objectives would then be further broken down into more specific targets for unit or departmental use, perhaps with an interpretation along the lines of, "This will be achieved by getting our people excited about what we do," or "We will establish closer links with our clients." Solutions for reaching these objectives can be as diverse as implementing employees' ideas, using flexible work hours, improving working conditions, investing in new equipment, providing improved training, establishing better reward systems, or a host of other *workable* ideas. A good way to determine if objectives are viable is for administrators (the people that determine a business's vision and mission) to walk the shop floor, talk to customers, ask questions, then shut up and *listen*. Doing so will provide a firsthand account of the match between the business's capabilities and the wants and needs of its external and internal customers. In the process, the language of everyone concerned is better learned and an understanding is reached of what best motivates the organization and how hard employees can be pushed.

An Example of Aiming High but Staying Grounded

Not long ago an industrial bakery in Great Britain decided that it wanted to become the country's leading manufacturer of bread and rolls *(vision)*. The idea for achieving this was to greatly improve customer service *(mission)*. To this end, new technology and equipment was purchased and employees were trained in new procedures in order to speed up operations *(objectives)*. Yet nothing much happened. Unable to explain why, the CEO decided to go on a fact-finding mission. To his surprise he discovered that the manufacturing side of the company was creating far more bread than the packaging section could handle. The result was a bottleneck of breathtaking proportions. Flabbergasted, he pointed to an old packaging machine and asked why it wasn't being used to help prevent the bottleneck. Nobody knew. As it turned out, when a new packaging machine had been purchased the old one had been shut down. Again, no one knew why, but when it was switched on it was found to be in excellent working order—and in the course of an afternoon the bottleneck was eliminated. The CEO decided then and there to make factory visits a part of his weekly routine. This led to him growing closer to his employees, which in turn enabled them to shed their fear of asking and answering questions. That resulted in most employees spontaneously generating new ideas and trying new things (work ownership). The result? The company is now one of the United Kingdom's leading bakery product distributors.

MANAGEMENT BY OBJECTIVES

One of the basic concepts of management by objectives is the elimination of ambiguity. Only then will employees understand what the business's objectives are as well as how and when they are expected to achieve these goals. Essentially, the procedure looks similar to the following:

1. Identify, discuss, and determine the organization's goals (i.e., its vision and mission).
2. Break the organization down into units. What is it that everyone in these units is supposed to be doing in relation to the company's overall goals?
3. Together with employees, establish *specific* goals for each unit and person. This should include both quantity and quality expectations for every task. Remember, these goals must be challenging but achievable.
4. Prioritize the goals. Employees may need help placing them in the company's preferential order.
5. Clearly state a realistic deadline for goal completion. As the old saying goes, without a timeline, goals are nothing more than dreams.
6. Build in feedback mechanisms so employees know exactly how they are doing.
7. Ensure that an appropriate reward system is linked to results.

That's It?

When you stop and consider that many organizations (1) place a wall between management and nonmanagement employees, (2) don't take the time to fully train employees, (3) don't do much of anything in regard to educating employees in the company's overall goals, (4) are satisfied when employees simply maintain the status quo, and (5) provide little or no feedback during an employee's workday, the value of managing by objectives becomes more obvious.

Warning! In Management, Panaceas Don't Exist

Managing by objectives is a fundamental management concept, but it does have its drawbacks. For example, goals can sometimes be seen as a ceiling rather than a floor. In other words, once targets have been obtained, employees have been known to stop performing.

Equally, setting objectives that are too demanding can encourage people to cheat. In fact, one of the problems inherent in management by objectives is that an emphasis can be too easily placed on quantity rather than quality. But fear not. There are solutions, and they can be found in the next chapter.

Chapter 12

Quality

Quality is the elimination of variation.

W. E. Deming

It must be said again that possibly no other word in the management lexicon is as misused as quality. Most business magazines or books are absolutely brimming with stories about how implementing quality resulted in massive savings, enormous efficiency improvements, and a sea change in employee performance. Unfortunately, in almost all cases, little if anything is mentioned about how this newfound quality was acquired. Therein lies the wrinkle, because quality isn't about a cost-saving idea or a spectacular work-check program. Rather, it's an all-out, do-or-die, in-your-face, bottom-line, fanatical way of thinking. But first, a little history.

ACHIEVING QUALITY

The father of managing quality is considered to be W. Edwards Deming. During World War II Deming established spectacular results in various lines of production (upwards of 200 percent improvement) by believing in the value of employees. He stated that most troubles faced by companies begin at the top by managers who place more emphasis on numbers than people and believe that superficial gimmicks and slogans can substitute for real improvement. He also said that the common workplace, riddled with fear and shortsightedness, often resists innovation and change through counterproductive internal competition (Deming, 1986).

Deming found that employee respect, input, and involvement unleashed the kinds of improvements that met the challenges of competition and a changing marketplace head on. Unfortunately, when the war ended and the troops came home, the age-old practice of dictating from the top resumed. During this same period, Japan was desperate to recover from its losses. For decades it had suffered a terrible reputation for making cheap, low-quality goods, so when it came time to rebuild, the country decided to change this reputation. In 1951, Deming was invited to Japan to explain quality-control techniques, and as a result, the quality of many Japanese products has become legendary. Today, the highest award a Japanese company can win is the "Deming Prize"—an honor so prestigious it's awarded on national television.

W. Edwards Deming's Points for Achieving Quality

- Create a culture that regularly asks for, and accepts, innovation.
- Invest heavily in training and research.
- Spend revenues on maintaining current equipment as well as acquiring new items.
- Work to improve every system—not just the end result of that system.
- Ask for statistical evidence of processes.
- Eliminate financial goals and quotas.
- Learn to motivate rather than give orders.
- Take the fear out of the workplace by providing an environment of constant learning.
- Break down barriers between departments and place an emphasis on communication.
- Eliminate superficial goals and slogans.
- Retrain people in new skills. (Deming, 1986)

Condensing the Master

Deming's concept of quality has since been reduced to three important concepts and rechristened *total quality management:*

1. *Quality is defined as the ability to meet customer needs 100 percent of the time.* Because this is a statistical impossibility, perhaps it's best to think about it this way: Quality is an ongoing process. In every conceivable way quality is a race without a finish line because it requires a dedicated commitment to continuous improvement. Perhaps one of the loftiest goals in the quest for quality is that of *zero defects*

(managing an operation that runs perfectly; creating a product that never needs improving, and so on). As with achieving customer satisfaction 100 percent of the time, obtaining zero defects is probably unobtainable. So why bother? Once again, it's better to view zero defects as a *means* to an end rather than an end in itself. For example, the reason why we educate ourselves and read management books isn't because we seek perfection but rather improvement. Most of us know that perfection is unobtainable, yet that doesn't prevent us from going through the perfection process. So it is with quality. Again, it's the unending *process* that counts.

2. *Quality revolves around making improvements in everything an organization does.* This requires an intense focus on the customer. Keep in mind our definition of the word *customer* (everyone an organization serves) and you'll start to understand the difficulty inherent in instilling quality into a business. Simply put, quality involves breadth and depth in its implementation. If you recall, this means every department in an organization must be made aware of the need for quality (breadth) and every individual within these departments must be actively involved in the quality process (depth). The entire concept of quality therefore hinges upon a shift in perspective from management to its workforce. Too many managers think it's their duty to determine quality work solutions. The error in this line of thinking is that quality isn't just a management issue—it's everybody's issue. In the search for quality, employees have to be trained to not only seek out problems but to continuously find their solutions as well. This takes time and effort.

3. *Quality must be viewed as a measurable degree of excellence.* Quality entails looking at all of an organization's systems and then breaking them down into countable units (the number of goods produced, the number of customers served, the time it takes to perform a task or service, the costs involved in a process, the number of errors made, etc.). Only when everyone has access to an accurate system of measurement can a determination be made as to whether or not what is being measured is good, bad, or average. Against this, improvements can be judged.

MEASURING QUALITY

The Eight Dimensions of Quality

According to D. A. Garvin (1987), competing on the basis of quality requires identifying and enhancing its various dimensions. Doing so will help a business gain a competitive advantage in the marketplace. Following are Garvin's eight dimensions of quality:

1. *Aesthetics:* how a product looks, feels, sounds, tastes, and/or smells
2. *Conformance:* the degree to which a product meets established standards
3. *Durability:* the amount of use a product provides before it fails
4. *Features:* the "bells and whistles" that supplement the function of a product or service
5. *Perceived quality:* the product's reputation
6. *Performance:* a product or service's main operating characteristics (i.e., how well does it do what it's supposed to do?)
7. *Reliability:* the time period in which a product malfunctions or fails
8. *Serviceability:* the speed and courtesy of attention given to customers as well as the competence and satisfaction with which a business offers repairs (Garvin, 1987)

Benchmarking

A term frequently used in connection with measurement and quality is **benchmarking.** To put it bluntly, benchmarking involves copying (or stealing) somebody else's ideas, the process of which follows:

1. It begins with a home business using another company's program(s) or idea(s) as a reference point.
2. A study is then carried out to determine what makes this program (or company) so successful.
3. An analysis is done to find out if ideas gathered from the other company will fit into the home business.
4. The challenge at this point is to try to implement the ideas of the successful company into the home business.

For example, a local health club may discover that a competitor has a big screen television mounted in its cardiovascular room so customers can watch programs while riding exercise bikes. The local health club then does the same thing. In a similar vein, major corporations routinely copy the services, operations, billing setups, and other systems of their rivals. Even unrelated industries can generate benchmarking ideas. Stories abound about how IBM used a Las Vegas casino's security systems as a benchmark to reduce employee theft. Another story involves a Chinese clothing manufacturer using a McDonald's menu format to simplify its product offerings. A colleague told me about an airline that once reviewed an Indy 500 pit crew to see if any ideas could be implemented in its quest to speed up baggage control systems.

PUTTING QUALITY INTO ACTION

Of all the areas that quality needs to permeate, one of the most important is customer service. Simply put, basic business survival is contingent upon providing *what* customers want, *how* they want it, and *where* they want it. If it's unknown what customers want, then they need to be asked (for a reminder of this concept, please review Chapter 4). Any attempt toward quality without the input of customers is a complete and utter waste of time—and could very well set a company marching off in the wrong direction.

Since quality is both a state of mind and a task-oriented concept, it can't and won't be achieved simply through an edict issued by senior managers. For quality to be all-encompassing, it must begin at both the top and bottom of an organization. Following are two plans to get you started. Keep in mind that for either of these plans to succeed, the determination of a zealot must be maintained, the patience of Job endured, and an extraordinary amount of persistence exhibited (you may also wish to refer again to Chapter 10).

Plan A

1. Gather your employees together and highlight a simple problem of which everyone is aware. Make sure the problem is work-related and is something that can be changed.

2. Become enthusiastic about finding a solution to the problem and look for a quick way to resolve it. This should be done with everyone's input.
3. Set a target and implement the solution.
4. When the solution has been implemented, praise and reward everyone.
5. Find another problem and repeat the previous steps (perhaps asking someone else to be the initiator).

Plan B

1. Formulate a weekly *quality circle* meeting. Quality circles are comprised of anywhere between two to twelve individuals from a department whose assignment is to make improvements.
2. Create an atmosphere in which employees are unafraid to voice their opinions and comments.
3. Provide your quality team(s) with the appropriate training or educational material on problem solving, group issues, and other quality related topics.
4. Establish a few basic ground rules outlining what you want to achieve.
5. Give your team(s) time to gather confidence.
6. Keep it going.

Again, it's of paramount importance that the establishment of quality involve *every* aspect of a business. Nothing should be overlooked because *everything* an organization does is interlinked and requires constant attention, upkeep, and care. Even an issue as seemingly trivial as the cleanliness of an organization's washrooms will reflect on the standards set in work areas, and that ultimately sends a message about the amount of respect given to both internal and external customers. This concept is aptly illustrated in a nursery rhyme:

For want of a nail, the horseshoe was lost
For want of the shoe, the horse was lost
For want of the horse, the rider was lost
For want of the rider, the battle was lost
For want of the battle, the kingdom was lost
And all for the want of a nail.

The Mother of All Battles

Quality is more than just a term—it's a commitment to undertake unending, backbreaking work. As an ongoing crusade it's also a long-term goal, and long-term success should always be given precedence over short-term gains. To establish quality, time must be devoted to making products or services that work right the first time. Staff training and development must never be sacrificed. Reliability should always take priority over speed. For each and every employee the pursuit of quality must become an unassailable state of mind, or the kingdom will be lost.

Chapter 13

Ethics

Pick up a newspaper or turn on a television or radio and nine times out of ten there'll be a story about a company being accused of dishonesty. The tobacco industry, for example, is reeling from their decades of lies. The Enron scandals of 2002 resulted in the bankruptcy of the world's seventh largest corporation, thousands of job losses, and the demise of Arthur Andersen, one of the largest and, up to then, most prestigious accounting firms on the planet. After the terrorist attacks in the United States on September 11, 2001, several local hotels raised their rates knowing that journalists and aid organizations would be arriving en masse. A few years ago a study concluded that *all* whitening toothpastes don't whiten teeth in the manner their manufacturers claim. Every year cosmetics companies are taken to court for producing materials that don't reverse the signs of aging or reduce cellulite. Other products kill or injure their users only to have the companies that produce them deny it or cover it up. Let's also not forget the clandestine polluters, the unfair competitors, the inside traders that leave the rest of us out in the cold, the cheaters, the greed mongers, and the fat-cat CEOs who destroy company market share and are rewarded with dismissal packages worth hundreds of millions of dollars.

But all is not lost. The reason these folks are in the news is because they got caught. Although the bad things we see may be just the tip of the iceberg, people who behave unethically usually get what they deserve.

ETHICAL BEHAVIOR

Learning Right from Wrong

Ethics can be defined as the factors that make a person or business good, moral, truthful, honest, and sincere. Behaving ethically means acting with integrity, thinking of others, saying what is meant, and meaning what is said. Similar to quality, ethics is an all-encompassing concept. You can't be "a little bit" ethical or "for the most part" ethical. You either are ethical or you aren't. Can ethics be learned or taught? Some people say yes, others say no. At the very least most of us do know the difference between right and wrong. Perhaps for many people the real question behind ethics is, "will I get away with it?" These days, the answer to that question is increasingly "no."

From a management perspective, therefore, behaving ethically is an integral part of long-term career success. Since customers today have access to more information and have more choices than ever before as to where to take their business, it only makes sense to behave ethically.

Reasons to Behave Ethically

From an internal customer's (employee's) standpoint, behaving ethically

- produces a sense of pride in the workplace (and that helps motivate workers);
- sets a good example (it's difficult to demand that employees be honest if managers aren't); and
- raises an organization's level of perceived fairness.

From an external customer's standpoint, a company's ethical behavior

- decreases the chances of being sued;
- provides another good reason to buy your products; and
- raises the level of social consciousness for all involved.

FOUR LEVELS OF ORGANIZATIONAL ETHICS

When making day-to-day decisions, every business consciously chooses to what extent it wishes to be responsible to its internal and external environments. There are four basic levels:

1. *Social disregard* occurs when a company, for the most part, does whatever it wants, regardless of the consequences.
2. *Social obligation* is when a company chooses to meet its legal responsibilities and nothing more.
3. *Social responsiveness* is when a company changes its policies and practices in regard to social conditions or pressures. For example, pressure from consumer groups was so strong that several tuna manufacturers eventually decided to buy tuna from fishermen who used dolphin-friendly harvesting methods. Now, whenever shoppers see the words "dolphin friendly" on a tuna label, the businesses providing that tuna benefit by selling what the public wants.
4. *Social responsibility* occurs when a company decides to pursue long-term goals that are good for society overall. An example of this is The Body Shop, a cosmetics company founded on the basis that cosmetics should not be tested on animals. For the company's founder, reducing animal cruelty helps make the world a better place.

UNETHICAL VERSUS ETHICAL DECISION MAKING

Rationalizing

How do otherwise intelligent people make unethical decisions? Usually by kidding themselves with the following justifications:

- *It's only a* little *unethical.* Perhaps the rationalization is that "everybody else is doing it," or the outcome seems trivial. Either way, it boils down to doing something wrong. Eventually someone will be held accountable for it—particularly if a scapegoat is being sought or someone is seeking ammunition against someone else.

- *No one will find out.* "Unless it's discovered," goes the argument, "it's not really unethical." Baloney. Little these days goes undetected and very few people are bright enough to commit the perfect crime. It may take a while, but someone, someday, will probably find out what was done and by whom. If you're stupid enough to do something unethical, you're stupid enough to get caught.
- *It's in everyone's best interest.* For example, if your business sells its products overseas and a buyer demands that a bribe be paid or else another supplier will be sought, what do you do? This is a very difficult dilemma. Overcoming this situation depends in part on the ability to look beyond short-term gains and address long-term implications.
- *My company will stand behind me.* Yeah, right. And so will Santa Claus, the Easter Bunny, and the Tooth Fairy.

How to Make an Ethical Decision

Make no mistake, people who act unethically do so at their own peril. Most of us do know the difference between right and wrong, however, when the world produces its myriad shades of gray, put yourself through both rounds of the following questions to ensure that a good decision is being made:

Round 1

1. *Legality:* Is what you wish to do legal?
2. *Fairness:* How will the decision's outcome affect the people who are involved with it?
3. *Self-respect:* Do you feel good about the decision and its outcome?
4. *Long-term effects:* Shortsighted solutions are rarely an answer. Will your decision create or destroy job security? What are the risks and dangers? How will your company's internal and external environments be affected?

Round 2

1. *Purpose:* Do you understand and accept the real reasons or intentions of what is being done?
2. *Perception:* Have you considered the feelings and well-being of those affected by your decision?
3. *Persistence:* Have you remained flexible to other people's viewpoints yet committed to your own faith and beliefs?
4. *Perspective:* Did you comprehend the whole picture and determine what is really important?
5. *Pride:* Will your superiors be happy with your decision? Does your organization want to be held accountable for it?

A Good Litmus Test

If you're ever in doubt as to whether something you wish to do is unethical, ask yourself the following question: "Would I do this in front of the boss (or my spouse or partner, or my children, or my friends)?" If the answer to this question is no, you have your answer to the first.

WHISTLE-BLOWING

Much of the world's unethical business practices are brought to light by **whistle-blowers:** people who expose the dishonest and/or criminal acts of others. Ironically, in many countries, whistle-blowers are detested and called a variety of names including snitches, rats, grasses, and other derogatory comments. Personally, as a manager, I used to both love and loathe the people who brought me information I might otherwise have never known about. At one end of the scale, these people were indeed tattletales. At the other end, they provided me with many under-the-surface-problems that could be resolved before they erupted, thereby preventing future catastrophes and ultimately improving the business (as well as my reputation as a manager). For the most part, despite all the good that whistle-blowers do, they tend to be stigmatized and often face impaired career development, termination from their jobs, and/or other forms of retaliation—

even when they save lives. Following are some "dos and don'ts" for whistle-blowers.

Dos

- Make certain a full understanding of what is happening is ascertained and that any allegations are *absolutely* correct.
- Talk to an attorney to ensure your rights will be protected and that proper procedures will be followed (*you* may be in trouble otherwise).
- Keep accurate records to support your claims. Make copies and keep them in different locations (not your office).

Don'ts

- Don't assume the law protects you.
- Don't talk to the media first.
- Don't expect a big financial windfall if you end up being correct, are fired, or are retaliated against.

THE BOTTOM LINE

Being ethical doesn't cost anything. Being unethical can cost dearly. Don't be fooled into thinking that unethical actions won't be discovered. Employees aren't stupid and they do know just about everything that's going on in an organization. It may sound trite, but unethical practices make us all poorer in almost every conceivable way. No one gets ahead in life by being unethical. What goes around comes around, and the bottom line is that if you're honest and can take pride in your life, your decisions, and your business—you *will* be repaid in kind.

Chapter 14

Leadership

Great leaders write new stories.

Carlos Ghosn, President
Nissan Motor Company

Leadership is a notoriously difficult concept to grasp, but it's not due to a lack of information on the subject. Most bookshops are literally bursting with material on leadership. What makes the subject difficult to pin down is that virtually everyone has an opinion regarding what constitutes effectiveness—and ultimately, being effective is what makes a leader. Add to this the too many people out there who seem to find no shame in calling themselves leaders and the concept becomes even more difficult to define.

LEADERSHIP VERSUS MANAGEMENT

For the most part, **leading** involves motivating people as well as building commitment toward a set goal (which in any business should be serving internal and external customers). So how does leadership compare with management? **Management,** it can be said, is about coping with complexity: bringing about order, consistency, and profit by drawing up and successfully implementing plans and structures, then measuring them. **Leadership,** on the other hand, is about coping with change: establishing a vision, effectively communicating it, and inspiring others to work consistently toward it. To put it more succinctly, *things* are managed. *People* are led. In fact, one of the more important aspects of leadership is that it doesn't occur unless others are willing to follow.

According to research, business leaders generally fall into two categories: those who place an emphasis on a *concern for task* (getting a job done by strictly meeting work objectives), and those who focus on a *concern for people* (getting things done via relationships and the consideration of others). Which is the most effective? In practice, good leaders probably combine both categories—using whichever method proves most reliable in the situation encountered at the time.

LEADERSHIP: ABILITIES AND ACTIONS

Beauty is in the eye of the beholder suggests an old saying. The same can be said about leadership. Indeed, one of the greatest determinants of leadership is hindsight. For example, American presidents Abraham Lincoln and Harry S Truman are today almost universally recognized as effective leaders, yet in their time they were widely derided. Conversely, think of the business leaders in the 1990s who were once held in high regard. Only later were some discovered to be liars, incompetent, scandalously greedy, and/or out-and-out crooks. Clearly, a rush to judgment, emotion, politics, public relations (spin), and a disregard of common sense often factor heavily when awarding leadership status. The following attributes, however, are more substantive when determining the characteristics of a leader.

Abilities

The following personal traits often lay the foundation for leadership success:

- *Above-average drive:* initiative, high energy, and a strong appetite for achievement
- *Motivation:* a desire to lead and influence others
- *Integrity:* honesty in dealing with others and consistency with words and deeds
- *Self-confidence:* being naturally decisive and confident with personal abilities
- *Intelligence:* able to gather, integrate, and interpret complex information
- *Vision:* a good understanding of present situations and how the future should be

- *Flexibility:* being willing and able to adapt to changes
- *Inspiring confidence in others:* to be measured, not necessarily by how many followers a leader has, but by how many leaders he or she creates

Actions

Successful leaders often possess the following result-producing styles:

- *Excellent communication abilities:* the ability to convey clear, short, understandable messages
- *A willingness to make sacrifices and display personal risk:* seen in televangelists who constantly remind everyone that their devotion costs them dearly (usually with the example of friends who abandoned them after they found God), or a politician's "I was born in a log cabin" type story, or an executive stating that he or she came up in the business the hard way
- *Exhibition of extraordinary behavior:* standing out in a crowd and making tough decisions
- *Instigating change:* leading changes rather than the other way around
- *Showing sensitivity:* being aware of the needs and wants of others
- *A willingness to be reliable and responsible at all times:* running a company is not unlike being the captain of a ship—even when not on the bridge, a captain is still on call and responsible for whatever happens
- *Handling adversity with grace:* remaining calm, professional, and polite under pressure

COMING TO GRIPS WITH LEADERSHIP THEORY

Among the dozens of tomes that try to explain leadership (one or two actually suggest that the loss of a parent is contributory), some of the more recognized have come to the following conclusions. Note that almost all of these theories appear to have their roots firmly entrenched in the concern for task versus concern for people categories mentioned previously.

- Fiedler's (1992) Contingency Model states that good leadership depends on matching or changing appropriate leadership styles (concern for task or concern for relationships) with the proper situation or best "fit."
- The Hersey-Blanchard (1998) Situational Theory suggests that successful leaders should adjust their styles (delegatory, participatory, persuasive, or forceful) depending on how ready and willing others are prepared to follow.
- House's (1990) Path-Goal Theory says that an effective leader is one who allows people to achieve their own task-related and/or personal goals (the leader helps set goals, removes barriers, and provides rewards).
- Blake and colleagues' (1964) Leadership Grid splits leaders into a grid with axes marked "concern for people" and "concern for production." Leadership styles are then marked accordingly, with the one at the upper right-hand corner being the most effective because it represents leaders who show a very high regard for both people *and* production.
- The Vroom-Jago (1998) Leader Participation Theory is designed to help leaders choose a decision-making method for solving problems. For example, with an *authority decision,* the leader makes the decision. With a *consultative decision,* the leader consults others and then decides. And with a *group decision,* both the leader and his or her followers participate and decide.

Drucker's Three Essentials of Leadership

Over the decades one of the more down to earth management writers has been Peter Drucker. The following list is Drucker's explanation of what constitutes leadership:

1. *Defining, communicating, and establishing a sense of mission in a way that's understandable to others.* This means establishing an organization's direction, priorities, and standards, and simply and effectively stating them. Put differently, a leader is someone who, in the midst of chaos, is "the trumpet that sounds a clear note."
2. *Treating leadership as a* responsibility *rather than a rank.* Good leaders accept their weaknesses and surround themselves with talented people. Doing so means they're not afraid to develop

strong and capable subordinates and they don't blame others when things go wrong. Although effective leaders do not normally treat all people similarly, they don't appear unfair when doing so.

3. *Earning and maintaining the trust of others.* Effective leaders display above-average levels of integrity despite evidence that suggests they sometimes lack in morals. For example, U.S. President Bill Clinton produced eight years of unprecedented growth and prosperity during his two terms in office, but severely tarnished his reputation after lying about a sex scandal and putting his country through needless embarrassment. His successor, George W. Bush, moved into the White House after a questionable election, decided to fight terrorism after initially ignoring it, created the largest debts in history, invaded Iraq while misleading the public, repeatedly changed his justifications for the Iraq invasion to suit current events, and pointlessly drove a wedge between America and its allies. Despite their faults, however, both men maintain devout—almost rabid—followers. Go figure.

The conclusion? Few, if any, leadership discourses mention winning-at-all-costs, arrogance, or ruthlessness as measures of leadership. Rather, in a statement that suggests most organizations are overmanaged, under led, and too public-relations oriented, Drucker suggests that effective leadership isn't based on being clever or deceiving; it's based on being ethical and consistent in word and deed.

THE NATURE OF LEADERSHIP

Leadership, Hype, and the Human Element

It's been said that the great leaders have great weaknesses. This means that leaders are all too human and that their strengths and weaknesses must be carefully considered to determine if and how they will best suit a business's needs. The successful manager of one company may prove disastrous as head of another.

For example, the founder of Chevrolet, Louis Chevrolet, left his firm after a heated disagreement with a financier. Later he beat Anton

Champion (of the spark plug company that bears his name) so badly Champion had to be hospitalized. Yet the Chevrolet company is still going strong, so fists-a-flying Louis must have done something right. That being said, would his tactics work elsewhere? Would you want to work for him?

Legendary manager Soichiro Honda, apart from reportedly liking a drink or two (or three) had a reputation for losing his temper with shoddy workmanship and hitting the responsible employees over the head with whatever tool was available. Yet he was also renowned for allowing workers to speak their minds and for listening to what they said.

Jack Welch, the former CEO of General Electric (GE), was proclaimed by many authorities to be the most successful manager of the last quarter century (1975-2000). However, when he retired in 2001, GE's stock price plummeted. In addition, the company's spectacular annual growth rates, which Welch regularly crowed about, fell under intense questioning because, according to some, they had been exaggerated and couldn't be proven. GE's accounting and risk management sections have since been accused of all kinds of business and accounting "shenanigans" (*The Economist,* 2002, p. 63). Welch was later further disgraced when upon divorcing his third wife it was revealed that he had wrangled a retirement package worth hundreds of millions of dollars (he has since rescinded the deal) that would have allowed him to be treated like a king, at GE's expense, for the rest of his life. If there's a lesson to be learned from all of this it must surely be that if you encourage an image of perfection, you'd better be perfect.

Last, consider Winston Churchill. Although a highly competent man, Churchill was notorious for making big mistakes that cost lives (the Gallipoli massacre being just one). He was also renowned for being sour and cruel to his subordinates and had a remarkable propensity to burst into tears. Despite this reputation, however, he was one of the few people in his day who understood that winning a war involves fighting and suffering losses. Ironically, just about everyone who put up with his surliness loved him (probably because he instilled in those around him a sense of genuine purpose). Nevertheless, immediately after he led the saving of the free world, British voters threw him out of office. Not because they disliked him but because they felt he wasn't sensitive enough to their needs after so many sacrifices had been made.

It cannot be overstated that the negative and positive aspects (the human elements) of an individual should be examined against a company's strengths, weaknesses, culture, and character before he or she is tapped to undertake a leadership position—and this must be done while keeping in mind that no one is, or ever will be, perfect.

Are You a Leader? A Practical Example and Exercise

Curiously, some people think that because they've been promoted to, or find themselves in, a leadership position, it automatically makes them a great leader.

Here is an exercise I give my students. It never fails to make an impact.

A few years ago, a female physician (Dr. Jerri Nielsen) volunteered to be the medical officer for a research facility in the Antarctic. The facility is situated in an extremely remote area that accommodates only a dozen or so scientists at a time. Because of the extreme cold (which has been deemed "searing") there are only a few weeks out of the year when a plane can land, pick up or unload passengers, and deliver supplies. At all other times aircraft fuel becomes gelatinous because of the cold. In other words, once someone commits to this project, they're stuck there for a full year.

Shortly after winter set in Dr. Nielsen discovered that she had a virulent form of breast cancer. Taking into account her surrounding resources she sat down with her colleagues and discussed the tasks each would have to perform in order for her to survive. One person would have to operate (incredibly, Dr. Nielsen remained awake during the surgery and told this person what to do *while it was being done*). Another person who knew how to work with chemicals had to learn to administer chemotherapy. Still others came up with a means to transmit pictures of blood and tissue samples to outside medical experts via a jury-rigged digital camera, a mobile phone, and a satellite hookup.

Thankfully, the story has a happy ending. Dr. Nielsen survived her ordeal and was eventually airlifted out of the Antarctic in a heroic rescue attempt weeks later. Needless to say, she learned many important lessons along the way.

When relaying this story, I ask my students to place the following list of people in the order of their importance to an Antarctic research station:

Manager (the person responsible for instilling teamwork, cooperation, and purpose)
Doctor (the person entrusted with saving lives)
Researcher (the person who checks facts and gathers information)
Chemist (the person who understands how chemicals and elements work)
Scientist (the person who conducts experiments and gathers data)
Mechanic (the person who fixes equipment)

For many by-the-book managers the logical answer would be to assume that everyone is equally important. But as we've seen before, management can be a contradictory subject.

So who is at the top of your list? The doctor? The manager? How about the bottom of your list? Did you select the researcher or the mechanic?

From her experiences, Dr. Nielsen identified the mechanic as perhaps the most important person in the group. Why? In the Antarctic, a good leader knows that the environment is the greatest enemy. Although each person in a scientific team is fully expected to pull his or her own weight, if something were to happen to the electrical generators or if the heating system shut down *everyone* would be dead in less than forty-eight hours unless a mechanic was available to fix the problem.

Dr. Nielsen went on to explain in her book, *Icebound: A Doctor's Incredible Battle for Survival at the South Pole,* that she also came to appreciate the sometimes conflicting interrelation between type A personalities (bold, aggressive, decision-making types), who turned into caged tigers during the Antarctic's dark months, as well as the importance of the quiet, type B personalities who exhibit patience, silence, and pragmatism. Once again, a good business leader fully understands concern for task versus concern for people situations and applies his or her leadership qualities accordingly to ethically achieve appropriate objectives and overcome adversity.

So, After All Is Said and Done, What Exactly Is Leadership?

Being named as the head of an organization does not automatically make someone a leader. Leading consists of convincing others to go places they have never gone, do things they have never done, and accept situations they have never encountered. Accomplishing this usually involves Handy's six methods of influence (described in Chapter 5) combined with the abilities and actions mentioned earlier in this chapter. With such a heady mix of conflicting traits and styles, not to mention the polarizing interpretations of followers, it's no wonder the subject continues to baffle so many. Perhaps leadership is best summed up with the famous words uttered years ago by a United States Supreme Court Justice (or Senator or a famous movie mogul, depending on who you believe said it first) when weighing a subject he was having difficulty grasping. "I may not know how to define it," he said, "but I know it when I see it."

Chapter 15

Management: Theory versus Practice

When I was a toddler, my mother used to place me in a playpen with my brother while she cleaned the house. One day, after she'd done this for the hundredth time, she heard me crying and rushed back to see what was wrong. To her surprise I was covered with bite marks—deep, angry, red-and-purple welts that sprouted over every inch of my body, including my face. She glared at my angelic-looking brother who quietly pretended that nothing was wrong. "Bad boy," she said, wagging her finger at him, "bad boy!"

Unfortunately, my brother decided he was onto a good thing. As time passed, whenever no one was looking, he continued to bite me. Not knowing quite what to do, my mother asked her local doctor for advice. "Maybe if I just bite him back it'll teach him a lesson and he'll stop," she said.

"No," replied the doctor, "don't do that. It'll cause more harm than good. Just be patient, continue to reprimand him, and he'll soon get tired of it."

But of course he didn't. Mom next sought the counsel of her friends.

"Maybe I should just bite him back," she pleaded.

"Oh, God no! You should never bite your child," replied one friend.

"Why not keep just them separated?" asked another.

Mom buried her face in her hands. She had had three boys in one year (yes, you read that correctly) and it was impossible to keep us separate. We simply had to learn to sit together peacefully. Although all the material on children who bite relayed calm, rational solutions, not to mention reams of explanatory theories, each was adamant about one thing: "Whatever the urge," they warned, "don't ever give in to the temptation of biting your child back."

Some time later, after watching my brother sitting silently beside me without any outward sign of mischief, she left the room, confident that the biting phase of childhood had finally passed him by. In less than a minute the sound of me crying filled the house. Infuriated, she stormed into the room, strode over to the playpen, grabbed my brother's arm, and bit him.

"And it wasn't just any old bite," she told me years later. "I bit him hard."

"Didn't he cry?" I asked, unfazed. My mother was a formidable woman in her day.

She reared her head back in amusement. "Oh my, yes! He was so loud I thought the windows would crack!" She leaned forward with a glint in her eyes. "But he *never* bit you again."

What does this story have to do with management? Read on.

In 1960, a man named Douglas McGregor published a book titled *The Human Side of Enterprise*. This was not just any book. *The Human Side of Enterprise* became one of the most important books on management ever published. In fact, some experts believe it's the most influential book on management that's ever been written. In it, McGregor formulated his X and Y theory of human nature. This theory states that people can be classified into two categories. The X category presents an essentially negative view of people. It suggests that individuals regularly avoid responsibility, dislike work, have little ambition, and need constant supervision. The Y classification takes the opposite approach. It assumes that people enjoy responsibility, like to work almost as much as they like to play, and when given the chance will exercise good judgment and self-direction. McGregor's conclusion is that Theory Y best captures the true nature of employees, and managers should practice the appropriate methods to take advantage of this type of behavior. In practice, McGregor's management motto can perhaps best be summed up as "softly, softly."

Unfortunately, the real world crept in. Make no mistake, McGregor was a very intelligent man (he taught at the Massachusetts Institute of Technology [MIT], which has been rated as the number one school in the United States for many years). Sometime after coming up with his theory he was offered the job of president of Antioch College. Naturally, he jumped at the chance to put his theories into practice, but after six years at Antioch, bravely admitting that his philosophy and management skills had failed, he resigned and returned to teaching at MIT. In his farewell address at Antioch, McGregor unabashedly explained that being a manager involved being authoritative—that meant enforcing policies, punishing slackers, playing politics, and facing responsibilities and difficult decisions with grit and resolve. Management was not, as he had thought and despite all his research, merely an advisory function.

To his credit, when McGregor returned to MIT he continued to advocate the Theory Y approach to management despite his own failings with it (i.e., he recognized that the fault lay with the messenger, not the message).

The point of these two stories is that the key to good management lies in maintaining a balance. Few if any management books seem to acknowledge that managing people is not always sunshine and sweetness (the words "hard work" are about as far as most authors go). When all is said and done, good management means having the backbone to use the stick approach when carrots cease to work. That's not to say this book advocates using unpleasantness as a management tool. Constant anger, threats, tantrums, and other dramatics in the workplace are self-defeating and usually nothing more than signs of insecurity. Yet when all other methods have failed, a little sterner stuff used within the boundaries of fairness and prudence sometimes goes a long way. Maybe a thousand years from now, when humanity has progressed to an age in which reason and a quiet word are enough to alter behavior, the anger and/or a raised voice in the workplace will become unnecessary. Until that happens, however, keep in mind that most employees are made of fairly resilient stuff. When they decide to test your resolve, which they inevitably will, your only option, after all else has failed, may be to bite back.

A PRACTICAL EXAMPLE

In 1994, a business I was managing acquired a new software system I'd ordered to improve customer service. Most of the company's employees were quite eager to learn this new system and several of them often stayed on in the evening past their shifts in order to become adept at its intricacies. One woman, however, held back. Realizing that fear was probably behind her excuses, I arranged for one of the staff to privately tutor her in the afternoons, but to no avail. She always insisted she had too much work to do. I then signed her up, at company expense, for a computer course located about a block from our offices. She never attended a single class. By then it became clear that no amount of persuasion was going to work. She'd simply decided that she wasn't going to use the new software program and she had quietly dug in her heels. Shortly thereafter I called her into my office, pointed out the different alternatives that had been provided to her, and issued an ultimatum. Her job required that she learn the new system, I explained. Everyone else had to gain these new skills (including myself) and she could not be the exception. In the meantime, the company had lost time and money because of her procrastination, not to mention her successful defiance of my authority in full view of everyone. "You have a choice," I said, "either you learn to use the new system within three weeks or you'll be fired."

Ironically, three weeks later, she was the employee that sang the praises of the new system the loudest. As I'd hoped, it had lightened everyone's workload considerably.

THEORY VERSUS PRACTICE: A METAPHOR

An adage states that "everything looks good on paper." Management theory is no exception. It almost always looks and sounds great—until it's applied. I'll use skiing to illustrate this point. Studying skiers, talking about skiing, watching ski films, reading books and articles, and conducting interviews is all very well and good, and necessary, when trying to understand the concept of skiing. Yet, until you strap on a pair of skis and set off down a snow-covered hill, fully appreciating the combined elements that constitute successful skiing will prove elusive. The next time you want to put theory into practice, replace the following skiing terms with the name of the theory and act accordingly.

- Skis are necessary for skiing. They are not wholly suitable for other purposes.
- Skis can be dangerous to those who do not know how to use them and even those who do. Avoid danger by regularly updating your knowledge as to how they work.

- Using skis properly and without malice provides consistent and immediate feedback. Learning to interpret that feedback is not a sign of failure—it leads to future success.
- Skis aren't designed to humiliate people, hold grudges, or accept excuses.
- Skis treat people equally; they do not play favorites.
- Skis are immune to power plays, whims, and emotions.
- If you're not using skis, you're not skiing—and you're not a skier.

For additional ideas on the subject of putting theory into practice as well as motivating and disciplining employees, please refer to Chapter 6, "Getting the Most from Employees"; Chapter 19, "Dealing with People in the Workplace"; and Chapter 28, "Tools for Developing External and Internal Employees."

Chapter 16

Managing in Different Cultures

There's much more to working in a foreign place than reading, memorizing, and conforming to stereotypes. Indeed, the quaint practices mentioned in many books have long since vanished in much of today's business world, especially when it comes to other countries. Examples include these:

Don't show the soles of your feet in the Middle East.
Don't touch the head of someone from Asia.
Burping after a meal in some countries is a way of showing satisfaction.
Don't talk business over lunch with the Spanish or Germans.

To make a long story short, if you're in doubt about how to behave in another nation or with a person from a different culture, do a bit of genuine research first. Some common sense wouldn't hurt either. Perhaps people from Asia don't like having their heads touched, but would you do this in a business setting in *any* country?

One Middle East business for which I had the pleasure of working contained more than fifty-two nationalities all under one roof (described at length in *Fundamentals of Leisure Business Success,* The Haworth Press, 1998). Since it's impossible to know the intricacies of fifty-two nationalities, most employees simply made the effort to be polite with everybody at work and that was all that was needed. Of course, that was at *work.* Many nonnationals, including quite a few Muslims, found it increasingly difficult to *live* day after day in a strict Islamic culture. In fact, throughout my tenure the number of individuals I met who sold their homes, left their jobs, and uprooted their families to move halfway around the world to a land they never bothered to investigate was astonishing. Incredibly, eleven individuals (and their families) were in my original orientation group, but after nine months only four of us remained. I shudder to think of the money, time, and energy this regularly costs both the company and the people who quit.

CULTURE AND HUMAN BEHAVIOR

What Is Culture?

Culture is a *learned* way of life that predominates a nation, society, or group. These learned behaviors include the following:

- Social organization (including class systems, caste systems, and social welfare or the lack of it)
- Religion (the inseparability of religion and government versus the secular approaches of the West)
- Customs, holidays, and rituals
- Values, attitudes, and education
- Political and legal systems (the last time I was in Singapore, for example, behavior as benign as chewing gum was against the law)
- Language
- Music, arts, and literature (conservative and liberal views are very different in different places)
- Work practices (for example, some cultures make it a rule to meet with several people at once rather than give one person a prearranged time of undivided attention)

Trying to Understand Human Behavior in Different Cultures

Generally speaking, we all tend to have similar wants: hope, a safe place to live and work, a future for our children, respect, and so on. What makes us different, as groups, is the way we attempt to achieve these wants. When we see others achieving their wants differently we usually cast a judgment. This can be explained via the **attribution theory.** In part, the attribution theory states that most people believe behavior is either *internally* caused (under the personal control of the individual) or *externally* caused (resulting from outside influences). A conclusion is dependent on three factors:

1. *Distinctiveness:* Is the behavior unusual?
2. *Consistency:* How often is the behavior displayed?
3. *Consensus:* Does everybody display the same trait?

Unfortunately, most of us have a built-in bias called the **fundamental attribution error.** This is based on the all-too-common belief that other people's behavior is almost always internally based rather than externally based. We'll readily believe that an employee's poor performance is due to laziness rather than faults with management or the company, or that the reason why someone appears aloof is because he or she is rude when it is instead due to a death in the family. Always judging others on an internal basis is tantamount to the joke about the English-speaking person who visits a non–English-speaking country and loudly laments that everyone there speaks a foreign language.

ERRORS IN CULTURAL PERCEPTIONS

Shortcuts in Judging Others

Whether internal or external, perceiving and determining why others do things differently is often a burden. As a result we tend to take shortcuts called **selective perception.** Sometimes these shortcuts can be valuable, but more often than not—particularly overseas—they can cause trouble. This is because humans generally react to their *perceptions* rather than to *reality.* Following are a few common misplaced perceptions:

- *Assumed similarity:* Assuming that other people are just like us and therefore go about their business the same way we do (all people are as ambitious, hardworking, have the same fears and concerns, and are as interested in something as we are).
- *Stereotyping:* Forming a general opinion based on a number of perceptions (real or otherwise) that we have of a particular group.
- *Halo effect:* Making a general impression based on one character trait. For example, we see or meet a man from an unfamiliar

place and assume that all people from that culture are just like him.

Emotions and Culture

Emotions are intense feelings directed at someone or something. Generally speaking, there are two types of recognized emotions:

1. *Felt emotions:* An individual's *actual* emotions.
2. *Displayed emotions:* Emotions that are expected or considered appropriate. In other words, displayed emotions, like cultural traits, are *learned.*

Felt and displayed emotions are often different in other cultures. When people working overseas for the first time begin to deal with employees and customers they sometimes naively assume that the emotions they're encountering are emotions these people actually feel. But again, that is a *perception.* Not long ago, a group of Americans was asked to match pictorial facial expressions with six basic emotions, and 86 to 97 percent of them agreed on the results. However when faced with the same pictures, the Japanese obtained only a 27 to 79 percent agreement. The point is that displayed emotions, like cultural differences, are *learned.* For example, in the United States it's considered normal for service-level employees to act overly cheerful and friendly with customers. However, in Israel this is sometimes interpreted as a sign of unprofessionalism. In Saudi Arabia it can be seen as a come-on that could land you in a lot of trouble.

CULTURE SHOCK

The Reality of Living Closely with a Different Culture

Culture shock is defined as the confusion, disorientation, and emotional upheaval that follows a move (not a visit) from one country to another. Every person that moves to another area of the world inevitably suffers through the following four stages, although most people deny that it ever happens to them.

Stage I: Excitement, pride, enthusiasm, and novelty characterize this stage. Being selected to represent your company in an international location is usually an attribute to your abilities and talents, and it's only natural to feel on top of the world during the first few weeks or months of the new job.

Stage II: Reality sets in. Factors such as not being able to speak the local language, which at first seemed somewhat humorous, now becomes a struggle. Menus, schedules, billboards, even radio and television programs are unintelligible. Simple conversation becomes a chore. In essence, everything you do requires much more effort than previously imagined and there seems to be no escape. (This can last two to three *long* months.)

Stage III: The struggle to adapt to a different language, foods, work patterns, schedules, customs, and so on turns into despair, depression, anger, or perhaps even defiance. Some people never quite get out of this stage. Symptoms include yearning for your place of origin, bad-mouthing everything, and generally being miserable. Turning to alcohol or any number of other self-destructive behaviors is not unusual for those who can't, or don't want to, cope during this period of adjustment.

Stage IV: The learning and acceptance process begins. At this stage the newcomer begins to understand what is and isn't important in the new culture and stops battling against all the differences being encountered. Instead, he or she learns to concentrate on maximizing the opportunities available in the new culture rather than focusing on what is different and/or unavailable.

Interestingly, once an individual leaves his or her adopted country and goes back home, this entire process is repeated—albeit much more quickly.

Smoothing the Transition

Here's how to smooth a move to another culture before leaving:

- *If possible, develop personal friendships.* This can be a slow and arduous process, and it isn't always realistic, but it can provide you with a good head start.

- *Conduct continuous research.* Undertake research for both general background information and basic business knowledge.
- *If possible, visit the country, region, or organization to which you plan to move.* This is invaluable for developing firsthand experience.
- *Talk to some born-and-bred locals.* People from the country you're moving to can be invaluable in teaching you the acceptable procedures. More often than not, when it comes to learning about their country, they'll be happy to help.
- *Use local distributors and agents.* National bureaucracy and distribution systems can be a nightmare. Again, since local people have a better understanding and familiarity of the marketplace, try to use them whenever possible.
- *Develop language skills.* Language is an essential part of a country's culture. Although mastering another language may not be feasible, attempting to learn as much as possible will impress others—and your initiative *will* be rewarded.
- *Use common sense.* Basic etiquette, common courtesy, speaking quietly, and showing respect will lessen most cross-cultural faux pas.

COMMUNICATING IN DIFFERENT CULTURES

Effective communication is difficult under the best of circumstances. However, four specific problem areas have been identified in relation to cross-cultural communication:

1. *Semantic barriers.* Words can have different meanings to different people. For example, the words *meeting, bizarre,* and *rendezvous* are more formal or are more powerful than most non-English speakers are aware.
2. *Word-connotation barriers.* Similarly, words can imply different meanings. In Japanese, the word *hai* translates as "yes," but it means that a person is listening, not that he or she agrees.
3. *Formality barriers.* In some cultures, language is changed when used in a formal sense rather than an informal one. Know the limits and correct uses of addressing others before you open your mouth.

4. *Perception barriers.* Different cultures view the world in different ways. For example, in some countries overpoliteness is sometimes seen as rude while in others too much casualness can be seen as lacking in manners. Again, familiarize yourself with local customs *before* you make a mistake.

The following tips will help minimize cultural misperceptions and misinterpretations:

- *Assume differences until similarity is proved.* You are far less likely to make an error if you assume that others are different rather than assuming they're similar.
- *Study what is said rather than your interpretation of it.* Interpretations are usually culturally sensitive. Delay making judgments until sufficient time has passed to think about what was said.
- *Empathize.* Before communicating, put yourself in the recipient's shoes.
- *Be careful with your conclusions.* When you think you've understood something, treat it as a hypothesis first. Be ready to modify your conclusion as time passes.

Being a Welcome Guest: The Art of Listening

Many people confuse hearing with listening, but the two are not similar. *Active listening* requires a listener to fully understand an intended message. Here's how it works:

1. Make eye contact and offer affirmative head nods and other appropriate expressions.
2. Listen for *message content*. What exactly is being said?
3. Ask questions, but don't interrogate. As the saying goes, "if you want to be interesting, be interested."
4. Try to understand the speaker's feelings.
5. Let the speaker know that his or her feelings are important.
6. Note any nonverbal cues. What does the speaker's body language suggest? Are any mixed messages evident?
7. Paraphrase and restate. Repeat to the speaker what you think you're hearing. Statistics state that 60 percent of American and

European companies identified poor or insufficient feedback as a primary cause of bad employee performance.

8. Don't overtalk.

IN CONCLUSION

Living in another country (or even another region of your own country) requires much restraint, hard work, and understanding, but it's also incredibly rewarding. My international experiences, both good and bad, have made my life immeasurably more interesting, humbled me, tested me beyond belief, and made me and my work more marketable. In addition, living abroad has broadened my mind and even changed a few of my political views, but the opportunities that have unfolded (and continue to unfold) have been breathtaking. Although I now feel comfortable just about anywhere, being surrounded by different cultures (which is an integral part of my work) is still an uphill climb. I still make mistakes, use the wrong words, and assume what I shouldn't—I just don't do it as often. It may sound corny, but poet Robert Frost was right when he said "I took the [road] less traveled by, and that has made all the difference." If you ever get the chance to work abroad and the offer is both legitimate and compatible with your personality and ambitions, go for it. Remember that good and bad are found every place you go—just as at home. After arriving in a new culture, let the air out of your ego, stop insisting that (and acting like) your culture is superior, lower your voice, concentrate on the good, avoid the bad, and don't compare everything to that tiny, closed-minded comfort zone you've created back home (I promise you that the fantasyland your nostalgia creates doesn't exist). Only then will you be well on the road to enriching yourself in ways you never thought possible.

PART III: THE BASIC SKILLS OF MANAGEMENT

Chapter 17

Managerial Decision Making and Problem Solving

Making decisions, both large and small, is a large part of a manager's daily life. In graduate school one of my finance teachers (a formidable man mentioned in this book's preface) started one of his lectures by proclaiming "If a good manager has ten decisions to make, he or she will probably get four right, two wrong, and the rest, well, it really doesn't matter."

It took me awhile to come to grips with that statement. What he meant was that not all decisions are necessarily right or wrong. In many instances, it is the *degree* to which they are right or wrong—as well as how an organization chooses to *deal* with its decision—that is just as important as the decision itself. A spectacular finish can be achieved after a bad start. It's up to each business to determine whether its decisions become successes or failures (i.e., the only true mistakes made in life are those allowed to continue as mistakes). Take a look at two examples:

The Tylenol poisoning crisis. In the 1980s a murderer opened a package of Tylenol pain capsules, poured out the contents of several, and replaced the ingredients with poison. Several people died as a result. Instead of distancing itself from its responsibility, the makers of Tylenol decided to inform the world about what had happened, ordered all its medications pulled from store shelves, assisted the FBI in its investigations, and made an effort to solve any future problems by developing tamper-proof packaging. As a result, the problem quickly disappeared. Shortly thereafter the company was widely praised for its response and it resumed business having earned an enormous amount of public respect.

The Firestone tire debacle. In the 1990s, reports accumulated suggesting that the tires Firestone made for sport utility vehicles (SUVs) had an inherent fault. Firestone publicly announced that it didn't really need to look into the situation. Instead, the company blamed the SUVs as the culprit. Of course, the SUV manufacturers blamed Firestone. Meanwhile, deaths from accidents resulting from tire blowouts continued to rise. In the end, as sales plummeted, the situation brought Firestone to the brink of ruin and several executives lost their jobs.

MAKING UP YOUR MIND

Several books claim that there's a big difference between managerial **decision making** (the process of finding and making a choice among alternative courses of action) and **problem solving** (the process of identifying and resolving the difference between what is actually happening and what should be happening). Any further elaborations will end here. Yes, problem solving and decision making are unique processes, but most decisions are made (or problems solved) in one of three ways:

1. *By avoiding the decision or problem:* ignoring the warning signs, doing nothing, and hoping the problem goes away (as Firestone did)
2. *By battling the problem:* taking action on problems as they arise (as Tylenol did)
3. *By preventing problems before they occur:* proactively finding ways to deal with future problems (as Tylenol also did with its innovative new packaging)

Two styles tend to be employed most when making decisions or solving problems. The first is called a *systematic approach*. This involves tackling problems in a rational and analytical fashion. It usually translates into breaking a problem down into small components and addressing each one in a logical manner. The second style is referred to as the *intuitive approach,* which allows for more flexibility and spontaneity. With the intuitive approach, experience and creativity are key.

Which style is the most effective? That depends upon the person involved in the decision making as well as the circumstances. Obviously it might be risky for an inexperienced manager to rely solely on gut feelings to make a decision. On the other hand, analyzing the minutiae of every decision option can be time consuming and tedious. In reality, most managers boil these processes down with a judgment call. So perhaps the overall question is: How good is your judgment?

GOOD PROBLEM SOLVING AND DECISION MAKING: A STEP-BY-STEP APPROACH

Several years ago I was appointed the general manager of a number of recreation facilities scattered across an area comprising more than two million people. One day early in my tenure a call came in from a cleaner at one of the swimming areas. A teenage boy had broken in and been caught swinging and jumping on a large canvas structure designed to provide shade. As a result, the structure had collapsed.

This was my wake-up call that vandalism was a rampant problem. Searching through the files later, it became apparent that my predecessors had done little to solve the problem. "These things just happen," was the attitude most of the staff had taken. Since we were located in the middle of a desert I cringed at the number of complaints we would receive because the shaded area was no longer available to our customers. In addition, the business was woefully short of cash, so our options were limited. I asked the cleaner to get the boy's correct name and address and send him on his way.

Sometime later, after visiting the scene, I telephoned the boy's parents with the hope of seeking reimbursement. By then the teen had been able to concoct a well-rehearsed lie. Imagine my surprise when I was informed that I had physically abused him (I hadn't come within miles of him) and his parents were considering taking legal action. Fed up with the attitude of "not-my-child" parents, I presented myself to the company's director. As I hoped, we began preparing for war.

To make a long story short, we let the matter drop. Simply put, doing nothing is sometimes the right decision. In every situation there comes a point when the effort and expense behind the process far outweighs possible conclusions. Besides, it rapidly dawned on me that I was ultimately to blame for the situation. Here's why, along with the steps that were taken to correct the problem:

1. *Every problem has a cause and every situation an alternative.* Find it. Investigate, dig deep, and get as many opinions as possible. Asking why five times is an old yet still an effective way of getting to the heart of the issue.

   Regarding the boy who pulled down the shaded structure I had to ask myself (and the staff) many questions and confront a series of highly unpleasant answers, among them:
   - Was the area supervised or unsupervised at the time? (unsupervised)
   - How did the vandal get into the pool area? (the gate lock was broken)
   - Had this happened before? (yes, but no one had bothered to report it)
   - How long was the lock broken? (possibly weeks, but again no one bothered to report it)

2. *Don't go it alone.* Gather as many creative solutions as you can. Get as many people involved in the decision-making process as possible (perhaps even external customers). Most important, be certain that the *cause* is being treated, not the symptom.

   The staff and I then came up with a number of possible solutions including:
   - Increase supervision of all pool areas before and after hours. If staff shortages make this impossible, assign a patrol.
   - Install "dud" security cameras (real cameras were too expensive).
   - Install/fix more sturdy locks on all pool gates.
   - Design more programs for teens (people rarely destroy what they are an active part of).

3. *Think ahead.* Whenever possible, choose the best long-term solution. Short-term solutions rarely solve anything and by definition must to be addressed over and over again.

   We then discussed the wider picture (the implications of our possible solutions) as well as putting the head of maintenance in charge of all the cleaners (it was his proposal). The idea was to train the cleaning staff to immediately report problems to the maintenance department before the facilities opened, thus ensuring that problems such as broken locks would not go unfixed or go unreported or get lost in the system.

4. *Take action.* Follow through with the decision. Often the difference between effective and ineffective managers is that effective managers are people of action.

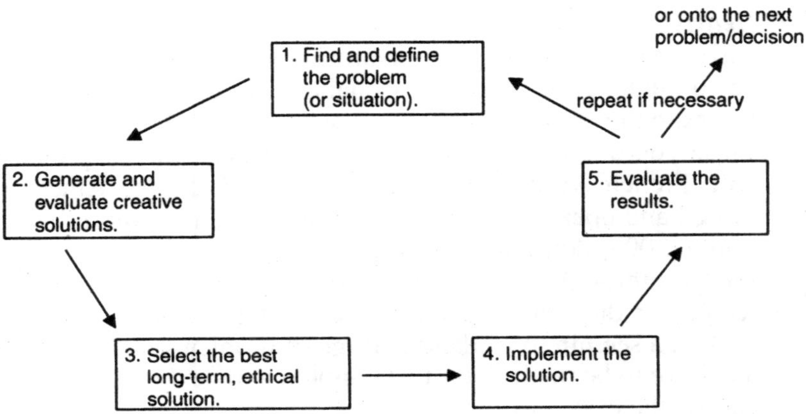

FIGURE 17.1. The Problem-Solving/Decision-Making Process

We decided to follow through with all the options we'd discussed (except installing the dud security cameras).

5. *Reevaluate the results of the decision.* Were the results effective? If not, repeat the process (see Figure 17.1).

   Our actions didn't resolve every future problem, but they did reduce the number significantly (as compared to earlier years), so we decided to maintain them.

PRACTICES TO AVOID WHEN MAKING DECISIONS

Everybody at some point must make a decision. The trick is to ensure that your decisions do as little damage as possible. The following practices typically result in bad decisions. Becoming aware of and avoiding them will improve the chances that a bad decision won't happen.

- *Escalating commitment* is the tendency to increase effort and apply more resources (people, materials, money, etc.) when the chosen solution is not working. This usually occurs when people can't admit that they're wrong.

- *Heuristics* are judgmental shortcuts in decision making often based on bias, stereotypes, misinformation, gossip, rumors, outdated thinking, or other unreasonable sources and experiences. For example, choosing not to buy products in red packaging because you don't like the color red or refusing to buy products with French words in their name, even if they're American owned and operated, because the French didn't want to invade Iraq in 2003 (don't laugh; it happened).
- *Rushing* through any problem or decision-making process is a recipe for disaster. Every manager suffers through days that present a seemingly endless barrage of problems and decisions that have to be made. Don't be tempted to race through them or choose the easy way out.
- *Not putting your customers first* is a rampant managerial mistake. The world's media is full of stories about managers who put self-interests before those of their customers. The classic example happened in the 1970s when Ford created an automobile called the Pinto. Somewhere along the line it became apparent that the Pinto had a tendency to burst into flames during collisions, thereby badly burning or killing its occupants. Instead of solving the problem, the company's executives made the astonishing decision to do nothing. Their conclusion was that the amount of damages they would have to pay as a result of court actions would actually be less than fixing the car's inherent design flaw. So people continued to die and, as is the case with most bad decisions, this one came back to haunt them. *Every* decision a manager makes must be geared toward customers. Anything else is just plain stupid.
- *Relying too much on statistics or mathematical formulas* is a bad idea. Collecting and analyzing data certainly has its place, but too many people seem to forget that the world doesn't always operate with mathematical precision. More to the point, management is more of a human endeavor (i.e., dealing with common sense) than a mathematical one. A specific example of this involves a famous vacuum cleaner manufacturer in Britain. The company decided to run an offer that included free plane tickets from London to New York (and back) with every purchase of their product—despite that the price of their product was virtually insignificant compared to the cost of the airline

tickets. "But," stated the marketing department, "statistics show that customers rarely take up such offers." Thinking that it would then be a good publicity exercise, the company decided to go ahead with the plan. Needless to say, they quickly became besieged with consumers who just wanted to get at the tickets. The company immediately withdrew its offer, but by then the die was cast. They were taken to court and they lost—the judge ruling that they had to provide the airline tickets just as their offer had promised. Sometime later the company went bankrupt and was bought out by its rival.

In 2003 the president of Red Lobster was fired after approving the promotion of an all-you-can-eat crab legs offer in the United States. Unfortunately, crab legs are very expensive and Red Lobster underestimated just how much Americans could eat. The result? Contrary to statistical evidence, Americans showed up in droves—costing the company millions.

- *Reinventing the wheel* is not a logical goal. Few managerial decisions are novel. Chances are that someone somewhere has had to make a decision similar to the one your organization is facing. Before making a wrong decision or inducing an ulcer trying to make the correct one, do a little research and find out what other people or companies did when they were faced with similar situations. It may save time, effort, money, embarrassment (when someone else points out that company X did it better) and a few sleepless nights.

CREATIVITY AND DECISION MAKING

"If you think that the solution to every problem is a hammer," goes the old saying, "then you'll probably see every problem as a nail." When it comes to finding an optimal resolution to a problem, most managers tend to (1) be too conservative and miss out on a full opportunity, (2) try the same old approach they've been using for years, or (3) happily settle for a *satisfactory* solution. To facilitate an *optimal* solution when making a decision, consider the following tips from *A Kick in the Seat of the Pants* by author Roger Von Oech (1986):

- *Believe in your creativity.* If you have the right attitude and think you can be innovative and creative, chances are that you will be.
- *Encourage nonconformity.* Allow differences to be presented.
- *Reach out beyond your specialization.* Use other people to expand upon ideas and assumptions.
- *Avoid too much logic.* Don't accept the way things have always been. Ask "why?" as often as possible.
- *Search for more than one right answer.* Don't get stuck in a closed-minded attitude.
- *Step back.* Take time to think, tinker, and play around with ideas.
- *Don't be afraid of trial and error.* Accept the fact that failure is often a path to success.

A FINAL THOUGHT

We're all continually faced with the need to choose—a process often subject to distortion and bias. Unfortunately, decision making is usually based on judgments rather than a planned, logical process. Concentrating on being proactive instead of reactive is a big step in reducing problems, but the next time you find yourself face to face with a big business decision, take a deep breath, think, and get others involved. You should also apply "Round 1" and "Round 2" of the questions posed in Chapter 13 on ethics. Doing so may bring you closer than you ever thought possible to an optimal solution.

Chapter 18

Managing Time

Time is a unique and precious resource. Once lost, it can never be replaced. Although the term *time saving* is frequently used, it's a misnomer. Time cannot be saved. It's either used or wasted. In the same vein, many people make the mistake of placing time in a category similar to money. Controlling time isn't controlling finances. Yes, two minutes or two hours can be "spent" on something, but whereas monetary units rarely vary (one dollar is the same as another dollar), two hours are never the same because different things always happen in different hours. For example, certain activities may be done at one hour but not another, or people may or may not be available during different hours.

Naturally, since time is valuable, it must be managed effectively. Not doing so often results in an organization characterized by high dramas, such as the following:

1. Lurching from one task or project to another
2. Last-minute rushes to meet deadlines
3. Days and/or hours that slip by with little or nothing to show for them
4. A general degradation of performance
5. A build-up of unnecessary stress
6. An environment in which everyone runs around constantly fighting fires

The good news is that time, like any resource, *can* be managed.

UNDERSTANDING EFFECTIVE TIME MANAGEMENT

The trick with most learned traits is to get into the habit of them—and the nice thing about habits is that the good ones are just as hard to break as the bad ones. Consider these five points:

1. *Time is allocated to everyone in equal measure.* Money, materials, and labor can be (and sometimes are) distributed unequally, but everyone has twenty-four hours in a day. With time management, the idea is to use those twenty-four hours the best way possible.
2. *Poor time management is often a symptom of overconfidence.* As with any management process, time must be planned, monitored, and reviewed. Once this is understood and *accepted,* a system can be devised to make the most of it.
3. *Work expands to fill the amount of time available (Parkinson's Law).* Put another way, if you're given an hour to perform a task that takes thirty minutes, you'll probably use the full hour. Likewise, if the task normally takes an hour and fifteen minutes, you may be able to squeeze it into an hour if that's all the time available.
4. *The most effective managers produce 80 percent of their results using 20 percent of their time.* Therefore, managers who use their time well often ensure that their most important responsibilities are included in that 20 percent of time. Everyone has a natural cycle. Some people work best in the morning, some in the afternoon. Use this cycle to its best advantage. Tackle the most demanding duties during your peak times and the routine tasks (answering e-mails, performing follow-ups, scheduling, etc.) at the slow points. Granted, this may be difficult if others have control over your time allocations, but do keep it in mind.
5. There is a major *distinction between action and accomplishment.* Being busy doesn't mean that something is being accomplished. Management involves focusing on results—not putting on a show.

Classifying Time

Two major types of time are found in most work environments:

1. *Response time:* The uncontrollable amount of time required to perform a task. For example, if a manager must attend a weekly meeting and that meeting typically lasts two hours, then that time can't be used for anything else.
2. *Discretionary time:* The amount of time that *is* under a manager's control. Sadly for many people at the low level of the management scale it doesn't amount to much, and what is available often occurs in blocks of five or ten minutes rather than hours. The trick is to learn to coordinate discretionary time so that it can be bundled into bigger and more useful units. Again, for the bottom-level manager this may be difficult—but don't despair. The suggestions in this chapter may prove helpful.

TIPS FOR MAXIMIZING YOUR TIME

Ranking Priorities

Learn to take control of your work before it takes control of you. Taking the time to think about and write a schedule may seem time-consuming and in itself a waste of time, but adopting this habit helps by

- planning each day (or week) efficiently;
- better allocating an appropriate amount of time for duties;
- eliminating the wasted time by providing time limits (remember Parkinson's Law);
- pointing out (and giving ammunition to refuse) excessive workloads;
- monitoring accomplishments; and
- being on time for appointments and meetings.

A good way to begin time management is to prioritize or rank work activities from the most important to the least important. Every workday contains many tasks that must be accomplished. Some are more important than others and some are more urgent. Taking ten or fifteen minutes to separate these tasks (the urgent from the important) and prioritize them will provide a good rough draft for the day ahead. Here's how to get started:

1. Make a list of your daily or weekly duties by ranking them in order of importance (those involving paying customers should come first).
2. Next to each duty write down the best or only time to perform it (e.g., some duties can be done only in the morning, others only in the evening, or on a Tuesday, etc.).
3. Determine how much time is *realistically* needed to accomplish each task.
4. Section your workday into units of time using a schedule notebook or desk diary.
5. Use the diary to fill in your *response times* first. Remember, response times are duties or obligations that can't be done at any other time.
6. Pencil in your most important or urgent tasks during the times that suit them best.
7. Last, fill in the rest of your available time slots as you go down your list of priorities. Be flexible. Nothing should be written in stone.

Avoid Classic Time Wasters

When making a schedule, two common managerial time wasters should be examined:

1. *Time spent between tasks:* Consider grouping together similar tasks to avoid having to start up each one independently.
2. *Time spent on personal or social matters:* Personal telephone calls, lengthy office conversations, playing solitaire on the office computer, and other unproductive activities have no place in a work environment. A good way to highlight this is to break down a salary into hourly increments. For example, $42,000 a year comes out to $875 a week or roughly $22 per hour. Would this amount of waste be tolerated if it involved other resources? Are all hours in a workday worth paying out $22? They should be.

Learn to Say No

One of the trickier aspects of time management involves understanding that everybody's time is valuable. Bottom-level employees may find this particularly difficult to communicate to superiors. A diplomatic way out of this predicament without being demoted or agreeing to take on more work is to show senior-level managers a copy of a typical work schedule to prove that time is indeed being used to its maximum. Otherwise, be firm but fair when you do the following:

- *Ask for clear goals and objectives.* Not long ago I was asked by the president of a small European college to set up a department based on a series of lectures I gave about entering foreign markets. His idea was to start a program that helped national businesses expand overseas. Yet when I asked him for a list of written objectives stating what he hoped to achieve he looked at me and said, "That's up to you. It'll be the first part of your job." So I turned him down. Why? Vague or ill-defined objectives waste time. When confronted with any task it's imperative that clarifications be made: What *exactly* is expected? What time limitations are involved? What resources are available? Such issues simply must be resolved before time is wasted on false assumptions.
- *Don't do the work of others.* Good employees know their responsibilities. Although it's important for people to chip in and cover shortfalls from time to time, constantly doing others' work shouldn't become a habit. This is not to say that an organization's staff shouldn't be enthusiastic and helpful to one another. Just keep in mind that help and enthusiasm don't add more hours to the day. For example, a manager shouldn't have to check a secretary's work for misspellings. The secretary shouldn't be required to cover the boss's forgotten duties. No one should have to mop up other people's messes.
- *Delegate.* Managers who refuse to delegate are likely to be frustrated people. It's simply not necessary for a manager to do everything, nor does it display good management skills by doing so. Good managers should regularly assign routine tasks to others. The bottom line: If an employee can do a job, let the employee perform it. In the process the manager may be surprised at how many "managerial tasks" are best suited to others.
- *Make appointments.* Throughout every workday a manager is beset by a host of people demanding chunks of time. One solution is to get these people in the habit of making appointments.

Although this is not necessary for every inquiry, the point is to ensure that time is being respected. Equally as important, when the appointee's time is up, politely say so.

Do the little things now. Twenty seconds spent jotting down an idea or request will help you later avoid wasting fifteen minutes trying to remember it and/or wasting someone else's time reminding you. Filing an important paper now may help you avoid spending ten minutes looking for it later. Phoning or contacting a person whose input is needed during an impromptu meeting rather than putting it off for later (and finding out that your plans need to be altered) usually avoids wasting hours of time. The moral of the story? Don't let little things pile up into a big mountain of time consumption.

THE END GAME: MAKING LIFE EASIER

Of course using time effectively isn't the answer to every problem, but it can reveal or eliminate a lot of managerial ills. One of the many positive side effects is the amount of stress it reduces. For many managers, thinking about all that must be done in a day (or week) is enough to unleash an unhealthy dose of anxiety. During one of my managerial positions I used to awaken at three or four o'clock in the morning with my brain racing into gear, focusing on everything that had to be done that day. For the next several hours I'd try to figure out how on earth everything could be accomplished. However, when I began using the desk diary that had previously sat unopened on the corner of my desk (it took a lot of discipline to make using it a regular habit), it became clear what had to be done by Wednesday, what couldn't be done on Friday, what was best done on Tuesday morning, and so forth. After this became apparent, that sinking feeling that all managers experience at one time or another began to evaporate. An unexpected bonus arose in discovering that not only was there enough time to do everything, but some left over to pursue other endeavors as well.

Chapter 19

Dealing with People in the Workplace

"My job might just be tolerable if it didn't involve people," a colleague of mine once confessed. To say the least, he was having a bad day. One of his employees had phoned in sick and his staff had spent the entire morning scrambling to cover her absence—knowing full well that she was suffering from nothing more than a hangover. That wasn't all. "Ever since the boss's wife had her baby," he continued, "he snaps and shouts at everyone because he's not getting enough sleep. Add to that the fact that our secretary's divorce has decreased her work output by at least 80 percent and it's a wonder we're getting anything done." He shook his head. Dark smudges rimmed his eyes. "People," he sighed, "who needs them?"

Well, the fact is we all need them, because, like it or not, work won't get done without them. The problem is that people invariably suffer through the ups and downs of life, and as a manager you must learn to deal with it. Some of these problems are beyond your control, some will test your character (would you fire an employee who has taken too much time off to attend to a sick child?), and some require the unpleasantness of discipline. Add to this the adage that for every negative comment leveled against an employee it takes three positive ones to negate it, and the process of dealing with people in the workplace can seem as if it were a minefield. This chapter is designed to help lead you around that minefield by getting you to think about creating a work environment that helps prevent *people problems* before they occur. It is not a definitive lesson in human psychology.

UNDERSTANDING EMPLOYEE BEHAVIOR (FOUR THEORIES)

Maslow's Hierarchy of Needs

In 1974, the *Academy of Management Journal* conducted a survey that sought to determine the most influential theories in management. Second place was awarded to Abraham Maslow and his "Hierarchy of Needs" pyramid (1943) (Matteson, 1974). (The first place winner is mentioned in Chapter 15.) Through his famous work, Maslow stipulated that people's needs can be classified into five different categories, as listed in Figure 19.1.

Maslow's theory is based on two underlying principles: (1) everyone starts at the bottom and attempts to move up the pyramid when they see that the need immediately above is not being fulfilled, and (2) a need cannot be activated until the one immediately below it has been met.

As with many groundbreaking ideas, Maslow's theory continues to be the subject of attack. For this chapter's purpose, however, it's

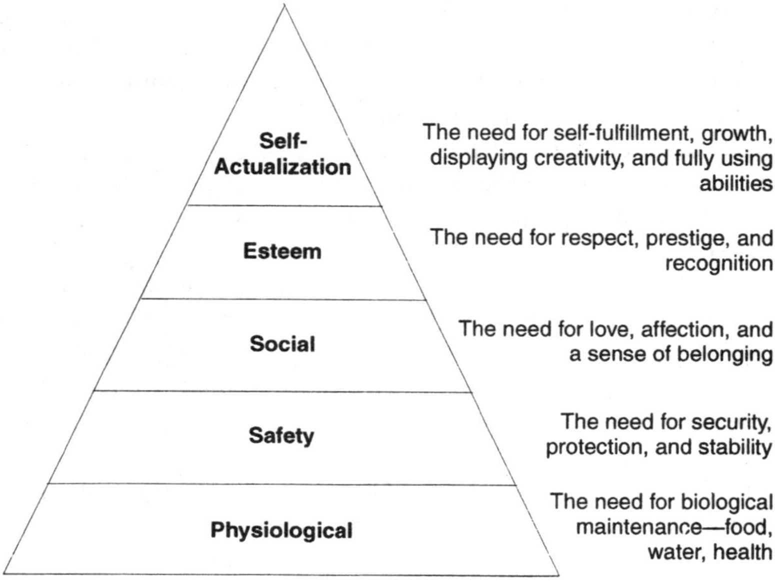

FIGURE 19.1. Maslow's Hierarchy of Needs

not important whether you agree or disagree with it. The point is that all people have basic needs and they seek to fill those needs. Smart managers, when searching for ways to keep their staff motivated and content, will find out what those needs are.

McClelland's Three Essential Human Motivation Needs

Later in that same decade, David McClelland more or less continued in the same vein by identifying three needs essential to human motivation:

1. *The need for achievement:* the desire to do better, solve problems, and master complexity
2. *The need for power:* the desire to control other people and influence their behavior
3. *The need for affiliation:* the desire to have friendly relations with people (McClelland, 1961)

McClelland argued that people, over time, acquire or develop different stages of these needs as a result of their experiences. Equally, each stage involves a distinct set of work environments. It is therefore a manager's duty to recognize the needs of employees and create appropriate work settings to satisfy them. For example, delegating to others can satisfy their need for achievement or power, and the creation of quality circles and/or the setting up of project teams may help to satisfy affiliation needs.

Herzberg's Two-Factor Theory

In 1967 Frederick Herzberg devised a two-factor theory based on a broad study of people at work. Herzberg concluded that there are two categories that directly relate to job satisfaction:

1. *Work content:* what people do while at work
2. *Work setting:* the actual environment in which work is done

Herzberg stated that these two areas must be handled separately. Work-content factors involve satisfying employees' sense of achievement, responsibility, and personal growth. Work-setting factors (or hygiene factors) deal with employees' work environment. Therefore, if productivity is down and improvements must be made, a manager needs to find out whether work content or work setting needs attention. Adding piped-in music and cleaning work areas may be fine for improving employee work settings but would be useless if the problem lies with work content. Likewise, improving job titles, handing out awards, and other intrinsic factors may not help much with environmental work concerns.

Alderfer's Existence-Related-Growth Theory

Later, in 1992, Clayton Alderfer sought to improve on Maslow's hierarchical pyramid by condensing its five categories into three:

1. *Existence needs:* the desire for physiological and material well-being
2. *Relatedness needs:* the desire to improve interpersonal relationships
3. *Growth needs:* the desire to pursue personal growth and fulfillment

Alderfer's existence-related-growth theory is meant to be more flexible than Maslow's. Alderfer says that people can move up and down his hierarchy of needs at any given time. If, for example, a higher need can't be fulfilled, a lower, previously satisfied need can then be reactivated in its place in what he calls *a frustration-regression* principle.

CORRECTIVE COMMUNICATION

Regardless of which human behavior theory you subscribe to, its application begins with effective measurement and communication. "If it can't be measured it can't be managed," a student once told me. She went on to confidently conclude that this statement, or variations of it, could be used to control almost anything pertaining to management. I agree. Prompt, precise measurement, placed in the context of **corrective communication** (i.e., guidelines, objectives, and results), is arguably one of the quickest ways to avoid or handle people problems.

Corrective communication (or feedback) can be provided at three stages of a work task:

1. Before the task begins
2. During the task
3. After the task

Use of corrective communication is contingent upon the situation and motivational factors of the people involved. However, whether formal or informal, it must remain timely (the fresher it is, the better), honest, simple, and constructive. It should also avoid personal comments as well as situations that are out of the recipient's control. The following sections give examples of different types of corrective measures that exist in most workplaces.

Establishing Norms

Acceptable perimeters of behavior are set by both management and employees and can be formally written down in a "codes of conduct" format or set in a more informal fashion. Once these norms have been established, organizational culture and peer pressure rather than managerial policing enforces corrective behavior. Norms are powerful shapers of human behavior and can work wonders, but if left completely on their own they can result in bullying or chaos.

Success and Failure System

Most managers at some point set employee targets and goals. If they're too high, they may result in failure with the subsequent eroding of future motivation. If they're too easy, a sense of accomplishment will be eluded. Ideally, goals should be lofty and be set in achievable stages. Progress (or a lack thereof) can then be verified and rewarded (or corrected) at each stage by

- highlighting something positive,
- pointing out what needs improving (without criticizing), and
- suggesting how an improvement can be made.

Recognition

Employees need to feel appreciated. If an employee does something well and he or she is recognized, then similar successful behavior can be expected in the future. If no recognition takes place, then a message is sent that no one cares. Bear in mind that recognition doesn't necessarily have to be award ceremonies or cash bonuses (although these can be appropriate). Sometimes a simple word of acknowledgment is all that's needed.

Evaluations

Regular **evaluations** are a necessary way to remind employees that the work they do is being monitored. However, yearly or biannual reviews should not become a tedious and banal formality during which little or no communication occurs. Employees and managers need to know how they are doing and the effect they are having on one another. In this regard, evaluations should be a constructive exercise that clears the air and lets all concerned know where they stand, what improvements need to be made, and where they are heading. For more on employee evaluations, consult Chapter 28.

BEHAVIOR MODIFICATION

On the face of it, Newton's third law of motion, which states that every action brings about an equal and opposite reaction, applies quite readily to humans. The beginning of this chapter relays the example of an employee who dishonestly phoned in sick to work. This is demonstrated via a simple model of human behavior:

trigger → action → payoff

The hungover employee may have been celebrating a holiday, blowing off steam, or suffering from a personal problem (trigger). The result is that she drank too much (action) and got a day off from work (payoff). How can a manager break this cycle and prevent it from happening again? One way is through a rather draconian-sounding process called **behavior modification,** explained in the following five steps:

1. *Recognize the behavior.* Find out who or what is influenced by the employee's behavior and whether the behavior is in fact worth correcting.
2. *Analyze the behavior.* Every action is preceded by a trigger and followed by a payoff. When analyzing behavior, dig deep and find the trigger. What is the resulting action? What is the payoff?
3. *Seek possible solutions.* Calmly sit down with the person(s) involved with, or influenced by, the behavior and get some feedback. Perhaps he or she wasn't aware of the problem. Mentioning the problem may be all that's necessary for it to end.
4. *Implement a solution.* People usually don't do something unless there is a payoff. In a calm and rational manner, modify the trigger or payoff by adding a consequence that is either positive or negative (ideally, it should be positive).
5. *Monitor the results.* If the results work, continue along the same lines and look for another solvable problem. If the results fail, go back and try something else.

Perhaps the hungover employee was drinking because it was her birthday. Therefore, her behavior may be singular (it happens rarely) or normal in that all employees do this on their birthday. It could be possible that the employee had a personal problem and sought solace in a few too many drinks. In that case, perhaps she needs some time off from work to sort out her problem. A few days off now may prevent weeks of additional problems later. Either way, a good response would be to sit down with her and calmly discuss the consequences of her actions (provide her with corrective feedback). She may not be aware of the difficulties she caused and may feel ashamed and embarrassed when she discovers that everyone had to perform extra duties to cover her absence. Peer pressure or group norms may then prevent future problems. Perhaps making her perform extra duties as compensation or docking her wages as a punishment will eliminate any future perceived payoff. The behavior selected to deal with the problem depends on the employee, the environment, the situation, and the manager.

SUMMING UP

Every workforce has unique needs, every behavior instigates a unique reaction, and every problem has a unique solution. When dealing with people in the workplace, time is of the essence because customers won't wait while an organization sorts out its people problems. Perhaps this is a good time to reconsider the problem prevention attributes inherent in the four employee behavior theories mentioned earlier in this chapter. In other words, keeping a workforce content, motivated, and moving in the right direction is contingent upon dealing with people problems *before* they occur.

Chapter 20

Oral Communication in the Workplace

Communication is about sending, receiving, and understanding information and meaning. The key words in this definition are *receiving* and *understanding*. Communication, particularly when it involves customers, is not just about transferring information from company to customer. That one-way street amounts to little more than advertising—and the problem with advertising is that there's so much of it in our lives that most people have learned, consciously or otherwise, to filter out what they think they don't want to see or hear. Therefore, if what's being conveyed isn't received properly, communication isn't taking place. Just as important, if what is said or written *has* been heard or seen yet *isn't understood,* communication still isn't taking place.

Two types of communication concern managers:

1. *Effective communication:* when the intended message of the sender and the interpreted meaning of the receiver are the same.
2. *Efficient communication:* when effective communication happens at a minimal cost to an organization. For this reason, managers sometimes e-mail messages or notices to employees instead of speaking with them (one of the more useful aspects of e-mail is that it allows a message to be delivered to hundreds of recipients as easily as it is to one).

DEALING WITH DIFFICULTIES AS THEY ARISE

Problems with communication usually involve human beings crossing wires, misunderstanding each other, or tuning out altogether. Welcome to the *problem zone* (see Figure 20.1)—an area filled with barriers and distractions, intentional and otherwise, that interfere with effective communication. Sometimes the problem zone is beyond the control of a manager, but for the most part the distractions within it can be greatly reduced with a little forethought.

The Problem Zone

Physical Distractions

Loud noises, telephone interruptions, drop-in visitors, lack of privacy, a dramatic workplace, etc., all contribute to distraction. Having the sender and recipient move to a quieter environment with specific instructions not to be disturbed can minimize many of these distractions.

Absence of Feedback

Letters, e-mails, memos, posted notices, reports, and voice messages are all examples of one-way communication. Dictatorial managers and large group gatherings in which feedback is unwelcome can also produce one-way communication. For managers, a solution could be to actively seek feedback from group representatives, or in the case of written material, ask recipients to initial it, comment, and send it back.

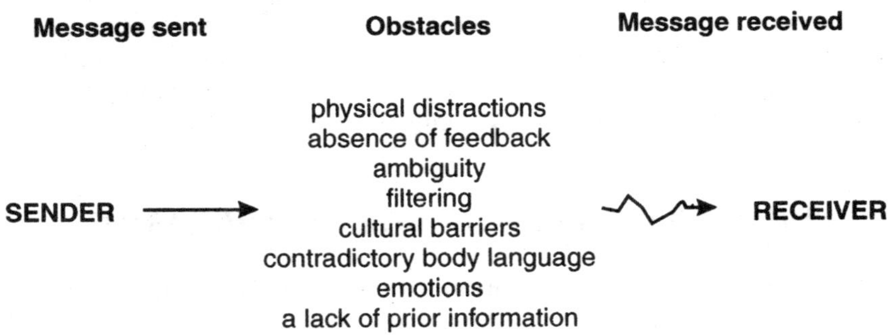

FIGURE 20.1. The Communication Problem Zone

Ambiguity

Ambiguity occurs when a message is unclear. This can be either unintentional or intentional. Unintentional ambiguity is often a result of misunderstanding and can arise due to a lack of leadership, too many people giving instructions, not thinking beforehand about the message being delivered, or the overuse of highbrow wording (I once overheard two department heads discuss "interfacing" with another employee—whatever that meant). However, ambiguity occurs sometimes on purpose. By being ambiguous, a manager (similar to a politician) can avoid questions and conflict, hide insecurities, make it easy to deny earlier statements, say several things at once, say no without actually uttering the word "no" and, in general, be all things to all people. The way to avoid sending an ambiguous message is to think carefully before sending it and to request confirmation of it immediately after it's been received by the recipient. The best method to avoid receiving an ambiguity is to ask the speaker for clarification.

Filtering

The intentional distorting of information to appease a recipient is known as filtering. In business this usually involves telling the boss what he or she wants to hear. Filtering has been described as one of the greatest enemies managers face. Whether the reasoning behind it is an unwillingness to identify personal mistakes, a desire to please, or a fear of retribution for delivering bad news, the results are the same. This includes making bad decisions based on distorted information as well as creating an environment that covers up errors. Wholehearted adoption of ethical policies as well as efforts toward eliminating fear from the workplace is essential for success.

Body Language

Body language is exhibited through facial expressions, eye contact, hand movements, posture, and sometimes voice intonation. Most listeners will watch a speaker's body movements (consciously or subconsciously) to discover if the movements coincide with what is being said. If not, confusion or mixed messages may result. Although this may sound trivial, inappropriate body language can unintentionally send signals of deception, dishonesty, mistrust, a lack of respect, or arrogance. Again, pay careful attention to *what* is being said and *how* it is being said. Asking for feedback is a good idea too.

Cultural Barriers

Cultural barriers exist mostly (but not exclusively) in international environments. This includes the disorientation that results from accents and/or words and actions that seem similar from region to region but aren't. For example, smiling, saying yes, and nodding when listening to a person from another culture may mean that either you agree with the subject or that you're merely listening. The best way to get around cultural barriers is to be attentive, let the other person talk freely, utilize the basic rules of etiquette, and politely ask a few questions. (Please reexamine Chapter 16.)

Emotions

Although losing self-control or displaying anger may feel good initially, it serves no purpose in the long run and is often counterproductive. Make it a rule never to address people when under emotional duress.

Lack of Prior Information

Missing information can result in a message's receiver being lost, confused, or sent off in the wrong direction. This usually happens when the sender assumes that a recipient fully understands (or doesn't need to know) the reasoning behind a message. The best way to avoid this is to remember the adage "if you assume anything, you will be wrong" before explaining something to someone.

A FEW COMMUNICATION BASICS

Years ago, when I was earning a teaching certification, an entire afternoon was spent learning to ask questions that elicited a response from students other than "yes" or "no." For those of us taking the course, this was more difficult than it sounded. Typical first attempts were similar to the following:

US: Do you understand?

THE STUDENTS: Yes.

US: Are you enjoying the class?

THE STUDENTS: Yes.

US: Is there anything you'd like us to repeat or discuss further?

THE STUDENTS: No.

The main reason we weren't getting any feedback was because of the questions we asked. Other reasons include never having shown a previous interest in the students wants and needs and therefore not yet having a trusting relationship with them. Simply put, effective communication can't start in a vacuum. It must first be *cultivated* by winning the attention and trust of the recipient. Once this has been established, asking questions that begin with the words *why, when, how, where,* and *what* will produce a greater chance of in-depth response. Try answering "yes" or "no" to them.

Silence As a Communication Instigator

Take a moment to consider using silence as a means of eliciting communication. People often become so preoccupied trying to answer someone or cut in on another's thoughts that they don't give silence a try. Most of us are usually wary of silence and try to fill it. Therefore, a way to use silence to advantage is to ask an open question (or an opinion), lean back, adopt an unthreatening posture, and await a response. The longer you remain quiet, the more detail the person will probably surrender just to fill the quiet.

A FINAL TIP

For more help developing your communication skills, as well as advice on how to establish a trusting bond with others, obtain a copy of the excellent book *How to Win Friends and Influence People* by Dale Carnegie. Don't be misled by the title. This timeless classic, first published in the 1930s and still widely available today, packs a potent message and offers a plethora of useful business advice dealing with communication, social intercourse, and their relationship in the workplace.

Chapter 21

Written Business Communication

Take a moment to study the following examples:

Example 1: In Australia, a successful businessman turns around a bankrupt company. When later asked how he accomplished this, he replies, "I forbid the writing of memos. Instead, I demanded that employees actually talk to one another."

Example 2: In Brazil, the chairman of the groundbreaking and successful company Semco describes in a best-selling book how he turned his company (and his life) around. Among the major contributing factors, he says, is the limitation of all company memos to one page in length.

Example 3: In the United States, a renowned novelist sits down to write a note to his daughter's teacher explaining the child's absence due to a medical appointment. After more than twenty minutes and numerous rough drafts, his frustrated wife finally grabs the pen from his hand and writes the note herself. It takes her less than fifteen seconds.

Example 4: Around the world, many couples forgo the option of marriage and simply live together instead. "It (the act of getting married) is just a piece of paper," many of them claim. In reply, most married people can only shake their heads, not at the act of living together, but at the absurdity of the statement.

Example 5: In the Middle East, a company manager sends out a memo to various department heads informing them of an upcoming event. Before the memo can wind its way around the organization, the event comes and goes.

Each one of these stories is true. When you get to the end of this chapter, try to ascertain the message behind each of them. For now, it's enough to know that writing is an essential managerial skill.

Among its purposes is the transfer of meaning and information from one person to another. Note, however, that differences exist between business writing and other forms of writing. Novels and stories, for example, are designed to enrich and entertain. In education, the emphasis is on imparting knowledge. With business, the point is to convey pertinent information via succinct, explanatory text.

Love it or loathe it, every manager must write competently, because the ability to write briefly, succinctly, and with clarity is considered a basic managerial strength. In fact, some estimates claim that up to 40 percent of a manager's time is spent writing.

THE ROLES OF BUSINESS WRITING

For the most part, writing in business fulfills four major roles:

1. *It conveys information.* Written words are used to communicate policies, rules, objectives, opinions, and ideas. Documentation provides a means to explain ongoing developments and plans for the future. In addition, the written word can be filed and reused as a form of definitive recording.
2. *It clarifies information.* If information or ideas aren't conveyed properly communication won't take place. Ironically, writing tends to eliminate this problem because of its complexity. No other action demands at the same time the use of the eyes (for registering what is being written), the ears (all people "hear" in their minds what they are writing as they write it), the brain (writing demands a high standard of perfection), and the hands (for the actual physical writing process). Writing forces a person to think about and plan what is being written as opposed to hiding behind the stammers, pauses, "umms," and "uhs" pervasive in verbal communication.
3. *It reflects seriousness on the part of the writer.* Some years ago I was asked to write an article for a business journal about pricing. "The first thing that must be done," I wrote, "is to get together with your colleagues and write down your business's objectives." Strangely, the journal's editors cut that sentence out—as well as the next sentence, which explained that taking the time and effort to write things down not only shows seriousness in the desire to deal with objectives but also provides a

guide that can be shared, compared, and used to measure thoughts with others (and against the future).

4. *It holds people accountable.* Poor communication is often blamed for problems or failures as diverse as (1) credibility issues concerning people who insist they were not involved with, or privy to, illegal or unethical behavior; (2) incompetence; and (3) value differences (differences in beliefs). In many of these situations initial problems may have been avoided if the use of clear, concise information was understood, agreed upon, and signed by all parties.

FORMS OF BUSINESS WRITING

E-mail

Two of the most obvious advantages of e-mail are that it's easy and it's cheap. These, however, are also its downside. With e-mail, it's easy to send hundreds of messages at the push of a button—thereby burdening employees who have to take the time to determine which messages are relevant: In this regard, e-mail has a tendency to be overused by people who don't want to communicate face to face (studies have shown that most office workers spend upward of two hours per day writing, reading, or sorting through e-mails). The cardinal rule behind e-mail (or any written business communication for that matter), apart from being considerate, is to refrain from being rude, aggressive, and/or unpleasant. Attempts at humor should also be avoided. The bottom line is that you shouldn't send an e-mail unless you can say what you've written in front of the boss. Remember, the written word, particularly on a computer screen, can be easily stored and used against you.

Memos

Internal communications designed to convey policy changes, company news, etc., can be effective in stating what actions need to be taken regarding certain issues. Generally speaking, the following format is often used as a heading:

To: (the recipient's name and job title)
Through: (the names and job titles of the individuals standing between you and the recipient in the company's chain of command)
From: (the sender's name and job title)
Date:
Subject: (a short statement describing *exactly* what the memo is about. For example, INSECTS FOUND IN OUR STRAWBERRY ICE CREAM PRODUCTS rather than INSECTS or ICE CREAM)

The golden rule behind memos is to keep their use to a minimum. Use them only when a written record is needed. Otherwise, they become an easy way to avoid people. Also be aware that many people use memos to cover their backsides (i.e., they're used as proof that information about something was given—making those who didn't heed it look bad).

Letters

Letters are more formal than e-mails, therefore extra precaution should be taken regarding spelling, grammar, layout, and style. All letters should state the name, title, and address of the writer, as well as the recipient, at the top of the page. Letters should begin with a proper salutation and date and conclude formally with a signature. After that, the basic rules of e-mailing apply.

Reports

Reports are little more than lengthy memos. However, because reports are research based (their purpose is usually to uncover information, solve a particular problem, or present solutions), they tend to contain headings and subheadings, the procedures and/or methods used to gather information, conclusions, and recommendations. Reports often take a long time to produce because the information they require must be analyzed and compiled. This doesn't mean they must be lengthy and take a long time to read. Keep reports short and to the point.

TIPS FOR BUSINESS WRITING

Regardless of what you're writing, most objectives can be accomplished with these simple steps:

1. *Determine the aim or focus.* Have a specific *and specified* reason why your document is being written:
   - What is the intention of the document? What is it supposed to accomplish?
   - What information is necessary in achieving that aim?
   - Can you summarize its aim in one sentence and then use that sentence as the main point?
2. *Know your customer.* Convey the message in a way that the recipient(s) will understand:
   - Exactly who will be reading the document?
   - What are their likes and dislikes?
   - Is the correct tone or attitude being used to address them?
   - How much do they already know about the topic?
   - Will they understand the terms and language used?
3. *Structure carefully.* Be organized and clear:
   - Does the document proceed in a logical and organized way?
   - Does every sentence and paragraph justify itself? (i.e., is it organized around a central theme?)
   - Have enough graphs, details, and/or explanations been included to support its main point?
   - Is everything that's been written necessary? (if not, remove it)
   - Is it clear to the reader what he or she needs to know or do?
4. *Revise.* Develop and edit the document:
   - Is the document's layout effective? (are its titles, spacing, and text well-balanced?)
   - Is the document's information and style easily accessible?
   - Has someone proofread the document?
   - Does the beginning statement have a resounding impact?

More Helpful Advice (and Reminders)

- Don't try to impress others with fancy jargon or overly technical wording. For example, a friend once told me about a résumé he'd been sent that included among the candidate's former jobs "Surface Textile Application Technician," otherwise known as a painter.

- Keep everything short and to the point. Avoid long sentences and long paragraphs.
- Don't be ambiguous. Ambiguity does not reduce opposition, hide your insecurity, cut down on questions, or allow you to be all things to all people. It just makes you look bad.
- Always be certain that a written format is your best option.

IN CONCLUSION

Remember the examples presented at the beginning of the chapter? Take a moment to review them and establish a moral for each one. Do your conclusions match the following?

Example 1: Don't let memo writing or e-mails become a barrier to interpersonal communications. There is a time and place for writing in business. Learn when and where that is. Few methods of communication win out over the give and take of face-to-face discussion.

Example 2: Time is a valuable commodity for every employee. Don't waste your employee's time (or yours) with lengthy written communications that take hours to prepare and read. In most businesses, more importance should be placed on *doing* things rather than writing about them.

Example 3: A clear and precise message is of utmost importance in all written communications, but in business, unless you're a best-selling novelist with a reputation to uphold, Pulitzer prize-winning prose isn't necessary. Trying to achieve literary merit in a business document wastes valuable time. In fact, many office documents are best delegated to an assistant or secretary.

Example 4: If you think that an official and binding agreement is "just a piece of paper," try explaining your view to anyone who's been involved in a contract dispute (or is married).

Example 5: Sometimes, written communication (writing, photocopying, collating, sending, and reading) takes much longer than expected. Ask yourself if writing the message is the most effective means of communicating it. Perhaps the company grapevine or a face-to-face meeting or a departmental meeting can do a more adequate job.

Chapter 22

Presenting Yourself and Your Ideas: Mastering the Skills of a Presentation

According to Gerard Blair, author of *Starting to Manage: The Essentials Skills,* presenting information is one of the most important skills in management. Whenever conveying plans, thoughts, or ideas to the boss, the board, or to customers, in effect a presentation is being made. Seen in this way, presentations can be formal or informal, yet in either case the basic objective remains the same: to communicate effectively.

First, the bad news. **Presentations,** by their very nature, put a person on display. Much rides on them. They convey a speaker's ability to be decisive, creative, and inspirational. In doing so they reflect leadership and managerial skills. When giving a presentation a speaker must convince others of the merits of his or her proposal as well as project enough confidence (and evidence) to motivate these people into giving their support.

Now the good news. Presentations provide a chance to speak freely and show your stuff. When someone holds the stage an audience is bound by good manners to sit and listen, so, at least at the beginning, the speaker should have everyone's attention. Most audiences respond to speakers who radiate a relaxed, informal manner, so it isn't necessary to approach a presentation as though life hangs in the balance. Put another way, a presentation provides an ideal format to *be yourself.* Since presentations are also mediums that foment discussion, using them as such establishes a connection with the people a speaker will be working with or against. Although it may not be suitable to hold a conversation with an audience during a presentation, providing a question-and-answer session at the end allows others to get involved by raising issues, presenting alternative views, and generating valuable input.

THE ALL-IMPORTANT GOAL: COMMUNICATION

The two most important factors in any presentation are (1) effective communication and (2) connecting with the audience. The entire preparation and content of a presentation should therefore be molded around its audience. Everything from words to charts and graphs should convey thoughts and ideas *in a way that is understandable to the people who are going to hear and see them.* Don't be fooled into thinking that a new suit or haircut will win the day—the presentation's message *and having it remembered* are the most important selling points. As one colleague of mine put it, "The six Ps of a presentation are: Proper Planning Prevents Piss-Poor Performance." The following steps, however, do a more specific job of conveying the planning process. Keep in mind the adage that for every five minutes planned in front of an audience, approximately one hour of preparation time is needed.

Step 1: Formulate Objectives

The first order of business when giving presentations is to write down the precise objectives you hope to achieve. This can take the form of a simple statement of intent. For example, the purpose of a presentation may be to gain permission, obtain funds, get approval of an idea, sell a product, or motivate employees. Whatever the objective, it's best to stick to one per presentation. If you remain unfocused on what it is you hope to achieve, you probably won't achieve it.

Step 2: Identify the Audience

Consider the audience and determine how the objective can best be achieved through them. If the presentation takes into account *their* fears, concerns, wants, or needs, then you're well on the way to achieving your objective. Understanding an audience shows that you've prepared and that you're on their side. For example, if motivation is the objective and employees are uneasy about the new technology your company is investing in, focus your presentation on the training that will be provided, explaining that job losses are not part of the business's plan. In the same vein, if you want to sell your company's senior management on a new idea and they're worried about cost overruns, focus on the amount of money your idea will create or save.

Step 3: Format the Presentation

All presentations must be structured. If they're not, the audience will not be able to follow them. When addressing others it's wise to choose a format that best displays an objective without being too dull, obvious, or complicated. Here are some examples:

- *The sandwich board* contains a simple, beginning-middle-end format. An introduction leads to a basic summary of the objective, which is then followed by a conclusion. This type of format is best used for short presentations.
- *Subheadings (hierarchical)* break down the main topic into subtopics and those subtopics are broken down further. This technique is very effective when using written presentations or visual aids. In a verbal context, the objective of the presentation should be kept simple so as to avoid reducing the objective down to too many pieces.
- *The journalistic approach* introduces the topic in an opening paragraph, then hammers the point home in subsequent paragraphs that further elaborate on the basic presentation objective. This approach relies heavily on repetition and is enhanced by anecdotes, facts, and other relevant bits of information. When done well, this can really keep an audience entertained and online.
- *The question-answer method* explains a topic by introducing it and providing any relevant background information, then showing the topic's various advantages and disadvantages. During the summary, everything is listed as to its pros and cons and a discussion follows. The trick is for the presenter to provide the criteria on which all options are judged beforehand, thereby allowing the desired outcome to be achieved.

MAKING OR BREAKING A PRESENTATION

The Introduction

Most audiences are won or lost in the first few minutes of a presentation. To ensure starting off on the right foot, begin with these five elements in mind:

1. *Ensure that you're the center of attention.* Wait until everyone is seated and has made themselves comfortable. Be patient while they finish acknowledging the person seated next to them. An effective way to do this (if circumstances allow) is to stand at the front of the audience and politely smile until they have silenced (disciplined) themselves. This avoids having to ask that everyone be quiet, which can start a speaker off on the wrong foot.
2. *State your theme.* Get the audience thinking about the presentation's objective by opening with an anecdote, question, or simple statement that illustrates the subject matter.
3. *Outline how you wish to proceed.* Let the audience know what to expect. Not only does this allow them to follow the structure of the presentation, it also promises an end to it.
4. *Make the connection.* If the audience is won over in the first minute or two of the presentation, it should be possible to hold them much longer. This can be accomplished by presenting yourself as an expert, a concerned colleague, or even a friend. Many people think that starting with a joke is essential, but this can lead to disaster if the audience isn't known well. Use jokes only if doing so comes naturally and if the subject demands it.
5. *End with a bang.* The final impression you make (apart from your opening gambit) is probably what an audience will remember most vividly. Keep this in mind when preparing your introduction. As with your opening statement, it's always necessary to gather the audience's attention at the presentation's end. Try not to close with a summary. This switches people off very quickly. Instead, focus on the main objective and introduce one final culminating thought or idea that brings the message home.

Making the Pitch

Of all elements discussed or shown in a presentation, the person doing the speaking is usually what's remembered most. Every presenter has the power to either kill the message or enhance it. The following tools will help to facilitate success:

1. *Appearance:* The motto "dress for success" is key. A good rule of thumb is to be yourself and not dress over or under what your audience will be wearing. Doing so will only distance you from your listeners, and if you look out of place, you've lost the game before it begins.
2. *Stance:* Use your body as a tool. Don't appear too casual (bored) or overpowering (threatening). Keep your movements smooth and natural and keep them in unison with your speech. If you mention "togetherness," then bring your hands slowly together. If you want to emphasize a point or two, don't thrust an index finger at the audience but instead raise it toward the sky or *gently* bring your hand to the lectern. Waving your hands in the air and pacing rapidly back and forth are disruptive, and usually have no place in a presentation. Last, *always* stand erect, but don't remain as stiff as a statue.
3. *Eyes and expression:* Throughout any presentation, most audience members will be watching the presenter's face, or more specifically, his or her eyes. If the speaker is enthusiastic, knowledgeable, and generally happy, then the audience will feel this and respond appropriately. The same applies if the speaker is bored, listless, speaks in a monotone, or makes some other negative impact. The point is for the presenter to establish eye contact with as many people as possible. This contact should last for two or three seconds (long enough to acknowledge the recipient). If contact is too short, the speaker will appear flippant. If the contact is too long, aggressiveness enters the picture. When addressing a large group, attention should be paid equally to every section of the audience—few things are as maddening to an assembly as a speaker who only appears to care about one or two listeners. Finally (and perhaps most important), *smile*—not like the Cheshire cat, but in a relaxed and casual way.

4. *Visual aids:* Most people expect a formal presentation to be reinforced with **visual aids** or slides. Since every presentation should be geared to what its audience wants, visual aids probably need to be incorporated. The essential factor to remember is that pictures really do say a thousand words. Few things bring a point home more effectively than an appropriate illustration or stage prop. Bear in mind that a simple statement projected onto a screen can also be used in this context. For example, if your talk is about safety, projecting that word onto a screen should keep everyone focused on that issue. If your talk is about generating profits, a picture of a pile of money may be effective (or it could be inappropriate—keep your audience's expectations in mind). Stage props such as models, examples of publications, or similar items can also highlight a topic. Just be sure they add to rather than distract from your message. Don't overburden your audience with too many words or pictures and don't think that visual aids will save a bad presentation. Ensure that every visual aid has a distinct purpose. If it doesn't, get rid of it.
5. *Common sense:* Most audiences are comprised of people who have a lot on their minds. Children, spouses, job responsibilities, doctor's appointments, debts—all these concerns and more present a potential distraction to your presentation. In order to prevent the audience's mind from wandering, keep your presentation short and to the point. This may sound like common sense, but common sense is often commonly ignored. Learn to crystallize your presentation in thirty seconds and you'll have the perfect ending or introduction from which to start. Equally as important, try not to use too many big words. Your audience will not be impressed.
6. *Repetition:* Make certain you present your point again and again without sounding like a parrot. To do this, repeat a point or reemphasize an issue utilizing different variations of what you've said. This allows people to better hear and understand your message. As author Gerard Blair says, the classic advice given by drill sergeants when addressing recruits is, "First tell 'em what you're going to tell 'em. Then tell 'em. Then tell 'em what you just told 'em!"
7. *Rehearsal:* Practice, practice, practice what you are going to say beforehand. If possible, give a trial run in front of others. If this

is not possible, practice in front of a mirror. Remember, practice *does* make perfect—but only when you make a positive effort to improve.

8. *Getting rid of the jitters:* It's normal and natural to feel nervous before giving a presentation. In fact, not being nervous is often a bad sign (overconfidence is a killer). The best ways to get a grip on too much nervousness are to
   - prepare well in advance—the more prepared you are the less chance there is of failure;
   - establish a genuine interest in what you're talking about—being enthusiastic about the subject of your presentation helps you focus on that rather than what you're doing; and
   - practice talking with and listening to people—the more time spent with people, the more accustomed you'll become in speaking to them collectively.

FINAL THOUGHTS

After the presentation is over and the audience has left, stop to think about what happened. Make a mental note of the high and low points. Ask others to provide feedback. Unless you make an effort to improve upon your weaknesses, you cannot realistically expect to make any future improvements.

Chapter 23

Making Meetings Matter

Although repetition is a necessary part of the learning process, the following information is not designed as a repeat of the previous three chapters. Instead, the objectives of this chapter are to (1) help determine if a **meeting** is necessary, (2) help with the meeting planning process, and (3) ensure meetings don't waste time.

More often than not, with the advent of easy-to-use color printers, eye-catching graphics, spreadsheet programs, and slide presentations, it's easy to lose sight of that fact that meetings are not supposed to merely convey information. That in itself can be accomplished by holding a conversation, using the phone, or writing a memo or e-mail. Instead, the purpose of business meetings is to be *task-oriented.* The idea is to achieve an objective that can be better obtained through group participation. The aim is to address an issue or set of issues and have everyone walk away with a viable solution (or at least be closer to one). Because this takes time and planning, too many routine meetings (those held at a specific time each week) are often cobbled together without much forethought, thereby becoming dreaded, ineffective, demoralizing, and time wasting. In fact, most meetings that don't have a preplanned, results-oriented objective often have the same effect.

TEN STEPS FOR PLANNING A SUCCESSFUL MEETING

Before calling a meeting, focus on the following points:

1. *Necessity.* Think about your meeting's justification. Is it really necessary? Will anyone's time be wasted? What could better be done in place of a meeting?

2. *Purpose.* What is the meeting's purpose? What are its goals? What is the desired outcome? Keep in mind that all business meetings must be customer oriented. If you can't figure out how your meeting relates to customers, you're wasting valuable time.
3. *People.* Who is best suited to lead the meeting? Who needs to be in attendance? Who doesn't need to be there? How will the meeting's planners avoid offending people who aren't invited? How will they encourage those who are needed, but don't want to attend?
4. *Planning.* Has the appropriate research been conducted to call a meeting? (Meetings should rarely involve the input of only one person.) Is there enough material for a complete agenda?
5. *Preparation.* Will any premeeting information be properly distributed (a short description of the topic, an outline of what is expected to happen, references to any pertinent information, etc.) at least three days before the scheduled date of the meeting? *All participants* should know *exactly* what is expected of them.
6. *Tools.* Are all the items necessary to conduct a meeting available (projectors, computers, software, paper, pens, white boards, etc.)? Is all the needed equipment in good working order?
7. *Practice.* Are the people involved with conducting the meeting practicing their presentation(s)?
8. *Introduction.* Will the meeting start on time? Will it end on time? When it begins, is the chair prepared to restate its purpose as well as the rules or procedures everyone is expected to follow? Will a rundown be provided on who will have the floor?
9. *Brainstorming.* After the initial presentations have ended, will the chair move quickly toward the brainstorming part of the meeting? (This is usually the reason why most meetings are called.) Is the chair (or someone else) prepared to write down conclusions, assign responsibilities, and determine time limitations? Will an appropriate amount of time be made available for a question-and-answer segment? Will the meeting conclude with a summarizing of the discussion, a restating of the conclusions, and a going over of the agreed-upon next step(s)?

10. *Follow-up.* Will everyone receive a copy of the meeting's minutes? Who will ensure that whatever has been agreed upon will be completed? Who will monitor or measure the meeting's results? How will this be done?

When it comes to meetings, the moral of the story, as with so much in management, is that adequate planning, examination, and follow-through are the essential elements behind success. If the previous ten steps are used and a positive answer can be found for most of the questions raised, you should be well on the way toward making your meetings productive, enlightening, and—miracle of miracles—perhaps even anticipated.

Chapter 24

An Outline for Project or Program Planning

> In every field, the progress of today is nothing more than the absurdity of yesterday.
>
> Luigi Barzini,
> *Corriere della Sera* (1910)

Imagine being handed a choice assignment at work that requires you to journey into uncharted territory. What will you do?

By its very nature, management constantly asks that people learn to do new things as well as familiar things in different ways. This can be frightening because planning, developing, and implementing new ideas and methods (venturing into the unknown) is usually a daunting process. But cheer up. It can be tackled. People do it every day. As with any large task, breaking down what needs to be done into manageable units is a good way to get started. Before beginning any new **project,** though, it's mandatory to do one thing first: the planning. The following outline should prove helpful.

I. Why? Before starting, clearly understand *why* you're doing whatever it is you're doing. This helps to define your task by explaining both the problem and, to some degree, the proposed solution. The result should be a *written* guideline describing what's needed as well as why and when. Bear in mind that everyone involved must be in agreement. If the crucial first step of writing everything down and agreeing with it isn't done, you'll pay dearly for it later. There are several reasons why this is so:

A. Agreeing in advance helps eliminate contradictory assumptions. In business you should never assume a common understanding because you'll probably be wrong. All it takes for a project to hit the skids is one new member (or manager) who is uninformed or not in agreement and the process may have to start all over again.
B. An agreement forces all concerned to read and think about what's being proposed. This includes setting reasonable time scales, deliveries, and so forth.
C. Written agreements help clarify issues and/or reveal misunderstandings, particularly with other departments or people.
D. A solid agreement helps expose practical and technical details as well as identify resources that will be needed (and perhaps the authority to use them).
E. Agreements help prevent people from changing their minds or coming up with new ideas halfway through the project (which almost always results in increases in cost and time).
F. Written specifications reveal the big picture by showing how everything fits together, thereby helping illuminate incompatibilities, inconsistencies, and duplications.

II. What? The *what* stage brings a project into focus by beginning the process at the point at which needs and ideas are joined together. The key word here is *structure*. Without structure, any project will become a tangled mess of seemingly unrelated tasks. By using your experience (and the experience of others) you should, at the very least, be able to make an educated guess for each of the following questions. *Don't attempt the planning process on your own.* A manager's duty is not to single-handedly come up with all the answers but to use everyone at his or her disposal to come up with the best possible solutions.
  A. Objectives
    1. What exactly do our customers want or need?
    2. How do we wish to serve them?
    3. What exactly do we (and our business) hope to accomplish?
    4. What are our financial capabilities? Our estimated labor needs? Equipment requirements?
    5. What will be the long-term effects of the project or program?

B. What Methods Will Be Used to Gain Our Objectives?
   1. What types of communication (or controls) will be used? How often will they be used?
   2. What type of management/organizational structures are most appropriate?

C. What Realistic Time Frames Will Be Set (or Have Been Set for Us)?
   1. What is the best time to start and finish each of the project's segments?
   2. Can clear, unambiguous, "milestone" targets be set?
   3. Are there any conflicts with other projects/dates/schedules?
   4. Are we being too optimistic or restrictive with our time estimations?
   5. Can certain segments be lumped together for maximum effect?
   6. Should segments be broken down further to facilitate successful completion?

D. Who Should Lead the Different Segments of the Project?
   1. Who is the best person for each job?
   2. How will people develop in their assignments?
   3. Should tasks be handled individually, in pairs, or in teams?
   4. Will we have to hire additional staff?
   5. Should tasks be handled in-house or will they be better accomplished through outside contractors?

III. How? The *how* phase constitutes the real-time planning of the project. This is the stage at which the manager sits down with his or her team and starts the process of actually managing. Continuing to obtain the feedback of others helps ensure that fewer mistakes will be made and allows for group ownership in the final plan. Again, remember that nothing can be assumed here (you will probably be wrong) and *everything must be put into writing and agreed upon*. The object at this stage is to establish the monitoring of the project and provide for a system that allows for the receiving of any early danger warnings. In doing so, the foundation for cooperation, as well as motivation, is fortified. Throughout, you must instill the notion that your team(s) is responsible for monitoring and controlling its own progress via tangible forms of measurement.

A. Financing the Project
    1. Have full costs been determined and necessary revenues been developed?
    2. Have financial resources been properly allocated?
B. Accumulation of Resources
    1. What type of people, equipment, facilities, schedules, and materials are needed?
    2. What type of training do the project's people and/or team(s) need?
    3. What are the project's insurance requirements?
    4. Have legalities, liabilities, and legal waivers been determined?
C. Distribution of Assignments
    1. Have we selected, consulted, and appointed the best person(s) for each job?
    2. Have the best outside contractors, suppliers, etc. been selected?
    3. Do we know when to make compromises?
    4. Have the standards of what constitutes quality been agreed upon?
    5. Have safety and ethical concerns been addressed?
    6. Have alternatives been penciled in or discussed?
D. Establishment of Communication Pathways
    1. When and how should problems and updates be reported?
    2. Who is responsible to whom?
E. Final Agreements
    1. Does everyone know about his or her duties, responsibilities, and contingency plans?
    2. Are current or foreseen problems being fixed or adjusted?
    3. Has reasonable time been scheduled for errors? (Don't fall into the trap of assuming that nothing will go wrong.)

IV. When? At last, you've started the ball rolling. The project is underway. Be attentive to what is going on and expect the unexpected. Keep in mind that when something does go wrong (which it inevitably will), the best way to approach the problem is to not immediately ask *why* it happened, but rather *how it can be corrected.*

A. Moving Forward

1. A point has been set on the horizon; now move toward it (keep in mind the old joggers' adage that the hardest step to take is always the first one out the door).
2. Stay informed as to what is going on without satisfying the desire to look over everyone's shoulder.
3. Provide and receive adequate feedback (including lots of praise and/or professional criticism and correction when needed).
4. Allow for flexibility.
5. Be patient and reasonable, and remember that any form of progress, no matter how small, is progress.
6. Self-doubt and momentary lapses of confidence are normal—just don't let them consume you or your team.

B. Quality Control

1. Are the project's people meeting the agreed-upon quality standards?
2. Should any changes be made?
3. Are any of the suggested changes really necessary? (Too many changes will slow your project down and add to its costs.)

C. Fighting for Time

1. If you find yourself falling behind schedule, *find out why* and *correct the problem immediately.*
2. If senior managers move a deadline forward and it can't be met, remind them of the original schedule and try for a compromise solution rather than flat-out saying no.

V. How did it go? After the project or program has been completed a review of what happened and the lessons learned should be made. This is best done in an open meeting through candid discussion and should include as many internal and external customers as possible. Summing up *always* proves invaluable and will help keep you on track in the pursuit of what should be the reason behind every project or program: increased customer satisfaction.

PART IV: THE BASICS OF BUSINESS

Chapter 25

Know Your Product

A timid man fears being bullied. As a result, he signs up for karate lessons at a local martial arts school. For three years he steadfastly sticks to the program, never missing a lesson. Day by day his confidence grows until, shortly after he graduates, a mugger demanding his wallet confronts him. The man strikes the classic kung fu pose, overjoyed at finally gaining control over his life. But his display is in vain. The mugger shrugs, pulls out a gun, and shoots him.

The message? Information, skills, and training are wonderful acquirements, but they aren't applicable to every situation. Equally as important, some situations aren't always as straightforward as they seem. **Products** are one example.

PRODUCT LEVELS

Every manager should be aware that every product (or service) has three distinct levels (see also Figure 25.1):

1. The *core product:* the actual benefit that consumers receive when they purchase a product.
2. The *actual product:* the attributes that separate one product from another in terms of quality, features, design, packaging, and so on.
3. The *augmented product:* additional services and benefits incorporated with the core product, such as installation, warranty, delivery, credit, or after-sales service.

Success in business greatly relies on finding out which level of a product is the most appealing to customers and then adjusting all pol-

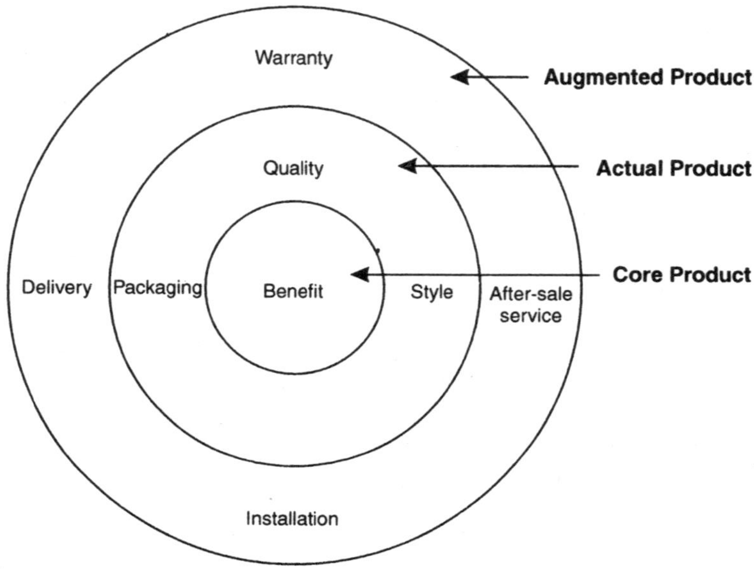

FIGURE 25.1. Product (or Service) Levels

icies and procedures accordingly in order to target specific customer groups and maximize sales.

The **core product** of McDonald's, for example, might be convenience (which is why so many McDonald's restaurants have great locations). Or it could be uniformity, hygiene, fast service, price, or some other *benefit* a patron *seeks* when choosing to eat there. The **actual product** is the burgers, fries, and foodstuffs. However, the next time you see a McDonald's advertisement, notice how little is said about the taste of the food. Instead, the **augmented product** is often used to make a sale, usually a coupon or movie tie-in taking the form of a toy that entices customers (or their children) into the restaurant.

Alternatively, the core product of a cosmetics company might be hope, sex appeal, sophistication, beauty, image, or whatever else it is that customers think cosmetics provide. This is then emphasized in a marketing campaign that focuses on youth, fighting age, career success, sassiness, sex appeal, trendiness, etc. The actual product, which is wrapped around the core product, is the brand name and physical product (lipstick, blush, mascara, etc.). The augmented product could be a money-back guarantee, a free sample, or something along similar lines that creates perceived extra value.

Which Product Level Results in the Most Sales?

Many experts concede that most business competition takes place at the augmented benefit level. The problem for managers is that augmented products (i.e., the added value in the form of freebies) have a tendency to become expected over time—and that costs money. A good example of this is British Airways wanting to place a small chocolate on the trays of its passenger meals to provide something a bit more special, but when a cost analysis was done, it was determined that this simple gesture would cost more than 1.5 million dollars a year!

UNDERSTANDING WHAT YOUR CUSTOMERS WANT

Years ago, while living in Nottingham, England, I watched a friend, a city center gym owner, as he struggled through a minor dilemma. As a small business manager with limited funds, he wanted to make certain that the $3,000 ad he was placing in the local yellow pages directory would attract customers. He had narrowed his decision to four different styles when he asked for my input. "Which one do you think is best?" he asked.

"It doesn't matter what I think," I replied. "What your customers think is more important. Do you know the reason why they chose this gym over the other ones in town?"

He shook his head and shrugged. "Convenience?" he suggested.

"Why don't you ask them?" I said. Before he could reply, I spread the four ads on the top of the reception desk and asked a woman signing in to select the one she thought was best. I then asked what had attracted her to the gym in the first place. During the following thirty minutes I did the same with each person that either entered or left. Far from being taken aback, everyone absolutely relished being asked for their opinion. Soon a line of persons had formed, each eager to give his or her input. In the end, more than 90 percent of them chose one ad as the most eye-catching, but more important, all of them mentioned price as the number one reason for joining. Incredibly, my friend hadn't mentioned price or value in any of his ads, so he took the selected advertisement back to the yellow pages and had BEST PRICES IN TOWN placed at the top in bold print. Since he now knows his core product is price and value, that's what he has to keep providing. Eventually this may change (customer wants usually do), but for now he knows what to focus on.

Sometimes It's Just So Simple

In 1997, I journeyed to Glasgow, Scotland, to investigate a PhD program into which I'd been accepted (I decided to write a novel instead). While there I spent a delightful afternoon listening to a man whose work provided most of the funding for one of the university's graduate schools. His office, literally piled to the ceiling with stacks of papers, was located in an ancient building's attic on the university campus. I immediately fell in love with the place. It was the office of a true business practitioner. "Why on earth do you want a PhD?" he asked in his thick Scottish accent. "Come work here with me instead."

For an hour or so we swapped stories about our work experiences. One of his better tales concerned a local museum that regularly lost money at its food service operation. For a time, the university sent dozens of graduate students and professors to research the problem, but despite their lengthy questionnaires and complicated data collections no firm conclusions were reached. That's when he decided to pay a visit. "Within a few minutes of arriving I knew exactly what the problem was," he explained, "it was the tables. The only option available to customers were long tables that everyone had to use together. Needless to say, most people don't want to sit among groups of complete strangers, so they ended up bypassing this area and going somewhere else to get a cup of tea."

He then suggested to the museum's management that they get rid of the long tables and buy smaller, more intimate ones. Soon after, the area filled up and began making money. "It all came down to providing what most people want after walking around all day looking at exhibits," he said, "and that is a few minutes of rest and calm. Tea and cake is an afterthought—it's the relaxation people want. Yet how can they do that if they're forced to share a table with a group of screaming schoolchildren?"

CONFRONTING COMPETITION

Being aware of your business's core product, actual product, and augmented product can help provide formidable ammunition against major competitors. But what can a local mom-and-pop grocery do to beat a Wal-Mart superstore opening just down the road? How can a hamburger stand take on a giant such as McDonald's? What can a local photocopying center do when a new Office Depot opens across the street? For the most part, you must know exactly what *benefits* customers need or want. More often than not, the way to successfully compete against a major rival, regardless of its size, is to offer what it can't—and that usually translates into individualized customer service. For example, my friend in the Nottingham gym story discussed earlier has been in business for seventeen years. During that time, six other fitness facilities have come and gone, yet his business keeps chugging along. The reason it does so becomes clear the moment you walk in the door and either he, or someone else on his staff, greets you as if you were a long lost friend. Simply put, customers are made to feel as if they belong, which plays a major role in customer retention. What's more, this type of focused, personalized service doesn't cost anything. His core product, as we saw, is price and value. His actual product though, apart from the gym itself, is service. From time to time he also runs sales and specials (particularly to students and groups) that many would classify as an augmented product.

In another example, a colleague of mine once relayed how a local photocopying center in his town was able to stay in business despite the existence of an Office Depot that opened across the street. Desperate to stay in the game, the small business owner decided to provide as many new services as possible that his rival couldn't, such as free pick up and delivery, while eliminating the retail side of his business with which he couldn't hope to compete.

Yet another tale is told about a small retail shop that found itself going head to head against a new Wal-Mart superstore. Rather than admit defeat, the small business owner cased his bigger rival and found out (1) specific products it didn't sell and (2) products it didn't sell well. After studying the buying habits of his customers, he then transformed his business to provide what Wal-Mart didn't. The result was that he became a local specialist in hardware and cleaning supplies—something Wal-Mart simply did not want to do.

Last, a host of small-time food stands competes against McDonald's and every other world-class fast-food restaurant in Warsaw, Poland, by providing what the big guns can't—*very* low prices. With hardly any overheads, these small businesses attract enough customers to pull a tidy profit, and none of the bigger chains can touch them.

KNOW YOUR MARKET

Ultimately, it's up to each business to find out exactly what its customers want and then decide the best means to deliver those needs (see Chapter 28, "Tools for Developing External and Internal Customers"). Knowing that every product has three distinct levels can provide a new perspective on what is being sought and what is being sold. Just as important, providing these benefits doesn't have to add substantially to a business's overheads. All it takes is a sincere desire to improve, a little common sense, the ability to listen (an open mind), and plenty of creativity. But be warned, because just like the man who thought many of his troubles would evaporate if he learned karate, if you don't know your customer's exact wants and needs you may end up doing your business more harm than good.

Chapter 26

Competitive Advantage Strategy

Strategy is not about predicting the future; it's about using the here and now to *prepare* for the future. In a business sense, this means developing an edge over rivals in order to secure customers and defend against competitors. In other words, strategy means creating a competitive advantage.

TYPES OF STRATEGIES

Generally speaking, there are three types of **competitive advantage** strategy:

1. A *low-cost strategy* strives to offer the lowest prices in town. The intent is to attract a broad cross section of the market. Low-cost strategies usually depend on offering few frills, having a limited selection, and extolling a somewhat acceptable quality. In a company that opts for a low-cost strategy, the emphasis is on continually seeking to keep costs down, year after year, in every aspect of the business, without sacrificing quality altogether. In the marketplace a focus is made on trying to make a virtue out of the product's features that lead to low prices. Of course, low prices are an extremely valuable asset when attracting consumers because, in part, it costs little for consumers to switch to a low-cost product line. In addition, standardized products can and do satisfy the needs of many customers, but these advantages can be neutralized if a competitor adopts similar low-cost methods. Similarly, concentrating on low costs can divert attention from other important aspects of a product that are dependant on the changing tastes of customers.

2. A *differentiation strategy* seeks to broaden customer choice by selling different variations of the same product. The *aim* is to attract a broad cross section of the market via the ability to offer variety (for

example, Procter & Gamble makes at least nine types of laundry detergents to satisfy its customers' different needs). The idea is to provide value for buyers by building in whatever differences customers want (such as quality). The company's goal therefore, is to communicate these differences in credible ways while charging a premium price since creating a line of different products usually results in higher costs. The manager's job is to stress constant improvement, invest in innovation, and concentrate on each product's distinct features. Doing so helps create buyer loyalty, but only if the company fully understands what customers consider as valuable. In other words, customers must see a distinct advantage with differentiated products or they'll go for lower priced alternatives.

3. A *focus* or *"niche" strategy* concentrates on a narrow part of a market rather than the whole market. The idea is to sell to a specific clientele whose preferences are known to be distinctly different from the rest of the market. The advantage of this is that lower costs are usually associated with serving a niche. The company's goal is to communicate the product's unique ability to its targeted buyers. A manager's job when using this strategy is to remain totally dedicated to serving the niche better than competitors while not damaging the company's image by selling out to other markets. The main reason for adopting a niche strategy is because big competitors don't usually like to cater to small markets. But make no mistake, if a niche market proves profitable, the big companies *will* move in. Examples of businesses using niche strategies include: easyJet airline company and Charles Schwab investment services.

Which Strategy Is Best?

Whenever I lecture about competitive strategy students inevitably ask why a company can't choose all three options. The answer is because it's *very* difficult for an organization to be all things to all people. For example, imagine three different career options: writer, athlete, and lawyer. As with any career choice, the literary world is full of competition. In fact, the odds of making a living as a writer are actually worse than winning the lottery. To put it mildly, it takes years of focused dedication, talent (or luck), and some form of interim financial backing to succeed as a writer. Now imagine a person who not only wants to become a writer, but also a professional athlete. If that isn't enough, try to visualize this same person wanting to become a lawyer too. Absurd? Absolutely. Each career option simply takes too much time, money, focus, and effort on its own. The same holds true for businesses when formulating a competitive strategy. Yes, some companies do succeed using two or three strategies, but they're the exception rather than the rule. The rest of us have enough on our hands just focusing on one.

Sometimes a Good Strategy Is So Obvious You Can't See It

Two hikers are walking through the woods. The first hears a noise, looks up, and sees a large, angry bear charging toward him. He turns to warn his colleague, only to find him sitting on a rock and putting on a pair of running shoes. "Are you crazy?" shouts the first hiker. "You can't outrun a bear!"

"I don't have to outrun the bear," the second hiker calmly replies. "I just have to outrun you."

As this joke suggests, good strategy can be both obvious and simple. For example, Canon's photocopying division used the phrase "beat Xerox" to describe its product differentiation strategy, and Wal-Mart, in its early days, stated that it simply wanted to "overtake Sears" via a low-cost competitive advantage. In Japan, a large construction-vehicle manufacturer named Komatsu made clear its strategic intent when it announced that it wanted to "encircle Caterpillar" with a broader product line.

The Ten Commandments of Business Strategy

1. Always think in the long term.
2. Never get stuck in the pack with no distinctive competitive position.
3. Always invest in a clear, proper, sustainable competitive advantage.
4. Avoid strategies that will succeed only in the best of circumstances.
5. Show caution when pursuing a rigidly prescribed or inflexible strategy—changing conditions may render it obsolete.
6. Never underestimate the reaction and commitment of rivals.

7. Remember that attacking a competitor's weakness is usually more profitable than attacking its strengths.
8. Don't cut prices without establishing a firm cost advantage over rivals.
9. Don't start something (a price war, a marketing offer, a new service, etc.) that you can't afford or stop.
10. Beware of attacking larger, stronger rivals without adequate resources. (Thompson and Strickland, 1993)

MATCHING STRATEGY TO THE BUSINESS

For any business, a winning strategy is the one that best matches the style and capabilities of the company with the wants and needs of its customers. Although that may sound patently obvious, it's based on the concept that a business must sell what customers want—not what the business wants to sell. How is this best done? Through the topics presented in Chapters 1 through 32 of this book. All of the principles and techniques mentioned in these chapters help lay the groundwork for business success. Again, strategy is about *preparing* for the future, not trying to predict it. The only way to prepare for the future is to strengthen your weaknesses (and those of your business), hone up on as many skills as possible, and remain adaptive and responsive to whatever is thrown your way.

Chapter 27

The Importance of Marketing

In 1991, only two companies in the world manufactured a special type of industrial flexible pipe. One was located in the United States, the other in France. Competition between the two companies was fierce. Then the Gulf War broke out, and it was quickly discovered that the products these companies made were perfect for helping to put out the oil-rig fires ignited by Saddam Hussein's fleeing forces. Soon both companies could barely keep up with demand.

Around this time one of the American company's young administrators, freshly armed with an MBA in finance (from Harvard), convinced his grandfather (who sat on the board of directors) that he could do a better job managing the company than the current team. In due course the old man persuaded the other board members that his grandson would take the company to a whole new level. That he did. Shortly after being named as the new president, the grandson decided to cut costs by eliminating a third of the workforce—including the *entire* sales and marketing department. To add insult to injury, guards with 9mm pistols were brought in on the day the pink slips were handed out to ensure any resultant anger didn't get out of hand. A year later he sat back scratching his head wondering why the company hadn't sold anything. How on earth could someone entrusted with running a company (and with a Harvard MBA to boot) be so stupid?

THE BASICS OF MARKETING

Hopefully by this point in the book you have arrived at the conclusion that few elements are more important to a business than marketing and sales. Contrary to popular belief, if you build a better mousetrap the world will not beat a path to your door. Just as important, good products do not sell themselves. One heart-wrenching situation I clearly remember involved watching a man (the first person to take a chance and hire me in my then chosen profession) lament the fact that he couldn't make a success of his enterprise despite it being a top-of-the-line establishment that stood head and shoulders above its competitors. "When I built this place," he told me, "I thought people would be lining up outside the door." His words, and the mournful way he stated them, still send a shiver down my spine to this day.

Marketing is a complex subject whose breadth makes it difficult to define. In essence, it involves *everything* an organization does. It's purpose however, is to bring a buyer and a seller together. Everything within a business plays its part in either encouraging or preventing marketing from happening. The product itself, its advertising, the way phones are answered, the cleanliness of an establishment, the training of employees, the sale, and everything afterward and in between, all comprise the basis of marketing.

THE MARKETING MIX

The most popular way to explain the multiple facets of marketing is to break the subject up into sections through an alliteration called the marketing mix, which includes the following:

- *Product:* the benefit of what is being sold or produced
- *Place:* the location (or time) where the product is sold or distributed
- *Price:* the perceived value of the product
- *Promotion:* communicating the product to potential customers
- *People:* the employees (and their knowledge or training) who make and/or sell the product
- *Physical environment:* the ambience or physical interior in which the product is sold
- *Processes:* the operational services that keep an organization running smoothly

The purpose of the marketing mix is to section the business into workable pieces that can be milled and sharpened in order to satisfy customers. Knowing what customers want beforehand helps identify opportunities. These opportunities are then researched to uncover any strengths or weaknesses and the results are matched with the business's abilities. The completed process is then targeted to a segment of the market in which success is envisioned because scattershot approaches are often highly ineffective. As seen in Chapter 25, "Know Your Product," marketers should focus on **benefit perception** (i.e., the benefits perceived by a potential customer), because all customers weigh in their minds the benefits they believe can be obtained by buying a product. They then act accordingly—if managers and employees are ready and able to finalize a sale.

THE PROMOTION MIX

Companies usually get their message to customers across via the promotion mix:

I. **Advertising** is any paid form of a nonpersonal presentation and promotion of a product.
   A. Pros
      1. It's a creative medium and its message can be repeated several times.
      2. It can be used diversely: from building up a long-term image to triggering quick sales.
      3. It can reach masses of people at a low cost per exposure.
      4. Consumers tend to view advertised products as legitimate.
      5. Large-scale advertising says something positive about a company's size and success.
   B. Cons
      1. It's impersonal and isn't necessarily persuasive.
      2. It carries only a one-way conversation with its audience.
      3. It can be very costly and ineffective if the wrong advertising medium is used. (One of the better lines from the world of marketing comes from a manager who stated, "I know half my budget is wasted on advertising; I just don't know which half!")

II. **Personal selling** is the use of oral presentation with one or more prospective customers for the purpose of making a sale and building a relationship.

A. Pros
   1. It involves personal interaction between two or more people so the needs and characteristics of a buyer can be determined quickly.
   2. It can create a relationship that leads to further sales.
   3. A buyer usually feels a greater need to listen and respond to a real live person.

B. Cons
   1. It can cost a lot to hire, train, and maintain a good sales force.
   2. It involves a long-term commitment (advertising can be turned on and off, but a sales force takes time to hire and train).

III. **Sales promotions** are short-term incentives designed to encourage the purchase of a product. Examples include coupons, contests, price reductions, offers, two-for-one-deals, and free samples.

A. Pros
   1. They attract immediate customer attention.
   2. They offer incentives to purchase or try a product by adding value for customers.
   3. They invite and reward quick response.

B. Cons
   1. They're short-lived and usually not effective in building long-run brand preference.

IV. **Public relations** (PR) is the building of good relations with the public by obtaining favorable publicity and creating a good image. This includes handling (or heading off) unfavorable rumors, stories, and events.

A. Pros
   1. It's very believable—PR news stories, features, and events seem real and convincing.
   2. It can reach those who avoid salespeople since the message gets to its audience as "news" rather than a sales pitch.

B. Cons
   1. PR can turn into a management nightmare if the company begins to believe its own PR, imagines that it's untouchable, and lowers its guard.

PRODUCT LIFE CYCLE

No matter how new or wonderful a product is, it will eventually go through phases akin to childhood, midlife, and old age. This is called **product life cycle.** Each phase requires a different marketing approach. Products can also "die" unless counteracted by an effective marketing campaign. In a product's introduction stage, advertising, promotion, and public relations are sometimes best for producing awareness. Personal selling, if used, might be geared toward convincing traders to carry the product or in attracting the interest of large centralized groups (such as clubs, professional organizations, companies, etc.). In the growth stage, advertising and promotion should probably dominate. In the mature stage, buyers are probably aware of the product and therefore may only need reminding, so advertising tends to cover the bill (although promotion can be used to boost interest and sales). In the decline stage, advertising is usually kept at a reminder level as promotions take over. However, since marketing should ultimately be customer led, any combination of the promotion mix may prove to be suitable at any time.

Increasing a Product's Marketing Life

One method of prolonging a product's life is to look at the product in different ways, based on the following viewpoints:

- *Uses:* This involves adapting (or promoting) different uses for a product. For example, a fitness center can use its aerobic studio for karate classes. Baking soda is marketed as being useful for cooking, cleaning, and refreshing refrigerator interiors (as well as teeth). But the classic case has to be the 1950s Colgate toothpaste advertising campaigns that stated that using Colgate freshens breath. Of course all toothpastes freshen breath, but no other company had ever said this before in their advertising. As a result of voicing this additional benefit Colgate's sales soared.
- *Users:* This involves increasing a product's appeal by targeting it to different groups. For example, I once worked at a resort that literally took the equipment from its outdoor children's camp activities and used them in corporate teamwork-promotion programs. In addition, variations of our exercise programs were

geared toward the fitness conscious (amateur athletes) and the health conscious (heart attack victims, the obese, and so on).

- *Usage:* This involves getting the customer to use a product more. The classic example is the instruction to "lather, rinse, repeat" on shampoo labels that supposedly resulted in double the product's usage overnight.

SOME MARKETING TIPS

Don't Go It Alone

There's no way around it: No business can succeed without selling something and sellers *must* search for buyers. In the process, the needs and wants of buyers must be determined and good products must be designed, promoted, delivered, stored, and their image constantly improved. It's an endless process, but there's no need to reinvent the wheel when marketing your business and selling your products. Information is widely available (much of it from the companies that make, sell, or distribute goods used in your business) as to how to attract buyer interest, display goods to maximum effect, and finalize a sale. Kraft, for example, sends representatives to show shop owners what products sell best according to local demographics as well as how to arrange cheeses and other products to maximize sales. The degree of accuracy regarding this type of information can be astonishing. In London, I once watched a news team challenge three marketers who claimed that they could determine a shopper's gender, age, profession, and first name (!) simply by looking at what the shopper had purchased. The marketers were then given three piles of goods and told to back up their claim. Forty minutes later, they correctly identified each shopper's sex, age, profession, and first name.

Marketing Doesn't Require Fancy Schemes or Costly Expenses

One of the best compliments I've ever been paid came from a friend who overheard a conversation in a shop. One of my competitors, a woman who'd been in business for twenty-five years, had earlier greeted my arrival in town with what can only be described via the words, "so what?" Six months later, I'd wrested most of her customers (and potential customers) away from her. "I've been here most of my life," she angrily told the shopkeeper, "yet now wherever I go I'm told that Jonathan Scott was here first."

Incredibly, I beat her in the marketplace with no advertising budget, no sales staff, no structured marketing campaigns, and—prepare yourself—no telephones (at the time we weren't accessible to a phone network). Realizing my limitations, I studied the programs we offered (an equestrian center, a sports club, a restaurant, and a golf course under construction) and did a great deal of research on potential customers. I then spent most of my free time visiting and introducing myself to consulates and embassies, local schools, apartment buildings, neighborhood community centers, and other places where people regularly gathered. You may find this hard to believe, but none of the other managers in the area, and there were quite a few, had ever done this before. Poster advertisements was about as far as they'd gone. Through repeated personal contact and the setting up of programs specifically designed for each targeted group *by* each targeted group, I established a client base that stuck with me through thick and thin as the business grew. Yes, we eventually got telephones, hired more staff, and printed fancy brochures, but our success was solidified through personal service and countless handshakes that cost no more than time, shoe leather, and elbow grease. The message couldn't be clearer. Today, marketing should be considered less of a broadcast medium and more of a customer-oriented dialogue.

Chapter 28

Tools for Developing External and Internal Customers

ESTABLISHING AN EXTERNAL CUSTOMER DATABASE

A good way to do more than pay lip service to servicing external customers is to establish a **customer database.** A database enables a business to study customer buying behavior and determine what may be needed in the future. Gathering this type of data is crucial, as is making it accessible. Working in their own departments, salespeople, accountants, and managers may not be aware of the whole customer picture, but working together they should be able to put one together. As always, if the answers to questions in the database are unknown—*ask the customer.* This is best accomplished through attentive contact that flatters customers by making them feel important. It needn't be (and shouldn't be) an interrogation. As with most good management practices, setting up a customer database isn't complicated (software programs are available). Most are quite simple and look similar to the following:

1. Customer specifics
   - Name, address, age, gender, profession, etc.
   - Geographic location and/or demographics of their business
   - Economic information (such as income level)
   - Basic needs and requirements
2. Purchasing history
   - Long term or short term
   - Amount purchased
   - Brand loyalty
   - Reason for buying (price, convenience, spur of the moment decision, etc.)

3. Future prospects
    - What are the customer's future plans?
    - What might he/she/they need in the future?
    - What type of future expenditures is the customer likely to make?
4. Other pertinent questions
    - How did the customer hear about us?
    - What does the customer need that we currently don't offer?
    - How can our service be improved?

MONITORING YOUR INTERNAL CUSTOMERS

Checking Progress: Evaluating Job Performance

Job evaluations are a valuable tool because they let employees know if they're going in the right direction and are doing what is expected of them. No evaluation style is superior; the varieties are endless and form should follow function. However, all evaluations should be written legibly to reflect seriousness on the part of the administrator as well as to have something substantial on file. Against this future progress can be measured. Also, don't look at evaluations as being negative. If they're done on a regular basis they're difficult to turn into reprimand sessions. When things are going well, they're also an excellent way to reward good performance. Just remember to keep them simple.

Work evaluations should take into consideration:

- Overall job performance
- Work output and quality
- Views from colleagues
- Social skills (including attitude toward work and co-workers)
- Punctuality and attendance
- Sometimes, the views or opinions of the person being evaluated

Work evaluations should avoid:

- Judgment on just one trait (good or bad)
- The ignoring of past performance by only judging recent work standards (this keeps the employee from "pouring on the goods" right before evaluation time)

- Personal bias
- Grading
- Marking everyone as average

Dealing with Consistently Poor Performance

When faced with an employee who shows consistently poor performance, find the answers to the following questions. All too often the blame for poor employee performance lays squarely on a manager's shoulders, and should therefore be rectifiable.

- Does the employee have a reason for his or her poor performance?
- Has proper training been provided?
- Is the employee being subjected to bullying by colleagues?
- Have proper motivational tactics and/or incentives been administered?
- Is the employee suffering from outside (personal) pressures?
- Is the employee working in a suitable department, field, or area?
- Is some form of punishment necessary? (*Note:* **Termination** is not a punishment. The process of firing an employee for poor performance is an act of finality that should be done only when all else has failed.)

A STITCH IN TIME SAVES NINE

Remember the old fable about the ant and the grasshopper? During the summer months the gadabout grasshopper sat back and laughed at the industrious ant. Then winter set in. Naturally, only the ant survived the cold because he had prepared for it. Likewise, whether your focus is on internal or external customers, forethought and effort will reap dividends. Proactivity is the key. With external customers, an updated customer database helps build a foundation from which further sales and contacts can be derived. With internal customers, keeping written records provides the measurement and information needed to develop your employees as well as possibly protect them (and you). The moral of the story couldn't be simpler: The work you do now may save your business in the future.

Chapter 29

Pricing

A dog walks into a bar and orders a beer. The bartender stares at the dog for a moment then gets him his order. "That'll be ten dollars," the bartender says. The dog produces the money from a pouch attached to his collar. "Sorry for staring," says the bartender, "but I have to admit that we don't get too many talking dogs in here."

"At these prices," says the dog, "I'm not surprised."

A *price* is the amount of money charged for a product or service, or the sum of values consumers exchange for the benefits of acquiring a product. Note the difference between price and value. *Price* is the monetary sum assigned to a product. *Value* is a customer's perception and may involve unseen costs such as the amount of money or time involved in switching over to your product.

Historically, prices for most goods were usually set through barter or negotiation. Prices therefore varied depending on a buyer's and seller's skills. However, in the early part of the twentieth century, F. W. Woolworth changed that by adopting a one-price policy in his stores. The practice soon spread.

FACTS ABOUT PRICING

- Price is the only component of the marketing mix that produces revenue. All others represent costs.
- Price is the most flexible element of the marketing mix. Unlike the other components, a price can be changed quickly.
- Pricing is often the most significant factor affecting buyer choice, but it's a double-edged sword. If a price is too high, buyers may turn away. If it's too low, they may sense something is wrong.

- Pricing often is not handled well (cut a price 10 percent and 50 percent of profits may be lost).

Common Mistakes in Pricing

- Setting prices that are too cost-oriented (i.e., customer value is not contemplated)
- Setting prices that do not reflect the current market (there could be high demand or a lack of demand)
- Not taking into account the other marketing mix components (again, the perception customers have of value may not be contemplated or may be misjudged)
- Not varying prices according to different products, different market segments, and/or promotions
- Slashing prices in the assumption that it will raise sales (the problem could be ineffective marketing, low perceived quality, or any number of other factors)
- Raising prices to increase revenues (again, the problem may lie somewhere else—and if it does, it won't be solved by upping prices and putting off customers)

THE PRICING PROCESS

Getting Started

Before the pricing process begins, it's necessary to consider what you want pricing to do for your business. The obvious answer is to generate revenue, but how will this be achieved? By being more competitive? By attracting a specific clientele? By getting more customers to try your products? A combination of one or more of these objectives? If you're serious enough about making the most of prices, then it's worth the time and effort to think about these questions, write them down, and discuss them with your colleagues.

Internal and External Factors Affecting Pricing

I. *Internal factors* are situations or determinants inside the company.

A. *Marketing objectives* are determined by the company's chosen target market and its position in the market overall. For example:
   1. Is the luxury market being sought?
   2. Is the economy market being sought?
   3. Is a survival strategy envisioned (selling below cost)?
   4. Will product prices be based on demand?
   5. Do research and development costs need to be covered?

B. The *marketing mix strategy* coordinates products along with production, distribution, and promotion to form a consistent and effective marketing program. Some examples include
   1. Target costing: Starting with the price the company wants to charge for a product then working backwards (changing production processes, simplifying systems, working with outside suppliers and distributors, deciding on a marketing campaign). Compaq did this years ago with their Prolinea personal computer line. First they determined what the production costs had to be in order to achieve the target price, then they changed their internal systems to meet the costs that would get them there.
   2. Value pricing: When the best strategy is not to charge the lowest price but to make the product different (or seem to be different) so that it's worth a higher price.

C. *Costs* are what the product actually costs to produce and market. **Fixed costs** are costs that do not vary with production, regardless of output (rent, heat, interest, depreciation, salaries, etc.). **Variable costs** vary according to output (labor, water, electricity, raw materials, etc.).
   1. **Cost-plus pricing** occurs when a standard markup is added after determining the fixed and variable costs of a product. This type of pricing is sometimes seen in construction companies or with lawyers, accountants, and other professionals who figure their costs then add 15 percent (or whatever).

II. *External factors* are situations or determinants outside the company.

A. *The market and demand*:
   1. Pure competition: Basing prices on "the going price" (everybody else is doing it so we will as well).

2. Oligopolistic competition: Having few sellers that are highly sensitive to one another's pricing strategies (if one company changes its prices so will the others).
3. Monopoly pricing: The producer pricing as he or she sees fit.

B. *Consumer perceptions* or basing prices on what customers think constitutes value (*Note:* This requires a *firm* understanding of consumer behavior).

C. *Price-demand relationship* involves setting prices according to market demand.

D. *Competitor's costs, prices, and offers* include basing prices on the overall selling environment.

Pricing in Action

The following list provides explanations of the different types of pricing strategies, with examples of their application:

- *Breakdown:* Prices are broken down into palatable segments. A $1,000 gym membership is sold in installments (four payments of $250 or only $2.75 per day).
- *Seasonal:* Price is adjusted for certain periods of time. Prices rise during peak seasons or are reduced during slow times.
- *Pay one price* or *pay as you go:* This label is self-explanatory. In amusement parks, either pay one fee and ride all the rides, or pay for each ride separately.
- *Bundling* or *unbundling:* Services or products sold as a package deal or split up and sold separately, such as activities sold in lots such as ten aerobics classes or five tennis lessons. Unbundling would sell these as single units.
- *Exclusivity:* Paying for "snob appeal." Setting premium prices for trendiness or what is perceived as social esteem.
- *Discount:* Low prices. Customers buy because the price is low.
- *Captive:* "Locking in" customers by initially selling cheap then charging a premium for necessary components. A classic example are computer printers that are cheap, but the ink cartridges are very expensive.
- *Psychological:* Prices do not approach what is perceived as too much. For example, charging $99 instead of $100, or listing member prices next to nonmember's.

- *Promotional:* Not paying a set price. This strategy means having constant sales or always bettering what the competition charges.
- *Value added:* Adding "freebies" or other incentives without charging for them. Two-for-one deals or a baker's dozen are two examples.
- *Trials:* Easing the perceived risk by encouraging participation before closing the sale. Customers are offered the first tennis lesson free, or a ninety-day trial period, or perhaps money-back guarantees.
- *Hidden costs:* Not displaying extra costs needed to complete the product or service. This is done by not including tips, taxes, labor, parts, batteries, etc.
- *Fixed to variable:* One price begins the process, the next price(s) is determined by use. For example, pay to get into the disco, then for each drink.
- *Differential:* Charging customers differently. Members pay one price, nonmenbers pay another.
- *Creative variable:* Setting prices according to demand, but in an imaginative way. This means altering the price depending on certain variables (e.g., selling rope by the inch).
- *Price performance:* Price determined by value perception. For instance, museums or exhibits may ask guests to leave a donation instead of charging an entrance fee.
- *Differing segments:* Same product/service sold at different prices. Children, senior citizens, groups, adults, etc., each pay a different price.
- *Product line:* Prices arranged to get customers to focus on "the deal." Expensive goods may be displayed next to reasonably priced goods.

SUMMING UP PRICING

When setting prices, don't sell yourself short. Think about how high you can reasonably go rather than how low. Always consider what your customers will perceive as fair and ethical. Never stop analyzing why and how your business came up with its prices and don't be afraid to try new ways to achieve pricing satisfaction.

Chapter 30

Business Marketing and Promotion: A Checklist

This checklist was developed from a variety of sources—particularly the school of hard knocks. Most frontline business managers strive to do many of the things listed in the following section. However, everyone needs a little reminding from time to time of the attributes and nuances that make up the big picture. Whether you're a student or a manager, study the categories discussed in this chapter. With a little imagination, many of the suggestions mentioned can be used or altered so that they'll achieve the ultimate objective in every business—a sale. Just bear in mind that there is no middle ground here. The answer to each question must be 100 percent yes. Anything else means no.

IN-HOUSE MARKETING

Point-of-Sale Area

The **point-of-sale area** is where maximum customer flow occurs. To ensure a peaceful, informative, and professional selling environment, evaluate whether your company meets the following criteria:

yes/no Adequate space to allow for efficient presentation of products on sale
yes/no A setup and service that minimizes delays and queues
yes/no Clean, well-lit display units allowing customers to examine products in a relaxed manner
yes/no Careful product arrangement to avoid too many distractions during the point of sale

yes/no Walls cleared of clutter and signs because employees either don't want to confront customers or don't want to do their job (i.e., clean area after use, we do not take credit, etc.)
yes/no Placing of essential products so that customers pass by when and where they are most likely to purchase them
yes/no Pleasing colors and background music that keeps with the image of the business

In-Store Promotion

This involves advertising on the premises. Indicate which promotions your company employs:

yes/no Special offers relating to specific product lines
yes/no Personalities invited to attend functions who will attract customers to the premises (don't laugh, there are plenty of well-known people in their field who'll come and give a seminar and/or sign a book for the publicity and the price of a train ticket)
yes/no Internal and external customer competitions offering attractive prizes or incentives (for example, the person bringing in the most paying customers wins)
yes/no Merchandise with company logo (can also be used for prizes and giveaways, such as a free key chain or T-shirt with every sale)
yes/no Provision of adequate promotional literature (leaflets, brochures, signs, coupons, etc.) (see section titled "Unique Selling Points")

In-Store Advertising

Evaluate whether your company fulfills the following requirements:

yes/no Professional posters with the name of a product and its advertising message
yes/no Staff uniforms neat, clean, and always worn
yes/no Professional posters or displays to promote products, deals, promotions, or services

yes/no A well-informed staff that knows what it's doing and what's going on

yes/no Well-stocked staff work areas (what message are you sending if a pen or other needed tool can't be found when and where it's needed?)

Internal Public Relations

Indicate which options your company has in place:

yes/no Introduction of a suggestion box where customers are not afraid to deposit their remarks

yes/no Introduction of a house journal, newsletter, or pamphlet

yes/no Arrangement of social events for customers and their families

yes/no Introducing incentives to reward employee productivity, customer loyalty, etc.

yes/no Offering special discounts or services to employees (if your employees buy and use your products they'll probably encourage others to buy them too)

yes/no Providing effective training opportunities for employees (including letting employees attend seminars, lectures, and personal-growth workshops)

yes/no Providing for employee participation in your business's decision making (particularly in setting up programs they envisioned or have a special interest in)

OUT-OF-HOUSE MARKETING

Unique Selling Points

Capitalize on what sets your business apart from others. Evaluate your company in terms of the following criteria:

yes/no Trained staff (Can/does your staff help sell your business outside of work hours? Do you have a champion or award winner on board? Is he or she mentioned in your advertising?)

yes/no Competitive prices
yes/no Good location (with ample parking)
yes/no Attractive peripheral service (late and early openings, delivery, installation, etc.)
yes/no Introduction of special events ("open house" days, sales, parties or get-togethers, etc.)
yes/no Provision of adequate promotional literature in the form of leaflets, brochures, signs, and coupons (It might be a good idea to have several different types, with each targeting a specific clientele. For example, one for walk-ins, one for corporate memberships, one for seniors or students, etc.)
yes/no Use of testimonials from satisfied customers

Community Relations

Indicate whether your company participates in the following initiatives:

yes/no Donations to local charitable causes (along with a story to the media stating this)
yes/no Development of good relations with local media owners
yes/no Introduction of your services to the local needy community (for example, a health club's facilities could be made available to a cardiac patient unit, physiotherapy businesses, a school or college, a community center, and so on)
yes/no Introduction of special events or special days during which the community can be exposed to your business's operations
yes/no Participation in local event sponsorship (and being allowed full advertising rights)
yes/no Favorable contacts with local council members and chamber of commerce members

Direct Sales Campaigns

Evaluate your company's performance on the following sales techniques:

yes/no Selling directly to the customer (direct mailings, personal visits, sales calls, etc.)

yes/no Target marketing select individuals with advertising paraphernalia (dropping off select-specific brochures at student unions, companies or corporations, sport shops, waiting/reception areas, the local tourist information center, etc.)

yes/no Target marketing groups (personal visits to local clubs, athletic teams, popular meeting places, company functions, and so forth to let them know of special group prices)

yes/no Having a booth at trade exhibits or fairs

yes/no Press releases (one or two hundred words sent to the media regarding information your business considers newsworthy)

yes/no Invitations to the media (or other notables) to come look over, try, and discuss your service

Indirect Sales Campaigns

Evaluate your company's use of these approaches:

yes/no Sponsorship/advertising space at local sports venues or with local team programs

yes/no Media advertising (*Note:* With television, radio, and newspapers, ascertain what demographic market they reach and if they match your target market. The operators of these mediums *do* have this information.)

yes/no Trade and technical journal advertising

yes/no Advertising in special-interest magazines or coupon booklets that reach your target audience (e.g., tourist pamphlets, student/university publications, etc.)

yes/no Neon/lighted signs (located outside and/or hanging over the sidewalk for all to see)

If you can't answer yes to the majority of these questions, you're selling yourself short, and something needs to be done about it.

TIPS FOR MARKETING THAT OBTAINS RESULTS

- *Don't make your task too complicated* and *don't go it alone.* Use your staff. The simpler the approach and the more people that are involved the better.

- *Have fun.* What you create will reflect the atmosphere and environment from whence it came.
- *Don't fall in love with your own advertising.* The point of advertising is to attract customers, not to design something that appeals to you and your staff. All marketing efforts should marry the benefits being sought by paying customers with what is being offered. Do you know why your current customers came to your business to begin with?
- *Don't count on cleverness to attract customers.* The most effective marketing campaigns don't come from dazzling advertisements and eye-catching slogans. The marketing campaigns that bring in the most customers are usually the ones for which the marketing team did the most work.
- *Learn from the results.* If your marketing is a success, find out why. Don't simply let your staff pat each other on the back and walk away with the notion that they'll win again in the future.
- *If your marketing isn't a success, find out why.* Sometimes only one ingredient is missing. As the saying goes, those who fail often never realize how close to success they came. Avoid the old chestnut "We tried that once and it didn't work." If you've done your research, know your customers, and everyone gets involved and pulls in the same direction, it *will* work. You'll never know until everyone stops talking about it or fighting it and actually *does* it.

Chapter 31

Advice

About twelve years ago I was exercising in a gym on the Red Sea coast when a friend entered and hopped on the adjacent exercise bike. This guy made a *lot* of money working for a management consulting firm, and at some point I steered our conversation toward exactly what it was a management consultant did. My previous experiences with consultants resulted in the conclusion that they charged enormous sums of money for doing basic research and/or stating the obvious. "Tell me," I said, "when a company calls on you to do a consulting job, do you start a unique analysis from scratch? Or do you have a set of prewritten concepts that are reworked and presented as if they were tailor-made?"

He contemplated his answer for a long time. "The latter," he finally replied.

I laughed. "Do you think it's fair to say that most consulting jobs involve little more than erasing the name of the last client from the pages of a prewritten text and inserting the name of the next one?"

"Mostly, yes," he said.*

THE PIG DANCE: DISCUSSION VERSUS ACTION

Too many companies are involved in what I call the PIG (perpetual information gathering) dance. All too often this dance is an illusion designed to fool everyone into thinking that continuous discussion,

---

*A friend who works in Africa recently e-mailed me with her opinion of consultants. "They use twenty-five words when one will do, they talk endlessly in circles, and they cringe whenever you ask them anything specific about practical application. Am I missing something?"

unending research, and infinite analysis is the raison d'être of management. Please understand that I'm not saying it's wrong to gather information in management; in fact gathering *pertinent* information is a basic necessity in every managerial position. What I'm talking about is the *dance*—the lining up at a company's trough to conduct endless analysis and partake in expensive trysts with consultants in order to produce reams of information that no one in the company bothers to do anything with. More often than not, the folks involved in the PIG dance are wallowing in procrastination at company expense, not to mention fobbing off their managerial duties onto someone else. For the most part, companies wishing to hire consultants should get off their backsides, get out of their offices, talk to their customers (not consultants), and do their own research. Remember, discussion, study, and analysis are a *part* of management—they're not supposed to be the end result. Equally as important, statistics should be seen as diagnostic tools, not operational blueprints. That being said, of course there are times when expertise may be needed in a specific area. For example, it would be foolish not to consult a lawyer when in need of legal advice or a safety expert for safety needs. Yet you should be *very* wary of those who give advice without ever having experienced its repercussions. The number of management consultants who have been fired from previous jobs because of incompetence, or were hired by a consulting firm fresh out of a university and can claim only "raking leaves" or "making french fries at a fast food restaurant" as experience, or who ran an amateurish (and now bankrupt) home business, is absolutely terrifying. Always do a thorough background check of a consultant, including contacting previous clients, before hiring one.

In most business environments, if you use the term *researcher* in place of *consultant* you're well on your way to understanding what it is that many people who call themselves consultants really do. The truth is that research isn't worth much if those who accumulate it can't, won't, or don't do anything with it. As the information technology director of a major United Kingdom bank once told me, "It's now an unwritten policy at my company to avoid hiring job candidates with PhDs." As he explained, his bank was fed up with people who could perform research but were clueless when it came to applying it (i.e., creating value).

Managing Is About Creating Value, Not Talking About It

Doing research and writing reports is easy. *Application* is what makes management difficult. The proof is in a story relayed to me by a seasoned practitioner. In fact, it's so well known I've even seen it dramatized on the BBC. Nevertheless, the obviousness of its message bears repeating.

One of the more notable consulting organizations in the world is McKinsey & Company. In fact, some estimates claim that almost two-thirds of the world's Fortune 1000 companies use McKinsey & Company when in need of a consultant. McKinsey & Company was founded in 1926, and took its name from its creator, James O. McKinsey. After several years of providing advice to some of the world's biggest corporations, Mr. McKinsey decided to crown his career by becoming the CEO of a major company. Such a move would not only solidify his reputation, he thought, but also the consulting business that bore his name. So in 1934, in the midst of the Depression, he accepted a position as chairman of the board of Marshall Field's, an acclaimed American retail institution. McKinsey began his chairmanship in earnest, quickly resorting to the cost-cutting measures and other astringent financial practices he'd been advising other companies to perform for years. Within two years after taking his post, however, it became apparent that these methods weren't working. Indeed, they seemed to have the opposite effect and Marshall Field's was soon brought to its knees. In desperation, the board of directors met behind McKinsey's back to determine how to get rid of him. McKinsey must have gotten wind of this meeting, for on the night it was conducted he collapsed and was rushed to hospital. He died a week later, but shortly before doing so he was overheard admitting to one of his assistants that in all the time he'd been a consultant *he'd never realized how difficult it was to be a manager* and *how wide the chasm was between management and consulting!*

IDEAS FOR IMPROVING YOUR BUSINESS

Along with just about everything else in this book, here are three more business improvement ideas that won't cost you the expense of a consultant. Bear in mind that these ideas aren't suitable for every business (*ideas* are found in books, not answers), but with a little creativity they can probably be reworked to suit one or two appropriate situations.

1. *Displaying productivity.* When I was in my twenties I heard about a factory foreman who regularly displayed what each of his employees had produced that day on a big board that everyone could see. The result was that everyone in the company knew who was pulling his or her weight and who wasn't. Ten years later I used a variation of this idea to keep track of sixty-two employees scattered across more than two dozen different work sites. The board was placed in the front office, and I displayed the names of those working off site, including where they were supposed to be, at what times, and several other bits of information. The result? Productivity tripled. An added benefit was that office workers could give customers detailed answers as to what was going on at these sites (something they'd had difficulty with before). It took a month to coax everyone into using the board, but once it became clear that it wasn't going away, it helped reduce my supervisory workload considerably. It also provided self-motivation and peer regulation for my employees.
2. *Multiple training.* There's a supermarket in my neighborhood that adheres religiously to this principle. Employees are rotated to different sections every week. The idea is to train each employee in several different jobs. That way, when someone is sick or quits, a temporary replacement can be found immediately from within. Rotating staff and having them perform many different tasks also has other benefits. It greatly reduces boredom, helps induce fresh new ideas, and tends to keep the pathways of communication open between employees.
3. *Saying yes.* Someone once asked me for the best piece of management advice I had. "Say *yes* more often than *no*," I replied. By prudently exploring all options and choosing the best one (saying yes), a manager explores new possibilities and constantly moves forward rather than standing still. Unfortunately, new and insecure managers are notorious for saying no. There are two reasons for this. The first is that they think saying no shows everyone who's boss (it doesn't). The second is that say-

ing yes translates into more work (as well as risk), which is true, but then again new ideas and practices always create more work initially. It's usually weeks or months afterward when the value of new ideas is most often seen—as well as the time and cost savings.

A BUSINESS NO-NO: LIVING IN THE SHORT TERM

Some companies (particularly large ones) seem to spend a lot of time and money concentrating on hype, spin, and media attention in order to appear successful. Unfortunately, these measures often do little more than strengthen a façade. Undoubtedly, glitz and showmanship do draw attention, but unless quality and service have increased in proportion to this hoopla, customers will wise up quickly. In other words, the major "paying-customer issues" (quality, service, value, speed, fairness, and convenience) that frontline managers and employees must contend with every day are the real building blocks of business. Just about everything else is window dressing. Businesses that build a strong foundation have a better chance of survival when economic or financial storms strike (which they inevitably do).

Living in the short term is seen in the leisure industry with bars or other venues that suddenly start charging an entrance fee for no apparent reason other than to get an extra five or ten dollars from paying customers. Of course, the ledger books look great the first week or so of this new policy, but after a while, if customers don't see any extra value connected with the new fee they'll take their patronage elsewhere. These business then have a very difficult time attracting both new and old customers once word spreads that they're just plain greedy.

Long-term business strategy revolves around earning money in exchange for a product or service and leaving customers with a desire to come back—not by making a lunge for the wallet of the first prospect who enters the door.

Chapter 32

An A-to-Z Business Success Primer

THE BASICS

AFFIRM YOUR PRIORITIES. Before succeeding in business, it's usually necessary to consider exactly what your company needs. The obvious answer is an increase in revenues, but how will this be done? Some options:

- Streamlining systems and/or operations
- Targeting a specific clientele
- Introducing a new product or service (or eliminating an old one)
- Improving customer service
- A combination of two or more of these (or other) objectives

If your organization is serious about succeeding then it's worth the time and effort to consider these questions, write them down, and then discuss them. By doing this, valuable input is gained from customers and a written guide can be formulated against which objectives can be measured.

BE PREPARED FOR RESISTANCE. Initiating changes not only means accepting that things will be done differently; it entails others accepting it too. Change is a difficult concept to preach. Few people like to abandon the comfort of the familiar and embrace the unknown. In most business situations, change is perceived as threatening because it involves accepting greater responsibilities.

Nonmanagerial employees' responsibilities include these:

- Accepting that the ownership of problems and solutions belongs to everyone in the business

- Understanding that work must equal value, and that it's not enough to show up and perform bottom-line duties
- Realizing that everyone must pull in the same direction (serve others)
- Caring about work by displaying integrity and trust

Managers must also face an expanded role and these responsibilities:

- Sharing information and providing complete and thorough training
- Viewing workers as assets
- Prudently choosing the right people for the right jobs
- Asking for, listening to, and then acting on other's viewpoints
- Rewarding good performance
- Ensuring that employees and departments endeavor to serve one another (pull in the same direction)

Make no mistake, the greatest difficulty in management often lies in providing employees with enough incentive to work hard. The good news is that management isn't rocket science. It doesn't take complex theories and formulas to succeed. Nor does it require a detailed set of blueprints. In fact, studies show that concrete plans and strict guidelines can be anathema to a business because they often result in a lack of flexibility and adaptability (and every organization *must* possess these qualities). So what does it take? To bolster the business arsenal and rediscover and awaken the human attributes that are found in every company, a need to work, the desire to excel, integrity, perseverance, loyalty, and fairness must exist. These are every company's greatest assets because they provide the impetus behind *every* success. Just as important, they cost nothing.

CUSTOMERS MUST BE THE FOCUS OF ALL WORK. All changes should lead to this concept. Keep in mind that the definition of a customer is *everyone that an organization serves*. In its broadest sense, this includes everyone encountered at work, not just people who exchange money for goods and services. In order for true customer care to be achieved, managers must get out of their ivory towers and walk along the front lines (the areas where customers are served). The idea is not to look over shoulders but to *listen,* learn, and formulate improvements and solutions from a whole new angle.

- Are all products, services, and systems designed based on what customers want and *how* they want them? (Don't think a business can dictate terms to paying customers.)
- Is the business concentrating so hard on one market that other potential markets are being excluded? (Customers have the ability to pick and choose. Businesses do not.)
- Do all attitudes thrive by the creed that it's everyone's job to serve both internal and external customers? (No one is too busy to help.)

It can't be made clearer—if customers don't like what they see or hear, they'll take their business elsewhere. Employees who know of their importance to the organization and who fully appreciate their responsibilities within it have the ability to provide good service. Customer care emanates best from people who feel they are genuinely part of a team.

DELEGATE. Encourage and train employees to handle problem-solving. Teach them to recognize and solve the *cause* of problems, not just the *effect*. Bear in mind that a common mistake made by many businesses is to-the-bone cost-cutting that squeezes the life out of the organization. Yes, regularly cutting expenses is paramount to every business, but doing so by reducing quality or laying off workers is not a viable long-term solution. *Revenues don't come from cost-cutting. Revenues come from customers—and customers must be sought and earned.* In other words, use your frontline employees to get closer to your paying customers and win them over. The buzzword here is *empowerment* (i.e., motivating employees for their own reasons, not the business's reasons).

- Provide employees with enough information and leeway to make decisions and formulate ideas.
- Work to harness the energy created by the inevitable conflicts that will arise.
- Join together to modify ideas so that (1) they will fit customer's needs and (2) the people who must work with these concepts *will* work with them.
- Delegate, don't abdicate, when employees think of, and apply, their own solutions.

The point is that a business should rely on itself for solutions because of its unique relationship with its customers. Be wary of consultants and the exorbitant fees that come with them. Don't eliminate boldness and risk and learn to handle conflict functionally (not dysfunctionally). Remember, there's a lesson in every objection and mistake. At the very least, failure or disagreement means that somebody had the courage to take action. If employees aren't performing to expectations, the fault usually lies with management for (1) not selecting the right person for the job, (2) providing insufficient information and training, or (3) not creating an atmosphere conducive to achievement.

ETHICS AND QUALITY ARE ESSENTIAL ELEMENTS IN ALL PHASES OF BUSINESS SUCCESS. It may be a cliché, but what goes around does come around. Never underestimate the intelligence of internal or external customers by shortchanging them. With so much choice available to customers these days, quality and ethics can't be overstated. When conducting business, be honest, say what you mean, mean what you say, and provide the very best. Reputations are priceless and, like customers, a good reputation must be earned. To enable ethical decision making, try these approaches:

- Understand the real reasons or intentions behind your company's decisions.
- Be aware of the outcome of every action or behavior.
- Show accountability with decision making.
- Comprehend the whole picture.

A good rule of thumb is to always think in the long term. Short-term solutions, by sheer design, are destined to cause trouble in the future. And the future is coming.

FORGE AHEAD. The missing catalyst in leading a successful business is often *action*—a decisive leap into uncharted waters. Don't let analysis lead to paralysis. Stick your neck out and get on with it!

- Divide goals into manageable, comprehensive steps.
- Communicate details clearly and often.
- Provide all the continuous training needed.
- Be patient and allow commitment to grow.

GALLANTRY. A good way to manage others successfully is to set a good example. I once managed a business that included several very large and busy facilities. Naturally, every hour produced some type of mess that had to be cleaned up, and I used to constantly needle the staff to make doing this a habit. Several employees came from countries in which this was considered demeaning, so one day, after asking them for the umpteenth time to clean up something and not getting any response, I did it myself. Within minutes the entire staff was helping. They never had to be asked again. The message? Authority works best when it radiates rather than is wielded.

H Sorry. But from here on out, you and your employees are on your own. Welcome to management.

AN ANALOGY

It might sound strange, but managing a business is comparable to entering an equestrian show-jumping competition. If you don't know much about show jumping, you're in good company. Most people who become managers have no idea what they're getting into either. Just as in business and management, in a show-jumping competition both horse and rider are attempting an untried situation for the first time. Nobody knows the outcome because steering a horse that might have other ideas over a series of formidable obstacles during the heat of competition is very different from boastfully envisioning the end result. The best advice on offer is to tackle each jump as it comes—one at a time.

Among the numerous obstacles that turn up on a course, there's usually one comprised of four or five (or more) hurdles set in a tight row. These are called bounce jumps. The difficulty with bounce jumps lies in the horse's ability to bound quickly over them. The solution is to aim for the center of the last jump and spur the horse on.

If you're serious about improving your business, your aim as a manager (that last hurdle) is to work toward becoming redundant—a difficult thing for insecure people to understand. In effect, it means setting up your business (or department) so that, as much as possible, it runs itself. The result is a workforce that prevents problems as well as responds to them, thereby avoiding the emotional and financial drain of being in a perpetual state of crises.

A popular adage states that several people, each wanting to pursue a separate destination, can be put on the back of a horse, but a horse can only go in one direction. Are you ready? Okay. Gather up your reins. The buzzer has sounded and your name's been called. It's time to exit the warm-up ring and enter the course. Keep in mind that in management there is no finish line—if you're in it, you're in it for the long haul. Yes, it's scary, but many times in life you must act even though you are afraid. And right now, the only obstacle standing between you and victory is that first leap.

Giddyup.

Glossary

accommodation: Letting someone else have his or her way in order to end a conflict.

actual product: What a business sells (and that which separates one product from another) in terms of parts, quality, features, design, and packaging that combine to deliver core product benefits.

adaptive organization: An organizational design that has little bureaucracy, reacts well to change and the environment, has few layers of management, and encourages the input of employees.

adjourning: The process of concluding a meeting or gathering.

administration: The people who set policies in a business and/or comprise the executive level of that business, or the management team of a public or nonprofit organization.

advertising: Any paid form of presentation and promotion of a product that does not involve personal selling.

attribution theory: A theory that helps explain the ways in which people interpret the behavior of others by, in part, suggesting that human actions are either internally or externally caused.

augmented product: The additional services and benefits incorporated with a core product (such as installation, after-sale service, sales, warranties, delivery, credit, and so forth).

autonomy: Independence or self-rule. In management, autonomy refers to the ability to act without constantly seeking approval or permission from superiors.

behavior modification: Changing people's behavior with rewards or punishment.

benchmarking: Comparing a product or business with another product or business to gain ideas that will result in an improvement.

benefit perception: The advantage, value, or profitable gain paying customers seek when buying a product or service.

brainstorming: The stimulation and free flow of opinions and ideas among people in a nonthreatening environment.

breadth: In business, a term that refers to the expansive layout of a company's hierarchical structure (i.e., all the departments) from top to bottom and left to right. *See also* DEPTH

bureaucracy: Usually seen today as an organization built on formality, a rigid chain-of-command authority, and many layers of management. Characteristically, bureaucracies tend to have many rules and regulations, reams of paperwork, and respond poorly to change.

bureaucratic organization: *See* BUREAUCRACY and MECHANISTIC ORGANIZATION

celebrity CEO: A chief executive officer who spends inordinate amounts of time and effort garnering attention.

chain of command: The uninterrupted direction a command or request takes through an organization, or a line of authority that links someone in an organization with someone else in that same organization.

change: To alter, vary, or modify something in some way.

communication: The sending, receiving, and understanding of meaning.

competitive advantage: An edge or trait that enables a business to do better than its competitors.

conflict: Disagreement, either seen or unseen, over an issue or issues of substance.

consultant: A person who is paid to give information, advice, or an opinion. In business, more often than not, a consultant is someone who produces research.

controlling: An act of responsibility and power that involves monitoring results and, if needed, taking action.

core culture: The aspects of an organization's culture that are not readily seen (how employees are judged, levels of worker involvement, quality of work life, etc.).

core product: The benefit consumers seek when they purchase a product.

corrective communication: Feedback designed to correct a behavior.

cost-plus pricing: Adding a standard markup to a product or service after determining fixed and variable costs.

culture: A learned set of beliefs, values, and patterns of behaviors common to groups or nations.

culture shock: The confusion, discomfort, and disorientation experienced by individuals after moving to another country or culture.

customer database: Information that explains a paying customer's details including address, economic description, buying habits, income level, possible future needs, and so on.

customers: Everyone whom an organization serves.

decentralization: Awarding managers the authority (autonomy) to make decisions without having to constantly consult a head office.

decision making: Identifying a problem then analyzing and choosing from corrective solutions.

delegation: Entrusting the completion of a task to one or more people by giving them the authority to think and act for themselves.

department: The separate divisions within an organization, or a group of people in an organization working as a unit and sharing a common duty or specialization under one manager.

depth: A term commonly associated with change management that refers to all the people in every department within a business. The term also implies that these people are aware of and fully involved in the functioning of the business. *See also* BREADTH

dysfunctional conflict: Always seeing conflict as a black-or-white issue or a battle that must be won. *See also* FUNCTIONAL CONFLICT

empowerment: The act of giving ongoing authority to an employee (or employees) by giving them the autonomy to think and act for themselves.

escalating commitment: Continuing to pour money, time, and effort into something that is not working.

ethics: Standards that determine what is acceptable or unacceptable in regard to behavior (i.e., what is good or bad or right or wrong).

evaluation: The formal judgment of an employee's performance.

external customers: The people who buy products or services who are not affiliated with or employed by the business.

feedback: The opinion, advice or correction given to someone who is performing, about to perform, or has just completed a task.

filtering: Altering information before passing it along to a superior or colleague to make it appear more favorable.

fixed costs: The costs of producing a product or service that do not change when production output volumes increase or decrease (rent, salaries, interest, heating and air conditioning, etc.).

forecast: An attempt to predict the future based on legitimate data.

formatting: To arrange in a particular order or way.

forming: Selecting people who will be assigned to work as a team.

functional conflict: Calmly encouraging, respecting, and listening to opposing views in order to reduce mistakes, clear the air, and come up with or improve ideas and solutions.

fundamental attribution error: Assuming that a person's behavior is the result of internal rather than external causes, or being wrong when trying to determine the cause of something.

goal: A specific result that an individual or organization expects to achieve.

group think: When a group's desire to reach agreement takes precedence over everything else and results in poor performance.

guidelines: Loose descriptions that dictate behavior and/or state what is or isn't expected.

heuristics: A process or strategy that oversimplifies decision making.

hierarchical pyramid: A triangle-shaped diagram showing either the chain of command of an organization or that ranks the importance or order of something.

humanism: The study of human personality and behavior in regard to motivation and the fulfillment of an individual's potential.

internal customers: The people who work within an organization (employees) and those who are a part of it (suppliers, contractors, shareholders, and other stakeholders) who need and rely on one another.

leadership: The influence of one person over another (or others) to strive toward the fulfillment of a goal or goals.

leading: Acquiring followers, maintaining morale, and motivating others while pursuing a common goal.

learning: The process of acquiring information that leads to permanent change.

management: Please refer to Chapter 1.

marketing: The act of bringing a buyer and seller together for the purpose of a sale or commitment.

mechanistic organization: Another term for bureaucracy (i.e., an organization built on formality, a rigid chain-of-command authority, many layers of management, many rules and regulations, reams of paperwork, and a poor response to change).

meeting: A gathering of people designed to convey information, brainstorm, and formulate possible answers or concrete solutions to customer-related problems.

mission statement: A broad outline briefly describing an organization as well as stating what it does, what it thinks is important, and where it's headed.

networking: Building and maintaining positive interrelationships with people.

norming: When a team settles down and begins to work.

norms: Informal rules adopted by a group to control behavior.

objectives: The specific results that a person or organization hopes to achieve (similar to goals).

observable culture: What one sees and hears when walking around a business that makes the business unique and instills it with a sense of character and unity.

organic organization: An organizational design that has little bureaucracy, reacts well to the environment, has few layers of management, and greatly encourages the input of employees.

organization: A group of people with formally designed roles who work together to achieve a common, agreed-upon purpose.

organizational culture: A learned set of traits and characteristics that establishes an organization's tone and practices and guides the behavior of its people.

organizational structure: The way an organization and its offices (chain-of-command authority and communication links) are arranged.

organizing: Clarifying, dividing, and arranging activities or work in order to produce a goal or goals.

performing: When a team agrees on a system that allows it to get to work and culminate individual efforts into a single shared outcome.

personal selling: The use of face-to-face oral presentation with one or more perspective customers for the purpose of making a sale and building a relationship.

plan: An idea and its implementation devised to accomplish a goal.

planning: Setting goals, courses of action, procedures, and the allocation of resources while forecasting future results.

point-of-sale area: The area in a business where money is exchanged for products or services.

presentation: A formal or informal display of information given by a person or a team of people that is designed to convey information and achieve a set goal.

proactive change: Preparing for change before it occurs.

problem solving: Identifying a discrepancy between an actual situation and a desired result and then taking action to rectify any problems.

product: The goods or services an organization manufactures, produces, and/or sells.

product life cycle: The course of a product's sales from development to its introduction and on to its growth, maturity, and decline.

project: A planned set of actions leading to a single (often marketable) result.

public relations: The building of relations with the public by obtaining favorable publicity and creating a good image.

quality: A degree of excellence that meets or exceeds customer expectations.

reactive change: Trying to deal with change after it occurs.

recession: A period of economic decline, usually identified when the gross national product falls for two successive quarters, characterized by sluggish product demand, the failure of real output to rise, and unemployment increases.

role: The position a person takes in an organization including what he or she is expected to perform.

rules: Strict and specific descriptions that dictate behavior and/or state what is or isn't expected.

sales promotion: Short-term incentives designed to encourage the purchase of a product.

selective perception: Looking at situations or problems from a limited point of view.

sensory adaptation: Becoming so accustomed to something that it's often taken for granted.

service: Assistance, aid, value, or cooperation given to others.

skill: An above-average ability to convert knowledge into action.

social loafing: The tendency of some individuals to reduce their input or effort when working in a group.

span of control: The number of people who report directly to a manager.

storming: The personality clashes, bids for domination, faction forming, and fights that typically arise shortly after a group of people has been assigned to work together.

strategy: Preparing for the future by doing everything possible to strengthen yourself and your organization in the here and now.

stress: A state of debilitating tension suffered when trying to cope with demands, situations, or constraints.

subculture: Small, independent cultures that exist within the larger culture of an organization.

synergy: When the end result of something is greater than the sum of its parts.

team: A group of people committed to a common purpose for which they work and hold themselves mutually accountable.

termination: A permanent and forced act that severs a person from an organization (usually due to incompetence, incompatibility, or illegal or unethical behavior).

value: The merit, caliber, or usefulness a person sees in something or someone else.

values: The underlying beliefs of what people feel is unimportant or important as well as what they should or should not do.

variable costs: The costs inherent in producing goods or services that vary according to production output (wages based on time, raw materials, electricity, etc.).

vision: In a business sense, vision refers to a simple and highly motivating means to unite people toward a common purpose and direction while invoking their emotions (lifting their hearts and minds).

visual aids: Items used to highlight or dramatize an issue or point in a presentation.

whistle-blowing: The practice of exposing the unethical or illegal behavior of others.

work: Effort partaken outside of personal time and usually done in exchange for money, favor, or validation, or activity that produces value for others.

work group: A group of people who share information, work together, and help one another to meet common goals and produce results (to a manager, a *work group* is more or less the same as a *team*).

Bibliography

Chapter 1

Collins Cobuild English Language Dictionary, William Collins and Co Ltd., London/Glasgow, 1988.

Kotter, J.P., "What Effective General Managers Really Do," *Harvard Business Review,* vol. 60, November-December 1974, pp. 156-157.

Longman Dictionary of Contemporary English, Longman Group UK Ltd., Harlow, 1988.

Merriam-Webster's Collegiate Dictionary (11th Edition), Merriam-Webster Inc., Springfield, MA, 2003.

The New Oxford English Dictionary, Oxford University Press, Oxford, 1993.

Schermerhorn, J.R., *Management* (Fifth Edition), John Wiley & Sons, New York, 1996.

Smith, A. *An Inquiry into the Nature and Causes of Wealth of Nations* (Fourth Edition). Edwin Cannon (Ed.), Methuen Publishing Ltd., London, 1925.

Chapter 2

Duncan, W.J., *Great Ideas in Management,* Jossey-Bass, San Francisco, 1989.

Fayol, H., *Industrial and General Administration,* Dunod, Paris, 1916.

Jones, S.R.G., "Was There a Hawthorne Effect?" *American Journal of Sociology,* November 1992, pp. 451-468.

Kanigel, R., *The One Best Way,* Viking Press, New York, 1997.

Linden, D.W., "The Mother of Them All," *Forbes Magazine,* January 16, 1995, pp. 75-76.

Roethlisberger, F.J. and Dickson, W.J., *Management and the Worker,* Harvard University Press, Cambridge, MA, 1939.

Weber, M., *The Theory of Social and Economic Organization,* Free Press, New York, 1947.

Chapter 3

"Back to Basics," Survey: Management, *The Economist,* March 9, 2002, pp. 3-18.

Boyatzis, R.E., *The Competent Manager,* John Wiley & Sons, New York, 1982.

Outcome Measurement Project of the Accreditation Research Committee, American Assembly of Collegiate Schools of Business, 1984.

Sorenson, R., "A Lifetime of Learning to Manage Effectively," *The Wall Street Journal,* February 28, 1983, p. 18.

Chapter 4

Kanter, R.M., "Transcending Business Boundaries," *Harvard Business Review,* May-June 1991, pp. 151-154.

Leonard, S., "Love That Customer," *Management Review,* October 1987, pp. 36-39.

Lorinc, J., "Now the Customer is Job 1," *Canadian Business,* July 1997, pp. 22-28.

"A Matter of Priorities," *The New York Times,* February 19, 1995, section F, p. 23.

Oakland, J., *Total Quality Management,* Butterworth-Heinemann, New York, 1993.

Scott, J.T., *Fundamentals of Leisure Business Success: A Manager's Guide to Achieving Success in the Leisure and Recreation Industry,* The Haworth Press, Binghamton, NY, 1998.

Chapter 5

Fishman, C., "The Wal-Mart You Don't Know," Fast Company, issue 77, December 2003, p. 68. Available at www.fastcompany.com/magazine/77/walmart.html.

Handy, C., *Understanding the Organization,* Penguin Books Ltd., London, 1993.

Katz, R.L., "Skills of an Effective Administrator," *Harvard Business Review,* September-October 1974, pp. 90-102.

Lau, A.W. and Pavett, C.M., "Managerial Work: The Influence of Hierarchical Level and Functional Specialty," *Academy of Management Journal,* March 1983, pp. 170-177.

Matteson, M.T., "Some Reported Thoughts on Significant Management Literature," *Academy of Management,* June 1974, pp. 386-389.

McGregor, D., *The Human Side of Management,* McGraw-Hill, New York, 1960.

Pascale, R.T., *Managing on the Edge,* Penguin Books, New York, 1991.

Wren, D.A., *The Evolution of Management Thought,* John Wiley & Sons, New York, 1994.

Chapter 6

Carnegie, D., *How to Win Friends and Influence People,* Simon & Schuster, New York, 1939.

Caudron, S., "Delegate for Results," *Industry Week,* February 6, 1995, pp. 27-28.

Lewicki, R.J., Bowen, D.D., Hall, D.T., and Hall, F.S., *Experiences in Management and Organizational Behavior* (Third Edition), John Wiley & Sons, New York, 1988.

Robbins, S.P. and Hunsaker, P.L., *Training in Interpersonal Skills* (Second Edition), Prentice-Hall, Saddle River, NJ, 1996.

Scott, J.T., *Fundamentals of Leisure Business Success: A Manager's Guide to Achieving Success in the Leisure and Recreation Industry,* The Haworth Press, Binghamton, NY, 1998.

Semler, R., *Maverick: The Success Story Behind the World's Most Unusual Workplace,* Warner Books, New York, 1995.

Whetton, D.A. and Cameron, K.S., *Developing Management Skills* (Third Edition), HarperCollins, New York, 1991.

Chapter 7

Burns, T. and Stalker, G.M., *The Management of Innovation,* Oxford University Press, Oxford, 1994.

Chandler, A.D., "Origins of the Organizational Chart," *Harvard Business Review,* March-April 1988, pp. 156-157.

Deal, T. and Kennedy, A., *Corporate Cultures,* Penguin Books, New York, 1988.

Harrison, R. "How to Describe Your Organization," *Harvard Business Review,* September-October 1972.

Hesselbein, F., Goldsmith, M., and Beckhard, R., *The Leader of the Future,* Jossey-Bass, San Francisco, 1996.

Hesselbein, F., Goldsmith, M., and Beckhard, R., *The Organization of the Future,* Jossey-Bass, San Francisco, 1997.

Schein, E.H., "Organizational Culture," *American Psychologist,* vol. 45, 1990, p. 109.

Sellers, P., "So you Fail . . . Now Bounce Back," *Fortune,* May 1, 1995, p. 49.

Chapter 8

Band, W., *Creating Value for Customers,* John Wiley & Sons, New York, 1991.

Chatwin, B., *Anatomy of Restlessness,* Picador, London, 1996.

Cole, G., *Management: Theory and Practice,* DP Publications, London, 1991.

Lewin, K., *Field Theory in Social Science,* Harper Press, New York, 1951.

Schein, E.H., *Process Consultation: Its Role in Organizational Development,* Addison-Wesley Press, 1969.

Strebel, P., "Choosing the Right Change Path," *The Financial Times* (part 14), February 9, 1996, p. 5.

Chapter 9

Filley, A.C., *Interpersonal Conflict Resolution,* Scott Foresman, Glenview, IL, 1975.

Kreitner, R., "Personal Wellness: It's Just Good Business," *Business Horizons,* vol. 25, May-June 1982, pp. 28-35.

Pascale, R.T., *Managing on the Edge,* Penguin Books, New York, 1991.

Peters, T.J. and Waterman, R.H., *In Search of Excellence: Lessons from America's Best-Run Companies,* Harper & Row, New York, 1983.

Robbins, S.P., "Conflict Management and Conflict Resolution Are Not Synonymous Terms," *California Management Review,* Winter 1978, p. 71.

Thomas, K.W. and Schmidt, W.H., "A Survey of Management Interests with Respect to Conflict," *Academy of Management Journal,* June 1976, pp. 315-318.

Walton, R.E., *Interpersonal Peacemaking: Confrontations and Third-Party Consultation,* Addison-Wesley, Reading, MA, 1969.

Chapter 10

Clegg, C.W., "Outcomes of Autonomous Workgroups," *Academy of Management Journal,* June 1986, pp. 280-284.

Cohen, S.G., Ledford, G.E., and Spreitzer, G.M., "A Predictive Model of Self-Managing Work Teams," *Human Relations,* May 1996, p. 644.

Robbins, H. and Finley, M., *Why Teams Don't Work,* Pacesetter Books, Princeton, NJ, 1995.

Tuckman, B.W., "Developmental Sequence in Small Groups," *Psychological Bulletin,* vol. 63, 1965, pp. 384-389.

Waterman, R.H., Peters, J., and Phillips, J.R., "Structure Is Not Organization," *Business Horizons,* vol. 23, no. 3, June 1980, pp. 14-26.

Chapter 11

Bart, C.K., "Sex, Lies, and Mission Statements," *Business Horizons,* November-December 1997, p. 11.

Kerr, S., "Overcoming the Dysfunctions of MBO," *Management by Objectives,* vol. 5, no. 1, 1976.

McConkey, D.D., *How to Manage by Results,* AMACOM, New York, 1976.

Robbins, S.P. and Hunsaker, P.L., *Training in Interpersonal Skills* (Second Edition), Prentice-Hall, Upper Saddle River, NJ, 1996.

Chapter 12

"Benchmarkers Make Strange Bedfellows," *Industry Week,* November 15, 1993, p. 8.

Deming, W.E., *Out of the Crisis,* The W. Edwards Deming Institute & The MIT Center for Advanced Engineering, Cambridge, MA, 1986.

Garvin, D.A., "Competing on the Eight Dimensions of Quality," *Harvard Business Review,* vol. 65, no. 6, 1987, pp. 101-109.

Lawler, E.E. and Mohrman, S.A., "Quality Circles After the Fad," *Harvard Business Review,* January-February 1985, pp. 65-71.

Main, J., "How to Steal the Best Ideas Around," *Fortune,* October 19, 1992, pp. 102-106.

Sashkin, M. and Kiser, K.J., *Putting Total Quality Management to Work,* Berret-Koehlor, San Francisco, 1993.

Chapter 13

Gellerman, S.W., "Why Good Managers Make Bad Ethical Choices," *Harvard Business Review,* vol. 64, July-August 1986, pp. 85-90.

Government Accountability Project as reported in "Blowing the Whistle Without Paying the Piper," *Business Week,* June 3, 1991, pp. 138-140.

Nash, L.L., "Ethics Without the Sermon," *Harvard Business Review,* November-December 1981, p. 81.

Otten, A.L., "Ethics on the Job," *The Wall Street Journal,* July 14, 1986, p. 17.

Chapter 14

Blake, R.R., Mouton, J.S., Barnes, L.B., and Greiner, L.E., "Breakthrough in Organization Development," *Harvard Business Review,* November-December 1964, p. 136.

Drucker, P.F., "Leadership: More Doing than Dash," *The Wall Street Journal,* January 6, 1988, p. 16.

Fiedler, F.E., "Time Based Measures of Leadership Experience and Organizational Performance," *Leadership Quarterly,* Spring 1992, p. 5.

Hersey, P. and Blanchard, K.H., *Management of Organizational Behavior,* Prentice-Hall, Englewood Cliffs, NJ, 1988.

House, R. (Goal Path Theory), see: Huber, G.P., "A Theory of Effects of Advanced Information Technologies on Organizational Design, Intelligence, and Decision Making," *Academy of Management Review,* vol. 15, 1990, p. 67.

"The Jack and Jeff Show Loses its Luster," *The Economist,* May 4, 2002, pp. 63-65.

Kirkpatrick, S.A. and Locke, E.A., "Leadership: Do Traits Matter?" *Academy of Management Executive,* vol. 5, May 1991, pp. 48-60.

Nielsen, J. and Vollers, M., *Icebound: A Doctor's Incredible Battle for Survival at the South Pole,* Hyperion, NY, 2001.

Vroom, V.H. and Jago, A.G., *The New Leadership,* Prentice-Hall, Englewood Cliffs, NJ, 1988.

Chapter 15

McGregor, D., *The Human Side of Enterprise,* McGraw-Hill, New York, 1960.

Wren, D.A., *The Evolution of Management Thought* (Fourth Edition), John Wiley & Sons, New York, 1994.

Chapter 16

Cox, T., "The Multi-Cultural Organization," *Academy of Management Executive,* vol. 5, May 1991, p. 34.

Emmons, S., "Emotions at Face Value," *The Los Angeles Times,* January 9, 1998, p. E1.

Gullahorn, J.T. and Gullahorn, J.E., "An Extension of the U-Curve Hypothesis," *Journal of Social Sciences,* January 1963, pp. 34-47.

Hofstede, G., "Cultural Constraints in Management Theories," *The Executive,* February 1993, pp. 81-99.

Mole, J., *Mind Your Manners: Culture Clash in the European Single Market,* Industrial Society Press, London, 1990.

Munter, M., "Cross-Cultural Communication for Managers," *Business Horizons,* May-June 1993, pp. 69-77.

Penrose, J.M., *Business Communication: Strategies and Skills,* Dryden Press, Chicago, 1988.

Rafaeli, A. and Sutton, R.I., "The Expressions of Emotion in Organizational Life" used in Cummings, L.L. and Staw, B.M., *Research in Organizational Behavior,* JAI Press, Greenwich, CT, vol. 11, 1989, p. 8.

Robbins, S.P. and Hunsaker, P.L., *Training in Interpersonal Skills* (Second Edition), Prentice-Hall, Upper Saddle River, NJ, 1996.

Schermerhorn, J.R., *Management and Organizational Behavior,* John Wiley & Sons, New York, 1996.

Scott, J.T., *Fundamentals of Leisure Business Success: A Manager's Guide to Achieving Success in the Leisure and Recreation Industry,* The Haworth Press, Binghamton, NY, 1998.

Chapter 17

Agor, W.H., *Intuition in Organizations,* Sage Publishing, Newbury Park, CA, 1989.

Hogarth, R.H., Kahneman, D., and Tversky, A., *Judgements in Managerial Decision Making* (Third Edition), John Wiley & Sons, New York, 1994.

Huber, G.P., *Managerial Decision Making,* Scott Foresman, Glenview, IL, 1975.
Pounds, W., "The Process of Problem Finding," *Industrial Management Review,* Fall 1969, pp. 1-19.
Simon, H.A., *Administrative Behavior,* Free Press, New York, 1947.
Von Oech, R., *A Kick in the Seat of the Pants,* Harper & Row, New York, 1986.

Chapter 18

Blair, G.M., *Starting to Manage: The Essentials Skills,* The Institute of Electrical & Electronics Engineers, Piscataway, NJ, 1996.
Drucker, P.F., *The Effective Executive,* Harper & Row, New York, 1967.
Griessman, B.E., *Time Tactics of Very Successful People,* McGraw-Hill, New York, 1996.
McCay, J.T., *The Management of Time,* Prentice-Hall, Englewood Cliffs, NJ, 1995.
Webber, R.A., *To Be a Manager,* Irwin Press, Homewood, IL, 1981.

Chapter 19

Alderfer, C.P., *Existence, Relatedness, and Growth,* Free Press, New York, 1992.
Herzberg, F., "One More Time: How Do You Motivate Employees?" *Harvard Business Review,* vol. 47, January-February 1968, pp. 54-63.
Luthens, F. and Kreitner, R., *Organizational Behavior Modification,* Scott Foresman, Glenview, IL, 1975.
Maslow, A.H., *Motivation and Personality* (Second Edition), Harper & Row, New York, 1970.
Matteson, M.T., "Some Reported Thoughts on Significant Management Literature," *Academy of Management Journal,* June 1974, pp. 386-389.
McClelland, D.C., *The Achieving Society,* Van Nostrand, New York, 1961.
Meyer, H.H., "A Solution to the Performance Appraisal Feedback Enigma," *The Executive,* February 1991, pp. 68-76.

Chapter 20

Berlo, D.K., *The Process of Communication,* Holt-Rinehart & Winston, New York, 1960.
Carnegie, D., *How to Win Friends and Influence People,* Simon & Schuster, New York, 1939.
Hall, E.T., *The Silent Language,* Doubleday, New York, 1973.
Kursh, C.O., "The Benefits of Poor Communication," *The Psychoanalytic Review,* Summer-Fall, 1971, pp. 189-208.
Peters, T. and Austin, N., *A Passion for Excellence,* Random House, New York, 1985.
Tannen, D., "The Power of Talk: Who Gets Heard and Why," *Harvard Business Review,* September-October 1995, pp. 138-148.

Chapter 21

Armstrong, M., *How to Be an Even Better Manager,* Kogan Page, London, 1990.

Filipczak, B., "Obfuscation Resounding: Corporate Communication in America," *Training,* July 1995, p. 36.

Gwynne, S.C. and Dickerson, J.F., "Lost in the E-Mail," *Time Magazine,* April 21, 1997, pp. 88-90.

Lengel, R.H. and Daft, R.L., "The Selection of Communication Media as an Executive Skill," *Academy of Management Executive,* vol. 2, Aug 1988, p. 225.

Semler, R., *Maverick,* Warner Books, New York, 1995.

Chapter 22

Blair, G.M., *Starting to Manage: The Essentials Skills*, The Institute of Electrical & Electronics Engineers, Piscataway, NJ, 1996.

Lahiff, J.M. and Penrose, J.M, *Business Communication: Strategies and Skills,* Dryden Press, Chicago, 1988.

Lengel, R.H. and Daft, R.L., "The Selection of Communication Media As an Executive Skill," *Academy of Management Executive,* vol. 2, August 1988, pp. 225-232.

Robbins, S.P. and Hunsaker, P.L., *Training in Interpersonal Skills: Tips for Managing People at Work* (Second Edition), Prentice-Hall, Upper Saddle River, NJ, 1996.

Chapter 23

Armstrong, M., *How to Be an Even Better Manager,* Kogan Page, London, 1990.

Hingston, P., *The Greatest Little Business Book,* Hingston, London, 1979.

Chapter 24

Blair, G.M., *Starting to Manage: The Essentials Skills,* The Institute of Electrical & Electronics Engineers, Piscataway, NJ, 1996.

Scott, J.T., *Fundamentals of Leisure Business Success: A Manager's Guide to Achieving Success in the Leisure and Recreation Industry,* The Haworth Press, Binghamton, NY, 1998.

Chapter 25

Kotler, P., Armstrong, G., Saunders, J., and Wong, V., *Principles of Marketing* (Second European Edition), Prentice-Hall Europe, London, 1999.

Murphy, P.E. and Enis, B.M., "Classifying Products Strategically," *Journal of Marketing,* July 1986, pp. 24-32.

Chapter 26

Coyne, K.P., "Sustainable Competitive Advantage: What It Is, What It Isn't," *Business Horizons,* vol. 29, no. 1, January-February 1986, pp. 54-61.
Porter, M.E., *Competitive Advantage,* Free Press, New York, 1985.
Porter, M.E., *Competitive Strategy: Techniques for Analyzing Industries and Competitors,* Free Press, New York, 1980.
Thompson, A.A. and Strickland, A.J., *Strategic Management* (Seventh Edition), Richard Irwin, Inc., Boston, 1993.

Chapter 27

Bennet, P.D., *Dictionary of Marketing Terms,* American Marketing Association, Chicago, 1988.
Farber, B. and Wycoff, J., "Customer Service: Evolution and Revolution," *Sales and Marketing Management,* May 1991, pp. 47-53.
Kotler, P., Armstrong, G., Saunders, J., and Wong, V., *Principles of Marketing* (Second European Edition), Prentice-Hall Europe, London, 1999.
Scott, J.T., *Fundamentals of Leisure Business Success: A Manager's Guide to Achieving Success in the Leisure and Recreation Industry,* The Haworth Press, Binghamton, NY, 1998.

Chapter 28

Scott, J.T., *Fundamentals of Leisure Business Success: A Manager's Guide to Achieving Success in the Leisure and Recreation Industry,* The Haworth Press, Binghamton, NY, 1998.

Chapter 29

Cateora, P.R., *International Marketing* (Seventh Edition), Irwin Press, Homewood, IL, 1990.
Nagle, T.T. and Holden, R.K., *The Strategy and Tactics of Pricing* (Second Edition), Prentice-Hall, Englewood Cliffs, NJ, 1995.
Schwartz, D.J., *Marketing Today: A Basic Approach* (Third Edition), Harcourt Brace Jovanovich, New York, 1981.
Scott, J.T., *Fundamentals of Leisure Business Success: A Manager's Guide to Achieving Success in the Leisure and Recreation Industry,* The Haworth Press, Binghamton, NY, 1998.

Chapter 30

Halloran, J.W., *The Entrepreneur's Guides to Starting a Successful Business* (Second Edition), McGraw-Hill, New York, 1992.
Schwartz, D.J., *Marketing Today: A Basic Approach* (Third Edition), Harcourt Brace Jovanovich, New York, 1981.
Scott, J.T., "Effective Marketing," *Recreation Magazine,* March/April 1996, pp. 5-6.
Scott, J.T., "Good Customer Care," *Hospitality,* August-September 1996, p. 15.
Tomkinson, L., "Tips for Improving Retail Sales," *Update,* July-August 1997, pp. 5-8.

Chapter 32

Scott, J.T., "Raising the Dead," *Entrepreneur,* February 2001, pp. 67-69.

Index

Page numbers followed by the letter "f" indicate figures.

The Fatimid Caliphate

The Institute of Ismaili Studies

Ismaili Heritage Series, 14

General Editor: Farhad Daftary

Previously published titles:

1. Paul E. Walker, *Abū Ya'qūb al-Sijistānī: Intellectual Missionary* (1996)
2. Heinz Halm, *The Fatimids and their Traditions of Learning* (1997)
3. Paul E. Walker, *Ḥamīd al-Dīn al-Kirmānī: Ismaili Thought in the Age of al-Ḥākim* (1999)
4. Alice C. Hunsberger, *Nasir Khusraw, The Ruby of Badakhshan: A Portrait of the Persian Poet, Traveller and Philosopher* (2000)
5. Farouk Mitha, *Al-Ghazālī and the Ismailis: A Debate in Medieval Islam* (2001)
6. Ali S. Asani, *Ecstasy and Enlightenment: The Ismaili Devotional Literature of South Asia* (2002)
7. Paul E. Walker, *Exploring an Islamic Empire: Fatimid History and its Sources* (2002)
8. Nadia Eboo Jamal, *Surviving the Mongols: Nizārī Quhistānī and the Continuity of Ismaili Tradition in Persia* (2002)
9. Verena Klemm, *Memoirs of a Mission: The Ismaili Scholar, Statesman and Poet al-Mu'ayyad fi'l-Dīn al-Shīrāzī* (2003)
10. Peter Willey, *Eagle's Nest: Ismaili Castles in Iran and Syria* (2005)
11. Sumaiya A. Hamdani, *Between Revolution and State: The Path to Fatimid Statehood* (2006)
12. Farhad Daftary, *Ismailis in Medieval Muslim Societies* (2005)
13. Farhad Daftary, ed., *A Modern History of the Ismailis* (2011)

The Fatimid Caliphate

Diversity of Traditions

Edited by
Farhad Daftary and Shainool Jiwa

B L O O M S B U R Y
NEW DELHI • LONDON • OXFORD • NEW YORK • SYDNEY

BLOOMSBURY INDIA
Bloomsbury Publishing India Pvt. Ltd
Second Floor, LSC Building No. 4, DDA Complex, Pocket C – 6 &
7, Vasant Kunj, New Delhi 110070

BLOOMSBURY, Bloomsbury Academic India and the Diana
logo are trademarks of bloomsbury Publishing Plc

First Published in India 2022
Published B.Tn 2018 bauriy I.Bs & C.Taouri. Lts & Cd o. Ltd

This edition is published with permission from Bloomsbury Publishing Plc.
50 Bedford Square, London WC1B3DP

A catalog record for this book is available from the Library of Congress.
A catalogue record for this book is available from the British Library.

ISBN: 978-93-56400-62-7

For sale in the Indian subcontinent only

Exclusively distributed in the Indian subcontinent by
Manohar Publishers & Distributors
4753/23, Ansari Road
Darya Ganj, New Delhi 110002
Tel.: 23284848, 23289100
Email: sales@manoharbooks.com, manoharbooks@gmail.com

Typeset in Minion Tra for The Institute of Ismaili Studies
Printed and bound in the India

The Institute of Ismaili Studies

The Institute of Ismaili Studies was established in 1977 with the object of promoting scholarship and learning on Islam, in the historical as well as contemporary contexts, and a better understanding of its relationship with other societies and faiths.

The Institute's programmes encourage a perspective which is not confined to the theological and religious heritage of Islam, but seeks to explore the relationship of religious ideas to broader dimensions of society and culture. The programmes thus encourage an interdisciplinary approach to the materials of Islamic history and thought. Particular attention is also given to issues of modernity that arise as Muslims seek to relate their heritage to the contemporary situation.

Within the Islamic tradition, the Institute's programmes promote research on those areas which have, to date, received relatively little attention from scholars. These include the intellectual and literary expressions of Shiʿism in general, and Ismailism in particular.

In the context of Islamic societies, the Institute's programmes are informed by the full range and diversity of cultures in which Islam is practised today, from the Middle East, South and Central Asia, and Africa to the industrialised societies of the West, thus taking into consideration the variety of contexts which shape the ideals, beliefs and practices of the faith.

These objectives are realised through concrete programmes and activities organised and implemented by various departments of the Institute. The Institute also collaborates periodically, on a programme-specific basis, with other institutions of learning in the United Kingdom and abroad.

The Institute's academic publications fall into a number of inter-related categories:

1. Occasional papers or essays addressing broad themes of the relationship between religion and society, with special reference to Islam.
2. Monographs exploring specific aspects of Islamic faith and culture, or the contributions of individual Muslim thinkers or writers.
3. Editions or translations of significant primary or secondary texts.
4. Translations of poetic or literary texts which illustrate the rich heritage of spiritual, devotional and symbolic expressions in Muslim history.
5. Works on Ismaili history and thought, and the relationship of the Ismailis to other traditions, communities and schools of thought in Islam.
6. Proceedings of conferences and seminars sponsored by the Institute.
7. Bibliographical works and catalogues which document manuscripts, printed texts and other source materials.

This book falls into category five listed above.

In facilitating these and other publications, the Institute's sole aim is to encourage original research and analysis of relevant issues. While every effort is made to ensure that the publications are of a high academic standard, there is naturally bound to be a diversity of views, ideas and interpretations. As such, the opinions expressed in these publications must be understood as belonging to their authors alone.

Ismaili Heritage Series

A major Shiʿi Muslim community, the Ismailis have had a long and eventful history. Scattered in many regions of the world – in Asia, Africa and now also in Europe and North America – the Ismailis have elaborated diverse intellectual and literary traditions in different languages. On two occasions they had states of their own, the Fatimid caliphate and the Nizari state of Iran and Syria during the Alamut period. While pursuing particular religio-political aims, the leaders of these Ismaili states also variously encouraged intellectual, scientific, artistic and commercial activities.

Until recently, the Ismailis were studied and judged almost exclusively on the basis of the evidence collected or fabricated by their detractors, including the bulk of the medieval heresiographers and polemicists who were hostile towards the Shiʿis in general and the Ismailis among them in particular. These authors in fact treated the Shiʿi interpretations of Islam as expressions of heterodoxy or even heresy. As a result, a 'black legend' was gradually developed and put into circulation in the Muslim world to discredit the Ismailis and their interpretation of Islam. The Christian Crusaders and their occidental chroniclers, who remained almost completely ignorant of Islam and its internal divisions, disseminated their own myths of the Ismailis, which came to be accepted in Europe as true descriptions of Ismaili teachings and practices. Modern orientalists, too, studied the Ismailis on the basis of these hostile sources and fanciful accounts of medieval times. Thus legends and misconceptions have continued to surround the Ismailis through the 20th century.

In more recent decades, however, the field of Ismaili studies has been revolutionized owing to the recovery and study of genuine Ismaili sources on a large scale – manuscript materials which through different means survived the destruction of the Fatimid and Nizari Ismaili libraries. These sources, representing diverse literary traditions produced in Arabic, Persian and Indic languages, had hitherto been secretly preserved in private collections in India, Central Asia, Iran, Afghanistan, Syria and Yemen.

Modern progress in Ismaili studies has already necessitated a complete rewriting of the history of the Ismailis and their contributions to Islamic civilisation. It has now become clear that the Ismailis founded important libraries and institutions of learning such as al-Azhar and the Dar al-ʿIlm in Cairo, while some of their learned *daʿis* or missionaries developed unique intellectual traditions amalgamating their theological doctrine with a diversity of philosophical traditions in complex metaphysical systems. The Ismaili patronage of learning and the extension of hospitality to non-Ismaili scholars was maintained even in such difficult times as the Alamut period, when the community was preoccupied with its survival in an extremely hostile milieu.

The Ismaili Heritage Series, published under the auspices of the Department of Academic Research and Publications of The Institute of Ismaili Studies, aims to make available to a wide audience the results of modern scholarship on the Ismailis and their rich intellectual and cultural heritage, as well as certain aspects of their more recent history and achievements.

Contents

Notes on the Contributors

Daniel Beben is an Assistant Professor of History at Nazarbayev University, Kazakhstan. He is preparing an edition and translation of the *'Ibrat-afzā* as well as a monograph on the history of the Ismailis in Central Asia.

Simonetta Calderini is a Reader in Islamic Studies at the University of Roehampton, London. She is at present completing a monograph on *Women as Imams: Classical Islamic Sources and Modern Debates on Leading Prayer*.

Delia Cortese is a Senior Lecturer in Religious Studies at Middlesex University, London. Her recent publications include *Women and the Fatimids in the World of Islam* (with S. Calderini, 2006).

Farhad Daftary is the Director of The Institute of Ismaili Studies. His recent publications include *A History of Shi'i Islam* (2013) and *Fifty Years in the East: The Memoirs of Wladimir Ivanow* (2015).

Maribel Fierro is a Research Professor at the Centre of Human and Social Sciences at the Council for Scientific Research (CSIC), Spain. Her recent publications include the second volume of *The New Cambridge History of Islam* (2010), of which she is the editor.

Shainool Jiwa is a Senior Faculty Member at The Institute of Ismaili Studies. Her publications include *The Founder of Cairo: The Fatimid Imam-Caliph al-Muʿizz and his Era* (2013).

Paul E. Walker is Deputy Director for Academic Programs, Center for Middle Eastern Studies at the University of Chicago. His publications include *Orations of the Fatimid Caliphs: Festival Sermons of the Ismaili Imams* (2009).

Note on Transliteration and Abbreviations

The system of transliteration used in this book for the Arabic and Persian scripts is essentially the same as that adopted in the second edition of *The Encyclopaedia of Islam*, with a few modifications, namely, ch for č, j for dj and q for ḳ.

There are no abbreviations in this book other than *EI* and *EI2* for the first and second editions, respectively, of *The Encyclopaedia of Islam*.

Introduction

Farhad Daftary and Shainool Jiwa

The foundation of the Fatimid caliphate in 297/909 marked the crowning success of the early Ismailis and their *da'wa* activities. The religio-political *da'wa* of the Ismailis had finally led to the establishment of a state, or *dawla*, headed by the Ismaili imam. This represented a great success not only for the Ismailis, who had come to possess for the first time an important state under the leadership of their imam, but also for the entire Shi'i Muslim community. Since the days of 'Alī b. Abī Ṭālib, this was the first time that an 'Alid imam from the Prophet Muḥammad's family, or the *ahl al-bayt*, had succeeded to the leadership of a major Muslim state. Fatimid victory, therefore, heralded the fulfilment of a long-awaited Shi'i ideal, frustrated and postponed for more than two centuries by numerous setbacks.

By acquiring political power, and then transforming the nascent Fatimid *dawla* into a vast empire, the Ismaili imam had at the same time presented his Shi'i challenge to the Abbasid hegemony and Sunni interpretations of Islam. Henceforth, the Ismaili Fatimid imam-caliph could readily and openly act as the spiritual spokesman of Shi'i Islam in general, much in the same way that the Abbasid caliph was the mouthpiece of Sunni Islam. The situation of the Fatimids remained unchanged when the Shi'i Būyids came to power in the 320s/930s, because the Būyids did not claim religious authority and they permitted the powerless Abbasid caliph to remain as the titular head of Sunni Islam. The status of the Abbasid caliphs was, in fact, strengthened when the ardently Sunni Saljūq Turks replaced the Shiʿi Būyids as the real masters of the Abbasid caliphate.

The Ismailis were able to practise their faith openly within Fatimid dominions, without the fear of persecution; while outside the boundaries of their state they were obliged to observe *taqiyya*, or precautionary dissimulation, as before. Furthermore, with the establishment of the Fatimid *dawla*, the need had arisen for promulgating a state religion and a legal code, even though Ismailism was never to be imposed on all the subjects of that state. Indeed, the Ismailis themselves continued to represent a religious minority within the Fatimid state. At any rate, Ismaili law, which had not existed during the earlier secret and revolutionary phase of Ismailism, was codified during the early Fatimid period, mainly through the efforts of Qāḍī al-Nuʿmān (d. 363/974), the foremost jurist of the Fatimid period. Thus the Ismailis came to possess their *madhhab* or school of religious law, relying on a variety of existing Sunni and other Shiʿi sources in elaborating their own legal system.

In line with their universal claims, the Fatimid imam-caliphs did not abandon their *daʿwa* activities upon assuming power. Aiming to extend their authority and rule over all of Muslim society, they retained a network of *dāʿī*s, operating on their behalf as religio-political missionaries both within and beyond Fatimid dominions. The Fatimids particularly concerned themselves with the affairs of their *daʿwa* after transferring the seat of their state from Ifrīqiya, in North Africa, to Egypt in 362/973. The conquest of Egypt itself in 358/969 represented an intermediary state in the Fatimids' strategy of eastern expansion.

Cairo, founded as a caliphal city by the fourth Fatimid imam-caliph al-Muʿizz (341–365/953–975), became the headquarters of the complex hierarchical Ismaili *daʿwa* organisation. Supreme leadership of the Ismaili *daʿwa* and the Fatimid *dawla* was the prerogative of the Fatimid imam-caliph. It is worth noting, however, that Ismailism had its greatest and most lasting success outside Fatimid dominions, especially in Yemen, Persia and Central Asia. The learned Ismaili *dāʿī*s of the Fatimid times, who were trained as theologians, were at the same time the scholars and authors of their community, producing what were to become the classical texts of Ismaili literature dealing with a multitude of exoteric (*ẓāhirī*) and esoteric (*bāṭinī*) subjects. The *dāʿī*s of this period elaborated distinctive intellectual traditions and made important contributions to Islamic theology and philosophy in general and to Shiʿi thought in particular.

Meanwhile, in the immediate aftermath of the Fatimid victory, the Abbasid-Sunni establishment launched an anti-Ismaili literary campaign. The overall aim of this systematic and prolonged campaign was to discredit the entire Ismaili movement from its origins onward, so that the Ismailis could be readily condemned as the *malāḥida*, heretics or deviators from the true religious path. Muslim theologians, jurists, historians and heresiographers participated variously in this campaign. In particular, Sunni polemicists fabricated the necessary evidence that would lend support to the condemnation of the Ismailis on specific doctrinal grounds. They concocted detailed accounts of the sinister teachings and immoral practices of the Ismailis, while denying the ʿAlid genealogy of their imams. These forgeries circulated widely and, in time, were used as source material by subsequent generations of Muslim authors.

By spreading these defamations, the polemicists and other anti-Ismaili authors gradually created a 'black legend'. Accordingly, Ismailism was depicted as the arch-heresy of Islam, carefully designed by non-ʿAlid impostors, who aimed at destroying Islam from within. By the end of the 4th/10th century, this fictitious account, with its elaborate details and stages of initiation leading towards atheism, was accepted as an accurate and reliable description of Ismaili motives, beliefs and practices, resulting in further anti-Ismaili polemics and intensifying the animosity of other Muslim communities towards the Ismailis. This 'black legend' also influenced the famous anti-Fatimid manifesto of Baghdad, issued in 402/1011. Sponsored by the reigning Abbasid caliph al-Qādir (381–422/991–1031), this declaration was a public denunciation of the ʿAlid descent of the Fatimid caliphs. The manifesto, most likely necessitated by the continued success of the Ismaili *daʿwa* in various parts of Iraq, and indeed at the very doorstep of the Abbasid capital, was read in mosques throughout the Abbasid caliphate, to the deep annoyance of the Fatimid imam-caliph, al-Ḥākim (386–411/996–1021).

The Fatimids pursued a policy of tolerance towards other religious and ethnic communities, a record hardly matched by any other Muslim dynasty of medieval times. The Fatimid officials, including viziers, were generally selected based on merit and qualification, without any particular regard to their religious affiliation or ethnic background. This policy explains why it was possible for several Christians, including Armenians, to succeed to the Fatimid vizierate, with numerous Jewish secretaries working in the Fatimid chancery (*dīwān al-inshāʾ*). It was also not unusual for Sunni jurists to head the Fatimid judiciary as supreme judge (*qāḍī al-quḍāt*). However, the Fatimids' liberal ethnic policy of utilising the services of Berbers, Turks, Sūdānīs, Daylamīs and Arabs led to intensive rivalries and factionalism in the Fatimid armies and administration, eventually contributing significantly to the demise of the Fatimid dynasty.

The Fatimids did not realise their universal ideals, perhaps ultimately because their Shiʿi identity and message existed in predominantly Sunni milieus. But they did manage, at least for a while, to have their suzerainty acknowledged from North Africa and Egypt to the Ḥijāz, Palestine and Syria. And for one full year, 450–451/1058–1059, the *khuṭba* at the Friday sermon in Baghdad itself, the Abbasid capital, was recited in the name of the Fatimid caliph reigning from Cairo.

Confronted with a multitude of internal and external problems, however, the Fatimid caliphate had already embarked on a steady path of decline by the second half of the 5th/11th century, almost one century before its actual collapse in 567/1171. By then, the Ismaili *dāʿīs* operating in the central and eastern lands of Islam, from Syria to Central Asia, had achieved lasting successes. They had won the allegiance of a growing number of converts throughout the Abbasid dominions, including regions ruled by the Būyids, Saljūqs, Ṣaffārids, Ghaznawids and other dynasties that emerged in the East. These Ismaili converts acknowledged the Fatimid caliph as the rightful 'imam of the time'. This explains why Ismailism outlived the downfall of the Fatimid dynasty and caliphate, also surviving the challenges posed by the Sunni revival of the 5th–6th/11th–12th centuries.

About This Volume

The Fatimid model of authority was based on universally held Muslim ideals of an imam as an incumbent necessity whose presence served as the focal point of communal unity, guidance and salvation. These ideals underpinned the various Muslim caliphates that arose after the death of the Prophet Muḥammad. In keeping with forms of government that had become characteristic of Muslim polities in the post-Prophetic era, the Fatimids instituted positions such as those of imam, caliph, *amīr*, *qāḍī* and *wazīr*. They likewise minted coins, regulated the marketplace, defended their frontiers, and directed the performance of communal rituals and the consecration of public spaces of worship.

Yet the Fatimid caliphate, as the crowning success of the Shiʿi Ismaili *daʿwa,* was predicated on distinct notions of legitimate authority, which upheld the Shiʿi belief in the ʿAlid succession to the caliphate, and the necessity for an authoritative imam as the divinely guided arbiter of law and doctrine. The positioning of the Fatimid imam-caliph at the apex of temporal and religious power thus culminated in a type of caliphate that was initially envisioned by the Abbasids but ultimately disregarded in the face of proto-Sunni opposition. The distinctive origins and doctrinal underpinnings of the Fatimid caliphate permeated the spectrum of interaction between state and society throughout the course of their two and a half centuries of rule.

Over the past several years, The Institute of Ismaili Studies (IIS) has sponsored a panel on Fatimid studies at the annual conference of the Middle East Studies Association (MESA). The studies presented in this volume represent a selection of papers originally presented at this forum.

Together, they investigate the distinctive nature of the Fatimid empire in a variety of areas. These include notions of authority, models of administration, the nature and context of regional and religious rivalries, the role of women in society as well as in the study of Sunni law, and the particular legacy of the Fatimid caliphate in the centuries after its demise.

In Chapter 1, Farhad Daftary traces the early movements that led to the establishment of the Fatimid state. He begins by charting the key developments that led to the formation of the various Shiʿi communities of interpretation in the formative period of Islam. He navigates the reader through the history of several strands of the Ismaili *daʿwa* across many regions of the Islamic world in the 3rd/9th century, which culminated in the establishment of the Fatimid state in Ifrīqiya. The chapter underscores the necessity in the Shiʿi world-view of the designated successor from the Prophet's family – the *ahl al-bayt* – as providing 'the sole authoritative channel for elucidating and interpreting the teachings of Islam'. The proclamation of ʿAbd Allāh al-Mahdī as the first Fatimid imam-caliph in 297/909 laid claim to this Shiʿi *sine qua non*.

The Fatimids were the only major medieval Muslim dynasty established in the heartlands of the Muslim world that claimed an ʿAlid ancestry. This challenge to Abbasid legitimacy is reflected in genealogical considerations which acquired an almost singular focus in relations between the Fatimids and their opponents. The issuing of the Baghdad Manifesto by the Abbasid caliph in 402/1011 became set in Sunni Muslim historiography as an indelible marker for denouncing Fatimid claims to ʿAlid lineage. In Chapter 2, on the Baghdad Manifesto, Shainool Jiwa examines the socio-political circumstances that led to the issuing of the Abbasid proclamation. Through a close reading of the surviving texts of the Manifesto and their signatories, she has been able to establish its various purposes. These reveal as much about the power dynamics in Abbasid circles between the caliph al-Qādir (381–422/991–1031) and his Būyid keepers, as well as the Sunni and Shiʿi notables of Iraq, as they do about the growing influence of the Fatimid *daʿwa* in the region. The enduring questioning of their ʿAlid descent among Sunni historians, long after the Fatimids had been politically vanquished, suggests that the Baghdad Manifesto itself had become emblematic of the larger mosaic of ʿAlid-Abbasid relations.

In Chapter 3, Paul E. Walker traces the origins of the title *amīr al-juyūsh*, held by Badr al-Jamālī (d. 487/1094), following his summoning from Syria to Egypt by the Fatimid imam-caliph al-Mustanṣir bi'llāh (427–487/1036–1094) in 466/1074. Through a calibrated analysis of the origins and evolution of the role of the *wazīr* in the Fatimid administration, Walker establishes the point that the military origins and functions of Badr al-Jamālī at the Fatimid court resulted in the formation of a unique type of vizierate, which had no precedence in the earlier Fatimid administration, or in that of any other Muslim dynasty. He notes that the *amīr al-juyūsh* came to wield absolute power over both the military and the civilian bureaucracy, and became the definitive model for the vizierate during the final century of Fatimid rule in Egypt.

Drawing upon three genres of writing – legal, ritual and esoteric – by Qāḍī al-Nuʿmān, in Chapter 4 Simonetta Calderini discusses the criteria and contexts that make it permissible for a woman to lead a congregation in prayer, an issue that remains topical today. Calderini points out that the legal and ritual position that was adopted by Qāḍī al-Nuʿmān, which is broadly in keeping with that of other Shiʿi scholars, is that a woman should not lead men in prayer (*ṣalāt*), but could lead women, provided she does so while standing in the middle of the congregation rather than in front of them. This is because a woman was not deemed to have the full legal capacity to act. However, in Qāḍī al-Nuʿmān's esoteric writings this issue is presented in a symbolic language, which does not concern itself with the physical reality of gender in a social context but focuses instead on states of knowledge, which are categorised in terms of the feminine recipient and the masculine giver of knowledge. She concludes that

> ultimately, all these perspectives, employing numerous levels of interpretation (*ẓāhir*, *bāṭin* and *bāṭin al-bāṭin* or *ḥaqq*), aim to link the social hierarchical structure of a given time, and the legal

> rulings pertinent to that context, to the higher spiritual and esoteric plane by means of which the hierarchical and political legitimacy of the Fatimid dynasty was justified.

The effect of Fatimid rituals and law as catalysts in the promulgation of positive assertions of aspects of Mālikī law is the subject of Maribel Fierro's thorough review in Chapter 5 of the biography, career and scholarship of the influential Mālikī scholar of al-Andalus, al-Ṭurṭūshī (d. 451/1059), who settled in Fatimid Alexandria during the later years of his life. Fierro examines al-Ṭurṭūshī's elucidation of the correct Mālikī practice of the *ʿibādāt* and establishes the fact that the principal purpose of his treatise entitled *Kitāb al-ḥawādith wa'l-bidaʿ* was to present a Mālikī corrective to Fatimid ritual practice, which he considered to be a reprehensible innovation. Fierro notes that al-Ṭurṭūshī's expertise on inheritance law, and his influence with the Fatimid vizier al-Baṭā'iḥī not only led to his rejection of the Ismaili law on inheritance, which eschews the superiority of male agnates as legal heirs, but also proscribed its application for Sunnis in Egypt. This is one of the various examples that she cites of al-Ṭurṭūshī's covert critique of Fatimid practice.

In Chapter 6, on the transmission of Sunni learning in Fatimid Egypt, Delia Cortese sets out to explore the role of women associated with *ḥadīth* scholarship in Egypt under the Fatimids. Through an exposition of the lives of specific female scholars, she assesses their contribution to the intellectual history of Egypt at this time. This provides Cortese with a platform from which to comment on those social and cultural norms that informed female agency in a scholarly Sunni community operating under an Ismaili Fatimid regime.

Cortese observes that, in contrast to the rest of the Muslim world, the institution of the madrasa arrived late in Alexandria and not at all in Cairo, leading male Sunni scholars to seek out other social signifiers for the validation of their authority as credible transmitters of knowledge. In these circumstances, learned Sunni women became 'bonding agents', fostering cohesion between Sunni learned networks in Egypt and beyond, and were useful links in the transmission and preservation of intellectual capital in scholarly lineages.

The volume concludes with Chapter 7 by Daniel Beben, in which he reviews the reception of the Fatimid legacy in the foundation of, and contemporary discourse on, the modern Nizārī Ismaili imamate. Tracing the cultural memory of the Nizārī Ismailis in the post-Mongol era, Beben argues that the import of the Fatimid era in present-day Nizārī articulations is rooted in the changes and developments that occurred in the community in the 18th and 19th centuries. He elucidates the way in which the emergence of the Nizārī imamate from a long period of concealment, along with its growing political and social prominence, led to 'a de-emphasis of the *qiyāma* and a renewed focus on the Fatimid era and its legacy'.

Beben argues that this reorientation of the Nizārī communal memory reflects a broader shift in the historical consciousness of the community, and a revision of the very notion of historical time, marking a transition from a cyclical to a linear presentation of history. He concludes that this illustrates 'a pattern of resilience and adaptability that has defined the Ismaili community throughout its long history'. The historical continuity with the Fatimid past is one such manifestation.

1

The Early Ismaili Imamate: Background to the Establishment of the Fatimid Caliphate

Farhad Daftary

Various Shiʿi communities of interpretation evolved during the formative period of Islam. They all believed that the Prophet Muḥammad himself had designated his cousin and son-in-law ʿAlī b. Abī Ṭālib, married to his daughter Fāṭima, as his successor. Furthermore, they held that this designation, or *naṣṣ*, had been instituted under divine command. Originally a minority, a group holding to this view had gradually expanded and so became generally designated as the *Shīʿat ʿAlī*, the party of ʿAlī, or simply as the Shiʿa. The Shiʿa also came to hold a particular conception of religious authority that set them apart from other Muslims. They held that the message of Islam as revealed by the Prophet Muḥammad contained inner truths that could not be comprehended directly through common reason. Thus, they recognised the need for a religiously authoritative guide, or imam as the Shiʿa have traditionally preferred to designate their spiritual leader. According to the Shiʿa, a person qualified for such an important task of spiritual guidance could belong only to the Prophet's family, the *ahl al-bayt*, whose members provided the sole authoritative channel for elucidating and interpreting the teachings of Islam.

By early Umayyad times, the Shiʿa were in disagreement among themselves regarding the precise definition and composition of the *ahl al-bayt*, causing internal divisions within Shiʿism. Initially, for some 50 years, Shiʿism had represented a unified community with limited membership comprised mainly of Arab Muslims. The Shiʿa had then recognised successively ʿAlī (d. 40/660) and his sons al-Ḥasan (d. 49/669) and al-Ḥusayn (d. 61/680) as their imams. This situation changed with al-Mukhtār's Shiʿi movement, organised in the name of ʿAlī's third son Muḥammad b. Ḥanafiyya as the Mahdi, the divinely guided messianic saviour imam and restorer of true Islam and justice in the world. The new eschatological concept of the Mahdi, used later by the Ismailis and other Shiʿi groups, proved particularly appealing to the *mawālī*, the non-Arab converts to Islam, who under the Umayyads were treated as second-class Muslims. The *mawālī* were now attracted to Shiʿism and played a key role in transforming it from an Arab party of limited membership and doctrinal basis to a dynamic movement.

Henceforth, different Shiʿi communities came to coexist, each with its own line of imams and elaborating its own ideas. However, the Shiʿism of Umayyad times developed mainly along two branches, the Kaysāniyya and the Imāmiyya, while another Shiʿi movement led to the foundation of the Zaydī branch of Shiʿi Islam. The Kaysāniyya, who followed an active anti-Umayyad policy, were eventually absorbed mainly into the Abbasid movement, and then disappeared after the Abbasid revolution of 132/750.

Meanwhile, the Imāmiyya, the common heritage of the Ismailis and the Ithnāʿasharīs, or Twelvers, had acknowledged a particular line of ʿAlids, descendants of al-Ḥusayn b. ʿAlī, as their imams; and they remained completely removed from any political activity against the establishment. It was in the imamate of al-Ḥusayn's grandson, Muḥammad al-Bāqir (d. ca. 114/732), that the Ḥusaynid ʿAlid line of imams and the Imāmī branch of Shiʿism began to acquire prominence. Imam al-Bāqir, too, refrained from any political activity and concerned himself with the spiritual aspects of his imamate. He is also credited with introducing the important principle of *taqiyya*, or precautionary dissimulation of one's true religious identity under adverse circumstances, which was later widely adopted by both the Ismailis and the Twelvers.

It was during the long and eventful imamate of al-Bāqir's son and successor, Abū ʿAbd Allāh Jaʿfar al-Ṣādiq, that the Imāmiyya expanded significantly and became a major religious community with a distinct identity. Imam al-Ṣādiq acquired prominence rather gradually during this turbulent period in early Islam when the Abbasids finally uprooted the Umayyads. He acquired a widespread reputation as a religious scholar. He was a reporter of *ḥadīth* and was later cited as such even in the chains of authorities accepted by Sunni Muslims. He also taught *fiqh*, or jurisprudence, and has been credited, after the work of his father, with founding the Imāmī Shiʿi school of religious law, or *madhhab*, named Jaʿfarī after him. Owing to the intense intellectual activities of Jaʿfar al-Ṣādiq and his circle of eminent scholars, the Imāmī Shiʿis came to possess a distinctive body of rituals as well as theological and legal doctrines. Above all, they now elaborated the basic conception of the doctrine of the imamate (*imāma*), which was essentially retained by later Ismaili and Twelver Shiʿis.[1] This doctrine enabled al-Ṣādiq to consolidate Shiʿism on a quietist basis.

The doctrine of the imamate was founded on the belief in the permanent need of mankind for a divinely guided, sinless and infallible (*maʿṣūm*) imam who, after the Prophet Muḥammad, would act as the authoritative teacher and guide of men in all their spiritual affairs. Although the imam, who could practise *taqiyya* when necessary, would be entitled to temporal leadership as much as to religious authority, his mandate did not depend on his actual rule. The doctrine further taught that the Prophet himself had designated ʿAlī b. Abī Ṭālib as his legatee (*waṣī*) and successor, by an explicit designation (*naṣṣ*) under divine command and that most of the Prophet's Companions had ignored this designation. After ʿAlī, the imamate would be transmitted from father to son by the designation of the *naṣṣ*, among the descendants of ʿAlī and Fāṭima; and, after al-Ḥusayn b. ʿAlī, it would continue in the Ḥusyanid ʿAlid line until the end of time. This ʿAlid imam, the sole legitimate imam at any time, is deemed to be in possession of special knowledge or *ʿilm*, and to have perfect understanding of the outward, or exoteric (*ẓāhir*), and the inward, or esoteric (*bāṭin*), aspects and meanings of the Qurʾan and the message of Islam. Indeed, the world could not exist for a moment without such an imam who would be the proof of God (*ḥujjat Allāh*) on earth.

Imam Jaʿfar al-Ṣādiq, the last imam recognised by both the Ismailis and the Twelvers, died in 148/765. The dispute over his succession caused historic divisions in Imāmī Shiʿism, leading to the eventual formation of independent Twelver and Ismaili communities. According to most of the available sources, Imam al-Ṣādiq had originally designated his second son, Ismāʿīl, the eponym of the Ismāʿīliyya, as his successor to the imamate by the rule of the *naṣṣ*. There cannot be any doubt regarding the historicity of this designation, which provides the basis of the Ismaili claims. However, matters are rather confused, as most of the sources report that Ismāʿīl predeceased his father and that three of al-Ṣādiq's other sons simultaneously claimed his heritage. According to the Ismaili religious tradition, Ismāʿīl succeeded his father in due course. However, most non-Ismaili sources relate that he died before his father, though some of these sources also state that Ismāʿīl was later seen in Baṣra. At any rate, Ismāʿīl was not present in Medina or Kūfa at the time of Imam al-Ṣādiq's death, when three other sons claimed his succession. As a result, the Imāmī Shiʿis now split into several groups, two of which may be identified with the earliest Ismailis, while another group eventually evolved into Twelver Shiʿism.

One of the two earliest Ismaili groups denied the death of Ismāʿīl during his father's lifetime and awaited his return as the Mahdi. The early Imāmī heresiographers al-Nawbakhtī and al-Qummī, who provide our main primary sources on the opening phase of Ismailism, designate this group as *al-Ismāʿīliyya al-khāliṣa*, or the 'pure Ismailis'.[2] The second splinter group of proto-Ismailis affirmed that Ismāʿīl predeceased his father and now they acknowledged his eldest son, Muḥammad b. Ismāʿīl, as their imam. They further held that Imam al-Ṣādiq had personally designated his grandson as the rightful successor to Ismāʿīl after the latter's death. The Imāmī heresiographers call this group the Mubārakiyya, named after Ismāʿīl's epithet al-Mubārak ('the blessed one').[3] The Mubārakiyya held that the imamate could not be transferred from brother to brother after the case of Imams al-Ḥasan and al-Ḥusayn; and this is why they could not accept the claims of any of Ismāʿīl's brothers.

Little is known about the life and career of Muḥammad b. Ismāʿīl, the seventh imam of the Ismailis. The relevant biographical information in the Ismaili sources was collected later by Idrīs ʿImād al-Dīn (d. 872/1468), the nineteenth Ṭayyibī Ismaili *dāʿī*.[4] Muḥammad was the eldest son of Ismāʿīl, and also the eldest grandson of Imam al-Ṣādiq. Born around 120/738, he was 26 at the time of al-Ṣādiq's death. Thus he was about eight years older than his uncle Mūsā al-Kāẓim, who was born in 128/745–746. Soon after the recognition of Mūsā al-Kāẓim's imamate by the majority of al-Ṣādiq's followers, Muḥammad's position became untenable in his native Ḥijāz, where Mūsā also lived. Due to his activist policies, Muḥammad also needed to avoid Abbasid persecution. Not long after 148/765 Muḥammad b. Ismāʿīl left Medina and went into hiding, initiating the *dawr al-satr*, or 'period of concealment', in early Ismaili history which lasted until the foundation of the Fatimid caliphate. Henceforth, Muḥammad b. Ismāʿīl acquired the epithet of al-Maktūm, 'the hidden one', in addition to al-Maymūn, 'the fortunate one'. However, he maintained contact with his Mubārakiyya followers who, like most other Shiʿi groups of the time, were based in Kūfa. Muḥammad b. Ismāʿīl seems to have spent the latter part of his life in Khūzistān, in south-western Persia, where he had some supporters. He died not long after 179/795, during the caliphate of Hārūn al-Rashīd, the year in which the Abbasid caliph arrested Mūsā al-Kāẓim and banished him from the Ḥijāz to Iraq. Muḥammad b. Ismāʿīl had several sons, including ʿAbd Allāh who, according to later Ismailis, was his rightful successor to the imamate.

On the death of Muḥammad b. Ismāʿīl, the Mubārakiyya themselves split into two groups. One small and obscure group apparently traced the imamate in the progeny of their deceased imam. However, most of the Mubārakiyya refused to accept Muḥammad b. Ismāʿīl's death. For these earliest Ismailis, identified by the Imāmī heresiographers as the immediate predecessors of the Qarmaṭīs, Muḥammad b. Ismāʿīl was regarded as their seventh and last imam.[5] He was expected to reappear imminently as the Mahdi or *qāʾim* (riser) – terms which were essentially synonymous in their early usage by the Ismailis and other Shiʿis. Almost nothing is known with certainty regarding the subsequent history of these earliest Ismaili groups until shortly after the middle of the 3rd/9th century, when a unified Ismaili movement emerged on the historical stage.

A variety of sources contain evidence that supports the idea that for almost a century after Muḥammad b. Ismāʿīl, one group of leaders which was well placed within the earliest Ismailis, worked secretly for the creation of a unified revolutionary movement against the Abbasids. Initially attached to one of the earliest Ismaili groups, and in all probability the imams of that obscure group that issued from the Mubārakiyya, who maintained the continuity of the imamate in the progeny of Muḥammad b. Ismāʿīl, these leaders did not openly claim the imamate for three generations. They had, in fact, hidden their true identity in order to escape Abbasid persecution. ʿAbd Allāh, the first of these hidden leaders, organised his campaign around the central doctrine of the majority of the earliest Ismailis, namely, the Mahdiship of Muḥammad b. Ismāʿīl. Be that as it may, the leaders in question were members of the same family who succeeded one another on a hereditary basis.

Ismaili tradition recognises three generations of leaders between Muḥammad b. Ismāʿīl and ʿAbd Allāh al-Mahdī, founder of the Fatimid caliphate and the last of the hidden leaders during the *dawr al-satr* of early Ismaili history.[6] The first of these leaders, ʿAbd Allāh, designated in later Ismaili sources as al-Akbar (the Elder), settled in ʿAskar Mukram in Khūzistān, where his father Muḥammad b. Ismāʿīl had spent his final years. He disguised himself as a merchant. It was from that locality that ʿAbd Allāh, who later received the epithet of al-Raḍī, began to organise a reinvigorated Ismaili *daʿwa*, sending *dāʿīs* to surrounding districts. Subsequently, at an unknown date in the first half of the 3rd/9th century, ʿAbd Allāh settled in Salamiyya, in central Syria, continuing to pose as a Hāshimid merchant. Henceforth, Salamiyya served as the secret headquarters of the early Ismaili *daʿwa*. The Ismailis now referred to their movement simply as *al-daʿwa*, the mission, or *al-daʿwa al-hādiya*, the rightly guiding mission.

The sustained efforts of ʿAbd Allāh and his successors began to bear fruit by the early 260s/870s, when numerous *dāʿīs* appeared in southern Iraq and other regions.[7] In 261/874, Ḥamdān Qarmaṭ was converted to Ismailism in the Sawād of Kūfa. Ḥamdān and his chief assistant ʿAbdān, a learned theologian, organised the *daʿwa* in southern Iraq. ʿAbdān trained numerous *dāʿīs*, including the Persian Abū Saʿīd al-Ḥasan b. Bahrām al-Jannābī, the future founder of the Qarmaṭī state of Baḥrayn. The Ismailis of southern Iraq became generally known as the Qarāmiṭa, after their first local leader. Later, this term was applied to other Ismaili communities not organised by Ḥamdān Qarmaṭ. At the time, there was a single Ismaili movement centrally directed from Salamiyya in the name of Muḥammad b. Ismāʿīl as the awaited Mahdi.

Meanwhile, the Ismaili *daʿwa* had appeared in many other regions. In southern Persia, the *daʿwa* was under the supervision of the *dāʿīs* in Iraq. Abū Saʿīd al-Jannābī (d. 301/913) was initially active there, before he was dispatched to eastern Arabia, then known as Baḥrayn, where he preached successfully among the Bedouin tribesmen and the local Persian community. The *daʿwa* in Yemen was initiated by Ibn Ḥawshab (d. 302/914), later known as Manṣūr al-Yaman (the Conqueror of Yemen), where he arrived in 268/881 accompanied by his chief collaborator, ʿAlī b. al-Faḍl (d. 303/915).[8] Both of these *dāʿīs*, like many other early *dāʿīs*, had been converted from Imāmī (Twelver) Shiʿism. By 293/905, almost all of Yemen had been brought under the control of the Ismaili *dāʿīs*. However, the Ismailis were later obliged to abandon the greater part of their conquests under pressure from the local Zaydī imams, who had established a state of their own in 284/897 in northern Yemen. Southern

Arabia also served as an important base for the extension of the *daʿwa* to remote lands, including North Africa and Sind. Indeed, by 280/893, on Ibn Ḥawshab's instructions, the *dāʿī* Abū ʿAbd Allāh al-Shīʿī (d. 298/911) was already active among the Kutāma Berbers of the Lesser Kabylia mountains in North Africa (in present-day eastern Algeria). Abū ʿAbd Allāh, too, had originally belonged to the Imāmī community of Kūfa.

It was in the same decade of the 260s/870s that the *daʿwa* was initiated in many parts of west-central and north-western Persia, the region called the Jibāl by the Arabs, and which included the cities Rayy, Qumm, Kāshān and Hamadān. Later the Ismaili *daʿwa* was extended to Khurāsān and Transoxania in Central Asia, where the *dāʿī* Muḥammad b. Aḥmad al-Nasafī converted the Sāmānid *amīr* Naṣr II and many of his courtiers. The *dāʿī* al-Nasafī, who was executed in Bukhārā in 332/943, has also been credited with introducing a form of Neoplatonic philosophy into Ismaili thought – a tradition of philosophical Ismailism further developed by other *dāʿī*s of the Iranian lands, notably Abū Yaʿqūb al-Sijistānī (d. after 361/971). The most detailed account of this phase of the early *daʿwa* is related by Niẓām al-Mulk (d. 485/1092), the learned Saljūq vizier who was a staunch enemy of the Ismailis.[9]

By the early 280s/890s, a unified and expanding Ismaili movement had replaced the earlier Kūfan-based splinter groups. This movement was centrally directed from Salamiyya by leaders who made every effort to conceal their true identity. The central leaders of the *daʿwa* were, however, in contact with the *dāʿī*s of different regions, propagating a revolutionary, messianic message in the name of Muḥammad b. Ismāʿīl as the Mahdi whose advent was eagerly anticipated.

In 286/899, soon after ʿAbd Allāh al-Mahdī, the future Fatimid caliph, had succeeded to the central leadership of the *daʿwa* in Salamiyya, Ismailism was rent by a major schism.[10] ʿAbd Allāh now felt secure enough to claim the imamate openly for himself and his predecessors, the same individuals who had organised and led the early Ismaili *daʿwa*. Later, in a letter sent to the Ismaili community in Yemen, he attempted to reconcile his doctrinal declaration with the actual course of events in early Ismaili history.[11] He explained that as a form of *taqiyya* the central leaders of the early *daʿwa* had adopted different pseudonyms, such as al-Maymūn, also assuming the rank of *ḥujja*, proof or full representative, of the absent Muḥammad b. Ismāʿīl. ʿAbd Allāh further explained that the earlier propagation of the Mahdiship of Muḥammad b. Ismāʿīl was itself another dissimulating measure, and that the Mahdi Muḥammad b. Ismāʿīl was in reality a collective code name for every true imam in the progeny of Jaʿfar al-Ṣādiq.

The doctrinal reform of ʿAbd Allāh al-Mahdī split the hitherto unified Ismaili movement into two rival branches. One faction remained loyal to the central leadership and acknowledged continuity in the Ismaili imamate, recognising ʿAbd Allāh al-Mahdī and his ʿAlid ancestors as their imams, which in due course became the official Fatimid Ismaili doctrine. These Ismailis allowed for three hidden imams (ʿAbd Allāh al-Akbar, Aḥmad, al-Ḥusayn), known as *al-aʾimma al-mastūrīn*, between Muḥammad b. Ismāʿīl and ʿAbd Allāh al-Mahdī. This loyalist faction included the majority of the Yemeni Ismailis and those communities in Egypt, North Africa and Sind founded by *dāʿī*s sent by Ibn Ḥawshab from Yemen. On the other hand, a dissident faction, led originally by Ḥamdān Qarmaṭ (d. 321/933) and ʿAbdān (d. 286/899), rejected ʿAbd Allāh's reform and maintained their belief in the Mahdiship of Muḥammad b. Ismāʿīl. Henceforth, the term Qarmaṭī came to be applied more specifically to the dissident Ismailis who did not acknowledge ʿAbd Allāh al-Mahdī and his predecessors and successors in the Fatimid dynasty as their imams. The dissident Qarmaṭīs, who lacked a central leadership, soon acquired their most important stronghold in Baḥrayn, where a Qarmaṭī state had been founded in the same eventful year, 286/899, by Abū Saʿīd al-Jannābī who had sided with Ḥamdān Qarmaṭ.[12] The Qarmaṭī state of Baḥrayn survived until 470/1077–1078. There were also Qarmaṭī communities in Iraq, Yemen, Persia and Central Asia.

Soon after the schism of 286/899, the *dāʿī* Zikrawayh b. Mihrawayh, who had remained loyal to Salamiyya, embarked on an adventurous campaign of his own on behalf of ʿAbd Allāh al-Mahdī. In 288/901, he began to send several of his sons as *dāʿīs* to Syria, where large numbers of Bedouins were converted. Zikrawayh, himself remaining in hiding, aimed to establish a Fatimid state in Syria for ʿAbd Allāh al-Mahdī, but without his authorisation.[13] Under the circumstances, Zikrawayh's sons, misled by their initial successes, summoned their Bedouin followers to proceed to Salamiyya and declare their allegiance to the imam, who was still guarding his identity. In the event, ʿAbd Allāh, his position now dangerously compromised, secretly and hurriedly left Salamiyya in 289/902 to escape the Abbasid agents who were sent to capture him.

Accompanied by his young son and future successor al-Qāʾim, a *dāʿī*, his chamberlain (*ḥājib*) Jaʿfar b. ʿAlī and a few attendants, ʿAbd Allāh first went to Ramla, in Palestine, where he stayed for some time awaiting the outcome of Zikrawayh's activities. However, Zikrawayh's success was short-lived. In fact, he briefly turned against al-Mahdī and established a separate wing of the dissident Qarmaṭī camp, before he was finally defeated and killed in 294/907 by the Abbasids. Meanwhile, ʿAbd Allāh travelled to Egypt in 291/904, then under the quasi-autonomous rule of the Ṭūlūnids. ʿAbd Allāh al-Mahdī's faithful chamberlain left a detailed account of his master's fateful seven-year journey (289–297/902–909), which ended eventually in Ifrīqiya, where he founded the Fatimid caliphate.[14] The rapid success of the early Ismaili *daʿwa* was thus crowned by the establishment of a state or *dawla* ruled by the Ismaili imam of the time as the Fatimid caliph; and the Ismaili imamate continued in the progeny of ʿAbd Allāh al-Mahdī (d. 322/934).

Notes

1 See Abū Jaʿfar Muḥammad b. Yaʿqūb al-Kulaynī, *al-Uṣūl min al-kāfī*, ed. ʿA.A. al-Ghaffārī (Tehran, 1388/1968), vol. 1, pp. 168–548, containing the earliest Shiʿi *ḥadīths* on the imamate, reported mainly from Jaʿfar al-Ṣādiq. Many of the same *ḥadīths* are reproduced in Qāḍī al-Nuʿmān, *Daʿāʾim al-Islām*, ed. Asaf A.A. Fyzee (Cairo, 1951–61), vol. 1, pp. 3–98; English trans., *The Pillars of*

Islam, tr. A.A.A. Fyzee, completely revised by I.K. Poonawala (New Delhi, 2002–2004), vol. 1, pp. 5–122.

2 Al-Ḥasan b. Mūsā al-Nawbakhtī, *Kitāb firaq al-Shī'a*, ed. H. Ritter (Istanbul, 1931), pp. 57–58; Sa'd b. 'Abd Allāh al-Qummī, *Kitāb al-maqālāt wa'l-firaq*, ed. M.J. Mashkūr (Tehran, 1963), p. 80.

3 Al-Nawbakhtī, *Firaq*, pp. 58, 62; al-Qummī, *al-Maqālāt*, pp. 80–81.

4 Idrīs 'Imād al-Dīn b. al-Ḥasan, *'Uyūn al-akhbār*, vol. 4, ed. M. al-Saghirji (Damascus and London, 2007), pp. 504–510; also his *Kitāb zahr al-ma'ānī*, ed. M. Ghālib (Beirut, 1411/1991), pp. 204–208; F. Daftary, 'Muḥammad b. Ismā'īl al-Maymūn', *EI2*, vol. 12, Supplement, pp. 634–635.

5 Al-Nawbakhtī, *Firaq*, p. 61; al-Qummī, *al-Maqālāt*, p. 83.

6 Aḥmad b. Ibrāhīm al-Nīsābūrī, *Istitār al-imām*, ed. W. Ivanow, in *Bulletin of the Faculty of Arts, University of Egypt*, 4, part 2 (1936), pp. 93–107; reproduced in *Akhbār al-Qarāmiṭa*, ed. S. Zakkār (2nd ed., Damascus, 1982), pp. 111–132; English trans., in W. Ivanow, *Ismaili Tradition Concerning the Rise of the Fatimids* (London, 1942), pp. 157–183; H. Halm, 'Les Fatimides à Salamya', *Revue d'Études Islamiques*, 54 (1986), pp. 133–149. See also Muḥammad b. Jarīr al-Ṭabarī, *Ta'rīkh al-rusul wa'l-mulūk*, ed. M.J. de Goeje et al. (Leiden, 1879–1901), series III, pp. 2124, 2126–2127; English trans., *The History of al-Ṭabarī*: Volume XXXVII, *The 'Abbasid Recovery*, tr. Philip M. Fields (Albany, NY, 1987), pp. 169, 171–173.

7 See F. Daftary, *The Ismā'īlīs: Their History and Doctrines* (2nd ed., Cambridge, 2007), pp. 107–116, where full references are cited.

8 Al-Nu'mān b. Muḥammad, *Iftitāḥ al-da'wa wa ibtidā' al-dawla*, ed. W. al-Qāḍī (Beirut, 1970), pp. 32–47; ed. F. Dachraoui (Tunis, 1975), pp. 2–18; English trans., *Founding the Fatimid State: The Rise of an Early Islamic Empire* (London, 2006), pp. 20–41; W. Madelung, 'Manṣūr al-Yaman', *EI2*, vol. 6, pp. 438–439.

9 Niẓām al-Mulk, *Siyar al-mulūk* (*Siyāsat-nāma*), ed. H. Darke (2nd ed., Tehran, 1347 Sh./1968), pp. 282–295, 297–305; English trans., *The Book of Government or Rules for Kings*, tr. H. Darke (2nd ed., London, 1978), pp. 208–218, 220–226. See also Samuel M. Stern, 'The Early Ismā'īlī Missionaries in North-West Persia and in Khurāsān and Transoxania', *Bulletin of the School of Oriental and African Studies*, 23 (1960), pp. 56–90; reprinted in his *Studies in Early Ismā'īlism* (Jerusalem and Leiden, 1983), pp. 189–233.

10 W. Madelung, 'Das Imamat in der frühen Ismailitischen Lehre', *Der Islam*, 37 (1961), pp. 59–65, 69 ff.; reprinted in his *Studies*

in Medieval Shiʿism, ed. S. Schmidtke (Farnham, 2012), article VII; F. Daftary, 'A Major Schism in the Early Ismāʿīlī Movement', *Studia Islamica*, 77 (1993), pp. 123–139; reprinted in his *Ismailis in Medieval Muslim Societies* (London, 2005), pp. 45–61.

11 Ḥusayn F. al-Hamdānī, ed. and tr., *On the Genealogy of Fatimid Caliphs* (Cairo, 1958); see also A. Hamdani and F. de Blois, 'A Re-examination of al-Mahdī's Letter to the Yemenites on the Genealogy of the Fatimid Caliphs', *Journal of the Royal Asiatic Society* (1983), pp. 173–207.

12 For the best modern account of relations between the Qarmaṭīs and the Fatimids, see W. Madelung, 'The Fatimids and the Qarmaṭīs of Baḥrayn', in F. Daftary, ed., *Mediaeval Ismaʿili History and Thought* (Cambridge, 1996), pp. 21–73; reprinted in his *Studies in Medieval Shiʿism*, article X.

13 H. Halm, 'Die Söhne Zikrawaihs und das erste fatimidische Kalifat (290/903)', *Die Welt des Orients*, 10 (1979), pp. 30–53; and his *The Empire of the Mahdi: The Rise of the Fatimids*, tr. M. Bonner (Leiden, 1996), pp. 66–88, 183–190.

14 Jaʿfar b. ʿAlī's eyewitness account of ʿAbd Allāh al-Mahdī's flight from Salamiyya and his eventual arrival in Ifrīqiya was dictated later to a certain Muḥammad b. Muḥammad al-Yamānī; see that author's *Sīrat al-ḥājib Jaʿfar b. ʿAlī*, ed. W. Ivanow, in *Bulletin of the Faculty of Arts, University of Egypt*, 4, part 2 (1936), pp. 107–133; English trans., in Ivanow, *Ismaili Tradition*, pp. 184–223; French trans., M. Canard, 'L'autobiographie d'un chambellan du Mahdî ʿObeidallâh le Fâtimide', *Hespéris*, 39 (1952), pp. 279–324; reprinted in his *Miscellanea Orientalia* (London, 1973), article V.

2

The Baghdad Manifesto (402/1011): A Re-Examination of Fatimid–Abbasid Rivalry

Shainool Jiwa

Just over a century after the Fatimids had established their caliphate in North Africa in 297/909, and four decades after the transfer of their capital to Cairo in 362/973, the Abbasid caliph al-Qādir bi'llāh (r. 381–422/991–1031) issued what became known in Muslim historiography as the Baghdad Manifesto. Proclaimed publicly in the Abbasid capital in 402/1011, and subsequently read out across the Abbasid lands, its principal purpose was to invalidate the ʿAlid lineage of the Fatimids and thus their claim to be the descendants of the Prophet, through his daughter, Fāṭima, and ʿAlī b. Abī Ṭālib; and by these means to render illegitimate their claim to be vested with the sole legitimate, universalist authority and leadership of the Islamic world.

Coverage of the Baghdad Manifesto acquired some prominence in early 20th-century Orientalist scholarship on the origins and early history of the Fatimid dynasty.[1] Limited access to Ismaili sources and an over-reliance on Sunni chronicles written after the 6th/12th century in which the Manifesto had become a valid source on the origins of the Fatimids were among the salient features of the scholarship in this period.[2] However, the discovery of further Sunni and especially Ismaili sources in the course of the 20th century saw scholarship on the early Fatimids base itself primarily on 3rd–4th/9th–10th-century texts, which were composed before the promulgation of the Manifesto.[3] As a result the Manifesto began to lose its importance in modern scholarship.[4] The fact that it was issued by the Abbasid caliph came to be variously understood as: the reproduction of particular forms of anti-Fatimid defamation which had begun earlier in the 4th/10th century;[5] an example of anti-Ismaili polemic and Abbasid propaganda against the Fatimid *daʿwa* during the reign of al-Qādir;[6] and as an aspect of al-Qādir's own pro-Sunni, anti-Fatimid and anti-Shiʿi strategy.[7]

The reduction of interest in the Manifesto in recent scholarship has left a lacuna regarding the context that led to the issuing of it and its subsequent reception in Muslim historiography. Through a close reading of particular Abbasid and Fatimid sources, this chapter aims to examine the relevant developments that led to the issuing of the Manifesto and its textual specificities. The exploration of the Manifesto will also serve as a vantage point from which to explore the social and religious caché of the ʿAlid lineage in the 4th–5th/10th–11th centuries.

By this time, the charismatic appeal of the ʿAlid lineage had transcended ethnic, social and sectarian divides, enabling the rise of the *ashrāf*, the descendants of the Prophet, as a unique social group across the Islamic world. The ʿAlid lineage also served as the cornerstone of all branches of Shiʿi Islam, and formed the bedrock of the Fatimid claim to the imamate.

The Historiography and Text of the Manifesto

The so-called Baghdad Manifesto has been provided either in full or referred to in several Arabic and Persian chronicles dating from the 6th to the 9th/12th to 15th centuries. These include the works of Ibn al-Jawzī (d. 597/1200),[8] Ibn al-Athīr (d. 630/1233),[9] Juwaynī (d. 681/1283),[10] Abu'l-Fidā (d. 732/1331),[11] Ibn al-Kathīr (d. 774/1373),[12] al-Dhahabī (d. 748/1348),[13] al-Ṣafadī (d. 764/1363),[14] Ibn Khaldūn (d. 784/1382),[15] al-Maqrīzī (d. 845/1442)[16] and Ibn Taghrībirdī (d. 874/1470).[17] Of these, Ibn al-Athīr, al-Ṣafadī and Ibn Khaldūn, while they extensively discuss the Manifesto and its signatories, do not quote the text. As Rosenthal pointed out, the earliest extant version of the Manifesto is that in Ibn al-Jawzī's *al-Muntaẓam*.[18]

The sources that quote the Manifesto present what is, by and large, a stable text. However, within these there are significant variations, including two distinct introductory segments and the inclusion of certain key passages which are found in some recensions but not in others. One such version is that of Ibn al-Jawzī, which Ibn al-Kathīr summarises, and al-Dhahabī and Ibn Taghrībirdī follow closely. This introduction ascribes a Khurramī origin to the Fatimids and includes passages that are not found in other versions.

The second version is that of Abu'l-Fidā, which al-Maqrīzī follows closely. Their introductory segment, which begins with the mention of the fourth Fatimid imam-caliph, al-Mu'izz li-Dīn Allāh, does not mention the Khurramīs, while their main text does not include key passages found in Ibn al-Jawzī's version.

The third version is that of Juwaynī, which is written in Persian and which shares the introductory segment found in the version of Abu'l-Fidā and al-Maqrīzī, but which also contains a few, though not all, of the passages from Ibn al-Jawzī's version that are not found in Abu'l-Fidā and al-Maqrīzī.

This suggests that by the 6th/12th century there were two or possibly three distinct recensions of the Baghdad Manifesto. In view of the fact that the Manifesto was reported to have been drafted in Baghdad in 402/1011, and that copies were then sent to adjacent regions, the different versions probably represent variant copies of the document made after its promulgation. The following section provides a translation of Ibn al-Jawzī's recension, as the earliest of the extant accounts, while indicating the differences found in the other versions.

Ibn al-Jawzī's introduction, seems to be an amalgam of a preamble to the Manifesto merged into the document itself.[19] It reads:

> In this month [of Rabī' al-Ākhir 402], written declarations (*maḥāḍir*) were drafted in the *dīwān* of the caliphate regarding the substance (*ma'nā*) of those in Egypt, to vilify (*qadḥ*) their lineage

> (*nasab*) and their *madhhab*.[20] A copy of it was read in Baghdad. Upon it were inscribed the signatures of the *ashrāf*, the judges (*quḍāt*), the jurists (*fuqāhā*), the pious (*ṣāliḥīn*), the legal witnesses (*shuhūd*), the trustworthy (*thiqāt*), and the exemplary (*amthāl*),[21] as regards their knowledge and comprehension concerning the lineage of the Dayṣāniyya – for their [the Fatimid] lineage is traced to Dayṣān b. Saʿīd al-Khurramī, the party of the infidels,[22] the seeds of the satans.
>
> [This was] a testimony to draw close to God the Almighty and Glorious, one [undertaken] in disappointment, for the sake of religion and for Islam,[23] and in belief [in the necessity] of disseminating what God Almighty has ordered upon the *ʿulamā'*, to make it evident to the people and not to conceal it. So they all together bore witness that …

The second introduction to the Manifesto reads more plausibly as the introductory passage to an actual document. It is provided by Abu'l-Fidā and al-Maqrīzī, and is also found in Juwaynī's Persian rendition:

> [In the name of God, the Merciful, the Compassionate][24] The witnesses bear witness that Maʿadd b. Ismāʿīl [the one who seized Egypt was Maʿadd][25] b. ʿAbd al-Raḥmān b. Saʿīd descends from Dayṣān b. Saʿīd, from whom come the Dayṣāniyya, [that the aforesaid Saʿīd went to the Maghrib, where he was called ʿAbd Allāh and received the *laqab* of al-Mahdī],[26] that …

Following these divergent introductory segments, the traditions merge into a common text. However, major passages found in Ibn al-Jawzī are omitted from Abu'l-Fidā's recension though two passages are present in Juwaynī. The common text is noted below, with indents indicating passages found in Ibn al-Jawzī's tradition but not in Abu'l-Fidā and al-Maqrīzī or Juwaynī.

> The one who has arisen (*nājim*) in Egypt,[27] is al-Manṣūr b. Nizār with the *laqab* al-Ḥākim (may the judgement, *ḥukm*, of God upon him be one of destruction, annihilation and humiliation, eradication and exemplary punishment), the son of Maʿadd,

the son of Ismāʿīl the son of ʿAbd al-Raḥmān the son of Saʿīd (may God give him no felicity, who having gone to the west was then called ʿUbayd Allāh and took the *laqab* al-Mahdī'), and those who preceded him of his foul and impure predecessors,[28] upon him and them the curse of God and the curse of all those who curse,[29] are false claimants (*adʿiyā'*) and *khawārij*, who do not have lineage (*nasab*) amongst the sons of ʿAlī b. Abī Ṭālib, nor do they have any claim of [filial] attachment to him, and it [the lineage of ʿAlī] is free from their falsehood.[30] What they claim in connection to this [lineage] is void and fabricated.

~ That they [the signatories] have no knowledge of anyone from the noble houses of the Ṭālibids[31] who has ever ceased pronouncing statements that these *khawārij* are pretenders (*adʿiyā'*). [Absent in Abu'l-Fidā and al-Maqrīzī.]

~ That this refutation, concerning their lies and [false] claims[32] is commonly known in the [lands] of the Two Sanctuaries (i.e., the *ḥaramayn*). [Absent in Abu'l-Fidā and al-Maqrīzī.]

~ From the onset of their affair (*amr*) in the west, it was made public (*muntashir*) and spread. [Absent in Abu'l-Fidā and al-Maqrīzī.]

~ [so as] to prevent their lie from deceiving anyone, or [prevent anyone from] embarking on a delusion that would lead to believing in them. [Absent in Juwaynī, Abu'l-Fidā and al-Maqrīzī.]

That this one who has arisen in Egypt, he and his predecessors, are infidels (*kuffār*), libertines (*fussāq*), debauchees (*fujjār*), deviators (*mulḥidūn*), and materialist Manicheans (*zanādiqa muʿaṭṭilūn*).[33] They do not believe in Islam.[34]

~ And [they] follow as their creed the *madhhab*s of the Dualists[35] and the Zoroastrians. [Absent in Juwaynī, Abu'l-Fidā, and al-Maqrīzī.]

They have abrogated the *ḥudūd* [of law], allowed sexual licentiousness,[36] permitted [the drinking of] *khamr*,[37] spilt blood, insulted the prophets, cursed the *salaf*,[38] and proclaimed divinity.

This was written in [the month of] Rabīʿ al-Ākhir in the year 402 [14 November 1011].

Almost all the extant versions mention the names or offices of those who signed the *maḥḍar* of 402/1011. While several different signatories appear in the various accounts, the list of signatories remains broadly consistent, including the mention of the names Sharīf al-Raḍī and Sharīf al-Murtaḍā. The full list collated across the sources include:

Among the ʿAlids: Sharīf al-Murtaḍā, Sharīf al-Raḍī,[39] Ibn Azraq al-Mūsawī,[40] Abū Ṭāhir b. Abī Ṭayyib,[41] Muḥammad b. Muḥammad b. ʿUmar, Ibn Abī Yaʿlā,[42] Ibn al-Baṭḥāwī.[43]

Among the judges: Abū Muḥammad b. al-Akfānī,[44] Abu'l-Qāsim al-Khazarī,[45] Abu'l-ʿAbbās al-Sūrī.[46]

Among the jurists: Abū Ḥāmid al-Isfarāʾinī,[47] Abū Muḥammad al-Kashfalī,[48] Abu'l-Ḥusayn al-Qudūrī,[49] Abū ʿAbd Allāh al-Ṣaymarī,[50] Abū ʿAbd Allāh al-Bayḍāwī,[51] Abū ʿAlī b. Ḥamkān.[52]

Among the legal witnesses: Abu'l-Qāsim al-Tanūkhī.[53]

Additionally, Ibn al-Athīr provides the names of Abu'l-Faḍl al-Nasawī and Abū Jaʿfar al-Nasafī.[54] Furthermore, Ibn al-Athīr, Abu'l-Fidā and Ibn Khaldūn also include the well-known Twelver Shiʿi theologian, Abū ʿAbd Allāh b. al-Nuʿmān, Shaykh al-Mufīd.[55]

The Context of the Manifesto

The Baghdad Manifesto of 402/1011 was a *maḥḍar* (decree) issued by the Abbasid caliph Aḥmad b. Isḥāq al-Qādir bi'llāh and was produced by the court chancellery (*dīwān*) in Baghdad. The *maḥḍar*'s principal message was the categorical public rejection of the ʿAlid descendancy of the Fatimids, who are then accused of heresy and immorality. This is apparent in the references to the Manifesto by authors such as Ibn al-Athīr and Ibn Khaldūn, who do not provide the text itself, but simply refer to it as a document denying the ʿAlid origins of the Fatimids.[56]

The promulgation of the Baghdad Manifesto has been discussed in scholarship primarily in the context of Fatimid–Abbasid rivalry. Central to the circumstances leading to its issuing was the potency of the ʿAlid lineage in the legitimisation of Fatimid claims to authority. It explains the use of lineage as a principal trope by pro-Abbasid sources from the early 4th/10th century onwards. The use of lineage by the Abbasids in the legitimisation of their caliphate and the emergence of the ʿAlid *ashrāf* as a charismatic social group by the 5th/11th centuries are also germane to this exploration.

Centrality of the ʿAlid lineage to the Fatimids

The establishment of the Fatimid caliphate in North Africa in 297/909 signalled a major shift in the socio-political and ideological dynamics of the medieval Mediterranean world. The move to Egypt in 362/973 placed the Fatimids at a central point in the Islamic world, and gave them a territorial proximity to the Abbasid heartlands of Iraq. Ideologically, the Fatimid claim to ʿAlid descent posed an unprecedented challenge to Abbasid claims of exclusive right to the caliphate, which reverberated long after the Fatimid caliphate had been vanquished.

The Fatimid caliphate was based on the Shiʿi doctrine which held that legitimate authority over the Muslim *umma* was the unique preserve of the divinely chosen imam from the descendants of ʿAlī b. Abī Ṭālib and Fāṭima, the daughter of the Prophet. The designation of the Fatimid imam-caliph as the Commander of the Faithful and the Imam of the Muslims thus negated the Abbasids' own claims and represented a direct challenge to their authority.

The activity of the Ismaili *daʿwa* (religio-political mission) which spanned the major regions of the Islamic world in the last decades of the 3rd/9th century, and which culminated in the formation of the Fatimid state, was predicated on the claim that rightful authority belonged solely to the designated imam from the descendants of ʿAlī and Fāṭima. The Ismaili Fatimid caliphate was based on this Shiʿi Imāmī axiom, with the Fatimid doctrine on the imamate receiving systematic exposition during the reign of the fourth imam-caliph al-Muʿizz li-Dīn Allāh.[57] The Fatimid imam-caliphs' right to rule as possessors of the inherent, divinely sanctioned imamate was traced from ʿAlī b. Abī Ṭālib through Jaʿfar al-Ṣādiq (d. 148/765) to his son Ismāʿīl, who was succeeded by Muḥammad b. Ismāʿīl, and then through the four generations of the 'concealed imams' during what came to be characterised as the 'period of concealment' (*dawr al-satr*), until the accession of ʿAbd Allāh al-Mahdī, whose public manifestation (*ẓuhūr*) marked the commencement of the Fatimid state.[58] The declaration of their ʿAlid lineage took a variety of forms, including books on law and doctrine, public orations, coinage and inscriptions on mosques, palaces and city gates, all serving as important features of the Fatimid state.

Inherent to the Fatimid claim of ʿAlid descent, and recognised by their detractors, was their assertion of descent from the Prophet himself. While ʿAlī b. Abī Ṭālib retained a central position in Fatimid articulations of legitimate authority, equally central was Fāṭima, the daughter of the Prophet, wife of ʿAlī and the eponym of the Fatimid dynasty.[59] It was through her that all the ʿAlids, the Shiʿi Imams and the Fatimid imam-caliphs in particular claimed descent, and therefore inheritance, from the Prophet Muḥammad.[60]

Reflecting the centrality of the daughter of the Prophet in Shiʿi doctrine, Fāṭima was given prominence in the public proclamations of the Fatimid imam-caliphs. This is evident in many of the transformative moments in Fatimid history. Fāṭima was named in the invocation of blessings upon the Prophet and his household in the first public Fatimid sermon in North Africa;[61] she was praised in al-Muʿizz li-Dīn Allāh's sermon announcing the demise of his father al-Manṣūr and his own accession;[62] and she was similarly invoked in the sermons in Egypt following the Fatimid takeover.[63] Fāṭima's name was also inscribed on Fatimid coinage,[64] and it is after her epithet, al-Zahrā' ('the illuminated'), that the Fatimids called the principal mosque in Cairo, al-Azhar which, as Brett notes, was named 'after the mother of the dynasty'.[65]

Based on their descent from Fāṭima, the Fatimid imam-caliphs referred to the Prophet Muḥammad as their grandfather (*jaddunā*), to whose legal, political and religious authority they were heirs, and whose *daʿwa* and commandments they had come to fulfil. Their supporters echoed these claims by referring to the Fatimid imam-caliphs as the 'sons of the Messenger'.[66] Fatimid diplomatic correspondence and dialogue with local notables, also reflected these claims.[67] The raison d'être of the Fatimid mission was linked to the mission of the Prophet. The Fatimids thus saw themselves as the protectors of their grandfather's community,[68] the revivers of his practices[69] and the continuators of his *daʿwa*.[70] Thus polemics against the ʿAlid descent of the Fatimids critically entailed the denial of their descent from the Prophet. This denial, therefore, also became a focal point of anti-Fatimid polemic by the Abbasids from the inception of Fatimid rule. Fundamentally, the Fatimid claim to ʿAlid descent directly impinged on the authenticity of the Abbasid claims to legitimacy.

Abbasid legitimisation: From ʿAlid to Abbasid primacy

The revolution that toppled the Umayyads in 132/750 had as its slogan 'the chosen one from the family of the Prophet Muhammad' (*al-riḍā min āl Muḥammad*) which was in effect a call for legitimate authority over the Islamic world to be restored to the Hāshimid clan. While the term encompassed all those who claimed to be of the family of the Prophet, in actuality it led to the establishment of the Abbasid dynasty after the assumption of power by the first Abbasid caliph, Abu'l-ʿAbbās al-Saffāḥ (r. 132–136/750–754).

Therefore, Abbasid legitimacy was originally positioned in a proto-Shiʿi belief in the primacy of ʿAlid succession. The earliest legitimisations of Abbasid authority held that rightful rule after the Prophet passed to ʿAlī, his sons and their successors, but was ultimately bequeathed to their Abbasid cousin in the well-known testimony of Abū Hāshim, a grandson of ʿAlī. It was following the aftermath of a major ʿAlid rebellion in 145/762–763 during the reign of the second Abbasid caliph, al-Manṣūr, that the Abbasid model of authority moved away from implicit articulations of ʿAlid legitimacy. Thereafter, the Abbasid claim was legitimised through legalistic, meritocratic and tribal notions of inheritance which proclaimed that the Prophet's uncle, al-ʿAbbās b. ʿAbd al-Muṭṭalib (d. ca. 32/653), the progenitor of the Abbasids, was the rightful successor to the Prophet, while rejecting the concept of inheritance through Fāṭima, the daughter of the Prophet. Subsequently, Abbasid claims that al-ʿAbbās and his descendants were the divinely sanctioned successors of the Prophet were based on traditions ascribed to the Prophet.

While the Abbasid model of legitimacy returned briefly to the notion of ʿAlid pre-eminence during the reign of al-Maʾmūn (r. 170–218/786–833), the concept of Abbasid primacy and succession remained dominant, despite the fact that 'their very rise to power had undermined the ideology by means of which they had risen'.[71] Central to this dominance was a compromise with the religio-juridical establishment whereby the *ʿulamāʾ* remained authoritative as expounders of law and doctrine, while the caliph retained his status as head of the *umma.* Following the failure of various attempts by different ʿAlids to overthrow Abbasid rule in the 2nd/8th century, the ʿAlid challenge to the Abbasids remained marginal for the following century, although scattered ʿAlid claimants secured political power in peripheral areas, such as the Zaydī imamates in the Caspian and Yemen.

The rise of the Fatimid caliphate in 297/909 proved, therefore, to be a major challenge to established Abbasid authority. For the first time, a large-scale and viable state positioned in the central Islamic lands legitimised its authority through ʿAlid claims to succession. Given that any refutation of ʿAlid legitimacy per se would need to be circumspect, the main thrust of the Abbasid anti-Fatimid propaganda over the next century sought to deny instead that the Fatimids were ʿAlids at all.

Ironically, it was the violent persecution of the ʿAlids following the Abbasid acquisition of political power that had compelled the descendants of Ismāʿīl b. Jaʿfar al-Ṣādiq to withdraw from public life. The concealment of the names and hiding places of the Ismaili imams for some 150 years before the Fatimids came to power, known in Ismaili history as the *dawr al-satr* (period of concealment), provided the Abbasids with their allegation that the Fatimids were upstarts whose ʿAlid ancestry could not be proved incontrovertibly with complete credence.[72]

Anti-Fatimid propaganda was produced by several parties that felt threatened by their rise.[73] These included Sunni theologians and heresiographers often patronised by the Abbasids, the Umayyads of al-Andalus, and the Ismaili Qarmaṭīs, who rejected the Fatimid claim to the imamate.

Pivotal to the framing of anti-Fatimid polemics were the works sponsored by the Abbasid caliphs or initiated by their supporters.[74] With one layer building upon another over the course of the 4th/10th century, their principal accusation was that the Fatimids were not of ʿAlid descent, and this eventually turned into defaming them as arch-heretics who harboured an enmity to Islam. One major milestone in the anti-Fatimid tradition was the accounts of Ibn Rizām and Akhū Muḥsin which began to circulate in the 4th/10th century. Their anti-Fatimid vitriol included the ascription of an alternative non-ʿAlid lineage to the Fatimid imam-caliphs, which were compounded by accusations of heresy as drafted in the Ibn Rizām-Akhū Muḥsin narrative, and these subsequently gained state validation in the Baghdad Manifesto.

The first anti-Fatimid alternative lineage

In a cursory mention of the rise of the Fatimids, which took place in the final decades of his life, Abū Jaʿfar b. Jarīr al-Ṭabarī (d. 310/923) refers to the first Fatimid imam-caliph, al-Mahdī bi'llāh, as Ibn al-Baṣrī.[75] Al-Ṭabarī's label indicates the first accretion of an alternative lineage in the pro-Abbasid circles of Baghdad which implicitly denied the validity of the ʿAlid origins of the Fatimids.

This early layer of anti-Fatimid accounts, propagating the notion that the Fatimids were not ʿAlids and that al-Mahdī was the 'son of a Basran', can be traced to investigations that were supposedly initiated in Baghdad by the Abbasid caliph around 301/914.[76] As reported by the Andalusī chronicler, ʿArīb b. Saʿd, after the first Fatimid campaign in Egypt, which took place in that same year, the Abbasid caliph al-Muqtadir (r. 295–320/908–932) set out to 'investigate the lineage (*nasab*) of ʿAbd Allāh al-Mahdī, who is called ʿUbayd Allāh al-Shīʿī', a derogatory diminutive that became customary among most later Sunni historians.[77] ʿArīb cited as his source the well-known Baghdadi scholar, Muḥammad b. Yaḥyā al-Ṣūlī (d. 335/947), who related it from Abu'l-Ḥasan ʿAlī b. Sirāj al-Miṣrī, known as a memoriser of reports (*akhbār*) regarding the Shiʿa. The Abbasid caliph's investigations concluded that:

> ʿUbayd Allāh, the one who has arisen (*al-qā'im*) in Ifrīqiya, is ʿUbayd Allāh b. ʿAbd Allāh b. Sālim – from the people of ʿAskar Mukram – Ibn Sindān al-Bāhilī, the chief of Ziyād's police and from his *mawālī*. Sālim, his grandfather, had been killed by [the Abbasid caliph] al-Mahdī because of his *zandaqa* (heresy).[78]

As noted by Madelung, in the literary biographical dictionary of the Andalusian Ibn al-Abbār (d. 658/1260) a similar version of this alternative lineage is traced to another Baghdadi scholar of the same period, the chronicler ʿUbayd Allāh b. Aḥmad b. Abī Ṭāhir Ṭayfūr.[79] The son of a literary figure, Ibn Abī Ṭāhir Ṭayfūr (d. 280/893), ʿUbayd Allāh b. Ibn Abī Ṭāhir Ṭayfūr continued his father's history of Baghdad (*Akhbār Baghdād*) before his own death in 313/925–926.[80] He was, therefore, a contemporary of both al-Ṭabarī and al-Ṣūlī, and a witness to this early version of an alternative Fatimid lineage circulating in the Abbasid court circles in Baghdad. ʿUbayd Allāh b. Abī Ṭāhir's alternative lineage approximates to that given by al-Ṣūlī.[81] Notably, this version omits the accusation that the grandfather was executed for *zandaqa*, which appears in al-Ṣūlī's later version.[82] The conjunction of an accusation of heresy among their forebears with an alternative non-ʿAlid lineage would, over the following century, become the staple features of anti-Fatimid Abbasid propaganda, culminating in the Baghdad Manifesto.

The Ibn Rizām/Akhū Muḥsin insertions

Writing in the first half of the 4th/10th century in Baghdad, the anti-Ismaili and anti-Fatimid Sunni polemicist Abū ʿAbd Allāh Muḥammad b. ʿAlī b. Rizām (or Razzām) al-Kūfī, composed the

Kitāb al-radd ʿalāʾl-Ismāʿīliyya (or *al-Naqḍ ʿalāʾl-Bāṭiniyya*), a work that professed to be a history of the Ismaili movement which had culminated in the Fatimid state.[83] Ibn Rizām's influential account posited another genealogy for the Fatimids that was traced to Maymūn al-Qaddāḥ and his son ʿAbd Allāh.[84] According to Ibn Rizām, both father and son were *dayṣāniyyūn* (Bardesanians, who followed a form of dualism), the latter a trickster and charlatan with pretentions to prophecy. ʿAbd Allāh b. Maymūn al-Qaddāḥ, succeeded by his son Muḥammad, is alleged by Ibn Rizām to have spearheaded the Ismaili movement which spread across the Islamic world and culminated in the emergence of a person he calls Saʿīd b. al-Ḥusayn b. ʿAbd Allāh b. Maymūn, that is, the Fatimid imam-caliph al-Mahdī bi'llāh.

Ibn Rizām added that ʿAbd Allāh b. Maymūn initially pretended to be a descendant of ʿAqīl, a brother of ʿAlī b. Abī Ṭālib,[85] but that this claim was altered when Saʿīd [i.e., al-Mahdī] went to Egypt and took to 'propagating the claim that he was descended from ʿAlī and Fāṭima, with the name ʿUbayd Allāh'.[86] Ibn Rizām recounts that seeing that his own claim was unsuccessful, Saʿīd then conjured up a young man, who he claimed was a descendant of Muḥammad b. Ismāʿīl, and who was to be his successor Abu'l-Qāṣim al-Qāʾim.

Ibn Rizām's account served as the basis for another major anti-Fatimid treatise by the *sharīf* Abu'l-Ḥusayn Muḥammad b. ʿAlī, more commonly known as Akhū Muḥsin.[87] Writing shortly after 372/983, Akhū Muḥsin asserted that his concern was to elucidate 'the matter of Ismāʿīl b. Jaʿfar … and his descendants, as much is being said about his son and he is being credited with descendants who do not belong to his family'.[88] He repeated the allegation that the Fatimids were, in fact, descendants of a non-ʿAlid by the name of ʿAbd Allāh b. Maymūn al-Qaddāḥ, a Dayṣānī dualist and the founder of their creed, all of whom were 'heretics' of the highest order who sought to destroy Islam from within.

In this same period, as Stern points out, the fraudulent publications and anti-Fatimid pamphlets that circulated in the Abbasid lands had a powerful influence on the shaping of anti-Ismaili public opinion.[89] They were alleged to be 'secret works' of the Ismailis and thus contained the 'hidden truths and goals' of the Ismaili *da'wa*. Prominent among them was the *Kitāb al-siyāsa*, the work of an 'able forger disseminated as the product of the cynical libertism of an Ismaili teacher'.[90] Though apparently based on an intimate knowledge of Ismaili doctrine, the work sought to portray how the *da'wa* instructed its adherents to 'capture souls' through seven steps of initiation that ultimately led to atheism.

The *Fihrist* of Ibn al-Nadīm, the famous book cataloguer of Baghdad, provides a snapshot of the layers of anti-Fatimid propaganda circulating in Baghdad in the last decades of the 4th/10th century. Though he disassociates himself from the calumny, Ibn al-Nadīm reproduced extracts from Ibn Rizām as well as other accounts circulating in this period which cumulatively claim to prove that the Fatimid imam-caliphs were descendants of Maymūn al-Qaddāḥ, a Bardesanian, who had 'contempt for the *sharī'a* and the basic teachings of prophecy', and whose secret books sought to beguile the naive into a system of initiation that led to atheism, which vilified the prophets and religion.[91] In the *Fihrist*, anti-Fatimid accusations also include claims that the founders of the Ismailis were aided by Magians who sought to restore the Sasānian state by means of figures such as the Persian anti-Muslim rebel Bābak Khurramī, who wanted the 'return of the government of the Persians and their religion as foretold in the stars'.[92] While the anti-Fatimid allegations of Ibn Rizām and Akhū Muḥsin gained credibility in Abbasid circles, it was al-Qādir who was instrumental in giving them the official Abbasid seal of approval by the reproduction of central elements of their polemic in the Baghdad Manifesto.

The Caliphate of al-Qādir: The Manifesto and the Abbasid Restoration

Thought to be a malleable replacement for his predecessor, the caliph al-Qādir was appointed by the Shi'i Būyid amir, Bahā' al-Dawla after he had unceremoniously deposed al-Qādir's cousin and predecessor, al-Ṭā'iʿ (r. 363–381/974–991).[93] The reign of al-Qādir is recognised in scholarship as a signal feature of what has been termed as the eastern Islamic world's 'Sunni revival', in which al-Qādir himself emerged as the champion of Sunni orthodoxy.[94] As summarised by Kennedy, al-Qādir was able to 'create a new and lasting role for the Abbasid Caliphate', for just as the Shiʿi Imam Jaʿfar al-Ṣādiq showed it was possible to be an imam without political power, 'al-Qādir showed that there was a religious role for the Abbasid caliphs, a role which they could fulfil even if their temporal power was non-existent'.[95]

The promulgation of the Baghdad Manifesto proved to be a pivotal moment not only in Fatimid–Abbasid rivalry but also in the resurgence of the Abbasid caliphate itself. Thus the Manifesto served a number of functions. First, it turned the accretions of a century of anti-Fatimid propaganda into an official document which, in addition to having the caliphal seal of approval, was allegedly endorsed by both leading Sunni and ʿAlid figures in Iraq. Moreover, through its co-option of leading ʿAlids in Iraq, the Manifesto deflected the potential for Fatimid-*ashrāf* alliances for which there were already precedents in Egypt and the Ḥijāz. Similarly, it sought to halt the spread of the Fatimid *daʿwa* and stem the recognition of Fatimid authority, particularly by local Iraqi rulers, such as the ʿUqaylids. Finally, the Manifesto became a major symbol of al-Qādir's own caliphal authority, through which he asserted his leadership over individuals and religious groups who were potential rivals by assembling their signatures in an official caliphal edict.

The manner of al-Qādir's accession in 381/991 exemplified the decline of Abbasid power, a process that had begun in the previous century. From the late 3th/9th century, endemic political instability and factional rivalries in Iraq saw the succession of five caliphs between 289 and 333/902 and 944, and this facilitated the arrival of the Būyid (or Buwayhid) dynasty in 334/945 in Baghdad, a Shiʿi dynasty of Daylamī chieftains whose power-base lay in northern Iran.[96] Yet while the Būyids eclipsed the Abbasids for half a century, relegating them to their palace complex to be deposed at will,[97] the caliphs nonetheless retained the critical function of legitimising the emerging model of the Būyid amirate.[98]

By al-Qādir's time, Būyid rule in Iraq had begun to unravel owing to a multitude of factors, presenting him with an opportunity to manipulate the web of religious and military factional alliances in Iraq such that he could assume power.[99] Amid the swift rise and fall of Būyid viziers, Sunni–Shiʿi urban riots, conflicts between the Shāfiʿī and Ḥanafī *madhhab*s for the judiciary, and between Daylamī and Turkish commanders for control of tax farms, the caliph al-Qādir remained 'the one stable figure in the politics of the era' and was gradually accorded 'increasing power that came to him as mediator in the fights of city factions and as court of appeal for army disputes'.[100]

The evolution of al-Qādir's caliphate over the four decades of his reign saw the gradual positioning of the Abbasid caliph as the spokesman of Sunni Islam and especially of its Ḥanbalī school of law.[101] This was finally realised with al-Qādir issuing *al-Risāla al-Qādiriyya*, which was read out from the Abbasid palace in 409/1018, and reinforced further by three public letters issued in 420/1029.[102] These represented al-Qādir's 'profession of faith', a pro-Ḥanbalī assertion which condemned Shiʿi, Muʿtazilī and Ashʿarī standpoints, while affirming veneration for the Prophet's companions and the first four caliphs.[103] The cumulative legacy of these pronouncements was an assertion of the truth of Sunni Islam as opposed to any form of Shiʿi Islam or Muʿtazilism.[104] While the period of the *miḥna* of the 3rd/9th century saw the Abbasid caliph al-Maʾmūn's endeavours to assert himself as the source of doctrine against the power of the Sunni *ʿulamāʾ*, including Aḥmad b. Ḥanbal, al-Qādir's reign in the 5th/11th century saw the caliph refashioned as the defender of doctrines that had been outlined earlier, particularly by the Ḥanbalī *ʿulamāʾ*.[105]

Al-Qādir's reign was thus marked by the evolution of religious and political policies through which the caliph consolidated his authority. The production and promulgation of the Baghdad Manifesto of 402/1011 can arguably be read as a testing of the waters by this redefined caliphate which served as the precursor of the public declaration of creed noted above. Yet the issuing of the Manifesto was motivated by an imminent concern to stem the rising Fatimid-ʿAlid influence in Iraq, and was fuelled by the potential for the Iraqi *ashrāf* to recognise the Fatimids as the true caliphs. In addition, concerns such as the pro-Fatimid turn that the Shiʿi-Sunni conflict of the urban population in Baghdad had taken, and significantly, the proclamation made in the Friday *khuṭba* by the ʿUqaylids that it was the Fatimids who were the rightful caliphs, which occurred in places as far apart as Mosul and Kūfa, also played an immediate role in the Manifesto's promulgation.

The role of the ʿAlid ashrāf in the Manifesto

In all the medieval Sunni chronicles that provide the list of signatories to the Manifesto, Sharīf al-Raḍī and his brother Sharīf al-Murtaḍā appear at the top of it. This is because it was the signatures of these two leading ʿAlid Shiʿi scholars, above all others, which, well into the 9th/15th century, were deemed to lend weight to the Manifesto. Accordingly, Sharīf al-Raḍī's career and his supposed expression of pro-Fatimid sympathies are discussed in several of these chronicles as an integral part of the immediate context of the Manifesto. While the presence of the ʿAlid *ashrāf* as signatories to the Manifesto has been mentioned in scholarship, the factors leading to the rise of the *ashrāf* in the 4th/10th century, and the impact on Fatimid-*ashrāf* relations of the proclamation of the Manifesto, remain to be explored.[106]

The ʿAlid *ashrāf* had, by this time, settled throughout the major regions of the Islamic world and they professed a cross-section of all the *madhhabs*.[107] Forming a distinct local nobility, they served as leaders, diplomats, mediators and local patricians who had the ability to span various social and religious groups. Their religious status was predicated on the belief in their blessed descent, which often led to their receipt of state pensions, as the certified inheritors of the Prophet's unique prerogative of receiving the *khums* (the one-fifth tax).[108] Moreover, the *naqībs* ('over-seers' or 'martials'), as the heads of the *ashrāf*, became the public guardians of the Prophet's lineage.[109] By the 5th/11th century, the regional *naqībs* had acquired the prerogative of publicly confirming a true ʿAlid descent and denouncing a false one by issuing a *maḥḍar*. So, for the Abbasids, the affirmation of the Fatimid ʿAlid lineage by the *ashrāf* would have been detrimental to their sustained propaganda effort. Conversely, co-opting the *ashrāf* to deny the validity of the ʿAlid lineage of the Fatimids gave the Manifesto a crucial seal of legitimacy.

There were precedents for Fatimid-*ashrāf* alliances in Egypt and the Ḥijāz, which had proved vital for buttressing Fatimid authority in the region. The symbiotic relationship between the Fatimids and the elite Egyptian and Ḥijāzī *ashrāf* had reinforced the Fatimid claim of being the ʿAlid imam-caliphs of a Shiʿi empire, and therefore, the champions of Shiʿi law and practice.[110] It also positioned the pro-Fatimid *ashrāf* as the privileged, state-patronised interlocutors with the various segments of the populace. The results of the Fatimid-*ashrāf* alliance are clearly evident in the relatively peaceful conquest of Egypt by the Fatimids,[111] as well as in the mention of the name of the Fatimid imam-caliph in the Friday *khuṭba* in Mecca and Medina from 362/973 onwards, displacing the Abbasids from the pulpits of the *ḥaramayn* for over a century.[112] Viewed in this light, al-Qādir's co-option of the ʿAlids was a necessary prerequisite for the reinforcing of the Manifesto's credentials, and for forestalling any potential reconciliation between the Fatimids and the Iraqi *ashrāf*.

The Mūsawī naqībs of Baghdad

Among the prominent *ashrāf* of Iraq during the reign of al-Qādir were the Mūsawī *ashrāf*, descendants of the seventh Ithnāʿasharī Shiʿi imam Mūsā al-Kāẓim b. Jaʿfar al-Ṣādiq. At the turn of the century, the head of the Mūsawīs of Iraq was Sharīf Abū Aḥmad Ḥusayn b. Mūsā al-Mūsawī al-ʿAlawī (304–400/916–1009), the father of Sharīf al-Raḍī and Sharīf al-Murtaḍā.[113] Abū Aḥmad al-Mūsawī's life illustrates the growing influence of the *ashrāf* in the region, and their own tussles of power with both the

Būyids and the Abbasids. Abū Aḥmad al-Mūsawī's appointment in 354/965 as the *naqīb* of the *ashrāf* by the Būyid amir Muʿizz al-Dawla marked the family's century-long ascent in Baghdad.[114] His appointment as the leader of the Pilgrimage for Iraq was significant, as the office was generally held by someone from the extended Abbasid family.

So substantive was Abū Aḥmad's social, political and economic standing that the Būyid amir ʿAḍud al-Dawla, coveting his wealth and fearing his growing power and prestige, had him imprisoned in his fortress in Shīrāz in 369/979. Following ʿAḍud al-Dawla's death in 372/983, Sharīf Abū Aḥmad was released from prison, reinstated as the *naqīb* and, in addition, appointed in charge of the *maẓālim* courts. The final years of his career proved to be ones in which he enjoyed unparalleled status and popularity. After being briefly dismissed, Abū Aḥmad was reinstated to the *niqāba* in 394/1004, with the exceptional honour of receiving an official title *al-Ṭāhir al-Awḥad Dhu'l-Manāqib*. In 397/1006, when Sharīf Abū Aḥmad was 93 years old, the office of the *niqāba* was bequeathed to his son Muḥammad, who came to be known as Sharīf al-Raḍī.

Sharīf al-Raḍī and the pro-Fatimid verses: Debate and reception

The life and legacy of Sharīf al-Raḍī exemplifies the charismatic role that the *ashrāf* fulfilled for all classes of society during this period.[115] Both al-Raḍī and his brother al-Murtaḍā were widely recognised as Ithnāʿasharī Shiʿis.[116] Yet al-Raḍī, like his father before him, often occupied a middle ground between various religious and factional groups in Iraq.

Thus accounts pertaining to the pro-Fatimid verses attributed to Sharīf al-Raḍī and the reactions that they provoked at the Abbasid court under al-Qādir provide an important angle in understanding the production and historiography of the Baghdad Manifesto.

The younger of the two brothers, Sharīf al-Raḍī, enjoyed unrivalled prestige during his life, which continued to reverberate through the centuries, owing in part to his distinct position but mainly because of his literary works. Having been educated under noted Arabic grammarians, as well as Mālikī and Muʿtazilī *ʿulamā*ʾ, al-Raḍī's production of verses from an early age led his contemporaries to call him the greatest poet of the Quraysh.[117]

Al-Raḍī's political career began when he was given responsibilities over the *niqāba*, the *maẓālim* and leadership of the *ḥajj*. For two decades his stature grew and the Būyid amir Bahāʾ al-Dawla granted him several titles, including *al-Raḍī Dhu'l-Ḥasabayn* in 396/1005, hence his sobriquet Sharīf al-Raḍī.[118]

Sharīf al-Raḍī is known to have presented himself as a viable candidate for the caliphate in his earlier years.[119] Although he wrote eulogies to the caliph al-Ṭāʾiʿ,[120] he also wrote 'audacious, impertinent, and provocative' verses against al-Qādir, including those that deny any difference in station between himself and the Abbasid caliph.[121] It is against this backdrop that in Abbasid circles the allegations were made that he had written pro-Fatimid verses.

At some point before 400/1009–1010, a series of verses, allegedly written by Sharīf al-Raḍī and in circulation in Baghdad, came to the attention of al-Qādir. These verses praise the Fatimids, hint at his possible migration to Egypt and affirm the ʿAlid lineage of the Fatimids. The commonly reproduced extract of the longer poem declaims:[122]

> [Why should] I bear humiliation in the land of the enemy, when in Egypt the Caliph is an ʿAlid
>
> His father is my father, his friend (*mawlāhu*) is my friend (*mawlāy*),
>
> if the distant stranger bears malice for me
>
> That which ties my neck to his neck, is the sayyid of all men, Muḥammad and ʿAlī.

Ibn al-Jawzī, Ibn al-Athīr and al-Maqrīzī report al-Qādir's reaction to these verses attributed to al-Raḍī, Ibn al-Athīr's version being nearly identical to that of Ibn al-Jawzī. Al-Maqrīzī uses excerpts from Hilāl b. al-Muḥassin al-Ṣābiʾ (d. 447/1055), thus providing a contemporary rendering of the event. Hilāl al-Ṣābiʾ and Ibn al-Jawzī's accounts share an identical narrative frame. Yet they also have notable variances, revealing some disagreement in the broader historical tradition concerning the Abbasid al-Qādir, Sharīf al-Raḍī and the signing of a *maḥḍar*.[123]

According to both versions, after al-Qādir became aware of these verses, his spokesman confronted al-Raḍī's father, Abū Aḥmad al-Mūsawī.[124] Among the issues that the spokesman raised was that if al-Raḍī were to go to Egypt, his status would be considerably reduced.[125] Abū Aḥmad later denied that the verses were composed by his son.[126] There is a notable variation between the two accounts that follows this denial. In Hilāl's version, al-Qādir said that if this denial was true, then 'let a *maḥḍar* be written denying the lineage of the rulers of Egypt, and let Muḥammad [i.e., al-Raḍī] sign it', at which point those in attendance at the Abbasid court, including Abū Aḥmad and Sharīf al-Murtaḍā, signed it.[127] Ibn al-Jawzī's account, however, has Abū Aḥmad promising al-Bāqillānī, who is acting as the caliph's spokesman, that he will secure an apology from al-Raḍī. Later, Abū Aḥmad asks al-Raḍī to write a letter in which the latter will deny the ʿAlid lineage of the Fatimids.[128]

The two accounts reconverge when Abū Aḥmad confronts his son, al-Raḍī, and the latter denies that he is the author of the verses. In both narratives, al-Raḍī refuses to publicly deny the validity of the Fatimids' ʿAlid lineage, either by refusing to sign the *maḥḍar*, as in Hilāl's version, or by not writing the letter, as in Ibn al-Jawzī's one.[129] Abū Aḥmad confronts his son's refusal to do this, upon which al-Raḍī professes that he is fearful of the *dāʿīs* of Egypt.[130] A bitter argument ensues between father and son, and the father swears an oath to either not speak to his son, as per Hilāl,[131] or not reside with him, as in Ibn al-Jawzī.[132] The matter ends with al-Raḍī swearing an oath that the poem was not his composition, and Hilāl adds that al-Qādir nonetheless had him removed from the *niqāba*, and replaced him with another *sharīf*.[133]

Several elements in the two narratives raise further questions. Although the narrative frames are identical, the variation in incidental details suggests a considerable reworking of traditions concerning al-Qādir, al-Raḍī and the *maḥḍar.* The supposed breakdown of relations between al-Raḍī and his father seems suspect in view of al-Raḍī's well-documented affection and reverence for his father, which can be seen in the fact that his earliest poems were written in praise of him and also that he wrote his biography.[134] One must also question why, in the contemporary version of Hilāl, Sharīf al-Raḍī is said to have refused to sign a *maḥḍar* produced at the Abbasid court, while in the later version of al-Jawzī the narrative has al-Raḍī refusing to write a new letter denouncing the Fatimids. Could it be that Ibn al-Jawzī's version is retrospectively adapted to validate the accounts in which Sharīf al-Raḍī is said to have signed the Baghdad Manifesto?

Between the accounts of the pro-Fatimid verses of al-Raḍī and those about the Baghdad Manifesto, two somewhat conflicting narratives present themselves in the extant sources. The first seeks to detach al-Raḍī from the pro-Fatimid verses, while also emphasising his refusal to sign a manifesto/letter. The second, on the Baghdad Manifesto itself, simply attaches al-Raḍī's signature to the Manifesto of 402/1011. Why al-Raḍī would sign the Manifesto, a year after his father's demise and despite his resistance to do so earlier, remains unanswered. The question therefore remains open to further exploration as to whether the pro-Fatimid verses were written by Sharīf al-Raḍī and whether or not he actually signed the Manifesto of 402/1011. Conversely, al-Qādir's motivations for securing al-Raḍī's denial of the pro-Fatimid verses, and his affirmation of the Manifesto, are evident.

While the validation of the Manifesto depended on the compliance of the *ashrāf,* its actual issuance was inextricably tied to the burgeoning influence of the Fatimid *daʿwa* in Iraq.

Al-Kirmānī, the Fatimid daʿwa in Iraq

Iraq had served as the crucible for Ismaili *daʿwa* activities during the *dawr al-satr* and into the 4th/10th century.[135] Conditions in the Abbasid heartlands were not conducive to preserving a detailed record of the Fatimid *daʿwa*'s activities there in this period. However, accounts of the diplomatic negotiations between the Būyid ruler ʿAḍud al-Dawla and the Fatimid imam-caliph al-ʿAzīz bi'llāh around 367–368/977–978, indicate how widespread in Iraq the *daʿwa* was during the last decades of the century.[136] The proscription of a prominent Fatimid *dāʿī* from Baṣra whom ʿAḍud al-Dawla accused of overstepping the mark, and who was consequently held to ransom at the Būyid court, pending the outcome of the Būyid-Fatimid overtures, is a case in point.[137]

The writings of the Fatimid *dāʿī* Ḥamīd al-Dīn al-Kirmānī (d. after 411/1020) provide an insight into the Fatimid *daʿwa* in Iraq during the years surrounding the issuance of the Baghdad Manifesto.[138] Known as *Ḥujjat al-ʿIrāqayn*, al-Kirmānī occupied the most senior position in the Fatimid *daʿwa* in the region. His works such as *al-Majālis al-Baṣriyya wa'l-Baghdādiyya* are also indicative of his activities for the *daʿwa* in Iraq.[139] However, it is his *al-Maṣābīḥ fī ithbāt al-imāma*, probably composed soon after the Baghdad Manifesto, which provides an insight into the approaches to belief and their expression in the Fatimid *daʿwa* at this time.[140]

Written for Fakhr al-Mulk, the Būyid vizier in Baghdad during this period (401–407/1010–1016), the principal aim of this work was to convince him of the veracity of the Fatimid claim to the imamate. That al-Kirmānī could compose such a work in a heightened anti-Fatimid environment, and address it directly to the Būyid vizier, suggests he may have had some patronage among the upper echelons of the Iraqi bureaucracy.[141] In his *al-Maṣābīḥ*, al-Kirmānī sets out to provide a series of cogently argued premises, so as to prove:

> the absolute necessity of the imamate and to indicate what it is as precisely as he could, all the while affirming the Fatimid position, and that of his imam, al-Ḥākim.[142]

In so doing, he disparaged the Abbasid al-Qādir as 'blatantly unqualified for the imamate'.[143] This is particularly significant because the Būyid vizier Fakhr al-Mulk was effectively in charge of relations with this caliph.

Al-Kirmānī delineates the criteria required for a valid claim to the imamate, the foremost of which is descent from al-Ḥusayn b. ʿAlī b. Abī Ṭālib. Consequently, he dismisses the claims of all the other contemporary Muslim rulers, beginning with the Abbasid al-Qādir and including the Zaydī and Khārijī imams of the time.[144] Al-Kirmānī reiterates the authentic ʿAlid lineage of the Fatimid imam-caliph al-Ḥākim:

> He is from the offspring of prophecy and is a descendant of al-Ḥusayn ... He has been designated by pure forefathers back through ʿAlī b. Abī Ṭālib, to Muhammad, the Chosen.[145]

Notably, al-Kirmānī makes no direct reference to the Baghdad Manifesto, which indicates that at the time of the issuing of the Manifesto, it may not have held any particular importance for the Fatimids.[146] Yet the fact that the entire work is concerned with affirming the imamate based on ʿAlid lineage reiterates its inviolable centrality for the Fatimid *daʿwa* in Iraq.

While al-Kirmānī's work demonstrates the prominent position of the leading Fatimid *dāʿī* in Iraq in the upper echelons of the Būyid administration, it was the manifestations of pro-Fatimid sentiment among the ordinary Shiʿi population of Baghdad, and especially the pronouncement of al-Ḥākim's name in the Friday *khuṭba* in several places around Baghdad, that may well have been the proverbial final straw which provoked al-Qādir's promulgation of the Manifesto.[147]

The proclaiming of al-Ḥākim by the Shiʿis of Baghdad

Kennedy has noted that the Būyid period was one of continuous crisis in Baghdad.[148] As a result of the breakdown of the Abbasid political order, a decline in trade and the emigration of wealthy families to Egypt, Baghdad had turned into a battleground for various military factions seeking control over the limited resources of the region. Clashes between rival Turkish and Daylamī contingents for supremacy produced 'the emergence of the Shīʿa and Sunnī as armed political groupings and the division of the city into Sunnī and Shīʿī quarters'.[149]

While the first signs of popular violence were evident in the anti-Shiʿi attacks by the Ḥanbalīs, which the Abbasid caliph sought to halt by a decree in 323/935,[150] the arrival of the Būyids in Baghdad was a catalyst for social rupture.[151] Then, in the aftermath of the political conflicts of 361/972, when Turkish regiments rebelled against the Būyids and their Daylamī regiments, there appeared what Donohue has termed a 'loose alliance' between the Turkish guards and the Sunnis on the one hand, and the Daylamī soldiery and the Shiʿis on the other.[152] Yet, though the political quarrels ended, as Kennedy notes, the 'arming of both factions and increasing division of the city into fortified quarters, each with its own sectarian character' became a permanent feature of the social landscape of the city until 'Baghdad was firmly divided between the adherents of the two rival sects, each armed and defending its own areas'.[153]

While various prominent figures, Sunni, Shiʿi and Būyid, sought to calm the violence, urban conflict became an endemic feature of 5th/11th-century Baghdad.[154] The eruption of Sunni–Shiʿi violence in 398/1008, however, took on new symbolic proportions when Shiʿi protestors publicly proclaimed their allegiance to the Fatimid ruler al-Ḥākim bi-Amr Allāh.[155] Citing several reasons for these clashes, Ibn al-Jawzī relates:

> The People of Karkh spoke about the one who was executed, for he was a Shiʿa. Then a battle ensued between them and the people of Bāb al-Baṣra, Bāb al-Shaʿīr and al-Qalāʾīn. The people of Karkh assaulted the home of Abū Ḥāmid (al-Isfarāʾinī) so he went to Dār al-Quṭn. There they [the people of Karkh] proclaimed: Yā Ḥākim Yā Manṣūr.[156]

The proclamation of loyalty to al-Hākim bi-Amr Allāh in the Abbasid capital appears to have jolted al-Qādir into action. In a seemingly unprecedented intervention, he instructed his palace guards to assist the Sunni partisans. This weakened the Shiʿa, whose leaders were compelled to seek the caliph's clemency.[157] While al-Qādir was increasingly recognised as the spokesman for the Sunnis, he sought to distance himself from the Sunni–Shiʿi fray. His personal intervention in this confrontation thus highlights his sensitivity to the growing success of the Fatimid *daʿwa*, which came to the fore some three years later in both northern and southern Iraq.

The khuṭba of Qirwāsh and the noose around Baghdad

It was recognition of Fatimid authority by the two major Bedouin Iraqi principalities in 401/1010 which provoked the issuing of the Baghdad Manifesto. The dynastic chieftains of the ʿUqaylids and the Mazyadids emerged as increasingly powerful among the array of factional leaders in Iraq and Syria during this period, and their recognition of the imamate of the Fatimid al-Ḥākim in 401/1010 proved to be a seminal moment in the history of Fatimid–Abbasid rivalry.

Following the decline of Ḥamdānid rule in Mesopotamia, the chieftains of the Arab tribe of ʿUqayl established their foothold in Mosul around 380/990. Six years later, their chieftain Qirwāsh b. al-Muqallid (d. 442/1050) extended their rule over the Jazīra (northern Iraq and eastern Syria), with Mosul as the capital for the next half-century.[158]

In southern Iraq, another Bedouin dynasty, that of the Banū Mazyad, established its rule following the waning of Būyid authority there. By 393/1003, ʿAlī b. Mazyad, the chief of the Mazyadid clan of the Banū Asad, had emerged as the unrivalled chieftain in the regions around Kūfa and south of Baghdad. In 397/1007, he was given the title Sanad al-Dawla in recognition of his stature.[159]

These two Bedouin principalities had large and cohesive nomadic armies upon which their polities had been built, and which gave them a distinct advantage over their factional rivals.[160] Though part of the Abbasid system of patronage, they had a notable affinity for Shiʿi Islam. Mazyadid patronage of Shiʿi scholarship at al-Ḥilla, originally their military encampment, eventually led to the emergence of the Ḥilla school of Ithnaʿasharī jurisprudence.

In 401/1010, the ʿUqaylid Qirwāsh b. al-Muqallid, publicly pronounced his allegiance to the Fatimid imam-caliph al-Ḥākim in the Friday *khuṭba* in Mosul on 4 Muḥarram/18 August.[161] Two months later, recognition of the imamate of al-Ḥākim bi-Amr Allāh was also declared in the sermon at Anbar, north of Baghdad. A week later, the same proclamations were made at al-Madāʾin (Ctesiphon) and Qaṣr Ibn Ḥubayra, south of Baghdad, and soon thereafter in Kūfa, the ancient bastion of Shiʿi Islam. Almost simultaneously, ʿAlī b. Mazyad, the chieftain of the Mazyadids, made similar public pronouncements in al-Ḥākim's name in southern Iraq.[162] Qirwāsh's change of allegiance effectively created what Walker has termed a Fatimid noose around Baghdad, placing the Abbasid caliph al-Qādir in a perilous position.[163] The ʿAlid descent of the Fatimids was declared in an unequivocal manner in the *khuṭba* of Qirwāsh:[164]

> O God, bless your radiant guardian and your greatest friend, ʿAlī b. Abī Ṭālib, the father of the rightly guided imams ... O God extend all Your blessings ... [to] the imam of the age, fortress of the faith, master of the ʿAlid *daʿwa* (*ṣāḥib al-daʿwa al-ʿalawiyya*) and prophetic religion (*al-milla al-nabawiyya*), Your servant and guardian on Your behalf, al-Manṣūr Abū ʿAlī al-Ḥākim bi-Amr Allāh, Commander of the Believers, just as You blessed his rightly guided forefathers.

The aftermath of this public declaration highlights the fact that despite al-Qādir's growing authority in Baghdad, he was compelled to turn to the Būyid military lords to repulse the pro-Fatimid stranglehold now around Baghdad. Following entreaties for aid from the Abbasid caliph, the Būyid amir Bahāʾ al-Dawla compelled Qirwāsh to rescind his recognition of the Fatimid *daʿwa* through threats and enticements.[165] Al-Qādir's military limitations being thus exposed, he turned in the following year to the soft power of propaganda and issued the Baghdad Manifesto.

The Baghdad Manifesto

Soon after the Baghdad Manifesto was issued from al-Qādir's court in 402/1011 it was read out publicly in Baghdad and Basra, as well as in other areas.[166] Seeking to definitively place the Fatimids outside the ʿAlid fold, the Manifesto placed them outside Islam altogether. It dredged up the central elements of the accumulated anti-Fatimid polemic of the 5th/11th century, especially as recounted in Ibn Rizām and Akhū Muḥsin, and gave them caliphal sanction. Most importantly, the attestation of the claims of the Manifesto by the prominent signatories in Baghdad set the seal on its validity.

The influence of the Manifesto lay as much in the fact that it was issued by the Abbasid caliph, as it did in the stature of the signatories underwriting its authenticity. An investigation of the key signatories as well as those whose names are absent from it, reveals that the Manifesto was conditioned as much by the dynamics of power in Baghdad, and al-Qādir's manipulation of them, as it was about forestalling the influence of the Fatimid *daʿwa* in the region.

The ʿAlids

In addition to Sharīf al-Raḍī and Sharīf al-Murtaḍā, whose significance to the signing of the Manifesto has been discussed above, there were several other major ʿAlid figures who were given as signatories. One of those listed by Ibn al-Jawzī and Ibn al-Athīr is Abū Ṭāhir b. Abi'l-Ṭayyib. A survey of the genealogical sources indicates that this is a reference to Abū Ṭāhir Aḥmad b. Abi'l-Ṭāyyib al-Ḥasan b. Muḥammad al-Ashtar, a descendant of the early Shiʿi Imam, ʿAlī Zayn al-ʿĀbidīn. Sharīf Muḥammad al-Ashtar is known as the progenitor of the Banū ʿUbayd Allāh, a large family of *ashrāf* whose predominance in Kūfa gave rise to the adage, 'The sky belongs to God, the earth to the Banū ʿUbayd Allāh.'[167] Over the 5th/11th century, major members of the *ashrāf* from this family held the *niqāba*s of Wāṣit, Kūfa, Baghdad and Mosul.[168] Furthermore, Muḥammad al-Ashtar's grandson, Abū ʿAbd Allāh Aḥmad (d. 398/1007) was close to Abū Aḥmad al-Mūsawī, the father of Sharīf al-Raḍī.[169] The signatory, Abū Ṭāhir Aḥmad b. Abu'l-Ṭayyib al-Ḥasan, was another grandson of Muḥammad al-Ashtar and a cousin of Abū 'Abd Allāh Aḥmad.[170] His signature on the Manifesto would have therefore served as a corroboration from one of the eminent *ashrāf* families of Iraq.

Also noted among the 'Alid signatories is Ibn al-Buṭḥāwī. In so far as this *nisba* is seemingly missing from the works of the genealogists, it is probably a transcription error for the *nisba* al-Buṭḥānī. The Buṭḥānīs were Ḥasanid 'Alids who had gained prominence as Zaydī imams and local notables generally throughout the eastern Islamic world.[171] Pre-eminent Buṭḥānīs included the two Zaydī imams, Abu'l-Ḥusayn Aḥmad al-Mu'ayyad bi'llāh (d. 411/1020) and his elder brother Abū Ṭālib Yaḥyā al-Nāṭiq bi'l-Ḥaqq (d. ca. 424/1033), both of whom, as Madelung notes, gained 'universal recognition among the later Zaidīs as Imams for their outstanding rank in religious scholarship'.[172] Notably, both studied in Baghdad before claiming the imamate.[173] Other Buṭḥānīs included the patrician families of Nīsābūr and Hamadhān.[174]

The possible mention of an anonymous Ibn al-Buṭḥānī in the Baghdad Manifesto can be linked to the career of another leading Zaydī in Baghdad, Abū 'Abd Allāh Muḥammad b. al-Ḥasan (d. 359/969) known as Ibn al-Dā'ī, who came from a collateral branch of the 'Alids. He came to Baghdad with the Būyid amir Mu'izz al-Dawla who had considered Ibn al-Dā'ī as a viable candidate for the caliphate, but appointed him instead as the *naqīb* over the *ashrāf*.[175] Thus there was a distinct Zaydī presence in Baghdad to be seen among the *naqīb*s. The signature of an anonymous Buṭḥānī on the Manifesto would have represented its validation by a distinguished Zaydī family in Iraq.

Among the other 'Alid signatories was Muḥammad b. Muḥammad b. 'Umar. Known as Abu'l-Ḥārith al-'Alawī, he was a *naqīb* of Kūfa who expended much of his wealth on leading the *ḥajj* caravans for over a decade.[176] Despite the Kūfan link and the mention of wealth, it is unclear if this figure is connected to the distinguished Iraqi *sharīf* who had died ten years earlier, Muḥammad b. ʿUmar.[177] If that is so, then the signature of his son, Muḥammad b. Muḥammad b. ʿUmar, on the Manifesto represented an endorsement by another major ʿAlid family in Iraq. Ibn Azraq al-Mūsawī and Ibn Abī Yaʿlā are also found among the ʿAlids, but little is known of them.

The judges

The signatories included also eminent judges. Qāḍī Abū Muḥammad ʿAbd Allāh al-Akfānī al-Asadī (316–405/928–1014) was the leading Ḥanafī judge of Baghdad at the time.[178] A major patron of traditionists, Ibn al-Akfānī served as the chief *qāḍī* of Baghdad after 396/1005–1006. After him is listed Abu'l-ʿAbbās Aḥmad b. Muḥammad b. ʿAbd al-Raḥmān al-Abīwardī (d. 425/1034), a *ḥadīth* narrator and poet, who later became a leading Shāfiʿī judge in Baghdad, under the patronage of his Shāfiʿī master al-Isfarāʾinī, as discussed in the section 'The jurists', below.[179]

The identity of the third judge remains uncertain, partly because of the variants of the name in the sources, either Abu'l-Qāṣim al-Khazarī or al-Jazarī.[180] There are seemingly no prominent contemporary *qāḍīs* with the *nisba* al-Jazarī or al-Khazarī of Baghdad in this era. It is likely, however, following Ibn al-Athīr's identification of him as Ibn al-Khazarī, that this *qāḍī* is the son of, or connected to, another eminent judge of Baghdad in the previous generation, who belonged to the Ẓāhirī *madhhab*, known as Qāḍī Abu'l-Ḥusayn ʿAbd al-ʿAzīz b. Aḥmad al-Khazarī. This *qāḍī* was appointed as one of the four deputy judges in Baghdad in 369/979 after ʿAḍud al-Dawla 'broke with tradition' and appointed a Ẓāhirī scholar from Shīrāz as the chief justice of Baghdad.[181] The contemporary Ibn al-Nadīm noted in his listing of Ẓāhirī jurists that ʿAbd al-ʿAzīz al-Isbahānī al-Khazarī was still serving as a judge in Baghdad in 376/987.[182] This al-Khazarī died in 391/1001, ten years before the Manifesto. While the connection of Abu'l-Qāṣim al-Khazarī with ʿAbd al-ʿAzīz al-Khazarī remains to be established, it would have fitted with the varied purposes of the Manifesto to have a leading Ẓāhirī's signature on it.

The jurists

The jurists listed as signatories to the Manifesto can be divided into Ḥanafīs and Shāfiʿīs with one exception, a major Shiʿi jurist. Foremost among the Shāfiʿī signatories is Abū Ḥāmid Aḥmad b. Muḥammad al-Isfarāʾinī (345–406/957–1016), the leader of the Shāfiʿīs of Baghdad from the end of the 4th/10th century and one of the capital's 'most important religious figures'.[183] Another Shāfiʿī signatory was Abū ʿAlī b. Ḥamkān (d. 405/1014).[184] Ibn al-Athīr also lists the Shāfiʿī *faqīh* Abu'l-Faḍl al-Nasawī.[185] The identities of two other listed jurists remains uncertain. It is likely that Abū ʿAbd Allāh al-Bayḍāwī, listed in Ibn al-Jawzī, was Abū ʿAbd Allāh Muḥammad b. ʿAbd Allāh al-Bayḍāwī al-Baghdādī (d. 424/1033), a Shāfiʿī jurist whose *nisba* may indicate the inclusion of a distinctly Baghdadi element.[186] One signatory, Abū Muḥammad al-Kashfalī, remains unidentified, though his *nisba* displays a Shāfiʿī connection.[187]

The Ḥanafī jurists who signed the Manifesto are named as Aḥmad b. Muḥammad al-Qudūrī al-Ḥanafī (d. 429/1037), the 'head of the Ḥanafī school of Iraq', a highly respected *faqīh* and teacher of al-Khaṭīb al-Baghdādī whose works are well known. Another leading Ḥanafī signatory was al-Ḥusayn b. ʿAlī b. Muḥammad al-Ṣaymarī (d. 436/1044), a leader of the Ḥanafīs of Baghdad as well as an important *faqīh* and judge. Ibn al-Athīr adds the name of an ascetic Ḥanafī scholar, Abū Jaʿfar al-Nasafī (d. 414/1023).[188]

Finally, included by Ibn al-Athīr and Ibn Khaldūn, and the only name of any signatory given by Abu'l-Fidā, is that of Abū ʿAbd Allāh b. al-Nuʿmān, the pre-eminent Ithnāʿasharī Shiʿi jurist of the era, Shaykh al-Mūfīd (336–413/948–1022). Regarded as 'a leading theologian and spokesman of the Imāmiyya', whose authority was widely recognised by Ithnāʿasharī Imāmīs beyond Baghdad, Shaykh al-Mufīd was a prominent figure in the intellectual life of Baghdad itself. Madelung adds that 'virtually all the leading Imāmī scholars of the following generation were his students', including Sharīf al-Raḍī and Sharīf al-Murtaḍā, the latter leading the funeral prayers over him in 413/1022.[189]

The legal witnesses (shuhūd)

Among the remaining figures listed as signatories can be found the legal witness Abu'l-Qāṣim ʿAlī b. al-Muḥassin al-Tanūkhī (365–447/976–1055), a son of Abū ʿAlī al-Tanūkhī (329–384/941–994), the famous littérateur and judge, who was the secretary and confidant of the Būyid amir, ʿAḍud al-Dawla. Ibn Khallikān says that, in addition to his scholarly endeavours, Abu'l-Qāsim ʿAlī was known for the soundness of his legal testimony before he became a *qāḍī*.[190]

An overview of the signatories highlights the point that the legitimacy of the Manifesto was conceived of strategically as a collectively signed legal testimony, with the signatories serving as public guarantors of its anti-Fatimid pronouncement. Moreover, their varied backgrounds reflect the three major sources of authority regarding the subject matter and claims of the Manifesto – genealogical, legal and doctrinal. The Iraqi *ashrāf* served as the genealogical validation of the document, the judges and *shuhūd* as the legal sponsors, and the representatives of the various legal and religious schools as the doctrinal verifiers.

Equally important in contextualising the relevance of the Manifesto is an analysis of the dynamics operating among the signatories. The most prominent figures noted in the Baghdad Manifesto were often at loggerheads with each other, and at times with al-Qādir. As leaders of the highly fragmented Sunni and Shiʿi communities of Baghdad, the Shāfiʿī Abū Ḥāmid al-Isfarāʾinī and Shaykh al-Mufīd found themselves as the de facto leaders of hostile Sunni and Shiʿi communities in Baghdad. A case in point is the urban violence in which the Shiʿi protestors invoked the Fatimid al-Ḥākim. Kindled by attacks against Shaykh al-Mufīd, the conflict culminated in an assault on the house of al-Isfarāʾinī for the role he played in effecting the burning of the *muṣḥaf* of Ibn Masʿūd.[191]

Relations between the Sunni signatories are similarly pertinent. The period of the signing of the Manifesto saw three of the major signatories pitted against each other in a dispute which also drew in Sharīf al-Raḍī and the Abbasid al-Qādir. As detailed by Donohue, a struggle for control of the office of *qāḍī* of Baghdad in the same year as the Manifesto led the Ḥanafī chief judge al-Akfānī to reject the attempt by the Shāfiʿī, al-Isfarāʾinī, to have his protégé al-Abīwardī appointed as the deputy.[192] When al-Akfānī rejected the caliph's order, al-Isfarāʾinī used his connections with al-Qādir to have him dismissed and replaced by al-Abīwardī. The appointment divided the *ʿulamāʾ*. Al-Akfānī was supported by the Ḥanafīs and by Sharīf al-Raḍī, while al-Abīwardī was upheld by the caliph's court and the Shāfiʿīs. The conflict spread beyond the city when al-Afkānī wrote to Maḥmūd of Ghazna complaining about al-Qādir's persecution of the Ḥanafīs. After the Būyid vizier, encouraged by Sharīf al-Raḍī, lent his weight to the Ḥanafīs, al-Qādir relented by reappointing al-Afkānī and dismissing al-Isfarāʾinī from the court. While its connection to this particular event is unclear, elsewhere potential Shāfiʿī hostility to al-Qādir is reflected in a story that claims Abū Ḥāmid al-Isfarāʾinī reputedly warned al-Qādir that he merely needed to write to Khurāsān to have the caliph removed from office.[193]

That al-Qādir was able to get these mutually hostile figures to sign the Manifesto reflects the fact that his attempts to position himself as the sole leading figure in Baghdad were ultimately successful. Just as later, in 408/1017, al-Qādir was to demand that the Ḥanafī Muʿtazila publicly renounce their creed, the Baghdad Manifesto of 402/1011 can be understood as a precursor to this success because he was able to persuade these rival factions to publicly denounce the Fatimids.

The fact that the Manifesto served a dual purpose, of anti-Fatimid propaganda and of reining in the leading figures in Bagdad under the authority of al-Qādir, is corroborated by the absence of one important segment of the Baghdadi leadership from the list of the signatories, namely, the Ḥanbalīs. This is significant considering their vociferous hostility to the Shiʿis, including the Fatimids, and their increasing affinity to al-Qādir. He could be sure of their support. A similar case is the absence of the signature of the Ashʿarī *qāḍī*, Abū Bakr al-Bāqillānī. A critical figure in the return of Qirwāsh to the Abbasid fold after his pro-Fatimid turn in 401/1010, al-Bāqillānī died three years after the production of the Manifesto. However, as the author of an anti-Ismaili tract his credentials were not under question, and therefore his signature on the Manifesto was perhaps deemed superfluous.

The Manifesto of 444/1052

Just over four decades after the promulgation of the Baghdad Manifesto of 402/1011, a second manifesto was issued from the court of al-Qādir's son and successor, al-Qā'im (r. 422–467/1031–1075), in 444/1052.[194] While a detailed review of the historical context of this second manifesto falls outside the purview of this chapter, it is noteworthy that it was issued during a time of great instability in Iraq and Iran, one which saw the end of Būyid rule and the westward advance of the Saljūq Turks across the Iranian plateau. Just as in the prelude to the first Manifesto, the period in which the second one was issued witnessed the growing influence of the Fatimid *daʿwa* in Iraq. Some six years after it appeared, the Turkish general Abu'l-Ḥārith Arslān al-Basāsīrī entered Baghdad and ordered that the Friday sermon be given in the name of the imam-caliph al-Muṣtanṣīr bi'llāh (427–487/1036–1094), which then occurred for 40 weeks in 450/1058.[195] The chief Fatimid negotiator in Iraq at the time, al-Mu'ayyad fi'l-Dīn al-Shīrāzī, who was instrumental in winning the Turkish general to the Fatimid cause, recounts at length in his autobiography the political manoeuvrings of the *daʿwa* leading up to this historic moment in the broader context of Fatimid–Abbasid rivalry.[196]

That the Manifesto of 444/1052 seemingly receives only cursory mention in the major sources indicates that it was essentially seen as a reproduction of the previous one of 402/1011, with two notable exceptions. First, this Manifesto, as preserved in Ibn al-Jawzī's recension, names Fāṭima, alongside ʿAlī, as the progenitor of the Fatimids. Secondly, while the first Manifesto reiterated the Dayṣānī accusations of the Ibn Rizām/

Akhū Muḥsin tradition, it left out the Qaddāḥid ancestry of the Fatimids. The Manifesto of 444/1052, however, added the attribution of Qaddāḥid origins to the existing anti-Fatimid polemic, giving these accusations validity in an official Abbasid proclamation. As a result, Ibn al-Jawzī's entry for the year 444/1052 reads:

> In this year, there were written *maḥāḍir* in the *dīwān* mentioning the ruler of Egypt (*ṣāḥib Miṣr*) and those who came before him from his forebears, rejecting the lineage which they claim and repudiating their link to the Prophet of God, and to ʿAlī and Fāṭima, and [instead] attributing them to the Dayṣāniyya of the Magians and the Qaddāḥiyya of the Jews. [It said] that they are outside [the fold] of Islam. And there occurred similar to what we had mentioned in the days of al-Qādir bi'llāh, whereby signatures were taken of the *ashrāf*, the *qāḍī*s, the witnesses and the *ʿulamā*ʾ in regard to this.[197]

The Sunni Reception and Ibn Khaldūn's Critique

The Baghdad Manifesto of 402/1011 was to be regularly deployed by medieval Sunni historians and polemicists from the 6th/12th century onwards as proof of the Abbasid claim that the Fatimids lacked ʿAlid descent. Its presentation as an authoritative document can be seen in works such as Juwaynī's *Ta'rīkh-i jahān-gushā* where the author employs it as part of his account of the advance of the Mongol ruler Hūlāgū (d. 663/1265) against the Nizārī Ismailis of Iran, in order to highlight the heresy of the latter and their belief in the 'false Mahdī'.[198] Meanwhile, Ibn al-Kathīr, in his own polemic against the ʿAlid origins of the Fatimids, gives the names of al-Isfarāʾinī and al-Qudūrī as signatories of the Manifesto in order to justify his rejection of the Fatimid lineage.[199]

The potency of the Baghdad Manifesto in medieval Sunni literature is most apparent in the fact that Sunni historians who accepted the ʿAlid lineage of the Fatimids felt it necessary to question the validity of the Baghdad Manifesto itself. Ibn al-Athīr, who affirms the ʿAlid descent of the Fatimids, rejects the validity of the Baghdad Manifesto because duress was employed to get individuals to sign it and because they included people who were not genealogists.[200] A sustained criticism of the veracity of the Manifesto was later offered by the renowned North African historian, Ibn Khaldūn. Writing some two centuries after the fall of the Fatimids, Ibn Khaldūn's assessment of them reflects his historian's cast of mind as well as his temporal and doctrinal distance from the Abbasids. His principal discussion of the Manifesto of 402/1011 occurs in his illustrious *Muqaddima*, which serves as his critique of Muslim historiography. In speaking about the 'eastern' Sunni historians' attitude towards the Fatimids, he points out: 'They deny their [i.e. the Fatimids] ʿAlid origins and attack their descent from Imam Ismāʿīl, son of Jaʿfar al-Ṣādiq' because they base their narratives on 'stories that were made up in favour of the weak Abbasid caliphs.'[201]

Ibn Khaldūn does not dwell on the religious considerations of lineal affinity, an angle which some 'eastern' Sunni historians invoked in declaring that the Fatimids could not be ʿAlids because of their supposed heresies. For Ibn Khaldūn, whose antipathy to several Shiʿi groups is evident in other parts of his work, this was an irrelevance because, as he argued, denying their descent would not invalidate any heresy they might have adhered to, nor would establishing their descent 'help them before God' if they were indeed heretical.[202]

Instead, Ibn Khaldūn's affirmation of the Fatimid lineage emerges from a pragmatic and rational exposé of the reaction of the Abbasids to the Fatimid venture. He points out that the empire of the Fatimids lasted for 270 years, that it spread from North Africa to the Ḥijāz and that 'they shared the realm of Islam equally with the Abbasids'; and he poses the question: 'How could all this have befallen a fraudulent claimant to the rulership?' He adds that the partisans of the Fatimid imam-caliphs 'showed them the greatest love and devotion ... [E]ven after the dynasty had gone and its influence had disappeared, people still came forward to press the claims.'[203]

For Ibn Khaldūn, it was the inability of the Abbasids and their supporters to resist the Fatimid advances that initiated the production of anti-Fatimid polemic in order to 'make up for their inability to resist and repel the Kutāma Berbers, the partisans and propagandists of the 'Ubaydids (Fatimids), who had taken Syria, Egypt, and the Ḥijāz away from the (Abbasids)'. It is in this vein that Ibn Khaldūn questions the validity of the Manifesto:

> The event took place on one memorable day in the year 402 [1011] in the time of al-Qādir. The testimony (of these witnesses) was based upon hearsay, on what people in Baghdad generally believed. Most of them were partisans of the Abbasids who attacked the 'Alid origin (of the 'Ubaydid-Fatimids). The historians reported the information as they had heard it. They handed it down to us just as they remembered it.

Ibn Khaldūn concludes his critique of the Manifesto by reflecting on how the vagaries of political circumstance affect the acquisition of knowledge:

> Dynasty and government serve as the world's market place, attracting to it the products of scholarship and craftsmanship alike. Wayward wisdom and forgotten lore turn up there. In this market, stories are told and items of historical information are delivered.[204]

Notes

1 For an overview and interpretation of the question of Fatimid origins in 20th-century scholarship, see Michael Brett, *The Rise of the Fatimids: The World of the Mediterranean and the Middle East in the Fourth Century of the Hijra, Tenth Century CE* (Leiden, 2001), pp. 29–49. The prevalence of the Manifesto as a document informing Fatimid origins culminated in Mamour's work, the motive of which was to refute the validity of the claims made in the document. See Prince P.H. Mamour, *Polemics on the Origin of the Fatimi Caliphs* (London, 1934; repr. Karachi, 1979). Mamour reproduces commentaries by earlier orientalists regarding the Manifesto, including those of

Margoliouth, Quatremère and Donaldson (ibid., pp. 21–22). See also Brett's comments on Mamour's defence (Brett, *Rise*, p. 34). For the label 'famous Baghdad Manifesto', see, for instance, Nabia Abbot, 'Two Būyid Coins in the Oriental Institute', *The American Journal of Semitic Languages and Literatures*, 56 (1939), pp. 350–364, p. 356; Bernard Lewis, *The Origins of Ismāʿīlism: A Study of the Historical Background of the Fāṭimid Caliphate* (Cambridge, 1940; repr. New York, 1975), pp. 3, 8; Farhad Daftary, *The Ismāʿīlīs: Their History and Doctrines* (2nd ed., Cambridge, 2007), p. 102; Farhad Daftary, *Ismaili Literature: A Bibliography of Sources and Studies* (London, 2004), p. 87; Paul E. Walker, ed. and tr., *Orations of the Fatimid Caliphs: Festival Sermons of the Ismaili Imams* (London, 2009), p. 5.

2 Lewis, *Origins*, p. 8, notes the pervasiveness of the Baghdad Manifesto in medieval Sunni chronicles.

3 For a sustained discussion on the progress in studies on the Ismailis, especially over the 20th century, see Daftary, *Ismāʿīlīs*, pp. 1–34.

4 For an exception, however, see Lewis who views the Manifesto as a milestone in what he characterises as three stages by which 'true knowledge' of Ismaili doctrine filtered to the Sunni world. The first is marked by knowledge based only on public activities, the second is based on some 'inklings', and the third on 'detailed' but not always accurate knowledge of the Ismailis and their origins. For Lewis, 'the third stage is marked by the famous Baghdad manifesto, denouncing the Fāṭimid caliphs as impostors and schematics': Lewis, *Origins*, pp. 1–3.

5 See, for example, Daftary, *Ismāʿīlīs*, p. 102.

6 See, for example, Hugh Kennedy, *The Prophet and the Age of the Caliphate: The Islamic Near East from the Sixth to the Eleventh Century* (London, 1986), pp. 241–242; Farhad Daftary, *The Assassin Legends: Myths of the Ismaʿilis* (London, 1994), p. 24; Paul E. Walker, 'The Ismāʿīlī Daʿwa and the Fāṭimid Caliphate', in M. W. Daly, ed., *The Cambridge History of Egypt*; Volume I, *Islamic Egypt, 640–1517*, ed. Carl F. Petry (Cambridge, 1998), pp. 145–146. Sadik A. Assaad, *The Reign of al-Hakim bi Amr Allah (386/996 – 411/1021): A Political Study* (Beirut, 1974), p. 16. Brett takes the Manifesto as an example of al-Qādir seeking to win the support of the Twelvers (as well as the Sunnis) of Baghdad against the Fatimid claim. See Michael Brett, "Abbasids, Fatimids and Seljuqs', in *The New Cambridge Medieval History*, Volume IV.

c. 1024–c. 1998 Part II, ed. D. Luscombe and J. Riley-Smith (Cambridge, 2004), p. 687.

7 See, e.g., D. Sourdel, 'al-Ḳādir Bi'llāh', *EI2*.

8 Ibn al-Jawzī, Abu'l-Faraj ʿAbd al-Raḥmān, *al-Muntaẓam fī ta'rīkh al-mulūk wa'l-umam*, ed. Muḥammad A. ʿAṭā and Muṣṭafā A. ʿAṭā (Beirut, 1412/1992), vol. 15, pp. 82–83.

9 Ibn al-Athīr, ʿIzz al-Dīn Abu'l-Ḥasan ʿAlī, *al-Kāmil fi'l-ta'rīkh*, ed. Muḥammad Yūsuf al-Daqqāq (Beirut, 1407/1987), vol. 6, pp. 447–448.

10 ʿAlā' al-Dīn ʿAṭā-Malik Juwaynī, *Ta'rīkh-i jahān-gushā*, tr. J.A. Boyle as *The History of the World-Conqueror* (Cambridge, MA, 1958), vol. 2, pp. 658–659.

11 Abu'l-Fidā, al-Malik al-Mu'ayyad ʿImād al-Dīn Ismāʿīl b. ʿAlī, *Mukhtaṣar ta'rīkh al-bashar* (Cairo, 1325/1907), pp. 142–143.

12 Ibn al-Kathīr, ʿImād al-Dīn Ismāʿīl b. ʿUmar, *al-Bidāya wa'l-nihāya*, ed. Ṣalāḥ Muḥammad al-Khaymī (2nd ed., Damascus, 2010), vol. 13, p. 9.

13 Al-Dhahabī, Shams al-Dīn Muḥammad b. Aḥmad, *Ta'rīkh al-Islām wa-wafayāt al-mashāhīr wa'l-aʿlām*, ed. ʿUmar ʿAbd al-Salām al-Tadmurī (Beirut, 1413/1993), vol. 28, p. 11.

14 Al-Ṣafadī, Ṣalāḥ al-Dīn Khalīl, *Kitāb al-wāfī bi'l-wafāyāt*, ed. Aḥmad Arnaʿūṭ and Turkī Muṣṭafā (Beirut, 1420/2000), vol. 19, p. 243.

15 Ibn Khaldūn, ʿAbd al-Raḥmān b. Muḥammad, *al-Muqaddima*, tr. Franz Rosenthal as *The Muqaddimah: An Introduction to History* (2nd ed., Princeton, 1980), vol. 1, p. 45. The Manifesto is also mentioned in the main body of Ibn Khaldūn's historical work. See his *Kitāb al-ʿibar*, ed. Khalīl Shaḥāda and Suhayl Zakkār as *Ta'rīkh Ibn Khaldūn* (Beirut, 1431/2001), vol. 3, p. 547.

16 Al-Maqrīzī, Taqī al-Dīn Aḥmad b. ʿAlī, *Ittiʿāẓ al-ḥunafā' bi-akhbār al-a'imma al-Fāṭimiyyīn al-khulafā'*, vol. 1, ed. Jamāl al-Dīn al-Shayyāl (Cairo, 1387/1967), pp. 43–44.

17 Ibn Taghrībirdī, Abu'l-Maḥāsin Jamāl al-Dīn Yūsuf, *al-Nujūm al-zāhira fī mulūk Miṣr wa'l-Qāhira* (Beirut, 1413/1992), vol. 4, p. 229.

18 Ibn Khaldūn, *al-Muqaddima*, tr. Rosenthal, vol. 1, p. 45, n. 129.

19 Ibn al-Kathīr's introductory passage is a summarised version of Ibn al-Jawzī as he himself notes at the end of his report on the Manifesto. It reads:

> And in Rabīʿ al-Ākhir of this year, written-declarations (*maḥāḍir*) were composed in Baghdad affirming the defamation (*al-ṭaʿn*) and public

> vilification *(qadḥ)* of the caliphs, that is, the kings (*mulūk*) of Egypt. They claim that they are Fāṭimiyyūn, but they are not so. Their lineage is from Dayṣān b. Saʿīd al-Khurramī. This was undersigned by a group of *ʿulamāʾ, quḍāt, fuqahāʾ*, the *ashrāf*, the *amthāl*, the *ḥadīth* transmitters, the legal witnesses, and the pious ones.

See Ibn Kathīr, *al-Bidāya*, vol. 13, pp. 9–10. The editors of this volume note that manuscripts of the *al-Bidāya* give ʿUbayd b. Saʿd al-Juramī instead of Dayṣān b. Saʿīd al-Khurramī. As it is unclear who this refers to, the editors corrected it to Dayṣān b. Saʿīd based on Ibn al-Jawzī's original. Ibid., vol. 13, p. 9, n. 2.

20 Al-Dhahabī's version begins: 'From the *dīwān* there was written a *maḥḍar* as to the substance (*maʿnā*) of the caliphs who were in Egypt, to publicly vilify their *nasab* and their creed (*ʿaqāʾidihim*).' al-Dhahabī, *Taʾrīkh*, vol. 28, p. 11. Ibn Taghrībirdī states: 'and in this year, in the month of Rabīʿ al-Ākhir, the ʿAbbāsid caliph al-Qādir wrote a *maḥḍar* as to the substance of the Egyptian caliphs, to publicly vilify their *nasab* and their creed.' Ibn Taghrībirdī, *al-Nujūm*, vol. 4, p. 229.

21 Al-Dhahabī, *Taʾrīkh*, vol. 28, p. 11, and Ibn Taghrībirdī, *al-Nujūm*, vol. 4, p. 229, only state 'and upon it were the signatures of *al-quḍāt waʾl-aʾimma waʾl-ashrāf*'.

22 Al-Dhahabī, *Taʾrīkh*, vol. 28, p. 11 and Ibn Taghrībirdī, *al-Nujūm*, vol. 4, p. 230, have *ikhwān* (the brothers of) rather than *aḥzāb* (the party of) – the orthography of *ikhwān* and *aḥzāb* without dots is similar, and these variants are probably a scribal error.

23 Al-Dhahabī, *Taʾrīkh*, vol. 28, p. 11, and Ibn Taghrībirdī, *al-Nujūm*, vol. 4, p. 230, only have: 'A testimony through which one seeks nearness to God.'

24 This *basmala* is found only in Juwaynī, *Jahān-gushā*, tr. Boyle, vol. 1, p. 659.

25 This addition about al-Muʿizz and Egypt is only noted in Juwaynī, ibid.

26 In this specific location, this segment is found only in Juwaynī, *Jahān-gushā*, tr. Boyle, vol. 1, p. 659. However, it is found in the main body of the text in Ibn al-Jawzī et al.

27 Boyle's translation from Juwaynī's Persian has 'this upstart in Egypt': Juwaynī, *Jahān-gushā*, tr. Boyle.

28 Ibn Kathīr, *al-Bidāya*, vol. 13, p. 10, omits 'of his foul and impure predecessors'.

29 Al-Dhahabī, *Ta'rīkh*, vol. 28, p. 11, and Ibn Taghrībirdī, *al-Nujūm*, vol. 4, p. 230, only have 'curses upon him and them.'

30 Only Ibn al-Jawzī, *al-Muntaẓam*, vol. 15, p. 83, and Ibn Kathīr, *al-Bidāya*, vol. 13, p. 10, have 'nor do they … falsehood.'

31 Al-Dhahabī, *Ta'rīkh*, vol. 28, p. 11, and Ibn Taghrībirdī, *al-Nujūm*, vol. 4, p. 230, only have 'of the Ṭālibids'.

32 'Concerning their false claims' is not in Ibn Kathīr, *al-Bidāya*, vol. 13, p. 10. Similarly, 'concerning their lies and false claims' is not in al-Dhahabī, *Ta'rīkh*, vol. 28, p. 11, and Ibn Taghrībirdī, *al-Nujūm*, vol. 4, p. 230.

33 *Muʿaṭṭil* here refers to the denial of God and of His attributes. See Juwaynī, *Jahān-gushā*, tr. Boyle, vol. 1, p. 660, n. 9. It is thus a shorthand for 'materialists' who deny God.

34 The order of invectives changes slightly across the variant sources though remaining generally stable. Abu'l-Fidā, *Mukhtaṣar*, vol. 2, p. 142, Juwaynī, *Jahān-gusha*, tr. Boyle, vol. 1, p. 660, and al-Maqrīzī, *Ittiʿāẓ*, vol. 1, p. 44, omit *fujjār*. Al-Dhahabī, *Ta'rīkh*, vol. 28, p. 12, does not have *fujjār, mulḥidūn, muʿaṭṭalūn*, while Ibn Taghrībirdī, *al-Nujūm*, vol. 4, p. 230, omits only *mulḥidūn*.

35 The editors of this edition of Ibn Taghrībirdī note that their manuscripts of the *al-Nujūm* have *Yahūdiyya* (Jews) instead of *Thanawiyya* (Dualists) but they adjusted it to correspond with Ibn al-Jawzī. Ibn Taghrībirdī, *al-Nujūm*, vol. 4, p. 230, n. 6.

36 Literally 'made available the orifices'.

37 'Permitting drink' is omitted in Ibn Taghrībirdī, *al-Nujūm*, vol. 4, p. 230.

38 Abu'l-Fidā, *Mukhtaṣar*, vol. 2, p. 142, Juwaynī, *Jahān-gusha*, tr. Boyle, vol. 1, p. 660, and al-Maqrīzī, *Ittiʿāẓ*, vol. 1, p. 44, omit 'cursed the *salaf*'.

39 Both al-Murtaḍā and al-Raḍī are mentioned in Ibn al-Jawzī, *al-Muntaẓam*, vol. 15, p. 83; Ibn al-Athīr, *al-Kāmil*, vol. 6, p. 448; Juwaynī, *Jahān-gusha*, tr. Boyle, vol. 1, p. 660; Ibn Kathīr, *al-Bidāya*, vol. 13, p. 9; al-Dhahabī, *Ta'rīkh*, vol. 28, p. 12; al-Ṣafadī, *al-Wāfī*, vol. 19, p. 243; Ibn Khaldūn, *al-Muqaddima* tr. Rosenthal, vol. 1, p. 46; Ibn Taghrībirdī, *al-Nujūm*, vol. 4, p. 230.

40 Ibn al-Jawzī, *al-Muntaẓam*, vol. 15, p. 83; Ibn al-Athīr, *al-Kāmil*, vol. 6, p. 448; Ibn Kathīr, *al-Bidāya*, vol. 13, p. 9; al-Dhahabī, *Ta'rīkh*, vol. 28, p. 12; Ibn Taghrībirdī, *al-Nujūm*, vol. 4, p. 230.

41 Ibn al-Jawzī, *al-Muntaẓam*, vol. 15, p. 83; Ibn Kathīr, *al-Bidāya*, vol. 13, p. 9.

42 The editions of the extant sources differ as to whether Muḥammad b. Muḥammad b. ʿUmar and Ibn Abī Yaʿlā are two separate persons, as in Ibn al-Jawzī, *al-Muntaẓam*, vol. 15, p. 83; Ibn Kathīr, *al-Bidāya*, pp. 9–10, or if Ibn Abī Yaʿla is the name of father of the former, as in al-Dhahabī, *Taʾrīkh*, vol. 28, p. 12; Ibn Taghrībirdī, *al-Nujūm*, vol. 4, pp. 230–231.

43 Only given in Ibn al-Athīr, *al-Kāmil*, vol. 6, p. 448 and Ibn Khaldūn, *al-Muqaddima* tr. Rosenthal, vol. 1, p. 45.

44 Ibn al-Jawzī, *al-Muntaẓam*, vol. 15, p. 83; Ibn al-Athīr, *al-Kāmil*, vol. 6, p. 448; Juwaynī, *Jahān-gusha*, tr. Boyle, vol. 1, p. 660; Ibn Kathīr, *al-Bidāya*, vol. 13, p. 9; al-Dhahabī, *Taʾrīkh*, vol. 28, p. 12; Ibn Khaldūn, *al-Muqaddima* tr. Rosenthal, vol. 1, p. 45; Ibn Taghrībirdī, *al-Nujūm*, vol. 4, p. 231.

45 Ibn al-Jawzī, Ibn al-Athīr, Ibn Kathīr, al-Dhahabī and Ibn Taghrībirdī oscillate between al-Khazarī, al-Jazarī and even al-Ḥarīrī. For a discussion of the possible identity of this individual, see the section on the signatories of the Manifesto above.

46 Ibn al-Jawzī, *al-Muntaẓam*, vol. 15, p. 83. Other sources call him al-Abiwardī. See Ibn al-Athīr, *al-Kāmil*, vol. 6, p. 448, Ibn Kathīr, *al-Bidāya*, vol. 13, p. 10 and Ibn Khaldūn, *al-Muqaddima* tr. Rosenthal, vol. 1, p. 45.

47 Ibn al-Jawzī, *al-Muntaẓam*, vol. 15, p. 83; Ibn al-Athīr, *al-Kāmil*, vol. 6, p. 448; Juwaynī, *Jahān-gusha*, tr. Boyle, vol. 1, p. 660; Ibn Kathīr, *al-Bidāya*, vol. 13, p. 9; al-Dhahabī, *Taʾrīkh*, vol. 28, p. 12; al-Ṣafadī, *al-Wāfī*, vol. 19, p. 243; Ibn Khaldūn, *al-Muqaddima* tr. Rosenthal, vol. 1, p. 45; Ibn Taghrībirdī, *al-Nujūm*, vol. 4, p. 231.

48 Ibn al-Jawzī, *al-Muntaẓam*, vol. 15, p. 83; Ibn al-Athīr, *al-Kāmil*, vol. 6, p. 448; Ibn Kathīr, *al-Bidāya*, vol. 13, p. 9; al-Dhahabī, *Taʾrīkh*, vol. 28, p. 12; Ibn Taghrībirdī, *al-Nujūm*, vol. 4, p. 231.

49 Ibn al-Jawzī, *al-Muntaẓam*, vol. 15, p. 83; Juwaynī, *Jahān-gusha*, tr. Boyle, vol. 1, p. 660; Ibn al-Athīr, *al-Kāmil*, vol. 6, p. 448; Ibn Kathīr, *al-Bidāya*, vol. 13, p. 9; al-Dhahabī, *Taʾrīkh*, vol. 28, p. 12; al-Ṣafadī, *al-Wāfī*, vol. 19, p. 243; Ibn Khaldūn, *al-Muqaddima* tr. Rosenthal, vol. 1, p. 46; Ibn Taghrībirdī, *al-Nujūm*, vol. 4, p. 231.

50 Ibn al-Jawzī, *al-Muntaẓam*, vol. 15, p. 83; Ibn al-Athīr, *al-Kāmil*, vol. 6, p. 448; Ibn Kathīr, *al-Bidāya*, vol. 13, p. 9; al-Dhahabī, *Taʾrīkh*, vol. 28, p. 12; Ibn Khaldūn, *al-Muqaddima* tr. Rosenthal, vol. 1, p. 46; Ibn Taghrībirdī, *al-Nujūm*, vol. 4, p. 230.

51 Only in Ibn al-Jawzī, *al-Muntaẓam*, vol. 15, p. 83; Juwaynī, *Jahān-gusha*, tr. Boyle, vol. 1, p. 660; Ibn Kathīr, *al-Bidāya*, vol. 13, p. 9.

52 Ibn al-Jawzī, *al-Muntaẓam*, vol. 15, p. 83; Ibn Kathīr, *al-Bidāya*, vol. 13, p. 9; al-Dhahabī, *Ta'rīkh*, vol. 28, p. 12; Ibn Taghrībirdī, *al-Nujūm*, vol. 4, p. 230.

53 Ibn al-Jawzī, *al-Muntaẓam*, vol. 15, p. 83; Ibn Kathīr, *al-Bidāya*, vol. 13, p. 9; al-Dhahabī, *Ta'rīkh*, vol. 28, p. 12; Ibn Taghrībirdī, *al-Nujūm*, vol. 4, p. 231.

54 Ibn al-Athīr, *al-Kāmil*, vol. 6, pp. 448–449.

55 He is referred to as Abū ʿAbd Allāh b. al-Nuʿmān, *faqīh* of the Shiʿa. See Ibn al-Athīr, *al-Kāmil*, vol. 6, p. 449; Abu'l-Fidā, *Mukhtaṣar*, vol. 2, p. 141; Ibn Khaldūn, *al-Muqaddima* tr. Rosenthal, vol. 1, p. 46.

56 See the introductory segments to the Manifesto in Ibn al-Athīr, *al-Kāmil*, vol. 6, p. 447 and Ibn Khaldūn, *al-Muqaddima* tr. Rosenthal, vol. 1, p. 45.

57 For a masterly survey of the evolution of doctrines on succession and the Imamate in early Ismaili history, see Wilferd Madelung, 'Das Imamat in der frühen ismailitischen Lehre', *Der Islam*, 37 (1961), pp. 43–135; reprinted in his *Studies on Medieval Shiʿism*, ed. S. Schmidtke (Farnham, Surrey, 2012), article VII.

58 More extensive expositions on the Fatimid notion of the imamate are provided in Daftary, *Ismāʿīlīs*, pp. 163–167; Brett, *Rise*, pp. 176–219; Heinz Halm, *The Empire of the Mahdi: The Rise of the Fatimids*, tr. M. Bonner (Leiden, 1996), pp. 346–355.

59 The question of the name of the dynasty and whether or not the Fatimids identified themselves by that appellation have been discussed in recent scholarship. Fierro's survey indicated that the term 'Fāṭimī' was not readily used by the leading authorities of the dynasty. See Maribel Fierro, 'On *al-Fāṭimī* and *al-Fāṭimiyyūn*', *Jerusalem Studies in Arabic and Islam*, 20 (1996), pp. 130–161. Walker points out that more recent scholarship has established that the term came into progressively increasing use during the history of the dynasty, so that 'by the end of the dynasty it was fairly common to call it *al-dawla al-fāṭimiyya* ("the Fatimid state" or "the Fatimid dynasty"), and thus later authors grew quite accustomed to the term.' He also adds that the terms *al-imām al-fāṭimī* and *al-fāṭimiyyīn* also appear in some early pro-Fatimid poetry, and in an occasional *khuṭba*. *Orations*, pp. 69–72.

60 Wilferd Madelung has argued that it was Fāṭima who was regarded as the true legal heir to the Prophet in the earliest phase of Muslim history. He bases his argument on Qur'anic regulations where the 'universally binding laws of inheritance' gave 'unconditional

precedence to direct descendants', and according to which, 'in the absence of a son, a daughter or daughters were sole primary heirs and could not be excluded by any rights of male kin'. 'Introduction', in F. Daftary and G. Miskinzoda, ed., *The Study of Shi'i Islam: History, Theology and Law* (London, 2014), pp. 3–16, p. 4. Considering the Qur'anic outlawing of adoption and the recognition of only blood relationships, Madelung argues that 'under the divine law of the Qur'an, Fāṭima was the Prophet's prime heiress and successor' (ibid., pp. 4–5). He adds that the crisis after the Prophet's death was brought on, 'by the exceptional circumstance that the legitimate successor to supreme leadership was a woman' and that the 'Caliphate of the Quraysh must be judged to have been a *coup d'état* in which the ruling house was overthrown'. 'Alī's position in this schema of succession was of a potential, though not confirmed, executor (*waṣī*) of the Prophet's will (ibid., pp. 5–7).

61 Qāḍī al-Nuʿmān, *Iftitāḥ al-daʿwa*, tr. Hamid Haji as *Founding the Fatimid State: The Rise of an Early Islamic Empire* (London, 2006), p. 178, p. 205.

62 Al-Muʿizz pronounced prayers for the 'rightly-guided imams' from the Prophet's family, who were elevated by their 'forefathers Muḥammad, the lord of the messengers, and 'Alī, the best of the legatees, and through their mother, the foremost of women, the fifth of the Companions of the Cloak'. Idrīs 'Imād al-Dīn, *'Uyūn al-akhbār*, trans., p. 71.

63 For Jawhar's inclusion of Fāṭima's name in the invocation of the public sermons of Egypt, see Idrīs 'Imād al-Dīn, *'Uyūn al-akhbār*, trans., pp. 230–231; al-Maqrīzī, *Ittiʿāẓ*, vol. 1, p. 117. See the translation of al-Maqrīzī's chapter on the reign of al-Muʿizz in the *Ittiʿāẓ* by Shainool Jiwa as *Towards a Shi'i Mediterranean Empire: Fatimid Egypt and the Founding of Cairo* (London, 2009), pp. 83–84.

64 For the Fatimid coin which declared "Alī b. Abī Ṭālib is the nominee of the Prophet and the most excellent representative and the husband of the radiant chaste one (*zawj al-zahrā' al-batūl*)', see W. Kazan, *The Coinage of Islam: Collection of William Kazan* (Beirut, 1983), no. 446.

65 Brett, *Rise*, p. 316.

66 See, for instance, al-Mahdī described in Abū 'Abd Allāh's message from Sijilmāsa to Qayrawān as 'son of the Messenger of God (*ibn rasūl Allāh*)'. Al-Nuʿmān, *Iftitāḥ*, trans., pp. 199–200. Note also, for

instance, the verses of Ibn Hāniʾ referring to the Prophet Muḥammad as al-Muʿizz's grandfather. Idrīs ʿImād al-Dīn, *ʿUyūn al-akhbār*, tr. Jiwa, p. 225.

67 On al-Muʿizz's reference to 'our grandfather, Muḥammad' in his correspondence with the Egyptian ruler Kāfūr al-Ikhshīdī see Idrīs ʿImād al-Dīn, *ʿUyūn al-akhbār*, tr. Jiwa, p. 184. In his first audience with the Egyptian notables, al-Muʿizz declared that he wanted to 'act upon what his grandfather had commanded' (ibid., p. 261).

68 In his eulogy to his deceased father al-Manṣūr, al-Muʿizz promised to safeguard the community 'of your grandfather, God's Messenger' (ibid., p. 73).

69 See, for example, al-Muʿizz's pronouncement on the eve of the state-sponsored circumcision ceremonies in North Africa that he wanted 'to revive the practise of our grandfather, His Messenger' (ibid., p. 172). Note elsewhere al-Nuʿmān stating that al-Muʿizz was the 'reviver of his grandfather's practice' (ibid., p. 83).

70 In al-Muʿizz's audience with the Idrīsids, he said: 'Who will you substitute for us? Whose *daʿwa* will you choose over ours, for this is the *daʿwa* of our grandfather Muḥammad?' (ibid., pp. 149–150).

71 Patricia Crone, *Medieval Islamic Political Thought* (Edinburgh, 2004), p. 89.

72 On the *dawr al-satr* and the Ismaili *daʿwa* activities during this period, see Daftary, *Ismāʿīlīs*, pp. 87–128.

73 For an overview of the origins and evolution of anti-Fatimid and anti-Ismaili propaganda, see Daftary, *Ismāʿīlīs*, pp. 7–10 as well as the introduction in Daftary, *Assassin Legends*, pp. 1–8.

74 Daftary argues that, as the most revolutionary wing of Shiʿism, the Ismailis 'from early on aroused the hostility of the ʿAbbāsid-Sunnī establishment of the Muslim majority'. Subsequently, 'the ʿAbbāsid Caliphs and the Sunnī *ʿulamāʾ* launched what amounted to an official anti-Ismaili propaganda campaign' whose aim was to discredit the Ismaili movement as heretics and deviators, a campaign which saw the participation of 'Muslim theologians, jurists, historians and heresiographers'. See Daftary, *Ismāʿīlīs*, p. 7.

75 Al-Ṭabarī's entry for 302/914–915 states that 'Ibn al-Baṣrī's man Ḥabāsah' entered Alexandria. See, *The History of al-Ṭabarī: Volume XXXVIII; The Return of the Caliphate to Baghdad*, tr. F. Rosenthal (New York, 1985), p. 205. Similarly, his entry for the year 301/913–914,

states that 'in this year, Ibn al-Baṣrī's Maghrībīs entered Barqah' (ibid., p. 202).

76 As noted by Madelung, 'Das Imamat', pp. 67–68.

77 'Arīb b. Sa'd, *Ṣilat ta'rīkh al-Ṭabarī*, ed. M. J. de Goeje (Leiden, 1897), p. 51.

78 Ibid., pp. 51–52.

79 See Madelung, 'Das Imamat', pp. 67–68. For the account, see Ibn al-Abbār, *al-Ḥulla al-siyarā'*, p. 49.

80 F. Rosenthal, 'Ibn Abī Ṭāhir Ṭayfūr', *EI2*. On the more famous father, see Shawkat M. Toorawa, *Ibn Abī Ṭāhir Ṭayfūr and Arabic Writerly Culture: A Ninth-Century Bookman in Baghdad* (London, 2005).

81 'Ubayd Allāh b. Abī Ṭāhir's version, as given in Ibn al-Abbār, says: 'The name of the one who emerged in Qayrawān is 'Ubayd Allāh b. 'Abd Allāh b. Sālim, *mawlā* of Mukram b. Sindān al-Bāhilī, the chief of the police of Ziyād and the one after whom 'Askar Mukram is named. 'Abd Allāh b. Sālim went to Salamiyya. He was an agent for merchants there, and it is said that he used to sell stones and [manifest] Shi'ism. When the Qarmaṭīs revolted in Syria, he was affected by him, seeking him out. So he ['Ubayd Allāh] went to the Maghrib and was known as Ibn al-Baṣrī.' See Ibn al-Abbār, *al-Ḥulla al-siyarā'*, p. 49.

82 Notably in al-Ḥimyari's (d. ca. 8th/14th century) *al-Rawḍ al-mu'ṭār fī khabar al-aqṭār*, another quotation directly from al-Ṣūlī is provided in which the accusation that his ancestor was executed for *zandaqa* is given. Thus al-Ṣūlī is quoted as saying: 'His father is 'Abd Allāh b. Sālim b. 'Abdān al-Bāhilī: his grandfather Sālim was crucified by al-Mahdī al-'Abbāsī because of his *zandaqa*, as was said by those people who had investigated (*faḥaṣū*) his affair.' See, *al-Rawḍ*, ed. Iḥṣān 'Abbās (Beirut, 1980), p. 308.

83 Ibn Rizām's work is not extant, but segments of his work are found in the *Fihrist* of Ibn al-Nadīm, and it also served as the main source for Akhū Muḥsin's work. See Daftary, *Ismā'īlīs*, pp. 8–9.

84 For a detailed exposition of the legend of Maymūn al-Qaddāḥ as the progenitor of the Fatimids and the role of Ibn Rizām and Akhū Muḥsin in propagating this myth, see Wladimir Ivanow, *Ibn al-Qaddah (The Alleged Founder of Ismailism)* (2nd ed., Bombay, 1957). Ivanow notes: 'One of the most extraordinary products of

anti-Ismaili propaganda is what may be called the myth of 'Abdu'l-lāh b. Maymūn al-Qaddāḥ' (ibid., p. i). He continues that the story of Ibn al-Qaddāh 'in its innumerable versions ... is nothing but an aetiological myth' (ibid., p. 2); but one that while 'incidentally invented' was 'later on gradually developed and polished in the course of long oral or written transmission, in the service of anti-Fatimid propaganda' (ibid.).

85 Ibn al-Nadīm, Muḥammad b. Isḥāq, *Kitāb al-Fihrist*, tr. Bayard Dodge as *The Fihrist: A Tenth Century Survey of Muslim Culture* (New York, 1970), vol. 1, p. 463.

86 Ibid., p. 465.

87 On Akhū Muḥsin, see Daftary, *Ismāʿīlīs*, pp. 8–10; Samuel M. Stern, 'The "Book of the Highest Initiation" and Other Anti-Ismāʿīlī Travesties', in his *Studies in Early Ismāʿīlism* (Jerusalem and Leiden, 1983), pp. 56–83; Wilferd Madelung, 'The Fatimids and the Qarmaṭīs of Baḥrayn', in F. Daftary, ed., *Mediaeval Ismaʿili History and Thought* (Cambridge, 1996), p. 42.

88 Madelung, 'Das Imamat', p. 58.

89 Stern, 'The Book of the Highest Initiation', p. 57.

90 Madelung, 'Das Imamat', p. 113.

91 See, Ibn al-Nadīm, *Fihrist*, tr. Bayard Dodge, p. 466.

92 Ibid.

93 The stigma of having been thus placed in the caliphate by a Shiʿi amir had plagued al-Qādir's early caliphate especially in lands outside Būyid rule. Ardent Sunni dynasties such as the Sāmānids and the Ghaznawids continued to produce coinage for al-Qādir's deposed predecessor al-Ṭāʾiʿ until around 390/1000. See K.V. Zettersteen [C.E. Bosworth]), 'al-Ṭāʾiʿ Li-Amr Allāh', *EI2*. The Fatimid *dāʿīs* in Iraq also capitalised on this to undermine al-Qādir's credentials.

94 John J. Donohue, *The Buwayhid Dynasty in Iraq: 334H./945 to 403H./102 – Shaping Institutions for the Future* (Leiden and Boston, 2003), p. 279. For an overview of the impact and legacy of the reign of the Abbasid al-Qādir, see Kennedy, *Age of the Caliphates*, pp. 241–242; Donohue, *Buwayhid*, pp. 277–288; D. Sourdel, 'al-Ḳādir Biʾllāh', *EI2*.

95 Donohue, *Buwayhid*, p. 279.

96 Kennedy, *Age of the Caliphates*, p. 242.

97 For an overview of the fractiousness of the post-3rd/9th century Abbasid polity, see Kennedy, *Age of the Caliphates*, pp. 187–212.

98 Note, however, Donohue's assertion that this isolation of the Abbasid caliphs by the Būyid amirs ultimately gave individual Abbasid caliphs security and a long reign as contrasted to those who preceded them. See Donohue, *Buwayhid*, pp. 262–263.

99 For a summary of the role of the Abbasids in the legitimisation of the Būyid system, which included the Abbasid official investiture of Būyid amirs, the granting of their titles and the approval of treaties see Donohue, *Buwayhid*, pp. 264–267.

100 Ibid., p. 278.

101 Ibid., pp. 278–281.

102 Kennedy notes that while the people of Baghdad 'might not fight to restore the political power of the 'Abbāsid caliph but many of them would support the Sunni cause against the pretensions of the Shia': Kennedy, *Age of the Caliphates*, p. 242.

103 Kennedy, *Age of Caliphates*, p. 242; Sourdel, 'al-Ḳādir', *EI2*.

104 Kennedy, *Age of the Caliphates*, p. 242. Kennedy here argues that Abbasid caliphs before al-Qādir cannot be described as Sunni 'in the modern sense' because of their emphasis on legitimisation through the *ahl al-bayt* and their Mu'tazilī leanings.

105 Ḥanbalī ideology became orientated to support the caliph. See Donohue, *Buwayhid*, p. 286.

106 Recent scholarship has explored the dynamics that gave rise to the 'Alid *ashrāf*, the name given to the collective descendants of al-Ḥasan and al-Ḥusayn b. 'Alī b. Abī Ṭālib, as a defined social group with institutional leadership. For a recent overview of this, see Shainool Jiwa, 'Kinship, Camaraderie and Contestation: Fāṭimid Relations with the Ashrāf in the Fourth/Tenth Century', *Al-Masāq*, 28 (2016), pp. 242–264. This article examines, in particular, the dynamics of Fatimid-*ashrāf* relations in 4th/10th century Egypt and the Ḥijāz.

107 The religious leanings of the *ashrāf* remained diverse, belonging to the varied Shi'i and Sunni traditions. They included several notable Sunni scholars, and many belonged to the Zaydī Shi'a. See Jiwa, 'Kinship', p. 247.

108 The Qur'anic verses adducing this prerogative of the Prophet are discussed in Roy Mottahedeh, 'Qurānic Commentary on the Verse of the Khums (an-Anfāl VIII:41)', in K. Morimoto, ed., *Sayyids and Sharifs in Muslim Socities: The Living Links to the Prophet* (London, 2012), pp. 37–48.

109 See Jiwa, 'Kinship', p. 245 and the references cited there.

110 For a detailed examination of reasons underpinning the alliances as well as rivalries between the Fatimids and the *ashrāf*, see ibid., pp. 247–249.

111 Ibid., pp. 252–259.

112 Ibid., pp. 251–252.

113 Abū Aḥmad's full lineage was Abū Aḥmad Ḥusayn b. Mūsā b. Muḥammad b. Mūsā b. Ibrāhīm b. Mūsā al-Kāẓim b. Jaʿfar al-Ṣādiq. See the entry on Sharīf al-Raḍī in Ibn Khallikān, *Wafayāt al-aʿyān*, ed. Iḥsān ʿAbbās (Beirut, 1967–1972), tr. M. de Slane as *Ibn Khallikān's Biographical Dictionary* (Paris, 1842–1871), vol. 3, p. 120.

114 Donohue, *Buwayhid*, p. 309.

115 As a Shiʿi Imāmī scholar and renowned literary figure of the 5th/11th century living in Iraq, Sharīf al-Raḍī has received extensive coverage in medieval Sunni and Shiʿi, as well as in contemporary scholarship. For major primary and secondary accounts, see the bibliography in Moktar Djebli, 'al-Sharīf al-Raḍī', *EI2*.

116 Both brothers were placed under the tutelage of the pre-eminent Iraqi Shiʿi scholar Shaykh al-Mufīd. Among the prose works of Sharīf al-Raḍī is his famed and widely reproduced *Nahj al-balāgha*, an anthology of sermons and sayings attributed to ʿAlī b. Abī Ṭālib. Sharīf al-Murtaḍā was an eminent Ithnā ʿasharī scholar and teacher of his age. See C. Brockelmann, 'al-Sharīf al-Murtaḍā', EI2.

117 See al-Thaʿālabī and al-Khaṭīb al-Baghdādī as cited in Ibn Khallikān, *Wafāyāt*, tr. de Slane, vol. 3, pp. 119, 121 and Ibn al-Jawzī, *al-Muntaẓam*, vol. 15, p. 116. Cross-sectional support for al-Raḍī is manifest in the highly eulogised and almost hagiographic coverage of his life by Sunni contemporaries. Ibn al-Jawzī, for instance, recounts al-Raḍī's piety and scholarship, provides anecdotes on his moral rectitude and generosity, before recounting praise for his poetry. See Ibn al-Jawzī, *al-Muntaẓām*, vol. 15, pp. 115–116. Ibn Khallikān follows suit, and praises al-Raḍī's work on the literary features of the Qurʾan: see Ibn Khallikān, *Wafayāt*, tr. de Slane, vol. 3, pp. 118–123.

118 On the granting of this title as well as that of al-Murtaḍā to his brother, see Ibn al-Athīr, *al-Kāmil*, vol. 8, p. 36. His other titles include al-Sharīf al-Jalīl granted in 388/988, and al-Sharīf al-Ajall in 401/1001. See Djebli, 'al-Raḍī', *EI2*.

119 As repeatedly asserted by his biographers, including the famous Muʿtazilī scholar and litterateur Ibn Abiʾl-Ḥadīd (d. ca. 655–656/

1257–1258). Djebli notes that this aspiration is expressed 'unequivocally' in Sharīf al-Raḍī's verses. 'Al-Raḍī', *EI2*. Donohue notes, however, that this question has 'prompted discussion on how an Imamite could ambition a position in direct conflict with his tenets'. See, *Buwayhid*, p. 312, n. 1490 for further references on discussions on al-Raḍī's ambition.

120 Ibn al-Athīr, *al-Kāmil*, vol. 8, p. 24.

121 The verses read: 'Alas, Amīr of the Believers! We are equal, at the summit of glory … Only the caliphate, of which you hold the reins, separates us': Djebli, 'al-Raḍī', *EI2*. De Slane in his translation of Ibn Khallikān's entry on Sharīf al-Raḍī provides an alternative translation of the same verses: 'I crave indulgence, Commander of the Faithful! We are not borne on different branches of the tree of glory! On whatever day we may vaunt our honours, no difference shall appear between us: we are both firmly rooted in our illustrious rank. The khalifate alone makes a distinction between us; you wear that noble collar, I do not': Ibn Khallikān, *Wafayāt*, tr. de Slane, vol. 3, p. 119.

122 For the fuller verses, see Ibn al-Jawzī, *al-Muntaẓam*, vol. 15, p. 118 and Ibn al-Athīr, *al-Kāmil*, vol. 6, pp. 446–447. Notably the 7th/15th-century Yemeni Ismaili historian and Ṭayyibī chief *dāʿī* Idrīs ʿImād al-Dīn also recounts a variant of these verses (note the term Fāṭimī instead of ʿAlawī), attributing them also to Sharīf al-Raḍī. See Idrīs ʿImād al-Dīn b. al-Ḥasan, *ʿUyūn al-akhbār*, tr. Jiwa, p. 263.

123 The variations mean that both the Hilāl al-Ṣābi' and the Ibn Jawzī/Ibn al-Athīr versions are relying on a common source or, as is more likely, they are based on a major rewriting of the Hilāl al-Ṣābi' original. Sharīf al-Raḍī was known to have been a particularly close friend of Hilāl al-Ṣābi''s grandfather, Abū Isḥāq Ibrāhīm. Djebli, 'al-Raḍī', *EI2*.

124 Al-Ṣābi''s account states that in a *majlis* of al-Qādir attended by Abū Aḥmad al-Mūsawī, his son al-Murtaḍā and other *ashrāf*, as well as judges and jurists, al-Qādir brought up the verses of al-Raḍī after which Abū Aḥmad was directly addressed by the court chamberlain (*ḥājib*). See al-Maqrīzī, *Ittiʿāẓ*, vol. 1, p. 33. In the later account of Ibn al-Jawzī as closely followed by Ibn al-Athīr, al-Qādir is informed of the verses and then becomes incensed, dispatches Qāḍī al-Bāqillānī with a letter to Abū Aḥmad al-Mūsawī, al-Raḍī's father. See Ibn al-Jawzī,

al-Muntaẓam, vol. 15, p. 118 and Ibn al-Athīr, *al-Kāmil*, vol. 6, p. 447.

125 In both accounts the spokesman (whether a *ḥājib* or al-Bāqillānī) rejects points raised in the pro-Fatimid verses of al-Raḍī, namely, what kind of humiliation was al-Raḍī referring to, had he not been given stewardship of the *niqāba*, the *ḥajj* (or as in Hilāl) the *maẓālim*. In Hilāl's version, the chamberlain says to Abū Aḥmad: 'We do not doubt that if he (al-Raḍī) were to reach him [the ruler of Egypt], he would merely have the status of one of the sons of the Ṭālibids in Egypt.' See, *Itti'āẓ*, vol. 1, p. 33. In Ibn al-Jawzī's version, al-Bāqillānī's letter asserts: 'If he were in Egypt, he would not be raised from the ranks of the subjects (*al-ra'iyya*)': *al-Muntaẓam*, vol. 15, p. 118.

126 Al-Ṣābi' has Abū Aḥmad denying al-Raḍī's authorship and mentions that his son's enemies may have done so, and ascribed them to him. *Itti'āẓ*, vol. 1, p. 33. Ibn al-Jawzī's version has a similar denial with a more elaborate admission of his son's recognition of the rights of the 'blessed *haḍra*', that is, the Abbasids and their own blessings stemming from them. *Al-Muntaẓam*, vol. 15, p. 119.

127 Al-Maqrīzī, *Itti'āẓ*, vol. 1, p. 33.

128 Ibn al-Jawzī, *al-Muntaẓam*, vol. 15, p. 119; Ibn al-Athīr, *al-Kāmil*, vol. 6, p. 447.

129 In al-Ṣābi', al-Raḍī writes a letter saying that it is not his poem (see al-Maqrīzī, *Itti'āz*, vol. 1, p. 34), while in Ibn al-Jawzī he says, 'I did not say these verses, nor do I know them': Ibn al-Jawzī, *al-Muntaẓam*, vol. 15, p. 119.

130 Thus: 'I fear the *dā'īs* of the ruler of Egypt' in al-Ṣābi' as quoted in al-Maqrīzī, *Itti'āẓ*, vol. 1, p. 33. Ibn al-Jawzī has al-Raḍī saying: 'I fear the Daylamīs, and the people of the *da'wa* in his land.' *Al-Muntaẓam*, vol. 15, p. 119. Ibn al-Athīr has: 'I fear the Daylamīs, and from the Egyptian I fear from the *dā'īs* in this land.' *Al-Kāmil*, vol. 6, p. 447. Both versions also project Abū Aḥmad's surprise that al-Raḍī fears the one who is distant (that is, al-Ḥākim), but not the one nearby (i.e., al-Qādir).

131 Al-Maqrīzī, *Itti'āẓ*, vol. 1, p. 34. Al-Ṣābi' adds here, however, that both al-Raḍī's father and his brother al-Murtaḍā did so in precautionary dissimulation (*taqiyya*) due to their fear of al-Qādir.

132 Ibn al-Jawzī, *al-Muntaẓam*, vol. 15, p. 119; Ibn al-Athīr, *al-Kāmil*, vol. 6, p. 447.

133 Ibn al-Jawzī adds that this was realised upon the intervention of al-Bāqillānī and al-Isfarā'inī. *Al-Muntaẓam*, vol. 15, p. 119.

134 Al-Maqrīzī, *Ittiʿāẓ*, vol. 1, p. 34.

135 Southern Iraq was particularly receptive to the Ismaili *daʿwa*, from where major early Ismaili *dāʿī*s, including Abū ʿAbd Allāh al-Shīʿī and Ibn Ḥawshab, entered the movement. The *sawād* region of Kūfa was also the locus of the Qarmaṭī Ismaili *daʿwa*, from where Ḥamdān Qarmāṭ led the movement. For a broader overview of *daʿwa* activities beyond the Fatimid realms, see Farhad Daftary, 'The Ismaili *Daʿwa* Outside the Fatimid *Dawla*', in M. Barrucand, ed., *L'Égypte Fatimide: Son art et son histoire* (Paris, 1999), pp. 29–43.

136 For an overview of this correspondence in the broader context of Fatimid-Būyid relations, see Shainool Jiwa, 'Fāṭimid-Būyid Diplomacy during the Reign of al-Azīz Billāh (365/975–386/996)', *Journal of Islamic Studies*, 3 (1992), pp. 57–71.

137 Varied accounts highlight the continued presence of pro-Fatimid *dāʿī*s in the 4th/10th century. In 315/927, as reported by Thābit b. Sinān, a Shīrāzī inhabitant of Baghdad declared his support for the Fatimid imam while on trial for Qarmaṭī links. See Madelung, 'Fatimids and the Qarmaṭīs', p. 41. Also see Donohue, *Buwayhid*, pp. 73–76.

138 The pre-eminent *dāʿī* of the era of the Fatimid imam-caliph al-Ḥākim, Ḥamīd al-Dīn Aḥmad b. ʿAbd Allāh al-Kirmānī was of Iranian origin and following his successful career as a leading *dāʿī* in Iraq was summoned to Cairo around 405/1014–1015 by the head of the *daʿwa*. Among the most prolific philosophers and theologians of the Fatimid age, al-Kirmānī's works cover a range of topics pertaining to Ismaili doctrine and philosophy. As well as his work on the Fatimid doctrine of the imamate discussed below, al-Kirmānī's works include *Mabāsim al-bishārāt bi'l-imām al-Ḥākim* and *al-Risāla al-wāʿiẓa*, written to articulate Fatimid doctrines on the imamate, but also to assert the official doctrines of the *daʿwa* in the light of claims made by dissident preachers who led the Druze movement. His magnum opus, *Rāḥat al-ʿaql*, composed after he returned to Iraq in 411/1020, provides a distinct metaphysical system, and is a milestone in the

development of medieval Ismaili cosmology. For a comprehensive biography of his life and scholarship, see Paul E. Walker, *Ḥamīd al-Dīn al-Kirmānī: Ismaili thought in the age of al-Ḥākim* (London, 1999). For a listing of his published works, see Daftary, *Ismaili Literature*, pp. 124–128. Also see Daniel de Smet, 'al-Kirmānī, Ḥamīd al-Dīn', *EI3*.

139 Walker, *al-Kirmānī*, p. 10.

140 De Smet, 'al-Kirmānī', *EI3*.

141 See Ḥamīd al-Dīn Aḥmad b. ʿAbd Allāh al-Kirmānī, *al-Maṣābīḥ fī ithbāt al-imāma*, ed. and tr. Paul E. Walker as *Master of the Age: An Islamic Treatise on the Necessity of the Imamate* (London, 2007).

142 See Walker, *al-Kirmānī*, pp. 14–15.

143 Al-Kirmānī, *al-Maṣābīḥ*, tr. Walker, p. 15.

144 Ibid.

145 Ibid., pp. 124–126.

146 Ibid.

147 Walker notes that on the subject of the Manifesto, 'al-Kirmānī seems to say nothing. In truth, the manifesto itself made so improbable a claim it was hardly credible. Those who signed could also insist they were coerced. It was in al-Kirmānī's interest not to make a point of it, especially as many leading Shiʿi authorities such as al-Raḍī and al-Murtaḍā were involved.' See al-Kirmānī, *Maṣābīḥ*, p. 17.

148 Kennedy, *Age of the Caliphates*, p. 225.

149 Ibid., p. 227.

150 Ibid., p. 229.

151 As Kennedy has demonstrated, integral to this rupture were the policies of the Būyid rulers which promoted the emergence of a distinct Shiʿi identity in the public sphere and the reaction of hostile Sunni elements to this. New elements in the public manifestation of Shiʿism in Iraq, as catalysed by Būyid rule, included notably the public performance of Shiʿi festivals such as ʿĀshūrā' on 10 Muḥarram and Ghadīr Khumm on 18 Dhu'l-Ḥijjā; the public cursing of the early caliphs and the development of public pilgrimage rituals around the tombs of the ʿAlids. See Kennedy, *Age of the Caliphates*, p. 228. In 351/962 Muʿizz al-Dawla gave orders that the public cursing of the first caliphs was to be painted on the city walls. In 353/964 he supported the performance of ʿĀshūrā' and Ghadīr Khumm ceremonies.

152 Donohue, *Buwayhid*, pp. 270–280.
153 Kennedy, *Age of the Caliphates*, pp. 231–235.
154 'Aḍud al-Dawla forbade 'inflammatory preaching', while Bahā' al-Dawla placed 'special stress on the abolition of provocative activities' and had the leading 'brigands' of the Abbasid and 'Alid factions executed. See Kennedy, *Age of the Caliphates*, pp. 236–237.
155 For varied accounts of this event, see Donohue, *Buwayhid*, p. 284; Walker, *al-Kirmānī*, p. 14. For a description of the event as described in a survey of the life and scholarship of Shaykh al-Mufīd, see Martin J. McDermott, *The Theology of al-Shaikh al-Mufīd* (d. 413/1022) (Beirut, 1978), pp. 18–19.
156 Ibn al-Jawzī accounts for two major flashpoints in the lead-up to the confrontation. First was an attack against the leading Iraqi Shi'i jurist, Shaykh Abū 'Abd Allāh Muḥammad b. al-Nu'mān [Shaykh al-Mufīd] which led to an angry reaction by his Shi'i supporters in Karkh who, in turn, led attacks against two Shāfi'ī scholars al-Akfānī and al-Isfarā'ini. Notably all three are listed among alleged signatories of the Manifesto. Secondly, these events were compounded by the burning of the *Muṣḥaf* of Ibn Mas'ūd, a variant Qur'anic recension, and the execution of a Shi'i who had publicly decried the burning, which further incensed the Shi'a in Baghdad. See Ibn al-Jawzī, *al-Muntaẓam*, vol. 15, pp. 58–59.
157 Ibn al-Jawzī reports: 'This [matter] reached the caliph, who was angered. He dispatched the guards at his gates to go in aid of the *ahl al-sunna*, and so the *ghilmān* helped them. The people of Karkh were weakened and the area beside Nahr al-Dajāj was set alight. Then the *ashrāf* and the merchants gathered at the gate of the caliph seeking forgiveness for what the rabble had done so he forgave them': *al-Muntaẓam*, vol. 15, pp. 59–60. As Donohoue notes: 'It is easy to imagine the fright which seized the Caliph' upon hearing the 'shibboleth of the Fatimid ruler': Donohue, *Buwayhid*, p. 284.
158 See C. E. Bosworth, 'Uḳaylids', *EI2*.
159 Kennedy, *Age of the Caliphates*, p. 295. On the political history of the Mazyadids, see C.E. Bosworth, 'Mazyad', *EI2*.
160 As Kennedy notes, with their 'power dependent on their tribal following' the rulers of the Bedouin principalities 'remained first and foremost Bedouin shaykhs even when they acquired the rights to collect taxes from settled areas and cities': Kennedy, *Age of the Caliphates*, p. 285.

161 The transfer of Qirwāsh b. al-Muqallid's allegiance is widely reported to have taken place in the year 401 [1010]. See Ibn al-Jawzī, *al-Muntaẓam*, vol. 15, pp. 74–77; Ibn al-Athīr, *al-Kāmil*, vol. 8, pp. 63–66; al-Maqrīzī, *Ittiʿāẓ*, vol. 2, p. 88. For discussion of Qirwāsh's allegiance also see Daftary, *Ismāʿīlīs*, p. 185; Walker, *al-Kirmānī*, p. 14; Walker, *Orations*, p. 3; Assaad, *al-Hakim*, pp. 111–112.
162 See Daftary, *Ismāʿīlīs*, p. 185; Assad, *al-Hakim*, pp. 111–112.
163 Walker, *Orations*, p. 3.
164 Ibid., p. 141. For the full text of the *khuṭba* of Qirwāsh, as transmitted, see Ibn al-Jawzī, *al-Muntaẓam*, vol. 15, pp. 74–77, and for an English translation, see Walker, *Orations*, pp. 138–141.
165 Al-Qādir reportedly dispatched Qāḍī al-Bāqillānī to the Būyid ruler Bahāʾ al-Dawla to deflect the threat. Bahāʾ raised a sum of 100,000 dinars either as a reward for Qirwāsh for renouncing the *khuṭba*, or to raise an army. Walker, *Orations*, p. 4.
166 Ibn al-Jawzī, *al-Muntaẓam*, vol. 15, p. 83 and Juwaynī, *Jahān-gushā*, tr. Boyle, vol. 1, p. 660.
167 Ibn ʿInaba, Jamāl al-Dīn Aḥmad b. ʿAlī, *ʿUmdat al-ṭālib fī ansāb āl Abī Ṭālib*, ed. Muḥammad Ḥusayn al-Ṭāliqānī (Najaf, 1380/1961), p. 323. The fullest lineage of Muḥammad al-Ashtar thus extracted from Ibn ʿInāba would be: Muḥammad al-Ashtar b. ʿUbayd Allāh al-Thālith b. ʿAlī b. ʿUbayd Allāh al-Thānī b. ʿAlī al-Ṣāliḥ b. ʿUbayd Allāh al-Aʿraj b. al-Ḥusayn al-Aṣghar b. ʿAlī Zayn al-ʿĀbidīn. Ibid., pp. 318–323.
168 Ibid., pp. 323 ff.
169 Abū ʿAbd Allāh Aḥmad is said to have led thirteen pilgrimages as *amīr al-ḥajj*, the deputy of Abū Aḥmad al-Mūsawī, and also served as the *naqīb* of Kūfa. Ibid., p. 328.
170 On him and his descendants, see ibid., p. 326.
171 The progenitor is Muḥammad al-Buṭḥanī b. al-Qāsim b. al-Ḥasan b. Zayd b. al-Ḥasan b. al-Ḥasan b. ʿAlī b. Abī Ṭālib. See ibid., pp. 72 ff.
172 See Wilferd Madelung, 'The Minor Dynasties of Northern Iran', in Richard N. Frye, ed., *The Cambridge History of Iran*, Volume 4: *The Period from the Arab Invasions to the Saljuqs* (Cambridge, 1975), p. 219.
173 See ibid. From 380/990 al-Muʾayyad biʾllāh sought to establish a Zaydī imamate in the Caspian region with varying degrees of success until his demise in 411/1020. Both he and his brother al-Nāṭiq biʾl-Ḥaqq were also noted as having studied under the

important Baghdadi Ḥanafī and Muʿtazilī theologian Abū ʿAbd Allāh al-Baṣrī. See, Gregor M. Schward, 'Abū ʿAbdallāh al-Baṣrī', *EI3*.

174 Richard W. Bulliet, *The Patricians of Nishapur: A Study in Medieval Islamic Social History* (Cambridge, MA, 1972), p. 234ff; Teresa Bernheimer, *The ʿAlids: The First Family of Islam, 750–1200* (Edinburgh, 2013), p. 32.

175 Ibn al-Dāʿī left Iraq to pursue the Zaydī imamate in the Caspian region, with the title al-Mahdī li-Dīn Allāh. See Donohue, *Buwayhid*, pp. 307–309.

176 Ibn al-Jawzī, *al-Muntaẓam*, vol. 15, p. 95; Ibn al-Athīr, *al-Kāmil*, vol. 8, p. 78. Also see al-Ṣafadī, *al-Wāfī*, vol. 1, p. 109.

177 Muḥammad b. ʿUmar b. Yaḥyā (d. 390/999) was a descendant of Imam Zayd b. ʿAlī Zayn al-ʿĀbidīn and undoubtedly one of the most influential *sharīf*s of the era, noted as the 'wealthiest man in Iraq', whose fortune was 'truly extraordinary' (Donohue, *Buwayhid*, p. 248), and which Ibn ʿInaba remarked was greater than that of any other ʿAlid: Ibn ʿInaba, *ʿUmdat al-ṭālib*, p. 278.

178 See J.J. Witkam, 'Ibn al-Akfānī', *EI2* and Donohue, *Buwayhid*, pp. 295–298.

179 Al-Akfānī's patronage of traditionists is noted in Ibn al-Jawzī, *al-Muntaẓam*, vol. 15, p. 107. Only Ibn al-Jawzī has him listed as Abu'l-ʿAbbās al-Sūrī, while Ibn al-Athīr, Ibn Kathīr and Ibn Khaldūn have him as Abu'l-ʿAbbās al-Abīwardī.

180 Though Ibn al-Jawzī, *al-Muntaẓam*, vol. 15, p. 83, has Abu'l-Qāsim al-Khazarī, the editors of this edition note that variant manuscripts of the *Muntaẓam* have al-Jazarī instead (ibid., vol. 15, p. 83, n. 2). Ibn al-Kathīr, *al-Bidāya*, vol. 13, p. 10 has Abu'l-Qāsim al-Ḥarīrī, but is the only source to have this and it could be a transcription error. Al-Dhahabī, *Ta'rīkh*, vol. 28, p. 12 adds the *kunya* and thus gives al-Qāḍī Abū Muḥammad Abu'l-Qāsim al-Jazarī. Ibn al-Athīr, *al-Kāmil*, vol. 6, p. 446, gives Ibn al-Khazarī while Ibn Taghrībirdī, *al-Nujūm*, vol. 4, p. 231, has Abu'l-Qāṣim al-Jazarī.

181 On the establishment of the Ẓāhirī chief judgeship, see Donohue, *Buwayhid*, p. 295.

182 See Devin Stewart, 'The Structure of the Fihrist: Ibn al-Nadim as Historian of Islamic Legal and Theological Schools', *International Journal of Middle East Studies*, 39 (2007), p. 371.

183 On al-Isfarāʾinī's career, see Donohue, *Buwayhid*, p. 323.
184 On Abū ʿAlī al-Ḥasan b. al-Ḥusayn b. Ḥamkān al-Hamadhānī, see Ibn al-Jawzī, *al-Muntaẓam*, vol. 15, p. 106, who does not recommend him as a *ḥadīth* narrator; see also Ibn Kathīr, *al-Bidāya*, vol. 13, p. 22.
185 Al-Ṣafadī, *al-Wāfī*, vol. 1, p. 97, calls him Muḥammad b. Muḥammad b. Ibrāhīm, Abu'l-Faḍl al-Nasawī, and says he lived and studied in Baghdad and narrated from al-Ṣāḥib b. ʿAbbād, and narrated to Abu'l-Qāṣim al-Tanūkhī, placing him therefore at the turn of the century.
186 Yaḥyā b. Abi'l-Khayr al-ʿImrānī, *al-Bayān fī madhhab al-imām al-Shāfiʿī*, ed. Qāsim al-Nūrī (Beirut, 2000), vol. 1, p. 42. Note also a Shāfiʿī jurist by the name Muḥammad b. Muḥammad b. Muḥammad b. ʿAbd Allāh al-Bayḍāwī was active during the reign of the Abbasid al-Muqtadī. See al-Ṣafadī, *al-Wāfī*, vol. 1, p. 213.
187 A certain Abū ʿAbd Allāh al-Ḥusayn b. Muḥammad al-Ṭabarī al-Kashfalī (d. 414/1023), known as a Shāfiʿī jurist of Baghdad who taught in the mosque of ʿAbd Allāh b. Mubārak after the death of Abū Ḥāmid al-Isfarāʾinī is mentioned in Ibn al-Athīr, *al-Bāb fī tahdhīb al-ansāb* (Baghdad, n.d.), vol. 3, p. 99.
188 M. Ben Cheneb, 'al-Ḳudūrī, Abu'l-Ḥusayn/al-Ḥasan Aḥmad', *EI2*. Donohue, *Buwayhid*, pp. 326–327. See Ibn al-Jawzī, *al-Muntaẓam*, vol. 15, p. 162.
189 See Wilferd Madelung, 'al-Mufīd', *EI2*.
190 On the father al-Muḥassin b. ʿAlī, see H. Fähndrich, 'al-Tanūkhī', *EI2*. Ibn Khallikān, tr. de Slane, vol. 2, pp. 567–568.
191 For the role of al-Isfarāʾinī in this affair, see Ibn al-Jawzī, *al-Muntaẓam*, vol. 15, pp. 58–59.
192 See Donohue, *Buwayhid*, pp. 297–298.
193 Ibid.
194 See Daftary, *Ismāʿīlīs*, p. 209.
195 On Abu'l-Ḥārith al-Basāsīrī, see Daftary, *Ismāʿīlīs*, pp. 195–197; Marius Canard, 'al-Basāsīrī', *EI2*.
196 Al-Muʾayyad fi'l-Dīn al-Shīrazī was a leading Fatimid *dāʿī*, an influential Fatimid statesmen and diplomat of the mid-5th/11th century. Born in Shīrāz in the last decades of the 4th/10th century, the rising influence of al-Muʾayyad at the Būyid court in Fārs culminated in the conversion of the Būyid amir Abū Kālījār, which unleashed hostility against him from the Sunni establishment in Baghdad, and ultimately provoked his

banishment. Arriving in Cairo in 438/1046, al-Mu'ayyad was appointed to the Fatimid chancery in 444/1052–1053. Two years later, he began to galvanise al-Basāsīrī to defeat the Saljūq army in 448/1057, which culminated in the conquest of Baghdad. In Cairo, al-Mu'ayyad eventually became the Chief *dāʿī*, whose *majālis al-ḥikma* ('sessions of wisdom') as well as his poetry continued to be venerated by the adherents of the Ismaili *daʿwa* in the centuries that followed. For a comprehensive outline of his biography and scholarly works, see Verena Klemm, *Memoirs of a Mission: The Ismaili Scholar, Statesmen and Poet al-Mu'ayyad fi'l-Dīn al-Shīrāzī* (London, 2003). See also, I. K. Poonawala, 'al-Mu'ayyad Fi'l-Dīn', *EI2*.

197 Ibn al-Jawzī, *al-Muntaẓam*, vol. 15, p. 336.

198 Juwaynī, *Jahān-gushā*, tr. Boyle, vol. 1, pp. 658–660.

199 Ibn al-Kathīr, *al-Bidāya*, vol. 12, p. 113.

200 Ibn al-Athīr initially rejects the aspersions against the 'Alid lineage of the Fatimids through the alleged attestation of al-Raḍī's signature upon the Manifesto. He notes that: 'there is no proof (*ḥujjā*) in what he [al-Raḍī] wrote in the *maḥḍar* which repudiated the lineage of the [Fatimid] caliphs, for fear brings forth [this and] even more': *al-Kāmil*, vol. 6, p. 447. He subsequently states: 'Those who claim the truthfulness of the [Fatimid] lineage say: the scholars who wrote in the *maḥḍar* did so out of fear and *taqiyya*, and [there were] those who had no knowledge of lineage. As to the pronouncement [of the correctness of the lineage] there is no protestation': *al-Kāmil*, vol. 6, p. 448.

201 Ibn Khaldūn, *al-Muqaddima*, tr. Rosenthal, p. 41.

202 Ibid., p. 44.

203 Ibid., p. 43. Subsequently, he notes: 'The partisans of the Abbasids made much use of this fact when they came out with their attack against the lineage of (the 'Ubaydid-Fatimids). They tried to ingratiate themselves with the weak (Abbasid) caliphs by professing the erroneous opinion that (the 'Alid descent of the 'Ubaydid-Fatimids was spurious).'

204 Ibid., p. 47.

3

Was the Fatimid *Amīr al-Juyūsh* in fact a *Wazīr*?

Paul E. Walker

From the coming to Egypt of Badr al-Jamālī[1] until the very end of the Fatimid state, the functioning head of government was, except for a few minor breaks in continuity, an *amīr al-juyūsh* (Commander of the Armed Forces). These men wielded all but absolute power over both the military and the civilian bureaucracy. Traditionally, the holders of this office, however, are referred to as *wazīr*s, although none were 'men of the pen' and thus hardly fit the classical mould of earlier Fatimid and non-Fatimid, or even contemporary, *wazīr*s in other regions of the Islamic world. Al-Maqrīzī, perhaps our best source, notes this discrepancy. The term *wazīr* appears to have fallen out of use in this period. And yet he also remarks that all these 'men of the sword' were nevertheless regarded as *wazīr*s, that title now having an informal rather than formal implication.

It is thus partly a matter of designation and titulary, not merely one of either theory or practice. Prior to Badr al-Jamālī the use of the title *wazīr* is well attested in the inscriptions on the *ṭirāz* fabrics which were produced under the supervision of the *wazīr* (as opposed to coinage which was the province of the *qāḍī*), and most importantly in the decrees (sing. *sijill*) of appointment to the office. The text of the decree elevating al-Jarjarā'ī to the wazirate in 418/1027 exists. It is a major piece of evidence for defining the Fatimid (or any other) wazirate. Its language is precise and it presents the complete rationale behind the institution. The evidence from the later period is much less clear in regard to use and definition of this term in this latter context. Still it is common to speak here of '*wazīr*s of the sword' or, even less appropriately, to apply to this situation al-Māwardī's two classes of *wazīr*, *tafwīḍī* (of delegation) and *tanfīdhī* (of implementation), although he died before it came into being and never observed a case like this, which was, at the time, unprecedented. The last century of Fatimid rule was organised according to a principle – a new institution – unlike any other before it. It represents, therefore, a unique development in the history of the Islamic wazirate.

In 466/1074 the imam-caliph al-Mustanṣir summoned Badr al-Jamālī, the commander of the Fatimid armies in Syria, to Egypt in effect to rescue him and the dynasty from almost certain collapse and extinction.[2] The invitation went out secretly but with the highest state authority behind it. Badr, a former *mamlūk* and ethnically Armenian,[3] was at the height of a long military career in service to the Fatimids. At that time he was stationed at Acre. He understood the difficult situation in Cairo and replied that he would come only on the condition that he be granted permission to bring with him an army. At the time there were no reliable troops in Egypt. Al-Mustanṣir agreed to the condition.

To avoid a protracted and well-observed march overland, Badr decided to risk an unprecedented mid-winter sailing from Acre. For 40 days he loaded 100 ships with troops and equipment and transported them successfully to Egypt,[4] landing safely at Damietta. No one could remember this having been achieved before. Once in the country, he marched to Cairo, which he entered soon after, welcomed by the local elite who knew little of why he had come. Not long after, he invited many of them to a day of festivities capped by a banquet at which he carefully staged the execution of his guests one by one, carried out on his orders by his own men, who in turn each inherited the possessions and position of the man he had personally killed. With all potential local opposition gone, Badr was accorded the powers of the *wazīr* – his rank, at least, now being obvious to all.

Next Badr led his army back into the eastern Delta to confront the Lawāta tribesmen who, with the exception of the major towns, dominated the region. The newly arrived Syrians decimated the Lawāta, killing a great many, including the leaders. Once the eastern Delta was put in proper order, Badr turned to the west, attacking renegade forces and finally capturing Alexandria. Following this victory he moved to Upper Egypt and routed a combined army of Arab Bedouin and Sudanese, the latter all formerly belonging to the Fatimid army but now independent supporters of various warlords. Badr's troops once again annihilated this opposition, in effect removing all resistance to the central government from Egypt, up to and including Aswān, where Badr dedicated a new mosque in the name of victory (*naṣr*). It was around this time that he received word that, at long last, the Saljūqs, who had threatened for two decades to conquer Egypt, had in fact invaded the country and were now moving through the Delta and threatening Cairo. Calmly, the Fatimid commander slowly marched back, passing the capital en route, and finally coming face to face with the Saljūq forces. By then he had assembled as many as 30,000 troops. The Saljūq army was much smaller and it, like all the others, was soon destroyed entirely, leaving only a handful to flee individually back towards Palestine.[5] The Saljūqs never invaded Egypt again. Badr al-Jamālī's hold on the land was secure and absolute. The Fatimid dynasty had been given a new lease of life.

The purpose of recounting in such detail the events associated with Badr al-Jamālī's advent in Egypt is to demonstrate, as clearly as possible, the military's role, that is, the role of his own militia, which he brought with him from Syria, and his personal command of it and its actions. Without it and his direct involvement in its operations, he could not have accomplished what he did. That he should be known above all as *amīr al-juyūsh*, the 'Commander of the Armed Forces' is absolutely appropriate. Yet once in power in Egypt he, and all those who were later to occupy this office, were said to be *wazīr*s, although most certainly Badr was not and had never been a bureaucrat. He was simply not from the clerical or scholarly class. Therefore, it is necessary to ask what, or where, was the precedent for a *wazīr* of this new type, if it in fact existed at all.[6] What did it mean to call Badr a *wazīr*, especially since he was never to use that title and was thus not formally designated as such.

It may be useful to stress the point again that Badr al-Jamālī came to the wazirate from the military, not merely by moving laterally from one office to another, but by ordering his own troops to seize control. And he remained in power on the strength of that same force. Is there a similar prior case among, say, the Abbasids?

Some background and context may be helpful at this point. Stepping back from 466/1074 to the watershed year of 450/1058–1059, the *wazīr* in Egypt at its beginning was al-Yāzūrī on behalf of the same Fatimid imam-caliph al-Mustanṣir. In Baghdad the *wazīr* was Ibn al-Muslima acting for the Abbasid caliph; the Saljūq grand sultan Ṭughril Beg had his own *wazīr*, al-Kundurī; and about that time, the future Saljūq sultan Alp Arslān began to rule Nīsābūr (in the name of his father), yet even then his *wazīr* was the later famous Niẓām al-Mulk. All four *wazīr*s were bureaucrats, strictly men of the pen. Note also that the two Saljūqs each had their own *wazīr*, as was fairly common for both the Saljūqs and the Būyids before them. There is no precedent in such examples of a 'military *wazīr*', or a *wazīr* of the sword, if that is the proper way to characterise the institution that Badr seems to have created.

As for the Fatimid dynasty, there were no *wazīr*s under the first four imam-caliphs in any sense. They all ruled personally and directly, and the delegation of substantial degrees of authority by them to underlings was relatively rare. The first true *wazīr* was Yaʿqūb ibn Killis, who was appointed to the office by al-ʿAzīz in 367/977–978. Aside from minor interruptions, once elevated to that rank, he remained *wazīr* from then until his death in 380/990–991. However, little primary evidence exists for this period: no documents, no inscriptions. Confirmation of his title – that he in fact was *wazīr* in name – comes from the *ṭirāz*. Coinage under the Fatimids was the domain of the *qāḍī*, not the *wazīr* (although only the name of the imam-caliph appeared on it).

But *ṭirāz*, following a practice that went back to the Abbasids, was the province of the *wazīr* and typically his name and titles were included in the inscription embroidered on each piece. Fortunately, we have examples bearing the name and title of *wazīr* for Ibn Killis.[7]

Ibn Killis was a man of many talents but they are all those of either a scholar or a bureaucrat.[8] After him, however, the Fatimid imam-caliphs appoint no more *wazīr*s for the next 38 years. Both al-ʿAzīz and his son al-Ḥākim preferred a lesser office, weaker and more malleable, that of *wāsiṭa*, a kind of quasi-wazirial 'intermediary'.[9] In the distinction between the offices of *wizāra* and *wasāṭa*, we may find some indication of how the Fatimids viewed the former. To be *wazīr* was obviously of greater significance; the rank was higher and carried more responsibility and independence. As long as the imam-caliph preserved a direct interest in the daily management of his empire, there were no *wazīrs*.

The next case is that of al-Jarjarāʾī, who became *wazīr* in 418/1027, after more than a quarter century of working his way up through the bureaucracy. With al-Jarjarāʾī, moreover, not only do we have *ṭirāz* that boldly proclaims him 'the Most Illustrious *wazīr* (*al-wazīr al-ajall*)', but the text of the decree, or *sijill*, appointing him to the office survives also.[10] This text is extremely important. It defines for us quite explicitly what the term *wazīr* meant to the Fatimids and what they expected of those who rose to this exalted office.

Although composed in the chancery, by yet another bureaucrat (in fact the head of the *dīwān al-inshāʾ*),[11] it surely reflects the attitude of the ruling authority and of the dynasty as a whole. In character with the Shiʿism of the government, it remarks first that ʿAlī b. Abī Ṭālib, the ancestor of the imam-caliph himself, was the *wazīr* of the Prophet.[12] It likewise cites the Qurʾanic proof-text for the term: Moses's request to God to appoint for him a *wazīr*, that person to be his own brother Aaron.[13] Yet, as obvious and as necessary as both citations appear in this situation – the brother connection of Aaron to Moses is parallel to that of Muḥammad and ʿAlī[14] – neither quite applies to al-Jarjarā'ī, who in contrast to 'Alī, was not of the same lineage and could in no way be expected to succeed to the caliphate. The notion implied in this designation – for the recipient eventually to take over and rule in place of the imam-caliph – was not acted upon for another century and a half when Saladin replaced those he had previously served as *wazīr* by becoming the sultan.

A better Qur'anic precedent – one also prominent in the text of this same *sijill* – is that of Joseph, who said to Pharaoh: 'Put me in charge of the storehouses of the land, for I am a guardian with great knowledge.'[15] Clearly, for the Fatimid rulers, Joseph represented the ideal *wazīr*, the management of money and resources being uppermost in their minds as functions of this post.[16]

Although these cases – Ibn Killis, al-Jarjarā'ī and al-Yāzūrī – illustrate and define the Fatimid wazirate quite well, they do not provide a precedent for that of Badr al-Jamālī, who, in contrast to them, did not come to office from the bureaucracy. He is thus not a 'Joseph'. But there are additional issues to consider in his case. One is that, unlike them, he was not given the title *wazīr* and may never have used it. Instead, he was the *amīr al-juyūsh*, a title held by him and all those who came after him. None of them were formally entitled *wazīr*, again, unlike all the earlier examples. Are we therefore to conclude that the term *wazīr* in itself denotes a man of the pen, a bureaucrat, and that *amīr al-juyūsh*, a new office, is a kind of military 'wazirate' but without the name?[17]

Here problems arise. For one, Badr al-Jamālī had held the title *amīr al-juyūsh* prior to his arrival in Egypt. It seems to have been used for and by the chief commander of the Fatimid armies in Syria. Others before Badr had the same title.[18] And, in any case, he was known in what may be contemporary accounts as Amīr al-Juyūsh Badr, not Badr, the *amīr al-juyūsh*.[19] Moreover, his personal militia bore the name 'al-Juyūshiyya' and his *mamlūk* commanders were called al-Juyūshī (similar to his having the name al-Jamālī, meaning the *mamlūk* of Jamāl, his original owner).[20] The oratory on the Muqaṭṭam hills is known locally as al-Guyūshī; the area of his residence in Cairo is still referred to as that of Mīrgūsh.

Even though subsequent holders of his rank all inherited his full list of titles, including *amīr al-juyūsh*, – the last of them, Saladin, was still the *amīr al-juyūsh* – each derived his basic claim to power from the militia he commanded and this force changed its name accordingly. The Juyūshiyya became the Afḍaliyya when al-Afḍal, the son of Badr, assumed command of it. The militia of Asad al-Dīn Shīrkūh was the Asadiyya until it was inherited by Saladin.

However, to follow the progression of the Fatimid wazirate in a technical sense – that is, of precise titulature and actual contemporary usage – we require more than anecdotal evidence. Yet that is difficult to find. Later chroniclers obviously had a tendency, as historians can do, to read what was true in their own time into the earlier situation. Unfortunately, for the era of Badr, which is so crucial for the transition to the period of military *wazīr*s, little exists. We know, for example, that a decree of appointment was issued for him and that it granted him control over all affairs of the government 'all except the throne of the caliph himself' (*mā warā' sarīr khilāfatihi*) – a standard phrase thereafter.[21] But, not having the whole text, we do not know what it said about the wazirate.[22] We also do not have such evidence as *tirāẓ*, although again we know it existed. Two surviving examples from Badr al-Jamālī's years are too fragmentary to yield a useful text.[23]

Ironically, however, in a major contrast with earlier periods of Fatimid rule, of which few if any inscriptions remain and there are no records of what they said, for Badr we have twenty, a large number by any standard in view of how little information exists for those years in any other form. These building inscriptions, coupled with references to Badr in a series of letters sent by the imam-caliph al-Mustanṣir to his *daʿwa* in the Yemen,[24] allow us, at least, to chart the use of formal titles in his case. We can see, for example, that Badr was not accorded titles denoting authority over the judiciary and the Ismaili *daʿwa* until 470/1077–1078 – in all likelihood because of the approaching death in that year of al-Mu'ayyad fi'l-Dīn al-Shīrāzī, the highly respected, longtime head of the *daʿwa*. Still none of these inscriptions, which nevertheless give the full titles of Badr, mentions the wazirate or refers to him as *wazīr*.[25]

What then is the actual evidence for regarding these *amīr*s as *wazīr*s, as is done regularly in both medieval and modern accounts of them? Al-Maqrīzī, for example, refers to them as '*wazīr*[s] of the sword' and he remarks in typical fashion: 'The *wazīr* of the sword from the era of Amīr al-Juyūsh Badr until the end of the dynasty, had become the sultan of Egypt, the real holder of power.'[26] His point about their being the sultans of Egypt seems to make good sense; their powers were certainly as formidable as those of either the Būyids or Saljūqs. Why were they not called sultans? Curiously, the same imam-caliph who invited Badr al-Jamālī to take charge of the government had, previously, granted the title 'sultan' to his vassal in Yemen, 'Alī b. Muḥammad al-Ṣulayḥī.[27] But in Egypt this never took place.

Here al-Maqrīzī's comments seem especially apropos. He explains:[28]

> The rank of *wazīr* in the time of the Fatimid caliphs was of the highest and most exalted up to the era of Amīr al-Juyūsh Badr al-Jamālī. When the above-mentioned *amīr al-juyūsh* came from Acre to the country of Egypt, at the invitation of the caliph, al-Mustanṣir bi'llāh, in the year 467 [1074–1075], al-Mustanṣir appointed Badr over all of his affairs and delegated to him the administration of everything save his own throne. The caliph depended on him in the slightest of matters as well as the most important and charged him with overseeing the grandest and the least of them. Thus his wazirate became a wazirate of delegation (*wizārat tafwīḍ*). The name for the holder of the wazirate thereby ceased at that time to be *wazīr*. He was called instead the *amīr al-juyūsh* and he became the *sulṭān* of Egypt. And the rest of the *wazīr*s thereafter were in the same position until the dynasty itself disappeared.

From the list of more than a dozen military *wazīr*s over the last century of Fatimid rule, four only – Ṭalā'i' b. Ruzzīk, Shāwar, Asad al-Dīn Shīrkūh and Ṣalāḥ al-Dīn Yūsuf (Saladin) – are the subject of a *sijill* of appointment, the text of which has been preserved for us. On the basis of this and other evidence (e.g., inscriptions), it is entirely possible to trace the history of the titles used by each in succession.[29] Ṭalā'i', for example, was the Most Illustrious Lord, Virtuous King, Aid to the Imams, Dispeller of Affliction, *amīr al-juyūsh*, Sword of Islam, The Succour of Mankind, Guarrantor of the Judges of Muslims, Guide of the Missionary of the Believers (*al-Sayyid al-ajall al-Malik al-ṣāliḥ Nāṣir al-a'imma Kāshif al-ghumma Amīr al-juyūsh Sayf al-Islām Ghiyāth al-anām Kāfil quḍāt al-muslimīn Hādī du'āt al-mu'minīn*). Several are titles added since the time of Badr al-Jamālī,[30] the most significant apparently being *malik*, though precisely what extra meaning it might have is not clear. And, even so, the title *wazīr* is not in evidence at any point.

The internal wording of these *sijill*s offers some help but is nevertheless not perfectly straightforward. There are phrases such as 'he [the caliph] entrusts you with his wazirate' (*fa qalladaka min wizāratihi*).

Ultimately, much more telling than this sort of indirect reference is a declaration in a slightly different type of document, one easily missed by looking only at inscriptions or the formal texts of the *sijill*s that were composed by the chancery. The other is what is called in Arabic a *tawqī'*, a signature. The decree of appointment was the formal document issued in the name of the caliph but, although worded as if he had written it, it was not actually by him. To add authenticity the caliph would append to it his own 'signature', a second text written in his own hand on the cover or overleaf (outer side?) – in Arabic the *ṭurra*. For Ṭalā'i' and the *sijill* issued for him in Rabī' II 549/June–July 1154 on behalf of the five-year-old caliph al-Fā'iz, we have the latter text and it states, as explicitly as one could wish, that the caliph addresses it to his *wazīr* – that is, Ṭalā'i'. It begins: 'For our *wazīr* (*li-wazīrinā*)' and ends 'May God … never cease to favour the days he spends in our wazirate.'[31] Another such *tawqī'*, one appended to the *sijill* appointing Asad al-Dīn Shīrkūh, reads in part: 'No other *wazīr* has had a commission (*'ahd*) like this one [given to you].'

The *sijill* appointing Saladin *amīr al-juyūsh*/*wazīr*, the last of its kind, contains a pointed reference to the first of them all, Badr al-Jamālī. And also to his son al-Afḍal, with the wish that may he be 'more excellent (*afḍal*) than even al-Afḍal'.[32]

Some conclusions are in order. Al-Maqrīzī is probably right when he says that the formal use of the term *wazīr* as a title of office fell out of use in the last century of Fatimid government. Apparently, it was understood as most properly signifying bureaucratic functions as performed previously by the men of the pen. The new 'wazirate', which combined both clerical and military command, a wazirate of both the pen and the sword in one person, required a designation that would distinguish it from all earlier examples, both under the Fatimids and under any other Muslim dynasty. But, for perhaps similar reasons, the notion of the sultanate, as in the cases of either the Būyids or the Saljūqs, had to be avoided. To have called Badr al-Jamālī *sulṭān* would have invited direct comparison between him and the Saljūq ruler whose independence from the Abbasid caliph was well known. The solution, however, was odd: not according Badr any meaningful title but rather and, less formally, still granting him all the accoutrements of the wazirate without the title. Perhaps Badr himself did not care; the power he gained was as near to absolute as it could be. He himself was ruthless; the niceties of protocol meant little; and all those who crossed him and happened to fall into his hands died. Future *wazīr*s of his type were not so secure but the powerful precedent he had set remained unchanged to the end.[33]

Notes

1 The importance of this event for the progress of Fatimid history has been noted and discussed by several modern authorities, among them particularly Michael Brett, 'Badr al-Ǧamālī and the Fatimid Renaissance', in U. Vermeulen and J. Van Steenbergen, ed., *Egypt and Syria in the Fatimid, Ayyubid and Mamluk Eras*, IV (Leuven, 2005), pp. 61–78, with citations to the author's previous studies as well; Johannes den Heijer, 'Le vizir fatimide Badr al-Ǧamālī (466/1074–487/1094) et la nouvelle muraille du Caire: quelques remarques préliminaires', in U. Vermeulen and K. D'Hulster, ed., *Egypt and Syria in the Fatimid, Ayyubid and Mamluk Eras*,

V (Leuven, 2007), pp. 91–107, also with citations of earlier studies by the author; and most especially Heinz Halm, 'Badr al-Ǧamālī – Wesir oder Militärdiktator?', in the same volume of *Egypt and Syria in the Fatimid, Ayyubid and Mamluk Eras*, V, pp. 121–127, which addresses directly many of the concerns explored in this chapter. See also Halm's *Kalifen und Assassinen: Ägypten und der Vordere Orient zur Zeit der ersten Kreuzzüge* (Munich, 2014), pp. 17–28, 35–37.

2 There are various sources for the advent of Badr in Egypt. See especially Taqī al-Dīn al-Maqrīzī, *Kitāb al-Muqaffā al-kabīr*, ed. M. al-Ya'lāwī (Beirut, 1991) (Badr); the same author's *Itti'āẓ al-ḥunafā' bi-akhbār al-a'imma al-Fāṭimiyyīn al-khulafā'*, ed. Jamāl al-Dīn al-Shayyāl and Muḥammad Ḥilmī Muḥammad Aḥmad (Cairo, 1387–1393/1967–1973); ed. A.F. Sayyid (Damascus, 2010); Tāj al-Dīn Muḥammad b. Muyassar, *al-Muntaqā min Akhbār Miṣr*, ed. A.F. Sayyid (Cairo, 1981) and Sibṭ b. al-Jawzī, *Mir'āt al-zamān fī ta'rīkh al-a'yān: al-Ḥawādith al-khāṣṣa bi-ta'rīkh al-Salājiqa bayna al-sanawāt 1056–1086*, ed. Ali Sevim (Ankara, 1968). The *Mir'āt al-zamān* has a different perspective and thus different information.

3 Information from Abū Bakr b. 'Abd Allāh b. al-Dawādārī, *Kanz al-durar wa jāmi' al-ghurar*, vol. 6, *al-Durra al-muḍiyya fī akhbār al-dawla al-Fāṭimiyya*, ed. Ṣ. al-Munajjid (Cairo, 1961), p. 372.

4 The number of ships is important because it is our only means of gauging how large a force he brought from Syria.

5 There are at least two accounts of this battle, one in Ibn Muyassar and al-Maqrīzī and the other in Sibṭ b. al-Jawzī, *Mir'āt al-zamān*, pp. 182–185.

6 Al-Maqrīzī, *Kitāb al-ma'rūf bi'l-mawā'iẓ wa'l-i'tibār bi-dhikr al-khiṭaṭ wa'l-āthār*, commonly known as *al-Khiṭaṭ* (Bulaq, 1270/1853), vol. 1, p. 440; ed. A.F. Sayyid (London, 2002–2004), vol. 2, p. 445, calls it *wazīr sayf* and remarks 'no one preceded him in [having] that [kind of] office (*wa lam yataqaddamhu fī dhalika aḥadun*)'.

7 Examples in the *Répertoire chronologique d'épigraphie arabe*, ed. Ét. Combe et al. (Cairo, 1933–). Hereafter *RCEA*.

8 Note the possibility that he planned to create a personal militia, the *wazīriyya*. See M. Brett, *The Rise of the Fatimids: The World of the Mediterranean and the Middle East in the Fourth Century of the Hijra, Tenth Century CE* (Leiden, 2001), p. 343.

9 Also called the *sifāra* (*safīr*). Shihāb al-Dīn Aḥmad al-Nuwayrī, *Nihāyat al-arab fī funūn al-adab*, vol. 28, ed. Muḥammad

Muḥammad Amīn and Muḥammad Ḥilmī Muḥammad Aḥmad (Cairo, 1992), p. 189 reports the appointment of one of these men in the year 401/1010–1011 using both: *taqlīduhu bi'l-sifāra wa'l-wasāṭa bayn al-nās wa bayn al-Ḥākim wa tafwīḍ al-umūr ilayhi.* Shihāb al-Dīn Aḥmad b. ʿAlī al-Qalqashandī, *Ṣubḥ al-aʿshā fī ṣināʿat al-inshā'* (Cairo, 1331–1338/1913–1920), vol. 10, pp. 478–479 says about the *wizāra*: 'Know that the *wizāra* in the Fatimid state was at times held by the lords of the sword (*arbāb al-suyūf*) and at others by the lords of the pen (*arbāb al-aqlām*) and in either of these two cases it was often so exalted a rank as to be a *wizāra* of delegation (*wizāra tafwīḍ*), equivalent to the *sulṭān* in the present, or close to it. In such cases it was called the *wizāra*, but when it was not so important and thus below that rank it was termed the *wasāṭa*.'

10 In Ibn al-Qalānisī, *Dhayl ta'rīkh Dimashq*, ed. H.F. Amedroz (Leiden and Beirut, 1908), pp. 80–83. See also al-Shayyāl, ed., *Majmūʿat al-wathā'iq al-Fāṭimiyya/Corpus Documentorum Fatimicorum* (Cairo, 1378/1958), and appendix 2 to A.F. Sayyid's edition of al-Ṣayrafī's *al-Ishāra ilā man nāla al-wizāra* (Cairo, 1990), pp. 113–118.

11 It was drafted by Walī al-Dawla Abū ʿAlī b. Khayrān, the supervisor of the chancery.

12 According to the boilerplate text for the appointment of a *wazīr*, which is found in ʿAlī b. Khalaf's *Mawādd al-bayān*, a manual for the use of clerks in the Fatimid chancery, ʿAlī b. Abī Ṭālib was the quintessential *wazīr*, '*akmal al-wuzarā'*', the most perfect of *wazīrs*. Published in al-Shayyāl, *Wathā'iq*, document no. 11.

13 Q 20:25–34. The use of the term in Q 25:35 is not cited in the *sijill*.

14 In the Shiʿa tradition Muḥammad said that ʿAlī was to him as Aaron was to Moses.

15 Q 12:55.

16 Al-Jarjarā'ī is particularly interesting in yet another regard. Years before his appointment as *wazīr* his hands had been cut off on the orders of al-Ḥākim who had charged him with gross malfeasance.

17 In his *Khiṭaṭ* (Bulaq ed., vol. 1, p. 440; Sayyid ed., vol. 2, p. 445), al-Maqrīzī explains, from the advent of Badr al-Jamālī, 'the wazirate from then onwards became a wazirate of delegation (*tafwīḍ*) and one called those who held the office *amīr al-juyūsh*. The term *wazīr* ceased to be used (*baṭala ism al-wizāra*).'

18 Al-Maqrīzī, *Khiṭaṭ*, Bulaq ed., vol. 1, p. 440; Sayyid ed., vol. 2, p. 445, in his discussion of Badr's own title, says that it had been used by the Fatimids for their governor of Damascus. Manjūtakīn

was *amīr al-juyūsh*; see Th. Bianquis, *Damas et la Syrie sous la domination fatimide (359–468/969–1076)* (Damascus, 1986 and 1989), pp. 188 and 193. Anūshtakīn al-Dizbarī also; see Abu'l-Maḥāsin b. Taghrībirdī, *al-Nujūm al-zāhira fī mulūk Miṣr wa'l-Qāhira* (Cairo, 1963–1971), vol. 4, p. 252.

19 By al-Maqrīzī and Sibṭ b. al-Jawzī.

20 Badr's governor of Syria in 486/1093 was Munīr al-Dawla al-Juyūshī (al-Maqrīzī, *Itti'āẓ*, Cairo ed., vol. 2, p. 328); Ibn al-Athīr, *al-Kāmil fi'l-ta'rīkh*, ed. C.J. Tornberg (Leiden, 1867; reprinted Beirut, 1965–1967), vol. 10, p. 77; Nāṣir (Naṣr) al-Dawla al-Juyūshī was sent to Syria with an army in 470/1077–1078 (*Itti'āẓ*, Cairo ed., vol. 2, p. 319) and 482/1089–1090 (*Itti'āẓ*, Cairo ed., vol. 2, p. 326); al-Maqrīzī, *al-Muqaffā*, p. 399, and Sibṭ (p. 200) must be referring to the same man as Naṣr Aftikīn (in Damascus, 470/1077–1078). Another appears on an inscription (*RCEA*, Year 473, p. 210) as Abū Manṣūr Sārtakīn al-Juyūshī.

21 It is used not only in later official proclamations but in the contemporary letters of the caliph to Yemen, one of which says in part '*wa qalladahu mā warā' al-khilāfa min al-da'wa al-hādiya wa maṣāliḥ al-umma*', in *al-Sijillāt al-Mustanṣiriyya*, ed. 'Abd al-Mun'im Mājid (Cairo, 1954), *sijill* no. 34 (partial trans. by M. Brett in the article cited above in note 1).

22 Phrases from it are given in the *Khiṭaṭ*, Bulaq ed., vol. 1, p. 440 and Sayyid ed., vol. 2, p. 445.

23 Reported in the *RCEA*.

24 *Al-Sijillāt al-Mustanṣiriyya.*

25 On the inscriptions in Cairo, see now Ayman F. Sayyid, *La Capitale de l'Egypte jusqu'à l'époque Fatimide (al-Qâhira et al-Fustât)—Essai de reconstitution topographique* (Beirut and Stuttgart, 1998), pp. 365–453 (the chapter on Badr's building activities). But note also the studies of G. Wiet, 'Une nouvelle inscription fatimide au Caire', *Journal Asiatique*, 249 (1961), pp. 13–20; his 'Nouvelles inscriptions fatimides', *Bulletin de l'Institut d'Égypte*, 24 (1941/1942), pp. 145–158 (a list of all of them appears on pp. 154–155).

26 Al-Maqrīzī, *Khiṭaṭ*, Bulaq ed., vol. 2, p. 305.

27 Idrīs 'Imād al-Dīn, *'Uyūn al-akhbār*, vol. 7, ed. and tr. A.F. Sayyid et al., as *The Fatimids and their Successors in Yaman: The History of an Islamic Community* (London, 2002), p. 22. Note the confirmation of such a title (*Sulṭān Amīr al-Mu'minīn*) in the *Sijillāt al-Mustanṣiriyya*, for example, nos 14 and 16 (pp. 58 and 66).

28 The following passage comes from the *musawwada* of the *Khiṭaṭ*, Sayyid ed., p. 258.
29 On the successive additions to the title, see al-Maqrīzī, *Khiṭaṭ*, Bulaq ed., vol. 1, p. 440; Sayyid ed., vol. 2, p. 445.
30 Badr was *al-Sayyid al-ajall Amīr al-juyūsh Sayf al-Islām Nāṣir al-imām Kāfil quḍāt al-muslimīn Hādī duʿāt al-muʾminīn.*
31 Al-Shayyāl, *Wathāʾiq*, p. 353; al-Maqrīzī, *Ittiʿāẓ*, Cairo ed., vol. 3, p. 218.
32 Items for further consideration as evidence of the less formal concept of *wazīr* in this late period are the residences, which were called the *dār al-wizāra*, and uniforms and clothing, such as the attire of a *wazīr* discussed by al-Maqrīzī in his *Khiṭaṭ*, Bulaq ed., vol. 1, p. 440, Sayyid ed., vol. 2, p. 445, with many details and comments like those by Idrīs ʿImād al-Dīn in his *ʿUyūn al-akhbār*, vol. 7, p. 178, were he says 'and bestowed him with the collar of the *wazīr*' *wa ṭawwaqahu ṭawqa al-wuzarāʾ*.
33 Halm's suggestion in the article referred to earlier in Note 1 that Badr in fact initiated a type of rule that continued in Egypt through the era of Saladin and on into the subsequent reigns up to the end of the Mamlūk sultanate has some serious merit, although it does not explain why there was no formal recognition of the new order, as would, for example, have been accorded by the application to him of the title *sulṭān*. Den Heijer makes an interesting case for Badr as the champion of a Fatimid caliphate experiencing a renewal of life. Badr may thus have preferred, or at least been satisfied, with the role of rescuer and reviver of an esteemed dynasty rather than the founder of a new form of rule.

4

'Leading from the Middle': Qāḍī al-Nu'mān on Female Prayer Leadership

Simonetta Calderini

Several past and recent studies on the Fatimid era have dealt with institutions, figures and roles at the centre of Fatimid religious life such as the *dāʿī*, the *qāḍī*, the Imam-caliph, but almost nothing is known about the roles played by the prayer leader or imam.* Historical references to imams of mosques during the Fatimid period, for example in Egypt, only seem to occur in relation to Sunni mosques and a broader Sunni environment.[1] As for the role of women in ritual prayer, little is known about female participation in public prayer and even less about female leadership of prayers; no references thus far have emerged in historical sources of any woman having led prayers during the Fatimid era.

The Ismaili jurisprudent Qāḍī al-Nuʿmān (d. 363/974) deals in several of his works with the role of imam as prayer leader from various, mainly theoretical, perspectives. In the passages on prayer leadership, he also discusses the criteria and contexts that make it permissible for a woman to lead a congregation in prayer. This chapter focuses on these references to female ritual leadership as presented and variously interpreted by Qāḍī al-Nuʿmān in three of his works, in which he states that a woman should not lead men in prayer but could lead women, provided she does not stand in front of them but in the middle of them.

It is argued here that at least three levels of interpretation (ritual, legal and esoteric) can be identified on the basis of the relevant passages. After an overview of attitudes to female prayer leadership in pre-modern Shiʿi jurisprudence, this chapter will conclude by showing Qāḍī al-Nuʿmān's dependence on, but also departure from, typically agreed interpretations adhered to by non-Ismaili Shiʿi groups.

The Role of Prayer Leader According to Qāḍī al-Nuʿmān

Qāḍī al-Nuʿmān, as the founder of Ismaili jurisprudence and long-standing judge 'in residence' of the Fatimid dynasty, witnessed and contributed first hand to the changes of emphasis and attitudes of the first four Imam-caliphs with regard to aspects of Islamic ritual and legal theories and practices. As a whole, his great works are the expression of the North African phase of the Fatimid dynasty and the more accomplished of them represent the vision and policies of the fourth Imam-caliph, al-Muʿizz (r. 341–365/953–975). Scholarly arguments vary regarding the origins of the Ismaili legal system that Qāḍī al-Nuʿmān formulated, when compared to Sunni and other schools of Shiʿi jurisprudence. While, for instance, some scholars argue that Ismaili law owes a great debt to Mālikī law,[2] and that Qāḍī al-Nuʿmān, or his father, was originally a Mālikī, it is commonly recognised that Ismaili law constitutes a synthesis, even a form of 'reconciliation' between different legal systems, notably between Imāmī and Zaydī Shiʿi, or Shiʿi and Mālikī jurisprudence.[3] This does not detract from the recognition that Ismaili law, in its distinctiveness and status, is one of the main Shiʿi *madhhab*s, alongside the Imāmī and Zaydī schools.[4]

Qāḍī al-Nuʿmān refers to ritual prayer and its leadership mainly in three of his works. Chronologically these are the *Kitāb al-īḍāḥ*, the *Daʿāʾim al-Islām* and the *Taʾwīl al-daʿāʾim*.

The *Kitāb al-īḍāḥ* is a compilation of legal *ḥadīth*s organised by topic, of which only the section on prayer is extant.[5] It can be defined as a *ḥadīth*-based work of *fiqh* which, given the variety of its sources, records several instances of *ikhtilāf*, or differences of opinion among scholars. It is believed to have been written under the first Fatimid Imam-caliph, al-Mahdī (r. 297–322/909–934),[6] possibly after 313/925–926, during the phase of the establishment and initial legal and doctrinal elaboration and consolidation of the Fatimid dynasty in Ifrīqiya.

The *Daʿāʾim*, written between 346 and 348/957 and 960 under the auspices of the Imam-caliph al-Muʿizz,[7] represents the epitome of Ismaili jurisprudence; it can be defined as a legal work on *furūʿ*, a compilation of legal rules supported by the authority of the Imam. The third work, which Qāḍī al-Nuʿmān edited and completed during the last decades of his life, is the *Taʾwīl al-daʿāʾim*, an esoteric interpretation of the *Daʿāʾim*, in fact a doctrinal work rather than one of *fiqh*.

The *Kitāb al-īḍāḥ* includes mainly Shiʿi *ḥadīth*s, each introduced with an *isnād* (chain of transmitters), predominantly based on the authority of Shiʿi Imams such as Muḥammad al-Bāqir (d. ca. 114/732) and Jaʿfar al-Ṣādiq (d. 148/765), and presents differing scholarly opinions about specific issues. One modern historian of the Fatimids, Heinz Halm, contends that the *Kitāb al-īḍāḥ* was a conciliatory work designed to be of broad appeal to Shiʿis, from Zaydīs to Imāmīs, which avoids quoting or referring to divisive figures such as the seventh Ithnāʿasharī Imam, Mūsā al-Kāẓim, as well as to controversial issues.[8] Even though the methodology and some of the sources used in the *Kitāb al-īḍāḥ* are different from those of the *Daʿāʾim*, both Wilferd Madelung and Ismail K. Poonawala argue that the two works present the same legal doctrine.[9] The section in the *Kitāb al-īḍāḥ* devoted to the *imāma* of a woman (fols. 94v–95v) supports all these scholarly statements about the work's inclusiveness and its content. Indeed, in the *Kitāb al-īḍāḥ*, Qāḍī al-Nuʿmān quotes sources ranging from well-known Kūfan Imāmī scholars such as Ḥammād b. ʿĪsā (d. 209/824–825) to Zaydī Shiʿis like Abū ʿAbd Allāh Muḥammad Ibn Sallām (ca. 235–287/850–900).

In the *Kitāb al-īḍāḥ* the point is progressively made that no woman can lead other women by standing in front of them. On the authority of the Imam Jaʿfar al-Ṣādiq, an exception is first mentioned of leading the prayer for the dead (as reported by

Ḥammād b. 'Īsā in his *Kitāb*) but only if there is no one else who is qualified to do so. In all other cases, the woman needs to stand in a row in the middle of other women and lead by reciting the *takbīr* and being followed in it by the other women.[10]

On the consensus of three of his main sources, two of which are Imāmī and one Zaydī,[11] and contrary to Mālikī law, Qāḍī al-Nu'mān indicates that a woman can indeed lead prayers. Specifically, she can lead women in the ritual compulsory prayer on the condition that she positions herself by standing in their midst so that the other women are on her right and on her left, implying no priority of position, no forefront and no behind. The precedent of the Prophet's wife Umm Salama is significantly adduced and supported by the authoritative words of the Prophet himself, who indicated to her the spatial position needed for the female imam in relation to the female congregation.[12] Qāḍī al-Nu'mān concludes this section in the *Kitāb al-īḍāḥ* by invoking again the authority of the Prophet Muḥammad on the matter, in the Book of Prohibitions (*Kitāb al-nahy*), with the statement that the Prophet affirmed that 'it is prohibited for a woman to lead a man in prayer'.[13] Qāḍī al-Nu'mān does not provide any explanation for this prohibition, except that there is consensus (*ijmā'*) in what he has learnt (but God knows best).

In the introduction to his magnum opus, the *Da'ā'im al-Islām,* Qāḍī al-Nu'mān states that such a book is intended to be comprehensive (*jāmi'*) but concise (*mukhtaṣar*),[14] easy to use, free from prolixity and inclusive only of the proven and authentic reports from the Imams and the *ahl al-bayt*. True to this statement, the section on a woman leading prayer is confined to one paragraph only, in contrast to two folios in the *Kitāb al-īḍāḥ*, and quotes only one report, with no *isnād*, on the authority of Imam Ja'far al-Ṣādiq in support of his stance on the subject.[15]

Being the normative book of Ismaili jurisprudence, there are no shades of interpretation here, no references to written sources and variants of *ḥadīths*,[16] nor to scholarly consensus,[17] but to the sole authority of the Imam as the source of knowledge and of ritual practice. As reported by the chief Ismaili historian Idrīs 'Imād al-Dīn, who wrote in the 9th/15th century, the *Da'ā'im* itself bore the official seal of approval of the Fatimid Imam-caliph al-Muʿizz, who is said to have commissioned the work and, after its compilation, also edited and revised it.[18] With such an endorsement, it is no wonder that, among Qāḍī al-Nuʿmān's works, the *Daʿāʾim* is by far the most successful and enduring, and to this day is the basis for the legal education of some contemporary Ismaili communities. It is in the *Daʿāʾim* that all the implications of the role of the Ismaili Imam-caliph as a source of law are made clear: after the Qurʾan and the *sunna*, the third source of legal authority is the infallible Imam.

The third work by Qāḍī al-Nuʿmān under consideration here, the *Taʾwīl al-daʿāʾim*, is what the modern scholar of Ismailism Farhad Daftary has defined as the *bāṭinī* companion to his *ẓāhirī* legal compendium, the *Daʿāʾim*.[19] The *Taʾwīl* differs in format, origin, scope and intended audience from all his other works. Organised as a commentary on the *Daʿāʾim*, sentence by sentence, as its allegorical interpretation, it is a collection of teaching sessions (*majālis al-ḥikma*) for Ismailis, which had been authorised by the Imam-caliph and were held by Qāḍī al-Nuʿmān, after the Friday *ʿaṣr* prayer, inside the Fatimid palace.[20]

The scope both of these sessions and of the *Taʾwīl* was to provide for the initiates (*al-awliyāʾ*) the inner meaning of the law as it had been expounded in the *Daʿāʾim*, and to present a different dimension of the understanding of legal prescriptions, in the case here of the ritual of prayer. Qāḍī al-Nuʿmān explains the gradual progression of knowledge from external (*ẓāhirī*) to esoteric/inner (*bāṭinī*) and then to *ḥaqq* (essence, truth) by providing parallels with the placenta of a newborn baby as an external envelope (the *ẓāhir* of the newborn) which is to be discarded, then with the umbilical cord which is cut and dries out after birth. The stage of *ḥaqq* represents the level of the initiate *muʾmin* who, after taking the oath, also discards the external layer of the People of the *bāṭin* (i.e., the Ismaili followers) to eventually grasp both the outer and the inner meaning of the people of *ḥaqq*.[21]

The inner meaning (*taʾwīl*) of *ṣalāt* is that it is an allegory (*mathal*) for the *daʿwa* (the invitation to the faith).[22] This is the call from the Prophet Muḥammad and, after him, the call from the Imam of the time; so the Prophet and the friends of God (i.e., the Ismaili Imams) are all *dāʿīs* (summoners).[23] Qāḍī al-Nuʿmān explains symbolically each aspect of *ṣalāt* (the daily prayers), from their number to their timings. He draws a parallel between, on the one hand, the Prophet and the Imam of the time and, on the other, the leaders of prayers, the imams, as day-to-day projections of the Prophet and the Imam. The Prophet and the Imam are the most excellent of the people of their era, while the prayer leaders are the most excellent of their community, performing the most excellent of rituals. Therefore, nobody can stand in front of them in prayer, hence the Prophet, the Imams and the leaders of prayer, all need to stand in front of the congregation. The imam as prayer leader is, in other words, the exoteric counterpart to the Ismaili Imam: the first leads the prayer, the second leads the *daʿwat al-ḥaqq*, or the call to the truth, to the Ismaili faith.[24] The 5th/11th century Ismaili writer and *dāʿī* al-Nīsābūrī, in his treatise on the code of conduct for the *dāʿīs*, extends this parallel between the prayer leader and the *daʿwa* by stating that the *dāʿī* should exhibit the same qualifications as the prayer leader, given that the *dāʿī* is the leader (*imām*) of the essential, most esoteric prayer (*al-ṣalāt al-ḥaqīqiyya*).[25]

As for female leadership of prayer, Qāḍī al-Nuʿmān clarifies his statement in the *Daʿāʾim*, by saying that a *maḥram*,[26] that is, a woman whom it is unlawful to marry (namely, a close relative), is not like a full *bāligh*, or a male with full legal capacity. At the esoteric level, the parallel is between, on the one hand, the woman and the rank of the *mustafīḍ*, that is, a student, a candidate for initiation or an ordinary initiate at the bottom of the Ismaili hierarchy, and, on the other, between the man and the rank of the absolute *mufīd*, that is, a teacher, a high rank.[27] As a woman cannot lead men, so the ordinary initiate cannot summon those who are in the highest ranks of the hierarchy, such as the *mufīd muṭlaq*.[28] In other words, the disciple cannot summon the master/guide. As in other works by Qāḍī al-Nuʿmān (and in Ismaili works written after his) the language of gender is here used not, or not only, to indicate the physical male and female, but to metaphorically express the relationship between the teacher as the possessor of knowledge and the pupil as the beneficiary of that knowledge.

According to the various examples of interpretative models of *ṣalāt* which Marion Katz discusses in her monograph on prayer,[29] Qāḍī al-Nuʿmān's treatment of prayer, as outlined above, falls within the cosmological and the educational models. The first assumes a homology between the rituals related to prayer and the cosmic hierarchy. This is possible because the spiritual hierarchy of the Ismaili *daʿwa* itself is a reflection of the physical cosmic hierarchy and of the religious hierarchy of the cycles inaugurated by specific prophets. The second interpretative model is educational in the sense that prayer and its rituals correspond to the instruction of knowledge that is imparted by the *dāʿīs* and the other ranks in the Ismaili *daʿwa* organisation.

In Qāḍī al-Nuʿmān's works, the levels of interpretation are not exclusive but converge and reflect various facets of the subject: the ritual, the legal and the esoteric. However, the exoteric ritual level is not discarded here. Qāḍī al-Nuʿmān is not an antinomian, nor are the other Fatimid Ismaili scholars, because for them the exoteric and the ritual are signs and symbolic representations of the esoteric spiritual realm. By using an allegorical language of gender, Qāḍī al-Nuʿmān further provides both the outer and the inner meanings of the statement that a woman cannot lead women from the front but only by standing in their midst. Not being able to be in a position of precedence among them, as they all share the condition of not being an absolute *dāʿī*, she cannot summon the initiates but is, with them, in a position of equality 'in status and rank'. This has a legal parallel in the status of women, actual women, not having full legal capacity, which would be seen as the equivalent of the high hierarchical ranks.[30]

This is, thus far, the most explicit reasoning and justification for the lack of permissibility for a woman to lead men *tout court*, and for leading other women, not from the front, but from the middle. The justification is legal, not ontological. Bearing in mind Qāḍī al-Nuʿmān's perspective and background, he is not speaking here in theological or philosophical terms, and he is not referring to the innate qualities of a real female, but to her legal capacity. One of the sources on which such an argument could be based might have been that which he refers to in a passage in his *Kitāb al-īḍāḥ* as the *Kutub* by the Zaydī, Abū 'Abd Allāh Muḥammad b. Sallām. Ibn Sallām, on the authority of the first Shi'i Imam 'Alī b. Abī Ṭālib, had stated that 'the woman does not call the *adhān*, does not contract marriage and does not lead the people in prayer (*lā ta'ummu al-nās*)'.[31] Unlike Imāmī Shi'is, Qāḍī al-Nu'mān agrees with Ibn Sallām (but also with Mālikīs and some other Sunni schools of law) in regard to a woman's legal inability to contract her own marriage without her guardian, irrespective of her age and status. In his *Da'ā'im* he selects the prophetic *ḥadīth* which considers a marriage contracted without the participation of the bride's guardian as invalid: 'There is no marriage without a guardian (*walī*) and two reliable witnesses.'[32] However, with regard to *adhān* and female *imāma*, Qāḍī al-Nu'mān's position as expressed in his *Da'ā'im* is at variance with Ibn Sallām's as well as that of all Mālikī scholars. According to al-Nu'mān, a woman can under certain circumstances give the call to prayer, in other words she can utter, if she wishes, the *adhān* and the *iqāma*,[33] as well as lead women in prayer. Nevertheless, the link is quite clearly established between ritual leadership and the full legal capacity of a woman, the one being the consequence of the other.

Similar to the case of marriage suitability (*kafā'a*), in a much later source analysed by Mona Siddiqui, the permissibility of a woman's ritual action such as calling the *adhān* or leading prayer can 'be interpreted as a legal argument carefully elaborated by a juristic desire to ensure control of social stratification'.[34] In the case of a more Ismaili doctrinal reading of the legal-ritual requirements, as found in the *Ta'wīl*, it is not only the social stratification which is at stake, but the very hierarchical structure of the spiritual line of transmission of knowledge and of the Ismaili *da'wa*.

The issue of legal capacity for a woman is a complex one. Even after having reached sexual and mental maturity (being both *bāligha* and *rashīda*), or attained her legal majority, in certain legal acts such as testimony and contracting her own marriage, Muslim legal scholars did not consider a woman's legal weight and authority to be the same as that of a man. As argued in her detailed study on women in Islamic law, the modern historian Judith Tucker posits that this kind of position on the part of jurists could have been 'a product of social context, specifically a disinclination to invite women into the public space of the court … or … deep-seated beliefs in the inferiority of women's mental powers'.[35]

More specifically, the issue of legal capacity and competence needs to be considered alongside that of the legal capacity to act. In her brief but thought-provoking article on medieval Mālikī sources, the medieval historian Cristina de la Puente argues that gender was a factor that could, and did, limit a woman's ability to exercise her legal capacity. Instances of this include the legal requirement of a 'complement', be it either a *walī* or a *wakīl*, for a woman to contract her marriage, to go out of the house when married and needing her husband's permission to do so and so on. This naturally has implications, for example, on her going to the mosque for the prayer, about which some Mālikī legal scholars repeatedly state that women not only are not obliged to go to the mosque to pray, but in fact are recommend not to go.[36]

Qāḍī al-Nuʿmān does not refer to the innate qualities of a female as compared to those of a male; his analogy of a woman as a pupil, a receiver rather than a giver of knowledge, though expressed in symbolic terms or in an esoteric context such as the *Ta'wīl*,[37] still begs the question as to whether a real woman could ever progress to higher hierarchical religious ranks, whether she could be a *mufīd*. Qāḍī al-Nuʿmān does not explicitly address this issue in either of the three works under examination here, even though, as rightly pointed out in a study by Karen Bauer, it could be inferred that as the *daʿwa* hierarchy was based on spiritual knowledge, it would be more flexible than the physical gender hierarchy, since a pupil might indeed progress to become a teacher.[38]

However, in another of his works, a historical insider's account of the establishment of Fatimid rule in North Africa, when praising the accomplishments and efforts of women in the promotion of the Ismaili mission, al-Nuʿmān goes as far as to say that some elderly women who had attended the educational sessions, achieved 'a rank in the *daʿwa*'.[39] This could be interpreted as evidence that women could and did reach the status of *mufīd*, given that the *mustafīd* or *mustajīd* are terms that denote the ordinary initiate, and are not ranks in the hierarchy of the *daʿwa*.

After Qāḍī al-Nuʿmān, other Ismaili scholars used gendered language with reference to spiritual hierarchy and continued to employ the male and female analogy of teacher and pupil. Almost two centuries later, towards the end of the Fatimid era, the Ismaili Ṭayyibī author al-Sulṭān al-Khaṭṭāb (d. 533/1138) referred positively to the ontological and spiritual equality of men and women to support the religious authority of a woman, Sayyida Arwā (d. 532/1138), the Ṣulayḥid queen in Yemen. The religious authority she embodied, or was claimed to have embodied, was not pertinent to ritual performance, but to a position of authority (religious/spiritual and dynastic at the same time) as the head of the Ismaili *daʿwa* in her region. To justify the queen's spiritual and religious status (and to legitimise the spiritual authority of the subsequent religious ranks in Yemeni Ṭayyibī Ismailism), specifically her status as *ḥujja*, a rank inferior only to that of the Ismaili Imam, al-Sulṭān al-Khaṭṭāb argued that it is not the external, physical form of male or female that gives an indication of the quality and spiritual achievement of a person, but rather the person's acts of devotion and good deeds.[40]

If the statements in Qāḍī al-Nuʿmān's works refer, above all, to the legal and ritual theory of women leading prayers, are there equivalent references about women's ritual practices during the Fatimid era? As far as *duʿāʾ* prayer was concerned, Qāḍī al-Nuʿmān himself provides the example of the so-called *tasbiḥat Fāṭima/tasbiḥat al-zahrāʾ* (Fāṭima's rosary), which was a series of invocations/blessings, consisting of 33 *subḥānas*, 33 *takbīrs* and 33 *taḥmīds*. These, with the addition of a *shahāda*, make 100 mentions of the name of God for which God will grant 1,000 good deeds.[41] However, there is thus far no evidence of this ritual being practised by women under the Fatimids.

With regard to the *ṣalāt* prayers at the mosque, it appears that women could and presumably did attend them. Some specific ritual stipulations were in place as to their proper attire, the wearing of jewellery and perfume and putting henna on their hands for these occasions. Such measures might have been in place so that women could be easily recognised as such and distinguished from men,[42] but also as expressions of religious Ismaili identity which were quite distinct from Sunni stipulations against, for instance, women wearing jewellery and perfume at public prayers,[43] or uttering the *adhān* and the *iqāma*. Qāḍī al-Nuʿmān also refers to the proper conduct of women in the mosque during the prayer, such as, how to attract attention in the case of an emergency.[44] Despite written norms and legal prescriptions being in place,[45] it is, however, very rare to find references in the chronicles to actual women attending the Friday prayer. During the Fatimid era, there is, nevertheless, more substantial evidence about elite women, such as the queen-mother, Durzān (d. 385/995), Queen Arwā and al-Āmir's consort, being patronesses of mosques or sponsors of ritual objects in mosques. Most references to women and ritual, however, concern less formal public settings, such as cemeteries, or informal sessions in the home.

The Imam as Prayer Leader in Qāḍī al-Nuʿmān's writings and other Shiʿi jurisprudence: Shared Roots and Departures

The task of establishing and developing an Ismaili formulation of legal rulings was undertaken by Qāḍī al-Nuʿmān in a context of some relative fluidity between Sunni and Shiʿi *madhāhib*. The legal foundations rested on *ḥadīth*s, especially those transmitted on the authority of the Imams, as well as on legal conventions and principles which were to some degree still being debated between the schools. Of these, especially relevant to him for geographical, historical and doctrinal reasons were the Imāmī and Zaydī Shiʿi and the Mālikī ones. Al-Nuʿmān's positions on prayer leadership, too, were the result of harmonisation and adaptation.

A telling example is the context for the discussion on the roles and characteristics of the prayer leader.

On the basis of statements in well-known *ḥadīth*s, some of the traits and roles of the imam – that is, the person leading the congregation in prayer – can be identified. In *ḥadīth* collections, basic descriptive assertions such as the following can be found: 'The imam is appointed so that he may be followed.'[46]

But there are also more complex statements with ritual and ethical implications about the role of the imam – 'The imam is a *junna* (a shield, a protection) for the believer'[47] – or assertions of a doctrinal-ethical nature – 'Your imam is your mediator/intercessor (*shafīʿ*) with God.'[48] Qāḍī al-Nuʿmān shares this understanding of the imam as a mediator between the believer and God by stating that 'the imam of the people is the one who ushers them into the presence of God'.[49] This and the other roles linked to or expected of the imam justify the widespread view that he should be the best person in the community.

There is indeed abundant evidence from the *sunna* of the Prophet that the person most qualified to be an imam is the one who has the best knowledge of the Qur'an.[50] Nevertheless, for most jurisprudents, several further characteristics, in some cases even prerequisites, came to be associated with the roles of imam. Majority was one of such conditions (*shurūṭ*), even a prerequisite for some scholars; other conditions, in the most reported order of priority, were being Muslim, sane, just and, significantly for this discussion, being male.

Jurisprudents, such as the influential 5th/11th-century Shāfiʿī jurist al-Māwardī and almost all Mālikīs, regarded being male as the first prerequisite for the office of imam, or prayer leader.[51] On the other hand, the Imāmī Shiʿis specify that maleness is a requisite only if the congregation being led includes men.[52] This is clearly explained by the 8th/14th-century jurisprudent al-Muḥaqqiq al-Ḥillī, who justifies female leadership of a female congregation by presenting as evidence the *ḥadīth* that the one who is best at reciting the Qur'an is the most qualified to lead in prayer. Al-Ḥillī argues that, as this *ḥadīth* does not specify male or female, it follows that it is permissible for a woman to lead other women in the compulsory prayers (*farīḍa*),[53] and this argument is shared by the majority of Shiʿi and several Sunni scholars.

Thus, while for an imam to be a male is a prerequisite in all cases for the Mālikīs, the other schools of Islamic law, both Sunni and Shiʿi, consider maleness to be required for a male-only or mixed male and female congregation. Jurisprudents discussed such cases within the framework of the validity of the prayer of the persons led by an imam. The prevalent rule for the validity of prayer is that the imam may lead a congregation which is similar in kind: a mute person may be the imam of mute people, a bisexual/hermaphrodite of a congregation of women or of bisexuals like himself, and a woman can be the imam of other women.[54] Yet while a physical condition, such as being mute or blind, is a biological and physical given (with social accretions), when it comes to gender, physical traits (apparent or not) are viewed and interpreted primarily through the lens of social contexts and constructs. Consequently, gender is viewed differently in relation to, for instance, the age of the woman and the place from where she leads other women in prayer.

I have argued elsewhere that the instances of unconventional imams and particularly female imams discussed by classical jurists, appear to be theoretical cases exhibited in legal manuals in order to demonstrate the writer's erudition rather than serving as evidence of actual practice.[55] To what extent was this the case for Qāḍī al-Nuʿmān's references to female leadership of prayer? This is by no means an agreed interpretation, as some scholars contend that the early developments of Islamic jurisprudence were in fact in response to practical cases.

Be that as it may, even in the theoretical cases in which women could lead other women in prayer, the very meaning of such 'leadership' needs to be specified for a more complete understanding of the context of al-Nuʿmān's argument. The verb *amma, taʾummu*, bears the specific connotation of 'leading from the front', that is, etymologically, the root of the term '*imām*'. However, to state that a woman cannot lead other women from the front, does not necessarily exclude women from being the imams of other women. This is evident in the wording of the *ḥadīth*, quoted by Qāḍī al-Nuʿmān, attributed to the sixth Imam Jaʿfar al-Ṣādiq and often included in other Shiʿi *ḥadīth* collections. When asked whether a woman could lead [from the front] (*taʾummu*) other women in prayer, Jaʿfar al-Ṣādiq's reply was positive in the case of the supererogatory prayer (*al-nāfila*); however, for the prescribed prayer (*al-maktūba*) his answer was that she should position herself in the middle of the female congregation.[56]

This and other *ḥadīth*s, also traced back to Jaʿfar al-Ṣādiq, are used as evidence for the permissibility of women leading (from the middle) other women in prayer. From exponents of the main 3rd/9th- and 4th/10th-century Shiʿi trends, those grouped among the *ahl al-ḥadīth*, such as Muḥammad al-Kulaynī (d. ca. 329/940–941) and the great Shaykh al-Ṭāʾifa al-Ṭūsī (d. 460/1067) in his *Mabsūṭ*, and in later centuries renowned Shiʿi scholars, all concur on this point.[57]

However, as is the case in a Sunni context, it does not mean that women are expected or encouraged to attend congregational prayers, especially in the mosque. The Imāmī Shiʿi authority Ibn Bābawayh (d. 381/991) quotes the well-known *ḥadīth*, often also found in Sunni collections, that for a woman to pray in her house is better than to pray in the mosque.[58] Even more restrictive is the advice, again on the authority of Jaʿfar al-Ṣādiq, that a woman's private chamber (*mikhdaʿuhā*) is a better place for her to pray than the rest of the house.[59] The opposite is the case for men: their prayers are worth more the wider, the more public and the more frequented the place of worship – better to pray in the great *jāmiʿa* mosque than the tribal mosque, or the market mosque and so on.[60]

In Shiʿi *ḥadīth* collections of the 4th–5th/10th–11th centuries, there reoccurs the habit of tracing back to Jaʿfar al-Ṣādiq those *ḥadīth*s in which his fellow men are advised not to allow women to leave their rooms/quarters (*ghuraf*), nor to teach them how to write or to teach them Sūrat Yūsuf, presumably because of its account of extra marital seduction and female guile. Instead, women should be taught Sūrat al-Nūr, with its rulings on adultery, marriage and modesty.[61] Is the recurrent presence of such 'restrictive' *ḥadīth*s to be read as an expression of a development in Shiʿi jurisprudence marked, among other trends, by increased restrictions on women in accessing public spaces? On the other hand, it could be argued that, given the variety of relevant *ḥadīth*s, textual precedents were already present from the early centuries of Islam, even though later jurists might have selected specific *ḥadīth*s to support varied social and legal attitudes towards women.

*Ḥadīth*s about restrictions on women have a direct impact on their attendance at the Friday or *jumʿa* prayer in a mosque. There are numerous extant works by the Twelver Shiʿi scholars about the status of the Friday prayer during the Occultation (*ghayba*) of their Twelfth Imam, which began in 260/874. They held contrasting opinions as to whether the Friday prayer itself ought to be prohibited, advisable or compulsory during the period of the Occultation. If they held it was not prohibited, then the issue discussed was whether or not the presence of a *mujtahid* acting as the Imam's representative was necessary.[62] In these circumstances leadership of the Friday prayer was seen as being representative, or suggestive, of a more encompassing leadership (political, religious and so on), whereby the qualities of the rightful prayer leader could be linked to those associated with the Shiʿis' supreme human leader, the Imam in a Shiʿi sense. For most Shiʿi jurists and scholars, particularly for Zaydīs, the quality of *ʿadāla* (righteousness) is so essential in a prayer leader for the legality of the prayer he leads, that its absence would make void (*bāṭil*) the prayer of the person being led. This is even more important in the case of the leader of the *jumʿa* prayer,[63] whose additional role is that of reading the *khuṭba* and therefore acting as the representative of the current government. From one Shiʿi perspective, the Twelfth Imam of the Ithnāʿasharīs being in *ghayba*, the imam of the *jumʿa* prayer convenes and performs the Friday prayer as his deputy.[64] It is because of this deputyship, according to several Shiʿi Imāmī scholars, that the prerequisites for a legitimate prayer leader become more numerous. In addition to faith, which as Ibn Bābawayh explains, means proactive Shiʿi faith and practice,[65] they include maleness, justice and intellect as well as purity (or legitimacy) of birth.[66]

As seen above, an analysis of Qāḍī al-Nuʿmān's three works shows that in many ways he shares Imāmī and Zaydī Shiʿi interpretations of prayer, along with the qualities needed to be a prayer leader. The ritual of prayer can be seen as an external exoteric ritual, one of the Pillars of Islam, but it also has an inner dimension which links it to the cosmic hierarchy and to the figure at its pole (*quṭb*), the Imam. Consequently, for Qāḍī al-Nuʿmān and many other Shiʿi scholars the prayer leader is the representative of the Imam (in a Shiʿi sense) and shares with him traits such as piety, justice, purity, including purity of birth, and attested excellence in the community. In the case of the Friday prayer, the prayer leader is the Imam's deputy and, like him, needs to be a man when the congregation is mixed.

As for female prayer leadership, Qāḍī al-Nuʿmān's position is in line with the broader Shiʿi focus on relationality. Unlike the Mālikī *madhhab*, which denies female *imāma* per se, irrespective of the congregation being led, Qāḍī al-Nuʿmān and Shiʿi scholars generally consider leadership of the ritual prayer by a woman as legitimate, provided she leads other women from the middle. Qāḍī al-Nuʿmān shares with other Shiʿi scholars interpretative approaches to ritual and to scripture, particularly relying on the inner interpretation on the authority of the Imam. But al-Nuʿmān departs from the Ithnāʿasharīs on account of the living presence of the Ismaili Imam, which makes him an active source of the law, in contrast to the Imāmī Shiʿi belief in the Occultation of their Imam and its lasting implications for the sources of law.

Conclusion

To conclude, on the basis of three of his works, Qāḍī al-Nuʿmān's short passages on female leadership of *ṣalāt* show that statements about female prayer leadership can be interpreted from different interlinked perspectives. A ritual and legal approach shows that a woman cannot lead men or lead other women from the front because she, like her female congregation, does not have the full legal capacity to act. But an esoteric reading of the same passages reveals that the language used is highly symbolic and does not necessarily refer to the physical reality of gender in a social context but to states of knowledge, seen in terms of the feminine recipient or the masculine giver of knowledge. Ultimately, all these perspectives, employing multiple levels of interpretation (*ẓāhir*, *bāṭin* and *bāṭin al-bāṭin* or *ḥaqq*), aim to link the social hierarchical structure of a given time, and the legal rulings pertinent to that context, to the higher spiritual and esoteric plane by means of which the hierarchical and political legitimacy of the Fatimid dynasty was justified.

These passages also show some development in Qāḍī al-Nuʿmān's Ismaili Shiʿi jurisprudence, from a summative, inclusive and harmonising initial phase of broad Shiʿi appeal as expressed in the *Kitāb al-īḍāḥ*, where a variety of opinions is displayed, to a normative Ismaili stance in the *Daʿāʾim*, and from there to concluding with an esoteric, selectively Fatimid Ismaili interpretation of the *Taʾwīl al-daʿāʾim*.

Notes

* For the sake of clarity, throughout this chapter, I use: the term Imam (with a capital 'I') to refer to the Shiʿi Imam, or what the Shiʿis identified as the leader of the Muslim community after the Prophet Muḥammad; the term Imam-caliph to refer to the spiritual and political leader of the Ismaili community during the Fatimid era; and imam (with a small 'i') to refer to the prayer leader within a congregation.

1 I am grateful to Dr Delia Cortese, Middlesex University, London, for providing the following references of a selection of mosque prayer leaders in Egypt contemporary or after Qāḍī al-Nuʿmān, from Ṭaqī al-Dīn al-Maqrīzī, *Kitāb al-muqaffā al-kabīr*, ed. Muḥammad al-Yaʿlāwī (Beirut, 1991), no. 1371: Abu'l-Qāsim b. Khāqān al-Muqrī (d. 402/1011), who was imam in a mosque and died in Miṣr; no 2792 Abū Bakr Ibn al-Jabbān (d. ca. 405/1014), who narrated in Tinnis from Abū Jaʿfar ʿUmar b. Abī Ṭāliq, who was imam of the Masjid Jāmiʿ (great mosque) of Tinnis; no. 3028: Ibn Nazīf al-Farrāʾ (341–431/952–1039), who spent seventy years praying for people in

the mosque of ʿAbd Allāh, was a Shāfiʿī and when he died the *imāma* was carried on by a Mālikī; no. 3426; the jurist al-Naḥḥās who was imam at the Jāmiʿ ʿAmr, and who died after 485/1092.

2 S. T. Lokhandwalla, 'The Origins of Ismaili Law' (D. Phil. thesis, Faculty of Oriental Languages, Oxford University, 1951).

3 Wilferd Madelung, 'The Sources of Ismāʿīlī Law', *Journal of Near Eastern Studies*, 35 (1976), pp. 32–33, considers Ismaili *fiqh* as presented in the *Kitāb al-īḍāḥ* as a compromise between Imāmī and Zaydī law, while Poonawala, when discussing the legal system expressed in the *Daʿāʾim al-Islām*, states that it aimed at a 'reconciliation of the Shīʿī Ismāʿīlī doctrine with that of the Sunni Mālikī *madhhab* of North Africa', in Ismail K. Poonawala, 'Al-Qāḍī al-Nuʿmān and Ismaʿili Jurisprudence', in F. Daftary, ed., *Mediaeval Ismaʿili History and Thought* (Cambridge, 1996), p. 129.

4 Al-Qāḍī al-Numān, *Minhāj al-farāʾiḍ*, ed. and tr. A. Cilardo as *The Early History of Ismaili Jurisprudence* (London, 2012), pp. 9–15.

5 Abū Ḥanīfa al-Qāḍī al-Nuʿmān, *al-Īḍāḥ*, ed. Muḥammad Kāẓim Raḥmatī (Beirut, 2007); this is not a critical edition and is based on the only manuscript (Tübingen) thus far recovered. During the 12th/18th century al-Majdū (d. 1183/1769), in his *Fihrist*, stated that of the whole work only a portion at the beginning of the 'Book on Prayer' was still extant.

6 For the compilation of *al-Īḍāḥ* during the reign of the Imam-caliph al-Mahdī, see references in Poonawala, 'Al-Qāḍī al-Nuʿmān', p. 121, especially n. 24.

7 For Poonawala's reasoning and sources on 349/960 as the composition date of the *Daʿāʾim*, see his 'Al-Qāḍī al-Nuʿmān', p. 127.

8 Heinz Halm, *The Empire of the Mahdi: The Rise of the Fatimids*, tr. M. Bonner (Leiden, 1996), pp. 370–371.

9 Madelung, 'The Sources of Ismāʿīlī Law', p. 32 and throughout, where a more accurate analysis of the *Kitāb al-īḍāḥ* is presented: Poonawala, 'Al-Qāḍī al-Nuʿmān and Ismaʿili jurisprudence', p. 128.

10 Al-Qāḍī al-Nuʿmān, *al-Īḍāḥ*, ed. Raḥmatī, p. 118; *al-Īḍāḥ*, Tübingen MS, fol. 95r.

11 The three sources referred to in *al-Īḍāḥ*, Tübingen MS, fols. 95r and 95v, are: the already mentioned *Kutub* by the Zaydī Muḥammad Ibn Sallām, on the authority of the Prophet; and the Imāmī works *al-Jamīʿ min kutub Ṭāhir b. Zakariyyāʾ*, by an unknown author but cited by the well-known Imāmī scholar Ibn Shahrāshūb (d. 588/1192) and the *Jamīʿ* by al-Thaʿālabī (d. ca. 765/1363).

12 Umm Salama Hind, of the Quraysh tribe, married the Prophet after her husband's death at the battle of Uḥud; over 300 *ḥadīth*s are transmitted on her authority. The passage in the *Īḍāḥ* is from the *Kutub* by Ibn Sallām, and narrates that the Prophet entered her house while the women were performing *ṣalāt* without being led, and, after Umm Salama questioned him on whether it is permissible for a woman to lead the women in prayer, the Prophet made it clear that it is if the female imam is in their midst. See al-Qāḍī al-Nuʿmān, *al-Īḍāḥ*, ed. Raḥmatī, p. 119; *al-Īḍāḥ*, Tübingen MS, fols. 95r and 95v.

13 Al-Qāḍī al-Nuʿmān, *al-Īḍāḥ*, ed. Raḥmatī, p. 119; *al-Īḍāḥ*, Tübingen MS, fol. 95v.

14 Al-Qāḍī al-Nuʿmān, *Daʿāʾim al-Islām*, ed. Asaf A. A. Fyzee (Cairo, 1951–1961), vol. 1, p. 2 and English trans. as *The Pillars of Islam*, by A.A.A. Fyzee, completely revised by Ismail K. Poonawala (New Dehli, 2002–2004), vol. 1, p. 2.

15 Al-Qāḍī al-Nuʿmān, *Daʿāʾim al-Islām*, ed. Fyzee, p. 153; English trans., *The Pillars of Islam*, vol. 1, p. 193.

16 The reference to the books from where Qāḍī al-Nuʿmān takes his quotes is one of the most useful characteristics of the *al-Īḍāḥ*. As Madelung says: 'In quoting the traditions of the *ahl al-bayt*, he [Qāḍī al-Nuʿmān] could not claim authorised oral transmission directly to himself but had to rely on literary sources available to him'; Madelung, 'The Sources of Ismāʿīlī law', p. 30, which makes the work a most valuable source on the written *ḥadīth* collections of the time.

17 On the redundancy and rejection of *ijmāʿ* and *ijtihād* as sources of law owing to the establishment of the Fatimid caliphate, see Poonawala, 'Al-Qāḍī al-Nuʿmān and Ismaʿili Jurisprudence', p. 126.

18 See Poonawala's introduction to the English translation of the *Daʿāʾim*, in *The Pillars of Islam*, vol. 1, p. xxx.

19 Farhad Daftary, *The Ismāʿīlīs: Their History and Doctrines* (2nd ed., Cambridge, 2007), p. 215.

20 For the development of the *majālis* and their location during and after Qāḍī al-Nuʿmān's lifetime, see H. Halm, 'The Ismaʿili Oath of Allegiance (*ʿahd*) and the "Sessions of Wisdom" (*majālis al-ḥikma*) in Fatimid times', in F. Daftary, ed., *Mediaeval Ismaʿili History and Thought* (Cambridge, 1996), especially pp. 101–112.

21 Al-Qāḍī al-Nuʿmān, *Taʾwīl al-daʿāʾim*, M.Ḥ. al-Aʿẓamī (Cairo, 1968–1969), vol. 1, pp. 47–48.

22 Ibid., pp. 176–177.

23 Ibid., p. 177.
24 Ibid., pp. 239–240.
25 From Aḥmad b. Ibrāhīm al-Nīsābūrī, *al-Risāla al-mūjaza*, ed. and tr. Verena Klemm and P.E. Walker as *A Code of Conduct: A Treatise on the Etiquette of the Fatimid Ismaili Mission* (London, 2011), p. 24 (Arabic text) and pp. 47–48 (English tran.).
26 *Maḥram* is a legal term indicating a non-marriageable person, that is, one who is related to another of the opposite sex within the forbidden degrees of marriage, or impediments to marriage based on relationship, such as one's female descendants or ascendants, one's mother-in-law and so on. Even though the term can be used for both men and women, I translated it as referring to a female *maḥram* because of the textual context.
27 Al-Qāḍī al-Nuʿmān, *Ta'wīl al-daʿā'im*, vol. 1, p. 245. See also, ibid., pp. 47–48, for another use of symbolic gender language. Like a first-born is examined after birth to establish whether it is a female or a male, the *dāʿī* needs to distinguish between the *mufīd*, who is equivalent to the male and the *mustajīb*, who is the equivalent to the female.
28 Al-Qāḍī al-Nuʿmān, *Ta'wīl al-daʿā'im*, vol. 1, p. 241: *wa qawluhu la ta'ummu al-mar'a al-rijāl huwa anna al-mustafīd la yajūzu lahu an yadʿū mufīdan muṭlaqan*.
29 Marion H. Katz, *Prayer in Islamic Thought and Practice* (Cambridge, 2013), pp. 114–116.
30 Al-Qāḍī al-Nuʿmān, *Ta'wīl al-daʿā'im,* vol. 1, p. 245.
31 Al-Qāḍī al-Nuʿmān, *al-Īḍāḥ*, ed. Raḥmatī, pp. 83–84.
32 Al-Qāḍī al-Nuʿmān, *Daʿā'im al-Islām*, ed. Fyzee, vol. 2, pp. 203-204. The woman's representative can be a *walī* (legal guardian) or a *wakīl* (an agent).
33 Al-Qāḍī al-Nuʿmān, *Daʿā'im al-Islām*, vol. 1, p. 184.
34 Mona Siddiqui, 'Law and the Desire for Social Control: An Insight into the Hanafi Concept of Kafa'a with Reference to the Fatawa 'Alamgiri (1664–1672)', in Mai Yamani, ed., *Feminism and Islam* (New York, 1996), p. 65.
35 Judith Tucker, *Women, Family, and Gender in Islamic Law* (Cambridge, 2008), p. 149; Tucker states: 'most jurists dealt with the issue of woman as a legal subject not just as a legal question, but also as a moral one … and/or an anthropological one.'
36 Cristina de la Puente, 'Juridical Sources for the Study of Women: Limitations of the Female's Capacity to Act According to Mālikī

Law', in M. Marín and R. Deguilhem, ed., *Writing the Feminine: Women in Arab Sources* (London, 2002), p. 106.

37 The association of the female with being a recipient rather than a giver of knowledge is present in a number of Ismaili texts but also in those of other Shiʿi groups such as the Qarmaṭīs, see *Kitāb al-rusūm*, attributed to the Qarmaṭī *dāʿī* ʿAbdān, where in a series of allegorical parallelisms associated with marriage, the bride is compared to the body (in the body-soul parallelism), the pupil and exoteric knowledge: see MS 1174 (ArI, ZA) in Delia Cortese, *Arabic Ismaili Manuscripts: The Zāhid ʿAlī Collection in the Library of The Institute of Ismaili Studies* (London, 2003), n. 65. To counter this, however, as an example of females as givers of knowledge is Qāḍī al-Nuʿmān's statement in his *Iftitāḥ*, see note 39, below.

38 K. Bauer, 'Spiritual Hierarchy and Gender Hierarchy in Fāṭimid Ismāʿīlī Interpretations of the Qur'an', *Journal of Qur'anic Studies*, 14 (2012), pp. 38–39. Bauer refers to the relational character of the spiritual hierarchy and adds that 'the strict rankings of the spiritual hierarchy indicate that a person maybe, spiritually, both "male" and "female"', in the sense that a *ḥujja*, for instance, is female in its relation to the superior rank of the imam but male if compared to the *dāʿī* (p. 39).

39 Al-Qāḍī al-Nuʿmān, *Iftitāḥ al-daʿwa*, ed. Farhat Dachraoui (Tunis, 1975), p. 132 (Arabic text). This statement has been interpreted to mean that these old women became *dāʿī*s; see Hamid Haji's annotated English translation of the *Iftitāḥ*, as *Founding the Fatimid State: The Rise of an Early Islamic Empire* (London, 2006), p. 109: 'There were some old women who followed these sessions and rose to the rank of *dāʿī*s (*ḥadd al-daʿwa*).' In his Arabic critical edition of the *Iftitāḥ*, Farhat Dachraoui states that the text in MS copy (a) reads *ḥadd al-daʿwa*, while in MS (b) the text is corrupt, see *Iftitāḥ al-daʿwa*, ed. Dachraoui, p. 132, n. 2 (Arabic text).

40 From *Ghāyat al-mawālīd*, in Ismail K. Poonawala, *al-Sulṭān al-Khaṭṭāb, ḥayātuhu wa-shiʿruhu* (Cairo, 1999), appendix 1, pp. 433–436. On Queen Arwā's status, see D. Cortese and S. Calderini, *Women and the Fatimids in the World of Islam* (Edinburgh, 2006), pp. 129–140.

41 Al-Qāḍī al-Nuʿmān, *Sharḥ al-akhbār fī faḍā'il al-a'imma al-aṭhār* (Qumm, 1409–1412/1988–1992), vol. 1, pp. 67–68.

42 Al-Qāḍī al-Nuʿmān, *The Pillars of Islam*, vol. 1, p. 221, if a woman does not have jewellery to wear, she 'should put on some kind of a

necklace, so that men can be distinguished from women', see also p. 222. For a more detailed account of Qāḍī al-Nu'mān's stipulations about women attending congregational prayer, see Cortese and Calderini, *Women and the Fatimids*, pp. 34–35.

43 See Prophetic *ḥadīth*s about slave women going to the mosque to pray 'unperfumed', quoted in the Ẓāhirī legal work *al-Muḥallā bi'l-āthār* in C. Adang, 'Women's Access to Public Space According to *al-Muḥallā bi'l-Āthār*', in Marín and Deguilhem, ed., *Writing the Feminine*, p. 83.

44 Al-Qāḍī al-Nu'mān, *The Pillars of Islam*, vol. 1, p. 216, where in case she needs something badly during prayer, a woman 'may clap her hands'.

45 Al-Qāḍī al-Nu'mān, *The Pillars of Islam*, vol. 1, p. 226, on the authority of the Imam 'Alī: 'If a woman or a slave attends the Friday prayer it is as though the obligation to say the *ẓuhr* prayer is fulfilled.'

46 Muslim b. al-Ḥajjāj al-Qushayrī, *Ṣaḥīḥ Muslim* (Cairo, 2000), vol. 1, *ṣalāt*, *bāb* 19, pp. 173–174.

47 Ibid., vol. 1, *ṣalāt*, *bāb* 19, *ḥadīth* 961, p. 175.

48 Ibn Bābawayh, *Man lā yaḥḍuruhu al-faqīh* (Tehran, 1390/1970), vol. 1, p. 247, adding the statement: 'do not make a fool or a sinful person (*fāsiq*) your intercessor.'

49 *Ḥadīth* on the authority of Ja'far al-Ṣādiq, from the Prophet, in al-Qāḍī al-Nu'mān, *Da'ā'im al-Islām*, vol. 1, p. 152; trans., *The Pillars of Islam*, vol. 1, p. 190.

50 See al-Bukhārī, *Ṣaḥīḥ al-Bukhārī*, ed. Muḥammad Muḥsin Khān (New Delhi, 1984), vol. 1, *bāb* 54, *ḥadīth* 661, p. 375, where the prayer is led by a slave, and heading to ch. 54, where the statement is made that it is permissible for a minor (or a slave, or an illegitimate child) to lead the prayer on the basis of the Prophet's statement that the imam is the one who knows the Qur'an better than others in the group. See also Abū Dāwud, *Sunan Abī Dāwud* (Ḥums, 1969), *kitāb al-ṣalāt*, 582, vol. 1, p. 390: 'the one who is most versed in the Book of God ... is the one who [should] lead the people in prayer.'

51 'Alī b. Muḥammad al-Māwardī, *The Ordinances of Government: A Translation of al-Aḥkām al-sulṭāniyya wa'l-wilāyāt al-dīniyya*, tr. Wafaa H. Wahba (Reading, 1996), p. 114. For al-Māwardī, to be a male is the first prerequisite condition for the office of judge (p. 72: 'women are not qualified to hold major government positions'); a woman cannot be a minister either, for 'it [the ministry] calls for more soundness of opinion and firmness of purpose than women

are capable of, and involves public performance of duty in a manner denied [to] them' (p. 29).

52 Al-Muḥaqqiq al-Ḥillī, *Sharā'i' al-Islām fī masā'il al-ḥalāl wa'l-ḥarām* (Tehran, 1389/1969), vol. 1, p. 124.

53 Al-ʿAllāma al-Ḥillī, *Mukhtalaf al-shīʿa fī aḥkām al-sharīʿa* (Qumm, 1371/1951–1952), vol. 2, *ṣalāt*, pp. 486–488.

54 Al-Māwardī, *The Ordinances of Government*, p. 112.

55 S. Calderini, 'Contextualizing Arguments about Female Ritual Leadership (Women Imams) in Classical Islamic Sources', *Comparative Islamic Studies*, 5 (2009), pp. 5–32.

56 Abū Jaʿfar Muḥammad al-Kulaynī, *al-Furūʿ min al-Kāfī* (Beirut, 1401/1980–1981), vol. 3, *kitāb al-ṣalāt*, *Bāb al-rajul ya'ummu al-nisāʿ*, *ḥadīth* 2, p. 376; same in Ibn Bābawayh, *Man lā yaḥḍuruhu al-faqīh*, vol. 1, *ṣalāt*, *bāb* 56, *ḥadīth* 86, p. 259.

57 Abū Jaʿfar Muḥammad b. al-Ḥasan al-Ṭūsī, *Tahdhīb al-aḥkām*, ed. Ḥasan al-Mūsawī Kharsān (Najaf, 1378/1959), vol. 3, *bāb* 3, *ḥadīth*s 111 and 112, p. 31 and al-Muḥaqqiq al-Ḥillī, *Sharā'i' al-Islām fī masā'il al-ḥalāl wa'l-ḥarām*, vol. 1, pp. 123–124.

58 Ibn Bābawayh, *Man lā yaḥḍuruhu al-faqīh*, vol. 1, *ṣalāt*, *ḥadīth* 8, p. 245.

59 Ibid., vol. 1, *ṣalāt*, *ḥadīth* 88, p. 259. Note the degree of spatial restriction: better the inner chamber/bedchamber than the home/house (*bayt*), better the house than the larger dwelling (*dār*, often with courtyard). For a general explanation of the difference between *bayt* and *dār*, see Marçais, 'Dār', *EI2*, vol. 2, pp. 113–115; in some *ḥadīth*s, however, the two terms are interchangeable.

60 Al-Ṭūsī, *Tahdhīb al-aḥkām*, vol. 3, *bāb* 25 on *faḍl al-masājid*, cf. *ḥadīth* 694 on women and *ḥadīth* 698 on men's best places of worship, pp. 252–253. Cf. al-Qāḍī al-Nuʿmān, *The Pillars of Islam*, vol. 1, p. 186, on the authority of Jaʿfar al-Ṣādiq: 'the prayer in the greatest mosque (*al-masjid al-aʿẓam*) [is equivalent to] one hundred prayers, and in the tribal mosque, twenty-five prayers, and in the mosque in the market, twelve prayers.'

61 Ibn Bābawayh, *Man lā yaḥḍuruhu al-faqīh*, vol. 1, *ṣalāt*, *ḥadīth* 9, p. 245.

62 For some of the jurists' opinions about Friday prayer during the Safawid period, see D.J. Stewart, 'Polemics and Patronage in Safavid Iran: The Debate on Friday Prayer during the Reign of Shah Tahmasb', *Bulletin of the School of Oriental and African Studies*, 72 (2009), pp. 425–457.

63 Abū Ja'far Muḥammad b. al-Ḥasan al-Ṭūsī, *al-Mabsūṭ fī fiqh al-imāmiyya* (Tehran, 1378/1958), *kitāb ṣalāt al-jum'a* (143–151), pp. 146, 149.
64 A.A. Sachedina, *The Just Ruler in Shi'ite Islam* (New York, 1988), pp. 177–180; see in particular al-Ṭūsī's list of qualifications of the *imām al-jamā'a* in his *al-Mabsūṭ fī fiqh al-imāmiyya*, vol. 1, p. 157.
65 Ibn Bābawayh, *Man lā yaḥḍuruhu al-faqīh*, vol. 1, p. 257.
66 Al-Kulaynī, *al-Furū' min al-Kāfī*, vol. 3, *kitāb al-ṣalāt*, p. 371; Ibn Bābawayh, *Man lā yaḥḍuruhu al-faqīh*, vol. 1, p. 247; al-Muḥaqqiq al-Ḥillī, *Sharā'i' al-Islām*, vol. 1, p. 124.

5

Al-Ṭurṭūshī and the Fatimids*

Maribel Fierro

Mālikīs and Fatimids in Ifrīqiya

The French scholar Robert Brunschvig devoted a study to analysing the ritual divergences between Ismailis and Sunnis, focusing on the period of Fatimid rule in Ifrīqiya before the Fatimids moved to Cairo.[1] He used as his main sources lists by three different authors (al-Muqaddasī, Ibn Ḥamāduh and Ibn ʿIdhārī) in which they discussed the ritual 'innovations' (pl., *bidaʿ*) of the Fatimids. Although the lists present specificities and a few divergences, they are remarkable in their convergence. The practices mentioned in them are related to purification, fasting and most especially to prayer, such as the *adhān* and *iqāma*, or call to prayer, the hours for the obligatory prayers, the use of the *basmala* and other formulas, the *qunūt*,[2] the supplementary night prayers, and the prayer for the dead and for rain. For each of them, Brunschvig discussed what the Ismaili position was and how it diverged from that of the Sunnis without failing to point to intra-Sunni divergence of opinion (*ikhtilāf*). In fact, one of his sources – the 4th/10th-century geographer al-Muqaddasī – had already specified three different types of ritual practice: (1) those on which there was *ikhtilāf* among the Sunnis, such as the *qunūt*; (2) those that involved the return to the practices of the first Muslims, such as the double *iqāma* that the Umayyads had reduced to a single one; and (3) the practices that were particular to the Fatimids and that went against those of the Sunnis while lacking any clear precedent, such as the prayer of the eclipse with five inclinations (*rakʿas*) and two prostrations in each *rakʿa*.

The practices analysed by Brunschvig are all public rituals and thus susceptible to scandalised reaction or rejection on the part of those sectors of the population who, as Sunni Muslims, had been taught to behave otherwise. Now, in Ifrīqiya there were followers of both the Ḥanafī and Mālikī schools. The Ḥanafīs are generally considered to have been more inclined towards Fatimid positions and in fact some eventually became Ismailis. Generally speaking, the Mālikīs resisted Ismailism in a variety of ways, and while the Ḥanafīs eventually disappeared from the scene the Mālikī *madhhab* became predominant and hegemonic after the disappearance of Ismailism.[3]

In his study, Brunschvig quotes the *Risāla* by Ibn Abī Zayd al-Qayrawānī (d. 386/996), a famous Mālikī scholar who lived in Ifrīqiya under Fatimid rule and who wrote his Epistle in order to offer, in a condensed and easy-to-consult form, what every Mālikī should believe and do.[4] In it, a concerned Muslim living under Fatimid rule could rapidly find the Mālikī counterpart of the Fatimid-sponsored ritual practices. Thus Ibn Abī Zayd's *Risāla* could be seen as one among the varied Mālikī reactions to the danger they felt was represented by Ismailism, in the sense of providing the Mālikī community with a doctrinal and educational resource. To what extent by writing it Ibn Abī Zayd contributed, by imposing his own selection of legal and religious materials on the Mālikī canon, is something to be explored as there were internal divergences in the Mālikī *madhhab*, with positions that could come close to those of other schools. The construction of the Mālikī legal school – on which a book needs to be written – was a process in which certain doctrines and practices were brought to the centre and others relegated to the periphery or even rejected, although what was located in the centre could be still the subject of debate. The main issue always concerned determination of the legitimising authority onto whom the doctrines and practices that some scholars wanted to push to the centre could be projected back, an issue that occupied Mālikīs – as well as the members of other legal schools –

throughout the centuries, and to which Robert Brunschvig devoted an illuminating study that is still valid.[5]

Mālikīs and Fatimids in Egypt

The ensuing lively and contentious interplay of different legal and religious trends inside the Mālikī school, and between this and other schools, can be studied through different phases. In the case of the encounter between Mālikīs and Ismailis/Fatimids, the first phase took place in Ifrīqiya, for which we have a number of sources that document Mālikī resistance to Ismaili ritual 'innovations', apart from those studied by R. Brunschvig.[6] If we now move to Egypt, a few studies have addressed how the Sunnis of Egypt reacted to Fatimid rule, how they tried to ensure the transmission of Sunni learning and how they fostered it, and also how polemics between Shiʿis and Sunnis left traces in Egyptian popular culture.[7] The extent to which the Fatimids influenced the Egyptian religious scene is still debated, with some scholars pointing out that Ismaili law held a privileged position and Ismaili ritual was compulsory on public occasions,[8] that the 'tenor and character of religious life in Fatimid Egypt was unmistakably Ismaili',[9] that 'Shiism was adopted by a significant segment of the population and not only a small group centred around the Fatimid caliph and his court, as is commonly believed',[10] and that the imam-caliphs, especially al-Ḥākim (r. 386–411/996–1021), tried to impose on their subjects an Ismaili understanding of Islamic rituals (*ʿibādāt*).[11] After the Fatimid conquest, the general Jawhar had given an *amān* to the Egyptian population, guaranteeing in the name of al-Muʿizz (r. 341–365/953–975) that Sunnis could carry out the *ʿibādāt* in their own fashion. Al-Ḥākim attempted to impose the Ismaili *ʿibādāt* on different occasions (in 397/1006, as well as two and four years later),[12] but afterwards the Sunnis were allowed to perform their ritual practices according to their own traditions. Thus Cortese concludes: 'If politically and religiously, Sunnism had to wait until the advent of the Ayyūbids in 567/1171 in order to be restored in Egypt, from a scholarly and intellectual point of view it had never gone away.'[13] Did the Sunnis produce polemical texts against Fatimid ritual practices during the two centuries of Fatimid rule in Egypt (from 358 to 567/969 to 1171)?[14] We have seen that a Sunni such as Ibn Abī Zayd al-Qayrawānī could counteract Fatimid doctrine and practice just by writing a Mālikī legal and theological text in which desired doctrine and practice were explained without reference to the Ismailis. But to what extent was it possible for Sunnis living under Fatimid rule to challenge Fatimid beliefs and practices in more open ways and claim that they were wrong? In what follows the way in which an Andalusī settled in Fatimid Alexandria did precisely that will be analysed.

Al-Ṭurṭūshī's Biography

The Andalusī's name is Abū Bakr Muḥammad b. al-Walīd b. Muḥammad b. Khalaf b. Sulaymān b. Ayyūb b. Abī Randaqa al-Fihrī al-Ṭurṭūshī. He is mostly known by his geographical *nisba* al-Ṭurṭūshī, as he was born in the town of Ṭurṭūsha, in northern al-Andalus (in what is now part of Catalonia) towards the year 451/1059. He died in Alexandria in 520/1126.[15]

Al-Ṭurṭūshī started his studies in the Taifa kingdom of Zaragoza, where one of his teachers was the Mālikī scholar Abu'l-Walīd al-Bājī (d. 474/1081), famous among other things because his knowledge of *uṣūl* methodology had aided him to successfully engage in polemics against the redoubtable Ẓāhirī scholar Ibn Ḥazm. Following in his teacher's footsteps – al-Bājī had studied in the East for thirteen years – al-Ṭurṭūshī left al-Andalus in 476/1083. He first stopped in Alexandria and Antioch (shortly before it was conquered by the Muslims from the Byzantines); he then moved to Baghdad, Basra and Wāsiṭ between the years 477 and 480/1084 and 1087; and in this last year he undertook the pilgrimage to Mecca.[16] Next, he went to Syria, living in Jerusalem and Damascus between the years 481 and 490/1087 and 1096, that is, on the eve of the Crusader conquest of Jerusalem. He then moved to Egypt, settling in Rashīd (Rosetta) and afterwards in Alexandria in the year 490/1097.

The teachers with whom al-Ṭurṭūshī studied during his stay in the East were many, the most famous being al-Ghazālī, whose life and work had a profound influence on him. Al-Ghazālī's staunch opposition to what he called *al-bāṭiniyya* (Batinism) was undoubtedly one particular aspect of his influence,[17] although al-Ṭurṭūshī was critical of the fact that al-Ghazālī's doctrine and thought had been, as he thought, excessively penetrated by both philosophy and mysticism.

Like some of his contemporaries, al-Ṭurṭūshī had gone through spiritual crises – one of them while living in Jerusalem – that led him to pursue a retired and ascetic life. But once he had settled in Fatimid Egypt, where he married a rich widow who helped him found a madrasa, he devoted the rest of his life to teaching. During the time he spent in Egypt, the viziers of the Fatimid caliphs were al-Afḍal and al-Baṭā'iḥī. While al-Ṭurṭūshī seems to have had some trouble with the former, who kept him under surveillance in Cairo, during the vizierate of the second (515–519/1121–1125) he was able to return to Alexandria; he dedicated to him his 'mirror for princes', the *Sirāj al-mulūk*. However, it should be noted that during his time in Cairo al-Ṭurṭūshī received a daily or monthly allowance from the viziers.

Al-Ṭurṭūshī's stay in the East coincided with the First Crusade, while in al-Andalus, Toledo fell into Christian hands in the year 478/1085. In 479/1086, the Almoravids were called upon by some of the Taifa kings seeking help to check the Christian military advance (their eventual failure in doing so resulted, e.g., in the loss of Tortosa to the Christians temporarily in 512/1118 and definitively in 543/1148). Although he never returned to his homeland, al-Ṭurṭūshī was influential with the Almoravids, to whom he wrote a letter counselling them on how to rule, as al-Ghazālī had done. The Sevillan scholar Abū Bakr b. al-ʿArabī (d. 543/1148) – who was a pupil of both al-Ghazālī and al-Ṭurṭūshī – took their letters to the Almoravid amir. Al-Ṭurṭūshī called on him and his fellow Muslims to undertake *jihād*. Both external and internal threats (Christian advances and Ismailism) motivated al-Ṭurṭūshī's concern for the need to reform the practices and beliefs of the Muslims, as well as his views about strengthening the restrictions on Jews and Christians and exalting the sacredness of Jerusalem. Ibn Khaldūn said he was a decisive influence in making Andalusī Mālikism known in the East, while al-Ṭurṭūshī disseminated Eastern Mālikī doctrines among the many pupils who studied with him in Egypt. There were many Andalusīs among them and through them al-Ṭurṭūshī's teachings were influential in the Islamic West during the Almoravid and Almohad eras. Ibn Tūmart, the founder of the Almohad movement, is said to have studied with him. Al-Ṭurṭūshī's grave in Alexandria attracted many visitors down the centuries after his death and is still renowned.

Al-Ṭurṭūshī's Scholarly Career

During his stay in Alexandria, al-Ṭurṭūshī fought against what he considered to be the legal and religious innovations brought about by the Fatimids, this being the reason that kept him from returning to his native land: the people, he was convinced, needed his *ʿilm*, his learning. Thus al-Ṭurṭūshī wrote a commentary on Ibn Abī Zayd al-Qayrawānī's *Risāla*, a text which was closely connected to the protection of Sunnism, as has already been mentioned, while al-Ṭurṭūshī's knowledge of inheritance law (*farā'iḍ*) made him oppose Fatimid practice. Ismaili law firmly rejects the principle of superiority which Sunni law grants to male agnates as legal heirs, this having to do with Shiʿi claims to legitimate authority through the inheritance of Fāṭima, the Prophet's daughter.[18] It is said that al-Ṭurṭūshī succeeded in stopping Ismaili law in this domain being applied to the Sunnis as a result of having obtained the agreement of the vizier, al-Baṭā'iḥī.[19] He also made sure that the government would not confiscate property that lacked legal inheritors.[20]

The *Kitāb al-ḥawādith wa'l-bidaʿ*

While living in Alexandria, and appalled by the innovations he had witnessed among his contemporaries,[21] al-Ṭurṭūshī wrote his treatise against innovation (sing., *bid'a*), a work that can be understood as a polemical tract against Fatimid ritual practices and a defence of Sunni – and more particularly Mālikī – positions.[22] For writing such a treatise, al-Ṭurṭūshī could draw on precedents in a well-developed Mālikī tradition, starting with the letters between Mālik b. Anas and Ibn Farrūkh from Qayrawān on how to fight against innovators,[23] and continuing with the tract against innovation by the Cordoban Muḥammad b. Waḍḍāḥ (d. 287/900),[24] and the interest in the subject shown by Ibn Abī Zayd al-Qayrawānī (d. 386/996),[25] al-Qābisī (d. 403/1012)[26] and Abu'l-Walīd al-Bājī. Al-Ṭurṭūshī's contribution to this tradition was crucial. He produced a systematic and well-organised tract that was quoted by later Mālikī and non-Mālikī authors alike. Although in his writings al-Ṭurṭūshī never renounces his Mālikism, when he deals with the discrepancy of opinion among the Sunnis he tends to put more emphasis on the existence of consensus than on divergence of opinion.

Further, al-Ṭurṭūshī was not so much interested in the detailed description of the innovations he condemned (as the Maghribī/Egyptian Ibn al-Ḥājj later provided in his *Madkhal*),[27] but in the conceptual framework that demonstrated why those practices lacked any legal foundation. For al-Ṭurṭūshī, *bid'a* had a negative meaning: it was either reprehensible (*makrūha*) or prohibited (*muḥarrama*), with one exception as shall immediately be seen. Later, the Egyptian Mālikīs 'Izz al-Dīn b. 'Abd al-Salām (d. 660/1262) and al-Qarāfī (d. 684/1285) would apply to *bid'a* the five legal qualifications: obligatory (*wājib*), recommended (*mandūb*), permitted (*mubāḥ*), reprehensible (*makrūh*) and forbidden (*muḥarram*).[28] Because of his negative view of *bid'a*, al-Ṭurṭūshī felt obliged to devote a great deal of space to the problem represented by the innovation of the second caliph, 'Umar b. al-Khaṭṭāb, relating to the prayer performed during the nights of Ramaḍān (*ṣalāt al-tarāwīḥ*), an innovation that the caliph had himself qualified as 'excellent' (*ni'mat al-bid'a hādhihi*). Al-Ṭurṭūshī's solution to the problem was to say that it was not really a *bid'a*, because what 'Umar did as a distinguished

Companion of the Prophet was to apply the spirit of what Muḥammad had established.[29]

The Organisation of the Treatise

In his introduction, al-Ṭurṭūshī explains that his aim is to deal with those innovations introduced in Islam that have no foundation in the Qur'an, the Prophet's tradition (*sunna*) or consensus (*ijmāʿ*), nor in any other pillar of Islam. Such innovations could be divided into two types: (1) one group was formed of those innovations that are known to be such both by the scholars and the ordinary people; (2) the other was formed of those innovations that, in spite of being such, both scholars and the people believed to be religious duties, pious acts and traditional practices. Al-Ṭurṭūshī decided to concentrate on the second group, as it was in respect of these that he felt that Muslims should be aware and alert. Because there are many such innovations, in his *Kitāb al-ḥawādith wa'l-bidaʿ* he says he will refer only to a selection, organising the book into four sections: the first three analyse the censuring of innovation in the Qur'an, moving on to the Prophet's *sunna* and in the third part to the sayings and acts of the Companions of the Prophet, while the fourth part is devoted to innovations existing in al-Ṭurṭūshī's own time.

Part One of the *Kitāb al-ḥawādith wa'l-bidaʿ*

In the first part, al-Ṭurṭūshī quotes the Qur'anic verses 7:163–166, 2:98/104, 6:108, 24:31 to show how acts and words that appear to be licit were forbidden by God because they could lead to perdition. This is the foundation of the Mālikī principle *sadd al-dharāʾiʿ* (to close those paths leading to dangerous ends), a recurrent theme throughout the *Kitāb al-ḥawādith.*[30] Some of these Qur'anic verses deal with the precept of *al-amr bi'l-maʿrūf wa'l-nahy ʿan al-munkar*, more specifically, with the following issue: given that God is going to punish the transgressors, are Muslims free from the duty of admonishing and correcting them?[31] The answer of course is negative, thus justifying the need for composing the kind of book al-Ṭurṭūshī is writing. The other verses quoted (7:161–162, 6:65) make reference to the punishment prepared by God for the innovators, as well as to the inevitable division of the Muslim community into sects. Thus in the same way that the Qur'an indicates that acts or words that are apparently licit can lead to, or can be used for, illicit ends, there are innovations that are not recognised as such by the Muslim community, which instead considers them pious practices. And in the same way that the Qur'an forbids or alerts one against such words and deeds, al-Ṭurṭūshī, making use of the Mālikī principle of *sadd al-dharāʾiʿ*, decided to carry out the duty of commanding good and forbidding evil, unveiling the dangerous consequences that await the Muslims if they do not abandon the innovations they are practising. God's punishment would be the result of any deviation from Islamic norms, and the division of the community into sects is part of such a punishment.

Part Two of the Treatise

The second part, divided into three chapters, starts by focusing on the main Prophetic traditions that advise against the opinions dictated by fantasy (*ahwāʾ*) and against innovations. Of paramount significance is the *ḥadīth*, 'Islam started as a stranger and will become one again; blessed be the strangers': the first Muslims felt like strangers among their fellow men and in later generations the true believer will continue feeling like a stranger among the so-called Muslims.[32] And this would be so because he would be following the straight path that leads to salvation. Those who deviate from the path fall into error and thus put their salvation at risk. Muḥammad forewarned that such deviants would appear among Muslim believers as they had appeared among the Jews and Christians. If these split into seventy-one or seventy-two sects, the Muslims would split into seventy-three, of which only one would be saved.[33] All innovations stem from the four main ones, those of the Khārijīs, Rāfiḍīs, Qadarīs and Murjiʾīs, deriving from them are the seventy-two sects that will end up in Hell. Al-Ṭurṭūshī exemplifies this with the case of the

Qadarīs/Muʿtazilīs. He then returns to the admonishments of the Prophet and his Companions against innovation. Some of these were of a general character, while others related to specific cases. All the examples quoted by him refer to *ʿibādāt*. Thus the Prophet had alerted the Muslims against the pagan practice of venerating a tree (*dhāt anwāṭ*) and against exaggeration in pious practices such as fasting on Fridays or preferring the right hand over the left. Finally, al-Ṭurṭūshī defines what *bidʿa* is, quoting two of the three Qur'anic verses where the root appears (2:117; 46:9).[34] According to these verses, it has a positive meaning when applied to God's actions, but a negative one when applied to those of a created being, thus Muḥammad as a prophet was not an innovator. Only God can innovate.

Part Three of the Treatise

The third part, divided into thirteen chapters, has as its main theme the concern shown by the Companions of the Prophet to put an end to innovation and the methods they used to achieve this objective. The first generations of Muslims had had to confront the existence of innovations early on, to the extent that Abu'l-Dardā', the father of Abū Suhayl b. Mālik, Anas b. Mālik, al-Ḥasan al-Baṣrī and Ibn al-ʿAbbās could not recognise the practices established by the Prophet in those of their contemporaries. The concept of *fasād al-zamān*, the corruption of the Muslim community brought by the passage of time, lay behind this: if that could happen already in the early times of the Muslim community, what could one expect from later times? Among the procedures followed by the Companions to put a stop to any innovation that did not appear to be such was their abstention from doing things that could appear inoffensive or even good practice in order to make sure that Muslims would not consider them obligatory. Thus ʿUthmān stopped abbreviating the prayer when travelling (*ṣalāt al-safar*), in spite of the precedent established by the Prophet, out of fear that the Bedouin would consider that this was an obligatory precept for prayer in general.[35] For the same reason women were denied access to mosques, in spite of the fact that the Prophet had said that mosques should be accessible to them, because they were introducing innovations there.[36]

Nine chapters of this third part are devoted to the origins and characteristics of the *ṣalāt al-tarāwīḥ*, and in them the transmissions from ʿĀʾisha are particularly abundant. The Prophet had stopped performing the night prayers of Ramaḍān out of fear that his acts would be misunderstood and what was a recommended practice would end up being considered obligatory. His Companions were aware that this was the reason. For the Mālikīs, in effect, this prayer is a recommended practice and the fact that the Prophet acted in a seemingly contradictory way (exhorting the people to perform this prayer and then abstaining from doing it) was motivated by his fear that either the Muslims would consider it an obligatory practice or that they would try to imitate him in things that he was able to do but ordinary human beings were not. After the Prophet's death and the short interval corresponding to the caliphate of Abū Bakr and the beginning of that of ʿUmar, the latter put an end to the indeterminate state in which the practice had remained. The fact that ʿUmar qualified his decision as an 'innovation' gave rise to different interpretations, but in any case it had to be accepted: either this 'innovation', ʿUmar being a Companion, had to be necessarily good, or it was not in fact a true innovation from a legal point of view, since what ʿUmar did was to act as the Prophet would have done. Al-Ṭurṭūshī adopted this second position and it is in this context that he quoted the third Qurʾanic verse where mention is made of the root *b-d-ʿ*.[37] The remaining chapters on the *ṣalāt al-tarāwīḥ* are devoted to treating specific aspects of it. The actions performed during this kind of prayer are valid only for the night prayers during Ramaḍān and cannot be extended to other supererogatory prayers. A discussion follows on whether the prayer should be performed only in the mosque or at home, whether a copy of the Qurʾan can be used, and whether or not the *qunūt* is allowed. Real innovations have been introduced, such as the elevation of pulpits from which the Qurʾan is recited, sermons are delivered and stories are told (Chapter 10 is devoted to such innovations).[38] Al-Ṭurṭūshī refuted the argument that these innovatory practices were followed in Qayrawān, a centre of religious learning in the Maghrib,[39] as if that being the case such practices could be legitimised, retorting that Medina is the only town whose practice can be considered a legal foundation and this only for the Mālikīs.[40] He adds that in Cordoba such practices do not exist; moreover, in Qayrawān they are followed by the ordinary people, not by the scholars who are the only ones who can be imitated. In connection with this, Chapter 13 is devoted to showing that corruption originates among the ignorant, not among those who know; for this reason, the *ʿulamāʾ* should keep apart from the powerful, but at the same time cannot abandon the world completely, as they have a duty to teach Muslims what is right and what is wrong.[41]

Al-Ṭurṭūshī also shows that the principle of *sadd al-dharāʾiʿ* is not exclusively Mālikī, and that not only Mālik but also Abū Ḥanīfa believed that licit acts may be avoided when they can lead to dangerous consequences. Abū Ḥanīfa was against the supererogatory fast of the month of Shawwāl, in spite of a *ḥadīth* in favour of it, out of fear that such fasting would be considered obligatory, thus leading to an increase of precepts as had happened among the Christians. Al-Shāfiʿī was in agreement with Mālik that the sacrifice of the Feast of Sacrifice was recommended, not obligatory. While the *ṣalāt al-tarāwīḥ* is not an innovation per se, the innovated practices that had been introduced into it needed to be abandoned.[42] The argument that they were widespread and that most Muslims believed that they were correct was not a valid reason to legitimise them, and Chapter 12 is devoted to giving other examples illustrating this point. Among the widespread practices that were nevertheless innovations, the following are mentioned: to sell broad beans cooked with their peelings,[43] to pay a person to undertake the Pilgrimage as a substitute for oneself,[44] to wear the turban without passing one of the ends below the chin,[45] to wear clothes that trailed on the ground, to wrap oneself in clothes covering the head with them.[46]

The Main Aim of the Treatise

The fourth part contains 22 chapters devoted to the main aim: alerting the Muslims against specific innovations – almost all of them belonging to the *ʿibādāt* – that are considered pious and correct practice not only by the ordinary people but also by scholars, and that have to do with Qurʾanic recitation and learning, mosques, story-tellers, the celebrations for certain days and months, the prayer, funerals, women, dress and food. Behind their censorship there is the rejection of exaggeration in religion, which is what caused previous communities to perish.[47]

Qurʾanic Recitation

Among the innovations related to Qurʾanic recitation, more space is devoted to the *qirāʾa biʾl-alḥān*.[48] Al-Ṭurṭūshī distinguishes what he calls *taṭrīb* and *alḥān* from the correct form of Qurʾanic recitation (*tartīl* or *tarsīl*), consisting in reciting the Qurʾan in a slow and deliberate form, pronouncing each word in a clear and distinctive way, caring for the pronunciation and using a serious and sad intonation. The wrong way, invented by musicians, consists of singing and using melodies. Al-Shāfiʿī is said to have supported the legitimacy of this way of recitation, but al-Ṭurṭūshī shows that there are contradictory transmissions regarding al-Shāfiʿī's doctrine,[49] and that his doctrine could be shown to coincide with that of Mālik, who was adamant in his opposition to the *qirāʾa biʾl-alḥān*, as Ibn Ḥanbal was. Al-Ṭurṭūshī, following Abuʾl-Walīd al-Bājī, is aware that men have different abilities, with some being unable to recite the Qurʾan in the appropriate way (*tartīl*). These individuals are allowed to recite it in an imperfect way (*hazz*), because if people are obliged to do what they cannot do, they will end up doing it reluctantly and with difficulty which will result in them abandoning the recitation of the Qurʾan.[50] The censorship of the *qirāʾa biʾl-alḥān* is determined not only by the fact that it lacks precedent but also because it causes Muslims to pay more attention to form than to meaning; also, it evokes non-Islamic practices.[51] In any case, it was an old practice, attributed by some to a successor, ʿAbd Allāh b. Abī Bakra al-Thaqafī, and attested in North Africa and al-Andalus already in the 2nd–3rd/8th–9th centuries,[52] with a long history of prohibition that points to its widespread and enduring popularity. According to al-Ṭurṭūshī, however, it would have been invented in the 4th/10th century, perhaps suggesting a Fatimid invention.

Another practice related to the recitation of the Qur'an is the *qirāʾa biʾl-idāra*, an innovation located in Alexandria and consisting of the simultaneous recitation performed by several persons so that they cannot listen to each other, contrary to what the Qur'anic verse 7:204 stipulates. Censored as well is earning money from the recitation of the Qur'an, as well as reciting it in the roadways, the market or the *ḥammām*, and also learning the Qur'an without learning its meaning.[53] Regarding the writing of the Qur'an, divisions in the text should not be established, the number of verses in each chapter should not be written down and punctuation is not allowed. This does not apply to children when they write the Qur'an on their tablets, as they can even write the *basmala* at the beginning of *sūra* 9, which lacks it. But this is unacceptable when a copy (*muṣḥaf*) of the Qur'an is made because the Sacred Book should be written as it was the first time.[54] Gold should not be used to write the Qur'an; it cannot be divided in ten parts (using gold), nor adorned.[55] To single out one verse above the rest is also wrong. The most famous case relates to the Qur'anic verse 112:1, a practice that seems to be supported by a *ḥadīth* in which the Prophet exalts it saying that its recitation equals that of a third of the Qur'an.[56] But it should not make one forget the rest, nor give rise to innovations such as the *alfiyya*, a prayer with 100 *rakʿas*, in which *sūra* 1 is recited once and then verse 112:1 ten times, making in this way 1,000 repetitions. The *alfiyya* was performed on the night in the middle of Shaʿbān and it would have had al-Ghazālī's approval. Other censored practices include reciting in the mosques following a *muṣḥaf* (a practice innovated by al-Ḥajjāj b. Yūsuf), gathering in the mosque to recite the Qur'an on Thursdays or other days, reciting the

Qur'an starting at the end and moving forwards to the beginning, and the *khatm* (complete recitation) in Ramaḍān.

Mosques

As regards mosques, according to al-Ṭurṭūshī the *miḥrāb* is an innovation,[57] especially if the imam places himself in it to lead the prayer.[58] Al-Ṭurṭūshī also reminds his reader that according to Mālik, the *miḥrāb* should not be decorated with inscriptions from the Qur'an.

The decoration of mosques is censored as an imitation of Jewish and Christian practices and because it distracts the believers.[59] Mosques should be like the booth of Moses.[60] God revealed to Isaiah the injunction that temples should be constructed only in order to remember and praise God in them, as He does not care for adornments. However, adornments could be excused as they demonstrated to the infidels the grandeur of Islam; this is what happened with the mosaic decoration in the mosque of Damascus.[61]

Ibn al-Qāsim stopped visiting a mosque built with illicit money. But even if this is not the case, all mosques are the same, none is better than the other and one should not deliberately go to pray in a specific one. The only exceptions are the mosques of Mecca, Medina and Jerusalem,[62] not even Qubā' in spite of its association with the Prophet, and this is in order to avoid the possibility that visiting it could be turned into a festival (*'īd*) or an obligatory precept.[63] Mālik was against intentionally visiting an Egyptian mosque called al-Khalūq of which wonders were told, such as that the prophet al-Khiḍr had been seen in it.[64] 'Umar made it clear that he was against going to pray intentionally in places with a special meaning, such as those where the Prophet had prayed or as in the case of the tree of Ḥudaybiyya.[65] Mālik also censored the visiting of the places in Medina associated with the Prophet, excepting only the mosque of Qubā'. Chapter 15 of the fourth part discusses whether it is more meritorious to recite the supererogatory prayers in those places where the Prophet had prayed than elsewhere. Mālik has two contradictory views, one based on 'Umar's censorship and the other in favour, this one legitimised by the authority of Ibn 'Umar and Salama b. al-Akwaʿ, who often went to pray at those places where the Prophet was known to have prayed.[66] Al-Ṭurṭūshī explains this by arguing that the solution to this issue requires one to establish first if the time, the place and the circumstances of an act determine it, that is, if an act (i.e., prayer) is more meritorious for being performed in a specific place, at a specific moment and in a specific way; if the answer is positive then it has to be established whether it becomes obligatory or merely commendable to perform it always under the same conditions.[67] Al-Ṭurṭūshī does not seem to regard the place occupied by Jerusalem among the 'exceptional' mosques, that is, those which can be visited ex profeso, as a polemical position which might be related to the fact that in his time Jerusalem had fallen into Christian hands.[68]

Chapters 8 and 9 are devoted to good manners in mosques following Qur'an 24:36–37. Coffers for collecting alms should not be deposited in mosques, and alms should not be asked for.[69] Eating and drinking should be avoided, although to hang up bunches of dates for the poor to eat is acceptable. Breaking the fast in a mosque is not acceptable, but drinking water is permissible.[70] Mālik disliked the fans that could be found at the entrances of mosques, and he also disliked speaking foreign languages in them as they are deceptive, as well as people cutting their nails and hair, and cleaning their mouths.[71] Equally reprehensible is adopting the upper part of mosques as dwelling places, and spending the night in them – something that is only licit for foreigners and the poor – although taking a nap in one is acceptable. The exceptions concern those who are performing a spiritual retreat (*muʿtakif*) and those who stay for the night prayers, but they have to leave the precincts of the mosque to attend to their personal hygiene.[72] Cushions and pillows should not be used for sitting in a mosque, although it is admissible to use mats and carpets to obtain a more uniform floor and to protect people from the cold of the flagstones. Lice and fleas should not be killed; spitting is forbidden, although if the spittle can be hidden below a pebble it is acceptable. Selling goods is completely forbidden, except if unpremeditated and this is so because transforming a mosque into a market is one of the signs of the Last Hour and because it causes noise and fuss. Announcing in a loud voice that something has been lost is wrong, also reciting poetry, and for this reason ʿUmar b. al-Khaṭṭāb built a courtyard near the mosque (*al-baṭḥāʾ*) where such things could take place. ʿUmar and Mālik strongly disliked people raising their voices in the mosque in Medina. But it is possible to transmit news of war and also *ḥadīth*s in a mosque in an acceptable tone of voice. God annihilated those who talked about mundane matters in the mosque and Jesus used to beat those who engaged in polemic. Copies of the Qurʾan can be transcribed in the mosque, but teaching children is to be rejected, as it involves gain and also because children are dirty. It is licit to apply light corporal punishment involving a few lashes in mosques.[73] Then there follows some norms regarding the mosques in Mecca and Medina that prohibit raising one's hands in front of the Kaʿba, touching the *maqām Ibrāhīm* (destroyed because of that)[74] and touching the grave and the *minbar* of the Prophet. Together with other recommendations, al-Ṭurṭūshī says that the mosques of the innovators should be destroyed.[75]

Story-Tellers (*quṣṣās*)

One of the strongest condemnations is reserved for story-tellers to which Chapter 7 is devoted.[76] Mālik was one of the scholars who opposed performances by *quṣṣāṣ* taking place in mosques. The first *quṣṣāṣ* appeared during the caliphate of ʿUthmān, which is a reminder of the role they played in the early political and religious conflicts. They clearly represented a reprehensible innovation because they did not exist at the time of Muḥammad, or that of Abū Bakr or of ʿUmar, and because they brought about innovations, such as raising one's hands and one's voice in the invocation in addition to the fact that what they say is false. They invent traditions about the Prophet and they corrupt religion. Not every story-teller, however, is necessarily an innovator. ʿAlī distinguished between those *quṣṣāṣ* who were innovators and al-Ḥasan al-Baṣrī. Thus al-Ṭurṭūshī differentiates between the bad *qāṣṣ* and the good one, who is the 'admonisher' (*wāʿiẓ*), whose function is to remind the believers of death and the punishment of the grave. ʿUmar b. ʿAbd al-ʿAzīz was the first to name an official story-teller in Medina.[77]

The *ṣalāt al-tarāwīḥ*

In the third part, al-Ṭurṭūshī refuted the idea that the *ṣalāt al-tarāwīḥ* was an innovation as it was based on a Prophetic precedent and the alleged innovation by ʿUmar merely consisted of fixing and formalising certain characteristics by following what he knew the Prophet had in mind.[78] But al-Ṭurṭūshī condemned certain practices associated with the *ṣalāt al-tarāwīḥ*, such as the elevation of pulpits for sermons, story-telling and invocations. These practices would be acceptable if they occurred in private and discretely; what is wrong is that they become public and multitudinous manifestations, leading to the dangerous mixing (*ikhtilāṭ*) of men and women.[79]

Laylat al-qadr and the Month of Shaʿbān

The *laylat al-qadr* is mentioned in Qur'an 97:1, and this gave rise to an intense debate about which date it corresponded to.[80] Usually it is believed that this night in which the Qur'an was revealed belongs to the month of Ramaḍān. But others consider it equivalent to the 'blessed night' mentioned in Qur'an 44:1–4, and some identify it with the middle of Shaʿbān. Al-Ṭurṭūshī categorically rejected this last possibility.[81] Chapter 11 is devoted to the merits of the night of the middle of Shaʿbān (*laylat al-niṣf min Shaʿbān*) and its celebration, an issue related to the identification of the *laylat al-qadr*, because the middle of Shaʿbān had been identified with the 'blessed night' mentioned in Qur'an 44:2, while others identify this night with the *laylat al-qadr*.[82] It is believed that on the night of the middle of Shaʿbān God determines everything that will happen in the coming year.[83] Among the Mālikīs there is a long tradition of disapproval of singling out the night of the middle of Sha'bān and its celebration.[84] Ibn Taymiyya and al-Suyūṭī were not so strict, although both disapproved of the *alfiyya* prayer being performed on that date.[85] In connection with this night, al-Ṭurṭūshī discusses an innovation associated also with the month of Rajab, the *ṣalāt al-raghā'ib*. He says that, in the year 448/1056, Abū Muḥammad al-Maqdisī told him that a man from Nablus, called Ibn Abi'l-Ḥamrā', performed this prayer in the mosque of Jerusalem being followed by many who thought it was *sunna*.[86] This prayer is already mentioned in *Qūt al-qulūb* by Abū Ṭālib Makkī (d. 386/996) and in al-Ghazālī's *Iḥyā' 'ulūm al-dīn*. Abū Shāma attributed its invention to the Sufi Ibn Jahḍam (d. 414/1023).[87] Ibn Taymiyya, who opposed the *ṣalāt al-raghā'ib*, managed to have it forbidden in Syria, but when he was imprisoned in Cairo it continued to be performed in the great mosque of Damascus.[88]

The Month of Rajab

Chapter 13 is devoted to matters pertaining to another month, that of Rajab, one of the sacred months mentioned in Qur'an 9:36.[89] Among the innovations associated with this month, fasting was a practice from the Jāhiliyya that Abū Bakr and 'Umar fought against in order to avoid any possibility of Rajab rivalling Ramaḍān.[90] Their efforts were unsuccessful. Neither the Prophet nor 'Umar forbade fasting in Rajab, but made it clear that excess in it was wrong. The reasons for disapproval are threefold: because it was a pagan practice; because it could rival Ramaḍān; and because the ignorant might think that fasting in this month was an obligatory precept (*farḍ*) or a commendable act firmly established at a specific time (*sunna thābita muwaqqata*) and therefore that it could become a festival (*'īd*).[91] Thus, even if there were traditions in favour of fasting in Rajab, because of the reasons given the first Muslims and the following generations disapproved of it so as to convince the believers that it was not obligatory as was the Fast of Ramaḍān and it did not form part of the meritorious works (*al-faḍā'il*) as did the fast of 'Āshūrā'. He who so desires may perform fasting in that month out of devotion,[92] but it was better to do it privately or publicly announce that it was not to be considered an obligation.

Yawm ʿArafa

Chapter 10 is devoted to the disapproval of celebrating Yawm ʿArafa (9 Dhu'l-Ḥijja) in places other than ʿArafa, visiting the local mosque and making an invocation, practices that are referred to as *taʿrīf bidʿa*.[93] The disapproval of this is attested in the 1st–2nd/7th–8th centuries, Mālik being one of those who censured it.[94] To stop people engaging in this celebration, scholars are urged not to go to the mosque on that day but to stay at home instead. He who wants to make the invocation may do it, but alone.[95] Al-Ṭurṭūshī reports how he witnessed the prayer on the day of ʿArafa in Jerusalem and there he learned that people believed that making four *wuqūf*s or assemblies on that day in Jerusalem was equivalent to the pilgrimage to Mecca.

Friday and Religious Observances

As regards Friday, Mālik reported that the Companions were against Muslims not working on Fridays in imitation of the practice of the Jews and Christians on Saturdays and Sundays.[96] Al-Ṭurṭūshī then moves on to the matter of prayer and starts with the innovation called *tathwīb*, censured by Mālik, and consisting of the muezzin adding, between the call to prayer (*adhān*) and its repetition (*iqāma*), a series of formulae (*qad qāmat al-ṣalāt, ḥayya ʿalā'l-ṣalāt, ḥayya ʿalā'l-falāḥ*) to urge believers to carry out the five daily prayers. In al-Ṭurṭūshī's time, the formula was *al-ṣalāt al-ṣalāt*.[97] Mālik transmitted a *ḥadīth* to the effect that ʿUmar was against continuing praying after the *ʿaṣr* prayer, connecting it with the *maghrib* prayer.[98] Al-Ṭurṭūshī was also against a number of innovations introduced in the invocation,[99] such as raising the voice and the hands (*taqlīṣ*).[100] Disapproval of these elements had a long tradition in the Mālikī school because this practice was considered to be of Jewish origin, and to have been popularised by the *quṣṣāṣ*.[101] The Mālikī school also disapproved of making the invocation after the complete recitation of the Qur'an[102] and, on the authority of Mālik, of using rhymed prose in the invocation or in any other circumstances. Mālik also deemed it preferable to make the invocation using words from the Qur'an.[103]

Funeral Rites

The last chapters of *Kitāb al-ḥawādith* are devoted to funeral rites.[104] According to a transmission by al-Bājī, ʿUmar was present at a funeral and, when he saw that the ceremony was being delayed, threatened to leave. Sepulchres should not be built over graves.[105] Mālik said that stones should not be put on graves, referring according to Ibn Shaʿbān to the inscribed slabs placed at the head of grave.[106] Al-Bukhārī, however, transmitted a *ḥadīth* which said that the Prophet put a stone near the grave of ʿUthmān b. Maẓʿūn to indicate that he was buried there so that his family could be buried near him. This does not really contradict Mālik's dictum, as he was referring to the fact that graves should not be built of stone: the graves of the Prophet, Abū Bakr and ʿUmar were dug outside in the red earth of a flat piece of land (*baṭḥā'*). The grave of the Prophet should not be touched.[107] In a quotation by al-Wansharīsī, we are informed that al-Ṭurṭūshī was against people making *tasbīḥ* near the grave during the seven days after a burial, considering this, as well as reciting the Qur'an, an innovation.[108]

Announcing a funeral so that large numbers of people may attend it was also disapproved of, as was raising the voice while the corpse was being carried to the grave. Funerals should not be announced near the gates of the mosque nor along the roadways, according to Mālik, Abū Ḥanīfa and al-Shāfiʿī. But there is nothing wrong in telling people confidentially.[109] Al-Ṭurṭūshī disapproved of what was done in Egypt in his time – people shouting in the funeral procession from the moment they left the house until the end of the funeral rites – his disapproval being based on a report from the Prophet.[110]

A Muslim should not be comforted by an unbelieving relative or neighbour.[111] But consoling is a recommended *sunna* that will be rewarded in the afterlife. According to al-Shāfiʿī, consolation should last from the moment of death until burial and also continue afterwards. According to Abū Ḥanīfa and Sufyān al-Thawrī, it should not be continued after the burial and also if much time has passed, and on this last point al-Shāfiʿī agreed. Al-Ṭurṭūshī agreed with al-Shāfiʿī's doctrine, especially regarding consoling after a burial as it is then that affliction increases. The most beautiful words of consolation were those that al-Khiḍr directed to the Muslim community after the death of the Prophet. Consolation should be extended to everyone, independent of social status, age and gender. However, in the case of a woman, she should only be consoled by those with whom she has the degree of kinship that forbids marriage. To expose oneself to people in expectation of consolation is an innovation. There is nothing wrong, however, in staying at home or in the mosque in sorrow as the Prophet did after the death of Jaʿfar, ʿAlī's brother. On that occasion, the Prophet also asked for food to be sent to the family, a practice accepted by Mālik. But it is wrong if the family of the deceased prepares the food and invites people to partake of it, according to both Mālik and al-Shāfiʿī.[112]

Mourning ceremonies (*al-maʾātim*) are forbidden, according to the consensus of scholars. Al-Shāfiʿī disliked them because they renew sorrow.[113] The *maʾtam* consists of gathering together on the morning after burial, then on the second, third and seventh day, as well as a month after and a year after. This is an innovation and needs to be firmly rejected, as Abū ʿImrān al-Fāsī said to one of his pupils who had taken part in one of these ceremonies. To light candles and burn incense in the mourning ceremonies is wrong: it is a wasteful expenditure and an excess; the guardian will have to answer for it, and will lose his honourable record as a person of probity (*ʿadāla*).[114] Women should not leave the house to attend funerals. Mālik only admitted the performance of this practice in the case of the burials of parents, husbands, children and brothers. If a woman attends a burial, she can recite the prayer for the dead.[115] Graves should not be watered after burial; the dead can be buried with their shoes and story-telling is acceptable during a funeral.[116] Camels should not be sacrificed, as this is a practice of the Jāhiliyya designed to thank the dead for their generosity when alive and also because it was then believed that the deceased would be mounted on camels on the day of Resurrection.[117]

It is wrong to perform lamentations because resignation is obligatory.[118] Sorrow and a sense of desolation for the loss of a beloved are natural feelings among human beings and it is acceptable to cry, as the Prophet did when his son Ibrāhīm died. But the crying should stop when the person dies. If crying is licit, lamentations for the dead are absolutely forbidden. The Prophet cursed wailing women and those who listened to them, including those who slap their cheeks and rip their clothes.[119] Lamentations for the dead are wrong because they could be interpreted as a censure of or accusation against God, whereas every Divine decision is truth and justice.[120]

Women

Women make frequent appearances in treatises against innovations.[121] We have already seen that al-Ṭurṭūshī refers to the prohibition on women attending mosques, in spite of the report from the Prophet forbidding this prohibition, claiming it became necessary because of the innovations fabricated by women.[122] The worst of all things is the mixing (*ikhtilāṭ*) of men and women when the recitation of the Qur'an in its entirety takes place during the nights of Ramaḍān, because it leads to immoral practices.[123] The caliph 'Umar prohibited slave women from wearing the *izār* (a type of veil) in order to prevent them being confused with free women.[124]

A Covert Criticism of the Fatimids

It is clear from this review of the innovations mentioned by al-Ṭurṭūshī that there is a certain tension between the fact that some of these practices are acts of devotion (prayer, invocations) and thus good in principle, and the concern that if they are allowed to proliferate they can alter the normative system of the *sharīʿa*. As we have seen, following the Mālikī tradition of treatises against innovations, al-Ṭurṭūshī explicitly states that he composed his book to alert his fellow Muslims to the point that practices which were seemingly good and pious were in fact dangerous innovations. His final aim is thus to stop the increase in the ritual practices of the Muslim community. Scholars were in fact entrusted with the task of avoiding the introduction of any innovation (*bidʿa*) in rituals (*ʿibādāt*), something aptly and concisely described by al-Shāṭibī as 'an invented path, parallel to that of the *sharīʿa*, that when followed leads to exaggeration (*mubālagha*) in the worship (*taʿabbud*) of God'.[125] In general terms, the most salient point about the innovations included by al-Ṭurṭūshī in his book is that they are 'old' innovations, as most of them had already been disapproved of or prohibited by Mālik b. Anas (d. 179/795) or by later generations of mostly Mālikī scholars. In any case, they had been labelled 'innovations' before al-Ṭurṭūshī gave them any attention. Another salient point is that some well-known 'innovations' are not mentioned, such as the use of the rosary, the visiting of graves and the *mawlid* of the Prophet – this being a festival considered by some modern scholars to have been started by the Fatimids. It was celebrated in Egypt, for example, in the year 516/1122, four years before al-Ṭurṭūshī's death in 520/1126.[126] A third point is that behind such innovations, according to al-Ṭurṭūshī, there was the imitation of Jewish or Christian practices,[127] popular practices,[128] or their invention by specific individuals (such as the infamous Umayyad governor, al-Ḥajjāj b. Yūsuf)[129] or families (e.g., the Abbasids).[130] Regarding groups, it should be noted that when dealing with the division of the Muslim community into denominations, al-Ṭurṭūshī chose the example of the Qadarīs, not that of the Shiʿa (whom he calls '*al-rāfiḍa*') who were much closer to home as far as he was concerned. In fact, apart from this instance, he does not explicitly refer to the Shiʿis. Nonetheless, some of the innovations dealt with can clearly be related to Fatimid Ismaili doctrines and practices.

The most obvious case is the ritual practice to which al-Ṭurṭūshī devotes most attention. The Fatimids had forbidden the *ṣalāt al-tarāwīḥ* in Qayrawān with the result that people stopped performing it, as documented by the geographer al-Muqaddasī.[131] For his part, the North African historian Abū Bakr ʿAbd Allāh al-Mālikī says that Muḥammad b. ʿUmar al-Marrūdhī, the *qāḍī* of the first Fatimid caliph, prohibited the people of Ifrīqiya from performing this prayer.[132] That this was an issue of Sunni/Shiʿi contention is proved by the fact that when the amir of Fez – who had formerly paid allegiance to the Fatimids – became an ally of the Umayyads in Cordoba, the caliph al-Ḥakam II (r. 350–366/961–976) insisted that the *ṣalāt al-tarāwīḥ* had to be performed in his territory.[133] The Fatimids continued to oppose this practice when they moved to Egypt. In fact, it was forbidden by the imam-caliph al-ʿAzīz (r. 365–386/975–996), and a man was executed for performing it.[134] ʿUmar's innovation was attacked by both Shiʿis and Muʿtazilīs,[135] but the performance of the *ṣalāt al-tarāwīḥ* became well established in Sunni North Africa and Egypt,[136] as well as in the rest of the Islamic world where Sunni practices prevailed.[137]

Another innovation that is clearly related to Fatimid practices is the *tathwīb*. The term *tathwīb* was employed by Ibn Waḍḍāḥ al-Qurṭubī in his *Kitāb al-bidaʿ* to indicate the pronunciation of the formula *al-ṣalāt khayr min al-nawm* ('Prayer is better than sleep') in the call (*adhān*) to the morning prayer. The introduction of this formula – in substitution of the repetition of the *adhān* – was attributed to ʿUmar b. al-Khaṭṭāb. It did not enjoy immediate acceptance among the Sunnis, and while the Ibāḍīs accepted it, it was rejected by the Shiʿis.[138] The term *tathwīb* is also applied to the second call to prayer or *iqāma*, which consisted of a repetition of the *adhān* with the addition of a new phrase, *qad qāmat al-ṣalāt*, a practice mostly associated with the Shiʿis.[139] The Andalusī Ibn Ḥafṣūn (d. 305/918), who paid allegiance to the Fatimids from his fortress of Bobastro, south of Cordoba, supported the performance of this practice.[140] Al-Ṭurṭūshī and al-Shāṭibī also used the term *tathwīb* in this sense, namely, to introduce, between the first and the second call to prayer, a number of exhortations (*qad qāmat al-ṣalāt*, *ḥayya ʿalāʾl-ṣalāt*, *ḥayya ʿalāʾl-falāḥ*) in order to urge the believers to perform the prayer.[141] In al-Ṭurṭūshī's time, the formula employed was *al-ṣalāt al-ṣalāt*; in the times of Ibn Rushd al-Jadd (d. 520/1126), the formula was *ḥayya ʿalāʾl-ṣalāt*. For the Almohads the *tathwīb* was a *sunna*, and they employed exhortations not only in Arabic (*aṣbiḥ wa li-llāh al-ḥamd*), but also in Berber. Al-Shāṭibī heard the Arabic formula in Granada where it was still being employed in the 8th/14th century. Therefore, in the *kutub al-bidaʿ* written by Mālikīs, the *tathwīb* which is considered an innovation consists of proclaiming between the call to prayer and its repetition certain formulae which urge the believers to perform the prayer. In spite of its early condemnation by Mālik, it was an extremely persistent practice, so that al-Wansharīsī, himself a Mālikī, ended by accepting it, calling it *bidʿa mustaḥsana* (that is, approved or commendable).

As regards funeral ceremonies, al-Ṭurṭūshī's disapproval has to do with practices that are documented among the Sunnis but also strongly associated with the Shiʿis: shrines built over graves;[142] wailing over the dead;[143] and the performance of *maʾtam* consisting in gathering on the morning after burial, on the second, third and seventh day, as well as a month and a year after the death or burial of the individual.[144] The Fatimids are known to have paid handsomely for Qurʾan reciters at dynastic funerals.[145]

Al-Ṭurṭūshī's remark that camels should not be sacrificed can also be connected to the Fatimid practice of sacrificing camels and more specifically she-camels at the Feast of Sacrifice. They had done so while in Ifrīqiya and continued to do so in Egypt.[146] Although the following event happened after al-Ṭurṭūshī's death, it reflects this practice: at the mosque of al-Ḥusayn whose remains were discovered in ʿAsqalān and brought to Cairo on 8 Jumada II 548/31 August 1153, it became customary for the people to slaughter camels, cows and sheep, to wail and weep profusely and curse those who had killed al-Ḥusayn.[147]

The censuring of the *quṣṣāṣ* by al-Ṭurṭūshī may have been addressed to the well-documented presence of story-tellers in Islamic society including in Egypt,[148] but it may also have had as its main target the Fatimid *munshidūn*, known to have made their presence felt in different public places reciting praises of the descendants of the Prophet, the story of al-Ḥusayn's death and imprecations against the pious ancestors.[149]

Al-Ṭurṭūshī also designates as wrong the practice of wearing the turban without passing one of the fringes below the chin. To wear the turban passing one of the fringes below the chin or fastened under the chin was a fashion – called *taḥnīk* – closely associated with the Mālikīs and also with North Africa. It was followed by some of the North Africans who became followers of the Fatimids, and there are some indications that the early imam-caliphs may have adopted this style at least on some occasions, but the predominant Fatimid way of wearing the turban was different and as North Africans lost their early influence in the Fatimid caliphate the *taḥnīk* seems to have also receded as a fashion.[150]

Thus some of the innovations discussed by al-Ṭurṭūshī can be clearly connected to a Sunni/Shiʿi divide, but there are others that, while reflecting that connection, can also be linked either to intra-Sunni divergence of opinion or simply to Sunni popular practice. The singling out of certain mosques or other sites for prayer on certain days with certain specific rituals may refer to the mosques built by the Fatimids to commemorate their imams and other members of the Prophet's family, but also to Sunni popular practice. The night of mid-Shaʿbān was the object of devotion and celebration among the Sunnis, as we have seen, and also among the Shiʿis.[151] Under the imam-caliph al-ʿAzīz, mid-Rajab and mid-Shaʿbān were celebrated with gatherings at al-Azhar led by the Ismaili chief *qāḍī*, Ibn al-Nuʿmān. Al-Azhar was brightly lit and meals supplied by al-ʿAzīz were served. In the time of al-Ẓāhir (r. 411–427/1021–1036), all the mosques were lit up and the ruler with his wives and entourage attended the celebrations. Given that the common people participated in these celebrations, this means that they were also held in old Cairo (Fusṭāṭ), and in fact the gatherings were held mostly in the cemeteries. The first days, as well as the dates of mid-Rajab and mid-Shaʿbān, became known as the 'nights of the lights' (*layālī al-wuqūd*), because funds were allocated by the state for lighting the congregational mosques and shrines.[152]

Al-Ṭurṭūshī dates an innovation associated with the month of Rajab, the *ṣalāt al-raghā'ib*, to the year 448/1056 when it was first performed in Jerusalem. This means that this happened under the Fatimids who, it is thus implied, allowed it to happen, perhaps as part of new Ismaili rituals given that the month of Rajab was much respected in Fatimid circles.[153]

In some cases, the connection – if any – of the practices censured with the Fatimids is not immediately apparent. Al-Ṭurṭūshī states that the *qirā'a bi'l-alḥān* was invented in the 4th/10th century, which may suggest a link with the establishment of the Fatimid caliphate. Regarding the innovations related to the copying of the Qur'an, al-Ṭurṭūshī's criticisms may reflect Fatimid practice, but this is something still to be explored as not much is known about Fatimid *maṣāḥif*, apart from the famous Blue Qur'an in which the use of gold in the script is documented, this being one of the innovations censured by al-Ṭurṭūshī.[154]

Other practices may also be related to Fatimid practices: did the imam-caliph or his representative stand in the *miḥrāb* to lead the prayer? In order to collect some of the special taxes required by the Fatimids, were special coffers for alms put in mosques? Was Friday declared to be a rest day?

Specific contentious issues between Sunnis and Shiʿis, such as the determination of the beginning and the end of Ramaḍān,[155] the cursing of the Companions,[156] and the mourning on ʿĀshūrā',[157] are not mentioned, but this is because they were clearly non-Sunni practices, while al-Ṭurṭūshī had decided to devote his attention only to those practices that the Sunni Muslims might either discard or follow as a result of an inadequate degree of knowledge.[158] Going back to al-Muqaddasī's categories quoted at the beginning of this chapter, al-Ṭurṭūshī generally gave his attention to those practices on which there was an apparent *ikhtilāf* among the Sunnis, in order to prove that the reality was that a Sunni consensus existed either in favour or against, and also to those practices that could be interpreted as involving a return to what the first Muslims did, in order to prove that the Mālikī position was in accordance with the Prophet's *sunna*, and therefore that the Mālikī position had to be acceptable, for example, to the Shāfiʿīs.[159] But mostly al-Ṭurṭūshī's aim was to warn against practices that not only the ordinary people but even some scholars thought were good. In this domain he seems to have had in mind Sunni scholars whose doctrinal positions made them agree with Ismaili practices.

In recent studies about Christian literary production under the Fatimids it has been shown how certain texts can be interpreted as containing a 'hidden transcript',[160] that is, the conquerors and the conquered apparently cooperated in creating a 'clean public transcript', but there are hidden scripts 'through which the dominated can operate without exposing themselves to the gaze of the oppressors and which enable them to develop a blunt dissonant political culture'.[161] Al-Ṭurṭūshī's text may be considered to fall under the same category and this would explain why he did not directly mention the Ismailis and their practices.[162] He did include some statements about the need for activism in order to condemn wrong practices and also about the religious and social consequences for those who indulged in them: Ibn al-Qāsim stopped visiting a mosque built with illicit money; the mosques of the innovators should be destroyed; Muslims should not be consoled by an infidel relative or neighbour; and to light candles and burn incense in the mourning ceremonies is wrong – it is wasteful spending and an excess, and the guardian will have to answer for it, losing his *ʿadāla*. The fact that his contemporary readers must have understood that Fatimid practices were also being targeted may explain why al-Ṭurṭūshī spent some years under surveillance in Cairo.

Notes

* This chapter was first read at MESA 47th Annual Meeting, 10–13 October 2013, at the panel *Integration and dissent: the challenge of Fatimid rule*, organised by P. Walker and sponsored by the Institute of Ismaili Studies.

1 R. Brunschvig, 'Fiqh fatimide et histoire de l'Ifriqiya', in *Mélanges d'histoire et d'archéologie de l'occident musulman II: Hommage à Georges Marcais* (Algiers, 1957), pp. 13–20; reprinted in his *Études d'Islamologie* (Paris, 1976), vol. 1, pp. 63–70. See also his

'Argumentation fāṭimide contre le raisonnement juridique par analogie (*qiyās*)', in R. Arnaldez and S. van Reet, ed., *Recherches d'Islamologie. Recueil d'articles offert à Georges C. Anawati et Louis Gardet par leur collègues et amis* (Louvain, 1977), pp. 75–84.

2 The term *qunūt* refers to different practices as documented by A.J. Wensinck in *Encyclopaedia of Islam,* 2nd ed., online. It mostly refers to an invocation during prayer in which enemies are cursed.

3 On the troubled relations between Mālikīs and Ismailis in Ifrīqiya, see W. Madelung, 'The Religious Policy of the Fatimids toward their Sunnī Subjects in the Maghrib', in M. Barrucand, ed., *L'Egypte Fatimide: Son art et son histoire* (Paris, 1999), pp. 97–104; M.T. Mansouri, 'Les *'ulamā'* en rupture avec le pouvoir en Ifrīqiya d'après le *Kitāb al-miḥan*', *Mélanges de l'École française de Rome. Moyen Âge*, 115 (2003), pp. 565–580.

4 There are many editions of the *Risāla*, a work that has enjoyed uninterrupted diffusion through the centuries in the Islamic West as can be checked in *HATA* (Historia De Los Autores y Transmisores Andalusíes) and *HATOI*. It has also been translated into other languages, first into French (ed. and tr. L. Bercher, Algiers, 1949).

5 R. Brunschvig, 'Polémiques médiévales autour du rite de Mālik', *Al-Andalus*, 15 (1950), pp. 377–435.

6 See Note 3, above, and M. Yaloui, 'Controverse entre le Fatimide al-Mu'izz et l'Omeyyade al-Nāṣir, d'après le *Kitāb al-Majālis wa-l-Musāyarāt* du Cadi Nu'mān', *Cahiers de Tunisie*, 26 (1978), pp. 7–33, at p. 9 on lamenting the dead.

7 Gary Leiser, *The Restoration of Sunnism in Egypt: Madrasa and Mudarrisūn 495–647/1101–1249* (Philadelphia, 1976); Leiser, 'The *Madrasa* and the Islamization of the Middle East: The Case of Egypt', *Journal of the American Research Center in Egypt*, 22 (1985), pp. 29–47; Delia Cortese, 'Voices of the Silent Majority: The Transmission of Sunni Learning in Fātimī Egypt', *Jerusalem Studies in Arabic and Islam*, 39 (2012) pp. 345–366; Devin Stewart, 'Popular Shiism in Medieval Egypt: Vestiges of Islamic Sectarian Polemics in Egyptian Arabic', *Studia Islamica*, 84 (1996), pp. 35–66.

8 S.M. Stern, 'Cairo as the Centre of the Ismā'īlī Movement', in *Colloque international sur l'histoire du Caire* (Cairo, 1972), pp. 437–450; reprinted in his *Studies in early Ismā'īlism* (Leiden, 1983), pp. 234–256.

9 Yaacov Lev, 'The Fāṭimid Imposition of Ismā'īlism on Egypt (358–386/969–996)', *Zeitschrift der deutschen Morgenländischen*

Gesellschaft, 138 (1988), pp. 313–325; Yaacov Lev, *State and Society in Fatimid Egypt* (Leiden, 1991).

10 Stewart, 'Popular Shiism in Medieval Egypt', p. 65.

11 Daniel de Smet, 'Comment déterminer le début et la fin du jeûne de Ramadan? Un point de discorde entre sunnites et ismaéliens en Égypte fatimide', in U. Vermeulen and D. de Smet, ed., *Egypt and Syria in the Fatimid, Ayyubid and Mamluk eras* (Leuven, 1995), pp. 71–84.

12 De Smet, 'Comment déterminer', p. 73.

13 Cortese, 'Voices', p. 348.

14 Was there any anti-Ismaili polemical production afterwards, when the Ayyūbids (564–648/1169–1250) and the Mamlūks (648–923/1250–1517) did their best to extirpate Shiʿism from the country?

15 What follows is a summary of the extensive study on al-Ṭurṭūshī's biography included in Abū Bakr al-Ṭurṭūshī, *Kitāb al-ḥawādith wa-l-bidaʿ (El libro de las novedades y las innovaciones)*, tr. M.I. Fierro (Madrid, 1993). Summaries are provided in other publications: M. Fierro, 'al-Ṭurṭūshī', in *Christian-Muslim Relations: A Bibliographical History (1050–1200 CE)*, vol. 3, ed. D. Thomas, et al. (Leiden and Boston, 2011), pp. 387–396; Fierro, 'al-Ṭurṭūšī, Abū Bakr', *Biblioteca de al-Andalus*, vol. 7, *De al-Qabrīrī a Zumurrud*, ed. Jorge Lirola Delgado (Almería, 2012), pp. 500–531, no. 1791.

16 In spite of this experience, al-Ṭurṭūshī is known for having been opposed to the Andalusīs performing the Pilgrimage: al-Wansharīsī (d. 914/1508), *al-Miʿyār al-muʿrib wa'l-jāmiʿ al-mughrib ʿan fatāwī ahl Ifrīqiya wa'l-Andalus wa'l-Maghrib* (Rabat, 1401/1981), vol. I, p. 433. This doctrinal position was connected with the need to concentrate on *jihād* against the Christians: Dominique Urvoy, 'Sur l'évolution de la notion de gihād dans l'Espagne musulmane', *Mélanges de la Casa de Velázquez*, 9 (1973), pp. 335–371.

17 Farouk Mitha, *Al-Ghazālī and the Ismailis. A Debate on Reason and Authority in Medieval Islam* (London, 2001).

18 A. Hajji, 'Institutions of Justice in Fatimid Egypt (358–567/969–1171)', in A. al-Azmeh, ed., *Islamic Law. Social and Historical Contexts* (London, 1988), pp. 198–214, p. 199. Cf. Asaf A.A. Fyzee, 'The Fatimid Law of Inheritance', *Studia Islamica*, 9 (1958), pp. 61–69 and 'Aspects of Fāṭimid Law', *Studia Islamica*, 31 (1970), pp. 81–91, pp. 90–91; A. Cilardo, *Diritto ereditario Islamico delle scuole giuridiche Ismailita e Imamita* (Rome, 1993).

19 The Mālikī judge of Cairo had been ordered to rule according to the doctrine of the *ahl al-bayt* in matters of inheritance, divorce and the new moon, see Paul Walker, 'The Relationship between Chief *Qāḍī* and Chief *Dāʿī* under the Fatimids', in G. Kramer and S. Schmidtke, ed., *Speaking for Islam: Religious Authorities in Muslim Societies* (Leiden, 2006), pp. 70–94, p. 79.

20 Al-Maqrīzī (d. 845/1442), *al-Muqaffā*, ed. M. Yaʿlāwī (Beirut, 1411/1991), vol. 7, pp. 409–416, no. 3493; al-Wansharīsī, *Miʿyār*, vol. 3, p. 149; ibid., vol. 9, p. 282, vol. 10, p. 142. See also Jamāl al-Dīn al-Shayyāl, *Aʿlām al-Iskandariyya fi'l-ʿaṣr al-Islāmī* (Cairo, 1965), p. 79; Lev, *State and Society*, p. 138 and n. 21 (under Badr al-Jamālī it had already been ordered that cases of inheritance had to be handled according to the legal school to which the deceased person had belonged), and p. 197.

21 He refers to such wrong practices of which he had personal experience in *Kitāb al-ḥawādith* (see next footnote), nos 51, 106, 110, 112–114, 118, 119, 166, 238, 250, 313; cf. no. 40.

22 The treatise was first edited M. Talbi (Muḥammad Ṭālibī) (Tunis, 1959); there is a second edition by A.M. Turki (Beirut, 1410/1990), based on the four known MSS. My Spanish translation (see note 15, above) is based on Turki's edition, but also takes into account Talbi's.

23 On these letters see Qāḍī ʿIyāḍ (d. 544/1149), *Tartīb al-madārik li-maʿrifat aʿlām madhhab Mālik*, 8 vols (Rabat, 1983), vol. 3, pp. 110–111. See also A.M. Turki, 'Défense de la tradition du prophète (*sunna*) et lutte contre l'innovation blâmable (*bidʿa*) dans le mālikisme: du *Muwaṭṭa'* de Mālik (–179/795) au *K. al-Gāmiʿ* d'Ibn Abī Zayd al-Qayrawānī (–386/996)', *Studia Islamica*, 87 (1998), pp. 5–34; Rüdiger Lohlker, '*Bidʿa* in der Malikitischen Rechtsschule. Weitere Überlegungen zu Strukturen des Feldes des islamischen Rechts', *Zeitschrift der deutschen Morgenländischen Gesellschaft*, 152 (2002), pp. 95–112.

24 Muḥammad b. Waḍḍāḥ al-Qurṭubī (d. 287/900), *Kitāb al-bidaʿ (Tratado contra las innovaciones)*, ed. and tr. M.I. Fierro (Madrid, 1988). To Ibn Waḍḍāḥ's slightly older contemporary, the North African Muḥammad b. Saḥnūn (d. 256/870), a number of works are attributed that seem to be related to the censuring of innovators, but they have not been preserved, see the preliminary study in Ibn Waḍḍāḥ's *Kitāb al-bidaʿ*, pp. 24 and 97, n. 193.

25 In his *Kitāb al-jāmiʿ fi'l-sunan wa'l-ādāb wa'l-maghāzī wa'l-ta'rīkh*, ed. M. Abu'l-Ajfān and ʿUthmān Baṭṭīkh (Beirut and Tunis, 1402/1982).

26 H. R. Idris, 'Deux juristes kairouanais de l'époque zīrīde: Ibn Abī Zayd et al-Qābisī', *Annales de l'Institut d'Études Orientales* (1954), pp. 173–198: 'Iyāḍ mentions among his works a *Risāla fi'l-bida'*.

27 Among the many editions and studies on Ibn al-Ḥajj (d. 737/1336), *Madkhal al-shar' al-sharīf*, see the edition in 4 vols, Cairo, 1380/1960, and H. Lutfi, 'Manners and Customs of Fourteenth- century Cairene Women: Female Anarchy versus Male Shari'i Order in Muslim Prescriptive Treatises', in N.R. Keddie and B. Baron, ed., *Women in Middle Eastern History: Shifting Boundaries in Sex and Gender* (New Haven, CT, 1991), pp. 99–121.

28 Ignaz Goldziher, *Muslim Studies*, tr. S.M. Stern (London, 1967–1971), vol. 1, pp. 17–37; French trans. of the part devoted to *bid'a* by G.H. Bousquet and H. Pérès under the title 'La *bid'a*', *Bulletin d'Études Arabes*, 2 (1942), pp. 131–134; M. Talbi, 'Les *Bida'*', *Studia Islamica*, 12 (1960), pp. 43–77; M. Fierro, 'The Treatises Against Innovations (*kutub al-bida'*)', *Der Islam*, 69 (1992), pp. 204–246; Rachel Ukeles, 'Innovation or Deviation: Exploring the Boundaries of Islamic Devotional Law' (PhD thesis, Harvard University 2006).

29 Al-Ṭurṭūshī, *Kitāb al-ḥawādith*, no. 60. See A.J. Wensinck, 'Arabic New Year and the Feast of Tabernacles', *Verhandelingen der Koninklijke Akademie van Wetenschappen te Amsterdam*, 25 (1925), pp. 1–41, where he proposes that the *ṣalāt al-tarāwīḥ* be substituted for the practice of the spiritual retreat (*i'tikāf*) associated with Ramaḍān, and where he also proposes a possible Jewish precedent.

30 M.I. Fierro, 'El principio mālikí *sadd al-darā'i'* en el *Kitāb al-ḥawādiṯ wa-l-bida'* de Abū Bakr al-Ṭurṭūšī', *Al-Qanṭara*, 2 (1981), pp. 69–87.

31 On this precept, see Michael Cook, *Commanding Right and Forbidding Wrong in Islamic Thought* (Cambridge, 2000).

32 Maribel Fierro, 'Spiritual Alienation and Political Activism: The *ghurabā'* in al-Andalus during the Sixth/Twelfth Century', *Arabica*, 47 (2000), pp. 230–260.

33 On this topic, see Josef van Ess, *Der Eine und das Andere. Beobachtungen an islamischen häresiographischen Texten*, 2 vols (Berlin, 2011).

34 The third one (Qur'an 57:27) is mentioned later (no. 61).

35 Al-Ṭurṭūshī, *Kitāb al-ḥawādith*, no. 41. On this issue, see J. Burton, 'The "Travel-prayer": *ṣalāt al-safar*', *Occasional Papers of the School of Abbasid Studies*, 2 (1988), ed. D.E.P. Jackson et al. (Edinburgh, 1990), pp. 57–87, p. 68.

36 Al-Ṭurṭūshī, *Kitāb al-ḥawādith*, nos 46–50. On this issue, see Christopher Melchert, 'Whether to Keep Women out of the Mosque: A Survey of Medieval Islamic Law', in B. Michalak-Pikulska and A. Pikulski, ed., *Authority, Privacy and Public Order in Islam* (Leuven, 2006), pp. 59–69; Marion Katz, *Women in the Mosque: A History of Legal Thought and Social Practice* (New York, 2014).

37 Al-Ṭurṭūshī, *Kitāb al-ḥawādith*, nos 53–59, 60–66, 72. See Note 33, above.

38 Such innovations are also treated in the treatise on innovations by the Shāfiʿī Abū Shāma (d. ca. 665/1268), *al-Bāʿith ʿalā inkār al-bidaʿ wa'l-ḥawādith*, ed. ʿUthmān Aḥmad ʿAnbar (Cairo, 1398/1978), p. 39; by the Mālikī al-Shāṭibī (d. 790/1388), *Fatāwā*, ed. M. Abu'l-Ajfān (Tunis, 1405/1984), pp. 207–208, and by ʿUthmān b. Fūdī/ Usumanu dan Fodio (d. 1232/1817), *Iḥyā' al-sunna wa ikhmād al-bidʿa* (Cairo 1381/1962), p. 139.

39 Al-Ṭurṭūshī, *Kitāb al-ḥawādith*, nos 110, 115–118.

40 On this, see Brunschvig, 'Polémiques médiévales autour du rite de Mālik', and Umar F. Abd-Allah Wymann-Landgraf, *Mālik and Medina: Islamic Reasoning in the Formative Period* (Leiden, 2012).

41 Al-Ṭurṭūshī, *Kitāb al-ḥawādith*, nos 122–129, 260.

42 Ibid., nos 102–104, 105, 106–109.

43 The consumption of such kinds of food is associated with summer festivals to obtain a good harvest: Wensinck, 'Arabic New Year', p. 33.

44 A practice approved by ʿAlī: see W. Ivanow, *Ibn al-Qaddah* (2nd ed., Bombay, 1957), p. 35. See also L.P. Harvey, 'The Moriscos and the Hajj', *BRISMES Bulletin*, 14 (1988), pp. 11–24 and J. Sourdel-Thomine and D. Sourdel, 'Nouveaux documents sur l'histoire religieuse et sociale de Damas au Moyen-Age', *Revue des Études Islamiques*, 32 (1964), pp. 1–25 and 33 (1965), pp. 73–85.

45 See Note 150, below.

46 Al-Ṭurṭūshī, *Kitāb al-ḥawādith*, nos 110–113.

47 Ibid., nos 254, 267, 268 and 261.

48 Ibid., nos 130–159. See M. Talbi, 'La *qirā'a bi-l-alḥān*', *Arabica*, 5 (1958), pp. 183–190; F.M. Denny, 'The Adab of Qur'ān Recitation: Text and Context', in A.J. Johns and S.H.M. Jafri, ed., *International Congress for the Study of the Qur'ān*, Series 1 (Canberra, 1982), pp. 143–160; Kristina Nelson, *The Art of Reciting the Qur'an* (Cairo and New York, 2001).

49 Al-Ṭurṭūshī, *Kitāb al-ḥawādith*, nos 150–158 and cf. al-Shāfiʿī (d. 204/820), *Kitāb al-umm* (in the margins, al-Muzanī's *Mukhtaṣar*) 7 vols. in 3 (Cairo, 1321–1326/1903–1908), vol. I, pp. 95, 147–148.

50 Al-Ṭurṭūshī, *Kitāb al-ḥawādith*, no. 157. Cf. R. Brunschvig, 'Devoir et pouvoir, histoire d'un problème de théologie musulmane', *Studia Islamica*, 20 (1964), reprinted in his *Études d'Islamologie* (Paris, 1976), vol. 1, p. 183.

51 Al-Ṭurṭūshī, *Kitāb al-ḥawādith*, no. 138, where a type of melody imitating those performed by monks is mentioned. Cf. Henri Pérès, *La poésie andalouse en arabe classique au XI*[e] *siècle: Ses aspects généraux, ses principaux thèmes et sa valeur documentaire* (2nd ed., Paris, 1953), p. 281. In their turn, the melodies of the Muslims would have influenced the Jews: M. Perlmann, 'A Seventeenth Century Exhortation Concerning al-Aqṣā', *Israel Oriental Studies*, 3 (1973), pp. 261–292, p. 266, n. 18, mentions that the Andalusī rabbis (10th–12th centuries) condemned the infiltration of Arabic melodies in the synagogues.

52 Abu'l-ʿArab Muḥammad. b. Aḥmad b. Tamīm al-Qayrawānī (d. 333/945), *Ṭabaqāt ʿulamāʾ Ifrīqiya wa Tūnis*, ed. ʿAlī al-Shābbī and N.H. al-Yāfī (Tunis, 1968), p. 141; Yaḥyā b. ʿUmar (d. 289/901), *Kitāb aḥkām al-sūq*, ed. M.A. Makkī, *Revista del Instituto Egipcio de Estudios Islámicos*, 4 (1956), pp. 59–152, trans. E. García Gómez as 'Unas *Ordenanzas del zoco* del siglo IX', *Al-Andalus*, 22 (1957), pp. 252–316, no. 31, English trans., p. 29; Ibn al-Abbār (d. 658/1259), *Takmila*, ed. M.A. Alarcón and A. González Palencia, *Miscelánea de Estudios y Textos Árabes* (Madrid, 1915), pp. 147–690, nos 2676, 2680, 2783, biographies of Qur'an reciters in Cordoba who followed the technique of *alḥān* in their recitation (one of them died in 209/824). The same recitation is mentioned by al-ʿUtbī (d. 255/869) in Ibn Rushd al-Jadd (d. 520/1126), *Kitāb al-bayān wa'l-taḥṣīl wa'l-sharḥ wa'l-tawjīh wa'l-taʿlīl fī masāʾil al-mustakhraja*, ed. M. Hajji et al. (2nd ed., Beirut, 1988–1991), vol. 1, p. 275.

53 Al-Ṭurṭūshī, *Kitāb al-ḥawādith*, nos 169–173.

54 Ibid., nos 174–175.

55 Ibid., no. 272, translation corrected according to Alain George, 'Calligraphy, Colour and Light in the Blue Qur'an', *Journal of Qur'anic Studies*, 11 (2009), pp. 75–125, n. 125. Cf. Ibn Taymiyya (d. 728/1328), *Kitāb iqtiḍāʾ al-ṣirāṭ al-mustaqīm mukhālafat aṣḥāb al-jaḥīm* (Cairo, 1369/1950), tr. M. Umar Memon, *Ibn Taymīya's*

Struggle against Popular Religion (Paris, 1976), pp. 297–298, trans. p. 245, and G.H.A. Juynboll, 'The Attitude towards Gold and Silver in Early Islam', in M. Vickers, ed., *Pots and Pans: A Colloquium on Precious Metals and Ceramics* (Oxford, 1986), pp. 107–115, p. 112.

56 'Abd al-Razzāq (d. 211/827), *al-Muṣannaf fi'l-ḥadīth*, ed. Ḥabīb al-Raḥmān al-A'ẓamī (Beirut, 1390–1392/1970–1972), vol. 3, p. 371, nos 60003–60006 and vol. 1, pp. 148–149, no. 2853; Mālik b. Anas (d. 179/795), *al-Muwaṭṭa'*, recension by Yaḥyā b. Yaḥyā (Beirut, 1401/1981), pp. 166–167, nos 333–335; Ibn al-Jawzī (d. 597/1200), *Kitāb al-mawḍū'āt*, ed. A.R.M. 'Uthmān (Medina, 1386–1388/1966–1968), vol. 1, pp. 249–50.

57 See, G. Fehérvári, 'Miḥrāb', *EI2*, vol. 7, pp. 7–15: the concave *miḥrāb* was used for the first time by 'Umar b. 'Abd al-'Azīz when he rebuilt the mosque of the Prophet in 87–88/706–707, when he was governor of Medina.

58 This is what the governor 'Abd al-'Azīz b. Mūsā b. Nuṣayr – the son of the Arab conqueror of the Iberian Peninsula – did in al-Andalus: Ibn al-Qūṭiyya, *Ta'rīkh iftitāḥ al-Andalus* (Madrid, 1926), p. 8. Cf. Ibn al-Jawzī, *Talbīs Iblīs*, ed. Khayr al-Dīn 'Alī (Beirut, n.d.), p. 276.

59 Al-Ṭurṭūshī, *Kitāb al-ḥawādith*, nos 180–182.

60 Ibid., no. 179. Cf. Meir J. Kister, '"A Booth like the Booth of Moses ...": A Study of an Early *ḥadīth*', *Bulletin of the School of Oriental and African Studies*, 25 (1962), pp. 150–155.

61 Al-Ṭurṭūshī, *Kitāb al-ḥawādith*, nos 188 and 183; Maribel Fierro, 'Sobre la decoración con mosaicos de las mezquitas omeyas', in *Homenaje al Prof. Jacinto Bosch Vilà* (Granada, 1991), vol. 1, pp. 131–144; also, al-Wansharīsī, *Mi'yār*, vol. 2, p. 423.

62 Meir J. Kister, '"You shall only set out for three mosques": A Study of an Early Tradition', *Le Museón*, 82 (1969), pp. 173–196.

63 Al-Ṭurṭūshī, *Kitāb al-ḥawādith*, nos 185–186. Cf. Ibn Taymiyya, *Iqtiḍā'*, ed. 1369/1950, pp. 429–432, trans. pp. 314–315; Robert Brunschvig, 'Le culte et le temps dans l'Islam classique', *Études d'Islamologie*, vol. 1, p. 172.

64 Al-Ṭurṭūshī, *Kitāb al-ḥawādith*, no. 187. Al-Ḥārith b. Miskīn ordered the destruction of a mosque where people gathered with the intent to perform certain pious practices: Ibn Farḥūn (d. 799/1397), *al-Dībāj al-mudhhab fī ma'rifat a'yān 'ulamā' al-madhhab* (Cairo, n.d.), vol. 1, p. 339.

65 Al-Ṭurṭūshī, *Kitāb al-ḥawādith*, nos 252, 265, 281. Cf. Ibn Taymiyya, *Iqtiḍā'*, ed. 1369/1950, p. 306, trans. p. 250.

66 Al-Ṭurṭūshī, *Kitāb al-ḥawādith*, nos 280–282. Cf. Ibn Taymiyya, *Iqtiḍā'*, ed. 1369/1950, pp. 387–389/300–302 and especially p. 423, trans. p. 311.

67 Al-Ṭurṭūshī, *Kitāb al-ḥawādith*, no. 283.

68 E. Sivan, 'Le caractère sacré de Jerusalem dans l'Islam aux XIIe–XIIIe siècles', *Studia Islamica*, 27 (1967), pp. 149–182; Amikam Elad, *Medieval Jerusalem and Islamic Worship: Holy Places, Ceremonies, Pilgrimage* (Leiden and New York, 1995); Lev, *State and Society*, p. 51.

69 Al-Ṭurṭūshī, *Kitāb al-ḥawādith*, nos 199, 212, cf. 197. Cf. al-Wansharīsī, *Mi'yār*, vol. 1, p. 147.

70 Al-Ṭurṭūshī, *Kitāb al-ḥawādith*, nos 200, 206–209.

71 Ibid., nos 200–202, 210.

72 Ibid., nos 202–204. Cf. al-Wansharīsī, *Mi'yār*, vol. 1, p. 23, vol. 11, p. 13.

73 Al-Ṭurṭūshī, *Kitāb al-ḥawādith*, nos 205, 210–211, 213–218, 220–224.

74 A. Guillaume, 'Stroking an Idol', *Bulletin of the School of Oriental and African Studies*, 27 (1964), p. 430.

75 Al-Ṭurṭūshī, *Kitāb al-ḥawādith*, nos 274, 260.

76 Charles Pellat, *Le milieu basrien et la formation de Ǧāḥiẓ* (Paris, 1953), pp. 108–116; J. Pedersen, 'The Criticism of the Islamic Preacher', *Die Welt des Islams*, NS, 2 (1952), pp. 215–231; J. Pauliny, 'Zur Rolle der *Quṣṣāṣ* bei der Entstehung und Überlieferung der populären Prophetenlegenden', *Asian and African Studies*, 10 (1974), pp. 125–141; A. Hartmann, 'La prédication islamique au Moyen Age', *Quaderni di Studi Arabi*, 5–6 (1987–1988), pp. 337–346; Jonathan Berkey, *Popular Preaching and Religious Authority in the Medieval Islamic Near East* (Seattle, 2001).

77 Al-Ṭurṭūshī, *Kitāb al-ḥawādith*, nos 189–198, cf. 275.

78 He was not alone in focusing on this prayer: Ibn Rushd (Averroes), *Bidāyat al-mujtahid wa nihāyat al-muqtaṣid* (Cairo, n.d.), vol. 1, pp. 202–203; Abū Shāma, *Bā'ith*, pp. 85–87; Ibn Taymiyya, *Iqtiḍā'*, ed. 1369/1950, Arabic pp. 103, trans. p. 156; Arabic, p. 275, trans. p. 231; Arabic, pp. 276–277, trans. pp. 234–236; p. 360, n. 279; Ibn al-Ḥājj, *Madkhal*, ed. 1380/1960, vol. 2, pp. 298–314; al-Turkumānī (8th–9th/14th–15th centuries), *al-Luma' fi'l-ḥawādith wa'l-bida'*, ed. S. Labib (Stuttgart, 1986), vol. 1, p. 232; al-Shāṭibī (d. 790/1388),

al-I'tiṣām, different editions reproducing the one prepared by M. R. Riḍā and published in *al-Manār*, 17 (1333/1913), vol. 1, pp. 39, 193–195. Al-Suyūṭī (d. 911/1505) is the author of a work entitled *al-Maṣābīḥ fī ṣalāt al-tarāwīḥ* (MSS in Baghdad, *Awqāf*, no. 13741/15; Yale, no. 776; Ahlwardt, vol. 3, pp. 319, 389). See also al-Wansharīsī, *Mi'yār*, vol. 1, pp. 147–149, 156, 158–159, 162, 172, 216; vol. 12, p. 68; Ibn Fūdī, *Iḥyā' al-sunna*, pp. 22, 25, 13–15, 197.

79 For an historical example, see Robert Brunschvig, *La Berbérie Orientale sous les Ḥafṣides, des origines à la fin du XV*[e] *siècle* (Paris, 1940–1947), vol. 2, pp. 308–309.

80 Al-Ṭurṭūshī, *Kitāb al-ḥawādith*, nos 232–237.

81 Wensinck, 'Arabic New Year', includes a discussion of the different identifications proposed for such a night; for Wensinck, it was originally the night of New Year. See also the materials collected in Mālik, *Muwaṭṭa'*, pp. 262–264, nos 11–17; 'Abd al-Razzāq, *Muṣannaf*, vol. 4, pp. 246–255; Ibn Abī Shayba (d. 235/849), *Kitāb al-muṣannaf fi'l-aḥādīth wa'l-āthār*, ed. 'Abd al-Khāliq Khān al-Afghānī (Hyderabad, 1386–1390/1966–1970), vol. 2, pp. 511–515 and vol. 3, pp. 75–77; Saḥnūn (d. 240/854), *al-Mudawwana al-kubrā* (Cairo, 1323/1905), vol. 1, p. 239; al-Bayhaqī (d. 458/1066), *Kitāb al-sunan al-kubrā* (Hyderabad, 1344–1355/1925–1936), vol. 4, pp. 306–314; al-Haythamī (d. 807/1404), *Majma' al-zawā'id* (Cairo, 1352–1353/1933–1934), vol. 3, pp. 174–179; Ibn Ḥazm, *al-Muḥallā* (Cairo, 1348/1929), vol. 7, p. 33; al-Wansharīsī, *Mi'yār*, vol. 11, p. 114; al-Nābulusī (d. 1143/1730), *Faḍā'il al-ẓuhūr wa'l-ayyām wa yalīhi al-Lu'lu' al-maknūn fī ḥukm al-ikhbār 'ammā sayakūn*, ed. M.A.Q. 'Aṭā' (Beirut, 1406/1986), pp. 51–54.

82 Al-Nābulusī, *Faḍā'il*, pp. 33–8; Wensinck, 'Arabic New Year', p. 11; Meir J. Kister, '"Sha'bān is my month": A Study of an Early Tradition', *Studia Orientalia memoriae D.H. Baneth dedicata* (Jerusalem, 1979), pp. 15–37; Vardit Rispler-Chaim, 'The 20th Century of an Old *bid'a*: *laylat al-niṣf min Sha'bān*', *Der Islam*, 72 (1995), pp. 82–97.

83 Abū Bakr b. al-'Arabī (d. 543/1148), *Aḥkām al-Qur'ān*, ed. 'Alī Muḥammad al-Bijawī (Cairo, 1376–1378/1957–1958), vol. 4, p. 1678.

84 Ibn Waḍḍāḥ, *Bida'*, vol. 7, pp. 1–2; Ibn al-Ḥājj, *Madkhal*, ed. 1380/1960, vol. 1, pp. 292–307 and vol. 2, p. 19; al-Shāṭibī, *I'tiṣām*, vol. 1, pp. 227, 229, 230; see also Abū Shāma, *Bā'ith*, pp. 34–41. The celebration seems to have been already widespread at the time of the successors especially in Syria: Kister, 'Sha'bān', p. 29, for whom

it was a survival from the Jāhiliyya (p. 34). See also Ibn al-Ḥājj, *Madkhal*, ed. 1380/1960, vol. 1, pp. 302–303 (Kister, 'Sha'bān', p. 30).

85 Ibn Taymiyya, *Iqtiḍā'*, ed. 1369/1950, pp. 302–303, trans. pp. 248–249; al-Suyūṭī (d. 911/1505), *al-Amr bi'l-ittibā' wa'l-nahy 'an al-ibtidā'*, ed. M.A.Q. 'Aṭā' (Beirut, 1408/1988), p. 61. See also al-Nābulusī, *Faḍā'il*, pp. 39–43; Ibn al-Jawzī, *Mawḍū'āt*, vol. 2, pp. 127–130; al-Suyūṭī, *al-Amr bi'l-ittibā'*, p. 65.

86 Al-Ṭurṭūshī, *Kitāb al-ḥawādith*, no. 238. See also Abū Shāma, *Bā'ith*, p. 34; Ibn Taymiyya, *Iqtiḍā'*, ed. 1369/1950, pp. 292–293/241; Ibn al-Ḥājj, *Madkhal*, ed. 1380/1960, vol. 1, pp. 286–288 and vol. 4, pp. 261–297; al-Turkumānī, *Luma'*, p. 53; al-Suyūṭī, *al-Amr bi'l-ittibā'*, pp. 59–60; Ibn Fūdī, *Iḥyā' al-sunna*, p. 100; al-Wansharīsī, *Mi'yār*, vol. 1, p. 300 and vol. 2, pp. 508–509. Ibn al-Jawzī considered the *ḥadīths* in favour of this kind of prayer to be false: *Mawḍū'āt*, vol. 2, pp. 124–126.

87 Abū Shāma, *Bā'ith*, pp. 42–43.

88 Memon, introd., *Iqtiḍā'*, p. 12.

89 Al-Ṭurṭūshī, *Kitāb al-ḥawādith*, nos 240–251. See al-Nābulusī, *Faḍā'il*, pp. 27–32 and M.J. Kister, '"Rajab is the month of God...": A Study in the Persistence of an early Tradition', *Israel Oriental Studies*, 1 (1971), pp. 191–223. See also Abū Shāma, *Bā'ith*, p. 52; Ibn Taymiyya, *Iqtiḍā'*, ed. 1369/1950, pp. 301–302, trans., p. 248; al-Suyūṭī, *al-Amr bi'l-ittibā'*, pp. 60–66; Ibn Ḥajar, *Tabyīn al-'ajab bi mā warada fī faḍl Rajab* (Beirut, 1988).

90 Kister, 'Rajab is the month of God', as well as the study in Ibn Waḍḍāḥ, *Bida'*, pp. 111–112. For the Prophetic materials praising the fast in this month, see Ibn al-Jawzī, *Mawḍū'āt*, vol. 2, pp. 205–208; al-Haythamī, *Majma' al-zawā'id*, vol. 3, p. 191. The Prophet of the Berber Barghawāṭa established fasting in the month of Rajab: M. Dernouny, 'Aspects de la culture et de l'Islam du Maghreb médiéval: Le cas de l'hérésie Bargwāṭa', *Peuples méditerranéens: revue trimestrielle*, 34 (1986), pp. 89–97.

91 See note 63, above.

92 As the Moriscos did: Longás, *Vida religiosa de los moriscos* (Madrid, 1915), p. 230.

93 Al-Ṭurṭūshī, *Kitāb al-ḥawādith*, nos 225–231. On 'Arafa see A.J. Wensinck-H.A.R. Gibb in *EI2*, vol. 1, p. 604; s.v. A.J. Wensinck-J. Jomier 'Ḥadjdj', *EI2*, vol. 3, pp. 33–37; al-Nābulusī, *Faḍā'il*, pp. 61–65; Fierro, 'The Treatises against Innovations'.

94 Ibn Waḍḍāḥ, *Bida'*, ch. VIII; al-Bayhaqī, *Sunan*, V, pp. 117–118; Gaudefroy-Demombynes, *Le pèlerinage à la Mekke* (Paris, 1923), pp. 253–255. For Fatimid Egypt, see Lev, *State and Society*, p. 51 and n. 50.

95 Al-Ṭurṭūshī, in his *Kitāb al-du'ā'*, ed. M.R. al-Dāya (Beirut, 1988), includes traditions exalting the *du'ā'*... said on the day of 'Arafa (pp. 66, 145, 186).

96 Al-Ṭurṭūshī, *Kitāb al-ḥawādith*, no. 255 and cf. Meir J. Kister, 'Do not assimilate yourselves...', *Jerusalem Studies in Arabic and Islam*, 12 (1989), pp. 321–371, p. 325, n. 13. Innovations related to this day are dealt with by Abū Shāma, *Bā'ith*, pp. 96–102; Ibn Taymiyya, *Iqtiḍā'*, ed. 1369/1950, p. 287, trans. p. 239; Lyall R. Armstrong, *The quṣṣās of early Islam* (Leiden-Boston, 2017).

97 Cf. 'Abd al-Razzāq, *Muṣannaf*, I, 475, nos 1821, 1832; Ibn Waḍḍāḥ, *Bida'*, vol. 5, pp. 13–14; al-Shāṭibī, *I'tiṣām*, vol. 2, pp. 53, 69–70 and vol. 1, pp. 256–257; al-Wansharīsī, *Mi'yār*, vol. 1, p. 278 and vol. 2, pp. 462–463.

98 Al-Ṭurṭūshī, *Kitāb al-ḥawādith*, no. 253.

99 Cf. al-Ṭurṭūshī, *Kitāb al-du'ā'*, pp. 53–57, 154, 66, 65, 209 for the right way of raising one's voice and the invocations performed on *laylat al-qadr*, the recitation of the Qur'an and the *qiyām*.

100 Al-Ṭurṭūshī, *Kitāb al-ḥawādith*, no. 100; cf. Ibn Waḍḍāḥ, *Bida'*, ch. II, no. 41; Abū Shāma, *Bā'ith*, pp. 17, 87-88; al-Shāṭibī, *al-I'tiṣām* (Beirut, n.d.), vol. 1, p. 358; al-Suyūṭī, *al-Amr bi'l-ittibā'*, p. 68; M. Fierro, 'La polémique á propos de *raf' al-yadayn fī l-ṣalāt* dans al-Andalus', *Studia Islamica*, 65 (1987), pp. 69–90.

101 Kister, 'Do not assimilate yourselves', p. 332, n. 40; Pedersen, 'The Islamic Preacher', p. 233 and 'Criticism of the Islamic Preacher', pp. 218–219.

102 Al-Ṭurṭūshī, *Kitāb al-ḥawādith*, no. 99; cf. al-Wansharīsī, *Mi'yār*, vol. 1, p. 284.

103 Al-Ṭurṭūshī, *Kitāb al-ḥawādith*, nos 275–276.

104 Ibid., ch. 18–22. Cf. Abū Shāma, *Bā'ith*, pp. 91–93; Ibn al-Jawzī, *Kitāb al-mawḍū'āt*, ed. 'A.R.M. 'Uthmān (Medina, 1386–1388/1966–1968), vol. 3, pp. 216–229, 231–243; al-Turkumānī, *Luma'*, pp. 214–229; Ibn al-Ḥājj, *Madkhal* (Cairo, 1380/1960), vol. 3, pp. 243–296; al-Suyūṭī, *al-Amr bi'l-ittibā'*, pp. 99–100; al-Wansharīsī, *Mi'yār*, vol. 2, p. 484; Ibn Fūdī, *Iḥyā' al-sunna*, pp. 118–119.

105 Al-Ṭurṭūshī, *Kitāb al-ḥawādith*, no. 272. Cf. Ibn Taymiyya, *Iqtiḍā'*, ed. 1369/1950, pp. 108, 329/160, 262; al-Wansharīsī, *Mi'yār*, vol. 1, pp. 317–319, 320–324, and vol. 11, p. 152; Ibn Fūdī, *Iḥyā' al-sunna*, p. 126.

106 Cf. Ibn al-Ḥājj, *Madkhal*, ed. 1380/1960, vol. 3, p. 286, and al-Haythamī, *Majmaʿ al-zawāʾid*, 10 vols. in 5 (Cairo, 1352–1353/1933–1934), vol. 3, p. 61.
107 Al-Ṭurṭūshī, *Kitāb al-ḥawādith*, no. 274.
108 Al-Wansharīsī, *Miʿyār*, vol. 1, p. 328 and vol. 2, p. 509. Cf. al-Shāṭibī, *Fatāwā*, pp. 209–210. However, al-Ṭurṭūshī seems to have participated in the recitation of the Qurʾan for seven days at the grave of the judge of Alexandria, Ibn Ḥadīd: see the study that accompanies Fierro's trans. of *Kitāb al-ḥawādith*, p. 72.
109 Al-Ṭurṭūshī, *Kitāb al-ḥawādith*, nos 277, 312–313.
110 Ibid., no. 313. Cf. Ibn al-Ḥājj, *Madkhal*, ed. 1380/1960, vol. 2, pp. 225–256; al-Wansharīsī, *Miʿyār*, vol. 1, p. 317.
111 Al-Ṭurṭūshī, *Kitāb al-ḥawādith*, no. 277.
112 Ibid., nos 296–301.
113 Cf. al-Suyūṭī, *al-Amr biʾl-ittibāʿ*, p. 112.
114 Al-Ṭurṭūshī, *Kitāb al-ḥawādith*, no. 309. Leiser, 'The *Madrasa* and the Islamization of the Middle East', p. 34, mentions the use of incense in the funeral procession of a Christian.
115 Al-Ṭurṭūshī, *Kitāb al-ḥawādith*, no. 311. On the role of women in funerals see Leor Halevi, *Muhammad's Grave: Death Rites and the Making of Islamic Society* (New York, 2006).
116 Al-Ṭurṭūshī, *Kitāb al-ḥawādith*, no. 277.
117 Ibid., no. 302.
118 For the dismissal of lamenting the dead as a *jāhilī* practice see Kister, 'Do not assimilate yourselves', p. 323, n. 6.
119 G.H.A. Juynboll, *Muslim Tradition: Studies in Chronology, Provenance and Authorship of Early ḥadīth* (Cambridge, 1983), pp. 102–108; Nadia El Cheikh, 'Mourning and the Role of the Nāʾiḥa', in C. de la Puente, ed., *Identidades marginales* (Madrid, 2003), pp. 395–412.
120 Al-Ṭurṭūshī, *Kitāb al-ḥawādith*, nos 303–306. Al-Ṭurṭūshī devoted one of the chapters of his *Sirāj al-mulūk* to patience and resignation.
121 Al-Maqdisī (d. 643/1245), *Ittibāʿ al-sunan wa ijtināb al-bidaʿ*, ed. M. Badr al-Dīn al-Qahwajī and M. al-Arnāʾūṭ (Damascus and Beirut, 1407/1987), pp. 37–57; Ibn al-Jawzī, *Mawḍūʿāt*, II, 255; Ibn al-Ḥājj, *Madkhal*, ed. 1380/1960, I, 238–76 and *passim*; Ibn Taymiyya, *Iqtiḍāʾ*, ed. 1369/1950, pp. 224–220; see also, al-Wansharīsī, *Miʿyār*, vol. 2, pp. 499–500 and 505.

122 See note 36, above.
123 Al-Ṭurṭūshī, *Kitāb al-ḥawādith*, nos 51, 118, 185, 260, 277, 309. Cf. al-Suyūṭī, *al-Amr bi'l-ittibā'*, p. 65; al-Wansharīsī, *Mi'yār*, vol. 1, p. 500 and vol. 11, p. 228; Ibn Fūdī, *Iḥyā' al-sunna*, pp. 139–141. For Egypt, see Lev, *State and society*, pp. 169–170.
124 Al-Ṭurṭūshī, *Kitāb al-ḥawādith*, no. 262.
125 Al-Shāṭibī, *I'tiṣām*, vol. 1, p. 37.
126 Lev, *State and Society*, p. 146. See also J. Knappert, 'The Mawlid', *Orientalia Lovaniensia Periodica*, 19 (1988), pp. 209–215; N.J.G. Kaptein, *Muhammad's Birthday Festival: Early History in the Central Muslim Lands and Development in the Muslim West until the 10th/16th Century* (Leiden, 1993).
127 Kister, "Do not assimilate yourselves".
128 J. Waardenburg, 'Official and Popular Religion as a Problem in Islamic Studies', in P.J. Vrijhof and J. Waardenburg, ed., *Official and Popular Religion: Analysis of a Theme for Religious Studies* (The Hague, 1977), pp. 340–386; Jonathan Berkey, 'Tradition, Innovation and the Social Construction of Knowledge in the Medieval Islamic Near East', *Past and Present*, 146 (1995), pp. 38–65.
129 According to al-Ṭurṭūshī the caliph 'Umar is exempted from having started any 'bad' innovation as we have seen.
130 Al-Ṭurṭūshī, *Kitāb al-ḥawādith*, no. 101.
131 Al-Muqaddasī, *Aḥsan al-taqāsīm fī ma'rifat al-aqālīm*, ed. M.J. de Goeje (Leiden, 1967 [Bibliotheca Geographorum Arabicorum III]); English trans. Basil Collins, corrected by Mohammad Hamid Alta'i (Reading, 2001), pp. 186–187.
132 Al-Mālikī, *Riyāḍ al-nufūs*, ed. B. al-Bakkūsh et al., 3 vols (Beirut, 1401–1403/1981–1983), vol. 2, pp. 55–56; R. Brunschvig, '*Fiqh* fatimide et histoire de l'Ifriqiya', in *Mélanges d'histoire*, pp. 13–20 reprinted in his *Études d'Islamologie*, vol. 1, p. 68.
133 Ibn Ḥayyān, *Muqtabis*, ed. A.R. Ḥājjī (Beirut, 1965), p. 174. On the contrasting policies by which the Cordoban Umayyads and the Fatimids expressed their rivalry, see M. Fierro, 'Espacio sunní y espacio šī'í', in *El esplendor de los omeyas cordobeses. La civilización musulmana de Europa Occidental. Exposición en Madīnat al-Zahrā' 3 de mayo a 30 de septiembre de 2001* (Granada, 2001), pp. 168–177.
134 Lev, *State and Society*, p. 143 and n. 48, quoting his previous study 'The Fāṭimid Imposition of Ismā'īlism on Egypt (358–386/969–996)', pp. 313–325.

135 The Muʿtazilī, al-Naẓẓām, accused ʿUmar of having invented the prayer: al-Baghdādī (d. 429/1037), *al-Farq bayn al-firaq* (Beirut, 1978); trans. as *Moslem Schisms and Sects* by A.S. Halkin (Tel Aviv, 1935), p. 99.

136 For Egypt, see al-Kindī (d. 350/961), *Kitāb wulāt Miṣr*, ed. R. Guest (Leiden and London, 1912), p. 210; al-Ṣubkī (d. 771/1369), *Ṭabaqāt al-shāfiʿiyya al-kubrā* (Cairo, 1383–1396/1964–1976), vol. 8, pp. 251–252; Ibn Taghribirdī (d. 874/1470), *al-Nujūm al-zāhira fī mulūk Miṣr wa'l-Qāhira* (Cairo, 1351/1932), vol. 2, p. 338; E.W. Lane, *An Account of the Manners and Customs of the Modern Egyptians* (London, 1846), vol 1. pp. 475–478. For North Africa, see ʿIyāḍ, *Madārik*, vol. 5, p. 147 and vol. 6, p. 218 (Ibn Abī Zayd wrote a *Kitāb faḍl qiyām Ramaḍān*); al-Maqqarī (d. 1041/1631), *Nafḥ al-ṭīb min ghuṣn al-Andalus al-raṭīb wa dhikr wazīrihā Lisān al-dīn Ibn al-Khaṭīb*, ed. I. ʿAbbās (Beirut, 1398/1968), vol. 7, p. 75. For al-Andalus, see Ibn ʿAbdūn, 'Risāla fī'l-qaḍā' wa'l-ḥisba', in É. Lévi-Provençal, ed., *Trois traités hispaniques de ḥisba* (Cairo, 1955), pp. 1–65; tr. E. García Gómez and E. Lévi-Provençal as *Sevilla a comienzos del siglo XII. El tratado de Ibn ʿAbdūn* (Madrid, 1948), p. 83; Ibn al-Abbār, *al-Takmila li-kitāb al-Ṣila*, ed. I. al-ʿAṭṭār al-Ḥusaynī (Cairo, 1956), nos 305, 423, 703, 930, 1524; Ibn Saʿīd (d. 685/1286), *al-Mughrib fī ḥulā'l-Maghrib*, ed. Sh. Ḍayf (Cairo, 1964), vol. 1, p. 331.

137 A.J. Wensinck, *The Muslim Creed: Its Genesis and Historical Development* (Cambridge, 1932), pp. 219–220; G. Makdisi, *Ibn ʿAqīl et la résurgence de l'Islam traditionniste au XIe siècle* (Damascus, 1963), p. 446.

138 I.K.A. Howard, 'The Development of the *adhān* and *iqāma* of the *ṣalāt* in Early Islam', *Journal of Semitic Studies*, 26 (1981), pp. 219–228, especially p. 221.

139 See Th.W. Juynboll, '*Iḳāma*', *EI2*. For another practice in the *adhān* associated with the Shiʿis, see Liyakat A. Takim, 'From *bidʿa* to Sunna. The *wilāya* of ʿAlī in the Shīʿī *adhān*', *Journal of the American Oriental Society*, 120 (2000), pp. 166–177.

140 Ibn Ḥazm, *Naqṭ al-ʿarūs*, ed. C.F. Seybold, *Revista del Centro de Estudios Históricos de Granada y su reino*, 1 (1911), pp. 160–180 and 237–248, pp. 179–180; Spanish trans. by L. Seco de Lucena (Valencia, 1974), p. 111.

141 Al-Ṭurṭūshī, *Kitāb al-ḥawādith*, no. 269 (cf. ʿAbd al-Razzāq, *Muṣannaf*, vol. 1, p. 475, nos 1821–1832); al-Shāṭibī, *Iʿtiṣām*, vol. 2,

pp. 53, 69–70 and vol. 1, pp. 256–257 (cf. Ibn Rushd al-Jadd, *Kitāb al-bayān*, I, 435–436). See also al-Wansharīsī, *Mi'yār*, vol. 1, p. 278 and vol. 2, p. 462–463.

142 Al-Ṭurṭūshī, *Kitāb al-ḥawādith*, no. 272. Such shrines lead to *ziyārat al-qubūr*: Lev, *State and Society*, pp. 149–152.

143 See note 6, above.

144 For the Shi'i practices, see Th. Leisten, 'Between Orthodoxy and Exegesis: Some Aspects of Attitudes in the Shari'a Toward Funerary Architecture', *Muqarnas*, 7 (1990), pp. 12–22; Muhammad Ayoub, *Redemptive Suffering in Islam: A Study of the Devotional Aspects of 'Āshūrā' in Twelver Shī'ism* (The Hague, 1978). For the convergence with popular practices, see Juan Campo, 'Muslim Ways of Death: Between the Prescribed and the Performed', in K. Garces-Foley, ed., *Death and Religion in a Changing World* (New York, 2006), pp. 147–177.

145 Cortese, 'Voices', p. 360.

146 Heinz Halm, *The Empire of the Mahdi: The Rise of the Fatimids*, tr. M. Bonner (Leiden, 1996), p. 320; Paula Sanders, *Ritual, Politics and the City in Fatimid Cairo* (Albany, NY, 1994), pp. 49–50; H. Halm, *Die Kalifen von Kairo: Die Fatimiden in Ägypten 973–1074* (München, 2003). According to Ibn Baṭṭa, the Rāfiḍa forbade eating the meat of the sacrificed she-camel: Henri Laoust, *La profession de foi d'Ibn Baṭṭa* (Damascus, 1958), pp. 135–137; cf. Ṣā'id al-Ṭulayṭulī (d. 462/1070), *Ṭabaqāt al-umam*, tr. R. Blachère (Paris, 1935), pp. 92–93.

147 Stewart, 'Popular Shiism in Medieval Egypt', p. 55.

148 Boaz Shoshan, *Popular Culture in Medieval Cairo* (Cambridge, 1993).

149 Stewart, 'Popular Shiism in Medieval Egypt', pp. 54–55.

150 A thorough discussion of these issues may be found in Maribel Fierro, 'The Turban and Its Meanings in the Medieval Islamic West', paper read at University of California, Santa Barbara, May 2014 and at the 27th Congress of the Union Européenne des Arabisants et Islamisants (UEAI 27), Helsinki, June 2014.

151 Kister, 'Sha'bān', p. 27; Lev, *State and Society*, p. 144.

152 Lev, *State and Society*, pp. 144–145.

153 As noted by M.J. Kister in his review of Talbi's edition of the *Kitāb al-ḥawādith wa'l-bida'* by al-Ṭurṭūshī in *Journal of Semitic Studies*, 6 (1961), pp. 137–142, p. 140, n. 3, quoting *al-Majālis al-mustanṣiriyya*; Lev, *State and Society*, p. 144.

154 On the Blue Qur'an – the date and place of production of which are still subject to debate – see Jonathan Bloom, 'The Early Fatimid Blue Koran Manuscript', *Graeco-Arabica*, 4 (1991), pp. 171–178; Yasser Tabbaa, 'The Transformation of Arabic Writing: Part I: Qur'ānic Calligraphy', *Ars Orientalis*, 21 (1991), pp. 119–148, and Alain George, 'Calligraphy, Colour and Light in the Blue Qur'an', *Journal of Qur'anic Studies*, 11 (2009), pp. 75–125, who argues it was produced under the Abbasids (see especially p. 100 on the correct way to understand Mālik's view on the writing of the Qur'an as quoted by al-Ṭurṭūshī).

155 De Smet, 'Comment déterminer', pp. 45–61.

156 Stewart, 'Popular Shiism in Medieval Egypt', p. 37 ('While the Imamate became a major issue in Islamic theological doctrines, the cursing, deprecation and vilification of Companions of the Prophet was one of the most prominent popular manifestations of Shi'i identity throughout medieval Islamic history'), referring to Etan Kohlberg, 'Some Imāmī Shī'ī Views on the Ṣaḥāba', *Jerusalem Studies in Arabic and Islam*, 5 (1984), pp. 143–175.

157 Maribel Fierro, 'The Celebration of 'Āshūrā' in Sunnī Islam', *The Arabist (Proceedings of the 14th Congress of the Union Européenne des Arabisants et Islamisants)*, 13–14 (1994), pp. 193–208. For disturbances in Egypt opposing Shi'is and Sunnis on that day, see Stewart, 'Popular Shiism in Medieval Egypt', pp. 53–54.

158 Cortese, 'Voices', p. 355, has pointed out that: 'a notable feature of Egypt was the lack of religious-ideological barriers between traditionists in pursuit of knowledge. Ḥadīths and ideas continued to circulate and be exchanged irrespective of *madhhab* as shown by the variety of persuasions held by the people listed in any given Egypt-related scholarly pedigree.'

159 Leiser, 'The *Madrasa* and the Islamization of the Middle East', p. 44, has pointed out the tendency to highlight Sunni convergence in Egypt: al-Qāḍī al-Fāḍil (an indirect student of al-Ṭurṭūshī) founded a madrasa for both Mālikīs and Shāfi'īs, as he 'apparently wanted to emphasise a certain unity of purpose in strengthening the link between the government and the orthodox religious community'. The *madrasa* possessed a Qur'an that had belonged to 'Uthmān.

160 A concept developed by James C. Scott, *Domination and the Arts of Resistance: Hidden Transcripts* (New Haven, CT, 1990). For its application to the relations between *dhimmīs* and Muslims in

Egypt, see *Medieval Encounters* (Special edition: Proceedings of 'Non-Muslim Communities in Fatimid Egypt' colloquium).

161 M. Frenkel, 'Adaptive Tactics: The Jewish Communities Facing a New Reality', *Medieval Encounters*, 21 (2015), pp. 364–389 (I would also like to thank the author for allowing me to quote from her unpublished study).

162 Leiser, 'The *Madrasa* and the Islamization of the Middle East', pp. 36, 40, points to the fact that the greatest challenge the Sunnis faced in Egypt was not heterodoxy but a large and powerful Christian community: 'Nowhere within the context of the appearance and spread of madrasas in Alexandria do the sources give the slightest hint of any concern for combating Shi'ism.' This silence can be understood in different ways, one is through the concept of 'hidden transcript'.

6

Transmitting Sunni Learning in Fatimid Egypt: The Female Voices

Delia Cortese

The contribution of Sunnism to the social, intellectual and cultural history of Egypt during the Fatimid period has remained thus far the elephant in the room in the field of Fatimid studies.* The privileged attention paid by contemporary scholarship to the Shiʿi Ismaili character of the Fatimid dynasty and aspects of its regime has caused the scholarly activities of Sunnis to be largely ignored despite the Sunnis being the majority religious community in Egypt before, during and after the 4th/10th to 6th/12th centuries. A lack of cross-fertilisation between disciplines penalises not only our knowledge of the Fatimids but also that of the social and intellectual history of medieval Sunni Islam as a whole. In this history, the role of women as participants has also long been ignored and it is only in recent times that women's contribution to the transmission of learning has become the subject of increasing systematic investigations. In contrast to a time when Ignaz Goldziher treated the existence of female transmitters of *ḥadīth*s (pl. *muḥaddithāt*) as a curiosity,[1] today – thanks to recent research – we are now aware of some 8,000 female contributors belonging to the early, classical, pre-modern and modern periods of Islamic history.[2] Broadly speaking, recent studies on *muḥaddithāt* consist of either general, mostly quantitative analyses, or of contextualised biographical accounts of prominent female personalities. In the latter category, research has mostly focused either on the formation and transmission of *ḥadīth*s by women who lived at the time of the Prophet Muḥammad and the Companions' generation or on women of the Ayyūbid and Mamlūk periods, hailed as an epoch of revival in female participation in *ḥadīth* learning. Yet, as Asma Sayeed puts it: 'We still lack analyses that synthesize the fragmented historical evidence to reconstruct more complete portraits.'[3]

In the eastern lands of the Abbasid empire, a precipitous decline in female *ḥadīth* transmitters from the mid-2nd/8th to the mid-4th/10th centuries has been mooted on the basis of a lack of any record of them in early and medieval Islamic sources. In the second half of the 4th/10th century, however, women re-emerged in the sources as vehicles of learning and transmission. From this period until well into the Mamlūk era, the sources show that an increasing number of women acquired exemplary reputations.[4] Against the grain of these data, in Egypt, the period of history stretching from the 4th/10th to the late 6th/12th centuries (coinciding with the Fatimid era) has been typically regarded as a time of decline in *ḥadīth* scholarship in general,[5] and even more so in the relative female participation in the transmission of Prophetic traditions.[6] This consideration has been largely based on the, so-far unchallenged, assumption that the Shiʿi character of the Fatimid dynasty must have automatically meant a lesser relevance in Egypt of Sunni Islam and its intellectual traditions.[7] We can, therefore, see how the oversight that has resulted in the absence of comprehensive studies on the activities of Sunni scholars in Egypt during the Fatimid period, has also – by default – generated a neglect of any investigation of *muḥaddithāt* in Egypt in this era, thus rendering our knowledge of the history of medieval *ḥadīth* scholarship somewhat incomplete.

In response to A. Sayeed's call, the purpose of this chapter is therefore to re-inscribe the role of those women associated with *ḥadīth* scholarship, who were active in Egypt under the Fatimids, in the history of the female contribution to *ḥadīth* sciences; to acknowledge the place that these women occupied in the intellectual history of Egypt during the period; and to revisit, through the reports of these women's experiences, the social and cultural norms that informed female agency within a Sunni scholarly community operating under a regime that was officially Shiʿi Ismaili. In the context of the Sunni learning environment in Egypt in the 5th/11th and 6th/12th centuries where, in contrast to the rest of the Muslim world, the institution of the madrasa arrived late (in Alexandria) or not at all (in Cairo), male scholars had to resort to a variety of social signifiers to affirm and advertise their prestige and authoritativeness as credible transmitters of knowledge. The argument in this chapter is that, in this male-dominated environment, learned Sunni women played an important role as 'bonding agents' in the fostering of cohesion between Sunni scholarly networks in Egypt and beyond while under a Shiʿi regime, and as useful 'genealogical links' in the transmission and therefore preservation of intellectual capital in family lineages. Thus women emerge here primarily as agents in the varied social applications of religious knowledge rather than as contributors to it.[8]

The engagement with learning of these Sunni women will also be contrasted broadly with that of their female Ismaili contemporaries. Throughout most of their reign, the Fatimid imam-caliphs were credited with instructing high-ranking *dāʿīs* to deliver lectures and hold preaching sessions specifically designed for the women of the court and Ismaili female followers at large. In most cases, these sessions are reported to have taken place in formal settings, in accordance with procedures that were officially approved and based on gender-specific pedagogical methods.[9]

The most important sources on the *muḥaddithāt* of Egypt during Fatimid rule are two biographical dictionaries by two Egypt-based Sunni *ḥadīth* scholars who lived during and immediately after the Fatimid era. The first is the *Muʿjam al-safar* (*The Dictionary of Travel*) by Abū Ṭāhir al-Silafī (b. Iṣfahān in 472/1079; d. Alexandria in 576/1180), arguably the most famous Sunni educator of the 6th/12th century in Egypt. A prolific author and meticulous recorder of his own learned lineage, al-Silafī compiled the *Muʿjam* mostly as a personal record of the teachers and students he had met throughout his career. Covering the period from 511/1117 to 560/1164, the *Muʿjam* can be regarded as a digest of intellectual life in late Fatimid Alexandria.[10] The second dictionary is *al-Takmila* (*The Supplement*) by Zakī al-Dīn al-Mundhirī (b. Fusṭāṭ in 581/1185; d. Cairo in 656/1258). A prominent figure in the history of education in pre-modern Egypt, his *al-Takmila* is the supplement to *Wafayāt al-naqla* by Abu'l-Ḥasan al-Maqdisī (d. 611/1214), a student of al-Silafī. Written by men for men, these works are the product of authors who reported selectively on women scholars on the basis of their own personal experiences, interests and agendas. Notwithstanding this limitation, the *Muʿjam* and *al-Takmila* are the only extant extensive biographical dictionaries dealing with Egypt where the authors were contemporary with, or at least chronologically close to, the time in which the women they describe lived.

Early *muḥaddithāt* in Egypt

In a wide variety of accounts reported in Islamic biographical dictionaries the earliest known female *ḥadīth* transmitters in Egypt are consistently traced back to the time of the Prophet Muḥammad. Hagiographical and anachronistic owing to the nature of the genre in which they appear, these narratives include among the *muḥaddithāt* the Prophet's concubine, Maryā the Copt, and her sister, as well as wives or daughters of the Companions of the Prophet who followed their male relatives to Egypt at the time of the conquests. Of the latter group the best known among them are Umm Dharr, wife of Abū Dharr al-Ghiffārī (d. 31 or 32/652–653), Fāḍila al-Anṣāriyya, wife of Ibn Unays al-Juhānī and Sawdā' al-Juhāniyya.[11] A century later, the woman who is given prominence in the sources as a transmitter of Prophetic traditions in Egypt was the ʿAlid Sayyida Nafīsa, the daughter of al-Ḥasan b. Zayd b. al-Ḥasan b. ʿAlī b. Abī Ṭālib (d. 208/823–824). Nafīsa had come to Egypt with her husband, Isḥāq al-Mu'taman, a son of Imam Jaʿfar al-Ṣādiq. Praised for her generosity, piety and asceticism, she is credited with having helped Muḥammad b. Idrīs al-Shāfiʿī (d. 204/820) in Egypt, who in turn is reported to have sometimes led her in prayer. Her status as a *ḥadīth* transmitter rests on the claim that al-Shāfiʿī heard *ḥadīth*s from her. As testimony to the close association between the two, it is related in a number of sources that when al-Shāfiʿī died the funeral cortege stopped at her house so that she might pray over his body.[12] In the first quarter of the 4th/10th century, when the Fatimids were well established in North Africa but already preparing for the conquest of Egypt, the best-known female transmitter of *ḥadīth* in Fusṭāṭ was Fāṭima bint ʿAbd al-Raḥmān b. Abī Ṣāliḥ al-Ḥarrāniyya Umm Muḥammad, described as *ṣūfiyya*, *ṣāliḥa* and *mutaʿabbida* (ascetic, virtuous and devout). She was born in Baghdad, but travelled to Fusṭāṭ where she died at an advanced age. She became known for her renunciation practices, sleeping only in her prayer room. Fāṭima is credited with having heard *ḥadīth*s from her father, and one of her nephews, ʿAbd al-Raḥmān b. al-Qāsim, transmitted traditions based on her authority. She died in 312/924.[13]

In the early phase of Fatimid rule in Egypt, Umm Ḥabīb Ṣafwā (d. 377 or 379/987 or 989) was the matron at the heart of the only named scholarly family from Fusṭāṭ in which the contours of what is arguably the first network of female members as transmitters of *ḥadīth* can be clearly recognised. Nicknamed *al-ṣaghīra* ('the small one'), Umm Ḥabīb was the mother of the renowned scholars ʿAbd al-Raḥmān al-Ṣadafī (d. 399/1008) and Ḥasan b. ʿAlī al-Ṣadafī.[14] Her father was a *muḥaddith* and her sons and her sisters transmitted *ḥadīth*s from her. A knowledge of many traditions was ascribed to her, particularly those concerning the *ahl al-bayt*.[15] Her contribution to the transmission and dissemination of ʿAlid traditions at this particular time was in keeping with the people's ongoing fascination with and devotion to ʿAlid descendants of the Prophet who had settled in Egypt, such as the already-mentioned Nafīsa. As claimants to ʿAlid descent, the Fatimids promoted the circulation of ʿAlid traditions, irrespective of the *madhhab*. For example, in 380/990 the Fatimid imam-caliph al-ʿAzīz (d. 386/996), seeking to counter popular discontent about Jews and Christians occupying high positions at the court, commissioned the eminent Sunni scholar ʿAbd al-Ghanī b. Saʿīd (d. 409/1018) to compile a collection of the *faḍāʾil*, or virtues, of ʿAlī b. Abī Ṭālib. In 385/995 the Ismaili jurist Muḥammad b. al-Nuʿmān (d. 389/999) was giving lectures on the *ahl al-bayt* to large crowds.[16]

The Fatimid historian al-Musabbiḥī (d. 420/1030), best known for his detailed chronicling of the events in the reign of the imam-caliph al-Ḥākim (r. 386–411/996–1021), lists several women in his obituary notes for the years 414–415 (1023–1025). Several of these women were closely linked to the court. Others were ladies from the broader society of Cairo/Fusṭāṭ, who were associated with famous scholars. The fact that, as reported, the funerals of these women attracted large crowds indicates that they had somehow earned a reputation for piety and respectability above and beyond that of their male relatives. One of these women was the wife of the historian Ibn Zūlāq (d. 386/997). Of note among them was also the daughter of Ibn Bakār, a relative of al-Musabbiḥī, nicknamed *al-ʿābida* ('the devout'), who died at the age of 100.[17] Given their familial contexts, it is safe to assume that the popularity of these women must have been based on a display of piety that often took the form of acquiring a reputation as learned persons in religious matters.

However, the woman of this period who appears to have earned the most prestige was Umm al-Khayr al-Ḥijāziyya (active ca. 415/1024). She became famous as a preacher (*wāʿiẓa*) at the Mosque of ʿAmr and was praised for her piety and probity. A *ribāṭ* was eventually dedicated to her in the Qarāfa cemetery.[18] Likewise renowned for her piety was her contemporary Fāṭima bint al-Ḥusayn b. ʿAlī b. al-Ashʿath b. Muḥammad al-Baṣrī whose mausoleum became a well-known site of popular piety.[19]

In the period from the reign of al-Mustanṣir (427–487/1036–1094) to the caliphate of al-Āmir (495–524/1101–1130), the most distinguished Cairo-based female scholar that we know of was the daughter of the celebrated savant and erudite, Mubashshir b. Fātik Abu'l-Wafāʾ. Originally from Damascus, Mubashshir spent most of his life in Egypt. Possibly linked to the ruling elite, he wrote – among other works – a biography of the imam-caliph al-Mustanṣir, now lost. If his wife comes across in anecdotal accounts as a petty woman who, at Mubashshir's death, threw his books in a fountain in retaliation for the neglect she suffered as a result of her husband's dedication to his studies, his daughter by contrast is portrayed as Mubashshir's scholarly heir. Probably born in Damascus, al-Khafrita bint Mubashshir b. Fātik was also known as al-Jadīda. Abū Ṭāhir al-Silafī, who claimed to have recounted traditions based on her, dedicated two entries to al-Khafrita in his *Muʿjam al-safar*. Al-Silafī not only reports the details of her scholarly lineage, of which he claims she informed him, but also lists the Prophetic traditions that she had transmitted. Al-Silafī must have met her at her family home in Cairo between 515/1121 and 516/1122, the only period in which he left Alexandria after his move to Egypt, as he states that he had already benefited from listening to her father among the group of shaykhs he met in the Fatimid capital. According to al-Silafī's records, al-Khafrita's informers included Muḥammad b. al-Ḥusayn b. al-Ṭaffāl al-Nīsābūrī (d. 448/1056)[20] and Abū Ṭāhir b. Saʿdūn al-Mawṣilī.[21] Her death, in 528/1133, must have been a noteworthy event in Cairo as al-Silafī states that he was informed of it in writing by Abu'l-Ḥusayn b. al-Ṣawwāf.[22]

Female Contributions to Sunni Scholarship in 6th/12th-Century Alexandria

In the 6th/12th century we witness the growing visibility of women engaged in *ḥadīth* transmission, coinciding with the rise of Alexandria as the most important centre of Sunni learning in late Fatimid Egypt.[23] Though not immune from bloody rebellions, which were all suppressed by the regime and which profoundly affected the local scholarly community during the second half of the 5th/11th century, Alexandria had been, on the whole, less affected by the major upheavals that had hit the Fatimid capital hard and by the vicissitudes that affected the Fatimid regime in this period. In economic terms, violent swings between prosperity and want escalated into a total socio-economic collapse (*al-shidda al-mustanṣiriyya*) that marked the reign of al-Mustanṣir. Politically speaking, the rise of the military vizier as the effective holder of power debased once and for all the authority of the imam-caliph. Dynastically, disputes gave way to irreversible factionalism. In religious terms, the pre-eminence of Ismailism as the *madhhab* at the heart of the regime was declining. As far as commerce was concerned, trade and pilgrimage routes that had passed through Egypt were reconfigured. Internationally, the Fatimids found themselves in the crucible of major geopolitical changes. They suffered major territorial losses outside Egypt; in the east, the Saljūqs advanced westward; and they also suffered as a result of the Byzantine empire's shift in alliances and the arrival of the Crusaders in the Holy Land. In the western Mediterranean they saw the Normans conquering Sicily and, in Spain, the beginning of the Christian advance pushing southwards, reducing the area of Muslim rule in al-Andalus.

In 4th/10th-century Egypt, Sunni learning – elsewhere an urban phenomenon mostly sustained by a cosmopolitan network of trading communities – had remained a constant in the religious, legal and scholarly life of the country, thriving particularly in commercially important cities such as Fusṭāṭ and Tinnīs. However, from the late 5th/11th century onwards, with the gradual decline of the Fatimid regime in Cairo, and the consequent loss of the mercantile prestige of Tinnīs, Sunni scholarly elites found Alexandria a more congenial place to work and live in. Several factors worked in Alexandria's favour as a destination: there was the long-established presence of Mālikīs resulting from both the proximity to North Africa and the activities of Spanish Muslims who had settled there, driven there by the Christian advance southwards in Spain.[24] Shāfiʿī Sunnis from the eastern lands of the Muslim world came to Alexandria for trade and on pilgrimage or were impelled there by political volatility and conflict. Alexandria also became an abode of refuge for those people forced to escape Cairo during the years of the *shidda al-mustanṣiriyya*. The city enjoyed a favourable strategic position as a stopping place on the international trade route between East and West. Especially from the late 5th/11th century onwards, at Alexandria one could come and go by sea with relative ease and, if through circumstance one was stuck there, the place itself was not disagreeable. Interestingly, the vast majority of Sunni scholarly families active in the Fatimid period are reported to have lived in the port (*thaghr*) area of the city.

This new phase of female participation in *ḥadīth* scholarship coincided with the arrival in Egypt around 490/1097 of the Mālikī scholar from al-Andalus, al-Ṭurṭūshī (451–520/1059–1126). Al-Ṭurṭūshī – or rather his wife – can be credited as the founder of the first de facto madrasa in Egypt. After extensive travelling, al-Ṭurṭūshī arrived in al-Rashīd (Rosetta) around 490/1097 with his companion ʿAbd Allāh al-Sāʾiḥ. Committed to a life of probity, both sustained their quest for learning and a pious life by eking out a modest living by selling salt and firewood.[25] By the time of al-Ṭurṭūshī's arrival in Egypt, crucial positions in the state administration were increasingly in the charge of Sunnis and this was particularly so in Alexandria where the chief judge of the city – a Mālikī of Andalusī origins, al-Makīn b. al-Ḥadīd – invited him to settle. There al-Ṭurṭūshī married a wealthy and devout woman, which brought him a large two-storey house. The upper floor was used as living quarters, while al-Ṭurṭūshī used the reception hall and the rest of the lower floor as a de facto madrasa where he taught jurisprudence.[26] Al-Ṭurṭūshī's wife – probably a widow since she had a son who had so disapproved of her marriage to him that he had attempted to kill them both – was not only instrumental in giving her husband the financial means to establish himself as a scholar but also ensured that he established important familial links with the Alexandrian scholarly elite.[27] Notably, she was the aunt of Abū Ṭāhir b. ʿAwf al-Zuhrī who became al-Ṭurṭūshī's foster son and arguably his most distinguished pupil.[28] Secure in the financial, domestic and social stability he had achieved by means of, among other things, his marriage, al-Ṭurṭūshī's scholarly reputation grew until he became one of the most sought-after teachers of his time, particularly among the Mālikī Andalusīs who travelled to Egypt on a regular basis for trade, refuge or pilgrimage.

If al-Ṭurṭūshī's wife seems to have played a purely supportive role in promoting the transmission of Sunni learning, women in the household of his most prominent student, Ibn ʿAwf, are known to have been active participants in the process. Ibn ʿAwf was born in Alexandria in 485/1092 but his ancestry went back to the Arab tribe of Zuhra, a branch of the Quraysh. There had been women in the ʿAwf family of this tribe who came to be identified as transmitters of traditions since ancient times.[29] Ibn ʿAwf was put in charge of the first full purposely endowed madrasa to have been built in Egypt, to which he was assigned by Riḍwān b. al-Walakhshī, the first Sunni vizier of the Fatimids in 532/1137–1138. It became known as the ʿAwfiyya, after Ibn ʿAwf, who became the first Mālikī *mudarris* to teach in what was most probably the first Mālikī madrasa anywhere. He taught there until his death in 581/1185. Throughout this formative period of madrasa-led learning in Egypt, the houses of reputable shaykhs continued to be the preferred setting for scholarly gatherings. Ibn ʿAwf's house by the port of Alexandria was a well-known intellectual centre where jurists used to gather in groups of seven at a time.[30] Abū Ṭāhir al-Silafī took notes at these events.[31] Ibn ʿAwf's daughter Zaynab became known as a *shaykha*, that is a teacher of *ḥadīth* and a student of jurisprudence (*fiqh*). Born in Alexandria in 528/1133, she died there in 597/1200. Zaynab must have married, as she is known as Umm Aḥmad and Umm Muḥammad. Although, as one would expect, she learned *ḥadīth*s from her father, she also received *ijāzāt* (diplomas) from a wide range of scholars who were active in the main centres of *ḥadīth* scholarship of her time, such as Khurāsān, Iṣfahān and Baghdad.[32] Prominent personalities are recorded as having given her *ijāzāt*, including al-Ḥusayn b. ʿAbd al-Mālik al-Khallāl, ʿAbd al-Jabbār b. Muḥammad al-Ḥuwayrī and Saʿīd b. Abiʾl-Rajāʾ al-Ṣayrafī.[33] As there is no evidence of extensive travelling by Zaynab or her family, nor of her meeting in person the scholars mentioned above, the most likely scenario is that these licences were brought to her as gifts or – according to a customary practice of the time – sent to her on request through correspondence. This, however, does not diminish her status, but on the contrary, it testifies to the fact that she must have acquired a reputation as a learned woman well beyond Alexandria.

Al-Ṭurṭūshī's and Ibn ʿAwf's scholarly status was somewhat overshadowed by the arrival in Alexandria, in 511/1117, of the Shāfiʿī Abū Ṭāhir al-Silafī. Once in Egypt, al-Silafī became the most celebrated and sought-after scholar of his day. As his *Muʿjam al-safar* shows, seekers of knowledge came from everywhere to learn from him. Al-Sakhāwī points him out as the person who single-handedly revived *ḥadīth* scholarship in Alexandria.[34] It is in association with al-Silafī that we find the most extensive, complex and diverse family network of women involved in the transmission of Prophetic traditions in Fatimid Alexandria.

Al-Silafī travelled extensively for 40 years in quest of *ḥadīth* before settling in the Egyptian port city. In his youth al-Silafī attended the preaching sessions of ʿUrwa bint Muḥammad, a leading *muḥadditha* from his family who died in 480/1087.[35] He started to devote himself to the study of *ḥadīth* in 488/1095 and within a short period of time he learned from hundreds of scholars of whom at least 17 were women.[36] In the course of his travels, al-Silafī had the opportunity to learn from more women, particularly in Baghdad which he went to in 493/1099 and where he resided on and off for several years.

According to his *Mashyakha Baghdādiyya* and his *Muʿjam al-safar* he learned *ḥadīth* from the following women:[37] Umm al-Faḍl Rābiʿa bint ʿAbd Allāh Ibrāhīm al-Ḥibrī, Sitt al-Balad al-Rūmiyya, Sitt al-Ahl bint ʿAlī al-Bahimashī, Karīma bint Abī Bakr al-Daqqāq and Maryam bint ʿAbd al-Raḥmān b. al-Ḥasan al-Būsīriyya.[38] In Alexandria, in 544/1149, the Shāfiʿī al-ʿĀdil b. Salār, a governor of Alexandria who became vizier to the Fatimid al-Ẓāfir, ordered the building of a madrasa for al-Silafī. This was the second madrasa to be built in Egypt and the first Shāfiʿī one. Though formally named al-ʿĀdiliyya, after its founder, it came to be typically referred to as al-Silafiyya.[39] Quite apart from his relationship with al-ʿĀdil b. Salār, al-Silafī was generally held in high esteem by the Fatimid regime as a whole. Like al-Ṭurṭūshī, in Alexandria al-Silafī married an affluent woman who eased his hitherto stringent and difficult way of life. From his *Muʿjam al-safar* we learn that his wife was called Sitt al-Ahl. Described by al-Silafī as a pious woman, Sitt al-Ahl belonged to a family of distinguished scholars, particularly on her mother's side. Sitt al-Ahl was the daughter of the shaykh Abū ʿAbd Allāh Muḥammad b. Abī Mūsā al-Khalwānī, who died before al-Silafī arrived in Egypt, and his wife Turfa (d. 534/1139–1140), also known as ʿĀʾisha. The latter was one of the daughters of Abu'l-ʿAbbās Aḥmad b. Ibrāhīm al-Rāzī (d. 491/1097–1098), an eminent Shāfiʿī traditionist and jurisconsult.[40] According to the testimony of his son Muḥammad the family had previously lived in Cairo but moved to Alexandria because of the *shidda* in the Fatimid capital between 459/1066 and 464/1069. Aḥmad performed the Pilgrimage in 414/1023–1024 and met many prominent scholars during his travels.

Once back in Cairo he systematically assembled and organised the extensive material he had gathered from meeting with and attending the lessons of a great number of scholars either living in Cairo or passing through it. According to his son, however, all this material was looted – together with the family belongings – when the family moved to Alexandria.[41] Al-Maqrīzī comments on the dispersal of the libraries of Cairo during this crisis and gives details of how many books eventually found their way to Alexandria. For example, one of Aḥmad al-Rāzī's former students, the Alexandrian *muḥaddith* ʿAlī b. al-Musharraq al-Anmāṭī (d. 518/1124)[42] was the source of the books that came to form the library of Abū Ṭāhir al-Silafī.[43]

Turfa, described as a woman of sound faith, transmitted *ḥadīth*s to al-Silafī after listening to her father. When she was still in Cairo, her informants included Abū ʿAbd Allāh Muḥammad b. Jaʿfar b. Muḥammad al-Māristānī. She also learned *ḥadīth*s transmitted by, among others, Aḥmad b. ʿAlī al-Marwazī and ʿAbd al-Wārith b. Saʿīd.[44] Al-Silafī recounted based on her, shortly before she died in 534/1139.[45] Tarifa had a brother and a sister. Turfa's sister, Khadīja, also called Mulayḥa (d. 526/1131–1132) was described by al-Silafī as an ascetic woman who remained celibate. Anecdotes of her piety reflect the reputation she had acquired. The serving woman of one of al-Silafī's scholarly acquaintances told her master that she had observed Khadīja practising all-night vigils, absorbed in prayer. Khadīja was a traditionist of some stature who also transmitted *ḥadīth*s to al-Silafī. Beside her father, her informants included Abu'l-Ḥusayn Muḥammad b. Ḥamūd b. al-Dalīl al-Ṣawwāf (d. ca. 480/1087) in Cairo,[46] who transmitted from Muḥammad b. Aḥmad b. Muḥammad al-Wāsiṭī in Jerusalem,[47] who in turn transmitted from ʿUmar b. ʿAlī b. al-Ḥasan al-ʿAtakī (d. 360/970–971).[48] She had an *ijāza* from Abu'l-Walīd Ay Muḥammad.[49] When she died in 526/1131, al-Silafī led her funeral as she had stipulated. Turfa and Khadīja's brother, Muḥammad b. Aḥmad b. Ibrāhīm al-Rāzī (434–525/1042–1131), came to be regarded as one of the great transmitters (sing., *musnid*) in Egypt.[50]

The father of al-Silafī's wife, al-Khalwānī, was described as a pious man who, besides Sitt al-Ahl, had a son named Abu'l-Barakāt ʿĪsā who worked as a notary for the *qāḍī* of Alexandria. Al-Silafī's marriage to Sitt al-Ahl was officiated by her brother, probably in the year 512/1118. It is not clear when Sitt al-Ahl died, though it probably occurred after 570/1174 but before al-Silafī's death, as in the *Muʿjam* he refers to her as deceased. It was reported that the memorisers ʿAbd al-Qādir (536–612/1141–1215) and ʿAbd al-Ghanī al-Maqdisī (541–600/1146–1203) – the latter one of al-Silafi's most eminent students – wanted to study a particular work under al-Silafī's tutelage but he kept fending them off until his wife interceded with him on their behalf. If this was the case, since ʿAbd al-Ghanī visited Alexandria in 566/1170 and again in 570/1174, we may assume that al-Silafī's wife might have been alive at least until the latter date.[51]

Al-Silafī's and Sitt al-Ahl had a daughter, Khadīja, who married the scholar Abu'l-Ḥarām Makkī b. ʿAbd al-Raḥmān al-Ṭarabulsī and gave birth to a son, Abu'l-Qāsim ʿAbd al-Raḥmān, in 570/1174. This child grew up to become a prominent traditionist in Alexandria. Khadīja (d. 623/1226), in keeping with her family lineage of distinguished female *ḥadīth* scholars, also achieved fame as *shaykha*. She learned from her father, from whom she obtained an *ijāza*, and she taught *ḥadīth*. After the death of her father, she moved to Cairo where she was admired for her kindness. Khadīja then returned to Alexandria where al-Mundhirī went to visit her, although he did not hear traditions from her. He nevertheless claimed that she granted him an *ijāza* which he had eagerly desired.[52] Such was the lasting fame and prestige of al-Silafī, that after his death subsequent generations of transmitters sought ways of tracing their scholarly lineage back to this eminent Shāfiʿī and found, in claiming to hold an *ijāza* from his daughter Khadīja, a useful way to establish a direct 'link' to al-Silafī's authority.

In addition to being the pupil and relative of female traditionists, al-Silafī was also a teacher of women. His best-known female student in Egypt was Umm ʿAlī Taqiyya bint Abi'l-Faraj Ghayth b. ʿAlī b. ʿAbd al-Salām b. Muḥammad b. Jaʿfar al-Sulamī al-Armanāzī al-Ṣūrī, also known as Sitt al-Niʿm. Born in Damascus in 505/1111, she died, most likely in Egypt, in 579/1183–1184. She must have moved to Egypt after 511/1118, given that she was a disciple of Abū Ṭāhir al-Silafī who arrived in Alexandria in that year. She was certainly living in the port area of the city before 568/1172, since this is given as the year in which her husband died there. However, the most likely time for her arrival must be around 520/1126, as her son, Abu'l-Ḥasan ʿAlī b. Fāḍil b. Ḥamdūn al-Ṣūrī (d. 603/1206), is reported to have been born in Ṣūr before that year. Several sources acknowledge her as a woman of talent and wit who composed *qaṣīda*s and short poems. Described as a literary personage, *adība*, she famously wrote in praise of Taqī al-Dīn ʿUmar b. Shāhinshāh, a nephew of Ṣalāḥ al-Dīn, on the subject of wine and conviviality. When he commented that she must have written from experience, she rebuked him with another poem on war, asking him whether he thought she had written these verses from experience too. She knew Ibn ʿAwf, who wrote a poem in response to her verses,[53] and eulogised her mentor, al-Silafī, excusing him for dismissing her son from his sessions.[54] In turn al-Silafī praised her for her verses and her devotion to him on an occasion when he had injured his foot, and so she took him into her house and bandaged the foot with a piece of cloth cut from her headdress. Although better known for her poetry, she was also a *ḥadīth* transmitter, as well-known scholars such as Abu'l-Ḥasan ʿAlī b. al-Mufaḍḍal al-Muqaddasī[55] and others acknowledged they had listened to *ḥadīth*s from her. She belonged to a family of distinguished *ḥadīth* transmitters: her father, Abu'l-Faraj (d. 509/1115), was an authoritative traditionist and so was her grandfather, ʿAlī b. ʿAbd al-Salām (d. 478/1085) in Tyre. Taqiyya's son, Abu'l-Ḥasan ʿAlī, became a well-known grammarian, reciter and calligrapher. Her husband, Fāḍil, born in Damascus in 490/1097, was also a man of scholarly reputation.[56]

The other prominent female scholar said to have been a pupil of al-Silafī in Egypt was the *shaykha* Umm Muḥammad Khadīja (d. 618/1221), a daughter of the *qāḍī* Abu'l-Mukarram b. ʿAlī b. Mufarrij b. Ḥātim b. Ḥasan b. Jaʿfar b. Ibrāhīm Ahamm b. al-Ḥasan. Although the family was originally from al-Quds, she was born in 550/1155 in Alexandria and spent her life there. She was the sister of the already-mentioned Abu'l-Ḥasan ʿAlī b. al-Mufaḍḍal al-Muqaddasī. Umm Muḥammad is said to have received *ijāzāt* from al-Silafī and Fakhr al-Nisā' Shuhda bint Abī Naṣr (482–574/1089–1178)[57] – a rare instance in this period of a woman granting another woman an *ijāza*. She transmitted *ḥadīth*s and al-Mundhirī claimed to have heard *ḥadīth*s from her. Al-Mundhirī described her as extremely generous, saying that she gave everything she had in the name of piety and that she was respected by all the scholars and those in quest of purity. Al-Dhahabī, however, adds a detail to her biography, perhaps deliberately overlooked by al-Mundhirī, saying that Umm Muḥammad had received al-Silafī's *ijāza* in the year of her birth.[58]

References in biographical dictionaries to transmitters receiving *ijāzāt* from famous scholars at a very early age are not infrequent. It is obvious that the granting of *ijāzāt* to infants, whether girls or boys, was intended as a symbolic gesture or as a gift to a child in order to honour their distinguished parents, rather than the actual certification of any learning acquired by the recipients. The embellishing of the scholarly lineages of female scholars by associating them with famous scholars might have – on occasion – also served a practical purpose for the biographers who reported on them. Since al-Mundhirī claimed to have heard *ḥadīth*s from Umm Muḥammad, showing that his female informant was herself the pupil of an outstanding scholar, reflected well on him. Since al-Mundhirī could not claim to have learnt directly from al-Silafī, as he had been long dead when al-Mundhirī began to study *ḥadīth* in 591/1194–1195, the best he could do was to 'extend' his association to the celebrated scholar via his proximity to al-Silafī's 'certified' students. What raises suspicions about al-Mundhirī's claim of a direct association between Umm Muḥammad and al-Silafī is the fact that there is no mention of her in al-Silafī's otherwise meticulous *Mu'jam*.

Female Contributions to Sunni Scholarship in 6th/12th-Century Cairo

While formally restored as the state *madhhab* on the fall of the Fatimids in 567/1171 at the hands of Ṣalāḥ al-Dīn, Sunni Islam had already been dominating the political and institutional life of Cairo for several decades. Yet, before 567/1171, it was probably the fact that Ismailism was still the official religion of Fatimid Egypt, at least formally, which prevented the establishment of madrasas in Cairo. Unlike in Alexandria, Sunni learning in Cairo was still an exclusively private affair, conducted in the circles of highly reputed scholars who did not enjoy the visibility that madrasas accorded to al-Ṭurṭūshī, Ibn 'Awf and al-Silafī. However, there is no evidence that the presence of madrasas in Egypt, or rather the lack of them, in the Fatimid period had any direct impact on women either as students or as teachers. In Cairo, as in Alexandria, the home was the place where their scholarly activities took, and continued to take, place.

In Cairo, arguably the most prominent female *ḥadīth* transmitter of the late Fatimid period, bridging into the Ayyūbid era, was Fāṭima bint Sa'd al-Khayr (b. 522 or 525/1128–1130; d. 600/1203). Born in Iṣfahān (although China, probably Kashghar, has also been suggested), she lived in Baghdad and Khurāsān, before moving to Egypt from Damascus, following her husband. He was the preacher Abu'l-Ḥasan 'Alī Ibrāhīm b. Najā (b. 508/1114; d. after 584/1188), one of her father's students who eventually became the secretary of the Ayyūbid sultan, al-Malik al-Afḍal Nūr al-Dīn.[59] Fāṭima's father was Abu'l-Ḥasan Sa'd al-Khayr b. Muḥammad b. Sahl al-Anṣārī al-Andalusī al-Balansī, a distinguished scholar who had travelled from his native city of Valencia to the east, as far as China.[60] Fāṭima's son, ʿAbd al-Karīm, was also a scholar of some repute. Abu'l-Ḥasan Saʿd al-Khayr had several daughters whom he reportedly made study *ḥadīth* and whom he also taught himself.

The sources describe Fāṭima as a precocious child who was accustomed to listening to *ḥadīth* transmitters from a very young age. Apparently she listened to al-Dāraquṭnī in 529/1134 and al-Khaṭīb al-Baghdādī in the same year. Reportedly, she received *ijāzāt* from many scholars in Baghdad, Iṣfahān and Khurāsān. Al-Mundhirī, who received an *ijāzā* from her, says that her father used to take her to listen to the same shaykh up to three times to ensure that she had learned the *ḥadīth*s he recited. While in Iṣfahān he took Fāṭima to study with, among others, Umm Ibrāhīm Fāṭima bint ʿAbd Allāh al-Juzdāniyya, the most prestigious female narrator of the day.[61] In Baghdad, where her father took her in 525/1130, her female mentor was the memoriser Karīma, daughter of the memoriser Abū Bakr Muḥammad b. Aḥmad b. ʿAbd al-Bāqī known as Ibn al-Khadība (or al-Khadīʿa).

It was, however, in Damascus and then Cairo that Fāṭima was acknowledged as an authoritative transmitter and many scholars are reported to have travelled especially to study with her. The list of her students also confirms her rank as a respected *muḥadditha*. Her pupils included Abū Mūsā, son of the already-mentioned memoriser ʿAbd al-Ghanī, the transmitter ʿAbd al-Raḥmān b. Muqarrab al-Tajībī,[62] the jurist Abū ʿAbd Allāh Muḥammad b. Muḥammad b. al-Wazzān. Ibn al-Khīmī (d. 642/1244), who arrived in Cairo in 584/1188, listened to *ḥadīth*s from her and her husband,[63] as did the Ḥanbalī scholar Ibn al-Naḥḥās al-Miṣrī (d. 643/1245).[64] Besides al-Mundhirī, those who received her *ijāza* included Aḥmad b. al-Khayr.[65]

Female Contributions to Sunni Learning at the End of Fatimid Rule and the Onset of the Ayyūbid Period

The number of female transmitters in Cairo appears to have increased during the period marked by the end of the Fatimid rule and the start of Ayyūbid dominance. On the one hand this trend could be seen as the start of a process of steady female engagement in Prophetic transmission that culminated in the 'renaissance' of female *ḥadīth* scholarship in the Ayyūbid and Mamlūk periods. One could be tempted to claim that this impetus went hand in hand with the restoration of Sunni Islam in Egypt. On the other hand, the greater availability of information could simply be owing to the fact that the generational gap between these women and the biographers who wrote about them was narrower, thus making late Fatimid–early Ayyūbid female scholars more directly relevant to the interests of narrators and also more directly familiar to the writers and therefore easier to collect and report data on. Therefore, the relative growth of records about women scholars at the end of the Fatimid period might not necessarily have been a by-product of the institutional reassertion of Sunnism that took place with the demise of the Fatimid regime. Even al-Maqrīzī, when it came to female scholars, only listed in his *al-Muqaffā* the ones who lived closer to his time.[66]

The following list of female traditionists, born under Fatimid rule but who died in Ayyūbid times, is emblematic of how the personal experience of the biographers could have an impact on the precedence given to some personalities over others in their writings. Al-Mundhirī claims to have been acquainted with the following women:

Ṣafā' al-'Aysh (d. 627/1229), daughter of 'Abd Allāh and al-Ashrafiyya al-Ḥamziyya al-Qaṣriyya, and known as Shamsa, was the manumitted slave of the *qāḍī* Abu'l-Qāsim Ḥamza b. 'Alī b. 'Uthmān al-Makhzīmī. Al-Mundhirī, who heard from her, asked her about her birth and she recalled events that pointed to her birth occurring in 557/1161. Besides the *qāḍī* she also heard from Abū Ṭāhir Ismā'īl b. Ṣāliḥ b. Yāsīn.[67]

Umm al-Khayr Futūḥ (d. 625/1227), the daughter of Shaykh Abū Isḥāq Ibrāhīm b. 'Uthmān b. Abi'l-Qāsim, originally from Shām, was born around 562/1166 and grew up in Cairo. She narrated to al-Mundhirī, from Shaykh Abu'l-Qāsim 'Abd al-Raḥmān b. Muḥammad al-Musaybānī.[68]

Umm Ḥasan Ghudayba (d. 635/1237) called ʿIzziyya or ʿAzīza, was the daughter of ʿInān b. Ḥumayd al-Saʿdiyya and the wife of al-Mundhirī's shaykh, Abu'l-Ḥasan Murtaḍā b. al-ʿAfīf b. al-Jūd al-Muqaddasī. Besides her husband, she heard *ḥadīth*s from Abu'l-Qāsim ʿAbd al-Raḥmān b. Muḥammad b. Ḥusayn al-Sabiyy, Abu'l-Maʿālī Munjib b. ʿAbd Allāh al-Murshidī and the *ḥadīth* memoriser, Abū Muḥammad al-Qāsim b. ʿAlī al-Dimashqī. She must have been born well into Fatimid times as al-Mundhirī, who heard from her, states that she was very old when she died.[69]

Finally, there was Umm al-Faḍl Karīma (d. 641/1243), who can be considered to be linked to the Fatimid period more for her distinguished ancestry than for chronological reasons. She was the granddaughter of the famous Shāfiʿī *qāḍī* in the service of the Fatimid caliphs, Hibat Allāh al-Quḍāʿī. Al-Mundhirī, who heard *ḥadīth*s from her, paid tribute to her scholarly and familial lineage as the daughter, granddaughter and sister of traditionists. Her brother, Abū ʿAbd Allāh Muḥammad, was known as al-Zunbūrī after the Zunbūr mosque outside Cairo.[70]

Conclusion

The overall picture that emerges from this collation of fragmentary data reflects general trends already observed by R. Roded and M.L. Avila in their quantitative analyses of the portrayal of women in Islamic biographical dictionaries.[71] By and large, the *muḥaddithāt* of the Fatimid period acquired their reputations more as learners than as teachers. Their mentors and their pupils were mostly men. Their learning experiences were mediated by the environment of the male-dominated scholarly families in which they lived. In these families, women appear to have functioned as a genealogical link for the retention and transmission of knowledge within male family lines: mothers and sisters as transmitters to sons and nephews and daughters as learners from fathers and brothers feature more prominently than wives.[72] It was through intermarriage, however, that scholarly families merged, forming or reinforcing social, cultural and economic networks founded on shared *madhhab*s, geographical provenance and class. The reliability and rigour of these women as 'retainers' and 'transmitters' of learning is never questioned by the narrators who reported on them but none of them are acclaimed as 'producers' of theological knowledge.[73] They received *ijāzāt*, but only rarely issued them to men, and even more rarely bestowed them on other women. In a social world dominated by rules of gender seclusion and decorum, female scholars are shown to have acted in seemingly close proximity to men. The sources do not tell us – outside the context of familial relationships – what mechanisms were in place to ensure that gender boundaries were maintained or negotiated between male mentors and female students or vice versa. Since youth, seniority and commitment to celibacy or asceticism rendered women sexually unthreatening to the social order, in some cases these factors might have facilitated the *muḥaddithāt*'s interactions with their male counterparts, as epitomised by the encounter between al-Silafī and his mature pupil, Umm ʿAlī Taqiyya.

Besides the practical and logistic implementation of gender boundaries,[74] the methods of learning through which knowledge was exchanged did not necessarily demand physical proximity: *ijāzāt* could be issued by correspondence and the *samāʿ* system did not necessarily imply listening to the reading of a book directly in the presence of its author. On occasion, the reporting on women as *ḥadīth* informants with a focus on their distinguished scholarly lineages betrays the narrators' real intention behind the mention of women, which was to establish an association between themselves and prestigious scholars whom they had had no opportunity to meet in person.

The above picture points to the fact that dispensation from the formalism imposed by the Fatimid regime on Ismaili women as learners actually allowed greater fluidity in the possibilities that Sunni women enjoyed as participants in the sharing and dissemination of learning within Sunni circles in Egypt and beyond.[75] The Fatimids are rightly hailed as pioneers in promoting the formal education of women. But it is the formality of the male-led Ismaili lectures (*majālis al-ḥikma*) that obscures the role that Ismaili women might have played not just as receivers of knowledge but as its shapers too.[76]

The *muḥaddithāt* of Fatimid Egypt affirmed themselves in a region that was, by and large, outside the madrasa system. The late establishment of madrasas in Fatimid Alexandria and their absence in Cairo meant that the personal prestige that elsewhere in the Muslim world came with being formally attached to an academic institution was not as powerful a signifier of social status in Fatimid Egypt as it was elsewhere. Over a period of time, the Sunnis living under a Shiʿi regime – but not necessarily serving it – devised their own internal categories for qualifying social distinction and priority. The savant-traders emerged as the elite whose scholarly reputation (and the social and economic prestige that derived from it) relied upon building extensive international contacts with other Sunni scholars-cum-traders. It was the presence in Fatimid Egypt of representatives of this international network that helped to popularise there the fame of *muḥaddithāt* who had acquired prestige in other regions of the Muslim world.

To report traditions from famous *muḥaddithāt* of Baghdad, Iṣfahān or Mecca was a mark of prestige, but to have a *muḥadditha* in the family became an even stronger signifier of class distinction, respectability and trustworthiness communicated – among other means – through the displays of piety and theological knowledge of female relatives. Women linked to savant-merchants could function as 'repositories' of the family's intellectual capital. With the establishment of madrasas in Alexandria, the learned and pious mother, daughter and wife became necessary figures in shaping the public image of the professional (male) scholar. Through marriage to daughters of local notables, foreign savants eased their entree into new social milieus.[77] All in all, the *muḥaddithāt* of the Fatimid period, whether agents in or the content of biographical narratives, ultimately served purposes designed to fit with a male world and fulfil male agendas. Rather than the female voices, what we hear are the voices of the men who spoke for them. Yet, without such spokesmen, the memory of these women might have never been preserved.

Notes

* Parts of this chapter were presented at the 26th conference of the Union Européenne des Arabisants et Islamisants (UEAI), Basel, September 2012 and the 46th annual conference of the Middle East Studies Association (MESA), Denver, November 2012.

1 Cf. I. Goldziher, *Muslim Studies (Muhammedanische Studien)*, tr. C.M. Barber and S.M. Stern (London, 1967–1971), vol. 2, pp. 366–368.

2 This figure is given in M.A. Nadwi, *al-Muḥaddithāt: The Women Scholars in Islam* (Istanbul, 2007), p. xv.

3 A. Sayeed, 'Women and Ḥadīth Transmission: Two Case Studies from Mamluk Damascus', *Studia Islamica*, 95 (2002), pp. 71–72. For a comprehensive discussion on women as transmitters of knowledge in the pre-modern Islamic world, see A. Sayeed, *Women and the Transmission of Religious Knowledge in Islam* (Cambridge, 2013).

4 This periodisation is extensively discussed throughout in Sayeed, *Women and the Transmission of Religious Knowledge.*

5 See the statement of the Egyptian scholar and prosopographer Shams al-Dīn Muḥammad al-Sakhāwī (d. 902/1497) in his *al-I'lān bi'l-ṭawbīkh li-man dhamma ahl al-ta'rīkh* (Damascus, 1349/1930), p. 138.

6 Nadwi, *al-Muḥaddithāt*, pp. 268–269.

7 For a challenge to this view, see D. Cortese, 'Voices of the Silent Majority: The Transmission of Sunnī Learning in Fāṭimī Egypt', *Jerusalem Studies in Arabic and Islam*, 39 (2012), pp. 345–366.

8 For a brief discussion on the sociology of knowledge in the context of women in the medieval Islamic world, see Sayeed, *Women and the Transmission of Religious Knowledge*, pp. 4–5.

9 See D. Cortese and S. Calderini, *Women and the Fatimids in the World of Islam* (Edinburgh, 2006), pp. 28–36.

10 This work has been the subject of extensive studies and partial as well as complete editions. Among the most important, see U. Rizzitano, 'Akhbār 'an ba'ḍ muslimī ṣiqillīya alladhīna tarjama la-hum Abū Ṭāhir al-Silafī', *Annals of the Faculty of Arts, University of 'Ayn Shams*, 3 (1955), pp. 49–112; I. 'Abbās, *Akhbār wa tarājim Andalusiyya al-mustakhraja min Mu'jam al-safar li al-Silafī* (Beirut, 1963); S.M. Zaman, 'Abū Ṭāhir al-Silafī al-Iṣbahānī: His Life and Works with an Analytical Study of His *Mu'jam al-safar*' (PhD thesis,

Harvard University, Cambridge, MA, 1968); Ḥ. Ṣāliḥ, 'The Life and Times of al-Ḥāfiẓ Abū Ṭāhir al-Silafī Accompanied by a Critical Edition of Part of the Author's *Muʿjam al-safar*' (PhD thesis, University of Cambridge, 1972); B. al-Ḥasanī, *Muʿjam al-safar*, vol. 1 (Baghdad, 1978); B.A. Maʿrūf, 'Muʿjam al-safar li-Abī Ṭāhir al-Silafī', *al-Mawrid*, 8 (1979), pp. 379–383. The full text was published by S.M. Zaman, *Muʿjam al-safar* (Islamabad, 1988). For this chapter I have used B. al-Ḥasanī's edition and S. M. Zaman's PhD thesis.

11 Jalāl al-Dīn al-Suyūṭī, *Ḥusn al-muḥāḍara fī akhbār Miṣr wa'l-Qāhira*, ed. Khalīl al-Manṣūr (Beirut, 1418/1997), vol. 1, pp. 208–209.

12 Nadwi, *al-Muḥaddithāt*, p. 268.

13 Al-Suyūṭī, *Ḥusn*, vol. 1, p. 421.

14 He is listed in the chain of transmitters of Ibn Muṣliḥ al-Māsargisī (d. ca. 384/994), a Shāfiʿī jurist originally from Nīshābūr, who came to Cairo. Taqī al-Dīn Aḥmad b. ʿAlī al-Maqrīzī, *Kitāb al-muqaffā al-kabīr*, ed. M. Yaʿlāwī (Beirut, 1991), vol. 6, no. 2753.

15 Shams al-Dīn Abū ʿAbd Allāh Muḥammad al-Dhahabī, *Ta'rīkh al-Islām wa wafayāt al-mashāhīr wa'l-aʿlām* (Beirut, 1987–1999), vol. for the decades 351–380, pp. 644–645 and Ibrāhīm b. Saʿīd ʿAbd Allāh al-Ḥabbāl, *Wafayāt al-Miṣriyyīn (375–456)*, ed. Abū ʿAbd Allāh Maḥmūd b. Muḥammad al-Ḥaddād (Riyadh, 1408/1987), p. 31 and year 399.

16 See Cortese, 'Voices', pp. 352, 354 and F. Daftary, *The Ismāʿīlīs: Their History and Doctrines* (2nd ed., Cambridge, 2007), p. 215.

17 Muḥammad al-Musabbiḥī, *Akhbār Miṣr*, ed. W.G. Millward (Cairo, 1980), p. 239.

18 Taqī al-Dīn al-Maqrīzī, *Kitāb al-mawāʿiẓ wa'l-iʿtibār fī dhikr al-khiṭaṭ wa'l-āthār* (Būlāq, 1270/1853–54), vol. 2, p. 450.

19 Muḥammad b. Muḥammad, Ibn al-Zayyāt, *al-Kawākib al-sayyāra fī tartīb al-ziyāra fī al-Qarāfatayn al-kubrā wa'l-ṣughrā* (Baghdad, 1968), p. 79.

20 Cf. ʿAlī b. Muḥammad, Ibn al-Athīr, *al-Lubāb fī tahdhīb al-ansāb* (Cairo, 1938–1949), vol. 2, p. 136. Ibn al-Ṭaffāl was a silk merchant from Fusṭāṭ, al-Maqrīzī, *al-Muqaffā*, vol. 5, no. 2149.

21 Son of a well-known transmitter, listed among al-Ḥabbāl's informants, al-Maqrīzī, *al-Muqaffā*, vol. 1, no. 147.

22 Abū Ṭāhir Aḥmad b. Muḥammad, al-Silafī, *Muʿjam al-safar*, part one, ed. Bahīja Bakr al-Ḥasanī (Baghdad, 1398/1978), entries

106 and 120, pp. 224, 236–237, and al-Dhahabī, *Ta'rīkh*, vol. for decades 521–530/531–540, entry 118, p. 167.

23 For an overall discussion, see Paul E. Walker, 'Fāṭimid Alexandria as an Entrepôt in the East–West Exchange of Islamic Scholarship', *Al-Masāq: Journal of the Medieval Mediterranean*, 26 (2014), pp. 36–48.

24 For a discussion on this trend, see Abd al-Aziz Salem, 'Alexandria to Almeria. Banū Khulayf: An Alexandrian Family in the Middle Ages', *Journal of the Muslim West and the Mediterranean*, 46 (1987), pp. 64–70.

25 Y. Lev, 'Piety and Political Activism in Twelfth Century Egypt', *Jerusalem Studies in Arabic and Islam*, 31 (2006), p. 294.

26 See G. Leiser, 'Muslims from al-Andalus in the *madrasas* of the Late Fāṭimid and Ayyūbid Egypt', *Al-Qantara*, 20 (1999), p. 147; al-Ṭurṭūshī, *Kitāb al-ḥawādith*, ed. and Spanish tr. Maribel Fierro as *El Libro de las novedades y las innovaciones* (Madrid, 1993), pp. 23, 52; Ibrāhīm b. 'Alī b. Muḥammad Ibn Farḥūn, *al-Dībāj al-mudhahhab fī ma'rifat a'yān 'ulamā' al-madhhab* (Cairo, 1423/2003), vol. 2, no. 504, pp. 226–227; al-Suyūṭī, *Ḥusn*, vol. 1, p. 377.

27 For a discussion on al-Maqrīzī's biography of al-Ṭurṭūshī and his Alexandrian *'ulamā'*'s milieu, see Lev, 'Piety and Political Activism', p. 296.

28 Leiser, 'Muslims from al-Andalus', p. 146; al-Ṭurṭūshī, *Kitāb al-ḥawādith*, p. 23; Ibn Farḥūn, *al-Dībāj*, vol. 1, no. 169, p. 259; Ibn Khaldūn, *The Muqaddima: An Introduction to History*, tr. F. Rosenthal (London, 1958), vol. 3, pp. 17–18.

29 Ṣalāḥ al-Dīn Khalīl b. Aybak al-Ṣafadī, *Kitāb al-wāfī bi'l-wafayāt*, ed. H. Ritter et al. (Istanbul, 1931—), vol. 16, nos 5433 and 5434, pp. 98–99.

30 Ibn Farḥūn, *al-Dībāj*, vol. 1, no. 169, p. 259.

31 Ibn Khallikān, *Ibn Khallikan's Biographical Dictionary*, tr. W. MacGuckin de Slane (Paris, 1842–1871), vol. 2, no. 2, p. 197. On Ibn 'Awf, see also al-Maqrīzī, *al-Muqaffā*, vol. 2, no. 783.

32 Zakī al-Dīn Abū Aḥmad al-Mundhirī, *al-Takmila li-wafayāt al-naqala*, ed. Bashshār 'Awwād Ma'rūf (Najaf, 1401/1981), vol. 1, no. 632, p. 406.

33 Al-Dhahabī, *Ta'rīkh*, vol. for the decade 591–600, no. 360, p. 283.

34 Al-Sakhāwī, *al-I'lān*, pp. 138–139.

35 Shams al-Dīn Abū 'Abd Allāh Muḥammad al-Dhahabī, *Siyar a'lām al-nubalā'*, ed. Shu'ayb al-Arna'ūṭ et al. (Beirut, 1410/1990), vol. 8, p. 21.

36 Beside many references in al-Silafī's *Muʿjam*, see al-Dhahabī, *Siyar*, vol. 8, p. 21.
37 For information about extant manuscripts of this work, see F.N. Hashimi, 'A Critical Edition of *Kitab al-Wajiz fi Dhikr al-Mujaz wa al-Mujiz* by Abu Tahir Ahmad B. Muhammad B. Ahmad B. Muhammad al-Silafi, al-Isbahani (d. 576/1181)' (PhD thesis, University of Glasgow, 1989), pp. 11–12.
38 Al-Silafī, *Muʿjam*, Introduction, p. 27.
39 Ibn Khallikān, *Biographical*, vol. 1, pp. 86–89.
40 On him, see G. Vajda, 'La Mašyaḫa d'Ibn al-Ḥaṭṭāb al-Rāzī. Contribution à l'histoire du Sunnisme en Égypte faṭimide', *Bulletin d'Études Orientales* 23 (1970); reprinted in N. Cottard, ed., *La transmission du savoir en Islam (VIIe–XVIIIe siècles)* (London, 1983), article 5, p. 32, no. 1. His students included the Shāfiʿī jurist Ibn al-Ṣanūbrī al-Nīsābūrī (d. after 507/1113) who arrived in Egypt in 490/1096, al-Maqrīzī, *al-Muqaffā*, vol. 5, no. 2340.
41 G. Vajda, 'La Mašyaḫa', p. 22.
42 His pupils included the famous Sevillan traditionist Abū Bakr b. al-ʿArabī (d. 543/1148) who listened to him in Alexandria, al-Maqrīzī, *al-Muqaffā*, vol. 6, no. 2553. See also I. ʿAbbās, 'al-Jānib al-siyāsī min riḥlat Ibn al-ʿArabī ilā al-mashriq', *al-Abḥāth*, 16 (1963), pp. 217–236 and J. Robson, 'Ibn al-ʿArabī', *EI2*, vol. 3, p. 707. In turn al-Anmāṭī, like al-Rāzī's children, Muḥammad and Tarifa, had been a student of Ibn al-Dalīl, a *qāḍī* of Bilbays. On Ibn al-Dalīl, see al-Maqrīzī, *al-Muqaffā*, vol. 5, no. 2177 and Vajda, 'La Mašyaḫa', pp. 62, 86.
43 G. La Viere Leiser, 'The Restoration of Sunnism in Egypt: Madrasas and Mudarrisūn 495–647/1101–1249' (PhD thesis, University of Pennsylvania, 1976), p. 176. See also H. Halm, *The Fatimids and their Traditions of Learning* (London, 1997), p. 77.
44 Unlike the case of her sister Khadīja, none of the names linked to Tarifa appear in the *mashyakha* of her brother Muḥammad.
45 Al-Silafī, *Muʿjam al-safar*, no. 102, p. 221.
46 See note 40, above.
47 Also listed in the brother's *mashyakha*. See Vajda, 'La Mašyaḫa', p. 87.
48 Shams al-Dīn Abū ʿAbd Allāh Muḥammad al-Dhahabī, *ʿIbar fī khabar man ghabar*, ed. Ṣalāḥ al-Dīn al-Munajjid (Kuwait, 1960–1966), vol. 2, p. 322; ʿAbd al-Ḥayy b. Aḥmad, Ibn al-ʿImād, *Shadharāt al-dhahab fī akhbār min dhahab* (Beirut, 1350/1982), vol. 3, p. 38. In the *mashyakha*

of Khadīja's brother he is indicated as the author of a *kitāb al-qurba*, which Khadīja's brother (and very likely Khadīja as well) memorised. There is no mention, however, of this work in the sources mentioning al-ʿAtakī. As the chain in Khadīja's *mashyakha* continues backward, after al-ʿAtakī, with 'Umar b. ʿAbd Rabbihi al-Daʿā' and ʿAbd Allāh b. Muḥammad al-Qurashī, it is possible that the latter, rather than al-ʿAtakī, was the actual author of this work.

49 Al-Silafī, *Muʿjam al-safar*, no. 121, pp. 237–239.

50 Interestingly, Muḥammad does not mention his sisters in his *mashyakha*.

51 S.M. Zeman, 'Abū Ṭāhir Aḥmad b. Muḥammad al-Silafī al-Iṣbahānī: His Life and Works with an Analytical Study of his *Muʿjam al-Safar*', pp. 60–65.

52 Al-Mundhirī, *al-Takmila*, vol. 3, no. 2120, p. 187.

53 Al-Maqrīzī, *al-Muqaffā*, vol. 2, no. 783.

54 Muḥammad b. ʿAlī b. al-Sabūnī, *Takmilat ikmāl al-ikmāl fi'l-ansāb wa'l-asmā' wa'l-alqāb* (Beirut, 1986), p. 50.

55 He is listed among the pupils of the Alexandrian Muḥammad b. ʿAbd al-Raḥmān al-ʿAlā'ī al-Ṣiqillī (d. 579/1183), Abu'l-Qāsim al-Ḥijāzī (d. 574/1178) and al-Kamāl b. al-Jalājilī al-Baghdādī (d. 612/1215). See, respectively, al-Maqrīzī, *al-Muqaffā*, vol. 6, nos. 2441, 2740 and 2798.

56 Al-Silafī, *Muʿjam*, no. 101, pp. 220–221 and n. 1. There is also a biography of her in Ibn al-ʿImād, *Shadharāt*, vol. 4, no. 265, p. 220. In al-ʿImād al-Iṣfahānī, *Kharīdat al-qaṣr wa jarīdat al-ʿaṣr* (Damascus, 1955–1959), vol. 2, p. 223, it is stated that her verses were good. Ibn Khallikān, *Biographical*, vol. 1, pp. 276–277.

57 On Shuhda al-Kātiba, see Sayeed, *Women and the Transmission of Religious Knowledge*, pp. 149–159.

58 Al-Mundhirī, *al-Takmila*, vol. 3, no. 1803, pp. 41–42 and al-Dhahabī, *Ta'rīkh*, volume for the decade 611–620, no. 520, pp. 399–400.

59 About ʿAlī Ibrāhīm b. Najā, see G. La Viere Leiser, 'Ḥanbalism in Egypt before the Mamlûks', *Studia Islamica*, 54 (1981), pp. 168–169. He is listed among those who transmitted to Nabīh al-Dīn al-Anṣārī al-Kātib (d. 613/1216) who was placed in charge of the *dīwān al-awqāf* and Abu'l-Khayr Badal al-Tabrīzī (d. 631/1233); see, respectively, al-Maqrīzī, *al-Muqaffā*, no. 767 and no. 1012.

60 His pupils included the merchant erudite Ibn Taghlib al-Āmadī (d. 557/1161) who was born in Baghdad but travelled to Cairo and Alexandria, al-Maqrīzī, *al-Muqaffā*, vol. 5, no. 1688.

61 Ibn Khallikān, *Biographical*, vol. 1, p. 191.

62 Listed among those who, in the Mosque of ʿAmr in Fusṭāṭ, met the important *qāḍī* al-Jawwānī Nassāba (d. 598/1201), a prolific scholar who had been in charge of the union of the *ashrāf* in Cairo. Among those he listened to was also Muḥammad b. ʿAbd al-Raḥmān al-ʿAlāʾī al-Siqillī (d. 579/1183), an Alexandrian already mentioned in connection to Umm ʿAlī Taqiyya earlier in this chapter. See, respectively, al-Maqrīzī, *al-Muqaffā*, vol. 5, no. 1893 and vol. 6, no. 2441.

63 Al-Maqrīzī, *al-Muqaffā*, vol. 6, no. 2790.

64 Ibn al-Zayyāt, *al-Kawākib al-sayyāra*, p. 222.

65 Al-Mundhirī, *al-Takmila*, vol. 2, no. 773, p. 15; al-Dhahabī, *Taʾrīkh*, volume for the decade 591–600, no. 612, pp. 469–470; M.A. Nadwi, *al-Muḥaddithāt*, pp. 268–269, pp. 93–96.

66 See for example al-Maqrīzī, *al-Muqaffā*, vol. 5, nos. 1562, and 1572.

67 Al-Mundhirī, *al-Takmila*, vol. 3, no. 2320, pp. 275–276.

68 Ibid., no. 2202, p. 226.

69 Ibid., no. 2776, pp. 465–466.

70 Ibid., no. 3146, pp. 632–633. On her see also the biographies of Ibn al-Sabūnī, *Takmila*, pp. 284–285; al-Dhahabī, *Taʾrīkh*, f. 8. She is listed among the authorities in the *mashyakha* of ʿAbd al-Muʾmin al-Dimyāṭī (b. 613/1217). See G. Vajda, *Le dictionnaire des autorités (Muʿjam al-suyūḫ) de ʿAbd al-Muʾmin ad-Dimyāṭī* (Paris, 1962), p. 102.

71 R. Roded, *Women in Islamic Biographical Collections: From Ibn Saʿd to Who's Who* (Boulder, CO, and London, 1994), ch. 4. See also M.L. Avila, 'Women in Andalusi Biographical Sources', in M. Marin and R. Deguilhem, ed., *Writing the Feminine: Women in Arab Sources* (New York, 2002), pp. 149–163.

72 This observation challenges the assertion made by M.L. Avila on Andalusian women according to which: 'When a female link appears in the chain, it very frequently marks the beginning of a dead end. The woman does not normally pass her knowledge to anybody. If she does so, it is to another woman until sooner or later – most probably sooner – one of the women breaks the chain': Avila, 'Women', p. 159.

73 Issues regarding the reliability of women as *ḥadīth* transmitters are discussed in A. Sayyed, 'Gender and Legal Authority: An Examination of Early Juristic Opposition to Women's Hadīth Transmission', *Islamic Law and Society*, 16 (2009), pp. 115–150.

74 See examples of practical devices to separate male teachers from female learners (and vice versa) in al-Andalus in Avila, 'Women', pp. 156–157, 158.

75 This view is somewhat corroborated by A. Sayeed's analysis on the curtailing effects of 'professionalism' on women participation in the dissemination of knowledge. See A. Sayeed, 'Women and Ḥadīth Transmission in Islamic History (First to Eighth Centuries') (PhD thesis, Princeton University, 2005), p. 3.

76 For an indication of active engagement in religious debates by Ismaili women during the North African phase of the Fatimid dynasty, see D. Cortese, '"A Woman's Work is Never Done": Women and Da'wa in Early Ismā'īlism', in U. Vermeulen and K. D'Hulster, ed., *Egypt and Syria in the Fatimid, Ayyubid and Mamluk Eras*, V (Leuven, 2007), pp. 68–72. It should be observed that, under the Fatimids, there is no indication that – on a day-to-day basis – the realms of Ismaili and Sunni women (or non-Muslim women for the matter) were mutually exclusive. In fact one can expect that interaction at most levels must have taken place in the public spaces typically frequented by women.

77 On the function of women as part of the kinship networks of the *'ulamā'* in a broader Abbasid context, see A. Sayeed, *Women and the Transmission of Religious Knowledge in Islam*, pp. 113–114.

7

The Fatimid Legacy and the Foundation of the Modern Nizārī Ismaili Imamate

Daniel Beben

The Fatimid era is ubiquitous today in the discourse of the Nizārī Ismaili imamate.[1] Yet this was not always the case. As with other societies and religious communities the world over, the arrangement and presentation of history in the Ismaili tradition has evolved in the course of time, with new historiographical agendas and subjects of emphasis emerging or receding in response to changes in the political and social contexts. In this chapter the place of the Fatimids in the cultural memory of the Nizārī Ismailis in the post-Mongol era will be explored.[2] It will be argued that the emphasis placed on the Fatimid era in present-day Nizārī discourse is a relatively recent development, rooted in the dynamic changes that occurred in the social and political context of the community in the 18th and 19th centuries. Rather than the Fatimids, the primary locus of Nizārī communal memory in the earlier period from the 7th/13th to the 12th/18th centuries was the Alamūt era, and particularly the declaration of the *qiyāma* (spiritual resurrection) under Imam Ḥasan *ʿalā dhikrihi'l-salām* at Alamūt in 559/1164. It was only in the 18th century, when the Nizārī imamate emerged from a long period of concealment and entered into a new-found position of political and social prominence, that we see the first signs of a de-emphasis of the *qiyāma* and a renewed focus on the Fatimid era and its legacy.

This reorientation of the locus of Nizārī communal memory away from the events of the *qiyāma* and towards the Fatimid era was facilitated by an even more dramatic shift in historical consciousness that saw a revision in the very notion of historical time. In an article published in 2014, Shahzad Bashir called for greater attention to emic conceptions of time and chronology in Muslim societies and texts.[3] This chapter aims to respond to this challenge through presenting a closer examination of conceptions of chronology in Nizārī literature and their shift over time. While the notion of time in the Ismaili tradition has received some consideration in scholarship, to date these studies have focused primarily on presentations found in the 'classical' period of Ismaili literature from the Fatimid era, with little attention given to the manner in which these conceptions have changed over the course of time or with consideration to the social and political contexts that informed these shifts. We shall explore how the cyclical model of history presented in Ismaili works of the Fatimid era was revised in the light of the declaration of the *qiyāma*, and then ultimately discarded entirely in the new Nizārī historiographical tradition established in the 19th century. These developments facilitated a major shift in the place of the Fatimid era in the historical imagination of the Nizārīs.

The *Qiyāma* and Communal Memory in the Nizārī Tradition

The events surrounding the declaration of the *qiyāma* in 559/1164 and its significance have long been the subject of scholarship and debate, and hence do not merit an extensive elaboration here.[4] Both contemporary Sunni sources and later Nizārī sources concur that in that year the Nizārī lord of Alamūt, Ḥasan, publicly declared his status as the awaited imam. Up to this time, the Nizārīs had lived without direct access to their imams, who had remained in hiding following the death of the Fatimid Imam-caliph Mustanṣir bi'llāh in 487/1094 and the schism in the Ismaili community arising from a dispute between the supporters of his sons, Nizār and Must'alī. This schism led to the execution of Nizār a year later and the dominance of the Must'alī faction at the Fatimid court.

Contemporary Sunni sources relate that Ḥasan initially declared himself to be merely the representative (*khalīfa*) of the hidden imam, only later revealing that he was in fact the descendant of the Fatimid imam Nizār b. al-Mustanṣir bi'llāh, whose son and successor al-Hādī had been secretly escorted to Alamūt before Nizār's murder, and hence was the awaited imam himself. Thereafter Imam Ḥasan II became known among the Nizārīs with the honorific *ʿalā dhikrihi'l-salām* ('upon whose mention be peace'), a sobriquet by which he is still known among Nizārīs today.

For many contemporary Sunni authors, the declaration of the *qiyāma* constituted little more than an abolition of the *sharīʿa*, that is, the legal structure of Islam, and a brazen excuse to indulge in libertinism. For Nizārī authors, however, the *qiyāma* in Ḥasan's declaration, beyond an immediate declaration of his personal imamate, amounted more broadly to an unveiling of the true, spiritual essence of the imam and the revelation of the esoteric reality of religion, one with profound consequences that would be felt long after the Mongol conquests and the end of the Alamūt era. Moreover, for Nizārīs living in the post-*qiyāma* era, the declaration constituted not simply a new stage in the linear unfolding of history, but a historical rupture of cosmic significance. From an early period, Ismaili writers had propounded a cyclical model of history in which each cycle (*dawr*) of human history is defined by the presence of a prophet, or 'annunciator' (*nāṭiq*).[5] The *nāṭiq*s of the first six eras of human history were Adam, Noah (Nūḥ), Abraham (Ibrāhīm), Moses (Mūsā), Jesus (ʿĪsā) and Muḥammad, each of whom were in turn accompanied by a successor, or 'silent one' (*ṣāmit*), who was entrusted with the esoteric knowledge of his teaching, corresponding to the function of the imam in Ismaili thought. With Muḥammad (the *nāṭiq*) and his successor ʿAlī b. Abī Ṭālib (the *ṣāmit*) humanity had entered the sixth cycle, the last one before the day of resurrection.

This model was given a revision in Nizārī literature following the declaration of the *qiyāma* under Imam Ḥasan *ʿalā dhikrihi'l-salām*, which was presented as the initiation of a seventh historical cycle. This new historical model is illustrated in a text that is among the oldest Nizārī works known to survive from the period following the Mongol conquests, namely the *Risāla-yi ṣirāṭ al-mustaqīm*, tentatively dated to the late 8th/14th or early 9th/15th century. The author of the anonymous *Risāla* writes:

> These are the six cycles (*dawr*s) of the six Annunciators (*nāṭiq*s). In truth, after that they were uninterrupted and successive 'descendants, one after the other' (Qur'an 3:34) reaching the time of the noble [Ḥasan] *'alā dhikrihi'l-salām*, the Lord of the Resurrection (*qā'im al-qiyāmat*), which is the seventh cycle. From the time of Mawlānā Ismā'īl until the time of Mawlānā Mahdī 'Abd Allāh, the imams were concealed ... Mawlānā Mahdī manifested in the lands of the Maghrib and the succeeding imams were manifest until the time of Mawlānā Mustanṣir of Egypt. Mawlānā Mustanṣir of Egypt had several children but the imamate was with Mawlānā Nizār. Must'alī falsely claimed the imamate, but it was cut off with his descendant 'Āḍid. They martyred Mawlānā Nizār and the following imams were concealed until the time of Mawlānā Ḥasan *'alā dhikrihi'l-salām*, the Lord of the Great Resurrection. The imam's manifestation reached the entire world. Since then, the imams have been in concealment until our day. However, this concealment was for the exotericists, not for the esotericists (*ahl-i bāṭin*). Even when there is concealment for the esotericists, it is not for all of them, for it is decreed that the epiphany of the Universal Intellect, who is the proof (*ḥujja*) of the imam, always has access to the Imam of the Age and Time in the spiritual world.[6]

The enduring relevance of the *qiyāma* for the historical memory of the Nizārīs is further illustrated in a late 9th/15th-century source, the *Haft bāb* of Abū Isḥāq Quhistānī. In the third chapter of his work, Quhistānī provides a historical and genealogical overview of the imams. This account offers a fairly straightforward historical chronology of the imamate down through the Fatimids and the early Nizārī imams, until arriving at the mention of Ḥasan *'alā dhikrihi'l-salām*, of whom he writes:

> He [Ḥasan] was the *Qā'im* of the Resurrection (*qiyāmat*). It was in his time that the ties and fetters of *sharī'at* fell from the necks of his slaves. By that time, 180,000 years had passed since the 'Great Date'

> (*tārīkh-i aʿẓam*). [This was] the date indicated by the Prophet, who said, 'I will remain in the grave no more than half a day.' And what Jesus predicted in the Gospels (*Injīl*), Moses in the Torah (*Tūrat*), Zoroaster in the Book of Zand (*Kitāb-i Zand*), in the *Kitāb-i anhigliyūn* of Abū Saʿīd Yūnānī,[7] and all other predictions of the prophets all came true with him.[8]

This emphasis on the pivotal nature of the imamate of Ḥasan II is a defining element of most of the Nizārī literature produced down to the 19th century.[9] Broadly speaking, Nizārī authors of this same period displayed little interest in the Fatimid era; it is generally referred to only in passing, and almost invariably only in the context of accounts of the genealogy of the imams.[10] Hence, while the genealogical connection between the Nizārī and Fatimid imams continued to be emphasised, the Fatimid era itself quickly lost its relevance as a primary point of historical reference, having been superseded in Nizārī communal memory by the *qiyāma* and the imamate of Ḥasan *ʿalā dhikrihiʾl-salām*. This lack of emphasis on the Fatimid era was facilitated by a broader sense of a detachment between the Nizārī and Fatimid literary legacies; while the question has yet to be explored at any depth in scholarship, it would appear overall that very little of the Fatimid literary heritage was preserved among the Nizārī communities in pre-modern times, being reintroduced to the Nizārī tradition only in the 20th century via modern scholarship.[11] In their writings, Nizārī authors of the post-Mongol era reveal little knowledge of the Fatimids beyond the broadest outlines of this era, and in fact display little interest in the period aside from the genealogy of the imams of the era. It is telling that when Nizārī authors of the late 19th and early 20th century, such as Fidāʾī Khurāsānī (discussed in the section 'A New Vision of History' below), set about writing a history of this period they were forced to rely primarily on non-Ismaili sources.

It should be emphasised, however, that the absence of any attention to the Fatimids in pre-modern Nizārī literature did not reflect a lack of interest in history per se, as has sometimes been claimed, but rather is reflective of the overwhelming impact on communal memory of the *qiyāma* and its legacy, which was seen as having superseded the Fatimid era in the historical vision of the Nizārīs. The enduring relevance of the *qiyāma* for Nizārī historical memory is rooted also in the social and political reality of the Ismailis of the post-Mongol era. For most of the period between the Mongol conquests in the 7th/13th century and the public re-emergence of the imamate in the 18th century, the Nizārī imams generally lived in a state of relative concealment. While the extent of this concealment varied according to the specific time and circumstances, throughout most of this period the Nizārīs by and large had little direct contact with their imams. As a result, authority in the community devolved to the local representatives of the imams, known as *pīr*s and *khalīfa*s. Accordingly, this state of affairs produced an environment that was uniquely suited to the appeal of the *qiyāma*, which emphasised the spiritual nature of the imam as a reality that transcends his physical form, and hence provided a plausible model of authority for those who lacked direct contact with the imams. Conversely, this context may also explain the lack of attention paid to the Fatimid era, as the model of direct political and social authority employed by the imamate in this period would have certainly appeared alien and anachronistic to later Nizārī observers. But, as will be seen, beginning in the 18th century a series of geopolitical transformations occurred that once again placed the Nizārī imams in a position of public authority. In time, these transformations would lead to a wholesale reassessment of the historical vision of the Nizārī community, which reduced the emphasis on the *qiyāma* and once again turned the focus of memory towards the Fatimids.

The 18th-Century Transformation in Ismailism

This section will briefly outline a series of developments, beginning in the 18th century, which led to a drastic shift in the status of the Nizārī imamate and its political and social standing in the Islamic world. These developments provide the context for understanding the transformation of communal history and the role of the Fatimids in the Nizārī literature of the 19th century. The destruction of Alamūt and the murder of the Imam Rukn al-Dīn

Khurshāh by the Mongols in 655/1257 initiated 200 years of the utmost level of concealment for the Nizārī imamate. The history of the imamate for most of this period remains almost entirely obscure and little is known of it beyond the barest outlines.[12] While the decentralised political climate of late 9th/15th-century Iran permitted a brief public re-emergence of the imamate in the period known in Ismaili history as the 'Anjudān revival', the Safawid conquests of the early 10th/16th century once again forced the imams into a more guarded position. Despite their Shiʿi disposition, the Safawid rulers were largely hostile to the Nizārī imams, seeing in them a challenge to their own claim to be heirs to the authority of the earlier twelve imams of the Ithnāʿasharī tradition. At least one of the Nizārī imams from this period, Murād Mīrzā, was executed by the Safawids on the charge of spreading heresy, while others were forced into hiding or exile.[13]

The collapse of the Safawid state in the early 18th century and the subsequent rise to power in Iran of Nādir Shāh provided the opportunity for a critical change in the status of the Nizārī imamate under Ḥasan ʿAlī (known also as Sayyid Ḥasan Beg). This shift in the status of the Nizārī imamate had its roots in a close personal relationship that formed between Imam Ḥasan ʿAlī and Nādir Shāh. According to a number of accounts of this relationship, Nādir Shāh employed the imam as a commander in his army, in which many Nizārīs also served in the ranks.[14] It would appear, moreover, that Nādir Shāh made this appointment while entirely aware of Ḥasan ʿAlī's status as the Nizārī imam. According to some accounts of their relationship, Imam Ḥasan ʿAlī also accompanied Nādir Shāh on his invasion of India, after which he was rewarded with the governorship of the region surrounding his ancestral village of Maḥallāt. After some time, however, intrigues were fomented at court by enemies of the imam who accused him of heresy, leading Nādir Shāh to blind him. However, Nādir Shāh later apologised to Imam Ḥasan ʿAlī and reinstated him to his former position.[15] Despite its hesitant beginnings, the relationship between the Nizārī imams and the Afshārid dynasty outlived Nādir Shāh and was strengthened significantly under his successors, as will be outlined shortly.

Nādir Shāh's cultivation of a relationship with the Nizārī imamate was reflective of the broader political and religious agenda he pursued in the course of his short-lived effort to rebuild and expand the Safawid empire. Lacking the genealogical or religious claims to legitimacy afforded to the Safawids, Nādir Shāh instead made use of a series of alternative bases of legitimation in order to establish his rule in Iran.[16] Given his efforts to combat the influence of the Ithnāʿasharī Shiʿi *ʿulamāʾ* and to displace them from the privileged position they held under the Safawids, it is likely that Nādir Shāh would have seen a useful ally in the Nizārī imamate.[17] Nādir Shāh also replaced Twelver Shiʿism with Sunnism as the official religion of his realm, while according Twelver Shiʿism the status of a *madhhab*. In this context he sought to have the Jaʿfarī *madhhab* recognised as the fifth school of Islamic jurisprudence, alongside the four Sunni schools. This particular endeavour entailed an effort not only to reduce the barriers between Shiʿi and Sunni interpretations of Islam, but also, and equally, to efface distinctions in Shiʿism under the common umbrella of a single Jaʿfarī *madhhab*, hence creating a space for Ismaili participation in the project.[18] While this effort met with considerable resistance from both the Shiʿi and Sunni *ʿulamāʾ*, leading to its ultimate failure, it nonetheless provides a context for understanding Nādir Shāh's motivations in seeking the support of religious constituencies outside the structure of the Twelver *ʿulamāʾ*.

Nādir Shāh's cultivation of the Nizārīs came on the heels of another significant development concerning the religious and social context of the imamate. From the beginning of the Nizārī era to the end of the 9th/15th century the imams had operated in a largely Sunni environment. In the wake of the Mongol conquests this environment became increasingly marked by the presence of the Sufi traditions that flourished in this period, and the imams elaborated their claims to religious authority accordingly within this context.[19] The Safawid conquest ushered in a dramatically revised religious environment in Iran. Consequently, for the first time in history, the Ismaili imamate found itself situated within a majority-Shiʿi environment. As noted above, initially this development did not prove favourable to the imams, who suffered greatly under the repressive ideological regime of the Safawids. The position of the Nizārīs was alleviated somewhat beginning in the late 10th/16th century during the reign of Shāh ʿAbbās and there is evidence suggesting that the imams actually adopted Ithnāʿasharī Shiʿism as a form of *taqiyya* during his reign.[20] Following the collapse of the Safawid state it would appear that the Nizārī imams were no longer under pressure to practise *taqiyya*. As the sources of this period illustrate, the Ismaili identity of the imams was clearly known to observers during the reign of Nādir Shāh and after, indicating a cessation of *taqiyya* practices.[21] From this point forward the imams asserted new claims to legitimacy on the basis of appeals to a pan-Shiʿi heritage. It was this context that saw an increasing emphasis on the imams' descent from Jaʿfar al-Ṣādiq and on the legacy of the Fatimids as the first Shiʿi polity in history.

One of the major developments that accompanied the public emergence of the Nizārī imamate under Nādir Shāh was the shift of the seat of the imamate from the Qumm region, where it had been based since at least the 9th/15th century, to the province of Kirmān in south-eastern Iran. The main sources chronicling this development are the writings of Aḥmad ʿAlī Khān Vazīrī (d. 1295/1878), among whose works are the *Tārīkh-i Kirmān*, a history of Kirmān from pre-Islamic times to the early Qājār period, completed in 1293/1876, and a historical geography of the Kirmān region titled *Jughrāfiyā-yi Kirmān*. While Kirmān had not historically been an important centre of Ismaili activity, the imamate had maintained a following there since at least the late 11th/17th century. During the imamate of Sayyid Ḥasan Beg's grandfather, Shāh Nizār (d. 1134/1722), a group of nomadic Khurāsānī tribesmen known as the ʿAṭāʾ Allāhīs (after the *takhalluṣ* of Shāh Nizār, ʿAṭāʾ Allāh), who were followers of the imam, were resettled in the province of Kirmān, in the region of Sīrjān. One interesting characteristic of this group was that they are explicitly identified in the sources as not having been Ismaili, but nonetheless as followers of the imam, drawn to his charismatic authority as a sayyid and a descendant of Jaʿfar al-Ṣādiq. According to Vazīrī,

> this group maintained complete faith and sincerity in the sayyids of the line of Ismāʿīl, son of Ḥaḍrat-i Imām, to speak correctly, Jaʿfar Ṣādiq ... from that time forward the Khurāsānī and ʿAṭāʾ Allāhī communities have been believers and followers of this *silsila*, but like the Ḥaydarābādīs, they are neither Sevener Shiʿas nor Ismailis.[22]

The Khurāsānī and ʿAṭāʾ Allāhī communities continued to be steadfast supporters of the imams down to the time of Ḥasan ʿAlī Shāh (Aga Khan I), who made use of the tribesmen as a military force in the course of his campaign, on the orders of the Qājār ruler Muḥammad Shāh, to pacify the province of Kirmān and expunge it of the invading Afghāns and Balūchīs.[23] The presence of the ʿAṭāʾ Allāhīs offers one of the earliest signs of the gradual growth and extension of the political and social authority of the Nizārī imams in the 18th century, which saw the development of new constituencies for the imamate outside the context of narrowly defined Ismaili communities. This development should also be understood in the context of a broader phenomenon witnessed in the Indo-Iranian border regions in this period, as well as in many other areas of the Islamic world, in which, in the absence of any firm state authority, sayyids and other individuals of revered or sacred status, come to occupy positions as political intermediaries and as mediators in conflicts.[24] This role was illustrated most vividly during the imamate of Ḥasan ʿAlī Shāh, who was charged with mediating between the Qājār government and various tribal groups in the border regions of Sīstān and Balūchistān. Critically, the authority assigned to the imams among these groups was given not on the basis of their position as Ismaili imams, but rather on their charismatic status as sayyids.

The decision under Imam Sayyid Ḥasan Beg to move the seat of the imamate from the village of Kahak, near Qumm, to Kirmān was made primarily out of concern for the imamate's relationship with its followers in India. According to Vazīrī, who introduced the imam as 'from the lineage of Nizār who was, at several degrees removed, among the ancestors of Ismāʿīl b. Imām Jaʿfar al-Ṣādiq', owing to the disorder in Iran following the fall of the Safawids the Nizārīs in India faced increasing difficulty in travelling to visit and pay tribute to the imams in northern Iran.[25] Many of their caravans were plundered by the Bakhtiyārī tribesmen and the flow of tithes to the imamate was blocked. Thus towards the end of the reign of Nādir Shāh the decision was made by Imam Sayyid Ḥasan Beg to move the seat of the imamate to the town of Shahr-i Bābak in Kirmān in order to position himself closer both to the overland routes from India and to the port of Bandar ʿAbbās, which was also used by many Indian Ismailis, or Khojas, coming to Iran in this period. The flow of tithes from his followers in India resumed and increased, and the imam soon became a major landholder in Kirmān, maintaining a winter home in the capital city of Guvāshīr (now the city of Kirmān) and spending his summers in Shahr-i Bābak. Vazīrī further relates that, following the death of Nādir Shāh, Imam Sayyid Ḥasan Beg developed a close relationship with Nādir Shāh's grandson, Shāhrukh Khān, the governor of Kirmān, and that the imam gave one of his daughters in marriage to Shāhrukh Khān's son, Luṭf ʿAlī Khān.

The sources relate few details regarding Imam Sayyid Ḥasan Beg's successor, Qāsim ʿAlī, whose imamate evidently was quite brief. Much more information is available on the next imam, Sayyid Abu'l-Ḥasan ʿAlī.[26] During Sayyid Abu'l-Ḥasan's imamate, control of Kirmān passed from the Afshārids to the Zands. The imam also enjoyed a close relationship with the Zand governor of the region, Mīrzā Ḥusayn Khān, who reaffirmed his position in the area and eventually appointed him to the positions of *beglerbegi*, or governor, of the province of Kirmān.[27] The imam successfully repelled a major Afghān invasion of Kirmān in this period, which brought him many accolades from the Zands. In addition, he patronised the construction of a public square adjacent to the Friday mosque as well as several other prominent buildings in the city of Kirmān, displaying a predilection for the patronage of public architecture that had defined the rule of the Fatimids and which remains a priority for the modern Nizārī imamate. Following the death of the Zand ruler Karīm Khān in 1193/1779, Imam Abu'l-Ḥasan ʿAlī continued to receive the support of his successors and governed the province as a virtually autonomous ruler. However, he crucially switched his support to Āghā Muḥammad Khān Qājār during the latter's conflict with the Zands and repelled an effort by the Zand ruler Luṭf 'Alī Khān to capture the city of Kirmān in the winter of 1790–1791.[28] This switch in allegiance proved to be remarkably prescient, as it laid the foundations for a very close and profitable relationship between the Nizārī imamate and the Qājār establishment for the next half century.

The Fatimid Legacy under Aga Khan I

Imam Abu'l-Ḥasan 'Alī died in 1206/1792 and was succeeded by his son Shāh Khalīl Allāh.[29] The new imam decided to transfer the seat of imamate to its former location in Kahak in the region of Qumm, on account of the violent upheavals that continued to take place across Kirmān following the imposition of Qājār authority there,[30] and the Qājār ruler Āghā Muḥammad Khān obligingly appointed Shāh Khalīl Allāh as mayor of the town and granted his family new holdings there. It was here in Kahak that Ḥasan 'Alī Shāh, the future Aga Khan, was born in 1804. In 1815 Shāh Khalīl Allāh moved his headquarters to the city of Yazd in central Iran which lay along the trade routes to and from India, a move made once again in order to situate the seat of the imamate more conveniently for the Indian Ismailis who brought with them a significant amount of revenue each year. In 1817, two years after the shift of the imamate to Yazd, Imam Shāh Khalīl Allāh and his residence were attacked by an angry mob instigated by some members of the local Shi'i clergy, who murdered the imam and several of his followers. This incident clearly illustrates the fact that the Nizārī imamate's position in Iranian society continued to be contested in this period. Yet, at the same time, the incident also reveals the remarkable degree of affinity between the imamate and the political elite of Iran that had developed over the previous century. The Qājār monarch of the period, Fatḥ 'Alī Shāh, had the cleric responsible for inciting the murder severely punished. In further compensation, Fatḥ 'Alī Shāh appointed Shāh Khalīl Allāh's son and successor to the imamate, Ḥasan 'Alī Shāh, governor of Qumm and bestowed on him the honorific title of Aga Khan which has become a hereditary title for the Nizārī imams.

Little more is known about this period of Aga Khan I's life until the death of Fatḥ 'Alī Shāh in 1834 and the accession of his grandson Muḥammad Shāh to the Qājār throne. The Aga Khan endeared himself to the new ruler and soon afterwards was appointed governor of Kirmān, the same position that his grandfather had held under the Zands. The Aga Khan's appointment as governor of Kirmān came with considerable responsibility, as the province had evidently fallen into disorder and was plagued by a series of tribal uprisings. The Aga Khan agreed to accept this appointment without any stipend. By his own account, he carried out this task with great success, and succeeded in restoring the province to the Qājārs.[31] Very quickly, however, the relationship between the Aga Khan and the Qājār government took a decisive turn for the worse, and less than two years after his appointment as governor of Kirmān the Aga Khan was dismissed from his position and recalled to Tehran. This dismissal led to a chain of events culminating in the permanent departure of the imamate from Persia, severing the long-established relationship between the Nizārī imamate and the rulers of Iran.[32]

Following his arrival in India, the Aga Khan quickly cultivated a reputation as a patron of various pan-Shi'i constituencies, sponsoring the *ta'ziya* commemorations in the city of Jamnagar in Muḥarram 1845 during a period of residence there and then again two years later in Calcutta. Following the permanent re-establishment of the seat of the imamate in Bombay in 1848, the Aga Khan composed a memoir of his career under the Qājārs, entitled *'Ibrat-afzā*.[33] In this work the Aga Khan declared his continued loyalty to the Qājār dynasty and defended his record of service to the court. At the same time, the text reveals an effort to establish new political relationships, most notably among the British.[34] Most importantly, the work reveals a renewed effort on the part of the Aga Khan to draw upon the imamate's Fatimid legacy as a means of broadening the basis of his claim to religious authority. In one telling passage in the text the Aga Khan poignantly reminds the reader of his own illustrious lineage and claims to religious legitimacy:

> Since it was and is known to God and his shadow, His Highness the King, that in my mind there was and is no thought of the rule of Kirmān, much less that of Īrān and Tūrān, I simply obeyed the royal order and carried out the imperial wishes and decrees. All know that due to the blessings of God and the grace of my ancestors and pure forefathers, I consider rulership with utter contempt in the breadth and extent of my dervishhood …
>
> It is known to all that material and spiritual kingship has belonged to my ancestors and forefathers since eternity, and is in perpetuity, and will be so. But despite the fact that my great forefathers were the firm handle of religion and the strong cord of God, 'in which there is no split', [as is written] in the Clear Book, [or] 'there is no splitting the twain and no cutting the twain' in the famous tradition of my ancestor, the Master of the Messengers, peace be upon him and upon his family, I am not attached in the slightest detail to this world and what is in it. Yes, efforts have been exerted as far as possible in spreading the faith and religious law of the final prophet in imitation of the pure ancestors. Likewise, is it evident that in Egypt several generations of my ancestors held the positions of kingship and the caliphate, and they carried out the joining of the Jaʿfarī Shiʿi community to the law of the Ithnāʿasharī, which today is attributed to Shāh Ismāʿīl Ṣafawī. I am a descendant of that family.[35]

The Aga Khan's statement here may be interpreted on many levels. First, it may be understood within the context of the immediate background to his dispute with the Qājār throne and in relation to Qājār claims to symbolic succession (if not dynastic succession) to the Safawid throne.[36] The Qājār claim to Safawid inheritance not only was advanced through historiographical production, but was also manifested in visual and material culture, through what Priscilla Soucek terms the 'neo-Safavid' style displayed in the coinage and medals of the era.[37] Given the importance of the Safawids for the history of Shiʿi Islam in Iran, a claim to this heritage was vital for establishing the religious legitimacy of the dynasty. In the words of Hamid Algar:

> The Qajar dynasty was tribal in its origins; whereas the Safavids claimed descent from the Imams, the Qajars could point only to the Mongols for the origin of their line. They raised no religious claims, even if they inherited, consciously or unconsciously, many of the assumptions concerning regal power implicit in the Safavid monarchy. Under the Safavids, a close alliance of the state and the religious body had existed, with the former as the dominant partner; under the Qajars, there would never be more than an uneasy and fitful coalition.[38]

The Aga Khan's statement in *ʿIbrat-afzā*, therefore, may be seen as a forthright retort to Qājār claims. Notably, the Aga Khan presents the Fatimid legacy not merely within the context of Ismaili history, but as part of a Jaʿfarī and 'pan-Shiʿi' heritage. While not denying Qājār claims to the Safawid legacy, the Aga Khan instead lays claim to an even older legacy and precedent for religious authority in Shiʿi history, hence dispensing with the need for his reliance on the Qājār court for the legitimation of his authority.

Beyond this, the Aga Khan's statement here is indicative of the broader and more nuanced manner in which the Fatimid legacy has been adduced by the Nizārī imams. As this example illustrates, the Fatimid legacy has not been evoked as a basis for claims to direct political or territorial authority; rather, the Aga Khan in his statement explicitly denies any pretences to territorial rule, evoking in its place a claim to religious and charismatic authority. This statement has been echoed repeatedly by his successors. For example, the current Ismaili imam, Shah Karim al-Husayni, Aga Khan IV, in a speech to the Canadian parliament in 2014 stated:

> Although there was a time when the Ismaili Imams were also caliphs, that is to say the heads of state – for example in Egypt during the Fatimid period – my function today is apolitical; every Ismaili is primarily a citizen of his or her country of birth or adoption. However, the scope of the Ismaili Imamat is considerably greater than that distant time, since today it operates in many parts of the world.[39]

Rather than claims to territorial rule, the Fatimid legacy has been evoked by the modern Nizārī imamate as a precedent for a broader claim to social and religious leadership within the Muslim *umma* extending beyond the boundaries of the Ismaili community.[40] Over the past century and a half, the Fatimids have been repeatedly evoked by the imams as precedents for their patronage of educational and cultural institutions, and have been cited particularly vigorously by the present imam in the context of his work as a patron of architectural projects. In the discourse of the modern Nizārī imamate, the Fatimids are recalled not for the glory of their military victories or for the extent of their territorial sovereignty, but rather as a dynasty that oversaw remarkable advancements in areas such as education, cultural and artistic production, and public works. In particular, the role of religious tolerance and pluralism under the Fatimids has been repeatedly emphasised and cited as a model for present-day forms of governing and as a precedent for the imamate's engagement with a wide range of political and religious constituencies.[41] The connection between the modern imamate and the Fatimids was solidified by the decision of the previous imam, Sultan Muhammad Shah, Aga Khan III, to be buried in Aswān along the banks of the Nile, his ancestral Fatimid land. More recently, the present imam has supervised a 20-year project (completed in 2005) to create the Azhar Park and renovate its surrounding structures in Cairo, which has become a potent symbol of the modern Nizārī imamate's claim to the Fatimid legacy.[42]

A New Vision of History

In the second half of the 19th century a new genre of historical writing was developed by the Nizārī community under the patronage of Aga Khan I and his successors. To date, this body of historiography has been almost exclusively used as a repository of historical information on the imams with little attention being given to their historiographical concerns or their context. Yet this new body of historical works displays a number of remarkable departures from previous literary and historiographical practices in the Ismaili tradition. Most conspicuously, these new texts completely disregard the cyclical model of history found in older Nizārī writings, emphasising in its place a continual and linear genealogical chain of imamate stretching from the present imam back to the Prophet Muḥammad. Furthermore, this body of work is devoid of any reference to the events of the *qiyāma*, once again marking a radical departure from previous Nizārī literature.

The earliest example of this new historiographic approach may be seen in the *Khiṭābāt-i ʿāliya*, a collection of discourses by Pīr Shihāb al-Dīn Shāh Ḥusaynī (d. 1302/1884), a grandson of Aga Khan I and elder brother of Aga Khan III, composed sometime before the former's death in 1298/1881.[43] While not formally a historical work, the *Khiṭābāt-i ʿāliya* is nonetheless noteworthy for including a historical and genealogical overview of the Nizārī imams, which standardised the official genealogy of the imams accepted by the Nizārī community down to the present day.[44] This same arrangement is found in a later work, the *Hidāyat al-muʾminīn al-ṭālibīn* of Fidāʾī Khurāsānī (d. 1342/1923), which was composed around the turn of the 20th century under the patronage of Aga Khan III.[45] This text is noteworthy for being the first work in the Nizārī tradition to be explicitly designated as a work of history (*tārīkh*).[46] In the introduction to his work, Fidāʾī Khurāsānī laments the absence of histories of the imams and outlines how he was compelled to rely upon non-Ismaili historical works, such as the late medieval histories *Rawḍat al-ṣafāʾ* and the *Ḥabīb al-siyar*, in composing his work, particularly for the Fatimid era.[47] Most importantly for our purposes, both the *Khiṭābāt-i ʿāliya* and the *Hidāyat al-muʾminīn al-ṭālibīn* entirely dispense with the cyclical arrangement of history found in the older Nizārī tradition, replacing it instead with a linear chronological overview of the imams, with a substantial emphasis on the Fatimid period. In addition, both works likewise omit any mention of the *qiyāma* in their accounts of Imam Ḥasan *ʿalā dhikrihiʾl-salām*.[48]

Consequently, the events of the *qiyāma*, which had had such a predominant influence on the historical imagination of earlier generations of Nizārīs, by the first decades of the 20th century had largely receded from communal memory, having been replaced by a renewed focus on the legacy of the Fatimids. The shift of focus away from the *qiyāma* in the historical record was also accompanied by a shift in the very conception of historical time itself, marked by the transition from a cyclical to a linear presentation of history. The reconceptualisation of communal history found in these works, along with the renewed focus placed on the Fatimid era, emerged as a response to the dramatically new context encountered by the Nizārī imamate in the modern era, illustrating a pattern of resilience and adaptability that has defined the Ismaili community throughout its long history. While the notion of the spiritual and transcendental reality of the imam inherent in the concept of *qiyāma* remains an essential element in the conceptualisation of the imamate among the Nizārī Ismailis today, the view of the *qiyāma* itself as a historically significant event has now been almost entirely displaced in favour of a narrative emphasising historical continuity with the Fatimid past.

Notes

1 As an illustration of this point, the collection of the present Nizārī Ismaili imam's speeches and interviews archived at http://www.nanowisdoms.org (accessed 25 January 2017) presents over 60 separate occasions in which the term 'Fatimid' or 'Fatimids' was referenced. In contrast, the name 'Alamūt' appeared on only one occasion, in which it was mentioned by the interviewer, while no references were found to the term '*qiyāma*' or its variants.

2 On the notion of 'cultural memory', see Jan Assmann, *Religion and Cultural Memory: Ten Studies*, tr. Rodney Livingstone (Stanford, 2006).

3 Shahzad Bashir, 'On Islamic Time: Rethinking Chronology in the Historiography of Muslim Societies', *History and Theory*, 53 (2014), pp. 519–544.

4 Among studies on the *qiyāma*, see Jorunn J. Buckley, 'The Nizârî Ismâ'îlîtes' Abolishment of the Sharî'a during the "Great Resurrection" of 1164 A.D./559 A.H.', *Studia Islamica*, 60 (1984), pp. 137–165; Delia Cortese, 'Eschatology and Power in Mediaeval Persian

Ismailism' (PhD thesis, School of Oriental and African Studies, University of London, 1993), pp. 129–190; Cortese, 'The Ismāʿīlī Resurrection of Alamūt: A Bid for Spiritual Awakening or a Statement of Political Authority?', in S.E. Porter et al., ed., *Resurrection* (*Journal for the Study of the New Testament*) Supplement 186 (1999), pp. 249–262; Farhad Daftary, *The Ismāʿīlīs: Their History and Doctrines* (2nd ed., Cambridge, 2007), pp. 358–367; Marshall G.S. Hodgson, *The Order of Assassins: The Struggle of the Early Nizārī Ismāʿīlīs Against the Islamic World* (The Hague, 1955), pp. 148–184; M. Hodgson, 'The Ismāʿīlī State', in John A. Boyle, ed., *The Cambridge History of Iran*, vol. 5, *The Saljuq and Mongol Periods* (Cambridge, 1968), pp. 457–463; Christian Jambet, 'La grande résurrection d'Alamût d'après quelques textes Ismaéliens', in *Apocalypse et sens de l'histoire*, being *Cahiers de l'Université Saint Jean de Jerusalem*, no. 9 (Paris, 1983), pp. 113–131; C. Jambet, *La grande résurrection d'Alamût: Les formes de la liberté dans le shî'isme ismaélien* (Lagrasse, 1990); Liudmila V. Stroeva, '*Den' voskreseniia iz mertvykh i ego sotsial'naia sushchost'*, *Kratkie soobshcheniia Instituta Vostokovedeniia, AN SSSR* (Moscow) 38 (1960), pp. 19–25; L. Stroeva, *Gosudarstvo ismailitov v Irane v XI–XIII vv.* (Moscow, 1978), pp. 171–198. The declaration of the *qiyāma* became the focal point of the earliest studies on the Ismailis by Western scholars dating back to the early 19th century; for example, see Joseph von Hammer-Purgstall, *The History of the Assassins*, tr. O.C. Woods (London, 1835), pp. 105–138. See also the critique of this work by Farhad Daftary, 'The "Order of the Assassins": J. von Hammer and the Orientalist Misrepresentations of the Nizari Ismailis', *Iranian Studies*, 39 (2006), pp. 71–82.

5 For an overview of this system and its symbolism, see Henry Corbin, *Cyclical Time and Ismaili Gnosis*, tr. R. Manheim and J.W. Morris (London, 1983); Farhad Daftary, 'Cyclical Time and Sacred History in Medieval Ismaili Thought', in K. D'Hulster and J. Van Steenbergen, ed., *Continuity and Change in the Realms of Islam: Studies in Honour of Professor Urbain Vermeulen* (Leuven, 2008), pp. 151–158.

6 Shafique N. Virani, '*The Right Path*: A Post-Mongol Persian Ismaili Treatise', *Iranian Studies*, 43 (2010), p. 211 (English trans.), pp. 219–220 (Persian text).

7 Probably a garbled reference to the Gospel of St John.

8 Abū Isḥāq Quhistānī, *Haft bāb*, ed. and tr. Wladimir Ivanow (Bombay, 1959), p. 23 (English trans.), pp. 23–24 (Persian text). I have amended Ivanow's translation here. This account is also reproduced in the third chapter of the *Kalām-i pīr*, a later text that was partially adapted from the *Haft bāb*; see *Kalāmi pīr: A Treatise on Ismaili Doctrine, also (wrongly) called Haft-Bābi Shah Sayyid Nāṣir*, ed. and tr. Wladimir Ivanow (Bombay, 1935), p. 44 (English trans.), p. 51 (Persian text).

9 One noteworthy exception to this paradigm is a 16th-century text from Central Asia produced within the community of the rival and now defunct Muḥammad-Shāhī lineage of Nizārī imams, titled the *Irshād al-ṭālibīn fī dhikr a'immat al-Ismā'īliyya*. In this work, the bulk of which consists of a genealogy of the Nizārī imams, the mention of Ḥasan *'alā dhikrihi'l-salām* passes without further comment or reference to the *qiyāma*. In this regard, the organisation of the work resembles much more closely the presentation found in the later Nizārī historiography of the 19th and 20th centuries, discussed further in the section entitled 'A New Vision of History'. Too little is known of this rival line of Nizārī imams to enable us account for this omission, but it may be related to the particular genealogical claims and legitimising paradigm it sought to uphold. I have consulted MSS 1959/24 (dated 1144/1732–1733) and 1963/12 (dated 1327/1909–1910) in the Institute of Oriental Studies of the Academy of Sciences of Tajikistan (the former copy is not included in the catalogue description of the manuscript). MS 1963/12 contains a lacuna in this section, omitting the name of Imam Ḥasan II and his immediate successor, while the sobriquet *'alā dhikrihi'l-salām* is erroneously assigned here to a later imam, 'Alā' al-Dīn Muḥammad.

10 It should be emphasised here that the study of Nizārī history in the post-Mongol era remains in its infancy, and many of the essential manuscript collections for this period in Iran, India and, in particular, Central Asia still remain largely unexplored. Hence, it is not inconceivable that new textual discoveries in the future may provide additional nuance to this argument. For studies reviewing the Nizārī literature of the post-Mongol era, see Daniel Beben, 'The Legendary Biographies of Nāṣir-i Khusraw: Memory and Textualization in Early Modern Persian Ismā'īlism' (PhD thesis, Indiana University, 2015); Shafique N. Virani, *The Ismailis in*

the Middle Ages: A History of Survival, a Search for Salvation (Oxford, 2007).

11 The primary exception here is the work of Nāṣir-i Khusraw, who appears to be the only Fatimid-era author whose writings were preserved in the Nizārī communities. For a further discussion of this issue, see Beben, 'The Legendary Biographies of Nāṣir-i Khusraw', pp. 114–119.

12 For an overview of this era, see Daftary, *The Ismāʿīlīs*, pp. 403–422; Virani, *Ismailis in the Middle Ages*.

13 On Safawid persecution of the Nizārī imams, see Said Amir Arjomand, *The Shadow of God and the Hidden Imam: Religion, Political Order and Societal Change in Shiʿite Iran from the Beginning to 1890* (Chicago, 1984), pp. 112–116; Farhad Daftary, 'Shāh Ṭāhir and the Nizārī Ismaili Disguises', in T. Lawson, ed., *Reason and Inspiration in Islam: Theology, Philosophy and Mysticism in Muslim Thought: Essays in Honour of Hermann Landolt* (London, 2005), pp. 395–406; Daftary, *The Ismāʿīlīs*, pp. 435–436.

14 For a further discussion of the relationship between Imam Ḥasan ʿAlī and Nādir Shāh and its sources see Beben, 'The Legendary Biographies of Nāṣir-i Khusraw', pp. 257–264.

15 Muḥammad Taqī b. ʿAlī Riḍā Maḥallātī, *Āthār-i Muḥammadī*, MS 919, Institute of Ismaili Studies, pp. 15–16.

16 On this see Ernest Tucker, *Nadir Shah's Quest for Legitimacy in post-Safavid Iran* (Gainesville, FL, 2006).

17 On Nādir Shāh's religious policies, see Hamid Algar, 'Religious Forces in Eighteenth- and Nineteenth-Century Iran', in P. Avery, G.R.G. Hambly and C. Melville, ed., *The Cambridge History of Iran*, vol. 7: *From Nadir Shah to the Islamic Republic* (Cambridge, 1991), pp. 706–710; Ḥ Algar, 'Shiʿism and Iran in the Eighteenth Century', in T. Naff and R. Owens, ed., *Studies in Eighteenth Century Islamic History* (Carbondale, IL, 1977), pp. 288–302; Ernest Tucker, 'Nadir Shah and the Jaʿfari *Madhhab* Reconsidered', *Iranian Studies*, 27 (1994), pp. 163–179.

18 This notion of Ismailism as an element of the Jaʿfarī *madhhab* has more recently been evoked by Aga Khan IV, who gave his support on behalf of the Nizārīs to the Amman Declaration of 2004, which established the Jaʿfarī *madhhab* as one of eight recognised schools of Islamic law. In his message of support for the declaration, the Aga Khan declared that: 'Our historic adherence is to the Jafari Madhhab and other Madhahib of close affinity, and it continues, under the leadership

of the hereditary Ismaili Imam of the time.' See http://ammanmessage.com/letter-from-h-h-the-aga-khan/ (accessed 25 January 2017).

19 On the Nizārī relationship with the Sufi orders in the post-Mongol era, see Farhad Daftary, 'Ismaili-Sufi Relations in post-Alamut Persia', in F. Daftary, *Ismailis in Medieval Muslim Societies* (London, 2005), pp. 183–203.

20 Daftary, 'Shāh Ṭāhir and the Nizārī Ismaili Disguises', pp. 395–406.

21 For example, see Muḥammad Kāẓim Marvī, *'Ālamārā-yi Nādirī*, ed. Muḥammad Amīn Riyāḥī (Tehran, 1364 Sh./1985), vol. 3, p. 1182.

22 Aḥmad 'Alī Khān Vazīrī, *Jughrāfiyā-yi Kirmān*, ed. Muḥammad Ibrāhīm Bāstānī Pārīzī (Tehran, 1340 Sh./1961), p. 265. The reference to the Ḥaydarābādīs in this account most probably refers to the town of Ḥaydarābād in the province of Sindh in present-day Pakistan, where the Nizārī imams likewise have had a strong community of followers since the early modern era.

23 Aga Khan Maḥallātī, Ḥasan 'Alī Shāh, *Tārīkh-i 'ibrat-afzā*, ed. Ḥusayn Kūhī Kirmānī (Tehran, 1325 Sh./1946), p. 10.

24 Nile Green, 'Blessed Men and Tribal Politics: Notes on Political Culture in the Indo-Afghan World', *Journal of the Economic and Social History of the Orient*, 49 (2006), pp. 344–360. For the classic study of this phenomenon in the context of highland Morocco, see Ernest Gellner, *Saints of the Atlas* (London, 1969). This claim to broader social and religious authority on the basis of sayyid status echoes practices from the Fatimid era as well; see Shainool Jiwa, 'Kinship, Camaraderie and Contestation: Fāṭimid Relations with the *Ashrāf* in the Fourth/Tenth Century', *Al-Masāq*, 28 (2016), pp. 242–264.

25 Aḥmad 'Alī Khān Vazīrī, *Tārīkh-i Kirmān*, ed. Muḥammad Ibrāhīm Bāstānī Pārīzī (Tehran, 1340 Sh./1961), pp. 332–333.

26 On this imam, see also Sayyid 'Alī Āl-i Dāvud, 'Abū al-Ḥasan Khān Beglerbegī Maḥallātī', *Encyclopaedia Islamica*, vol. 2, pp. 29–32; Heribert Busse, 'Abu'l-Ḥasan Khan Maḥallātī', *Encyclopaedia Iranica*, vol. 1, p. 310; Daftary, *The Ismā'īlīs*, pp. 459–462.

27 Vazīrī, *Tārīkh-i Kirmān*, pp. 334–341. On Zand rule in Kirmān see John R. Perry, *Karim Khan Zand: A History of Iran, 1747–1779* (Chicago, 1979), pp. 134–136; James M. Gustafson, 'Kerman viii: Afsharid and Zand Period', *Encyclopaedia Iranica*, (online).

28 On these events, see also Riḍā Qulī Khān Hidāyat, *Rawḍat al-ṣafā-yi Nāṣirī* (Tehran, 1339 Sh./1960), vol. 9, pp. 250–252.

29 On the imamate of Shāh Khalīl Allāh, see Daftary, *The Ismāʿīlīs*, pp. 462–464.
30 On Kirmān in the early Qājār era, see James M. Gustafson, 'Kerman ix: Qajar Period', *Encyclopaedia Iranica*, (online).
31 Aga Khan Maḥallātī, *Tārīkh-i ʿibrat-afzā*, pp. 9–10.
32 On these events, see Hamid Algar, 'The Revolt of Āghā Khān Maḥallātī and the Transference of the Ismāʿīlī Imāmate to India', *Studia Islamica*, 29 (1969), pp. 55–81; Daftary, *The Ismāʿīlīs*, pp. 464–473.
33 *ʿIbrat-afzā* was originally published by the Aga Khan's lithograph press in Bombay in 1278/1862. An edition of the text, with numerous typographical errors, was published by Ḥusayn Kūhī Kirmānī (Tehran, 1325 Sh./1946). Another version of the text, evidently based on the Kūhī Kirmānī edition but with several critical alterations (on which see below note 35) was published by Muḥsin Sāʿī in his *Āqā Khān Maḥallātī va firqa-yi Ismāʿīliyya* (Tehran, 1329 Sh./1950). A new edition and English translation of the text is currently in preparation by the present author. On *ʿIbrat-afzā* and its connection with the broader religious project pursued by the Aga Khan in this period, see also Nile Green, *Bombay Islam: The Religious Economy of the Western Indian Ocean, 1840–1915* (Cambridge, 2011), pp. 155–160.
34 Aga Khan Maḥallātī, *Tārīkh-i ʿibrat-afzā*, p. 56.
35 Ibid., pp. 20–21. This passage has been curiously altered in Sāʿī's edition of the text (p. 35), which reads here: 'Likewise, is it evident that in Egypt several generations of my ancestors held the positions of kingship and the caliphate, and they revived the Shiʿi faith, which up to that time had fallen into despondency', omitting the reference to the Safawids (perhaps out of concern for the sensibilities of his Iranian Ithnāʿasharī readers).
36 On this claim, see Abbas Amanat, *Pivot of the Universe: Nasir al-Din Shah Qajar and the Iranian Monarchy, 1831–1896* (Berkeley, 1997), p. 2.
37 Priscilla Soucek, 'Coinage of the Qajars: A System in Continual Transition', *Iranian Studies*, 34 (2001), pp. 51–87; P. Soucek, 'The Visual Language of Qajar Medals', in D. Behrens-Abouseif and S. Vernoit, ed., *Islamic Art in the 19th Century: Tradition, Innovation, and Eclecticism* (Leiden, 2006), pp. 308–310. On Qājār appropriation of the Safawid legacy, see also Sussan Babaie, 'In the Eye of the Storm: Visualizing the Qajar Axis of Kingship', *Artibus Asiae*, 66 (2006), pp. 35–54.

38 Hamid Algar, *Religion and State in Iran, 1785–1906: The Role of the Ulama in the Qajar Period* (Berkeley, 1969), p. 41.

39 *Même s'il fut une époque où les Imams ismaïlis étaient aussi Califes, c'est-à-dire chefs d'Etats — par exemple en Egypte à l'époque fatimide — ma fonction est aujourd'hui apolitique; tout ismaïli étant avant tout un citoyen ou une citoyenne de son pays de naissance ou d'adoption. Le champ d'action de l'Imamat ismaïli est pourtant considérablement plus important qu'à cette époque lointaine, puisqu'il déploie aujourd'hui ses activités dans de nombreuses régions du monde.* See: http://www.akdn.org/speech/his-highness-aga-khan/address-both-houses-parliament-canada-house-commons-chamber (accessed 25 August 2016).

40 On this point, see further the recent study by Daryoush Mohammad Poor, *Authority without Territory: The Aga Khan Development Network and the Ismaili Imamate* (New York, 2014).

41 On the role of religious pluralism in Fatimid governance see Shainool Jiwa, 'Inclusive Governance: A Fatimid Illustration', in A.B. Sajoo, ed., *A Companion to the Muslim World* (London, 2009), pp. 157–176.

42 On this project, see http://www.akdn.org/publication/aga-khan-trust-culture-al-azhar-park-cairo-and-revitalisation-darb-al-ahmar (accessed 25 January 2017). Similar efforts to lay claim to the Fatimid heritage in Egypt have also been pursued in modern times by the Bohra Ismaili community, on which see Paula Sanders, *Creating Medieval Cairo: Empire, Religion and Architectural Preservation in Nineteenth-Century Egypt* (Cairo, 2008), pp. 115–142.

43 The text was published as Shihāb al-Dīn Shāh Ḥusaynī, *Khiṭābāt-i ʿāliya*, ed. Hushang Ojaqi (Bombay, 1963). On this work, see also Farhad Daftary, *Ismaili Literature: A Bibliography of Sources and Studies* (London, 2004), p. 152.

44 Shihāb al-Dīn Shāh, *Khiṭābāt-i ʿāliya*, pp. 37–45.

45 On the work and its author, see Farhad Daftary, 'Fedāʾī Ḵorāsānī', *Encyclopaedia Iranica*, vol. 9, p. 470; Daftary, *Ismaili Literature*, p. 112. Several later copies of this work are preserved among the Nizārīs in Central Asia. According to Daftary, these copies, which formed the basis for Semenov's edition, demonstrate numerous corruptions from the original text of Fidāʾī Khurāsānī's work preserved in Iran, which remains unpublished. On this see Daftary, 'Kitābī na-chandān muhimm dar tārīkh-i Ismāʿīliyya',

Nashr-i Dānish, 4 (1984), pp. 32–37. I have compared Semenov's edition with one manuscript of the text made available to me in Dushanbe, MS 1960/17, dated 1343/1924–1925. The Iranian manuscripts of Fidā'ī Khurāsānī's original work were not available to me.

46 While an earlier historiographical tradition was maintained under the Fatimids, these sources were almost entirely lost in subsequent centuries and were evidently not available to medieval Nizārī authors. Several chronicles and biographies were composed by individuals in the early Nizārī community of the Alamūt period, but none of these are known to have survived, although some of them were consulted by the non-Ismaili historians of the Mongol era, such as Juwaynī and Rashīd al-Dīn; on this, see F. Daftary, 'Persian Historiography of the Early Nizārī Ismā'īlīs,' *Iran: Journal of the British Institute of Persian Studies*, 30 (1992), pp. 91–97.

47 Muḥammad b. Zayn al-'Ābidīn Fidā'ī Khurāsānī, *Hidāyat al-mu'minīn al-ṭālibīn*, ed. A.A. Semenov (Moscow, 1959), p. 4.

48 Shihāb al-Dīn Shāh Ḥusaynī, *Khiṭābāt-i 'āliya*, p. 39; Fidā'ī Khurāsānī, *Hidāyat al-mu'minīn al-ṭālibīn*, pp. 110–111.

Bibliography

ʿAbbās, I. ʿal-Jānib al-siyāsī min riḥlat Ibn al-ʿArabī ilā al-mashriqʾ, *al-Abḥāth*, 16 (1963), pp. 217–236.

Abbot, Nabia. ʿTwo Būyid Coins in the Oriental Instituteʾ, *The American Journal of Semitic Languages and Literatures*, 56 (1939), pp. 350–364.

ʿAbd al-Razzāq. *al-Muṣannaf fiʾl-ḥadīth*, ed. Ḥabīb al-Raḥmān al-Aʿẓamī. Beirut, 1390–1392/1970–1972.

Abū Dāwūd al-Sijistānī, Sulaymān b. al-Ashʿath. *Sunan Abī Dāwūd*. Ḥums, 1969.

Abū Isḥāq Quhistānī. *Haft bāb*, ed. and trans. W. Ivanow. Bombay, 1959.

Abuʾl-ʿArab Muḥammad b. Aḥmad b. Tamīm al-Qayrawānī. *Ṭabaqāt ʿulamāʾ Ifrīqiya wa Tūnis*, ed. ʿAlī al-Shābbī and Naʿīm Ḥasan al-Yāfī. Tunis, 1968.

Abuʾl-Fidā, al-Malik al-Muʾayyad ʿImād al-Dīn Ismāʿīl b. ʿAlī. *Mukhtaṣar taʾrīkh al-bashar*. Cairo, 1325/1907.

Abū Shāma, Shihāb al-Dīn. *al-Bāʿith ʿalā inkār al-bidaʿ waʾl-ḥawādith*, ed. ʿUthmān Aḥmad ʿAnbar. Cairo, 1398/1978.

Adang, C. ʿWomen's Access to Public Space According to *al-Muḥallā biʾl-Āthār*ʾ, in M. Marín and R. Deguilhem, ed., *Writing the Feminine: Women in Arab Sources*. New York, 2002, pp. 75–94.

Aga Khan Maḥallātī, Ḥasan ʿAlī Shāh. *Tārīkh-i ʿibrat-afzā*, ed. Ḥusayn Kūhī Kirmānī. Tehran, 1325 Sh./1946.

Al-i Davud, Sayyid Ali. ʿAbū al-Ḥasan Khān Beglerbegī Maḥallātīʾ, *Encyclopaedia Islamica*, vol. 2, pp. 29–32.

Algar, Hamid. *Religion and State in Iran, 1785–1906: The Role of the Ulama in the Qajar Period*. Berkeley, 1969.

———. ʿReligious Forces in Eighteenth- and Nineteenth-Century Iranʾ, in P. Avery, G.R.G. Hambly and C. Melville ed., *The Cambridge*

History of Iran, Volume. 7: *From Nadir Shah to the Islamic Republic*. Cambridge, 1991, pp. 705–731.

———. 'Shiʿism and Iran in the Eighteenth Century', in T. Naff and R. Owens, ed., *Studies in Eighteenth Century Islamic History*. Carbondale, IL, 1977, pp. 288–302.

———. 'The Revolt of Āghā Khān Maḥallātī and the Transference of the Ismāʿīlī imamate to India', *Studia Islamica*, 29 (1969), pp. 55–81.

Amanat, Abbas. *Pivot of the Universe: Nasir al-Din Shah Qajar and the Iranian Monarchy, 1831–1896*. Berkeley, 1997.

al-ʿArabī, Abū Bakr Muḥammad b. ʿAbd Allāh al-Maʿāfirī. *Aḥkām al-Qurʾān*, ed. ʿAlī Muḥammad al-Bijawī. Cairo, 1376–1378/1957–1958.

ʿArīb b. Saʿd. *Ṣilat taʾrīkh al-Ṭabarī*, ed. M.J. de Goeje. Leiden, 1897.

Assaad, Sadik A. *The Reign of al-Hakim bi Amr Allah (386/996–411/1021): A Political Study*. Beirut, 1974.

Avila, M.L. 'Women in Andalusi Biographical Sources', in M. Marin and R. Deguilhem, ed., *Writing the Feminine: Women in Arab Sources*. New York, 2002, pp. 149–164.

Ayoub, Muhammad. *Redemptive Suffering in Islam: A Study of the Devotional Aspects of ʿĀshūrāʾ in Twelver Shīʿism*. The Hague, 1978.

al-Baghdādī, Abū Manṣūr ʿAbd al-Qāhir b. Ṭāhir. *al-Farq bayn al-firaq*, ed. Muḥammad Muḥyī al-Dīn ʿAbd al-Ḥamīd. Beirut, 1978; English trans., *Moslem Schisms and Sects*, Part II, tr. A.S. Halkin. Tel Aviv, 1935.

Bashir, Shahzad. 'On Islamic Time: Rethinking Chronology in the Historiography of Muslim Societies', *History and Theory*, 53 (2014), pp. 519–544.

Bauer, Karen. 'Spiritual Hierarchy and Gender Hierarchy in Fāṭimid Ismāʿīlī interpretations of the Qur'an', *Journal of Qurʾanic Studies*, 14 (2012), pp. 29–46.

al-Bayhaqī, Abū Bakr Aḥmad b. al-Ḥusayn al-Khusrawjirdī. *Kitāb al-sunan al-kubrā*. Hyderabad, 1344–1355/1925–1936.

Ben Cheneb, M. 'al-Ḳudūrī, Abu'l-Ḥusayn/al-Ḥasan Aḥmad', *EI2*.

Berkey, Jonathan. *Popular Preaching and Religious Authority in the Medieval Islamic Near East*. Seattle, 2001.

———. 'Tradition, Innovation and the Social Construction of Knowledge in the Medieval Islamic Near East', *Past and Present*, 146 (1995), pp. 38–65.

Bernheimer, Teresa. *The ʿAlids: The First Family of Islam, 750–1200*. Edinburgh, 2013.

Bianquis, Thierry. *Damas et la Syrie sous la domination fatimide (359-468/969-1076)*, Damascus, 1986–1989.

Bloom, Jonathan. 'The Early Fatimid Blue Koran Manuscript', *Graeco-Arabica*, 4 (1991), pp. 171–178.

Bosworth, C. E. "Uḳaylids', *EI2*.

———. 'Mazyad', *EI2*.

Brett, Michael. *The Rise of the Fatimids: The World of the Mediterranean and the Middle East in the Fourth Century of the Hijra, Tenth Century CE*. Leiden, 2001.

———. 'Badr al-Ǧamālī and the Fatimid Renaissance', in U. Vermeulen and J. Van Steenbergen, ed., *Egypt and Syria in the Fatimid, Ayyubid and Mamluk Eras*, IV. Leuven, 2005, pp. 61–78.

———. "Abbasids, Fatimids and Seljuqs', in *The New Cambridge Medieval History,* Volume IV. *c. 1024–c. 1998 Part II*, ed. D. Luscombe and J. Riley-Smith. Cambridge, 2004, pp. 675–721.

Brockelmann, C. 'al-Sharīf al-Murtaḍā', *EI2*.

Brunschvig, R. *La Berbérie Orientale sous les Ḥafṣides, des origines à la fin du XVe siècle*. Paris, 1940–1947.

———. *Études d'Islamologie*. Paris, 1976.

———. 'Argumentation fāṭimide contre le raisonnement juridique par analogie (*qiyās*)', in R. Arnaldez and S. van Riet, ed., *Recherches d'Islamologie. Recueil d'articles offert à Georges C. Anawati et Louis Gardet par leur collègues et amis*. Louvain, 1977, pp. 75–84; reprinted in his *Études sur l'Islam classique et l'Afrique du Nord*. London, 1986.

———. 'Le culte et le temps dans l'Islam classique', *Revue d'histoire des religions*, 177 (1970), pp. 183–193; reprinted in his *Études d'Islamologie*, vol. 1, pp. 183–193.

———. 'Devoir et pouvoir, histoire d'un problème de théologie musulmane', *Studia Islamica*, 20 (1964), pp. 5–46; reprinted in his *Études d'Islamologie*, vol. 1, pp. 179–220.

———. 'Fiqh fatimide et histoire de l'Ifriqiya', in *Mélanges d'histoire et d'archéologie de l'occident musulman II: Hommage à Georges Marcais*. Algiers, 1957, pp. 13–20; reprinted in his *Études d'Islamologie*, vol. 1, pp. 63–70.

———. 'Polémiques médiévales autour du rite de Mālik', *Al-Andalus*, 15 (1950), pp. 377–435; reprinted in his *Études d'Islamologie*, vol. 2, pp. 65–120.

Buckley, Jorunn J. 'The Nizârî Ismâ'îlîtes' Abolishment of the Sharî'a during the "Great Resurrection" of 1164 A.D./559 A.H.', *Studia Islamica*, 60 (1984), pp. 137–165.

al-Bukhārī, Muḥammad b. Ismā'īl. *Ṣaḥīḥ al-Bukhārī*, ed. Muḥammad Muḥsin Khān. New Delhi, 1984.

Bulliet, Richard W. *The Patricians of Nishapur: A Study in Medieval Islamic Social History*. Cambridge, MA, 1972.

Busse, Heribert. 'Abu'l-Ḥasan Khan Maḥallātī', *Encyclopædia Iranica*, vol. 1, p. 310.

Calderini, S. 'Contextualizing Arguments about Female Ritual Leadership (Women Imams) in Classical Islamic Sources', *Comparative Islamic Studies*, 5 (2009), pp. 5–32.

Campo, Juan. 'Muslim Ways of Death: Between the Prescribed and the Performed', in K. Garces-Foley, ed., *Death and Religion in a Changing World*. New York, 2006, pp. 147–177.

Canard, Marius. 'al-Basāsīrī', *EI2*.

Cilardo, A. *Diritto ereditario Islamico delle scuole giuridiche Ismailita e Imamita*. Rome, 1993.

Combe, Ét., et al., ed., *Répertoire chronologique d'épigraphie arabe*. Cairo, 1933–.

Cook, Michael. *Commanding Right and Forbidding Wrong in Islamic Thought*. Cambridge, 2000.

Corbin, Henry. *Cyclical Time and Ismaili Gnosis*. tr. R. Manheim and J.W. Morris. London, 1983.

Cortese, Delia. *Arabic Ismaili Manuscripts: The Zāhid 'Alī Collection in the Library of The Institute of Ismaili Studies*. London, 2003.

———. 'Voices of the Silent Majority: The Transmission of Sunnī Learning in Fāṭimī Egypt', *Jerusalem Studies in Arabic and Islam*, 39 (2012), pp. 345–366.

———. '"A Woman's Work is Never Done": Women and the Da'wa in Early Ismā'īlīsm', in U. Vermeulen and K. D'Hulster, ed., *Egypt and Syria in the Fatimid, Ayyubid and Mamluk Eras*, V. Leuven, 2007, pp. 63–72.

———. 'The Ismā'īlī Resurrection of Alamūt: A Bid for Spiritual Awakening or a Statement of Political Authority?', in S.E. Porter et al., ed., *Resurrection (Journal for the Study of the New Testament)*, Supplement 186 (1999), pp. 249–262.

——— and Calderini, S. *Women and the Fatimids in the World of Islam*. Edinburgh, 2006.

Crone, Patricia. *Medieval Islamic Political Thought*. Edinburgh, 2004.

Daftary, F. *The Ismā'īlīs: Their History and Doctrines*. 2nd ed., Cambridge, 2007.

———. *Ismaili Literature: A Bibliography of Sources and Studies*. London, 2004.

———. *The Assassin Legends: Myths of the Isma'ilis*. London, 1994.
———. 'The Ismaili *Da'wa* Outside the Fatimid *Dawla*', in M. Barrucand, ed., *L'Égypte Fatimide: Son art et son histoire*. Paris, 1999, pp. 29–43.
———. 'Cyclical Time and Sacred History in Medieval Ismaili Thought', in K. D'Hulster and J. Van Steenbergen, ed., *Continuity and Change in the Realms of Islam: Studies in Honour of Professor Urbain Vermeulen*. Leuven, 2008, pp. 151–158.
———. 'The 'Order of the Assassins': J. von Hammer and the Orientalist Misrepresentations of the Nizari Ismailis', *Iranian Studies*, 39 (2006), pp. 71–81.
———. 'Shāh Ṭāhir and the Nizārī Ismaili Disguises', in T. Lawson, ed., *Reason and Inspiration in Islam: Theology, Philosophy and Mysticism in Muslim Thought, Essays in Honour of Hermann Landolt*. London, 2005, pp. 395–406.
———. 'Ismaili-Sufi Relations in post-Alamut Persia', in F. Daftary, *Ismailis in Medieval Muslim Societies*. London, 2005, pp. 183–203.
———. 'A Major Schism in the Early Ismā'īlī Movement', *Studia Islamica*, 77 (1993), pp. 123–139; reprinted in F. Daftary, *Ismailis in Medieval Muslim Societies*. London, 2005, pp. 45–61.
———. 'Persian Historiography of the Early Nizārī Ismā'īlīs', *Iran: Journal of the British Institute of Persian Studies*, 30 (1992), pp. 91–97.
———. 'Kitābī na-chandān muhim dar tārīkh-i Ismā'īlīya', *Nashr-i Dānish*, 4 (1984), pp. 32–37.
———. 'Muḥammad b. Ismā'īl al-Maymūn', *EI2*, vol. 12, Supplement, pp. 634–635.
———. 'Fedā'ī Ḵorāsānī', *Encyclopædia Iranica*, vol. 9, p. 470.
———. 'Isma'ilism ii: Isma'ili Historiography', *Encyclopædia Iranica*, vol. 14, pp. 176–178.
De la Puente, Cristina. 'Juridical Sources for the Study of Women: Limitations of the Female's Capacity to Act According to Mālikī law', in M. Marín and R. Deguilhem, ed., *Writing the Feminine: Women in Arab Sources*. New York, 2002, pp. 95–110.
De Smet, Daniel. 'Comment déterminer le début et la fin du jeûne de Ramadan? Un point de discorde entre sunnites et ismaéliens en Égypte fatimide', in U. Vermeulen and D. de Smet, ed., *Egypt and Syria in the Fatimid, Ayyubid and Mamluk eras*. Leuven, 1995, pp. 71–84.
———. 'al-Kirmānī, Ḥamīd al-Dīn', *EI3*.
Denny, F.M. 'The Adab of Qur'ān Recitation: Text and Context', in A.J. Johns and S.H.M. Jafri, ed., *International Congress for the Study of the Qur'ān*. Canberra, 1982, pp. 143–160.

Dernouny, M. 'Aspects de la culture et de l'Islam du Maghreb médiéval: Le cas de l'hérésie Bargwāṭa', *Peuples méditerranéens: revue trimestrielle*, 34 (1986), pp. 89–97.

al-Dhahabī, Shams al-Dīn Abū ʿAbd Allāh Muḥammad. *al-ʿIbar fī khabar man ghabar*, ed. Ṣalāḥ al-Dīn al-Munajjid. Kuwait, 1960–1966.

———. *Siyar aʿlām al-nubalāʾ*, ed. Shuʿayb al-Arnaʾūṭ et al. Beirut, 1410/1990.

———. *Taʾrīkh al-Islām wa wafayāt al-mashāhīr waʾl-aʿlām*. Beirut, 1987–1999; ed. ʿUmar ʿAbd al-Salām al-Tadmurī. Beirut, 1413/1993.

Djebli, Moktar. 'al-Sharīf al-Raḍī', *EI2*.

Donohue, John J. *The Buwayhid Dynasty in Iraq: 334H./945 to 403H./102 – Shaping Institutions for the Future*. Leiden and Boston, 2003.

El Cheikh, Nadia. 'Mourning and the Role of the Nāʾiḥa', in C. de la Puente, ed., *Identidades marginales*. Madrid, 2003, pp. 395–412.

Elad, Amikam. *Medieval Jerusalem and Islamic Worship: Holy Places, Ceremonies, Pilgrimage*. Leiden and New York, 1995.

van Ess, Josef. *Der Eine und das Andere. Beobachtungen an islamischen häresiographischen Texten*. Berlin, 2011.

Fehérvárí, G., 'Mihrāb', *EI2*.

Fidāʾī Khurāsānī, Muḥammad b. Zayn al-ʿĀbidīn. *Kitāb-i hidāyat al-muʾminīn al-ṭālibīn*, ed. A.A. Semenov. Moscow, 1959.

Fierro, M. 'al-Ṭurṭūšī, Abū Bakr', *Biblioteca de al-Andalus*, vol. 7, *De al-Qabrīrī a Zumurrud*, ed. Jorge Lirola Delgado. Almería, 2012, pp. 500–531.

———. 'al-Ṭurṭūshī', in *Christian-Muslim Relations: A Bibliographical History (1050–1200 CE)*, vol. 3, ed. D. Thomas, et al. Leiden and Boston, 2011, pp. 387–396.

———. 'Espacio sunní y espacio šīʿí', in *El esplendor de los omeyas cordobeses: La civilización musulmana de Europa Occidental. Exposición en Madīnat al-Zahrāʾ 3 de mayo a 30 de septiembre de 2001*. Granada, 2001, pp. 168–177.

———. 'Spiritual Alienation and Political Activism: The *ghurabāʾ* in al-Andalus during the Sixth/Twelfth Century', *Arabica*, 47 (2000), pp. 230–260.

———. 'The Celebration of ʿĀshūrāʾ in Sunnī Islam', *The Arabist (Proceedings of the 14th Congress of the Union Européenne des Arabisants et Islamisants)*, 13–14 (1994), pp. 193–208.

———. 'The Treatises Against Innovations (*kutub al-bidaʿ*)', *Der Islam*, 69 (1992), pp. 204–246.

———. 'La polémique á propos de *raf' al-yadayn fī l-ṣalāt* dans al-Andalus', *Studia Islamica*, 65 (1987), pp. 69–90.

———. 'El principio mālikí *sadd al-darā'i'* en el *Kitāb al-ḥawādiṯ wa-l-bida'* de Abū Bakr al-Ṭurṭūšī', *Al-Qanṭara*, 2 (1981), pp. 69–87.

Fyzee, Asaf A. A. 'Aspects of Fāṭimid Law', *Studia Islamica*, 31 (1970), pp. 81–91.

———. 'The Fatimid Law of Inheritance', *Studia Islamica*, 9 (1958), pp. 61–69.

Gellner, Ernest. *Saints of the Atlas*. London, 1969.

George, Alain. 'Calligraphy, Colour and Light in the Blue Qur'an', *Journal of Qur'anic Studies*, 11 (2009), pp. 75–125.

Goldziher, I. *Muslim Studies (Muhammedanische Studien)*, tr. S.M. Stern. London, 1967–1971.

Green, Nile. *Bombay Islam: The Religious Economy of the Western Indian Ocean, 1840–1915*. Cambridge, 2011.

———. 'Blessed Men and Tribal Politics: Notes on Political Culture in the Indo-Afghan World', *Journal of the Economic and Social History of the Orient*, 49 (2006), pp. 344–360.

Guillaume, A. 'Stroking an Idol', *Bulletin of the School of Oriental and African Studies*, 27 (1964), p. 340.

Gustafson, James M. 'Kerman viii: Afsharid and Zand Period', *Encyclopædia Iranica*, online edition, 2014.

al-Ḥabbāl, Ibrāhīm b. Sa'īd 'Abd Allāh. *Wafayāt al-Miṣriyyīn (375–456)*, ed. Abū 'Abd Allāh Maḥmūd b. Muḥammad al-Ḥaddād. Riyāḍ, 1408/1987.

Hajji, A. 'Institutions of Justice in Fatimid Egypt (358–567/969–1171)', in A. Al-Azmeh, ed., *Islamic Law. Social and Historical Contexts*. London and New York, 1988, pp. 198–214.

Halevi, Leor. *Muhammad's Grave: Death Rites and the Making of Islamic Society*. New York, 2006.

Halm, H. *Kalifen und Assassinen: Ägypten und der Vordere Orient zur Zeit der ersten Kreuzzüge, 1074–1171*. Munich, 2014.

———. *Die Kalifen von Kairo: Die Fatimiden in Ägypten 973–1074*. Munich, 2003.

———. *The Fatimids and their Traditions of Learning*. London, 1997.

———. *The Empire of the Mahdi: The Rise of the Fatimids*, tr. M. Bonner. Leiden, 1996.

———. 'Badr al-Ǧamālī—Wesir oder Militärdiktator?', in U. Vermeulen and K. D'hulster, ed., *Egypt and Syria in the Fatimid, Ayyubid and Mamluk Eras*, V. Leuven, 2007, pp. 121–127.

——. 'The Isma'ili Oath of Allegiance (*'ahd*) and the 'Sessions of Wisdom (*majālis al-ḥikma*)' in Fatimid Times', in F. Daftary, ed., *Mediaeval Isma'ili History and Thought*. Cambridge, 1996, pp. 91–115.

——. 'Les Fatimides à Salamya', *Revue d'Études Islamiques*, 54 (1986), pp. 133–149.

——. 'Die Söhne Zikrawaihs und das erste fatimidische Kalifat (290/903)', *Die Welt des Orients*, 10 (1979), pp. 30–53.

Hamdani Abbas and F. de Blois, 'A Re-examination of al-Mahdī's Letter to the Yemenites on the Genealogy of the Fatimid Caliphs', *Journal of the Royal Asiatic Society* (1983), pp. 173–207.

al-Hamdānī, Ḥusayn F., ed. and tr. *On the Genealogy of Fatimid Caliphs*. Cairo, 1958.

Hammer-Purgstall, Joseph von. *The History of the Assassins*, tr. O.C. Wood. London, 1835.

Hartmann, A. 'La prédication islamique au Moyen Age', *Quaderni di Studi Arabi*, 5–6 (1987–1988), pp. 337–346.

Harvey, L. P. 'The Moriscos and the Hajj', *BRISMES Bulletin*, 14 (1988), pp. 11–24.

al-Haythamī, 'Alī b. Abī Bakr. *Majma' al-zawā'id wa manba' al-fawā'id*. Cairo, 1352–1353/1933–1934.

den Heijer, Johannes. 'Le vizir fatimide Badr al-Ğamālī (466/1074–487/1094) et la nouvelle muraille du Caire: quelques remarques préliminaire', in U. Vermeulen and K. D'Hulster, ed., *Egypt and Syria in the Fatimid, Ayyubid and Mamluk Eras*, V. Leuven, 2007, pp. 91–107.

Hidāyat, Riḍā Qulī Khān. *Rawḍat al-ṣafā-yi Nāṣirī*. Tehran, 1339 Sh./1960.

al-Ḥillī, al-'Allāma Jamāl al-Dīn al-Ḥasan Ibn al-Muṭahhar. *Mukhtalaf al-shī'a fī aḥkām al-sharī'a*. Qum, 1371/1951–1952.

al-Ḥillī, al-Muḥaqqiq Abu'l-Qāsim. *Sharā'i' al-Islām fī masā'il al-ḥalāl wa'l-ḥarām*. Tehran, 1969.

al-Ḥimyarī, Muḥammad b. 'Abd al-Mun'im. *al-Rawḍ al-Mu'ṭār fī khabar al-aqṭār*, ed. Iḥṣān 'Abbās. Beirut, 1980.

Hodgson, Marshall G. S. *The Order of Assassins: The Struggle of the Early Nizārī Ismā'īlīs Against the Islamic World*. The Hague, 1955.

——. 'The Ismā'īlī State', in J.A. Boyle, ed., *The Cambridge History of Iran*: Volume 5, *The Saljuq and Mongol Periods*. Cambridge, 1968, pp. 422–482.

al-Ḥusaynī, Aḥmad b. Muḥammad. *Ṣilat al-takmila li-wafayāt al-naqala*, ed. Bashshār 'Awwād Ma'rūf. Beirut, 2007.

Ibn ʿAbdūn, 'Risāla fi'l-qaḍāʾ wa'l-ḥisba', in É. Lévi-Provençal, ed., *Trois traités hispaniques de ḥisba*. Cairo, 1955, pp. 1–65; tr. E. García Gómez and É. Lévi-Provençal as *Sevilla a comienzos del siglo XII. El tratado de Ibn ʿAbdūn*. Madrid, 1948.

Ibn Abī Shayba, Abū Bakr ʿAbd Allāh b. Muḥammad. *Kitāb al-muṣannaf fi'l-aḥādīth wa'l-āthār*, ed. ʿAbd al-Khāliq Khān al-Afghānī. Hyderabad, 1386–1390/1966–1970.

Ibn al-Abbār, Muḥammad b. ʿAbd Allāh. *al-Takmila li-kitāb al-ṣila*, ed. M.A. Alarcón and A. González Palencia in *Miscelánea de Estudios y Textos Árabes*. Madrid, 1915.

Ibn al-Athīr, ʿIzz al-Dīn Abu'l-Ḥasan ʿAlī. *al-Kāmil fi'l-ta'rīkh*, ed. C.J. Tornberg. Leiden, 1851–1876; reprinted Beirut, 1965–1967; ed. Muḥammad Yūsuf al-Daqqāq. Beirut, 1407/1987.

——. *al-Lubāb fī tahdhīb al-ansāb*. Cairo, 1938–1949.

——. *al-Bāb fī tahdhīb al-ansāb*. Baghdad, n.d.

Ibn Bābawayh, Abū Jaʿfar Muḥammad b. ʿAlī al-Ṣadūq. *Man lā yaḥḍuruhu'l-faqīh*. Tehran, 1390/1970.

Ibn al-Dawādārī, Abū Bakr b. ʿAbd Allāh. *Kanz al-durar wa jāmiʿ al-ghurar*, part six, *al-Durra al-muḍiyya fī akhbār al-dawla al-fāṭimiyya*, ed. Ṣ. al-Munajjid. Cairo, 1961.

Ibn Farḥūn, Ibrāhīm b. ʿAlī b. Muḥammad. *al-Dībāj al-mudhahhab fī maʿrifat aʿyān ʿulamāʾ al-madhhab*. Cairo, 1423/2003.

Ibn Ḥajar al-ʿAsqalānī, Aḥmad b. ʿAlī. *Tabyīn al-ʿajab bi mā warada fī faḍl Rajab*. Beirut, 1988.

Ibn al-Ḥajj. *Madkhal al-sharʿ al-sharīf*. Cairo, 1380/1960.

Ibn Ḥayyān, Abū Marwān Ḥayyān b. Khalaf. *al-Muqtabis fī akhbār balad al-Andalus*, ed. A.R. Ḥājjī. Beirut, 1965.

Ibn Ḥazm, Abū Muḥammad ʿAlī b. Aḥmad. *al-Muḥallā bi'l-āthār*. Cairo, 1348/1929.

——. *Naqṭ al-ʿarūs fī tawārikh al-khulafāʾ*, ed. C. F. Seybold, in *Revista del Centro de Estudios Históricos de Granada y su reino*, 1 (1911), pp. 160–180 and 237–248; Spanish trans. by L. Seco de Lucena. Valencia, 1974.

Ibn al-ʿImād, ʿAbd al-Ḥayy b. Aḥmad. *Shadharāt al-dhahab fī akhbār min dhahab*. Beirut, 1350/1982.

Ibn ʿInaba, Jamāl al-Dīn Aḥmad b. ʿAlī. *ʿUmdat al-ṭālib fī ansāb āl Abī Ṭālib*, ed. Muḥammad Ḥusayn al-Ṭāliqānī. Najaf, 1380/1961.

Ibn al-Jawzī, ʿAbd al-Raḥmān b. ʿAlī. *Kitāb al-mawḍūʿāt*, ed. A.R.M. ʿUthmān. Medina, 1386–1388/1966–1968.

——. *al-Muntaẓam fī ta'rīkh al-mulūk wa'l-umam*, ed. Muḥammad A. ʿAṭā and Muṣṭafā A. ʿAṭā. Beirut, 1412/1992.

——. *Talbīs Iblīs*, ed. Khayr al-Dīn ʿAlī. Beirut, n.d.

Ibn al-Kathīr, ʿImād al-Dīn Ismāʿīl b. ʿUmar. *al-Bidāya waʾl-nihāya*, ed. Ṣalāḥ Muḥammad al-Khaymī. 2nd ed., Damascus, 2010.

Ibn Khalaf, ʿAlī. *Mawādd al-bayān*, published in fascimile, Frankfurt, 1986; ed. Ḥusayn ʿAbd al-Laṭīf. Tripoli, Libya, 1982.

Ibn Khaldūn, ʿAbd al-Raḥmān b. Muḥammad. *al-Muqaddima*, tr. F. Rosenthal as *The Muqaddimah: An Introduction to History*. London, 1958; 2nd ed., Princeton, 1980.

——. *Kitāb al-ʿibar*, ed. Khalīl Shaḥāda and Suhayl Zakkār as *Taʾrīkh Ibn Khaldūn*. Beirut, 1431/2001.

Ibn Khallikān, Aḥmad b. Muḥammad. *[Wafayāt al-aʿyān] Ibn Khallikan's Biographical Dictionary*, tr. W. MacGuckin de Slane. Paris, 1842–1871.

Ibn Muyassar, Tāj al-Dīn Muḥammad. *al-Muntaqā min Akhbār Miṣr*, ed. A. F. Sayyid. Cairo, 1981.

Ibn al-Nadīm, Muḥammad b. Isḥāq. *Kitāb al-Fihrist*, tr. Bayard Dodge as *The Fihrist: A Tenth Century Survey of Muslim Culture*. New York, 1970.

Ibn al-Qalānisī, Abū Yaʿlā Ḥamza. *Dhayl taʾrīkh Dimashq*, ed. H.F. Amedroz. Leiden and Beirut, 1908.

Ibn Rushd, Abū Walīd Muḥammad b. Aḥmad, al-Jadd. *Kitāb al-bayān waʾl-taḥṣīl waʾl-sharḥ waʾl-tawjīh waʾl-taʿlīl fī masāʾil al-mustakhraja*, ed. M. Hajji et al. 2nd ed., Beirut, 1988–1991.

Ibn Rushd (Averroes) al-Ḥafīd, Aḥmad b. Muḥammad. *Bidāyat al-mujtahid wa nihāyat al-muqtaṣid*. Cairo, n.d.

Ibn Saʿīd al-Maghribī, ʿAlī b. Mūsā. *al-Mughrib fī ḥulāʾl-Maghrib*, ed. Sh. Ḍayf. Cairo, 1964.

Ibn al-Ṣayrafī, Abuʾl-Qāsim ʿAlī. *al-Ishāra ilā man nāla al-wizāra*, ed. ʿA. Mukhliṣ. Cairo, 1924; ed. Ayman F. Sayyid. Cairo, 1990.

Ibn Taghrībirdī, Abuʾl-Maḥāsin Jamāl al-Dīn Yūsuf. *al-Nujūm al-zāhira fī mulūk Miṣr waʾl-Qāhira*. Cairo, 1348–1392/1929–1972; Beirut, 1413/1992.

Ibn Taymiyya, Taqī al-Dīn Aḥmad. *Kitāb iqtiḍāʾ al-ṣirāṭ al-mustaqīm mukhālafat aṣḥāb al-jaḥīm*. Cairo, 1369/1950; tr. M. Umar Memon as *Ibn Taymīya's Struggle against Popular Religion*. Paris, 1976.

Ibn al-Zayyāt. *al-Kawākib al-siyāra*. Baghdad, [19–].

Idris, Hady R. 'Deux juristes kairouanais de l'époque zīride: Ibn Abī Zayd et al-Qābisī', *Annales de l'Institut d'Études Orientales*, 12 (1954), pp. 173–198.

Idrīs ʿImād al–Dīn b. al-Ḥasan. *ʿUyūn al-akhbār*, vol. 4, ed. M. al-Saghirji. Damascus and London, 2007; vol. 7, ed. Ayman F. Sayyid. London,

2002; tr. Shainool Jiwa as *The Founder of Cairo: The Fatimid Imam-Caliph al-Mu'izz and his Era. An English translation of the section on al-Mu'izz from Idrīs 'Imād al-Dīn's 'Uyūn al-akhbār.* London, 2013.

———. *Kitāb zahr al-ma'ānī*, ed. M. Ghālib. Beirut, 1411/1991.

al-'Imād al-Iṣfahānī, Muḥammad b. Muḥammad. *Kharīdat al-qaṣr wa jarīdat al-'aṣr.* Damascus, 1955–1959.

Ivanow, Wladimir. *Ibn al-Qaddah (The Alleged Founder of Ismailism).* 2nd ed., Bombay, 1957.

———. *Ismaili Tradition Concerning the Rise of the Fatimids.* London, etc., 1942.

Jambet, Christian. *La grande résurrection d'Alamût: Les formes de la liberté dans le shî'isme ismaélien.* Lagrasse, 1990.

———. 'La grande résurrection d'Alamût d'après quelques textes Ismaéliens', in *Apocalypse et sens de l'histoire*; being *Cahiers de l'Université Saint Jean de Jerusalem*, 9 (1983), pp. 113–131.

Jiwa, Shainool. 'Kinship, Camaraderie and Contestation: Fāṭimid Relations with the Ashrāf in the Fourth/Tenth Century', *Al-Masāq*, 28 (2016), pp. 242–264.

———. 'Inclusive Governance: A Fatimid Illustration', in A.B. Sajoo, ed., *A Companion to the Muslim World.* London, 2009, pp. 157–176.

———. 'Fāṭimid-Būyid Diplomacy during the Reign of al-Azīz Billāh (365/975–386/996)', *Journal of Islamic Studies*, 3 (1992), pp. 57–71.

Juwaynī, 'Alā' al-Dīn 'Aṭā-Malik. *Ta'rīkh-i jahān-gushā*, tr. John A. Boyle as *The History of the World-Conqueror.* Cambridge, MA, 1958.

Juynboll, G.H.A. *Muslim Tradition: Studies in Chronology, Provenance and Authorship of Early ḥadīth.* Cambridge, 1983.

———. 'The Attitude towards Gold and Silver in Early Islam', in M. Vickers, ed., *Pots and Pans: A Colloquium on Precious Metals and Ceramics.* Oxford, 1986, pp. 107–115.

Kalāmi Pīr: A treatise on Ismaili Doctrine, also (wrongly) called Haft-Bābi Shah Sayyid Nasir, ed. and tr. Wladimir Ivanow. Bombay, 1935.

Kaptein, N.J.G. *Muhammad's Birthday Festival: Early History in the Central Muslim Lands and Development in the Muslim West until the 10th/16th Century.* Leiden, 1993.

Katz, Marion H. *Prayer in Islamic Thought and Practice.* Cambridge, 2013.

Kennedy, Hugh. *The Prophet and the Age of the Caliphate: The Islamic Near East from the Sixth to the Eleventh Century.* London, 1986.

al-Kindī, Abū ʿUmar Muḥammad. *Kitāb wulāt Miṣr*, ed. R. Guest. Leiden and London, 1912.

al-Kirmānī, Ḥamīd al-Dīn Aḥmad b. ʿAbd Allāh. *al-Maṣābīḥ fī ithbāt al-imāma*, ed. and tr., Paul E. Walker as *Master of the Age: An Islamic Treatise on the Necessity of the Imamate*. London, 2007.

Kister, Meir J. '"Do not assimilate yourselves ..."', *Jerusalem Studies in Arabic and Islam*, 12 (1989), pp. 321–371.

———. '"Shaʿbān is my month": A Study of an Early Tradition', *Studia Orientalia memoriae D.H. Baneth dedicata*. Jerusalem, 1979, pp. 15–37.

———. '"Rajab is the month of God ...": A Study in the Persistence of an early Tradition', *Israel Oriental Studies*, 1 (1971), pp. 191–223.

———. '"You shall only set out for three mosques": A Study of an Early Tradition', *Le Museón*, 82 (1969), pp. 173–196.

———. '"A Booth like the Booth of Moses ...": A Study of an Early *ḥadīth*', *Bulletin of the School of Oriental and African Studies*, 25 (1962), pp. 150–155.

Klemm, Verena. *Memoirs of a Mission: The Ismaili Scholar, Statesmen and Poet al-Mu'ayyad fi'l-Dīn al-Shīrāzī*. London, 2003.

Knappert, J. 'The Mawlid', *Orientalia Lovaniensia Periodica*, 19 (1988), pp. 209–215.

Kohlberg, Etan. 'Some Imāmī Shīʿī Views on the *Ṣaḥāba*', *Jerusalem Studies in Arabic and Islam*, 5 (1984), pp. 143–175.

al-Kulaynī, Abū Jaʿfar Muḥammad b. Yaʿqūb. *al-Furūʿ min al-Kāfī*. Beirut, 1401/1980–1981.

———. *al-Uṣūl min al-Kāfī*, ed. ʿA.A. al-Ghaffārī. Tehran, 1388/1968.

Lane, E.W. *An Account of the Manners and Customs of the Modern Egyptians*. London, 1846.

Laoust, Henri. *La profession de foi d'Ibn Baṭṭaṭa*. Damascus, 1958.

Leiser, Gary. *The Restoration of Sunnism in Egypt: Madrasa and Mudarrisūn 495–647/1101–1249*. Philadelphia, 1976.

———. 'Muslims from al-Andalus in the Madrasas of the Late Fāṭimid and Early Ayyūbid Egypt', *Al-Qantara*, 20 (1999), pp. 137–159.

———. 'The *Madrasa* and the Islamization of the Middle East: The Case of Egypt', *Journal of the American Research Center in Egypt*, 22 (1985), pp. 29–47.

———. 'Ḥanbalism in Egypt before the Mamlûks', *Studia Islamica*, 54 (1981), pp. 155–181.

Leisten, Th. 'Between Orthodoxy and Exegesis: Some Aspects of Attitudes in the Shariʿa Toward Funerary Architecture', *Muqarnas*, 7 (1990), pp. 12–22.

Lev, Yaacov. *State and society in Fatimid Egypt*. Leiden, 1991.

——. 'Piety and Political Activism in Twelfth century Egypt', *Jerusalem Studies in Arabic and Islam*, 31 (2006), pp. 289–324.

——. 'The Fāṭimid Imposition of Ismāʿīlism on Egypt (358–386/969–996)', *Zeitschrift der deutschen Morgenländischen Gesellschaft*, 138 (1988), pp. 313–325.

Lewis, Bernard. *The Origins of Ismāʿīlism: A Study of the Historical Background of the Fāṭimid Caliphate*. Cambridge, 1940; repr. New York, 1975.

Lohlker, Rüdiger. '*Bidʿa* in der Malikitischen Rechtsschule. Weitere Überlegungen zu Strukturen des Feldes des islamischen Rechts', *Zeitschrift der Deutschen Morgenländischen Gesellschaft*, 152 (2002), pp. 95–112.

Lutfi, H. 'Manners and Customs of Fourteenth-century Cairene Women: Female Anarchy versus Male Shariʿi Order in Muslim Prescriptive Treatises', in N. R. Keddie and B. Baron, ed., *Women in Middle Eastern History: Shifting Boundaries in Sex and Gender*. New Haven, CT, 1991, pp. 99–121.

McDermott, Martin J. *The Theology of al-Shaikh al-Mufīd (d. 413/1022)*. Beirut, 1978.

Madelung, W. 'Introduction', in F. Daftary and G. Miskinzoda, ed., *The Study of Shiʿi Islam: History, Theology and Law*. London, 2014, pp. 3–16.

——. 'The Religious Policy of the Fatimids toward their Sunnī Subjects in the Maghrib', in M. Barrucand, ed., *L'Egypte Fatimide: Son art et son histoire*. Paris, 1999, pp. 97–104.

——. 'The Fatimids and the Qarmaṭīs of Baḥrayn', in F. Daftary, ed., *Mediaeval Ismaʿili History and Thought*. Cambridge, 1996, pp. 21–73; reprinted in his *Studies in Medieval Shiʿism*, ed. S. Schmidtke. Farnham, UK, 2012, article X.

——. 'The Sources of Ismāʿīlī Law', *Journal of Near Eastern Studies*, 35 (1976), pp. 29–40; reprinted in his *Religious Schools and Sects in Medieval Islam*. London, 1985, article XVIII.

——. 'The Minor Dynasties of Northern Iran', in Richard N. Frye, ed., *The Cambridge History of Iran*, Volume 4: *The Period from the Arab Invasions to the Saljuqs*. Cambridge, 1975, pp. 198–249.

——. 'Das Imamat in der frühen Ismailitischen Lehre', *Der Islam*, 37 (1961), pp. 43–135; reprinted in his *Studies in Medieval Shiʿism*, ed. S. Schmidtke. Farnham, UK, 2012, article VII.

——. 'al-Mufīd', *EI2*.

——. 'Manṣūr al-Yaman', *EI2*.

Makdisi, Georges. *Ibn ʿAqīl et la résurgence de l'Islam traditionniste au XIe siècle*. Damascus, 1963.

Mālik b. Anas. *al-Muwaṭṭaʾ*, recension by Yaḥyā b. Yaḥyā. Beirut, 1401/1981.

Mansouri, M. T. 'Les *ʿulamāʾ* en rupture avec le pouvoir en Ifrīqiya d'après le *Kitāb al-miḥan*', *Mélanges de l'École française de Rome. Moyen Âge*, 115 (2003), pp. 565–580.

al-Maqdisī, Muḥammad b. ʿAbd al-Wahīd. *Ittibāʿ al-sunan wa ijtināb al-bidaʿ*, ed. M. Badr al-dīn al-Qahwajī and M. al-Arnāʾūṭ. Damascus and Beirut, 1407/1987.

al-Maqqarī, Abu'l-ʿAbbās Aḥmad. *Nafḥ al-ṭīb min ghuṣn al-Andalus al-raṭīb wa dhikr wazīrihā Lisān al-dīn Ibn al-Khaṭīb*, ed. I. ʿAbbās. Beirut, 1398/1968.

al-Maqrīzī, Taqī al-Dīn Aḥmad b. ʿAlī. *Ittiʿāẓ al-ḥunafāʾ bi-akhbār al-aʾimma al-fāṭimiyyīn al-khulafāʾ*, vol. I, ed. Jamāl al-Dīn al-Shayyāl and vols II-III, ed. Muḥammad Ḥilmī Muḥammad Aḥmad. Cairo, 1967-1973; new edition, ed. A. F. Sayyid, 4 vols. Damascus, 2010; partial tr. Shainool Jiwa, as *Towards a Shiʿi Mediterranean Empire: Fatimid Egypt and the Founding of Cairo; The reign of the Imam-caliph al-Muʿizz, from al-Maqrīzī's Ittiʿāz al-ḥunafāʾ*. London, 2009.

———. *Kitāb al-mawāʿiẓ waʾl-iʿtibār bi-dhikr al-khiṭaṭ waʾl-athār*, commonly known as *al-Khiṭaṭ*. Bulāq, 1270/1853–1854; Beirut, n.d.; ed. of *musawwada*, A.F. Sayyid. London, 1995. Complete edition by A.F. Sayyid. London, 2002–2004.

———. *Kitāb al-muqaffā al-kabīr*, ed. M. Yaʿlāwī. Beirut, 1411/1991.

Marçais, G. 'Dār', *EI2*, vol. 2, pp. 113–115.

al-Māwardī, ʿAlī b. Muḥammad. *The Ordinances of Government: A Translation of al-Aḥkām al-sulṭāniyya waʾl-wilāyāt al-dīniyya*, tr. Wafaa H. Wahba. Reading, 1996.

Mitha, Farouk. *Al-Ghazālī and the Ismailis. A Debate on Reason and Authority in Medieval Islam*. London, 2001.

Mottahedeh, Roy. 'Qurānic Commentary on the Verse of the Khums (an-Anfāl VIII:41)', in K. Morimoto, ed., *Sayyids and Sharifs in Muslim Socities: The Living Links to the Prophet*. London, 2012, pp. 37–48.

al-Mundhirī, Zakī al-Dīn Abū Aḥmad. *al-Takmila li-wafayāt al-naqala*, ed. Bashshār ʿAwwād Maʿrūf. Najaf, 1401/1981.

al-Muqaddasī, *Aḥsan al-taqāsīm fī maʿrifat al-aqālīm*, ed. M.J. de Goeje. Leiden, 1967; English trans. by B. Collins, corrected by Mohammad Hamid Altaʾi, as *The Best Division for Knowledge of the Regions*. Reading, 2001.

al-Musabbiḥī, Muḥammad. *Akhbār Miṣr*, ed. W.G. Millward. Cairo, 1980.

Muslim b. al-Ḥajjāj al-Qushayrī, *Ṣaḥīḥ Muslim*. Cairo, 2000.

al-Mustanṣir bi'llāh, Abū Tamīm Ma'add. *al-Sijillāt al-Mustanṣiriyya*, ed. 'Abd al-Mun'im Mājid. Cairo, 1954.

al-Nābulusī. *Faḍā'il al-ẓuhūr wa'l-ayyām wa yalīhi al-Lu'lu' al-maknūn fī ḥukm al-ikhbār 'ammā sayakūn*. ed. M.A.Q. 'Aṭā'. Beirut, 1406/1986.

Nadwi, M.A. *al-Muḥaddithāt: The Women Scholars in Islam*. Istanbul, 2007.

al-Nawbakhtī, al-Ḥasan b. Mūsā. *Kitāb firaq al-Shī'a*, ed. H. Ritter. Istanbul, 1931.

Nelson, Kristina. *The Art of Reciting the Qur'an*. Cairo and New York, 2001.

al-Nīsābūrī, Aḥmad b. Ibrāhīm. *Istitār al-imām*, ed. W. Ivanow, in *Bulletin of the Faculty of Arts, University of Egypt*, 4, part 2 (1936), pp. 93–107; reproduced in *Akhbār al-Qarāmiṭa*, ed. S. Zakkar. 2nd ed., Damascus, 1982, pp. 111–132.

———. *al-Risāla al-mūjaza*, ed. and tr. Verena Klemm and P. E. Walker as *A Code of Conduct: A Treatise on the Etiquette of the Fatimid Ismaili Mission*. London, 2011.

Niẓām al-Mulk, Abū 'Alī Ḥasan b. 'Alī. *Siyar al-mulūk* (*Siyāsat-nāma*), ed. H. Darke. 2nd ed., Tehran, 1347 Sh./1968; English trans., *The Book of Government or Rules for Kings*, tr. H. Darke. 2nd ed., London, 1978.

al-Nu'mān b. Muḥammad, al-Qāḍī Abū Ḥanīfa. *Da'ā'im al-Islām*, ed. Asaf A.A. Fyzee. Cairo, 1951-61; English trans., *The Pillars of Islam*, tr. A.A.A. Fyzee, completely revised by I.K. Poonawala. New Delhi, 2002–2004.

———. *al-Īḍāḥ*, ed. Muḥammad Kāẓim Raḥmatī. Beirut, 2007.

———. *Iftitāḥ al-da'wa wa ibtidā' al-dawla*, ed. W. al-Qāḍī. Beirut, 1970; ed. F. Dachraoui. Tunis, 1975; tr. H. Haji as *Founding the Fatimid State: The Rise of an Early Islamic Empire*. London, 2006.

———. *Minhāj al-farā'iḍ*, ed. and tr. A. Cilardo as *The Early History of Ismaili Jurisprudence: Law under the Fatimids*. London, 2012.

———. *Sharḥ al-akhbār fī faḍā'il al-a'imma al-aṭhār*. Qumm, 1409–1412/1988–1992.

———. *Ta'wīl al-da'ā'im*, ed. M.Ḥ. al-A'ẓamī. Cairo, 1967–1972.

al-Nuwayrī, Shihāb al-Dīn Aḥmad. *Nihāyat al-arab fī funūn al-adab: al-Juz' al-thāmin wa'l-'ishrūn*, ed. Muḥammad Muḥammad Amīn and Muḥammad Ḥilmī Muḥammad Aḥmad. Cairo, 1992.

Pauliny, J. 'Zur Rolle der *Quṣṣāṣ* bei der Entstehung und Überlieferung der populären Prophetenlegenden', *Asian and African Studies*, 10 (1974), pp. 125–141.

Pedersen, J. 'The Criticism of the Islamic Preacher', *Die Welt des Islams*, NS, 2 (1952), pp. 215–231.

Pellat, Charles. *Le milieu basrien et la formation de Ǧāḥiẓ*. Paris, 1953.

Perry, John R. *Karim Khan Zand: A History of Iran, 1747–1779*. Chicago, 1979.

Poonawala, Ismail K. *al-Sulṭān al-Khaṭṭāb, ḥayātuhu wa-shiʿruhu*. Cairo, 1999.

———. 'Al-Qāḍī al-Nuʿmān and Ismaʿili Jurisprudence', in F. Daftary, ed., *Mediaeval Ismaʿili History and Thought*. Cambridge, 1996, pp. 117–143.

———. 'al-Mu'ayyad fi'l-Dīn', *EI2*.

al-Qalqashandī, Shihāb al-Dīn Aḥmad. *Ṣubḥ al-aʿshā fī ṣināʿat al-inshā'*. Cairo, 1331–1338/1913–1920.

al-Qayrawānī, Ibn Abī Zayd. *Kitāb al-jāmiʿ fi'l-sunan wa'l-ādāb wa'l-maghāzī wa'l-ta'rīkh*, ed. M. Abu'l-Ajfān and ʿUthmān Baṭṭīkh. Beirut and Tunis, 1402/1982.

al-Qummī, Saʿd b. ʿAbd Allāh al-Ashʿarī. *Kitāb al-maqālāt wa'l-firaq*, ed. M.J. Mashkūr. Tehran, 1963.

al-Qurṭubī, Muḥammad b. Waḍḍāḥ. *Kitāb al-bidaʿ (Tratado contra las innovaciones)*, ed. and tr. M.I. Fierro. Madrid, 1988.

Rispler-Chaim, Vardit. 'The 20th Century of an Old *bidʿa*: *laylat al-niṣf min Shaʿbān*', *Der Islam*, 72 (1995), pp. 82–97.

Roded, R. *Women in Islamic Biographical Collections: From Ibn Saʿd to Who's Who*. Boulder, CO, and London, 1994.

Rosenthal, F. 'Ibn Abī Ṭāhir Tayfūr', *EI2*.

Sachedina, A.A. *The Just Ruler in Shiʿite Islam*. New York, 1988.

al-Ṣafadī, Ṣalāḥ al-Dīn Khalīl b. Aybak. *al-Wāfī bi'l-wafayāt, Das Biographische Lexicon des Ṣalāḥaddīn Ḫalīl Ibn Aybak Aṣ-Ṣafadī*, ed. H. Ritter et al. Istanbul, 1931–1999; ed. Aḥmad Arnaʿūt and Turkī Muṣṭafā. Beirut, 1420/2000.

Saḥnūn, Abū Saʿīd ʿAbd al-Salām al-Tanūkhī. *al-Mudawwana al-kubrā*. Cairo, 1323/1905.

Sāʿī, Muḥsin. *Āqā Khān Maḥallātī wa firqa-i Ismāʿīliyya*. Tehran, 1329 Sh./1950.

al-Sakhāwī, Shams al-Dīn Muḥammad. *al-Iʿlān bi'l-ṭawbīkh li-man dhamma ahl al-ta'rīkh*. Damascus, 1349/1930.

Salem, Abd al-Aziz. 'Alexandria to Almeria. Banū Khulayf: An Alexandrian family in the Middle Ages', *Journal of Muslim West and the Mediterranean*, 46 (1987), pp. 64–70.

Sanders, Paula. *Ritual, Politics and the City in Fatimid Cairo*. Albany, NY, 1994.

Sayyed, A. *Women and the Transmission of Religious Knowledge in Islam*. Cambridge, 2013.

——. 'Gender and Legal Authority: An Examination of Early Juristic Opposition to Women's Hadīth Transmission', *Islamic Law and Society*, 16 (2009), pp. 115–150.

——. 'Women and Ḥadīth Transmission: Two Case Studies from Mamluk Damascus', *Studia Islamica*, 95 (2002), pp. 71–94.

Sayyid, Ayman F. *La Capitale de l'Egypte jusqu'à l'époque fatimide, al-Qâhira et al-Fustât—Essai de reconstitution topographique*. Beirut and Stuttgart, 1998.

Schward, Gregor M. 'Abū ʿAbdallāh al-Baṣrī', *EI3*.

Scott, James C. *Domination and the Arts of Resistance: Hidden Transcripts*. New Haven, CT, 1990.

al-Shāfiʿī, Abū ʿAbd Allāh Muḥammad b. Idrīs. *Kitāb al-umm* (in the margins, al-Muzanī's *Mukhtaṣar*) 7 vols in 3. Cairo, 1321–1326/1903–1908.

al-Shāṭibī al-Gharnāṭī, Abū Isḥāq Ibrāhīm b. Mūsā. *Fatāwā*, ed. M. Abu'l-Ajfān. Tunis, 1405/1984.

al-Shayyāl, Jamāl al-Dīn, *Aʿlām al-Iskandariyya fi'l-ʿaṣr al-Islāmī*. Cairo, 1965.

——. ed. *Majmūʿat al-wathāʾiq al-Fāṭimiyya/Corpus Documentorum Fatimicorum*. Cairo, 1958.

Shihāb al-Dīn Shāh Ḥusaynī. *Khiṭābāt-i ʿāliya*, ed. H. Ojaqi. Bombay, 1963.

Sibt b. al-Jawzī, *Mirʾat al-zamān fī taʾrīkh al-aʿyān: al-Ḥawādith al-khāṣṣa bi-taʾrīkh al-Salājiqa bayna al-sanawāt 1056–1086*, ed. A. Sevim. Ankara, 1968 (also in *Belgeler: Türk Tarik Belgeri Dergisi* 14 [1989–1992], pp. 1–260).

Siddiqui, Mona. 'Law and the Desire for Social Control: An Insight into the Hanafi Concept of Kafa'a with Reference to the Fatawa ʿAlamgiri (1664–1672)', in M. Yamani, ed., *Feminism and Islam*. New York, 1996, pp. 49–68.

Sivan, E. 'Le caractère sacré de Jerusalem dans l'Islam aux XIIe-XIIIe siècles', *Studia Islamica*, 27 (1967), pp. 149–182.

al-Silafī, Abū Ṭāhir Aḥmad b. Muḥammad. *Muʿjam al-safar*, part one, ed. Bahīja Bakr al-Ḥasanī. Baghdad, 1398/1978.

Soucek, Priscilla. 'The Visual Language of Qajar Medals', in D. Behrens-Abouseif and S. Vernoit, ed., *Islamic Art in the 19th Century: Tradition, Innovation, and Eclecticism*. Leiden, 2006, pp. 305–331.

———. 'Coinage of the Qajars: A System in Continual Transition', *Iranian Studies*, 34 (2001), pp. 51–87.

Sourdel, D. 'al-Ḳādir Bi'llāh', *EI2*.

Stern, Samuel M. 'Cairo as the Centre of the Ismāʿīlī Movement', in *Colloque international sur l'histoire du Caire*. Cairo, 1972, pp. 437–450; reprinted in Samuel M. Stern, *Studies in early Ismāʿīlism*. Jerusalem and Leiden, 1983, pp. 234–256.

———. 'The Early Ismāʿīlī Missionaries in North-West Persia and in Khurāsān and Transoxania', *Bulletin of the School of Oriental and African Studies*, 23 (1960), pp. 56–90; reprinted in Samuel M. Stern, *Studies in Early Ismāʿīlism*. Jerusalem and Leiden, 1983, pp. 189–233.

———. 'The "Book of the Highest Initiation" and Other Anti-Ismāʿīlī Travesties', in Samuel M. Stern, *Studies in Early Ismāʿīlism*. Jerusalem and Leiden, 1983, pp. 56–83.

Stewart, Devin J. 'Polemics and Patronage in Safavid Iran: The Debate on Friday Prayer during the reign of Shah Tahmasb', *Bulletin of the School of Oriental and African Studies*, 72 (2009), pp. 425–457.

———. 'The Structure of the Fihrist: Ibn al-Nadim as Historian of Islamic Legal and Theological Schools', *International Journal of Middle East Studies*, 39 (2007), pp. 369–387.

———. 'Popular Shiism in Medieval Egypt: Vestiges of Islamic Sectarian Polemics in Egyptian Arabic', *Studia Islamica*, 84 (1996), pp. 35–66.

Stroeva, Liudmila V. *Gosudarstvo ismailitov v Irane v XI–XIII vv.* Moscow, 1978.

———. '*Den' voskreseniia iz mertvykh* i ego sotsial'naia sushchost', *Kratkie soobshcheniia Instituta Vostokovedeniia*, AN SSSR (Moscow), 38 (1960), pp. 19–25.

al-Ṣubkī, Tāj al-Dīn. *Ṭabaqāt al-shāfiʿiyya al-kubrā*, ed. Maḥmūd M. al-Ṭanaḥi and ʿAbd al-Fattāḥ al-Ḥilwī. Cairo, 1383–1396/1964–1976.

al-Suyūṭī, Abu'l-Faḍl ʿAbd al-Raḥmān Jalāl al-Dīn. *al-Amr bi'l-ittibāʿ wa'l-nahy ʿan al-ibtidāʿ*, ed. M.A.Q. ʿAṭāʾ. Beirut, 1408/1988.

———. *Ḥusn al-muḥāḍara fī akhbār Miṣr wa'l-Qāhira*, ed. Khalīl al-Manṣūr. Beirut, 1418/1997.

al-Ṭabarī, Muḥammad b. Jarīr. *Ta'rīkh al-rusūl wa'l-mulūk*, ed. M. J. de Goeje et al. Leiden, 1879–1901; English trans., *The History of al-Ṭabarī: Volume XXXVIII; The Return of the Caliphate to Baghdad*, tr. F. Rosenthal. New York, 1985; Volume XXXVII, *The ʿAbbasid Recovery*, tr. Philip M. Fields. Albany, NY, 1987.

Tabbaa, Yasser. 'The Transformation of Arabic Writing: Part I: Qurʾānic Calligraphy', *Ars Orientalis*, 21 (1991), pp. 119–148.

Takim, Liyakat A. 'From *bidʿa* to Sunna. The *wilāya* of ʿAlī in the Shīʿī *adhān*', *Journal of the American Oriental Society*, 120 (2000), pp. 166–177.

Talbi, M. 'La *qirā'a bi-l-alḥān*', *Arabica*, 5 (1958), pp. 183–190.

Toorawa, Shawkat M. *Ibn Abī Ṭāhir Ṭayfūr and Arabic Writerly Culture: A Ninth-Century Bookman in Baghdad*. London, 2005.

Tucker, Ernest. *Nadir Shah's Quest for Legitimacy in post-Safavid Iran*. Gainesville, FL, 2006.

——. 'Nadir Shah and the Jaʿfari *Madhhab* Reconsidered', *Iranian Studies*, 27 (1994), pp. 163–179.

Tucker, Judith. *Women, Family, and Gender in Islamic Law*. Cambridge, 2008.

al-Ṭulayṭulī (al-Andalusī), Saʿīd b. Aḥmad. *Ṭabaqāt al-umam*, tr. R. Blachère. Paris, 1935.

Turki, A.M. 'Défense de la tradition du prophète (*sunna*) et lutte contre l'innovation blâmable (*bidʿa*) dans le mālikisme: du *Muwaṭṭa'* de Mālik (-179/795) au *K. al-Gāmiʿ* d'Ibn Abī Zayd al-Qayrawānī (-386/996)', *Studia Islamica*, 87 (1998), pp. 5–34.

al-Turkumānī, Idrīs b. Baydakīn. *al-Lumaʿ fi'l-ḥawādith wa'l-bidaʿ*, ed. S. Labib. Stuttgart, 1986.

al-Ṭurṭūshī, Abū Bakr. *Kitāb al-ḥawādith wa bidʿa*, ed. and Spanish trans. Maribel Fierro, as *El Libro de las novedades y las innovaciones*. Madrid, 1993.

al-Ṭūsī, Abū Jaʿfar Muḥammad b. al-Ḥasan, 'al-Shaykh al-Ṭā'ifa'. *al-Mabsūṭ fī fiqh al-imāmiyya*. Tehran, 1378/1958.

——. *Tahdhīb al-aḥkām*, ed. Ḥasan al-Musawī Kharsān. Najaf, 1378/1959.

ʿUthmān b. Fūdī/Usumanu dan Fodio. *Iḥyā' al-sunna wa ikhmād al-bidʿa*. Cairo 1381/1962.

Vajda, G. 'La Mašyaḫa d Ibn al-Ḫaṭṭāb al-Rāzī. Contribution à l'histoire du Sunnisme en Égypte faṭimide', in N. Cottard, ed., *La transmission du savoir en Islam (VIIe-XVIIIe siècles)*. London, 1983, V, pp. 21–99 [originally published in *Bulletin d'Études Orientales* 23 (1970)].

——. *Le dictionnaire des autorités (Muʿjam al-suyūḫ) de ʿAbd al-Muʾmin ad-Dimyāṭī*. Paris, 1962.

Vazīrī, Aḥmad ʿAlī Khān. *Jughrāfiyā-yi Kirmān*, ed. Muḥammad Ibrāhīm Bāstānī Pārīzī. Tehranī, 1376 Sh./1997.

——. *Tārīkh-i Kirmān*, ed. Muḥammad Ibrāhīm Bāstānī Pārīzī. Tehran, 1340 Sh./1961.

Virani, Shafique N. *The Ismailis in the Middle Ages: A History of Survival, a Search for Salvation*. Oxford, 2007.

——. '*The Right Path*: A Post-Mongol Persian Ismaili Treatise', *Iranian Studies*, 43 (2010), pp. 197–221.

Walker, Paul E., ed. and tr. *Orations of the Fatimid Caliphs: Festival Sermons of the Ismaili Imams*. London, 2009.

——. *Ḥamīd al-Dīn al-Kirmānī: Ismaili Thought in the Age of al-Ḥākim*. London, 1999.

——. 'Fāṭimid Alexandria as an Entrepôt in the East–West Exchange of Islamic Scholarship', *Al-Masāq*, 26 (2014), pp. 36–48.

——. 'The Relationship between Chief *Qāḍī* and Chief *Dāʿī* under the Fatimids', in G. Kramer and S. Schmidtke, ed., *Speaking for Islam: Religious Authorities in Muslim Societies*. Leiden, 2006, pp. 70–94.

——. 'The Ismāʿīlī Daʿwa and the Fāṭimid Caliphate', in M.W. Daly, ed., *The Cambridge History of Egypt*, Volume I, *Islamic Egypt, 640–1517*, ed. Carl F. Petry. Cambridge, 1998, pp. 120–150.

Waardenburg, J. 'Official and Popular Religion as a Problem in Islamic Studies', in P. J. Vrijhof and J. Waardenburg, ed., *Official and Popular Religion: Analysis of a Theme for Religious Studies*. The Hague, 1977, pp. 340–386.

al-Wansharīsī. *al-Miʿyār al-muʿrib waʾl-jāmiʿ al-mughrib ʿan fatāwī ahl Ifrīqiya waʾl-Andalus waʾl-Maghrib*. Rabat, 1401/1981.

Wensinck, A.J. *The Muslim Creed: Its Genesis and Historical Development*. Cambridge, 1932.

Witkam, J.J. 'Ibn al-Akfānī', *EI2*.

Wymann-Landgraf, Umar F. Abd-Allah. *Mālik and Medina: Islamic Reasoning in the Formative Period*. Leiden, 2012.

Yaḥyā b. ʿUmar. *Kitāb aḥkām al-sūq*, ed. M.A. Makkī, in *Revista del Instituto Egipcio de Estudios Islámicos*, 4 (1956), pp. 59–152, tr. E. García Gómez as 'Unas *Ordenanzas del zoco* del siglo IX', *Al-Andalus*, 22 (1957), pp. 252–316.

Yalaoui, Mohammed. 'Controverse entre le Fatimide al-Muʿizz et l'Omeyyade al-Nāṣir, d'après le *Kitab al-Majalis w-al-Musāyarāt* du Cadi Nuʿman', *Cahiers de Tunisie*, 26 (1978), pp. 7–33.

al-Yamānī, Muḥammad b. Muḥammad. *Sīrat al-ḥājib Ja'far b. 'Alī*, ed. W. Ivanow, in *Bulletin of the Faculty of Arts, University of Egypt*, 4, part 2 (1936), pp. 107–133; English trans., in Ivanow, *Ismaili Tradition*, pp. 184–223; French trans., M. Canard, 'L'autobiographie d'un chambellan du Mahdî 'Obeidallâh le Fâṭimide', *Hespéris*, 39 (1952), pp. 279–324; reprinted in his *Miscellanea Orientalia*. London, 1973, article V.

Zetterstéen, K. V. [C. E. Bosworth]). 'al-Ṭā'i' Li-Amr Allāh', *EI2*.

Index